Prominent Architects and Engineers:

"In light of September 11, 2001, and the subsequent events which focus our well deserved attention on terrorism and security, Barbara Nadel's *Building Security: Handbook for Architectural Planning and Design* meets a critical need for lucid and straightforward design response to a wide range of threats that we can no longer ignore. It also acknowledges the responsibility of all design professionals to balance issues of security and openness as we reaffirm our belief in a free society."
—JOHN D. ANDERSON, FAIA, Senior Vice President, Anderson Mason Dale Architects, Denver, Colorado; 2001 President, The American Institute of Architects

"Nothing is more comforting than feeling secure in one's environment. Barbara Nadel's timely book, *Building Security: Handbook for Architectural Planning and Design* illustrates how to solve security challenges for commercial, institutional and industrial building types, from arenas to women's health centers. This reference is an essential security bible for any design professional, owner or public official seeking to balance security and design, along with crime prevention design solutions for safer communities."
—TERRANCE J. BROWN, FAIA, Senior Architect, ASCG Inc., Albuquerque, New Mexico; 2001 AIA Vice President, 2004 Whitney M. Young Jr. Award winner, The American Institute of Architects

"As the public increasingly looks to architects to address issues of security, Barbara Nadel's book will become an invaluable companion in our quest for balancing security with good design."
—THOMPSON E. PENNEY, FAIA, President and CEO, LS3P Associates, Ltd., Charleston, South Carolina; 2003 President, The American Institute of Architects

"Creating well-designed, safe, humane environments is a twenty-first century goal for architects, engineers, building owners and public officials. Rather than building bunkers, transparent security enhances design excellence in our society. Barbara Nadel's book, *Building Security: Handbook for Architectural Planning and Design* is an essential reference for all those responsible for security in the workplace and the built environment."
—EUGENE HOPKINS, FAIA, Senior Vice President, Group Director, Smith Group, Detroit, Michigan; 2004 President, The American Institute of Architects

"The difference between comfort derived from a security conscious design and comfort as a condition of freedom is very subtle, yet innately distinguishable. In her book, Barbara Nadel displays a depth of understanding, provides significant insights into this differentiation and reveals how design professionals, facility managers and building owners can simultaneously achieve the comfort from both."
—DOUGLAS L STEIDL, FAIA, Principal, Braun & Steidl Architects, Inc., Akron, Ohio; 2005 President, 2001 Vice President, The American Institute of Architects

"The increasing importance of security in architecture demands that architectural and engineering practitioners and students alike have increased familiarity with security design and operational issues. Barbara Nadel's book will be an essential resource for students and faculty of architecture, as they learn and teach about twenty-first century firmness, commodity, and delight."
—KATE SCHWENNSEN, FAIA, Associate Dean/Associate Professor, College of Design, Iowa State University, Ames, Iowa; 2003 Vice President, The American Institute of Architects

"Engineers and architects now have a new design challenge. In addition to making buildings safe for wind, seismic, gravity and thermal loads, and designing for normal air quality and environmental concerns, we now have the 'design threat,' the unexpected aggressive occurrence of explosive, chemical, biological and radiological terror attacks. Protective design against these threats must be accomplished in a way that makes the public feel safe entering, occupying and leaving our buildings. Barbara Nadel's book clearly defines this reality and helps owners and design professionals meet this challenge efficiently and economically."
— RICHARD L. TOMASETTI, PE, Principal, The Thornton-Tomasetti Group, New York, NY

"American history is defined by architecture. As architecture creates the fabric of our communities, we recognize the value of being assured a safe and healthy environment for the next generation of Americans. This book gives us lessons in how to sustain our communities and enhance our future through careful planning and thoughtful design."
— STEPHAN CASTELLANOS, FAIA, California State Architect, Valley Springs, California; 2001–2002 National Secretary, The American Institute of Architects

"A timeless architecture derives from many subtexts. In our time, security is a foreground subject and Barbara Nadel understands the importance of an architecture that quietly and effectively addresses this issue while communicating feelings of openness and invitation. In a thoughtful and persuasive way, she posits optimistic possibilities for buildings in a world where security in civic buildings could become the frightening conclusion of the design process. I highly recommend this balanced view of a twenty-first century reality."
— ANTOINE PREDOCK, FAIA, Principal, Antoine Predock Architect, Albuquerque, New Mexico

"Since September 11, 2001, security has become a strategic issue in our society. This book is an invaluable resource for everyone who is engaged in the design, construction and operation of buildings. It demonstrates that good design and good security can indeed go hand in hand, enhancing rather than restricting our quality of life."
— SCOTT SIMPSON, FAIA, President and CEO, The Stubbins Associates, Cambridge, Massachusetts, Coauthor of *How Firms Succeed—A Field Guide to Design Management*

"Security has become one of the chief considerations of any responsible architect today for a variety of building types. Barbara Nadel's book is sure to become a landmark publication in the aftermath of September 11, 2001, as design professionals and building owners work to understand how to design safe, secure buildings. This book is the best place to start."
— MICHAEL J. CROSBIE, PH.D., R.A., Senior Associate, Steven Winter Associates, Norwalk, Connecticut, Editor, *Time-Saver Standards for Building Types* (McGraw-Hill)

"*Building Security: Handbook for Architectural Planning and Design* tackles the key security issues relating to design and disaster planning—essential elements for every current and aspiring architect, engineer and client. With heightened public awareness about safety and security since September 11, 2001, architects, engineers and building owners must pay close attention to the evolving standards of care. *Building Security* is a comprehensive reference for professionals and students alike, and is a must-read for everyone responsible for ensuring public health, safety and welfare."
— BARRY Z. POSNER, PH.D., Dean and Professor of Leadership, Santa Clara University, Santa Clara, California. Coauthor, *The Leadership Challenge* and *Credibility: How Leaders Gain and Lose It, Why People Demand It*; 2002–2003 AIA Public Director, The American Institute of Architects National Board of Directors

Law Enforcement

"Some buildings are properly designed and built, eventually becoming classics or historical monuments. Too many buildings, especially government buildings, are poorly designed, use outdated technologies, and quickly become deteriorated old hulks. In today's political climate, with today's many complex workplace issues, it is imperative that buildings incorporate the best possible design and security technologies. We owe our employees, and we owe future generations, nothing less. Barbara Nadel's new book provides an interesting perspective for this growing area of concern."
—WILLIAM J. BRATTON, Chief of Police, Los Angeles Police Department
(and former New York City Police Commissioner)

"At the Nation's founding, Jefferson appreciated the important relationship between architecture and democracy. It is critical now more than ever for architects to get right the often conflicting demands of freedom and security to ensure that democratic ideals are not lost in the steel and stone of our edifices."
—RAYMOND W, KELLY, New York City Police Commissioner

"Given the ever looming specter of terrorism and other threats to the assets and well being of businesses and building owners alike, today's architect must now approach building design paying equal consideration to aesthetics, functionality, and nowadays, security. Ms. Nadel has written an insightful, sweeping book on security design that is a must-read for architects, landlords, security consultants and anyone else tasked with or interested in ensuring security and averting catastrophic loss."
—BERNARD B. KERIK, 40th Police Commissioner, New York City (Ret.)

Members of Congress:

"Our architects, engineers, and design and construction experts now play a critical role in protecting the American public. They are faced with the challenge of preserving comfort and convenience while integrating security mechanisms into our homes and offices. *Building Security: Handbook for Architectural Planning and Design* leads them through this delicate process, folding the post-September 11th reality into architecture and design."
—CONGRESSWOMAN NITA LOWEY (D-NY)

"As September 11th proved in the most tragic terms, the front line in the war on terror has moved to our buildings and skyscrapers. As a result, building designers find themselves playing a crucial role in our urban safety planning, and the stakes couldn't be higher. Barbara Nadel's *Building Security: Handbook for Architectural Planning and Design* promises to become one of the most important reference books in any architect, construction professional, or building owner's library."
—CONGRESSMAN ANTHONY WEINER (D-NY)

BUILDING SECURITY

BUILDING SECURITY

HANDBOOK FOR ARCHITECTURAL PLANNING AND DESIGN

Barbara A. Nadel

Editor in Chief

McGraw-Hill

New York   Chicago   San Francisco   Lisbon   London
Madrid   Mexico City   Milan   New Delhi   San Juan
Seoul   Singapore   Sydney   Toronto

The McGraw·Hill Companies

Cataloging-in-Publication data is on file with the Library of Congress.

Copyright © 2004 by The McGraw-Hill Companies, Inc. All rights reserved. Printed in the United States of America. Except as permitted under the United States Copyright Act of 1976, no part of this publication may be reproduced or distributed in any form or by any means, or stored in a data base or retrieval system, without the prior written permission of the publisher.

3 4 5 6 7 8 9 0 IBT / IBT 0 1 0 9 8 7

ISBN 978-0-071-41171-4
ISBN 0-07-141171-2

The sponsoring editor for this book was Cary Sullivan, the editing supervisor was David E. Fogarty, and the production supervisor was Pamela A. Pelton. This book was set in the HB1 design in Times Roman by Kim Sheran and Wayne Palmer of McGraw-Hill Professional's Hightstown, N.J. composition unit. The art director for the cover was Margaret Webster-Shapiro.

Printed and bound by IBT Global.

This book is printed on recycled, acid-free paper containing a minimum of 50% recycled, deinked paper.

McGraw-Hill books are available at special quantity discounts to use as premiums and sales promotions, or for use in corporate training programs. For more information, please write to the Director of Special Sales, McGraw-Hill Professional, Two Penn Plaza, New York, NY 10121-2298. Or contact your local bookstore.

To Ruth and George Nadel
In loving memory of Bruce Evan Nadel

To the victims of September 11, 2001, and all who died from acts of terrorism...

This book is dedicated to advancing the knowledge needed to prevent similar events from recurring.

CONTENTS

Contributors   xv
Foreword   xix
Preface   xxi
Acknowledgments   xxiii
About the Author   xxxi

Part 1   Achieving Transparent Security

Chapter 1. Lessons Learned from September 11, 2001, and Other
Benchmark Events   *Barbara A. Nadel, FAIA*   **1.3**

Chapter 2. Security Master Planning   *David V. Thompson, AIA and Bill McCarthy, AIA*   **2.1**

Chapter 3. Crime Prevention through Environmental Design   *Terri Kelly*   **3.1**

Part 2   Planning and Design

Chapter 4. Arenas, Sports Facilities, Convention Centers, Performing Arts
Facilities: Safety and Security after September 11, 2001
*Russ Simons, Gerald Anderson, AIA, and the International Association
of Assembly Managers, Safety and Security Task Force*   **4.3**

Chapter 5. Commercial High-Rise Egress Systems   *Carl Galioto, FAIA*   **5.1**

Chapter 6. Courthouse Security   *Kenneth J. Jandura, AIA
and David R. Campbell, PE*   **6.1**

Chapter 7. Federally Owned or Leased Office Buildings: Security Design
Terry L. Leach, AIA   **7.1**

Chapter 8. Health Care Security   *Thomas M. Jung, R.A.*   **8.1**

Chapter 9. **Historic Preservation Guidance for Security Design**
Sharon C. Park, FAIA, and Caroline R. Alderson   9.1

Chapter 10. **Hospitality Facility Security**   *Bradley D. Schulz, AIA*   10.1

Chapter 11. **Multifamily Housing: Security Checklist for Building Owners
and Real Estate Professionals**   *James W. Harris*   11.1

Chapter 12. **Home and Business Security, Disaster Planning, Response, and
Recovery**   *Barbara A. Nadel, FAIA*   12.1

Chapter 13. **Industrial Facilities and Office Buildings: Safety, Security, Site
Selection, and Workplace Violence**   *Barbara A. Nadel, FAIA*   13.1

Chapter 14. **Lobby Security Design: First Impressions**   *Casey L. Jones*   14.1

Chapter 15. **Museum and Cultural Facility Security**   *Arthur Rosenblatt, FAIA* 15.1

Chapter 16. **Perimeter Security: The Aesthetics of Protection**   *Deborah Bershad
and Jean Parker Phifer, AIA*   16.1

Chapter 17. **Religious Institutions and Community Centers**
Anti-Defamation League   17.1

Chapter 18. **Research Facilities: Security Planning**   *Regis Gaughan, PE,
Joseph Calabrese, PE, and Stanley Stark, AIA*   18.1

Chapter 19. **Retail Security Design**   *Jeffrey J. Gunning, AIA, and
Lance K. Josal, AIA*   19.1

Chapter 20. **School Security: Designing Safe Learning Environments**
Thomas Blurock, AIA   20.1

Chapter 21. **Women's Health Centers: Workplace Safety and Security**
Barbara A. Nadel, FAIA   21.1

Part 3 Engineering

Chapter 22. **Protective Design of Structures**   *Richard L. Tomasetti, PE,
and John Abruzzo, PE*   22.3

Chapter 23. Mechanical, Electrical, and Fire Protection Design
Andrew Hlushko, PE   **23.1**

Chapter 24. Chemical and Biological Protection   *Michael C. Janus, PE,*
and William K. Blewett   **24.1**

Part 4   Construction

Chapter 25. Construction Cost Estimating for Security-Related Projects
Elizabeth J. Heider, AIA   **25.3**

Chapter 26. Construction: Emergency Response Lessons Learned
from September 11, 2001   *Lewis J. Mintzer*   **26.1**

Part 5   Technology and Materials

Chapter 27. Security Technology   *William G. Sewell, RCDD*   **27.3**

Chapter 28. Selecting and Specifying Security Technology Products:
A Primer for Building Owners and Facility Managers
Francis J. Sheridan, AIA   **28.1**

Chapter 29. Glazing and Security Glass Applications   *F. John W. Bush,*
Sue Steinberg, Catherine Kaliniak   **29.1**

Part 6   Codes and Liabilities

Chapter 30. Codes, Standards, and Guidelines for Security Planning
and Design   *Walter "Skip" Adams, CPP, and*
Deborah A. Somers   **30.3**

Chapter 31. Liability Exposure after September 11, 2001
Michael S. Zetlin, Esq., and Noelle Lilien, Esq.   **31.1**

Index   I.1

CONTRIBUTORS

Never doubt that a small group of thoughtful, committed citizens
can change the world. Indeed, it's the only thing that ever has.
MARGARET MEAD (1901-1978)
U.S. anthropologist

AUTHORS

John Abruzzo, PE   *Vice President, LZA Technology, The Thornton-Tomasetti Group Inc., New York, N.Y.* (CHAP. 22)

Walter "Skip" Adams, CPP   *Senior Security Consultant, Sako & Associates, Inc., New York, N.Y.* (CHAP. 30)

Caroline R. Alderson   *Program Manager, Center for Historic Buildings, Office of the Chief Architect, U.S. General Services Administration Public Buildings Service, Washington, D.C.* (CHAP. 9)

Gerald Anderson, AIA   *Senior Principal and Director of the Event Division, HOK Sport + Venue + Event, Salt Lake City, Utah* (CHAP. 4)

Deborah Bershad   *Executive Director, Art Commission of the City of New York, New York, N.Y.* (CHAP. 16)

William K. Blewett   *Chief Engineer, Engineering Applications and Operations, Battelle Memorial Institute, Aberdeen, Md.* (CHAP. 24)

Thomas Blurock, AIA   *Principal, Thomas Blurock Architects, Costa Mesa, Calif.* (CHAP. 20)

F. John W. Bush   *Director of Laminated Products and Development, Oldcastle Glass, Sunrise, Fla.* (CHAP. 29)

Joseph Calabrese, PE   *Principal, Simon Rodkin Engineers, New York, N.Y.* (CHAP. 18)

David R. Campbell, PE   *Associate Principal, DMJM Technology, Colorado Springs, Colo.* (CHAP. 6)

Morris S. Casuto, MA   *Regional Director, The Anti-Defamation League, San Diego, Calif.* (CHAP. 17)

Carl Galioto, FAIA   *Partner, Skidmore, Owings & Merrill, New York, N.Y.* (CHAP. 5)

Regis Gaughan, PE   *Managing Partner, HLW International LLP, New York, N.Y.* (CHAP. 18)

Jeffrey J. Gunning, AIA   *Vice President, RTKL Associates, Inc., Dallas, Tex.* (CHAP. 19)

James W. Harris   *Vice President of Business Services, Registry-SafeRent, a First Advantage Company, Rockville, Md.* (CHAP. 11)

Elizabeth J. Heider, AIA   *Vice President, Skanska USA Building Inc., Alexandria, Va.* (CHAP. 25)

Andrew Hlushko, PE   *Senior Vice President, Flack + Kurtz Inc., New York, N.Y.* (CHAP. 23)

Kenneth J. Jandura, AIA   *Justice Principal, DMJM Design, Arlington, Va.* (CHAP. 6)

Michael C. Janus, PE   *Manager, Engineering Applications and Operations, Battelle Memorial Institute, Aberdeen, Md.* (CHAP. 24)

Casey L. Jones   *Architect and Director, First Impressions Program, Office of the Chief Architect, Public Buildings Service, U.S. General Services Administration, Washington, D.C.* (CHAP. 14)

Lance K. Josal, AIA   *Senior Vice President, RTKL Associates Inc., Dallas, Tex.* (CHAP. 19)

Thomas M. Jung, R.A. *Director, Bureau of Architectural and Engineering Facilities Planning, Division of Health Facilities Planning, New York State Department of Health, Albany, N.Y.* (CHAP. 8)

Catherine Kaliniak *Public Relations Consultant to Oldcastle Glass, McLean, Va.* (CHAP. 29)

Theresa "Terri" Kelly *Director, Community Outreach and Support, National Crime Prevention Council, Washington, D.C.* (CHAP. 3)

Terry L. Leach, AIA *Senior Security Specialist, DMJM Systems Solutions/DMJM Technology, Albuquerque, N.M.* (CHAP. 7)

Noelle Lilien, Esq. *Associate Attorney, Zetlin & De Chiara LLP, New York, N.Y.* (CHAP. 31)

Bill McCarthy, AIA *Associate Vice President, RTKL Associates, Inc., Baltimore, Md.* (CHAP. 2)

Lewis J. Mintzer *Director of Marketing, URS Corporation, New York, N.Y.* (CHAP. 26)

Barbara A. Nadel, FAIA *Principal, Barbara Nadel Architect, Forest Hills, N.Y.* (chaps. 1, 12, 13, 21)

Sharon C. Park, FAIA *Chief, Technical Preservation Services, National Park Service, Washington, D.C.* (CHAP. 9)

Jean Parker Phifer, AIA *Architect, Thomas Phifer & Partners, New York, N.Y.* (CHAP. 16)

Arthur Rosenblatt, FAIA *Principal of RKK&G Museum and Cultural Facilities Consultants, Inc., New York, N.Y.* (CHAP. 15)

Bradley D. Schultz, AIA *Principal, KGA Architecture, Las Vegas, Nev.* (CHAP. 10)

William G. Sewell, RCDD *Senior Vice President, DMJM Technology, Arlington, Va.* (CHAP. 27)

Steven C. Sheinberg Ph.D., J.D. *Coordinator, Security Awareness Programs, Special Assistant to the Director, The Anti-Defamation League, New York, N.Y.* (CHAP. 17)

Francis J. Sheridan, AIA *Director of Facilities Planning and Development, New York State Department of Correctional Services, Albany, N.Y.* (CHAP. 28)

Russ Simons *Principal, Operations and Facility Evaluations Group, HOK Sport + Venue + Event, Kansas City, Mo.* (CHAP. 4)

Deborah A. Somers *Senior Security Consultant, Sako & Associates, Inc., Arlington Heights, Ill.* (CHAP. 30)

Stanley Stark, AIA *Managing Partner, HLW International LLP, New York, N.Y.* (CHAP. 18)

Sue Steinberg *Vice President, Corporate Communications, Oldcastle Glass, Santa Monica, Calif.* (CHAP. 29)

David V. Thompson, AIA *Vice President, RTKL Associates, Inc., Baltimore, Md.* (CHAP. 2)

Richard L. Tomasetti, PE *Co-Chairman, The Thornton-Tomasetti Group Inc., New York, N.Y.* (CHAP. 22)

Michael S. Zetlin, Esq. *Partner, Zetlin & De Chiara LLP, New York, N.Y.* (CHAP. 31)

COVER DESIGN

David Schroer *President, Loudmouth Graphics, Venice, Calif.*

ARTISTS

Terrance J. Brown, FAIA *Senior Architect, ASCG Inc. Albuquerque, N.M.*

Francis J. Sheridan, AIA *Director of Facilities Planning, New York State Department of Correctional Services, Albany, N.Y.*

Stanley Stark, AIA *Managing Partner, HLW International LLP, New York, N.Y.*

PHOTOGRAPHY AND ARCHITECTURAL RENDERING

Peter Aaron *Photographer, Esto, Mamaroneck, N.Y.* (CHAP. 14)

Advanced Media Design *Architectural Rendering, Providence, R.I.* (CHAP. 1)

Richard Barnes *Photographer, San Francisco, Calif.* (CHAP. 21)

Bruce D. Eisenberg, AIA *Principal, Bruce Eisenberg Architects, New York, N.Y.* (CHAP. 1)

John Gillan *Photographer, John Gillan Photography, Inc., Ft. Lauderdale, Fla.* (CHAP. 6)

Mark Ginsberg, AIA *Principal, Curtis + Ginsberg Architects LLP, New York, N.Y.* (CHAP. 1)

Charles F. Harper, FAIA *Principal, Harper Perkins Architects, Wichita Falls, Tex.* (CHAP. 12)

Timothy Hursley *Photographer, Timothy Hursley Photography, Little Rock, Ark.* (CHAP. 14)

Jeffrey Katz *Photographer, CenterSpan Productions, LLC, Severena Park, Md.* (CHAP. 6)

Richard Meier, FAIA *Partner, Richard Meier & Partners, Architects, New York, N.Y.*
(CHAP. 14)

Milroy/McAleer *Architectural Photography, Costa Mesa, Calif.* (CHAP. 20)

Walt Roycraft *Photographer, Walt Roycraft Photography, Nicholasville, Ky.* (CHAP. 14)

FOREWORD

Leadership and learning are indispensable to each other.
JOHN F. KENNEDY (1917-1963)
*35th U.S. President, in a speech prepared
for delivery in Dallas the day of his
assassination, November 22, 1963*

We are facing a new horizon for leadership with many opportunities for fresh and innovative solutions to the emerging issues of the twenty-first century. In this post-9/11 world, security, sustainability and building community have become, and will continue to be, the main challenges driving public policy development.

Among the professions, architects are best suited to address and solve these important concerns. Architects are trained to logically grasp complex subjects and balance diverse competing interests. More importantly, architects have the inherent skills to engage the public in unique ways through their ability to build understanding and cooperation by use of the design process.

Enhancing security, sustainability and fostering community in the built environment provide the architectural and design professions with unprecedented opportunities for leadership and making important contributions to an increasingly global society. These challenges became apparent to me on a daily basis during my tenure as U.S. Ambassador to Denmark.

As the first licensed architect to serve as a U.S. ambassador in American history, I was one of many American diplomats living abroad managing the balance between evolving public policy, security, sustainability and national relations in an era of globalization. Stewardship of a post-World War II U.S. embassy, including the safety and productivity of the diplomatic staff, engaged my architectural training and professional experience. Being a diplomat and a designer called for merging two very different professional agendas, resulting in a greater understanding of the complex challenges necessary for creating a secure and productive environment.

The need for security is a condition that transcends all social, racial and cultural lines. When the built environment incorporates well-designed security, sustainability and community aspects into the places where we live, work, play and study, we can better appreciate the transformative power of building understanding and cooperation among diverse nations and societies. These places are where the integrative skills and leadership abilities of architects are most valuable and necessary.

One architect who has pursued this leadership role is Barbara A. Nadel, FAIA. She possesses the breadth of experience, expertise and skill to lead the building industry through the complicated maze of security design. As an architect of justice, health and institutional facilities, an accomplished journalist and an eloquent public advocate, Barbara has spoken and written extensively about the role of design in making our world a better, safer place.

Barbara has researched and written, in collaboration with many multi-disciplinary experts, the definitive opus on the subject of building security. This book most certainly is a seminal contribution to the profession of architecture, schools of architecture and engineering, and society in general.

What's more, Barbara truly understands the leadership role architects *must* play in addressing this critical challenge and demonstrates the ability to explain the difficult issues of security in a way that is understandable to professionals and laypeople alike, without technical jargon. She achieves a masterful balance.

This book is an important bridge to be used in connecting security measures with the freedoms enjoyed by an open and democratic society. Anyone who reads it, be they architects, engineers, academics, public servants, developers, facility managers, building owners or building occupants, will have an invaluable resource with which to create more livable environments and communities, leading ultimately to a safer society.

As we look to protect ourselves from the problems of the present, it is equally important to design solutions promoting the strongest possibility of a better, safer future. Barbara A. Nadel has stepped up and contributed her special talents and creative vision as her part in this new horizon of leadership.

AMBASSADOR RICHARD N. SWETT, FAIA
President, Swett Associates Inc.
Senior Counselor, APCO Worldwide
Senior Fellow, Design Futures Council
New Hampshire, New York, Washington, D.C.

PREFACE

Regardless of where you live and work, or what you do, it is never to early, or too late, to learn more about building security, disaster planning, and emergency response. The tragic events of September 11, 2001, underscored the need for everyone to be professionally knowledgeable and personally prepared to deal with emergencies of any kind.

My primary goal in editing and writing this book is to provide everyone involved in building security and public safety with practical information needed to protect people, buildings, and assets from catastrophe. Studying the lessons of September 11, 2001, and other events illustrates what can happen when the details of design, technology, and building operations are not thoroughly considered. Building security is, and will likely continue to be, a fundamental concern for the foreseeable future.

This volume is intended to be a handy reference for architects, designers, planners, engineers, facility managers, building owners, construction managers, real estate professionals, public officials charged with security, and public safety specialists seeking to create safe, secure, and well-designed environments. Over 20 building types and several disciplines are addressed. Additionally, information on home and business security, covering crime, disaster planning, response, and recovery, is provided. This volume should also be of interest and use to educators and students, especially within schools of architecture, engineering, and construction.

To reach this wide audience, I have collaborated with a stellar roster of renowned contributors, from 15 states, representing different areas of professional expertise. All contributors, and their organizations, have dealt successfully with security issues from distinct vantage points. The contributors include design and construction consultants, building owners, technology experts, disaster response experts, attorneys, and those from government agencies and not-for-profit organizations. Given the comprehensive scope of information, the book is organized in six parts, each covering an area of expertise, and enabling readers to find what they want at a glance. These areas are as follows:

1. Achieving Transparent Security
2. Planning and Design
3. Engineering
4. Construction
5. Technology and Materials
6. Codes and Liability

Three underlying themes are highlighted throughout the book, reflecting the concept that security and good design are compatible, essential elements in the built environment:

- *Learn from the past.* There are lessons to be learned from September 11, 2001, and other benchmark events, applicable to many building types, communities, and situations. As a unique feature of the book, notable examples of lessons learned are cited in each chapter, within specially marked tables. All the lessons learned are summarized in Chapter 1 for quick reference by chapter.

- *Integrate the approach.* Effective security relies on successfully integrating design and technology with building operations, policies, and procedures, which are typically established by building owners and facility managers. Many chapters address one or more of these vital components. In addition to a wealth of information for design professionals, several chapters contain specific guidance for facility managers, along with recommendations and handy checklists on technology, disaster planning, emergency management, and building operations.

- *Plan carefully for each situation.* Transparent security, invisible to the public eye, can be achieved through informed planning and design, to enhance the built environment. When appropriate, security planning for new construction and upgrades of existing facilities can explore ways to avoid the use of visible, unsightly barriers while maintaining public safety. There may be situations where security components need to be visible, and that is an important decision to be made by building owners and their project teams.

As for how to use this book, most readers will probably not read the book sequentially, as in a novel, one chapter at a time, but will skip around to the chapters they most need to know about at any given moment. For those who want the big picture before getting into the details, Chapter 1, "Lessons Learned from September 11, 2001, and other Benchmark Events," provides an overview, and serves as the executive summary of the entire book. Chapter 2, "Security Master Planning," provides overall context, and lays the groundwork for information presented within subsequent chapters, including a glossary of basic security terms.

Because of the many contributors, and their areas of expertise, each chapter is designed to be self-contained to address specific topics. There may be some overlap of broad concepts, and interested readers may be able to glean fresh ideas from different building types or disciplines for various applications. The index provides additional guidance.

This book is generously illustrated with 600 photographs, drawings, charts, tables, and checklists, to provide handy reference and highlight key points. Three architect contributors are also talented illustrators, and their pen and ink drawings appear in several chapters.

Along with the many lessons learned cited throughout the book, another unique feature consists of Internet Resources listed at the end of the chapters, offering additional information. Web site links to industry publications, organizations, and government agencies are provided.

It is my hope that this book will inspire you to think about security and design in new and different ways. Refer to this handbook often. Use the information contained within as a guide to creating secure and well-designed environments. Share it with your colleagues, clients, consultants, friends, and family. Encourage them to prepare for disasters and emergencies. Their lives may some day depend on your foresight and thoughtfulness.

BARBARA A. NADEL, FAIA
Queens, New York

ACKNOWLEDGMENTS

Noble deeds are most estimable when hidden.
BLAISE PASCAL (1623–1662)
French mathematician and philosopher

Writing is a solitary craft, but any successful creative project is a collaborative achievement, and this book is no exception. This project is the result of collaboration among over 100 friends, colleagues, and people whom, even as the completed manuscript goes to press, I've not (yet) met or spoken with. Through the power of technology, and the importance of the subject, security in the built environment, everyone from marketing coordinators to managing principals in offices across the country has generously dedicated his or her time and expertise.

I am indebted to all the contributing authors for their meticulous work and sharing their knowledge. Of the many who encouraged me from the beginning and were the bedrock support throughout the project, there is a special place reserved for the firm principals, public agency directors, colleagues and friends who recommended authors; the many contributing firms, agencies and organizations for their generous investment of staff time, resources, and commitment to the project; and to several national organizations that allowed adaptation and use of their materials. These collective contributions form the foundation of the book.

I owe a very special acknowledgment to Alexandra Spencer, Media Relations Officer, DMJM+HARRIS, Los Angeles, California, for her intuitive eye and generosity in tapping graphic artist David Schroer, President, Loudmouth Graphics, Venice, California, to provide the distinctive book cover design.

Many people worked diligently with me throughout the project, providing insightful comments and carefully pouring over each draft, and there were many overall to contend with. All photography in the book appears courtesy of the photographers, firms, agencies, and contributors of each chapter. I extend my thanks to everyone for providing publication rights to these images. The following honor roll acknowledges those behind the bylines who assisted me in creating each chapter, and bringing this book to fruition.

PART 1   ACHIEVING TRANSPARENT SECURITY

Chapter 1: Lessons Learned from September 11, 2001, and other Benchmark Events, by Barbara A. Nadel, FAIA. My thanks to Larry Silverstein, President and CEO, Silverstein Properties, Inc., New York, New York; Carl Galioto, FAIA, Partner, and Ken Lewis, Associate Partner, Skidmore, Owings & Merrill, New York, New York for granting permission to publish the photograph of Seven World Trade Center; Bruce D. Eisenberg, AIA, Principal, Bruce Eisenberg Architects, New York, New York and Mark Ginsberg, AIA, Principal, Curtis + Ginsberg Architects LLP, New York, New York, for permission to publish their photographs; and Nicholas Pearson and Tyrone Mitchell, artists, New York, New York, for providing public art information.

Chapter 2: Security Master Planning, by David V. Thompson, AIA, and Bill McCarthy, AIA. My sincere appreciation to Harold Adams, FAIA, RIBA, JIA, Chairman Emeritus, RTKL Associates, Inc., who was among the first to commit his firm to the book, and Lily Thayer, Public Relations Manager, RTKL Associates, Inc., Baltimore, Maryland, for her dedicated editorial efforts in Chapters 2 and 19.

Chapter 3: Crime Prevention Through Environmental Design, by Terri Kelly. I am grateful to the National Crime Prevention Council for granting permission to adapt material from *Designing Safer Communities: A Crime Prevention Through Environmental Design Handbook*; and John D. Ratliff, Esq., Assoc. AIA, Director & Counsel, Center for Livable Communities, The American Institute of Architects, Washington, D.C., who provided valuable resources.

PART 2   PLANNING AND DESIGN

Chapter 4: Arenas, Sports Facilities, Convention Centers, Performing Arts Facilities: Safety and Security after September 11, 2001, by Russ Simons, Gerald Anderson, AIA, and the International Association of Assembly Managers, Safety and Security Task Force. My heartfelt thanks to dear friend and colleague, Robert L. Watson, AIA, former Associate Principal, HOK Sport + Venue + Event, who recommended the firm's contribution; Russ Simons, for obtaining permission from IAAM to adapt material from the *Safety and Security Task Force Best Practices Planning Guide*; Erin Jones, Marketing Coordinator, HOK Sport + Venue + Event, who was a tremendous help as editor in chief; and Carrie Plummer, Brand Manager, HOK Sport + Venue + Event, Kansas City, Missouri for her assistance.

Chapter 5: Commercial High-Rise Egress Systems, by Carl Galioto, FAIA. My thanks to those at SOM, who assisted Carl in preparing the images for this chapter, and supported his contribution on behalf of the firm.

Chapter 6: Courthouse Security, by Kenneth J. Jandura, AIA, and David R. Campbell, PE, and *Chapter 7: Federally Owned or Leased Office Buildings: Security Design,* by Terry L. Leach, AIA. The three chapters by DMJMH+N (6, 7, and 27) appear due to the recommendation of fellow AIA Committee on Architecture for Justice colleague, Donald J. Dwore, FAIA, Principal, Spillis Candela DMJM, Coral Gables, Florida. I'm grateful to DMJMH+N for their generous firmwide commitment in contributing to this project.

Chapter 8: Health Care Security, by Thomas M. Jung, R.A. My thanks to Tom, the New York State Department of Health, and NYU Downtown Hospital for securing permission to publish emergency protocols, photographs and case studies from 9/11. Although their original submission was not used, I extend my thanks for the contributions and longstanding support of Ronald L. Skaggs, FAIA, FACHA, 2000 AIA President, and Chairman, HKS Inc., H. Ralph Hawkins, FAIA, FACHA, President and CEO, HKS Inc., and Joseph G. Sprague, FAIA, FACHA, Principal, Director of Health Facilities, HKS. Inc., Dallas, Texas; the significant work of Michael Pietrzak, M.D., Project Director, ER One, Washington Hospital Center, Washington, D.C.; and the efforts of Craig Beale, FAIA, FACHA, Principal, Senior Vice President, HKS Inc.; David R. Vincent, AIA, ACHA, Associate Principal, and Trish Martinek, Associate and Director of Communications, HKS Inc., Dallas, Texas.

Chapter 9: Historic Preservation Guidance for Security Design, by Sharon C. Park, FAIA, and Caroline R. Alderson. My heartfelt thanks to: Sharon, Caroline, and their respective agencies, the National Park Service and the U.S. General Services Administration, for authorizing Sharon and Caroline to collaborate and contribute their considerable expertise on behalf of the federal government; Edward A. Feiner, FAIA, Chief Architect, Public Buildings Service, GSA, for supporting GSA's contributions to Chapters 9 and 14; and the talented architects, designers, landscape architects, engineers, photographers, GSA and National Park Service personnel, and other individuals who so generously assisted Sharon and Caroline in developing this chapter.

Chapter 10: Hospitality Facility Security, by Bradley D. Schulz, AIA. My thanks to KGA Architecture, and Brad's wife, Patti Schulz, Las Vegas, Nevada, for supporting his contribution to the book.

Chapter 11: Multifamily Housing: Security Checklist for Building Owners and Real Estate Professionals, by James W. Harris. My thanks to Lisa E. Blackwell, Vice President, Housing Policy Initiatives, National Multi Housing Council/ National Apartment Association, Washington, D. C., for bringing this project to Jay's attention, resulting in his valued contribution, and adaptation of the NMHC/NAAA's operational guidelines.

Chapter 12: Home and Business Security, Disaster Planning, Response, and Recovery, by Barbara A. Nadel, FAIA. Few U.S. architects are more knowledgeable about disaster planning and response than Charles F. Harper, FAIA, Principal, Harper Perkins Architects, Wichita Falls, Texas, and my fellow 2001 AIA Vice President, Terrance J. Brown, FAIA, Senior Architect, ASCG Inc., Albuquerque, New Mexico. I am deeply grateful to Charlie for sharing his wisdom, wealth of resources, and compelling disaster photographs for publication. Terry has my enduring admiration and thanks for his contributions on disaster response, editorial reviews, and most notably, his distinctive pen and ink renderings used throughout the book. I appreciate the support of Frank D. Musica, Esq., Risk Management Attorney, and Paul V. Riccardi, Publications Specialist, Victor O. Schinnerer & Company, Inc., Chevy Chase, Maryland, who generously allowed adaptation and use of their material from *Schinnerer's Guidelines for Improving Practice*, concerning liability and emergency response.

Chapter 14: Lobby Security Design: First Impressions, by Casey L. Jones. I'm deeply grateful to Caroline Alderson for introducing me to Casey, who skillfully marshaled the cooperation of many talented firms, architects, and designers for use of their work in this chapter, and obtained GSA's permission to adapt material from *Design Notebook for Federal Building Lobby Security*, published by the U.S. GSA and the U.S. Marshals Service. My thanks to Frances Halsband, FAIA, Principal, R.M. Kliment & Frances Halsband Architects, New York, New York, whose firm developed the *Design Notebook* under contract to GSA, and granted use of the firm's photography; and Yetsuh Frank, RA (formerly with the same firm), Project Architect, Beyer Blinder Belle Architects & Planners LLP, New York, New York, who was helpful in organizing the many images. Additional thanks go to the firms and photographers whose work appears in this chapter, through GSA's permission, and especially to those who patiently worked with me to secure photography rights and provide images for the following projects: U.S. Courthouse, Covington, Kentucky—Newby Walters, Director of Business Development, Sherman Carter Barnhart, Lexington, Kentucky; Alfonse M. D'Amato U.S. Federal Courthouse, Islip, New York—Richard Meier, FAIA, Partner; Elizabeth Lee, Communications Coordinator; and Lisetta Koe, Director of Communications and Business Development, Richard Meier & Partners, Architects, New York, New York; Lloyd D. George U.S. Courthouse, Las Vegas, Nevada—Robert L. Newsom, FAIA, Principal, Cannon Design, Los Angeles, California. Special thanks to Katie Meyer, former Marketing Assistant, Cannon Design, Grand Island, New York, and Cynthia J. Hilliers, Director of Communications, Cannon Design, Grand Island, New York, for their timely assistance. Thomas F. Eagleton U.S. Courthouse, St. Louis, Missouri—Barbara Cronn, Senior Associate, HOK, St. Louis, Missouri, promptly coordinated images.

Chapter 15: Museum and Cultural Facility Security, by Arthur Rosenblatt, FAIA. My thanks to Arthur's partners at RKK&G Museum and Cultural Facilities Consultants, Inc., New York, New York, for supporting his contributions to the book.

Chapter 16: Perimeter Security: The Aesthetics of Protection, by Deborah Bershad and Jean Parker Phifer, AIA. I am grateful to Deborah and the Art Commission of the City of New York for the use of material adapted from their publication, *Designing for Security: Using Art and Design to Improve Security*, prepared in partnership with the Design Trust for Public Space.

Chapter 17: Religious Institutions and Community Centers, by The Anti-Defamation League. My heartfelt thanks to Myrna Shinbaum, Director, Media Relations & Public Information and Abraham H. Foxman, National Director, The Anti-Defamation League, New York, New York, for leading me to the chapter ghostwriters, Steven C. Sheinberg, Coordinator, Security Awareness Programs, Special Assistant to the National Director, The Anti-Defamation League, New York, New York, and Morris S. Casuto, Regional Director, The Anti-Defamation League, San Diego, California, who adapted their material, with permission, from ADL's *Keeping Your Jewish Institution Safe*.

Chapter 18: Research Facilities: Security Planning, by Regis Gaughan, PE, Joseph Calabrese, PE, and Stanley Stark, AIA. My sincere thanks to Leevi Kiil, FAIA, Chairman and CEO, HLW International LLP, New York, New York, who generously committed the firm as a contributor; Victoria Lewko, Account Manager, CarryOn Communication, Inc., New York, New York, who was always very responsive and a pleasure to work with; and contributor Stan Stark, AIA, who graciously allowed publication of his wonderful pen and wash drawings.

Chapter 19: Retail Security Design, by Jeffrey J. Gunning, AIA, and Lance K. Josal, AIA. I'm grateful to Harold Adams, FAIA, RIBA, JIA, and to Lily Thayer, for her diligent efforts in coordinating all RTKL contributing authors, graphic materials, and everyone who assisted in Chapters 2 and 19.

Chapter 20: School Security: Designing Safe Learning Environments, by Thomas Blurock, AIA. My thanks to Jennifer Schamberger, Marketing and Public Relations Manager, Thomas Blurock Architects, Costa Mesa, California, for her assistance in coordinating images.

Chapter 21: Women's Health Centers: Workplace Safety and Security, by Barbara A. Nadel, FAIA. A special thank you is owed to Anne Fougeron, AIA, Principal, Fougeron Architecture, San Francisco, California, for providing me with her Planned Parenthood Golden Gate projects, through Elizabeth Kubany, President, Kubany Communications, Maplewood, New Jersey, at the suggestion of Charles Linn, FAIA, Managing Senior Editor, *Architectural Record,* in New York. Dian J. Harrison, MSW, President and CEO, and Therese Wilson, Vice President, External Affairs, Planned Parenthood Golden Gate, San Francisco, California shared insights on operating health facilities, and granted permission to adapt their *Security Reference Guide* checklists. As a result, the International Archive of Women in Architecture (IAWA) awarded *Building Security: Handbook for Architectural Planning and Design* the 2003 Milka Bliznakov Prize Commendation, six months prior to publication, on the basis of advocating transparent, enhanced security for women's facilities and other buildings. My thanks to the jurors, especially Donna Dunay, AIA, Chair, Milka Bliznakov Prize, IAWA, and Professor in Architecture, and Marcia F. Feuerstein Ph. D., AIA, Chair, Board of Advisors, IAWA, and Associate Professor in Architecture, Virginia Tech, College of Architecture and Urban Studies, Blacksburg, Virginia, for bestowing this honor.

PART 3   ENGINEERING

Chapter 22: Protective Design of Structures, by Richard L. Tomasetti, PE, and John Abruzzo, PE. My thanks to those at The Thornton-Tomasetti Group, Inc. who assisted Richard and John in preparing their chapter.

Chapter 23: Mechanical, Electrical, and Fire Protection Design, by Andrew Hlushko, PE. I'm grateful to Norman Kurtz, PE, Chairman, Flack + Kurtz Inc., New York, New York, for providing the firm's support; Michelle Brady, former Administrative Assistant, and John Gerney, CADD Operations, Flack + Kurtz Inc., for their assistance in preparing the text and graphics.

Chapter 24: Chemical & Biological Protection, by Michael C. Janus, PE, and William K. Blewett. Sincere thanks go to the many people from Battelle Memorial Institute's Engineering Applications and Operations in Aberdeen, Maryland who generously assisted Mike and Bill in writing, reviewing and preparing their chapter.

PART 4   CONSTRUCTION

Chapter 25: Construction Cost Estimating for Security-Related Projects, by Elizabeth J. Heider, AIA. I'm grateful to those at Skanska USA Building Inc., and all those who supported Beth's contribution to the book.

Chapter 26: Construction: Emergency Response Lessons Learned From September 11, 2001, by Lewis J. Mintzer. My thanks to John D. Onnembo, Jr., Esq., Senior Vice President and General Counsel, AMEC Construction Management Inc., New York, New York, for granting permission to adapt material from *Lessons Learned: Emergency Responses to the World Trade Center and the Pentagon Attacks,* which Lewis originally authored; Josh Ofrane, former Marketing Coordinator, AMEC Construction Management Inc., for organizing AMEC's unforgettable photographs taken at both sites; Mitch Becker, former President and CEO, AMEC Construction Management Inc., New York, New York; Jake Bliek, Vice President, and Ed Brundage, Vice President Business Development, AMEC Construction Management Inc., both in Chantilly, Virginia, for assisting in the firm's contribution.

PART 5   TECHNOLOGY AND MATERIALS

Chapter 27: Security Technology, by William G. Sewell, RCDD. I am most grateful for the prompt and valued assistance from Lyna Shirley, Marketing and Business Manager, DMJM Technology, and Timothy O'Leary, Marketing Coordinator, DMJM Technology, Arlington, Virginia, for assisting Bill on preparation of text and images.

Chapter 28: Selecting and Specifying Security Technology Products: A Primer for Building Owners and Facility Managers, by Francis J. Sheridan, AIA. My thanks to Jane Carrara, Executive Assistant, New York State Department of Correctional Services, Division of Facilities Planning and Development, Albany, New York, who was tremendously helpful in preparing this chapter; and to Frank Sheridan, AIA for allowing publication of his wonderful pen and ink drawings.

Chapter 29: Glazing and Security Glass Applications, by F. John W. Bush, Sue Steinberg, and Catherine Kaliniak. I'm grateful to Peter Fillmore, President, and Moty Emek, Chief Technology Officer, Oldcastle-Arpal, LLC, Arlington, Virginia, for their support and contributions to this chapter.

PART 6   CODES AND LIABILITY

Chapter 30: Codes, Standards, and Guidelines for Security Planning and Design, by Walter "Skip" Adams, CPP, and Deborah A. Somers. I'm grateful to Joseph C. Razza, PE, Sako/Rolf Jensen & Associates, Inc., New York, New York, for recommending Skip and Deb as contributors, and to their colleagues who reviewed the chapter.

Chapter 31: Liability Exposure after September 11, 2001, by Michael S. Zetlin, Esq., and Noelle Lilien, Esq. A special debt of thanks goes to those at the firm who supported Michael and Noelle's efforts for this chapter, and especially to Ray Mellon, Esq., Partner; Michael Zetlin, Esq., Partner; and Michael De Chiara, Esq., Partner, Zetlin & De Chiara LLP, New York, New York, for their unwavering encouragement, guidance, and industry leadership.

My sincere appreciation to the friends and colleagues who assisted me in seeking grants: Harold Adams, FAIA, RIBA, JIA; John D. Anderson, FAIA, Senior Vice President, Anderson Mason Dale Architects, Denver, Colorado; Derek Bradford, AIA, RIBA, ASLA, Professor of Architecture, The Rhode Island School of Design, Providence, Rhode Island; Michael Crosbie RA, Ph.D., Senior Associate, Steven Winter Associates, Norwalk, Connecticut; Robert Ivy, FAIA, Vice President, Editor in Chief, *Architectural Record*, New York, New York; Jan Hird Pokorny FAIA, Principal, Jan Hird Pokorny Associates, Inc., New York, New York; James Stewart Polshek, FAIA, Senior Partner, Polshek Partnership Architects; Susan Strauss, Director of Communications, Polshek Partnership Architects, New York, New York; Mary Six Rupert, Program Officer and grant sponsor, New York Foundation for the Arts, New York, New York; the quintessential Queenser, Michael Schenkler, Publisher, Editor In Chief, *The Queens Tribune*, Fresh Meadows, New York; Linda Searle, FAIA, Principal, Searle & Associates, Chicago, Illinois; and Andrea Woodner, Co-Executive Director, Design Trust for Public Space, Inc., New York, New York. Special thanks to Bob Ivy and Mike Schenkler for providing me with many opportunities to write for their outstanding publications, and learn the art of magazine and newspaper journalism.

I am fortunate to have a wide national network of remarkably talented friends and gifted colleagues who have so generously offered encouragement and inspiration in ways they do not know. Among the many people at the American Institute of Architects in Washington, D.C. who have been invaluable friends and resources over the years, several deserve special mention. As a result of their seemingly routine activities, they provided this book with print and broadcast media exposure, early and often, long before the finish line or the final product was in sight, gestures always appreciated by a first time author. They include: Charles Hamlin, Hon. AIA, former Team Vice President, AIA Advocacy, for his insight on media, and mastery of print and broadcast advertising; and Tricia Chamblerlain Boone, Director, Media Relations, for interviews with the Wall Street Journal, WSJ Radio, the St. Louis Post-Dispatch, and others which lead to even more opportunities. As a result of the St. Louis Post-Dispatch interview, William Marler, CEI, CSI, Architectural Consultant, NMI

Associates, St. Louis, Missouri provided a generous keynote invitation in St. Louis. Other pre-publication opportunities came from Phil Simon, Managing Director, Marketing and Promotion; Anieca Lord, Project Manager, for her work with TISP; and Allison Clifford, Manager, Meetings and Exhibits, for a WSJ Radio interview with Ron Kilgore. All were generous in alerting me to media and industry outreach opportunities I would not otherwise have had. Brenda J. Henderson, Hon. AIA, Managing Director, Component Affairs, and Ray Rhinehart, Hon. AIA, Senior Director, Special Projects, The American Institute of Architects, Washington, D.C., provided many quotable words of wisdom, some of which appear in these pages.

During my five years of service and leadership on the American Institute of Architects Board of Directors, I gained a national perspective, through the many people I met and worked with, about what architects and the public want, and need, to create safe, secure, attractive, and eminently livable communities. To all those I (unintentionally) omit, be assured the debt I owe you is felt, even if not noted here. Those who provided insight, spirited encouragement and kind words during the process of writing this book include: 2001 AIA President John D. Anderson, FAIA (and his wife, Flodie); 2003 AIA President, Thompson E. Penney, FAIA (and his wife, Gretchen Penney, AIA), President and CEO, LS3P Associates, Ltd., Charleston, South Carolina; 2004 AIA President Eugene Hopkins, FAIA (and his wife, Jane), Senior Vice President, Group Director, Smith Group, Detroit, Michigan; 2005 AIA President/2001 Vice President, Douglas L. Steidl, FAIA (and his wife, Sue), Principal, Braun & Steidl Architects, Inc., Akron, Ohio; 2001 AIA Vice President Terrance J. Brown, FAIA (and his wife, Sandy), Albuquerque, New Mexico; 2002 AIA Vice President, Ed Kodet, FAIA (and his wife, Jan), Principal, Kodet Architectural Group, Ltd., Minneapolis, Minnesota; 2003 AIA Vice President Kate Schwennsen, FAIA, Associate Dean/Associate Professor, College of Design, Iowa State University, Ames, Iowa; my longtime friend, 2003 AIA New England Regional Director, Scott Simpson, FAIA, President and CEO, The Stubbins Associates, Cambridge, Massachusetts; 2001–2002 AIA National Secretary, Stephan Castellanos, FAIA (and his wife, Linda Derivi, AIA), California State Architect, Valley Springs, California; 2002–2003 AIA Public Director Barry Z. Posner, Ph.D., Dean and Professor of Leadership, Santa Clara University, Santa Clara, California; internationally renowned designer and educator, Antoine Predock, FAIA, Principal; Regina Harris, Managing Senior Associate, Antoine Predock Architect, Albuquerque, New Mexico; and Angel Saqui, FAIA (and his wife, Charo), Principal, Angel C. Saqui, FAIA, Architects, Planners, Interiors, Coral Gables, Florida.

A special recognition goes to: members of the 2000, 2001 and 2003 board classes (and spouses) that I served with, as 2000 and 2003 AIA New York Regional Director, and 2001 AIA Vice President; Norman L. Koonce, FAIA (and his wife, Sue), Executive Vice President/Chief Executive Officer; James Dinegar, Chief Operating Officer, The American Institute of Architects, Washington, D.C.; Rick Bell, FAIA, Executive Director, AIA New York Chapter; Stephen Suggs, Hon. AIA NYS, Deputy Director, AIA New York Chapter; and 2006 AIA New York Regional Director George H. Miller, FAIA, Managing Partner, Pei Cobb Freed & Partners, New York, New York for their continued encouragement and support.

Several leading national public figures in Congress and law enforcement provided early inspiration about the need for building security. My heartfelt appreciation to the following for their kind words: in Congress, sincere thanks to Congresswoman Nita Lowey, House Representative from Westchester (and formerly Queens), New York, Washington, D.C.; Pat Keegan, District Director, Congresswoman Nita Lowey's Office, White Plains, New York; Elizabeth Stanley, Communications Director, Congresswoman Nita Lowey's Office, Washington, D.C.; Congressman Anthony Weiner, House Representative from Queens and Brooklyn, New York, Washington, D.C.; and Anson Kaye, Communications Director, Congressman Anthony Wiener's Office, Washington, D.C.

I'm honored to have the encouragement of three current and former New York Police Commissioners, who serve on the front lines of making America, and the world, more secure. My deepest thanks to: Raymond W. Kelly, Commissioner, New York City Police Department, New York, New York; Paul Browne, Deputy Commissioner for Public Information, New York Police Department, New York, New York; Daniel S. Wilson, Senior Director, Federal Affairs, The American Institute of Architects, Washington, D.C; Judy Chesser, Director, City of New York Washington Office, Washington, D.C.; Bernard B. Kerik, CEO, Giuliani-Kerik LLC (and former Commissioner,

New York Police Department), New York, New York; Joslyn King, Executive/Personal Assistant, Giuliani-Kerik LLC, New York, New York; Sunny Mindel, Director of Communications, Giuliani Partners LLC, New York, New York; William J. Bratton, Chief of Police, Los Angeles Police Department (and former Commissioner, New York Police Department), Los Angeles, California; Mary E. Grady, Public Information Director, Los Angeles Police Department, Los Angeles, California; and Kristi Sandoval, Police Officer, Public Information Office, Los Angeles Police Department, Los Angeles, California.

Which brings me to those directly associated with the inception and production of this book. Cary Sullivan, my editor at McGraw-Hill Professional, New York, New York, supported this effort in innumerable ways, from inviting me to write the book, to her patience and ability to negotiate an extended schedule. David Fogarty, Editing Manager, consistently improved the text, and Lynn M. Grimes, MLS, LYNG, Inc., Bedford, Texas, provided indexing services on short notice.

Sincere thanks as well to those at McGraw Hill Construction in New York not previously noted, especially James H. McGraw IV, Group Publisher, Norbert W. Young, Jr., FAIA President; Deborah Smikle-Davis, Director, Marketing and Communications; and all the talented editors and managers I've been privileged to work with, and write for, at *Architectural Record* and *Engineering News Record* over the past decade. Those opportunities, in large part, prepared me for writing and editing this book. Thank you all.

I'm indebted to the many friends, family members, contributors, colleagues and clients who provided continued support and inspiration, and became accustomed to my extended absences and delays. Those not already mentioned include my dear friends Warren G. Nadel, Project Administrator, New York City Department of Correction, New York, New York; Sarelle T. Weisberg, FAIA, Principal, Sarelle Weisberg Architect, New York, New York; Bruce D. Eisenberg, AIA; Ann LoMonte, Hon. AIA NYS (and her family), Executive Director, AIA Long Island, Mineola, New York; 2004 AIA New York Regional Director Orlando T. Maione, AIA, Chief Architect, Hospital Architectural Services, Stony Brook University Hospital, Stony Brook, New York; 2005 AIA National Associate Director Jeremy S. Edmunds, Assoc. AIA, Design Consultant, NYC Design Solutions, New York, New York; James T. Martino, AIA, Principal, James Thomas Martino Architect PC, Port Washington, New York; my neighbors, Carol, and Ida Lippman, Shirley Schindler, Yvonne Acriche, of Spectrym, and my aunt, Beatrice Friedman, R.N. of Los Angeles, California.

Finally, these efforts would not have been possible without the wisdom and loving encouragement of my parents, Ruth and George, and my late brother, Bruce. Their unwavering support inspired me to follow my dreams, and reach for the sun, the moon, and the stars.

BARBARA A. NADEL, FAIA
Queens, New York

ABOUT THE EDITOR

BARBARA A. NADEL, FAIA, principal of Barbara Nadel Architect, specializes in planning and design of justice, healthcare, and institutional facilities. As an accomplished practitioner and journalist, Ms. Nadel's work on design, security, technology, and business has appeared in over 100 publications, including *Architectural Record, Engineering News Record,* and *Time Saver Standards for Building Types.* She has been interviewed and quoted in many publications and media outlets, including *The New York Times,* Fox News Channel, *The Wall Street Journal, Newsday, La Libre Belgique,* and others.

Well known in the architecture, design, and construction industry, Ms. Nadel was national 2001 Vice President of the American Institute of Architects, served twice on the national AIA Board of Directors, chaired the AIA Advertising Committee (responsible for creating a multimillion dollar print and radio advertising campaign), and chaired the AIA Committee on Architecture for Justice. She has received honor awards for outstanding leadership, service, and impact on the architectural profession.

Ms. Nadel is a graduate of the Rhode Island School of Design (Bachelor of Architecture, Bachelor of Fine Arts) and the State University of New York at Binghamton (Bachelor of Arts, Pre-Architecture). She has taught design and is a frequent guest lecturer and design award juror.

BUILDING SECURITY

P·A·R·T · 1

ACHIEVING TRANSPARENT SECURITY

CHAPTER 1
LESSONS LEARNED FROM SEPTEMBER 11, 2001, AND OTHER BENCHMARK EVENTS

Barbara A. Nadel, FAIA
Principal, Barbara Nadel Architect
Forest Hills, New York

Those who cannot remember the past are condemned to repeat it.
GEORGE SANTAYANA (1863–1952)
Spanish philosopher

The only thing we have to fear is fear itself - nameless, unreasoning, unjustified terror which paralyzes needed efforts to convert retreat into advance.
FRANKLIN D. ROOSEVELT (1882–1945)
32nd U.S. President, during his first inaugural speech, 1933

In 1933, President Roosevelt told the world that only by confronting the biggest challenges head-on could they be defeated. Years later, twenty-first century global communities, linked electronically and through air travel, challenge free societies to resist threats to freedom and attacks on personal safety. The events of September 11, 2001, changed the way Americans and global citizens go about their daily routines, from entering an office building or attending a popular sporting event to visiting a national landmark or arriving at an airport. Increased terrorist threat levels have focused greater attention on defeating these threats head-on, by successfully integrating design, aesthetics, and public safety throughout the built environment.

Building security is based on identifying threats and vulnerabilities in order to determine the most appropriate methods of protecting people, buildings, assets, and ongoing operations. The primary goals of security are preventing or mitigating damage from terrorism, crime, and disaster, so that communities can maintain the flow of commerce and continue the rhythm of daily life. Reconciling these realities is often difficult. However, until global terrorism and natural disasters cease to pose threats to free societies and the built environment, building security will remain an important public concern.

SEPTEMBER 11, 2001

We shape our buildings; thereafter they shape us.
SIR WINSTON CHURCHILL (1874–1965)
BRITISH LEADER

On the morning of September 11, 2001, four hijacked airliners on different flight paths crashed into three buildings: the Twin Towers at New York City's World Trade Center (Fig. 1.1) and the Pentagon in Washington, D.C. (Figs. 26.1 to 26.6). The fourth plane, reportedly bound for the U.S. Capitol or the White House in Washington, D.C., crashed into a field in Shanksville, Pennsylvania. Approximately 3000 civilians at three sites were killed in those highly coordinated terrorist attacks. The events of that clear September morning changed history, indelibly altering U.S. public policy, homeland security, and building design (Table 1.1).

FIGURE 1.1 World Trade Center towers on September 11, 2001, at 9:05 a.m., looking south from 6th Avenue and Washington Place, New York, N.Y. (*Architect: Minoru Yamasaki with Emory Roth and Sons; photographer: Bruce D. Eisenberg, AIA.*)

TABLE 1.1 **September 11, 2001, Timeline of Events**

8:45 a.m.	Plane crashes into the North Tower of the World Trade Center (WTC), tearing a deep gash in the building and setting it afire.
9:03 a.m.	Second hijacked airliner crashes into the South Tower of the WTC, and explodes.
9:21 a.m.	All New York area airports, bridges, and tunnels are closed.
9:43 a.m.	Third plane crashes into the Pentagon; immediate evacuation begins.
10:05 a.m.	South Tower of WTC collapses.
10:10 a.m.	Portion of the Pentagon collapses; a plane crashes in a field outside Shanksville, Pennsylvania.
10:13 a.m.	United Nations New York headquarters evacuates 11,700 people (Fig. 1.2).
10:28 a.m.	North Tower of WTC collapses.
10:45 a.m.	All federal buildings in Washington, D.C., are evacuated.
4:10 p.m.	Seven WTC, a 47-story building, and others in the area are reported on fire.
5:20 p.m.	Seven WTC collapses, from damage to WTC across the street.

Source:www.cnn.com

This book is dedicated to the memory of all those who died from terrorism, by advancing the knowledge needed to prevent similar events from recurring. Over 100 multidisciplinary experts from across the United States have generously shared their knowledge about security in the post-9/11 built environment. The information is set forth in 31 chapters, organized in six sections: Achieving Transparent Security, Planning and Design, Engineering, Construction, Technology and Materials, and Codes and Liability. This chapter includes a summary of each area of expertise and lessons learned from benchmark events.

BALANCING SECURITY AND OPENNESS IN A FREE SOCIETY

U.S. Senator Daniel Patrick Moynihan began a national conversation about terrorism on March 25, 1999, at the U.S. General Services Administration (GSA) Design Awards, when he challenged the design community and the public "to keep our nerve in the face of obvious but scarcely overwhelming threat." As a lifelong champion of architecture and design excellence in the civic realm, Senator Moynihan's call for balancing security and openness in public buildings, to represent the values of a democratic society, was significant, particularly at a time and place when concrete barriers were the most visible and pervasive forms of building security in Washington, D.C. Years earlier, on the night of November 7, 1983, he recalled, a bomb exploded in the U.S. Capitol, in the hallway outside the Senate Chamber. Had the Senate been in session, a massacre would have occurred, but no one was hurt. Upon arriving at the scene the next morning, Senator Moynihan said, "They can blow up the building. But they cannot blow up the democracy."

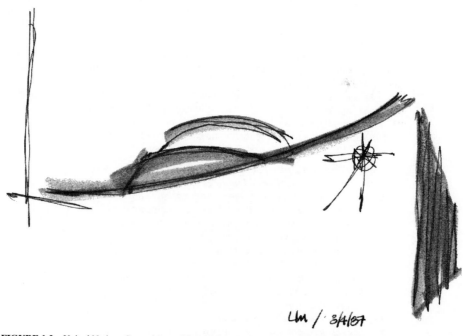

FIGURE 1.2   United Nations General Assembly Building, New York, New York. The graceful open-ended form, visible from the street and the East River, presents a courageous, simple, forthright face to the world. (*Architects: Le Corbusier, Wallace K. Harrison, Sven Markelius, 1950; pen and wash drawing by Stanley Stark, AIA.*)

*Architecture is inescapably a political art, and it reports faith-
fully for ages to come what the political values of a particular
age were. Surely ours must be openness and fearlessness in
the face of those who hide in the darkness. Precaution, yes.
Sequester, no. There is a risk to such a conversation. Call for
more openness, and the next day there may be a new atrocity.
But more is at stake than personal reputation. The reputation
of democratic government is at stake.*

DANIEL PATRICK MOYNIHAN (1927–2003)
*U.S. Senator from New York
"Resolved: A National Conversation on
Terrorism Is in Order," March 25, 1999.*

*The Guiding Principles for Federal Architecture
1. Producing facilities that reflect the dignity, enterprise,
   vigor, and stability of the federal government
2. Avoiding an official style
3. Incorporating the work of living artists in public buildings*

JOHN F. KENNEDY (1917–1963)
*35th U.S. President, proclaimed the
Guiding Principles, authored by Sen.
Daniel Patrick Moynihan, a member of the
Kennedy administration, on May 23, 1962.*

The *Guiding Principles for Federal Architecture* included a section, "The Redevelopment of Pennsylvania Avenue," calling for the revitalizing of Washington, D.C.'s grand axis (Fig. 1.3). President Kennedy proposed a thoroughfare that would be "lively, friendly and inviting, as well as dignified and impressive." Yet even in the 1960s, shortly after the Cuban missile crisis and the threat of nuclear war, a leaked internal draft document alleged that security in federal buildings was inadequate, and proposed that the buildings be closed to the public. During the 1960s, Washington, D.C., was an open city, and only the president and vice president received Secret Service protection. By the mid-1990s, after terrorist events in the United States and internationally, squad cars, armed officers, and concrete Jersey barriers routinely surrounded many federal buildings in Washington, D.C., and across the country.

Edward A. Feiner, FAIA, Chief Architect of the U.S. General Services Administration (GSA), the largest landlord, builder, and design client in the United States, has led the agency in advancing the Guiding Principles of Architecture, while promoting design excellence and implementing stringent security guidelines at federal courthouses and office buildings.

*Public policy must strike an appropriate balance between
security and openness. Public buildings must remain part of
the public domain. They must represent the positive attributes
of our democracy and our culture. They must welcome the
American people to their governmental institutions and provide services in an environment that enhances mutual respect.
Most importantly, public buildings are handed down from generation to generation. We should not convey to future citizens
of this nation, or the world, that ours was a society obsessed
with fear and that our government had to be cloaked in
secrecy and physically protected from its people. In the end,
the symbols of our institutions, cultural and governmental, are
a lasting testimony of our times. They also create our times.*

EDWARD A. FEINER, FAIA
*Chief Architect, U.S. General
Services Administration*

FIGURE 1.3 Federal Triangle and Old Post Office along Pennsylvania Avenue, Washington, D.C. (*Pen and ink drawing: Terrance J. Brown, FAIA.*)

With dangerous threats facing a global society, the need to balance security with openness, prudence, common sense, and preparation is crucial. Those responsible for public safety have a moral, professional, and legal obligation to remain cognizant of ways to ensure the greatest degree of security within the built environment. Highly effective security can be transparent or invisible to the public eye. Building security does not mean building bunkers or converting cities and national monuments into fortresses surrounded by concrete Jersey barriers.

Terrorist tactics have ranged from truck bombs, biochemical hazards, snipers, explosives, small missiles, and suicide bombers, to weapons of mass destruction and using civilian aircraft aimed at prominent buildings and locations. As the opportunities and means for inflicting damage upon civilians and military installations increase around the world, security design, technology, surveillance, data collection, and operational policies become more sophisticated and noticeable within environments unaccustomed to constant monitoring.

Disaster Planning and Emergency Preparedness

In many communities, terrorism may not appear to be, or is often not considered to be, the primary threat to public safety. However, the 1995 bombing of Oklahoma City's Alfred P. Murrah Federal Building illustrated that America's heartland, far from major cities, is not immune to acts of terrorism perpetrated by those seeking to inflict damage upon civilians. Natural disasters, such as hurricanes, floods, tsunamis, tornadoes, wildfires, and earthquakes, also present life-threatening situations. Regardless of the threat, emergency preparedness, through disaster planning, response, and recovery, should be an integral part of every home and business.

BUILDING SECURITY THEORY AND PRACTICE

Three concepts are important when developing effective building security programs:

1. *Learn from the past.* Previous acts of terrorism, violence, and disasters are instructive because they point out what happens due to lack of preparedness, when risks are not fully considered or addressed. During the twentieth century, most building codes and standards did not anticipate the range or likelihood of terrorist threats, or the magnitude of destruction from natural disasters. The examination of what happened and why brings about important changes to building codes and industry standards, thereby improving public health, safety, and welfare, and preventing loss of life.

2. *Integrate design, technology, and operations.* Building owners and project teams determine security requirements by conducting a risk assessment and vulnerability analysis. This information is used to establish priorities and solutions for protecting sites and facilities. The most successful security programs integrate good design and appropriate technology with building operational policies and emergency procedures.

3. *Plan and design transparent security.* Security need not be obtrusive, obvious, or restrictive to be effective. Installing concrete barriers in front of buildings may discourage vehicular bomb threats, but will not necessarily ensure greater security within buildings unless other elements are addressed. Transparent security, not visible to the public eye, can be achieved through informed planning, design, and facility operations.

ACHIEVING TRANSPARENT SECURITY

Designing for security presents architects and engineers with a new set of infrastructure challenges. Physical barriers and visible protective elements for buildings and sites have long been familiar, striving to maintain the philosophy of openness and welcoming, particularly critical to public sector structures. As technological security solutions are developed, the need to identify and address their requirements in the earliest planning stages confirms what we have learned from expanding communications and infrastructures. Retrofitting is so complex, costly and disruptive that specialized professionals are necessary from the outset.
SARELLE T. WEISBERG, FAIA
New York architect

Lessons Learned from September 11, 2001, and Other Benchmark Events

The analysis of circumstances surrounding significant, or benchmark, events forms a knowledge base to inform design professionals, building owners, public officials, and managers about how to build and maintain safer, more secure buildings. The lessons learned from domestic and international incidents provide best practices that are useful during policy and budgeting decisions aimed at prevention or response to terrorism and disasters (Tables 1.2 and 1.3).

World Trade Center, 2001

As of 2004, 2749 people were known to have died at the World Trade Center on 9/11. The planning, design, and construction decisions made in the mid-1960s, some 35 years before the Twin Towers fell, contributed to how both buildings collapsed after being hit by planes full of jet fuel. The design

TABLE 1.2   Notable Incidents of International Terrorism

Israeli Olympian athletes killed by terrorists, Munich, Germany	September 5, 1972
U.S. Embassy bombing, Beirut, Lebanon	April 18, 1983
U.S. Marine barracks bombing, Beirut, Lebanon	October 23, 1983
Pan Am 103 bombing, Lockerbee, Scotland	December 21, 1988
World Trade Center bombing, New York City	February 26, 1993
Sarin gas in Tokyo subway system, Tokyo, Japan	March 20, 1995
Khobar Towers bombing, Dhahran, Saudi Arabia	June 26, 1996
U.S. Embassy bombings in Kenya and Tanzania	August 7, 1998
USS Cole bombing, Yemen	October 12, 2000
Terrorist attacks on the World Trade Center, New York City, and the Pentagon, Washington, D.C.	September 11, 2001

TABLE 1.3   Notable Incidents of Terrorism, Violence, and Disasters within the United States

U.S. Capitol explosion near Senate Chamber, Washington, D.C.	November 7, 1983
Hurricane Andrew, South Florida and Louisiana	August 1992
World Trade Center bombing, New York City	February 26, 1993
Alfred P. Murrah Federal Building bombing, Oklahoma City	April 19, 1995
Olympic Park bombing, Atlanta, Georgia	July 27, 1996
Abortion clinic bombing, Birmingham, Alabama	January 27, 1997
Shooting of ob-gyn Dr. Barnett Slepian, Amherst, New York	October 23, 1998
Columbine High School shootings, Littleton, Colorado	April 20, 1999
Cerro Grande, New Mexico, wildfires	May 2000
Terrorist attacks on World Trade Center, Pentagon	September 11, 2001
Anthrax mailings, New York and Washington, D.C.	September 2001
Snipers, Washington, D.C., area	October 2002
Power blackout in six northeastern states and Canada	August 14, 2003
Southern California wildfires	Oct.-Nov. 2003

determined the available means of egress used by first responders and building occupants to evacuate the buildings. Significantly, both towers remained standing for at least an hour after impact, allowing thousands of people to evacuate the buildings and survive. This was a marked improvement from the 1993 World Trade Center bombing, when 50,000 people evacuated the towers in three to four hours. After that event, additional life safety features were installed, and building evacuation drills were practiced every six months.

Acts of terrorism, violence, and disasters, globally and in the United States, have provided design professionals with technical data about why buildings fail, and how to make them safer. These events serve as building performance case studies, for use in establishing building security requirements and disaster planning activities. Among the most significant events before 9/11 were bombings at the World Trade Center, in Oklahoma City, and at the Khobar Towers.

World Trade Center Bombing, 1993

In February 1993, eight years before the Twin Towers collapsed, a truck bomb exploded on the second underground level of the World Trade Center's parking garage. The blast produced a 150-foot-wide crater, five floors deep in the parking basement, killing six people and injuring more than a thousand.

The explosion ruptured two main sewage lines from both towers and water mains from the air conditioning system. Over two million gallons of water and sewage were pumped out of the area. Initial assessments determined that the structural integrity of the North Tower needed prompt attention. Several biological and material safety hazards put responders and rescue teams at risk: raw sewage from ruptured pipes, asbestos, mineral wool (a level 2 carcinogen), acid and gasoline from vehicles, small fires caused by short circuits, falling chunks of concrete, and sharp metal fragments from the building and the blast. The explosion also destroyed the underground chiller plant and backup emergency generator system. Primary and secondary systems were colocated underground, adjacent to each other, not remotely.

Lessons from WTC: Disaster Planning and Evacuation Practice Drills.   The 1993 bombing caused the original building owner at the time, the Port Authority of New York and New Jersey, to change all the evacuation procedures, so as to guarantee that more people would exit the building faster. Changes included adding loudspeakers, emergency lights, intercom systems, reflector exit lighting, and practice drills every six months. Because of this disaster planning response, many building occupants were able to exit from the towers within an hour after the planes hit on 9/11.

Lessons from WTC: Underground Parking and Emergency Generator Locations.   Public underground parking should not be located near critical building systems, emergency generators, or gas meters. After the 1993 bombing, WTC underground parking was limited to prescreened tenants and preauthorized deliveries at designated access points. Visitor, employee, and vehicular entry checkpoints were established, and all required identification. Locating emergency systems above grade, or on upper building floors, will avoid flood damage, but should a fire occur on upper floors, extinguishing the fire may be very difficult. Redundant building systems should be considered when possible in the event of an emergency or blast. Fire sprinklers should not branch off from main water supply lines where they might be vulnerable to failure in the event of an accident or explosion. Water mains and pumps should be plumbed so that if a break occurs in the main, water can reach the pumps by an alternate means.

Khobar Towers Bombing, 1996

In June 1996, a terrorist truck bomb explosion at the Khobar Towers, an American military installation in Dhahran, Saudi Arabia, caused 19 deaths and hundreds of injuries. According to an unclassified government report, Mylar window film was scheduled to be installed at the complex, but had been delayed because a commander believed the threats were not high enough to warrant immediate installation, and the fence barrier, combined with the building setback, would be adequate to mitigate damage from an explosion. Evacuation plans and warning systems had not been practiced, posing a security breach. Due to host nation concerns about noise from the complex, the building lacked a fire alarm and siren alert system, which made the building noncompliant with U.S. Air Force standards. The report estimated that flying glass shards from the blast caused up to 90 percent of the fatalities.

Lessons from Khobar Towers: Blast-Resistant Glazing Systems and Preparedness.   This incident raised awareness about the value of installing security window film, combined with laminated glass, to reduce fatalities in the event of a blast, especially for retrofits and existing buildings. Shatter-resistant window film can reduce injuries by holding glass pieces intact after they are broken, and preventing them from becoming lethal projectiles. Following applicable life safety regulations, building codes, and emergency preparedness procedures improves the chances that building occupants will survive and evacuate a building after a terrorist attack.

Oklahoma City Bombing, 1995

In April 1995, a truck bomb exploded in front of the Alfred P. Murrah Federal Building, killing 168 people and injuring hundreds of others. Shortly thereafter, the U.S. General Services Administration coordinated development of security guidelines for hardening buildings against blasts and other terrorist threats. The guidelines, *Vulnerability Assessment of Federal Facilities,* also known as *The Marshals Report,* were issued in June 1995. The findings resulted in a thorough evaluation of security measures for all federal buildings, and provided the initial road map for securing and classifying risks at over 1300 federal facilities owned or leased by the federal government. The guidelines contained in the report provided the basis for subsequent security measures and programs implemented by the federal government and other entities seeking security design standards.

Lessons from OKC: Security and Blast-Resistant Design.   The Oklahoma City bombing marked the beginning of a national, industrywide approach to security planning and building design to combat terrorism. Technical evaluation and research focused on several architectural, engineering, and landscape design elements, including site planning and access; vehicular circulation; standoff distance, which refers to building setbacks that mitigate truck bomb damage; hardening of building exteriors to increase blast resistance; glazing systems to reduce flying glass shards and fatalities; and structural engineering design to prevent progressive collapse.

Security Master Planning (Chapter 2)

Security master planning addresses the fundamental concepts of building security and is the basis for developing detailed security plans for every building project. This preliminary planning phase identifies threats, vulnerabilities, and recommendations to protect people, buildings, and assets.

In response to terrorist attacks, the U.S. government developed criteria to assess security risks and design responses at federal facilities (Fig. 1.4). David V. Thompson, AIA, Vice President, and Bill McCarthy, AIA, Associate Vice President, of RTKL Associates, Inc., examine how public agencies and private-sector organizations can adapt the federal guidelines and risk analysis process to other projects. Site planning, blast, architectural and engineering design, security personnel, staff training, and emergency planning are addressed, along with mitigation strategies and security solutions.

FIGURE 1.4 U.S. Capitol dome, Washington, D.C. (*Architects: William Thornton, Benjamin Henry Latrobe, and Charles Bulfinch, 1793-1829; pen and ink drawing: Terrance J. Brown, FAIA.*)

Crime Prevention through Environmental Design (Chapter 3)

In 1961, Jane Jacobs's classic, *The Death and Life of Great American Cities,* explored the correlation between safe, mixed-use, busy neighborhoods, and urban spaces designed with opportunities for residents to observe street activities. Ten years later, crime prevention through environmental design (CPTED) was defined as a technique to reduce fear and crime by promoting surveillance and safe neighborhoods (Fig. 1.5).

Terri Kelly, Community Outreach and Support Director of the National Crime Prevention Council (NCPC), describes how community-based CPTED partnerships increase the quality of life through good design. CPTED principles provide low-tech design solutions that have been adapted by many communities, and embraced around the world as effective strategies for solving neighborhood crime problems.

Lessons from CPTED Principles. The need for crime reduction, access control, surveillance, and territorial reinforcement is common to all building types and communities. Use of CPTED during early planning phases can result in long-term capital savings, through reduced neighborhood crime and maintenance costs, and greater operational efficiency.

PLANNING AND DESIGN

A day spent without the sight or sound of beauty, the contemplation of mystery, or the search for truth and perfection is a poverty-stricken day; and a succession of such days is fatal to human life.

LEWIS MUMFORD (1895–1990)
*U.S. urban planner, writer, and
architectural critic*

FIGURE 1.5 Old house, 1764, in historic neighborhood, Georgetown, Washington, D.C. (*Pen and ink drawing: Francis J. Sheridan, AIA.*)

Arenas, Sports Facilities, Convention Centers, Performing Arts Facilities (Chapter 4)

On September 5, 1972, at the Olympics in Munich, Germany, Palestinian terrorists entered the Olympic Village, killed two Israeli team members and later murdered nine other hostages. This act of terrorism illustrates the need for security at high-profile sports events. Before 9/11, most sports facilities had various internal security measures in place, tailored to the types of events and patrons anticipated, such as controlling the substances brought into a facility. Major league football and baseball events focused on in-house security to protect athletes and VIP attendees (Fig. 1.6).

Lessons from 9/11: Event Planning.   Large public assembly venues that accommodate thousands of people are considered terrorist targets. The magnitude and costs stemming from the potential loss of life, damage, and liability prompted members of the International Association of Assembly Managers (IAAM) to develop security guidelines for venue operational policies and design requirements. Russ Simons, Principal, and Gerald Anderson, AIA, Senior Principal, with HOK Sport + Venue + Event, discuss these guidelines, outlining how assembly managers and design teams can perform risk assessments and vulnerability analysis for their facilities. Security standards developed with federal agencies call for securing facilities from the outside in, and address screening and control of people and objects.

The U.S. Department of Homeland Security created a classification system to monitor domestic and international threat levels at special events, such as the Olympics. A National Security Special Event (NSSE) designation enables facility managers and federal and local law enforcement to assess risks and threats, and modify design and security operations accordingly. Law enforcement coordination is integral to major event planning and implementation.

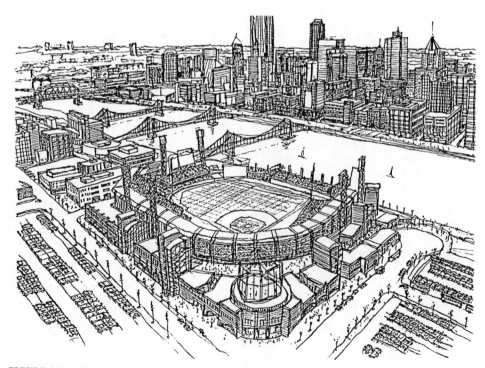

FIGURE 1.6   PNC Park, Pittsburgh, Pennsylvania. (*Architect: HOK Sports + Venue + Event; pen and ink drawing: Francis J. Sheridan, AIA.*)

Site and building security is subject to greater attention for large venues, and typically addresses perimeter site access, parking, and vehicular circulation policies; confirming and screening all deliveries; and prohibiting deliveries on event days. Building design issues include monitoring truck dock access; providing adequate public access, screening, and queuing areas to accommodate metal detectors; and rerouting underground building utilities away from loading docks and entries, in case of an explosion.

Commercial High-Rise Egress Systems (Chapter 5)

Since 9/11 and the collapse of the World Trade Center towers, few building types have received greater scrutiny for life safety and security improvements than commercial high-rises and related egress, or exiting, systems. Detailed design and engineering studies by public and private groups analyzed the factors that contributed to the challenges faced by first responders and occupants during evacuation before the buildings collapsed. In September 2003, the New York City Building Department and the New York City Task Force on Building Codes, composed of experts from government, and the design, construction, and real estate professions, issued a series of building design recommendations. Input was received from victims' families, World Trade Center attack survivors, academia, and special needs groups.

Carl Galioto, FAIA, Partner and Manager of the Technical Group at Skidmore, Owings & Merrill LLP, and a member of the task force, explains how to plan and design post-9/11 safety enhancements in a typical high-rise tower. Among the first new high-rise buildings to implement the building code recommendations will be Seven World Trade Center, replacing the building destroyed on 9/11, scheduled for late 2006 completion (Fig. 1.7).

FIGURE 1.7 Seven World Trade Center, New York, New York. (*Architect: Skidmore, Owings & Merrill. Image courtesy of Silverstein Properties, Inc., and Skidmore, Owings & Merrill. Rendering: Advanced Media Design.*)

Lessons from 9/11: Egress Systems. When completed, Seven WTC will include the following safety enhancements, developed in response to the events of 9/11: designed to prevent progressive collapse; reinforced concrete core; medium-density fireproofing; central fire-rated corridor; wider exit stairs; interconnected exit stairs; photoluminescent egress markings; battery-powered, low-level egress lights; internal antennae; and outside air filtration. Seven WTC will be a LEED- (Leadership in Energy and Environmental Design) certified high-rise building.

Lessons from 9/11: Building Codes Selected New York City Task Force on Building Code recommendations for high-rise construction include:[*]

1. Enhancing robustness and resistance to progressive collapse.

2. Prohibiting the use of open web bar trusses in new commercial high-rise construction.

3. Encouraging the use of impact-resistant materials in the construction of stair and elevator shaft enclosures.

4. Encouraging the inclusion of more stairwells or wider stairwells in buildings, as wide as 66 inches, to allow better building occupant exit flow.

5. Prohibiting the use of scissors stairs in high-rise commercial buildings with a floor plate of over 10,000 square feet.

6. Improving the marking of the egress path, doors, and stairs with photoluminescent materials and retrofitting existing exit signs with either battery or generator backup power.

[*]Sources: Zetlin & De Chiara, LLP; Carl Galioto, FAIA, Skidmore, Owings & Merrill.

7. Requiring controlled inspection to ensure that fireproofing is fully intact on all structural building members exposed by subsequent renovations to ensure continued compliance with applicable code requirements.

8. Requiring all high-rise commercial buildings over 100 feet without automatic sprinkler protection to install a sprinkler system throughout the building within 15 years.

9. Enhancing fire department emergency response communications in high-rise commercial buildings.

10. Requiring air intakes in all new construction to be located at least 20 feet above grade and away from exhaust discharges or off-street loading bays.

Courthouse Security (Chapter 6)

As symbols of government and icons of democracy, courthouses have always had a need for enhanced security. Courthouse violence can occur where prominent individuals are accessible to the public, or from internal threats within family or civil courts. Kenneth J. Jandura, AIA, Justice Principal with DMJM Design, and David R. Campbell, PE, Associate Principal with DMJM Technology, describe how separate circulation zones and entries eliminate security breaches for public, private, secure, and service areas. Distinct, monitored access points for judges and law enforcement personnel transporting defendants prevent the public from observing those entering and leaving the courthouse. During high-profile trials, anonymity is essential to jurors and witnesses, requiring alternative circulation routes.

Lessons from 9/11: Increased Security.   Federal courthouses are subject to federal security criteria, especially regarding site perimeters, restricted vehicular access, setbacks, which include hardened building exteriors, blast-resistant walls and windows; and prevention of progressive collapse. After 9/11, most state governments issued mandates for counties to implement screening and other security measures. These increased costs, during a period of declining revenues, have forced counties to allocate resources from other budget items to pay for security, posing a challenge for many jurisdictions.

Federally Owned or Leased Office Buildings (Chapter 7)

Federal building security guidelines, developed for use at federal facilities, may be applied to facilities owned and operated by state and local governments and privately owned buildings renting space to federal agencies and federal contractors requiring security clearance. Terry Leach, AIA, Senior Security Specialist with DMJM, reviews the design criteria, building systems, and performance levels required to meet federal building security standards.

Lessons from OKC: Security Design.   The Oklahoma City bombing resulted in security design criteria at federal facilities that focus on entry points; guard services and posts; parking; employee and visitor access; doors; walls, windows, and other openings; and lighting. Three protection levels—low and medium/low, medium, and higher protection—describe the characteristics and performance levels associated with each condition.

Lessons from 9/11: Technology.   Electronic security systems should be integrated through a security management system, enabling all subsystems to communicate with each other. System components include security management, intrusion detection, access control, closed-circuit television, video imaging and identification, communications, and intercoms.

Health Care Security (Chapter 8)

As first responders to disasters, health care facilities and providers must be prepared to treat those needing prompt attention. Hospitals and health care facilities have traditionally addressed security regarding infant abduction, crime, workplace violence, narcotics storage, and protection of dementia patients. After 9/11, providers added terrorism and biochemical warfare emergency preparedness criteria. Thomas M. Jung, RA, Director of the Bureau of Architectural and Engineering Planning, Division of Health Facilities Planning with the New York State Department of Health, describes how health care planning, regional response strategies, and decontamination facility design prepare health care facilities for terrorism, emergencies, mass casualties, and chemical, biological, and radiological attacks.

Lessons from 9/11: Hospital Response.   The New York University (NYU) Downtown Hospital received the first wave of victims on 9/11, injured rescue workers, and those seeking refuge. The facility is located a few blocks from ground zero, and was affected by debris, dust, loss of utilities, and security restrictions. The hospital's emergency response is a case study for medical facilities and personnel affected by a terrorist attack, as follows:

1. *Prepare for regional disaster response.* Many injured people escaped Manhattan and sought medical care at 97 hospitals, mostly in the metropolitan New York area, and as far away as Canada. All hospitals within the region of a major disaster should prepare to treat the injured and communicate with law enforcement agencies to determine needs and resources.

2. *Use compatible communications technology and equipment.* After 9/11, cellular communications and telephone lines throughout New York City were interrupted and unreliable. Police and fire department radios were incompatible, which complicated information sharing. Communications technology and equipment must be tested to ensure reliability and compatibility within and among public agencies, health care facilities, cities, areas, and regions.

3. *Communicate with rescue services and security checkpoints.* Police and National Guard troops at security checkpoints delayed delivery of vital fuel for the NYU Downtown Hospital's emergency generators, and off-duty staff recalled to duty had difficulty in clearing the same checkpoints. Communications among law enforcement and health facility personnel must be maintained on reliable, secure equipment and lines.

4. *Manage volunteers and credentialed professionals.* Many unaffiliated medical and nursing personnel converged upon the hospital to volunteer. Without any way of verifying credentials, volunteers required oversight by known, qualified medical and nursing staff. A database of credentialed staff should be maintained by public and private entities within a facility and health care system on a regional basis and through professional organizations.

5. *Maintain emergency generators.* The hospital's rooftop generators had to be constantly cleaned of dust and debris and gauges and indicators physically monitored on a 24-hour basis. Emergency generator locations should allow routine monitoring and protection from damage, whether underground or on rooftops.

6. *Maintain adequate medical supplies for mass casualties and injuries.* After 9/11, the hospital's supply of medical equipment, portable oxygen tanks, and paper goods used to treat victims was very low. Metropolitan hospitals must anticipate a large patient influx at once, types of emergency supplies required, and plan for storage and access on demand.

7. *Filter recirculated air to isolate interiors.* The hospital was forced to initiate a complete shutdown of the heating, ventilating, and air conditioning (HVAC) system to isolate the interior environment from outside contamination. If recirculated air is adequately filtered, health care services should be able to continue operations, subject to the buildup of carbon dioxide, which should be monitored. HVAC design should examine controlling extreme conditions of outdoor dust and debris.

8. *Ascertain presence of special needs populations near a disaster.* The loss of utilities and elevator service after the attacks was a hardship at the high-rise senior residence adjacent to the hospital. Staff provided meals and primary medical care to this dependent population for some time. Health care facilities should know their neighbors in the community and work with outreach groups to provide assistance.

9. *Prepare for extended post-disaster recovery time.* Long after 9/11, New York City area hospitals provided mental health services to survivors and rescue workers, especially for post-traumatic stress disorder and physical disabilities. Even after treating disaster victims, a high level of readiness and ongoing services may need to be maintained, to care for rescue personnel injured in the response and recovery efforts. Staffing plans must consider an extended response.

Lessons from 2003 Blackout: Disaster Planning.   During the August 2003 power outage that affected the northeastern United States and Canada, some problems occurred within health care facilities, primarily due to inadequate fuel for generators and equipment breakdowns. The post-9/11 attention to disaster planning minimized the impact at New York State hospitals and nursing homes. Hospitals and nursing homes reviewed the need for upgrades and repairs; extended emergency power and adequate capacity for anticipated demands; maintained minimum fuel levels; reviewed regional impact to area hospitals; and ensured that the emergency circuits support communication systems.

Historic Preservation Guidance for Security Design (Chapter 9)

Maintaining the unique character and features of historic structures is a challenging, costly hurdle to overcome during security retrofits. Successfully integrating new security features into existing buildings requires careful planning and attention to historic details, materials, spaces, and context. Balancing these diverse needs, while protecting occupants and operations within historic structures, is an ongoing concern.

Sharon C. Park, FAIA, Chief, Technical Preservation Services, National Park Service of the U.S. Department of the Interior, and Caroline R. Alderson, Program Manager, Center for Historic Buildings, U.S. General Services Administration, describe how successful approaches to security design for historic buildings have been achieved at federal buildings and landmarks. Established preservation standards and guidelines, along with methods for preventing and managing natural disasters at heritage sites, are a sound starting point for planning security improvements at historic properties (Fig 1.8).

Lessons after 9/11: Historic Properties.   The destruction of the World Trade Center and portions of the Pentagon, a registered National Historic Landmark, heightened awareness about the vulnerability of America's cultural icons and heritage properties, as follows:

1. *Document historic buildings and store copies off-site.* Several important landmark buildings were extensively documented using photo laser scanning, which an experienced team can usually accomplish within a week. Even buildings not of landmark status should be documented photographically with as much detail as possible for potential replacement of all or parts of the damaged building or artwork. Documents should be updated periodically and a copy kept off-site, along with other copies of drawings and photographs.

2. *Use tall, open spaces as smoke evacuation chambers.* When New York City's historic Tweed Courthouse, near City Hall, was completely renovated in the late 1990s, the historic rotunda was designated as a smoke evacuation chamber. This was useful on 9/11, as smoke engulfed Lower Manhattan. The rotunda's design features and fire shutters maintained building indoor air quality during evacuation. Mechanical vents should be closed to stop smoke from coming inside when heating and ventilating systems are shut down during evacuation.

3. *Reduce glass fragmentation casualties with blast-resistant windows, shades, and wall liners.* At the Pentagon, injury to employees occupying renovated areas was greatly reduced by blast-resistant windows and a proprietary fabric lining that had been installed under the new wall surfaces to prevent fragmentation. Reinforced columns remained in place and office

FIGURE 1.8 Clock tower at historic Independence Hall, where the Declaration of Independence was signed, Philadelphia, Pennsylvania. (*Pen and ink drawing: Terrance J. Brown, FAIA.*)

walls hardened in the renovations completed prior to 9/11, including areas immediately adjoining the area of impact, held for 35 minutes prior to collapsing, allowing employees time to vacate the building. Collapsing ceilings and fixtures caused most injuries.

Hospitality Facility Security (Chapter 10)

Hospitality properties, from hotels, motels, and casinos to conference centers and resorts, are designed to be open and welcoming to guests, visitors, and the public (Fig. 1.9). For these same reasons, they are vulnerable to crime, terrorism, and violence. Facility managers and owners must balance the need for security and make visitors and guests feel comfortable and safe.

Bradley D. Schulz, AIA, principal of KGA Architecture, observes that gaming properties must protect their operating license and meet strict requirements to ensure that the license is not jeopardized. Slot machines and gaming tables move large sums of money through the facility at all hours, and require closed circuit television (CCTV) and at least two employees during servicing and counting. Predictable routines make money more vulnerable to theft, and movement should occur at different times on different days.

Lessons from 9/11: Employee Background Checks.   After 9/11, terrorism became a major concern among hotel and gaming property owners, who often have a workforce of several thousand people, and a high turnover rate. Once considered a minor issue, background checks of five to ten years are conducted for many workplaces, as employees could be tied to terrorism, employee pilferage, and theft from guests.

FIGURE 1.9   Renaissance Vinoy Resort, St. Petersburg, Florida. (*Pen and ink drawing: Terrance J. Brown, FAIA.*)

Multifamily Housing (Chapter 11)

After 9/11, Lower Manhattan's Battery Park City and other residential properties near ground zero remained closed to tenants for months, forcing residents to find other places to live. Federal agency warnings later identified apartments as possible soft targets or potential terrorist staging grounds, causing landlords, real estate professionals, and apartment management executives to review property operating and security procedures. James W. Harris, former Vice President, Property Management, of the National Multi Housing Council/National Apartment Association Joint Legislative Program (NMHC/NAA JLP) developed operating guidelines as an industry resource.

Lessons from 9/11: Property Management.   Multifamily housing owners and real estate professionals should remain aware of activities by monitoring internal reporting, resident communications, unit inspections, contractors and employees, resident applicant verification, cooperation with law enforcement, and security for common, public, and community spaces (Fig. 1.10).

Home and Business Security, Disaster Planning, Response, and Recovery (Chapter 12)

Disaster planning and emergency preparedness are necessary activities for every home, workplace, and public facility (Fig. 1.11). Home and business security addresses various threats, from burglaries, terrorism, and power outages to natural disasters capable of leveling communities, such as floods, hurricanes, tornadoes, and wildfires. To avert personal and economic losses, disaster planning is best begun long before a crisis occurs, enabling individuals and business owners to recover and rebound quickly. Ongoing planning items should include reviewing insurance policies, life safety and building code compliance, and adequacy of safe room shelters, communications, evacuation plans, and emergency supplies.

Barbara A. Nadel, FAIA, explains how home and business security results from integrating design with disaster preparation, response, and recovery activities. Design professionals must under-

FIGURE 1.10 Multifamily housing complex (proposed), El Paso, Texas. (*Pen and ink drawing: Terrance J. Brown, FAIA.*)

FIGURE 1.11 Brick residence, Albuquerque, New Mexico. (*Pen and ink drawing: Terrance J. Brown, FAIA.*)

stand the scope of work and risks involved when volunteering professional services. Disaster planning experts Charles F. Harper, FAIA, Principal of Harper Perkins Architects, and Terrance J. Brown, FAIA, Senior Architect with ASCG, Inc., provide disaster response and recovery strategies for floods, hurricanes, tornadoes, and wildfires. Frank Musica, Esq., Risk Management Attorney, and Paul V. Riccardi, Publications Specialist with Victor O. Schinnerer & Company, Inc., provide information on professional liability, insurance coverage, emergency response, and managing a crisis through effective public relations for design and construction professionals, building owners, and public officials responsible for building security.

Lessons from 9/11: Records Protection. After 9/11, residents and businesses in Lower Manhattan were forced to evacuate their premises and relocate for months before being allowed to return to their buildings. Many lost all records and files and had to recreate information through clients, customers, and consultants, if duplicates did not exist. Backing up records and data, and off-site storage, expedite business continuity after a disaster.

Lessons from 2003 Blackout: Communications. The August 2003 power outage affected over 50 million people across 9300 square miles in six northeastern states and parts of Canada, leaving many without power for two days or more. Hard-wired, corded phones maintain phone service without electricity, when cell phones do not work. Homes and businesses should prepare for outages of 48 hours or longer, and maintain emergency supplies.

Lessons from Disaster Response: Providing Volunteer Services. Design professionals who volunteer after an emergency should be aware of potential liability. Many states lack volunteer protection acts, or Good Samaritan laws, affording immunity to licensed professionals who provide services during an emergency. Some professional liability policies may cover an insured firm in a volunteer capacity in the same way the firm would be covered when providing services for a fee. Firms should check professional liability coverage and state laws regarding volunteer services. Professional societies can advocate for Good Samaritan laws in state legislatures before disasters occur, to facilitate rapid emergency response when needed, protect the public health, safety, and welfare, and minimize liability risks to architects and engineers.

Lessons from 2000 New Mexico and 2003 California Wildfires.   Devastating wildfires caused billions of dollars in damages and destroyed thousands of homes, businesses, and buildings. Architects, homeowners, building officials, and insurers in fire-prone areas must be familiar with applicable codes, design criteria, and fire-resistant materials when rebuilding structures. The scale and duration of the fires emphasized the need for disaster and recovery planning.

Lessons from 1997 Great Plains Flood.   Rising tides from blizzards and spring floods inundated river valleys in Minnesota and the Dakotas, setting 100-year flood records, and devastating small, rural communities. Flooding disrupted water, sewage, and electrical services; blocked transportation routes; and caused power outages and evacuation of over 50,000 people. Protecting potable water supplies and sanitary systems was easier for communities with existing disaster plans. During recovery, the Midwest Assistance Program prepared a Flood Emergency Action Procedures (FEAP) manual, outlining tasks for flood preparation during fall of the previous year. The FEAP should be updated regularly to reflect infrastructure improvements, flood protection, equipment, emergency contacts, hazardous materials, and evacuation plans.

Industrial Facilities and Office Buildings: Safety, Security, Site Selection, and Workplace Violence (Chapter 13)

Security at industrial facilities, manufacturing plants, offices, and civic facilities relies on protecting people and assets, continuing operations, and preventing litigation. During the site selection process, building owners should review local crime statistics, adjacent land use, and liability concerns from relocation incentive programs. Integrating facility planning, design, and security policies will contribute to worker safety at site and building entries on large campuses, high-rises, and well-lit parking areas (Fig. 1.12).

Since the 1990s, workplace violence by employees and domestic partners has caused many employers to develop security procedures to protect against violence, industrial espionage, theft, and terrorism. Industrial employers are often concerned about threats from downsizing, layoffs, outsourcing, restructuring, striking workers, and replacing employees with temporary workers. Barbara A. Nadel, FAIA, describes how workplace safety can be improved by implementing crime prevention through environmental design principles, including layering security levels inward from site perimeters to building interiors, and communicating security procedures to all employees so they know what to do during a crisis or emergency.

Lessons from 2003 Blackout: Review Egress and Life Safety Systems.   During the blackout, many commercial buildings were dark and exit paths were not always apparent, especially where emergency power did not cover all building zones. Employers and facility managers should review all life safety codes and ensure that emergency generators and building egress systems are functional.

Lessons from 2003 City Hall Shooting: Security Screening Policy.   After 9/11, security screening was installed in most New York City government and high-rise buildings. In July 2003, a city councilman brought a visitor to City Hall. Despite high security and law enforcement presence, the visitor entered City Hall carrying a concealed handgun because by prior agreement, elected officials and guests were exempt from going through metal detectors. Shortly after arrival, the visitor used his concealed handgun to kill the councilman. A police officer in the council chamber immediately shot and killed the visitor. Until the facts were determined and terrorism ruled out, Manhattan mass transit networks were closed, causing great disruption. The policy was changed, requiring that everyone who entered City Hall go through metal detectors, with the goal of preventing future incidents.

FIGURE 1.12 Skyline, Chicago, Illinois. (*Pen and ink drawing: Terrance J. Brown, FAIA.*)

Lobby Security Design: First Impressions (Chapter 14)

Regardless of building type and function, lobbies provide visitors with their first impressions of an organization and facility (Fig. 1.13). Federal building lobbies are the initial line of defense against terrorism and violence directed at the government, federal employees, and the public. Although security screening stations have been installed in federal courthouses since the mid-1980s, screening stations in many federal office buildings were hastily pieced together to provide added security after the 1995 Oklahoma City bombing. Equipment and furniture in federal facilities were often haphazardly arranged to fit within a variety of vestibules and lobby configurations. This effort provided building security, but frequently looked chaotic.

GSA instituted the First Impressions program in 1998 to ensure that all federal facilities presented a positive first impression to those entering the building, conveying professionalism, conscientiousness, and security. Ten case studies of federal courthouses across the U.S., selected by Casey L. Jones, GSA's Director of the First Impressions Program, illustrate best practices of how lobby designs for new and renovated buildings ensure that design excellence and security standards are met.

Lessons from Oklahoma City and 9/11: Lobby Design.   Security screening and metal detectors installed within federal facilities after 1995 were enhanced after 9/11. Important design elements to review during lobby design include entrances, separation of entrance and exit paths; adequate queuing space; the free zone, or space between an exterior plaza and secure interior areas; screening station locations, arrangement, and operations; metal detectors and x-ray machines; and the secure area, which starts immediately after visitors pass through the security station.

FIGURE 1.13 The rich interior texture of the Palmer House Hotel lobby creates a welcoming first impression, Chicago, Illinois. (*Pen and ink drawing: Terrance J. Brown, FAIA.*)

Museum and Cultural Facility Security (Chapter 15)

Museums and cultural institutions are more than places to enjoy art; they are high-volume tourist destinations, offering restaurants, retailers, multimedia shows, film screenings, and receptions (Fig. 1.14). With so many scheduled activities, museum professionals are concerned about security of irreplaceable art, artifacts, and public safety during an emergency. Arthur Rosenblatt, FAIA, Principal of RKK&G Museum and Cultural Facilities Consultants, Inc., explains how museums can protect priceless art from theft and intruders with electronic technology to detect changing environmental conditions without compromising building aesthetics.

Lessons from 9/11: Electronic Technology. Twelve types of detectors are commonly used for museum security. Detectors do not protect anything, but identify an activity and issue an alarm to a security control center, which alerts security personnel to respond and investigate.

Perimeter Security: The Aesthetics of Protection (Chapter 16)

Security in the urban landscape can be achieved though innovative use of public art. After the Oklahoma City bombing, in response to vandalism, crime, and terrorism, visible security often consisted of installing concrete Jersey barriers in urban areas with high-risk buildings and landmarks (Fig. 1.15). Cumulatively, perimeter barriers can overwhelm attractive or imposing structures and turn pleasant streetscapes or plazas into oppressive spaces. Deborah Bershad, Executive Director, and Jean Parker Phifer, AIA, former President, of the Art Commission of the City of New York discuss how to successfully integrate perimeter security and urban design elements, through cooperation of city agencies and a Percent for Art Program.

FIGURE 1.14 The Castle, Smithsonian Institute, 1857, twelfth-century Romanesque-style national museum, Washington, D.C. (*Architect: James Renwick, Jr., pen and ink drawing: Terrance J. Brown, FAIA.*)

FIGURE 1.15 Concrete barrier limits vehicles at Federal Plaza, Duane Street, Lower Manhattan, New York. (*Photographer: Mark Ginsberg, AIA.*)

Lessons from 9/11: Integrating Security and Public Art. Bollards or barriers are generally installed near the curb of urban site perimeters. Artists and designers can intersperse bollards with planters, benches, or trees, where clearances allow, to deemphasize security and mitigate the repetition of identical elements. By commissioning artists and sculptors, unique design solutions engineered for security standards have been used effectively as bollards, walls, fences, and gates at many public facilities, including schools, subway stations, and courthouses.

Religious Institutions and Community Centers (Chapter 17)

Religious and community institutions provide social and spiritual services to people of all ages and backgrounds (Fig. 1.16). They are stabilizing influences in communities, operating over long hours, seven days a week, and must be secure and welcoming. Because of the open nature of most religious institutions and the range of employees and the visitors using them, security may be viewed as an affront to the organization's spiritual mission. Valuable religious items, books, documents, and cash are kept within religious facilities and need to be secured. Violent threats against religious groups, facilities, and members require a collaborative security effort.

Steven C. Sheinberg, Coordinator for Security Awareness Programs and Special Assistant to the National Director, and Morris Casuto, Regional Director with the Anti-Defamation League, describe how religious institutions and community centers can implement preventive security planning, design, and operational policies. An overview of indicators and emergency response procedures for car and truck bombs, suicide bombers, and weapons of mass destruction is also included.

FIGURE 1.16 The Franciscan Mission-style Memorial Chapel honors alumni killed in the nation's wars, University of New Mexico, Albuquerque, New Mexico. (*Pen and ink drawing: Terrance J. Brown, FAIA.*)

Lessons from 9/11: Target Hardening. Synagogues and Jewish institutions have long remained vigilant against terrorism, violent threats, explosions, suicide bombers, and vandalism. After 9/11, violence against religious facilities continued around the world, confirming the need for target hardening to discourage attacks. Institutions should not reveal security measures, but should provide clear evidence of security features. Target hardening tactics include visible alarm systems, security patrols, and vehicles; perimeter fencing and lighting; a well-maintained facility appearance; and regular presence of local law enforcement on or near the grounds.

Research Facilities: Security Planning (Chapter 18)

Research facilities must balance several security threats, such as preventing industrial espionage, containing hazards and risks, and keeping proprietary information inside the premises (Fig.1.17). Rapid advances in technology have made laboratories targets for outsiders and foreign governments attempting to acquire intellectual property, bypassing the costs of research and development. Controversy over some forms of research and the use of animals for experiments have led to vandalism by activist groups, primarily to disrupt operations. Research facility experts, Regis Gaughan, P.E., Managing Partner; Joseph Calabrese, P.E., former Principal; and Stanley Stark, AIA, Managing Partner of HLW International, LLP, address how to secure research facilities, create safe workplaces, and control access to hazardous functions through design and technology.

Lessons from 9/11: Airborne Contamination of Building Systems. Since 9/11, the federal government and scientific and technical communities have proposed or adopted heightened security measures for research facilities. In January 2002, the American Society of Heating Refrigeration and Air Conditioning Engineers (ASHRAE) issued a report, *Risk Management Guidance for Health and Safety under Extraordinary Incidents*, in response to terrorism and anthrax contamination. Findings

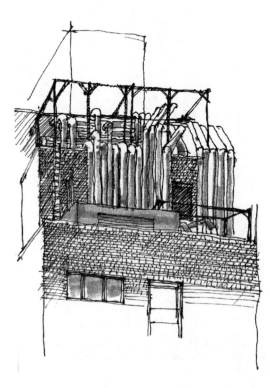

FIGURE 1.17 Biomedical research building infrastructure, Arnold and Marie Schwartz International Hall of Science, Memorial Sloan-Kettering Hospital, New York, New York. (*Pen and wash drawing: Stanley Stark, AIA.*)

include ways to minimize airborne contamination in building systems through HVAC system design, filtration, and enhanced building egress paths.

Retail Security Design (Chapter 19)

Regional malls, big-box retailers, and large public gathering places are vulnerable to terrorist threats, especially during crowded peak shopping season. Retail destinations must convey openness and hospitality to customers and employees, without making them feel vulnerable to terrorism, property crime, or violence. Terrorism is relatively new to American retailers, but property owners and security directors in Northern Ireland, Israel, and other countries have dealt with terrorism for decades. The majority of threats against retail facilities will likely remain traditional property or personal crimes, such as assault, criminal activities, robbery, theft, vandalism, and violence. Jeffrey J. Gunning, AIA, Vice President, and Lance K. Josal, AIA, Senior Vice President, of RTKL Associates, Inc., explain how to create welcoming and safe environments, while deterring terrorism and crime, through attention to risks, vulnerability, lighting, parking, entrances, technology, and operational security policies.

Lessons from 9/11: Terrorist Threats in Retail Environments.   After 9/11, emerging retail concerns in the United States expanded to include violent threats to intimidate shoppers and disrupt operations, armed raids, bombings, biochemical hazard contamination, shootings, mass violence, and property damage. Effective security strategies include applying CPTED principles and tenant participation to monitor commercial properties.

School Security: Designing Safe Learning Environments (Chapter 20)

The need for school security is illustrated by incidents of violence, guns, teenage street crime, and child abductions. School violence can be reduced through carefully designed grounds, playfields, building exteriors, and interior program spaces, using CPTED principles. Low-tech design strategies, such as site perimeter control, clear sight lines, good lighting, surveillance, landscaping, and low shrubs, will deter graffiti and improve neighborhood quality of life (Fig.1.18).

Thomas Blurock, AIA, Principal of Thomas Blurock Architects, observes that learning is directly related to the size of the school community, with smaller schools of 500 students or fewer providing more learning opportunities and greater security. Interaction improves when students take responsibility for each other, creating a safer learning environment. Thoughtful design of circulation areas, hallways, administration areas, common spaces, classrooms, toilet rooms, and locker rooms further enhances school security, in concert with school operational policies.

Lessons from 1999 Columbine High School Shootings.   Educational professionals consider this violent incident, in which several students and teachers were killed, to be an isolated case of psychological dysfunction. Early intervention by parents, teachers, and peers will prevent some tragedies from happening. Emergency preparedness, district policies, and school procedures should be implemented and shared with parents, students, and personnel.

Lessons from 9/11 and 2003 blackout: School Emergency Management Centers.   Disaster planning for large school systems includes creating emergency management centers to monitor activities and communicate with officials during a crisis. The New York City Department of Education created an emergency management center at the Lower Manhattan headquarters and a satellite facility at another location for crisis management at their 1200 facilities.

Women's Health Centers: Workplace Safety and Security (Chapter 21)

Violence has been a fact of life for women's health centers in the United States since the early 1970s. For years, health centers and clinics have fortified their facilities and operations to protect employees

FIGURE 1.18   Cooper Union for the Advancement of Science and Art, Astor Place, New York, New York. (*Architect: Frederick A. Peterson, 1859; pen and ink drawing: Francis J. Sheridan, AIA.*)

and patients from ongoing threats of violence, arson, firebombs, vandalism, assaults, blockades, death threats, anthrax, bioterrorism, snipers, and from killing health providers and their families. In the 1990s, in Canada and New York, snipers using rifles shot five doctors through a rear glass window or door at their homes. In October 1998, ob-gyn Dr. Barnett Slepian was murdered in his home outside Buffalo, New York. His killer was sentenced in 2003.

Barbara A. Nadel, FAIA, describes how women's health centers can successfully achieve a balance between security and accessibility, despite the challenges posed by groups and individuals. Patients and personnel entering and leaving clinics have been targeted for harassment and injury. The 1994 federal Freedom to Access Clinic Entrances (FACE) Act prohibits clinic violence by providing legal grounds for prosecuting those who threaten clinics and religious facilities. The FACE Act offers the same protection to pro-choice and pro-life crisis centers, abortion clinics, physicians' offices, health clinics, and access to places of worship without harassment. The law established criminal and civil penalties, including prison time and substantial fines.

Lessons from Clinic Violence: Clinic Security.   Nonprofit organizations have developed security design strategies and procedures to protect patients, staff, and daily operations. Dian J. Harrison, MSW, President and CEO, and Therese Wilson, Vice President, External Affairs at Planned Parenthood Golden Gate (PPGG) in San Francisco, California, created a security handbook for employees and volunteers, applicable to any workplace experiencing violent threats. Policies and checklists include staff training on handling incoming mail and suspicious packages, ensuring facility access, and documenting all threats in written reports to be filed with law enforcement agencies. Several PPGG clinics, designed by Anne Fougeron, AIA, of Fougeron Architecture, San Francisco, California, integrate design excellence with transparent and visible security to create welcoming and safe environments.

ENGINEERING

*It is the engineer's responsibility to be aware of social needs
and to decide how the laws of science can be best adapted
through engineering works to fulfill those needs.*

JOHN C. CALHOUN, JR., FASEE
*U.S. petroleum engineer,
Texas A&M University educator*

Protective Design of Structures (Chapter 22)

Notable incidents of terrorism and attacks on American facilities, and the thorough engineering
analysis performed after every event, have typically resulted in improved building performance, with
the goal of enabling a structure to withstand blast, and allow swift, complete building evacuation.
Progressive collapse is an initial local failure that spreads from element to element, eventually resulting
in the collapse of an entire or disproportionately large part of a structure.

Protective design of buildings occurs by integrating various means of mitigating threats and force
protection from blast, fire, ballistic attack, and illegal entry into architectural and engineering design
criteria. Protection is generally achieved through a combination of standoff, redundancy, and hardening. Standoff refers to building setbacks from public streets to mitigate the impact of truck bombs.
Redundancy is necessary for preventing progressive collapse. Hardening and energy absorptive
shields enhance critical structural elements where standoff alone is insufficient to reduce threats to tolerable levels. Each strategy alone can be effective, but the best solution combines all three (Fig. 1.19).
Structural engineers Richard L. Tomasetti, PE, Co-Chairman of The Thornton-Tomasetti Group, and
John Abruzzo, PE, Vice President, LZA Technology and The Thornton-Tomasetti Group, examine protective design and the lessons from three significant events involving damaged and collapsed structures.

FIGURE 1.19   Jacob K. Javits Convention Center structural frame under construction, 1983, New York, New York.
(Architect: I. M. Pei, pen and wash drawing: Stanley Stark, AIA.)

Lessons from Oklahoma City: Influence Area.   The collapse of a substantial part of the Alfred P. Murrah Federal Building showed that progressive collapse must be avoided. The loss of life due to the building collapse far exceeded the loss of life directly attributed to the blast. New designs should incorporate more redundancy to accommodate the loss of a perimeter column.

Lessons from 9/11: World Trade Center Collapse.   Redundant structural systems perform well under duress. The World Trade Center towers remained standing after the initial impact of the aircraft because their highly redundant perimeter tube structure redistributed the load around the damaged areas. The collapse of the towers indicates that other assumptions regarding the interaction of fire and structure need to be considered for future threats. It is generally acknowledged that steel frame buildings with fire protection will endure a building fire because the typical office environment does not provide enough fuel to sustain a fire for the duration needed to cause structural failure. Means of preventing large deliveries of fuel, either from aircraft or storage within the building, must be improved. Much of the spray-on fire protection was abraded from the steel during the aircraft impact and explosion, leaving the steel unprotected. For future terrorist threats, improved fire protection should be considered.

Hardening and increased redundancy of egress routes, emergency equipment, and emergency systems (electrical, mechanical, communication, and sprinkler) will enable a better emergency response. Typically, these systems are protected against fire by fire-rated drywall enclosures. Hardening these enclosures to blast and impact should be considered.

Lessons from 9/11, the Pentagon: Structural Design.   Areas of the Pentagon directly impacted by the aircraft exhibited severe and extensive damage to the columns. The collapse of the floor above was significantly more limited. This has been attributed to three factors: (1) Redundancy of the reinforced concrete floor framing systems in the form of flexural continuity of the beams and girders through the columns, along with the ability of the nonload-bearing exterior wall to carry floor load; (2) Short spans between columns that limit the remaining span should a column be removed; and (3) Spiral reinforcement of the concrete columns that increase the capability of the column to carry axial load after sustaining damage due to blast and impact.

Lessons from Oklahoma City: Brisance.   Brisance, the crushing or shattering effect of a high explosive on brittle materials, accounted for the failure or disappearance of the column closest to the blast at the Murrah Federal Building in Oklahoma City. This column segment was never recovered and is believed to have disintegrated. The dynamic blast pressures at this column were calculated to be well in excess of the compressive strength of the concrete. Because the quantity of the explosive was large, brisance occurred even though the column was nearly 20 feet from the bomb. However, much smaller bombs can produce similar effects when placed nearer to the columns. Increased standoff, a steel jacket, or a blast shield can provide an effective means of mitigating brisance.

Mechanical, Electrical, Fire Protection Design (Chapter 23)

As one of the most essential and transparent security building elements, engineering systems provide many aspects of life safety and security. System responsiveness depends on availability, design, use of appropriate technology, maintenance, and knowledgeable facility staff capable of operating sophisticated building systems. Emergency generators supply power to critical building and life safety systems that must maintain operations during utility power loss, including fire pumps, elevators, smoke management systems, emergency egress lighting, and fire alarm systems. Introducing fresh air through air intake louvers to the ventilation system provides a high level of indoor air quality. Ventilation systems could distribute airborne contaminants, biochemical hazards, and particles to all points throughout a building, posing serious health hazards, and therefore must be planned appropriately.

Andrew Hlushko, PE, Senior Vice President with Flack + Kurtz, discusses the impact of mechanical, engineering, and fire protection systems on building security and the life safety recommendations that arose from the events of 9/11. Fire command centers provide vital information to local fire departments that respond to emergencies. The fire command center is typically colocated with the central security control center at the main building entrance. Should this area become inaccessible due to an external or internal event, the emergency response team may not have access to necessary information.

Lessons from 9/11: Airborne Contamination.   Mechanical isolation of areas with dedicated HVAC systems, such as mailrooms and loading docks, will limit the likelihood of contaminants entering through these semipublic zones and infiltrating entire buildings. Systems serving these spaces should have dedicated air intakes, could be provided with higher ventilation rates, and should not transfer air to other building areas. Additional precautions include protecting air inlets, recording of visitors for future notification of exposure, and filtration only for extreme threats.

Lessons from 9/11: Air Intake Grilles.   Louvers and air intake grilles should be located high above grade level, where they will be inaccessible to those seeking to introduce hazardous materials into building air distribution system. GSA guidelines require louvers to be located at least 40 feet above grade. The New York City Department of Buildings WTC Building Code Task Force recommends locating air intakes in new construction at least 20 feet above grade, and away from exhaust discharges or off-street loading bays.

Lessons from 9/11: Building Information Cards.   The New York City Department of Buildings WTC Building Code Task Force recommended that all high-rise office buildings maintain a building information card, listing vital facility information. The information would be located at the fire command center, readily accessible to the responding fire department. Categories of information include: occupancy, building statistics, elevators, stairways, communications, fire safety, water supply, utilities, temporary considerations, hazardous materials locations, ventilation, and a schematic plan for indicating locations of elevators, mechanical equipment rooms, access stairs, and standpipes.

Chemical and Biological Protection (Chapter 24)

Chemical and biological (CB) terrorism is a challenging threat, due to the high level of uncertainty associated with the problem and the solution. CB agents unleashed in or near buildings, large gatherings of people, or within mass transportation systems are of greatest concern to cities and high-risk targets where small amounts can inflict widespread damage and fatalities. Air, water, food, or surfaces can be used to introduce CB agents and toxic industrial chemicals into building systems.

Michael C. Janus, PE, Manager of Engineering Applications and Operations, and William K. Blewett, Chief Engineer, at Battelle Eastern Science and Technology Center, examine CB building protection, including characteristics of CB agents, protection components affecting building design, and a prototype case study in Salt Lake City, Utah. Integrating building protection systems for chemical-biological hazards involves air filtration, detection, decontamination zones, and airflow management. Design elements affecting protective capabilities against CB agents include air intakes and penetrations; tight building envelope design; mailrooms, lobbies, receiving areas; entry screening areas; vestibules; mechanical rooms, and high-efficiency filter units.

Lessons from 1995 Tokyo Subway Sarin Gas Attack.   During the morning rush of March 20, 1995, members of a religious cult released sarin gas in the Tokyo subway system, killing 12 and hospitalizing over 5000. Sarin gas is a highly toxic nerve agent developed by Nazi scientists in the 1930s, believed to be more toxic than cyanide gas. The incident involved devices disguised as a soft drink can, briefcase, white plastic bag, and gas can wrapped in newspaper, set to go off on five subway cars on three different lines. This was the most serious terrorist attack in Japan's modern history, causing massive disruption and fear in a society with a low crime rate. The attack illustrated how easily a small group with limited means can engage in chemical warfare. Two lessons concerned the absence of decontamination plans or facilities, and lack of disaster planning, emergency response, and practice drills.

1. *Lack of decontamination facilities.* Over 1350 emergency medical technicians (EMTs) were dispatched after the attack, and 135 were secondarily affected. At a hospital, 23 percent of the medical staff complained of symptoms and secondary exposure signs. Had a 100 percent sarin solution been used instead of 30 percent, secondarily exposed EMTs and medical staff would have died. Decontamination facilities and personal protective equipment in the prehospital and hospital settings would have been useful in reducing additional exposure. Hospitals should provide staff with protective equipment and supplies enabling them to treat patients without getting contaminated, estimate the types and amounts of supplies needed to accommodate mass casualties at once, and store these items to allow rapid access on short notice.

2. *Lack of disaster planning.* Japan is a highly structured society, but the attack revealed a lack of coordination and confusion among agencies and organizations. Fire departments, police, metropolitan governments, and hospitals acted independently, without communications. After the attack, the Japanese government developed the Severe Chemical Hazard Response Team. Disaster planning for CB attacks, through interagency coordination and practice drills by all first responders, health care facilities, and public officials, is essential for emergency preparedness.

Lessons from 9/11: Anthrax Letters.   In the fall of 2001, several letters containing anthrax were sent to U.S. senators and the American media, in Washington, D.C., New York City, and Florida. Five people died, and 23 people contracted anthrax from the letters. As a result, many organizations created mailroom policies for package delivery and letter screening. The anthrax contamination of postal buildings and machinery caused widespread service disruption, highlighting the need for CB sensors and facility decontamination procedures.

CONSTRUCTION

> *Engineering is a great profession. There is the fascination of watching a figment of the imagination emerge through the aid of science to a plan on paper. Then it moves to realization in stone or metal or energy. Then it elevates the standard of living and adds to the comforts of life. This is the engineer's high privilege.*
>
> HERBERT HOOVER (1874–1964)
> *31st U.S. President and mining engineer*

Construction Cost Estimating for Security-Related Projects (Chapter 25)

After risk analysis and vulnerability assessments are conducted, and security recommendations are identified, building owners and the project team determine the costs for building security features. For new construction and renovations, identifying security costs should occur during early project phases to maintain budget control. The scope of work and related costs required for each proposed security measure, and an alternative, should be defined and evaluated.

Elizabeth J. Heider, AIA, Vice President, Skanska USA Building Inc., explains how to develop cost estimates for security design elements in new construction, based on the process used for hardening of federal buildings. Critical security elements include standoff distance, site perimeter with vehicular entry, site perimeter surveillance, lobbies; loading docks and mailrooms, progressive collapse; building exteriors and windows; roofing; and mechanical, electrical, fire protection, and life safety systems.

Lessons from 9/11: Cost Estimating   Hardening of buildings, and related security needs, often result in added costs for new construction and retrofit projects. Security-related costs address only the elements needed to secure a building from terrorist threats, as projects must comply with applicable building and life safety codes. A standardized approach to estimating security design elements allows building owners to determine the level of risk they wish to assume and to closely monitor construction costs.

Construction: Emergency Response Lessons Learned from September 11, 2001 (Chapter 26)

Within hours of the collapse of the World Trade Center towers, the City of New York asked AMEC Construction Management Inc. to assist in the demolition and cleanup of the WTC site and the Customs Building (WTC 6). The company mobilized on September 12, 2001, and established a round-the-clock operation to remove site debris.

AMEC had been working at the Pentagon before 9/11 on the renovation and restoration of Wedge One, and was on-site when the plane hit the building. Blast-resistant windows and a steel reinforcing system installed along the exterior wall were credited with saving lives at the time of impact. The company responded to the attack within minutes by rescuing survivors, constructing isolation barriers, installing shoring in portions of impacted areas; supplying debris removal equipment; and establishing an emergency communications system.

Both sites required coordination with hundreds of subcontractors, engineers, police, firefighters, city officials, and federal regulatory, military, and investigative personnel. Lewis J. Mintzer, former AMEC business development director, collected information gathered from employees at both sites and created an in-house emergency response handbook with detailed checklists for use where evacuation, rescue, and demolition are required. Several photographs, taken by AMEC at both sites, illustrate the mass destruction and dangerous conditions faced by construction crews at ground zero and the Pentagon.

Lessons from 9/11 for the Construction Industry   Construction companies, especially those working at government and high-profile sites which may be terrorist targets, should be prepared to provide emergency response services. Like any complex construction or demolition project, emergency response efforts must be carefully planned, scheduled, and managed. Implementing protocols for constant communication and coordination by all parties involved is essential for efficient response. A series of checklists, covering tasks throughout three phases of the response effort, can assist construction managers and project team members in navigating the complex sequence of events: (1) General activities are proactive measures applicable to any emergency response. (2) Immediate emergency response activities apply to the first 48 hours after a catastrophic event, especially for a rescue and recovery mission. (3) Follow-up emergency response activities can occur from 48 hours to two weeks after an event. Each of the three phases addresses scope, scheduling, budget, and cost; project management, resources, and communication; and quality assurance, quality control, and safety.

TECHNOLOGY AND MATERIALS

Where a new invention promises to be useful, it ought to be tried.
THOMAS JEFFERSON (1743–1826)
3rd U.S. President and architect

It is only with the heart that one can see rightly; what is essential is invisible to the eye.
ANTOINE DE SAINT-EXUPERY (1900–1940)
French pilot and poet

Security Technology (Chapter 27)

The best performing security sensor is a human being, but security personnel can be a costly component of facility operations (Fig.1.20). When vulnerabilities, risks, budgets, and security master

FIGURE 1.20   New World management meets Old World security personnel; the Conquistador-in-chief leading his armored executive team. (*Pen and wash drawing by Stanley Stark, AIA.*)

planning solutions are defined, building owners and design teams must determine which security technology applications meet their needs. Technology will deter, detect, delay, and assess an intruder or enemy attack. Sophisticated sensors and monitoring equipment provide continuous coverage, speed, and the ability to detect even the slightest change in an environment. Round-the-clock security patrols represent ongoing operational costs. Technology, coupled with good design allowing clear sightlines and observation capabilities, is a one-time capital investment. In the long term, advanced technology reduces operating costs, increases security coverage, and provides multiple functions and programming capabilities, such as sending alarms when further investigation is needed.

William G. Sewell, RCDD, Senior Vice President at DMJM Technology, describes the characteristics and applications for various types of security technology. These categories include passive and electronic site perimeter fencing; access control methods to deter intruders, biometric technology, to verify identity, revolving door portals, to limit entry access, weapons detection, such as metal detectors used at airports and in lobbies, industrial and transportation applications, to screen for explosive materials; and closed circuit television to record images. Manufacturers have refined and upgraded many types of technology to address terrorism threats, including video processing, detection sensor technology, and computer program monitoring systems.

Lessons from 9/11: Technology   During and after the World Trade Center evacuation, the handheld radio technology used by first responders failed to operate and was incompatible with other systems used in the vicinity. Firefighters and building occupants on upper floors did not know about the events unfolding on the ground and in the adjacent tower. First responders must be adequately trained to react in situations where communications are limited. Emergency response preparedness must include early coordination of equipment, before purchasing new systems. Thorough testing and compatibility of handheld portable radio technology, communication systems within a facility, and hard-line communications to law enforcement and medical response teams are also critical.

Lessons from 9/11: Pentagon Renovations.   On 9/11, smoke was a problem during egress, and exit signs were not visible. Arrow-shaped electro-luminescent floor strips along baseboards leading to exits were installed during renovations. The strips emit a nightglow light and remain on emergency power, like those on aircraft. Other security measures include chemical-biological sensors connected to the control center, highly redundant uninterrupted power service, and two complete communications systems for backup if one stops functioning.

Selecting and Specifying Security Technology Products: A Primer for Building Owners and Facility Managers (Chapter 28)

Owners and facility managers responsible for the purchase and installation of security technology face the daunting task of selecting and specifying products from many available options in the marketplace. Whether for a single building or a multi-site network of facilities seeking to standardize products and operations, managers must be aware that the technology they select may have future life and death implications in an emergency, and improper maintenance or failure to operate properly may result in litigation (Fig.1.21). Organizations will benefit from creating a structured process to identify, evaluate, and recommend appropriate technology products, rather than relying solely on subjective sales pitches by consultants, vendors, and manufacturers. Francis J. Sheridan, AIA, Director, Division of Facilities Planning and Development for the New York State Department of Correctional Services, describes how building owners can evaluate, select, and specify security technology products.

Lessons from the Corrections Industry.   The 1990's prison construction boom prompted development of new security products. Correctional facility administrators have installed sophisticated security products for decades, such as perimeter fencing, motion detectors, electronic locking systems, video monitoring, card access, communications systems, and security glazing. Establishing a product evaluation committee to review and field-test technology and equipment has proved to be cost-effective and oper-

FIGURE 1.21 Octagon Museum, American Architectural Foundation headquarters, Washington, D.C., www.archfoundation.org/octagon. (*Architect: Dr. William Thornton, built 1799-1801; pen and ink drawing: Francis J. Sheridan, AIA.*)

ationally efficient, especially for installations of a single product at multiple sites. Before investing in a technology system, owners should schedule a trial run to evaluate how products perform under heavy use or extreme climate conditions, and review maintenance and staff training agreements.

Glazing and Security Glass Applications (Chapter 29)

Glazing and window systems for all building types are selected based on potential threats and vulnerabilities (Fig. 1.22). The effects of blasts, burglaries, ballistics, hurricanes, and earthquakes can be mitigated with properly designed laminated glass construction, tailored to meet specific needs, such as energy conservation and sound reduction qualities. Blast windows are suitable for buildings considered terrorist targets and other adjacent structures that may also be impacted by the blast. These windows can significantly reduce or eliminate the need for building reinforcement, especially in retrofits, allowing installation to be completed in a short time with minimal disruption.

F. John W. Bush, Director of Laminated Products and Development; Sue Steinberg, Vice President, Corporate Communications, from Oldcastle Glass; and public relations consultant Catherine Kaliniak describe how to select the most appropriate type of laminated glass to protect against threats, while addressing aesthetics, security, and high-performance criteria.

Lessons from Hurricane Andrew, 1992.   Hurricane Andrew caused economic devastation in south Florida. The glazing industry learned that building pressurization following damage to windows and doors was the main cause of failure. Wind-borne debris caused windows to break, allowing high wind pressure to lift off roofs and destroy walls. After thorough testing to meet industry standards, hurricane-resistant glass is now accepted by all model building codes for high wind speed coastal areas.

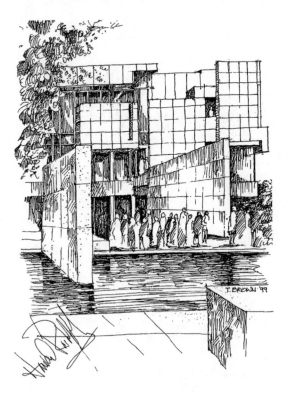

FIGURE 1.22   Rachofsky House, Dallas, Texas. (*Architect: Richard Meier & Partners, Architects; pen and ink drawing, Terrance J. Brown, FAIA.*)

Lessons from Oklahoma City Bombing, 1995.   After the explosion, shock from the blast wave impacted the area around the Murrah Federal Building. Many victims suffered severe cuts and lacerations because flying glass shards were blown out of windows. Use of laminated glass, as a component of blast-resistant glazing design, reduces glass-related injuries and protects building occupants.

CODES AND LIABILITY

Every man owes a part of his time and money to the business or industry in which he is engaged. No man has a moral right to withhold his support from an organization that is striving to improve conditions within his sphere.
      PRESIDENT THEODORE ROOSEVELT (1858–1919)
                                                     26th U.S. President

Codes, Standards, and Guidelines for Security Planning and Design (Chapter 30)

Despite the many nationally and locally accepted codes, standards, and guidelines covering design, construction, and life safety, no single security code exists, applicable to privately owned structures. Federal agencies generally have security design and operational standards, but most state and local government facilities do not. Without any binding codes or mandates addressing security systems in the private sector, building owners must decide on the level of risk they are willing to assume and pay for, and rely on recommendations from consultants and in-house security professionals. Many industry standards and security guidelines are available for adaptation to commercial buildings. Walter Adams, CPP, and Deborah A. Somers, Senior Security Consultants, at Sako & Associates, Inc., provide a survey of available building security industry resources and describe how to create a comprehensive security plan.

Lessons from 9/11: Security Planning.   Security plans mitigate risk and represent a tradeoff between operational freedom and restriction. Building security planning and design standards should be documented, in case proof is required for insurance or liability purposes. Records should be kept off-site from the building being covered.

Lessons from 9/11: Emergency Response Planning.   Emergency preparedness and planning should include worst-case scenarios, such as power outages, circumstances where key people are inaccessible, and building evacuation during life-threatening situations. Employees and tenants should be included in emergency practice drills and encouraged to be alert for unusual packages and surveillance attempts on properties.

Liability Exposure after September 11, 2001 (Chapter 31)

Since 9/11, design professionals have been forced to examine security issues and consider what steps they should take to protect themselves from liability risks. With limited exceptions, governmental entities have not revised building codes, and the courts have not addressed the extent to which the standard of care has evolved since 9/11. Informed design professionals can minimize their liability exposure by understanding sources of potential liability, appreciating how their responsibilities as design professionals may have changed since 9/11, and allocating risk during contract drafting and negotiation (Fig. 1.23).

FIGURE 1.23 New York City skyline, with World Trade Center and Brooklyn Bridge, before 9/11/01. (*Pen and ink drawing: Francis J. Sheridan, AIA.*)

Michael S. Zetlin, Esq., Partner, and Noelle Lilien, Esq., Associate Attorney with Zetlin & De Chiara LLP, identify issues related to security design and liability for design professionals, and provide sample letters to illustrate suggested steps to minimize future litigation risks.

Lessons from 9/11: Good Samaritan Laws. After 9/11, volunteer architects and engineers in and around New York City risked personal safety to help others. These volunteers faced substantial liability exposure because they were personally liable for any claims that may have arisen as a result of their services. As volunteers, they were not covered by their employers' professional liability policies. As of 2004, only 14 of 50 states in the United States provide immunity for volunteer design professionals responding to emergencies. In contrast, most states have enacted Good Samaritan statutes immunizing Certified First Responders, Emergency Medical Technicians (EMTs), and other medical professionals from liability if they render first aid or treatment during an emergency. Design professionals can support enactment of Good Samaritan laws for engineers and architects in their states and jurisdictions.

Lessons from 9/11: Terrorism Insurance Coverage. After 9/11, insurance companies excluded coverage for terrorism acts, rendering such coverage unobtainable or prohibitively expensive. To remedy this situation, the insurance industry and construction trade groups pushed for federal legislation to provide financial assistance from the federal government in the event of another terrorist attack. In November 2002, the Terrorism Risk Insurance Act, or H.R. 3210, was signed into law, providing coverage for catastrophic losses from terrorist attacks. The Act states that the federal government would create a one-year program (with a two-year extension) whereby the government would provide up to $100 billion in loans to the insurance industry to cover losses from future terrorist attacks.

CONCLUSION

> *Millions of men have lived to fight, build palaces and bound-*
> *aries, shape destinies and societies; but the compelling force*
> *of all times has been the force of originality and creation pro-*
> *foundly affecting the roots of human spirit.*
>
> ANSEL ADAMS (1902–1984)
> *U.S. photographer*

The body of knowledge contained in this volume is multidisciplinary and applicable to any number of building types and properties. By learning from the past; integrating design, technology and operations; and planning for transparent security where appropriate, everyone involved with public safety will be better equipped to create secure buildings that enhance the built environment and promote good design.

ACKNOWLEDGMENTS

- Edward A. Feiner, FAIA, Chief Architect, U.S. GSA, Washington, D.C.
- Ray Mellon, Esq., Partner, Zetlin & De Chiara, LLP, New York, New York
- Sarelle T. Weisberg, FAIA, Sarelle Weisberg Architect, New York, New York

Architectural Renderings

- Terrance J. Brown, FAIA, Senior Architect, ASCG, Inc., Albuquerque, New Mexico
- Francis J. Sheridan, AIA, Director, Facilities Planning and Development, New York State Department of Correctional Services, Albany, New York
- Stanley Stark, AIA, Managing Partner, HLW International, LLP, New York, New York

Photographs

- Bruce D. Eisenberg, AIA, Principal, Bruce Eisenberg Architects, New York, New York
- Mark Ginsberg, AIA, Principal, Curtis + Ginsberg Architects LLP, New York, New York

Seven World Trade Center

- Larry Silverstein, President and CEO, Silverstein Properties, Inc., New York, New York
- Carl Galioto, FAIA, Partner, Skidmore, Owings & Merrill, New York, New York
- Ken Lewis, Associate Partner, Skidmore Owings & Merrill, New York, New York

BIBLIOGRAPHY

Air Force, The Inspector General and The Judge Advocate General, *Report of Investigation-The Khobar Towers Bombing*, Conclusion, June 25,1996. www.fas.org/irp/threat/khobar_af/part4.htm

CNN.com/U.S., "September 11: Chronology of Terror," September 12, 2001, www.cnn.com/2001/US/09/11/chronology.attack/

Moynihan, Daniel Patrick, "Resolved: A National Conversation on Terrorism is in Order," March 25, 1999, speech, GSA Design Awards Ceremony, Washington, D.C.

Nadel, Barbara A., "Designing for Security," *Architectural Record*, March 1998, pp.145–148, 196–197.

Okumura, Tetsu; Kouichiro Suzuki; Shinichi Ishimatsu; Nobukatsu Takasu; Chiiho Fuiji; Akitsugu Kohama, Department of Acute Medicine, Kawasaki Medical School Hospital, Kurashiki-City, Okayama, Japan,"Lessons Learned from the Tokyo Subway Sarin Attack," *Journal of Prehospital and Disaster Medicine,* Univ. of Wisconsin, Madison, Wisc., July–Sept. 2000; 15(3):s30. http://pdm.medicine.wisc.edu/Okumura.htm.

Zalud, Bill, "Window Film's Capacity to Protect Glass," *Security Magazine*, June 2002.

INTERNET RESOURCES

American Institute of Architects
www.aia.org

Architectural Record
www.architecturalrecord.com

ArchitectureWeek™
www.architectureweek.com

Engineering News Record
www.enr.com

Great Buildings Collection
www.greatbuildings.com/gbc.html

Jane Jacobs Home Page at the University
of Virginia
Healthy Cities, Urban Theory, and Design:
The Power of Jane Jacobs
www.people.virginia.edu/~plan303

Lower Manhattan Development Corporation
www.renewnyc.com

National Memorial Institute for the
Prevention of Terrorism
www.mipt.org

New York New Visions
www.nynv.aiga.org

September 11, 2001
www.september11news.com

World Trade Center
www.greatbuildings.com/buildings/World_
Trade_Center.html

U.S. Department of Homeland Security
www.ready.gov

CHAPTER 2
SECURITY MASTER PLANNING

David V. Thompson, AIA,
Vice President,RTKL Associates, Inc.
Baltimore, Maryland

Bill McCarthy, AIA,
Associate Vice President,RTKL Associates, Inc.
Baltimore, Maryland

*Make no little plans; they have no magic to stir men's blood
and probably will themselves not be realized. Make big plans;
aim high in hope and work, remembering that a noble, logical
diagram once recorded will not die.*
DANIEL BURNHAM (1846–1912)
Chicago architect

Master planning addresses the future growth and physical character of an environment, while defining the design and functional criteria important to a campus or building. An effective master plan
provides the framework—or in Burnham's words, the logical diagram—for all future design decisions. Building owners and facility managers rely on master planning to meet long-term facility and
operational goals. The most effective master plans result from collaboration among architects, planners,
designers, engineers, construction professionals, and representatives of those who own, occupy, manage, and use a campus or facility. Architectural form, character, image, outdoor spaces, and indoor
environments are among the many criteria explored during site and facility master planning.

Security master planning is based on the same premise, but with a more narrow scope, focusing
primarily on threats and solutions required to protect people, buildings, and assets. The evaluation
criteria include broad, and even global concerns, as well as needs specific to a single building, neighborhood, site, or campus. A security master plan is most successful when balancing safety, function,
and aesthetics.

Two events served as benchmarks for public safety in the United States. Before the 1993 explosion of the World Trade Center, and the 1995 destruction of the Alfred P. Murrah Federal Building in
Oklahoma City, security planning and design was limited primarily to a few building types, such as
government buildings, correctional facilities, and financial institutions. After the Oklahoma City
bombing, building security took on new urgency nationwide, through the ongoing efforts led by the
federal government, public and private sector organizations, and individuals. After the September 11,
2001 attacks on the World Trade Center and the Pentagon, security planning has become an essential
tool for protecting the public in every building type, community, and metropolitan region.

Comprehensive security planning addresses terrorism, biohazards, crime, natural disasters, and
workplace violence. Natural disasters, such as earthquakes, hurricanes, and tornadoes, call for coordination of emergency services and local law enforcement to ensure that long-range public and private sector needs and anticipated responses are in place well before disaster strikes.

The elements discussed in this section were largely developed by the federal government in response to terrorist attacks, particularly on high-risk government installations. As design and construction professionals, building owners, and facility managers gain an understanding of the security planning process, they will be better equipped to consider and apply various strategies and solutions for any threat or potential disaster.

In a free and democratic society, security must be achieved without resorting to a bunker mentality. Balancing security with openness and aesthetics is a fundamental challenge of effective planning and design. Designing for transparent security—invisible to the public eye—is an important goal for building owners, landlords, and public agencies.

By applying widely accepted criteria and solutions for security master planning, building owners and design professionals can significantly enhance public safety and achieve transparent security in every type of building and site.

SECURITY MASTER PLANNING GOALS: PROTECTINGPEOPLE AND PROPERTY

Facility master plans address aesthetics, function, environmental impact, sustainability, codes and design guidelines, and budgets, and cover planning horizons spanning anywhere from one to ten years, often with annual validation of conditions. Security master plans are more specific in nature, and deal with operational and public safety issues (Fig. 2.1 and Tables 2.1 and 2.2). The goals of security master planning are to:

1. Prevent loss of life and minimize injury.
2. Protect critical assets.
3. Prevent loss of operation.
4. Deter criminals and terrorists from acting.
5. Enhance long-term security for personnel and assets.

Security requirements vary by project, scale, and building type. For example, government agencies renting several floors within a commercial building require different security measures than a large corporate or university campus owned and operated by a single entity. Despite varying security requirements for different building types, evaluation methods and criteria remain consistent.

Designers and building owners should be familiar with the types of threats stemming from terrorist attacks and criminal activities, and with determining preventative measures suitable for each scenario. Building owners and facility managers should understand the implications of design solutions, the best use of technology, and the need to develop policies and procedures, and they should be prepared to coordinate with local law enforcement agencies as needed.

Because threats change over the life of a facility, building owners and facility managers should be aware that security elements can be more economically integrated within structures during the early planning and design phases of new construction projects than during subsequent additions or renovations. Retrofits of existing facilities pose a greater challenge because building systems must be able to accommodate increased requirements and may not have the additional space or upgrade capacity.

The Security Planning Team

A security master plan requires coordination of facility stakeholders and professional disciplines. The most effective solutions are a combination of design elements, technology, and operational strategies.

From the beginning of every project, whether for new construction or renovation of existing facilities, the security planning team should include architects, engineers, specialty consultants, and members of the building owner and facility management team. Effective communication from the

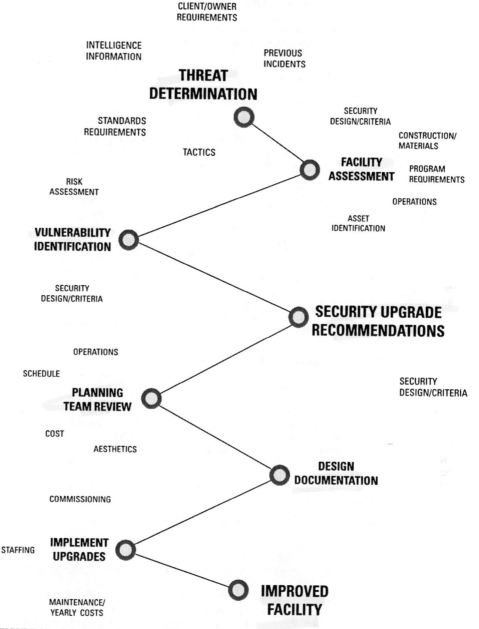

CLIENT/OWNER
REQUIREMENTS

INTELLIGENCE
INFORMATION

PREVIOUS
INCIDENTS

**THREAT
DETERMINATION**

STANDARDS
REQUIREMENTS

SECURITY
DESIGN/CRITERIA

CONSTRUCTION/
MATERIALS

TACTICS

**FACILITY
ASSESSMENT**

PROGRAM
REQUIREMENTS

RISK
ASSESSMENT

OPERATIONS

ASSET
IDENTIFICATION

**VULNERABILITY
IDENTIFICATION**

SECURITY
DESIGN/CRITERIA

**SECURITY UPGRADE
RECOMMENDATIONS**

OPERATIONS

SCHEDULE

SECURITY
DESIGN/CRITERIA

**PLANNING
TEAM REVIEW**

COST

AESTHETICS

**DESIGN
DOCUMENTATION**

COMMISSIONING

**IMPLEMENT
UPGRADES**

STAFFING

**IMPROVED
FACILITY**

MAINTENANCE/
YEARLY COSTS

FIGURE 2.1   Security planning process. (*Source: RTKL.*)

outset regarding goals, strategies, options, and costs will enhance the master plan by allowing greater input early on and minimizing surprises and omissions later.

In addition to design professionals, the security planning team should include those knowledgeable in technical and operational security, life safety, codes and standards, structural blast effects, and traffic engineering (Table 2.3). Each project is unique, and may require a different mix of expertise

TABLE 2.1   Security Master Planning Mission

1. Represent a multidisciplinary collaborative effort, tailored for each facility, site, and building owner's needs.
2. Combine three elements: design, technology, and operations.
3. Outline strategies for addressing perceived or potential threats.
4. Enable facility managers to anticipate a broad range of threat criteria, while remaining flexible enough to operate efficiently as threat levels increase or change.
5. Minimize costs by addressing security early in planning, programming, site selection, and conceptual design.

TABLE 2.2   Characteristics of a Successful Security Plan

1. Identifies potential threats
2. Identifies and prioritizes critical assets
3. Develops a comprehensive mitigation strategy
4. Meets current threats and plans for future modifications
5. Anticipates disasters, emergencies, and potentially damaging events
6. Eliminates single points of failure
7. Provides earliest detection of threats
8. Balances costs while acknowledging and accepting risk
9. Minimizes failure of building systems
10. Facilitates safe evacuation and rescue
11. Prevents intrusions and hostage situations
12. Protects people and assets
13. Facilitates early recovery of operations

TABLE 2.3   Security Planning Team Members

1. Building owner or landlord	11. Blast engineer
2. Client representatives from security and facility management	12. Mechanical and electrical engineer
	13. Fire protection or life safety engineer
3. Tenants or tenant group representatives	14. Telecommunications engineer
4. Local law enforcement representatives	15. Physical and technical security specialist
5. Government representatives and planners	16. Security staffing and operations specialist
6. Code officials	17. Traffic planner or engineer
7. Architect	18. Cost estimator
8. Landscape architect	19. Construction manager
9. Interior designer	20. Chemical, biological, and radiological specialist
10. Structural engineer	

and responsibilities for each discipline. For example, an urban site will likely encounter different issues than a suburban location, such as greater involvement by a blast engineer and less of a landscape architect.

Architects with an understanding of security and force protection planning are well qualified to lead security studies, especially if design of the built environment is a significant consideration. In traditional project roles, architects lead multidisciplinary teams and coordinate consultant efforts to create a final product and project for building owners. Ultimately, however, building owners must weigh all consultant recommendations and select a final approach.

Regardless of the circumstances driving the need for a security plan, such as an incident or a new project, building owners or client agencies should ideally designate a point person or liaison to coordinate in-house security needs with management, administration, and end-users. The liaison's role is to communicate these needs to the design team and ensure that all operational and technical criteria are thoroughly addressed during all work phases.

Crime Prevention through Environmental Design

Architect, urban planner, and author Oscar Newman established the principles of Crime Prevention Through Environmental Design (CPTED, pronounced, "sep-ted") in his book, *Defensible Space, Crime Prevention Through Urban Design* (1972). A decade earlier, in her landmark work, *The Death and Life of Great American Cities* (1961), author Jane Jacobs described how putting "eyes on the street" created safer urban environments. Jacobs understood how the complex social structure of urban life enhanced livability and personal safety. These ideas are the most basic aspects of security design.

These two important books discuss the role of environmental planning and design in creating safer urban environments, through a tiered, or layered, defense system, rather than high-tech solutions. Conceptually, defensive tiers, known as "rings of defense," move from neighborhoods, to site perimeters, facility exteriors, and interior zones, with different responses for each zone (Table 2.4).

Security planning establishes defensible layers by seeking opportunities to apply security at site perimeters and building entrances, within entry lobbies, and at stairwells, elevators, and tenant entries. Each layer should act as a ring of consistently applied security measures. For example, stationing a guard at the front door but leaving the loading dock open and unguarded is ineffective if both entries allow access to the same space. Different security techniques might be applied to separate areas, but they should achieve the same results.

The CPTED strategy of incorporating elements such as good lighting, clear, unobstructed sightlines, and physical landscape barriers during site planning may enhance security at relatively low cost (Table 2.5). In a highly competitive real estate market, commercial and residential property owners may also minimize liability and increase value by offering more security measures in place than other properties.

SECURITY ASSESSMENT

After the terror attacks during the 1990s, the federal government took action to ensure building safety, and both the public and private sectors have benefited from this public research and development on design, building materials, procedures, and protocols. The U.S. General Services Administration

TABLE 2.4 Defensive Tiers or Rings of Defense

1. Site perimeter
2. Building standoff
3. Inner perimeter
4. Building exterior
5. Building systems
6. Screening and access control zones
7. Safe interior areas for valuable assets or personnel safe havens

TABLE 2.5 Top 10 Security Design Considerations

1. Site issues
2. Access control
3. Parking
4. Building construction
5. Building systems
6. Infrastructure
7. Space planning
8. Operations
9. Technology
10. Cost

(GSA), Department of Defense (DoD), and other government organizations developed guidelines for construction and renovation of all buildings owned and occupied by the federal government. Corporate and commercial clients often have their own guidelines and security procedures to consider. The U.S. Department of Homeland Security, working with emergency planning agencies in states, counties, and major cities, is another resource for guidelines on regional threats and responses.

Private sector projects and organizations lacking specific security design criteria can turn to the security assessment process used by public agencies. The security planning team will be responsible for developing security "best practices" and applying appropriate design criteria. In all circumstances, building owners, tenants, and designers should remain aware of local developments and code issues within their state and city pertaining to Homeland Security. Terrorism insurance is a significant issue for facility owners and managers, along with assessing the cost benefits of mitigation against escalating premiums.

Performing Security Assessments

A security assessment provides an overview of threats and potential mitigating factors. The financial burden of security measures varies by threat level, acceptable risks, and desired protection. All team members should have a basic understanding of threats, applicable mitigation criteria, and the effects both will have on a security plan. Security assessment elements include the following:

1. Identification of critical assets
2. Threat assessment
3. Security survey
4. Vulnerability and risk assessments
5. Development of recommendations, security upgrades, and mitigation strategies
6. Refinement of solutions

Certain criteria may not be achievable in all situations, due to high costs or existing conditions. Documenting decisions and assumptions may prove to be important for future reference, providing alternative plans for mitigation when conditions change and insurance purposes in the event of a problem. Depending on the property and owner, the security assessment may be performed by law enforcement personnel, security specialists, the security planning and design team, or a combination of all involved (Table 2.6).

Implementing Solutions

Following the security assessment, building owners may decide to implement some or all of the proposed solutions. Phased implementation ensures operations and security are not compromised. The steps to implementing security solutions are as follows:

1. Documenting final design
2. Implementing project construction and upgrades
3. Communicating with and training personnel for operational policies and procedures
4. Revisiting design as needed to meet operational and threat requirements

Identifying Critical Assets

The security master planning team's first task is determining resources to be protected. The primary goal is protecting facility occupants and the general public from identified threats. The facility should

TABLE 2.6   Security Assessment Checklist

Public safety

1. Prevent threats from entering buildings, campus, and site perimeter, especially explosives
2. Upgrade existing conditions susceptible to threats such as explosives and ballistics
3. Maintain emergency and egress procedures
4. Establish procedures for admitting emergency vehicles onsite
5. Provide and maintain access to all building areas, including fire lanes

Access

1. Identify pedestrian and vehicular access requirements
2. Identify impact on external road network
3. Identify opportunities for separation of staff, visitor, and delivery entrances
4. Identify procedural and operational access requirements

Site

1. Determine owner requirements
2. Maximize standoff distances for critical structures
3. Conform to local, state and national codes, covenants, easements, and design guidelines
4. Verify security of site utilities and building connections
5. Identify and respect adjacent neighbors and property owners
6. Maintain aesthetic standards
7. Integrate security requirements with topography and other natural features

Design coordination

1. Minimize site visibility to the public
2. Consider impact on existing and future site development
3. Identify phasing responsibilities

TABLE 2.7   Typical Critical Assets to be Protected

1. Municipal, state, and regional emergency operations centers
2. Central building operations centers
3. Computer facilities
4. Building service utilities
5. Government installations
6. Technology facilities
7. Factories
8. Laboratories
9. Office buildings
10. Medical facilities
11. 911 call centers
12. Merchandise
13. Data

be located, designed and built to provide required resistance to design threats. For some project types, the critical asset may be the facility itself or certain program elements. The design should minimize potential damage and prevent loss of operations. Often, a combination of people, program space and operations will need to be protected (Table 2.7).

In retail facilities, merchandise is generally considered the asset to protect, and therefore theft is the major threat to be addressed. Industrial espionage may pose a threat for government, corporate or institutional facilities. For these instances, critical assets may include sensitive or classified information and scientific research developments.

Security planners often need to consider requirements encompassing an entire government installation, technology company campus, or individual factories, laboratories, and office buildings. Medical facilities, 911 call centers, and municipal emergency command centers are frequently designated as critical assets, because they protect the public, are essential during emergencies and disasters, and their building services must be maintained for round-the-clock operations.

Threat Assessment

After applicable security guidelines and critical assets are identified, actual, perceived and potential threats to a facility or campus are determined. For the most effective analysis, the building owner, landlord, tenants, and end user groups should collectively determine threats. Corporate criteria, industry standards, federal intelligence agencies, local law enforcement, community groups, and other trade organizations may be helpful in identifying threats to specific locations and building types.

Threats may be actual or perceived, and may relate to past incidents, current facility conditions, or postulated future event scenarios. Identifying all possible threats and their likelihood is crucial to the overall success of the security master plan. Omissions will compromise efficient use of the facility, complicate future upgrades, and cause undue hardship for security staffing and operations. The cost of mitigation measures will be directly attributable to the final threat design criteria selected. The most common threat types are terrorism, criminal, environmental, infrastructure failure, or service interruption (Tables 2.8 to 2.11).

SECURITY SURVEY

A security survey analyzes an existing space, individual building, or entire facility campus. The intent is to note all physical elements to be evaluated against threat criteria and to determine potential security vulnerabilities. The survey starts from the outer perimeter, includes public and outdoor areas, and works toward the center, or to the location of critical assets. All site areas are addressed, as well as building exteriors and internal program spaces. Building systems are identified, infrastructure is evaluated, and operational and staffing issues are documented. The process consists of interviewing owners, facility managers, and building users, and performing on-site inspections. The level of detail in each survey depends on project security requirements and owner concerns.

TABLE 2.8   Types of Terrorism Threats and Characteristics

Threat type	Characteristics
Explosive	• Vehicle outside the site perimeter • Vehicle within the site perimeter, adjacent to or below a building • Mail, package, or supply bombs
Forced entry	• At site perimeter • At building exterior • At internal program space
Ballistic	• Use of firearms
Chemical, biological, and radiological (CBR) weapons and agents	• Airborne contamination external to facility • Airborne contamination internal to building
Visual, acoustic, and electronic surveillance	• Cameras, wiretaps, computer hacking, industrial espionage
Aerial attack	• Airplanes as weapons or delivering weapons

TABLE 2.9 Criminal Threats

1. Theft of property or information
2. Assault
3. Vandalism
4. Protestors
5. Employee and workplace violence
6. Forged identification
7. Arson
8. Kidnapping and hostage taking

TABLE 2.10 Environmental Threats

1. Fire
2. Earthquakes
3. Floods, tsunamis
4. Hurricanes
5. Tornadoes
6. Snowstorms, ice storms

TABLE 2.11 Infrastructure Failure or Service Interruption Threats

1. Electricity—routine service and emergency power (blackouts)
2. Cooling systems
3. Heating systems
4. Water supply disruption or contamination
5. Telecommunications
6. Natural Gas

A successful survey ensures that all aspects are investigated, and is the result of a collaborative effort among all design disciplines. Owner, client, and user representatives should provide information throughout the interview process and during facility tours. Checklists and interview questions should be prepared in advance and tailored to each facility. Photographs of vulnerable areas and existing conditions throughout the facility are recommended for future reference and for insurance purposes. Documents from existing facilities, including as-built drawings, specifications, and lease agreements are helpful.

Security Survey Elements

Security is most effectively addressed during early program and schematic phases of new construction or renovation projects. Site planning and building elements can be more readily adjusted during early design phases than later on when major changes and additions may cost more and impact project scheduling (Tables 2.12 to 2.15).

VULNERABILITY AND RISK ASSESSMENTS

Vulnerability and risk assessments build on information developed through the threat assessment and security survey. The vulnerability assessment analyzes systems and individual elements.

TABLE 2.12   Secure Perimeter Security Survey Checklist

1. Adjacent properties and neighbors
2. Topography and vegetation
3. Surrounding roadways and vehicular entries
4. Parking
5. Fencing
6. Vehicular access
7. Pedestrian access
8. Existing structures
9. Sight lines and visibility
10. Existing or proposed infrastructure
11. Site utility access
12. Existing physical and technical security

TABLE 2.13   Site Planning Security Survey Checklist

1. Vegetation, visual obstructions, and hiding places
2. Vehicular access
3. Parking
4. Pedestrian access
5. Lighting
6. Existing physical and technical security

TABLE 2.14   Building Security Survey Checklist

1. Activities and tenant mix (commercial, retail, hospitality, government, and combination)
2. Circulation, life safety systems, and egress requirements
3. Exterior envelope constructions and glazing systems
4. Structural systems
5. Infrastructure locations and distribution
6. Space planning and program adjacencies
7. Air intakes and vents
8. Exterior doors and accessibility
9. Roofs and accessibility
10. Lobbies
11. Loading docks
12. Security operations and building control centers
13. System redundancies

Each must meet applicable design criteria and mitigate identified project threat criteria. Elements that fail or provide insufficient response are considered vulnerabilities and need to be upgraded (Table 2.16).

Certain vulnerabilities may be considered minimally significant while others may be too costly to mitigate. Either way, the decision not to remedy those defects implies an acceptance of risk. Risk assessment is performed by owners and tenants to review the probabilities and consequences of an event, and the level or amount of risk they are willing to assume if it occurs. The risks will be financial and may involve the loss of lives, operations, facilities, and future business.

TABLE 2.15 Operations Security Survey Checklist

1. Establishing owner and client protocols and standards
2. Developing an Emergency Operations Plan
3. Communication of policies and procedures to tenants and user groups
4. Emergency staff training, mobilization, and designation of team leaders
5. Practice drills for evacuation and familiarization with egress routes
6. Regular testing of building systems and alarms
7. Building systems monitoring and control capabilities
8. Operation of central security station, satellite checkpoints, and emergency response
9. Coordination with local law enforcement and government agencies
10. Insurance concerns for unforeseen situations and disasters
11. Secure maintenance and backup redundancy of important records, files, computer data, drawings, and documents

TABLE 2.16 Top 10 Security Deficiencies Found at Existing Facilities

1. Overgrowth of vegetation (notably at the fence lines)
2. Generic exterior glazing (neither blast nor ballistic resistant)
3. Insufficient CCTV coverage (for both the site and building)
4. Insufficient ballistic protection for security posts
5. Insufficient area for operations and implementation of badge inspection and visitor entry
6. Insufficient operations and implementation for delivery vehicle and material procedures
7. Insufficient security force relative to facility size and operational requirements
8. Lack of overall parking policies and vehicle identification procedures
9. Unknown response time to threat
10. Poor demarcation of property boundary

Risk Assessment Issues

The symbolic importance of national landmarks and large federal government facilities carries an inherent risk because they represent the U.S. government and are icons for democracy and freedom. Attacking symbols of the federal government is often a goal for both domestic and international terrorists. Major corporations and their executives may be susceptible to terrorist plots because of roles in the global marketplace, business practices, or other controversy.

Critical Nature

Functions occurring within a facility may be critical to maintaining services essential to society, government, a community, or business. Examples include:

- Hospitals, with designated areas for emergency power
- Telephone and computer centers providing critical data and communications
- Police, fire, emergency command centers, and 911 call centers communicating with central and satellite control centers during emergencies

- Financial institutions with data centers, computer networks, and communications for ongoing operations
- Public utilities and urban infrastructure, critical to public health, safety, and welfare

Consequences

Each owner must determine the consequences if people, goods, and services become temporarily or permanently unavailable. For example, if a hospital were to lose emergency power during an earthquake, patients could die. If a company were to lose its computer files and backups in a fire, as some did on September 11, 2001, the firm would be forced to consider whether copies could readily be retrieved from consultants and clients, or might be permanently lost.

Threat Type

Owners must determine if primary threats stem from criminal intent or terrorist attack, or a combination. Other factors include use and type of weapon.

Threat Verification

The increasing globalization of society has local consequences in the United States and at American installations abroad. As the national and global political climate and demographics change over time, so will the quantity and nature of threats, as well as to whom they will be directed. Building owners and occupants should remain alert to potential changes in society that may impact their facilities, operations, and personnel, and learn which agencies or organizations are best suited to help verify and avert potential threats.

Probability of Occurrence and Impact

Building owners, their staff, client agencies, and tenants should weigh the probability of an event occurring and the potential risks and impact to the organization and facilities. These issues should be assessed against the owner's or client's mission and goals. Training will enhance preparedness within organizations and assist in planning for effective emergency response.

Mitigation

During the facility master planning process, recommendations are developed after thoroughly analyzing all criteria. Similarly, for security master planning, recommendations are the result of the threat assessment, security survey, and vulnerability and risk assessments. Recommendations should be comprehensive and include solutions for all identified vulnerabilities. Solutions should incorporate all disciplines to achieve the most efficient, cost-effective design strategy that responds to, or exceeds, project threat criteria. Developing mitigation recommendations includes the following steps:

1. Formulate options and potential solutions.
2. Coordinate comments from entire project team, including owner, clients, users, facility managers, security personnel, designers, and consultants.
3. Provide flexibility for change and increased loads, capacities, special circumstances, one time situations, or occasional events.
4. Refine solutions.
5. Assess capital and operational costs of all options.

6. Determine priorities and phasing plan as needed.

7. Select desired options.

Recommendations should be reviewed by the planning team to ensure owner requirements are met, solutions are technically sound, and schedule, cost, and phasing issues are realistic. Frequently, more than one solution is possible and each should be evaluated to determine benefits and limitations. Once the entire team has reviewed and commented on the plan, some elements may need revisions to achieve a successful solution, such as additional site visits or reassessing threat criteria and acceptable risk levels.

Threat mitigation should provide a layered response, and incorporate design, technology, staffing, and operational requirements. Depending on project scope, the final design may be very simple and result in installing cameras or parking control devices, or could be complicated and involve construction of roads, fencing, structural upgrades, new glazing, and integrating new access control systems.

For maximum flexibility, addressing potential threats and mitigation solutions could be considered during planning for future expansion of buildings, system capacities, and secure perimeters. Examples include maintaining significant standoff distances during site design or incorporating empty conduits during construction.

Costs

Security measures are less costly to implement when factored into projects during early planning, programming, and schematic design phases, when critical decisions are made (Table 2.17). The importance of planning ahead cannot be overemphasized—entire building systems, site planning, floor layouts, room sizes, adjacencies, construction materials, and project schedules may be impacted by security design decisions.

In new construction or major renovation projects, architectural solutions are often the most cost effective. Correctional facility designers have found when planning secure facilities, that owners and managers must balance one-time construction costs against long-term operational costs and salaries for labor-intensive solutions, such as contracted security guards, staff officer posts, and around-the-clock security personnel. When salaries and benefits are tallied over a long range planning horizon, design and technology may turn out to be more effective, less costly solutions.

Security master planning is the first step toward developing a broad, comprehensive approach to designing secure facilities. The analyses and recommendations set the direction for all project components, from vehicular entry, building location, and parking layouts to curtain wall systems, infrastructure distribution, and total project costs.

As threats increase, professionals in every discipline within the public and private sectors should be able to generate and apply specific security solutions that:

TABLE 2.17   Top 10 Costs for Security Solutions*

1. Hardened construction
2. Exterior walls
3. Glazing
4. Structure
5. Vehicle standoff
6. Staffing
7. Perimeter systems
8. Vehicle control and roadway improvements
9. Access control systems
10. Security equipment

*Not ranked in order of magnitude.

- Weigh implementation costs against potential loss of lives, property, and assets.
- Balance transparency and design while avoiding a fortress mentality.
- Vary according to building type and potential threats.
- Consider past events and anticipate future scenarios, including those not considered before September 11, 2001.

The design team, in collaboration with building owners and facility managers, is well positioned to lead this effort, by combining design, technology, and operational expertise.

SOLUTIONS

Planning, design, and operational solutions should be applied as security mitigation measures, tailored to the needs of each building owner, building type, and individual project needs. Site planning elements and perimeter security are the first issues to be evaluated in any plan (Fig. 2.2 and Table 2.18). The role of perimeter security is to:

- Delineate legal property boundaries
- Limit site access
- Provide maximum distance between potential threats and assets to be protected
- Provide opportunities to assess and respond to intrusions

Design solutions may include multiple perimeters, as a layered defense to further prevent threats from reaching their targets. This approach requires coordinated facility operations and often results in higher design and operational costs.

Standoff distance is the closest a threat can come to an asset or building. For blast concerns, standoff is measured as the distance from a building's exterior to the nearest vehicle access, such as a road, parking lot, service yard, or unrestricted movements across the landscape. The area between is often referred to as the "vehicle exclusion zone."

Standoff is the primary protection against blast. The most critical assets are best located at the points farthest from the site perimeter, as blast effects decrease with distance. For blast effects on a structure, the ideal distance varies from 50 feet to 100 feet or more, depending on the threat, building type, owner, and function. Federal buildings, especially courthouses, have specific requirements for standoff and setbacks. The ability to achieve these distances is often a combination of vehicle weight and speed in relation to construction techniques.

Outer Perimeter

The outer perimeter is the first opportunity to mitigate threat requirements. Perimeter security is essential to prevent a moving or stationary vehicle bomb attack. Site planning criteria vary by building type, pedestrian, and vehicular circulation requirements. The 1995 bombing of the Alfred P. Murrah Federal Building in Oklahoma City provided several object lessons relating to site planning and design. (Table 2.19)

Inner Perimeter

The inner perimeter is the final line of defense before a threat reaches building exteriors. *Hardscape* (hardened landscaping) features are often used, consisting of site walls, bollards, boulders, planters, and other barriers to restrict vehicle access, or fencing to limit pedestrian access. These elements, along with roadways, provide protection from vehicular ramming and blast threats. When creating vehicle perimeters, operable features should allow emergency vehicle access.

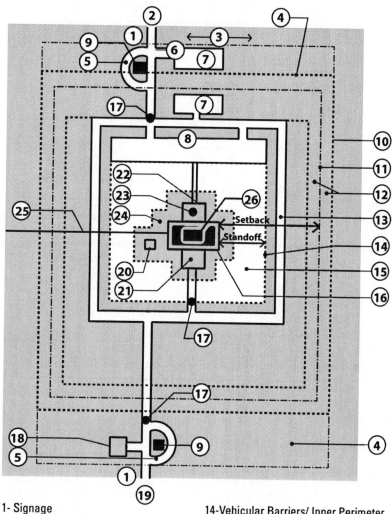

FIGURE 2.2   Planning concepts for site security. Not all elements are required for all facilities, based on outcome of threat and risk assessment. (*Source: RTKL.*)

1- Signage
2- Employee/ Visitor Access
3- Public Image
4- Uncontrolled Area
5- Reject Capabilities
6- Adequate Queuing Length
7- Visitor Parking (External or Internal)
8- Staff Parking
9- Security Post
10- Site Boundary/ Property Line
11- Perimeter Fence
12- Clear Zone
13- Inner Vehicular Circulation

14- Vehicular Barriers/ Inner Perimeter
15- Vehicle Exclusion Zone
16- Hardened Building Perimeter
17- Access Control
18- External Material Inspection Facility (Optional)
19- Service/ Employee Access
20- Redundant/ Emergency Utilities
21- Loading Dock
22- Building Lobby
23- Pedestrian/ Visitor Facility Access Control
24- Clear Zone
25- Incoming Utilities
26- Critical Asset

TABLE 2.18   Security Site Planning Elements

1. Site selection—location and suitability for use
2. Site edges and boundaries
3. Access control
4. Traffic and vehicular access
5. Fencing
6. Pedestrian access
7. Parking
8. Vegetation and topography
9. Plazas and landscaping
10. Guardhouses
11. Standoff distance
12. Setbacks

TABLE 2.19   Lessons Learned from the Oklahoma City Murrah Federal Building Bombing: Security Design Elements

The bombing and collapse of the Alfred P. Murrah Federal Building alerted design professionals to the importance of addressing:

1. Site access
2. Standoff distance
3. Setback requirements
4. Hardening of buildings to increase blast resistance
5. Glazing applications to reduce fatalities in a blast situation
6. Avoiding progressive collapse and implementing protective design of structures

Perimeter Fencing

Perimeter fencing defines a legal boundary around a site, and should be located as close to boundaries as zoning or existing site constraints allow. Fencing creates a barrier against outside encroachment or intrusion, whether intentional or unintentional (Table 2.20).

Many types of perimeter fencing and related technology are available. Correctional facilities and military installations have long been primary markets for electronic fencing and infrared movement sensors. Perimeter fencing prevents intruders from entering secure areas. Alarms, infrared movement sensors, lighting, and CCTV are often used with fencing to ensure greater observation and detection of intruders and unauthorized entries. Fence intrusion detection systems (IDS) are connected to a central control room with panels and TV monitors capable of zooming in on alarm zones. Facility operations should include procedures for responding to intrusions.

Fencing and all other high-technology products should be thoroughly tested and evaluated before major installations to ensure that they meet owner requirements, especially in harsh climates or extreme hot or cold temperatures. System sensitivities must be carefully calibrated to eliminate false alarms. As many facilities and agencies have learned through trial and error, weather, winds, and animals can impact effectiveness of perimeter fencing systems.

Use of several technologies within fencing components increases the time and effort intruders need to breach the secure perimeter, providing heightened antiram and antipersonnel resistance.

Vehicular Circulation

Individuals and vehicles should be checked, or vetted, before they enter a secure campus, office park, compound, or building. In some cases, names, vehicle descriptions, and license plate numbers are

TABLE 2.20   Fencing Design Criteria

1. Building codes, zoning standards, and design guidelines
2. Material selection and construction techniques
3. Finishes and durability
4. Height
5. Overall length and alignment
6. Topography
7. Climbability
8. Aesthetics
9. Signage
10. Infrastructure: power, alarms, lighting, CCTV
11. Cost
12. Vegetation
13. Clear zones
14. Sight lines
15. Adjacent property use and neighbors

required at least a day before visitors are scheduled to arrive. Traffic management and vetting operations could have a significant effect on staffing, length and design of ingress lanes, and traffic on surrounding roadways.

Vehicular circulation should be designed to separate employee traffic from visitors and deliveries. Roads should include turnaround opportunities for vehicles refused access to secure locations, known as rejection lanes. Nonemployee vehicles may require separate, off-site parking facilities until security clearances are arranged. Roadway planning criteria should include the following:

1. Queuing time and resulting queue lengths
2. Turnaround areas, rejection lanes, and exits
3. Separation of employees, visitors, VIP, services, and deliveries
4. Ability to bypass and separate entries
5. Multiple entries

To further screen and separate incoming traffic, high-security facilities and campus settings may include guardhouses, a Visitor Control Center (VCC), and a Mail Inspection Facility (MIF). Truck vetting areas should be designed for parking and inspection of delivery vehicles before they enter secure areas. Package drop-off and storage can also be provided within a VCC or MIF.

Parking

Design of parking lots and drop-off locations should consider the following criteria:

1. Zoned parking areas
2. Minimum standoff requirements
3. Separation of visitors and others
4. Drop-off points
5. Handicapped requirements

Hierarchy of parking areas may include restricted areas for staff and "trusted individuals" closer to the facility, and more remote visitor lots. Internal roads should be designed for efficient circulation between site access points and should never breach standoff areas or pass over areas of critical infrastructure distribution. Parking structure planning should address the following:

1. Avoiding progressive collapse and implementing protective design of structures
2. Distance and location to inhabited buildings
3. Blast wall design
4. Security personnel requirements
5. Open stairs for visibility

Vehicle Barriers

Standoff distance and perimeter security reduce the exponential effect of a vehicle bomb or explosive. Standoff can be combined with other features, such as natural topography, plaza setbacks, landscaping, trees, boulders, and street furniture to restrict vehicular access. Rock terracing or concrete retaining walls are also effective deterrents, particularly to motorcycles and small all-terrain vehicles, which can carry explosive materials.

Vehicle barriers manage traffic flow, but should not be the sole means of reacting to oncoming threats. Barriers can stop the vehicular movement at the point of contact, inflicting great damage to the vehicle's occupants, but site conditions do not always provide sufficient space for this type of operation. Many types of vehicle barriers are available; costs depend on performance criteria and automation requirements.

Barriers control access and egress during heightened emergency and off-peak hours by closing all but a single entry point. They can respond to reverse flow threats by keeping outbound gates in the up position during off-peak traffic hours. Use of barriers and access control technology can reduce staffing and operational needs, and provide additional threat response.

Vehicle barriers are most useful in the upright position (passive defense), such as at all vetting locations, off-hours at entrances, or during emergency lockdown. Various barrier types and their characteristics include:

- Pop-up wedges offer resistance throughout their cycle.
- Cable beams are only useful in the down and engaged position.
- Fixed bollards are often used in areas with pedestrian access and limited vehicular access.
- Tire shredders are installed where reverse traffic flow is a concern, but will not stop a vehicle.
- Trees, unless fully mature and within a densely wooded area, should not be relied on to stop approaching vehicles.

Vehicle barriers may be installed for use as operable, removable, or fixed. They may be manipulated remotely or at point of use, either manually or automated, typically hydraulic. Types of vehicle barriers include the following:

1. Fencing and rolling gates
2. Cable beams
3. Pop-up wedges/plates
4. Bollards—removable, fixed, and hydraulic
5. Landscape and hardscape elements—site walls, boulders, berms, moats, and curbs
6. Other—tire shredders, barrels, and aircraft cabling with "dead man" anchors

Closed Circuit Television

Closed Circuit Television (CCTV) is a common surveillance technology because incidents in remote areas can be assessed and recorded with minimal staff effort. By minimizing the need for personnel to monitor facilities around the clock, CCTV can reduce operational budgets. The types and numbers of cameras and monitors used should be selected to maximize coverage at access points and sensitive locations. Vegetation, topography and other site elements should be coordinated with the final design to ensure that all sight lines are maintained.

Exterior lighting should be planned and designed in tandem with CCTV specifications, since camera types, such as color, black and white, low light, and thermal, have different lighting requirements. When in a record and save mode, CCTV can track intruders and provide a post-incident analysis. Prominent camera placement is often a deterrent to intruders and criminals.

Security Posts and Guard Houses

Security posts and guardhouses provide protection for security officers and include weapons storage, toilets, and CCTV monitoring. A guardhouse may be custom designed or prefabricated. Guard house design criteria includes the following:

1. Site guard house to provide the greatest distance from critical structures and protected assets.
2. Provide good sight lines, observation, and visibility to surroundings.
3. Ascertain number of security staff per shift to be stationed at the post.
4. Provide protection from ballistic and ramming threats.
5. Include overhangs or canopies.
6. Meet heating and cooling requirements.
7. Provide staff toilet facilities.
8. Design for necessary wiring, space and lighting for CCTV monitors, consoles, alarms, and emergency distress systems.
9. Plan equipment with pass through drawers, speakers, intercoms, and vision panels.
10. Consider aesthetics of guardhouse location to blend into the landscape.

Berm and Blast Wall Construction

Blast barriers, either berms or blast wall, provide protection from an explosion, especially if a blast occurs in a confined zone, such as a vehicle vetting area. For berm or blast walls to be effective, the bomb has to be detonated near the barrier; otherwise, the same amount of damage could occur as if the barrier were not in place. The three most common barriers are: earthen berm, concrete wall or revetment, and a combination of the two (Table 2.21).

TABLE 2.21 Most Common Berm And Blast Wall Types

Type	Characteristics
Earthen berm	• Requires considerable space and soil to create gradual slope lines. • Not as efficient and effective as other types; generally not recommended.
Concrete wall or revetment	• Allows vehicle to get close to the vertical wall face. • Large amount of concrete needed to deflect the blast load can also become additional shrapnel and flying debris.
Combination	• Best solution. By placing a retaining wall in a partially buried vetting area, a vehicle is forced adjacent to the wall. • Soil can backfill and stabilize the retaining wall, while minimizing flying debris.

Security Operations Center (SOC)

The Security Operations Center (SOC) is the base for coordinating operations and technology throughout a building and site. Technology controls within the space typically include CCTV monitoring, alarm annunciation, vehicle barriers operations, and site lighting (Table 2.22). Construction of a redundant facility should be considered in the event one center is not available during an emergency.

Visitor Control Center (VCC)

The Visitor Control Center (VCC) is the central access point for all visitors entering a campus, compound, site, or major building with high traffic. It should be located adjacent to the secure perimeter, at the most distant location possible from protected assets, and planned to prevent unauthorized access onto the site, campus, or compound (Table 2.23).

Material Inspection Facility (MIF)

Mail, service deliveries, packages, and boxes containing harmful materials can enter a secure facility, campus, or compound, and then be distributed to other internal operations, causing damage. A Material Inspection Facility (MIF) increases security by providing a remote package drop-off and screening point for all incoming materials before packages arrive at occupied buildings through an internal delivery system (Table 2.24). The MIF ensures that all deliveries are unloaded from commercial vehicles at a remote onsite area, screened, and then delivered to main buildings and other facilities by the owner's vehicle fleet and staff.

Creating a MIF impacts staffing, operations, costs, and timely receipt of mail. Operational concerns must be weighed against benefits of increased package inspection and decreasing the chances of

---

TABLE 2.22   Security Operations Center Design Criteria

1. Locate the SOC near the main or official building entry, to oversee the employee "badge-in" process and clear visitors for entry into secure areas, or at an interior location on the grounds of a facility, further removed from the site perimeter.
2. Provide hardened construction to meet blast and ballistics threats and seismic requirements.
3. Allow clear observation and visibility to building access and entries for security officers.
4. Provide direct communication links from posted security officers to internal security officers, law enforcement, fire, emergency personnel, and public officials as required.
5. Secure telephones and mobile communications lines in the event of an emergency where service is cut off.
6. Allow video conferencing capabilities for larger central facilities.
7. Program spaces for tables and equipment needed to screen individuals and inspect packages.
8. Provide uninterrupted power supply (UPS) backup for the facility.
9. Plan parking locations to support operational requirements.
10. Consider food and sleeping accommodations for public agency security operations centers, as required.

TABLE 2.23   Visitor Control Center Design Criteria

1. Identify areas of hardened construction to protect occupants from threats.
2. Plan the Visitor Control Center for immediate and future demands.
3. Locate visitor parking area outside the secure perimeter.
4. Size the VCC parking to meet visitor demands.
5. Coordinate infrastructure with uninterrupted power supply backup and communication to the SOC.
6. Design the VCC to reflect the facility ambiance and the building owner's organizational, corporate, or public image.

TABLE 2.24   Material Inspection Facility Site Planning And Parking Design Criteria

1. Locate MIF adjacent to the secure perimeter, at the most distant location possible from assets and main buildings.
2. Prevent unauthorized access onto the campus or compound through or near the MIF.
3. Locate adjacent parking and loading areas outside the secure perimeter or fence line.
4. Provide parking and turn-around areas for 55-foot long semi tractor-trailers.
5. Use earth berms and blast walls for increased protection.
6. Provide vehicular circulation routes allowing trash and fuel delivery vehicles inspection upon site arrival. The size, routine scheduling, and close proximity of these vehicles to occupied buildings pose a real threat to secure facilities.
7. Plan for high hazard and detonation areas for suspicious packages.

TABLE 2.25   Material Inspection Facility Space Program Elements

1. Loading and unloading areas
2. Mail sorting and inspection areas
3. Suspicious package containment room
4. Safe haven
5. Staging areas
6. Storage, both air conditioned and not air conditioned
7. Offices
8. Lockers, toilets, and break room
9. Dog kennel for canine inspection team
10. Mechanical, electrical, communications, and security closets

TABLE 2.26   Material Inspection Facility Design Criteria

1. Provide hardened construction to protect building occupants and adjacent facilities from threats.
2. Provide areas of refuge in the event of a blast.
3. Design mechanical systems to withstand blast.
4. Consider sensors to detect hazardous substances.
5. Configure loading docks so blast pressures from an internal explosion vent away from the building.
6. Provide docks for incoming and outgoing materials, including waste handling and recyclables.
7. Provide dock levelers and dock seals.

unknown threats reaching densely populated areas or asset locations. Large companies, government agencies, and global organizations with critical assets, or those routinely subject to threats, will benefit from MIFs, as will organizations with high package delivery volumes. A central facility, containing storage and staging areas, may be shared by a several user groups or agencies.

The MIF should be programmed for screening equipment needed for high volume package inspection. In existing structures, loading dock perimeters and mailrooms can be lined with energy absorbing materials or additional concrete walls. The outside perimeter wall can be designed to be frangible (capable of blowing out to relieve blast pressures) under an explosive loading. These criteria may not be cost effective in existing buildings (Tables 2.25 and 2.26).

BLAST DESIGN

Blast analysis determines how a structure will respond to an explosion. Standoff distance and charge weight are the two most significant factors considered during blast analysis (Table 2.27). Blast pressures are functions of the standoff divided by the cube root of charge weight, known as the scaled

TABLE 2.27   Blast Design Criteria

1. Explosive charge weight
2. Explosive type
3. Distance to blast event
4. Angle of incidence
5. Site topography
6. Surrounding and adjacent structures
7. Building orientation
8. Building shape and configuration
9. Building size
10. Building exterior construction
11. Structural systems
12. Structural connection types

distance. The most effective method for minimizing blast pressures, aside from eliminating threats, is maximizing the standoff. Blast engineer specialists should be consulted if explosives are deemed credible threats, as not all structural engineers are familiar with the dynamics of blast design.

The standoff, or the radial distance between an explosive and a target, is measured from the minimum "keep out" distance surrounding the structure. For vehicle bombs, standoff is measured as the distance from the center of the vehicle at the edge of the keep out zone to the target. Although a terrorist threat may be an unsophisticated explosive composed of fertilizer and fuel, known as ammonium nitrate and fuel oil (ANFO), charge weight of explosives is typically measured in equivalent pounds of TNT.

Glazing and façade failure historically cause the most injuries to building occupants. Progressive collapse is responsible for the majority of fatalities. Structural blast analyses may be required to understand how structures nearest to the detonation location would respond to threats. Design of new building exteriors or upgrades to existing facilities may be needed to offset blast effects. Protection levels depend on available real estate, programmatic requirements, and the construction budget available for security countermeasures. For urban sites with minimal available standoff, building hardening is the only way to provide mitigation.

To achieve a balanced protection level, calculated risks and compromises may be required. Compromises from total protection address acceptable localized damage and minimized hazards to occupants to meet budget constraints. Danger to occupants cannot be eliminated, but personal injuries may be reduced and building damage minimized. Ultimately, informed owners are responsible for determining risk levels, and the extent and effectiveness of protective security measures. The amount of construction cost deemed appropriate for blast protection must be balanced against the ultimate cost of regret.

Construction costs are quantifiable, but the cost of injury and suffering of victims is not. Comparing protective costs against hazard reduction provides a basis for selecting budget allocations and mitigation design features. A cost estimating analysis will address the cost benefits for various proposed countermeasures, including structural hardening.

Blast Hazard Injuries

The extent of personal injuries to building occupants exposed to a blast depends on individual proximity to the explosion source. Blasts cause injury to soft tissue, such as skin, lungs, and eardrums. A person opposite a curtain wall may be shielded from some blast pressure, but flying and falling debris pose the most danger to personal safety. Falling pieces of exterior building material, glass shards, and falling floor slabs are the greatest hazards resulting from a blast. Severe injuries can also occur from being thrown to the ground or against an object.

Design against Progressive Collapse

Structural engineering design against blast damage is aimed at keeping structures intact to allow swift evacuation, isolating potential areas of collapse, and limiting overall damage. Progressive collapse refers to a localized failure causing adjoining structural members to be overloaded and fail, resulting in extensive damage disproportionate to the originating failure.

According to the American Society of Civil Engineers, ASCE 7, "Minimum Design Loads," progressive collapse is defined as the spread of an initial local failure from element to element eventually resulting in the collapse of an entire structure or a disproportionately large part of it. Some experts have defined resistance to progressive collapse to be the ability of a structure to accommodate, with only local failure, the notional removal of any single structural member. Aside from the possibility of further damage that uncontrolled debris from the failed member might cause, it appears prudent to consider whether the abnormal event will cause failure of only a single member.

An example of limited local damage would be the containment of damage to adjacent bays and within two or three stories of a higher structure. This damage may be the result of an explosion damaging the floor above and below the point of detonation and column failure. The restriction of progressive collapse requires containment of the damage to those areas directly loaded. Floors above should remain stable yet may sustain damage due to the loss of a column. Floor framing in bays not immediately adjacent the affected framing should also remain stable. Lastly, lateral load systems provided to carry wind and seismic loads should not be depleted, but must have sufficient alternative load paths to remain viable systems.

Security design criteria tries to avoid structural systems that facilitate or are vulnerable to progressive collapse resulting from the loss of a primary, vertical load-bearing structural member. Protective measures include elimination of external columns, elimination of cantilevers and exterior columns, and increased column construction (often composite constructions). It is possible to upgrade existing structures; however these methods are often costly, rely on specialized engineering analysis and new technology, and often require destructive testing and demolition to implement.

Building Structural Framing Systems

Cast-in-place concrete or steel framed buildings with wide flange beams are well suited for preventing progressive collapse. Buildings with large, open entrances, atria (particularly those exposed to exterior facades), or exposed or multistory unbraced columns are vulnerable to significant damage and failure. Load bearing walls are prone to progressive collapse failures if the lower floor walls are not properly reinforced. Prestressed concrete structures are prone to premature collapse due to the loss of tendon anchorage when the slab is damaged by a blast event.

Concrete reinforcement of slabs and beams, especially in outer structural bays, should be continuous at the top and bottom faces to permit reverse loading and large displacement in post-damage condition, though not complete failure. This will allow rescue access and evacuation of victims in the event of an attack. Column to beam connections are important when determining structural design systems against threat criteria. Other preferred building construction types include:

- Cast-in-place concrete buildings with either waffle slab or joist slab construction
- Sturdy steel frame structures with composite beam construction.

The least desirable structural systems include precast concrete construction or steel framed structures with open-web joists, because they do not provide the needed protection to occupants, will not stand up to low-level dynamic loads, and are prone to premature collapse or building failure.

BUILDING CONSTRUCTION ISSUES

Hardening of buildings against explosives and other threats refers to strengthening the building exterior, also known as the skin or building envelope, and structural systems, to resist collapse and damage from blast. Buildings and façades must be designed to transfer blast loads on the face of the structure to the lateral load-resisting system. When designing a new building, renovating an existing building, or evaluating an existing structure, the total system must be capable of gathering and transferring loads to the foundation.

Exterior Wall Construction

Building façades should be designed to meet threat requirements. For ballistic or forced entry, façade elements need to provide sufficient hardening. To resist blasts, they should be constructed of a rugged material sufficient to resist blast loads or designed to dynamically mitigate the effects of a blast attack.

The most effective protection is a façade that can fully resist blast loads, such as a cast-in-place concrete exterior wall. However, to be fully effective, the wall must be at least a foot thick, with increased reinforcement, and have only minimal window and door penetrations. This solution is very expensive and not aesthetically pleasing for most civic structures.

A more appealing solution is a semihardened façade, a system offering limited protection to building occupants, while attempting to mitigate flying glass hazards and debris. With this system, glass is designed to fail when damaged but remain secure within window frames, while walls are designed to accept localized damage. Suspended interior elements such as piping, VAV (variable air volume) boxes, and lighting may need additional attachment or bracing, similar to seismic detailing.

Windows

Splintered, flying shards of shattered annealed glass can inflict fatalities and serious injuries to building occupants. Laminated glass will, if properly anchored, remain in the frame in a failed condition and not become an airborne hazard. However, for this to occur, glass must be properly designed, anchored to the frame, and fail before the support system. Even at extremely high-pressure levels, this system will outperform standard glazing details used in commercial office buildings. Common types of window security glass include the following:

- Thermally tempered
- Annealed
- Heat strengthened
- Laminated
- Polycarbonate

Glass must be coordinated with the strength of the support system, mullion, anchor, and wall. Thermally tempered glass is the strongest, requiring the strongest mullion and support system, but fractures into tiny rock salt-like pieces, which may not adhere well to the laminate in a failed condition. This could result in flying glass shards or pieces causing serious personal injury.

Annealed and heat strengthened glass fails into much larger shards, and with an increased surface area, these pieces will remain attached to the laminate. Specifying laminated glass for the innermost window pane is the most effective measure to improve occupant safety. The glass will remain adhered to the polyvinyl butyral (PVB) interlayer when damaged, thereby limiting the extent of airborne shards projected into occupied spaces. Glazing material selection should be based on the nature of potential hazards, threats, and blasts in adjacent occupied spaces. Typical glazing hazards include the following:

- *Break-safe.* Glazing is retained in the frame or falls harmlessly to the floor.
- *Low hazard.* Damaged glass is thrown no greater than 10 feet from the window and impacts a vertical surface at a 10-foot distance no higher than 2 feet above the floor.
- *High hazard.* Damaged glass is thrown a distance of 10 feet or greater and impacts a vertical surface at a 10 foot distance a height of 2 feet above the floor.

Polycarbonate glazing is utilized in areas requiring ballistic resistance. Glazing thickness is associated with the type of firearm and ammunition utilized. Underwriters Laboratories (UL) standards rate ballistic protection from Levels 1-8.

Mullion and Window Support Systems

The final issue in creating a balanced façade is the strength of the mullion and window support system. Windows must fail before the support system, therefore the mullions and support system must be strong enough to resist blast loading, or be stronger than the glass.

Glass possesses a nominal strength used in glass design, and an actual strength, which is greater than the nominal strength and often not considered. When designing for guaranteed glass fail first, the framing system should match the strongest glass condition. When choosing glazing material, there is a distinct advantage to selecting the weakest glass available. This is true for blast loading, which overwhelms the capacity of the strongest available glass materials.

Glazing treatment, anchor details, and size will determine the minimum type of glass permitted. The protection is enhanced if the bite of the window frames is increased to retain the sheet of damaged laminated glass or a structural silicone sealant is used to adhere the laminated glass to the frame. This attention to the size of the bite and the sealant attachment will prevent the entire sheet of damaged laminated glazing from flying and becoming a large projectile.

In addition to the laminated glazing, flexibility of the framing members significantly affects the façade's blast loading resistance. Glazing retained within flexible framing members, such as curtain walls and storefront systems, is able to transfer significant portions of the blast energy to the more flexible supports. The interaction between the glazing and mullions will determine the increased blast loading resistance. However, the framing system must be designed to respond to highly impulsive dynamic loads with large inelastic deformations, and the system must be capable of sustaining these deformations without dismembering or dislodging the glass panes.

Window Film

Mylar or blast film can provide the same protection as laminated glass. However, the film life span is very short and requires replacement every five to seven years. In addition to this maintenance, the replacement film cannot be secured inside the profile of the window frame without removing the glass. Some mechanical anchorage systems offer better film attachment and thus better fragment retention; however these systems alter the window system aesthetics.

Blast Curtains

Blast net curtains were developed during World War II by the British to reduce glass hazards related to explosion incidents. The curtains consist of translucent KEVLAR®, a strong, lightweight material, sized longer and wider than the windows, with weights at the bottom. Excess curtain length is placed in a box at the window base. When a blast occurs, the curtains billow out, allowing the air blast to pass through, while collecting a portion of the glass fragments. For maximum effectiveness, curtains should be installed and kept closed. Leaving the curtains open defeats their purpose and renders them unable to function as intended. Exterior views, light transmission, visibility, and interior lighting need to be considered when blast curtains are used.

A catch bar is another alternative to blast curtains. A bar or grille is placed behind the window to stop filmed glass from flying into occupied spaces. Film must be thick enough to hold window fragments together in large pieces. However, this approach may not work with architectural design aesthetics and will not prevent glass shards from flying into spaces. To protect against projectile fragments of the façade or miscellaneous objects outside the building, the inside face of the exterior wall could be covered with materials such as Line-X, KEVLAR®, carbon fiber or fiberglass sheets, which capture falling debris.

Infrastructure

HVAC systems protect buildings from contamination, providing a means to remove any contamination caused by an internal event or prevent tainted air from entering the building, through building pressurization, purging exposed spaces, isolating critical areas, and protecting perimeter openings. Location of perimeter openings impacts site planning and architectural design.

Outside air intakes for all HVAC equipment must be protected against biohazards, by detecting chemical and biological pollutants and sealing openings. Air intake sensors should be located in or near these openings and tied to building controls. Motorized dampers should be installed in strategic locations to prevent contaminants from entering occupied spaces. Air intakes should not be located at grade level, where intruders can reach them. Recommended locations are several stories above grade, such as above the third floor roof or other inaccessible areas. Several areas require attention to HVAC systems, particularly lobbies, where most public access occurs. Other areas as previously discussed include loading docks, visitor control centers, mail inspection facilities, security operations centers, and any space with assembly or high occupancy rates, such as cafeterias, meeting rooms, and auditoria.

Infrastructure, such as generators and cooling towers, should be housed in structures meeting threat criteria. All structures outside a main facility or campus should be analyzed in the same manner for threat analysis. Equipment redundancies and alternate distribution paths should be considered for emergency operations.

Loading Docks

If a truck with explosives was parked and detonated next to a loading dock, the explosion could cause severe damage to a facility. The following design elements should not be located adjacent to loading docks:

- Incoming utility lines, above or below grade
- Emergency generators
- Fuel storage tanks or pipelines
- Building fire protection systems

Roofing

Roof access is sometimes overlooked during security planning. Roofing design criteria includes the following:

- Roofing levels can compromise building security if they are readily accessible due to grades, ladders, berms, or adjacent structures.
- Roof level access should be secured and monitored for authorized personnel only.
- Skylights should be designed to anticipate a blast incident.
- Critical equipment should be protected.

Building Planning

The most critical building spaces for security planning and design are lobbies, security operations centers, mechanical rooms, stairs and means of egress, loading docks, and mail rooms. Building lobbies are the most vulnerable program element. Emergency egress and life safety systems should be maintained separately, so that an incident does not prevent evacuation of building occupants. Design for critical and vulnerable spaces should address:

- Isolating critical spaces from populated areas with protective interior walls.
- Integrating critical spaces with frangible exterior materials.
- Providing sufficient space and infrastructure for inspection equipment.

TECHNOLOGY

Building owners, facility managers, and design professionals should be familiar with security technology systems when coordinating a security plan (Table 2.28).

TABLE 2.28   Overview of Security Technology Products

Security task	Products
Monitoring	• Closed circuit TV (CCTV), mounts, lenses, accessories (recorders, tracking, monitors) • Passive infrared • Glass break sensor
Inspection	• Turnstiles • X-Ray—package, palette, vehicle • Metal detector • Hand wand
Access control	• Electric locks • Magnetic contacts • Card readers • Biometrics • Combination locks

TABLE 2.29   Top 10 Operational Issues for Building Owners

1. Identifying security staffing levels, by shift, peak, and off-peak hours
2. Training and equipping security staff and all personnel for emergency procedures
3. Creating and training a rapid response team
4. Developing emergency policies and procedures
5. Communicating emergency policies and procedures to all personnel, including through a manual containing important contact phone numbers
6. Implementing access policies and procedures for staff, visitors, service, and maintenance personnel
7. Creating vehicle and truck vetting policies and procedures, including waste removal and fuel delivery
8. Establishing policies and procedures for screening mail and package deliveries
9. Creating a liaison with local law enforcement and public officials
10. Ensuring that insurance policies and premiums for premises and liability are in place, with copies maintained off-site

OPERATIONAL ISSUES

Operations refers to the day-to-day activities of personnel, security guards, employees, visitors, and deliveries within the facility. Operational considerations include hours of operation, delivery routines, building and ground maintenance, vetting of vehicles, and package inspection.

Even before design issues are addressed and technology systems are selected and installed, building owners are responsible for establishing and enforcing policies and procedures for daily operations within and around their facilities. These policies are developed in response to real and potential threat criteria (Table 2.29).

Security Officers and Personnel

Security staffing levels should be sufficient to defend against real or potential threats and respond to heightened security levels. Building owners and tenants must determine if in-house security personnel or outsourced companies provide the most cost-effective and efficient services, along with technology, to save operational costs. Contact information and ongoing communication with local law enforcement authorities, neighbors, and similar facilities should be part of emergency planning.

A facility-based rapid response team can provide quick and effective action in emergencies. For a campus, roving patrols may spend minimal time in one place and most of their time traveling between points, while monitoring site entrances. Personnel controlling site access points should do the following:

1. Verify valid identification of staff and visitors.
2. Check visitors against their driver's license photo identification.
3. Implement badge checks.
4. Require physical touching of badges for staff.
5. Install biometric scanners.
6. Schedule entry for maintenance, food service, and grounds personnel.

During simultaneous incidents or slow traffic, alarm response times may be very slow. Proper distribution of personnel throughout a facility, along with technology, will facilitate emergency response and more frequent patrols. Vehicular access control methods include the following:

1. Stop vehicles for vetting and inspection
2. Ensure that employee vehicles are registered and identifiable
3. Create reserved parking areas
4. Locate visitor parking outside the secure perimeter or at the most remote areas of parking lots

The jurisdiction of security officers is generally limited to within the legal property boundary of the campus or facility of their employer. When an off-site threat occurs, visible from on-site, such as on a public street or an adjacent property, security officers must alert local law enforcement and rely on them to respond. In some cases, a facility or building owner might enter a formal agreement with local law enforcement to respond immediately. A more aggressive approach, requiring advice from legal counsel, would be to seek an expansion of jurisdiction for officers to cover these situations.

Staff Training and Emergency Planning

Security is everyone's responsibility. Facility staff and employees should be trained to save lives and preserve operations during incidents and emergencies. Employees and security staff should be cognizant of suspicious activity. Training must be provided on recognizing, assessing, and reporting potential threats, and standard operating procedures must be developed for high threat environments. Building evacuation routes should be clearly marked and safe havens identified.

Some public agencies have established an Emergency Operations Manual (EOM), containing emergency control plans, telephone numbers, and contact information for management, staff, local law enforcement, public officials, and related procedures. The books are available to all personnel and are updated periodically.

CONCLUSION

Daniel Burnham's endorsement of big plans to be remembered and used over time is a valuable axiom for security master planning. The building project planning and design team must have a general understanding of security master plan components. Each element offers benefits and limitations to be carefully evaluated as standalone items and as part of an overall mitigation design strategy.

Establishing a comprehensive security master plan provides building owners and design professionals with the opportunity to enhance safety and security by evaluating, identifying, and selecting the best solutions for site planning, program adjacencies, architectural design, and engineering systems. Through a multidisciplinary collaboration and using the many design strategies available, operational efficiencies, cost savings, and transparent security approaches can be achieved. The net result will be measured in lives saved, and damage minimized during any subsequent terrorist attack, disaster, or emergency situation.

ACKNOWLEDGMENTS

- Harold Adams, FAIA, RIBA, JIA, Chairman Emeritus, RTKL Associates, Inc., Baltimore, Maryland
- Keith Kellner, Graphic Design, RTKL Associates, Inc., Baltimore, Maryland
- Lily Thayer, Public Relations Manager, RTKL Associates, Inc., Baltimore, Maryland

GLOSSARY

blast analysis   Determines how a structure will respond to an explosion.

CPTED   Crime Prevention Through Environmental Design is a planning concept to improve public safety by designing physical environments to influence human behavior in a positive way.

external factors   Those areas of concern located immediately adjacent to the campus, compound, or site, including external circulation, immediate neighbors, and site visibility.

hardening   The process of designing elements of the facility to withstand attack by various identified aggressor tactics.

infrastructure   The underlying critical support utilities for a facility, loss of which would result in mission failure and loss of security protection, such as power, water, and communications services.

operations   The day-to-day activities of guards, employees, visitors, deliveries, and intruders within the facility. Operational considerations include hours of operation, delivery routines, building and ground maintenance, vetting of vehicles, and package inspection.

perimeter and access points   Relates to definition of the site boundary, and means of access. Includes the hardening of areas immediately vulnerable to the facility and elements such as the perimeter fencing, alarm systems, gatehouses, and vehicle barriers.

policy   A statement explicitly dictating the daily interaction of employees and visitors to the facility. Policies evolve in keeping with the ongoing facility requirements and establish contingency plans for crisis situations.

progressive collapse   The failure of a building structure through removal of one column and the subsequent loss of bays both adjacent and above.

scaled distance   The cube root of the charge weight. Used to determine blast pressures during blast analysis. Blast pressure = standoff divided by scaled distance.

semihardened façade   A facade system offering limited protection to building occupants, while attempting to mitigate the hazard of flying glass and debris.

site   Elements, conditions, and characteristics of the property line protecting against threat criteria. Includes setbacks, parking improvements, signage, and implementation of physical barriers.

standoff   The distance maintained between a structure or asset from the potential location of a threat; threat criteria and building construction are both considered to determine the required separation.

technology or technical security   The utilization of hardware and software to deter, detect, and respond to threat criteria. Includes alarms, sensors, cameras, etc. to monitor specific areas of threat.

vehicle barrier   A device or element designed for traffic control; must be designed for the weight and speed parameters of the threat vehicle. May be passive or active.

vet   To examine carefully; to evaluate.

BIBLIOGRAPHY

ASCE 7-02, *Minimum Design Loads for Buildings and Other Structures,* American Society of Civil Engineers, Reston, Va., 2003.

Americans with Disability Act Standards for Accessible Design, U.S. GPO, Washington, D.C., July 1, 1994.

Building Design Criteria - GSA PBS-PQ-100 *Facilities Standards for the Public Buildings Service,* Dec. 23, 1993.

GSA, *Facility Standards for the Public Building Service,* PBS-P100, November 2000.

Hinman, Eve, *Upgrading Window for Blast Effects,* Hinman Consulting Engineers, San Francisco, www.hce.com/html/articles/glass.html#top.

ISC, *Security Design Criteria for New Federal Office Buildings and Major Modernization Projects,* May 28, 2001.

Jacobs, Jane, *The Death and Life of Great American Cities,* Random House, 1961.

Newman, Oscar, *Defensible Space, Crime Prevention Through Urban Design,* Macmillan, 1972. www.defensible-space.com.

U.S. Army Corps of Engineers, *Architectural and Engineering Instructions for the Designer,* November 21, 2000.

U.S. Department of Justice, *Vulnerability Assessment of Federal Facilities,* June 28, 1995.

Ventilation for Acceptable Indoor Air Quality, ASHRAE Standard 62, 1989.

INTERNET RESOURCES

American Institute of Architects (AIA)
www.aia.org

American National Standards Institute (ANSI)
www.ansi.org

American Planning Association (APA)
www.planning.org

American Society of Landscape Architects (ASLA)
www.asla.org

Architectural Record
www.architecturalrecord.com

Engineering News Record
www.enr.com

International CPTED Association
www.cpted.net

Landscape Architecture
www.asla.org

National Fire Protection Association (NFPA)
www.nfpa.org

Planning
www.planning.org/planning

RTKL Associates, Inc.
www.rtkl.com

Urban Land
www.urbanland.uli.org

Urban Land Institute (ULI)
www.uli.org

CHAPTER 3
CRIME PREVENTION THROUGH ENVIRONMENTAL DESIGN

Terri Kelly
Director, Community Outreach and Support
National Crime Prevention Council
Washington, D.C.

"The first thing to understand is that the public peace...is not kept primarily by the police, necessary as police are. It is kept by an intricate, almost unconscious, network of voluntary controls and standards among people themselves...No amount of police can enforce civilization where the normal, casual enforcement of it has broken down.   JANE JACOBS (b. 1916)
*Death and Life of Great
American Cities (1961)*

Streets and their sidewalks, the main public places of a city, are its most vital organs. If a city's streets are safe from barbarism and fear, the city is thereby tolerably safe from barbarism and fear...To keep the city safe is a fundamental task of a city's streets and its sidewalks.   JANE JACOBS
*Death and Life of Great
American Cities (1961)*

The relationship between crime, fear of crime, quality of life, and the built environment increasingly is of primary concern to the public, business leaders, and crime prevention practitioners. Communities experiencing problems with disorder, thefts, robberies, assaults, and other crimes often claim their neighborhoods and workplaces don't feel safe because streets are empty, properties are abandoned, graffiti covers the sides of buildings, or trash collection is erratic. The intersection of crime prevention, planning, and design addressing these issues is called crime prevention through environmental design, commonly abbreviated as CPTED (pronounced "sep-ted").

Criminologist Dr. C. Ray Jeffrey, of Florida State University, who coined the term in his landmark 1971 book, *Crime Prevention Through Environmental Design*, defined CPTED as: "The proper design and effective use of the built environment that can lead to a reduction in the fear and incidence of crime, and an improvement in the quality of life."

The built environment can be designed and modified to reduce vulnerability. CPTED programs examine access control, surveillance, and territoriality, providing residents and business leaders with opportunities to improve public safety. Collaboration among law enforcement, government agencies, local residents, planners, design professionals, and business people can identify crime and quality of life issues before they became serious and address public safety and security concerns during renovation and new construction projects.

CPTED examines decisions about:

- Absolute and relative locations of specific land use
- Relative siting of buildings and open spaces
- Interior and exterior design details such as color, lighting, entrances, exits, and landscaping
- When to use indoor and outdoor spaces, and for what purposes

In Bridgeport, Connecticut's Phoenix Project to control street-level drug trafficking, street barriers were constructed in areas adjacent to highway exits. Bridgeport developed a ten-point CPTED plan, with traffic control devices, one-way street design, increased tactical enforcement, and mobilization of area businesses and residents. The initiative resulted in a 75 percent crime decrease, the lowest crime rate in the area since 1972.

In Toronto, a program to prevent assaults and robberies changed local law to increase security standards for existing parking structures, the site of many incidents. Within a year of passing the CPTED-related law, providing security reminders to drivers and supporting driver escort programs, over 97 percent of the garages had adopted the security measures.

CPTED BASICS

CPTED encourages communities to be proactive in fighting crime. Environmental design decisions by planners, architects, designers, and law enforcement officials, along with residents and businesses, can affect a community by influencing human behavior and public perception of community safety. By evaluating urban design elements contributing to crime, decision makers can assess where problems might occur and implement changes before they become permanent in a building or neighborhood.

CPTED involves city agencies, community members, and economic interests, by providing alternative methods of addressing crime and underlying problems, instead of expending energy on patchwork responses to individual incidents. CPTED differs from other crime prevention strategies by emphasizing the role of design within the environment.

Traditionally, crime prevention emphasized opportunity reduction through property. Bars on windows and doors, alarm systems, cameras, gates, and other so-called "target hardening" techniques were used to protect people and property and reduce the potential for revictimization. These measures are essential for residents and businesses, and some facilities, such as banks, cannot function without them. Beyond a certain level, hardening of potential crime targets can be expensive and disruptive. Alarms, cameras, and school guards can mask symptoms, but cannot successfully address causes if criminal opportunity results from the design of a building or property.

As a crime control strategy, CPTED uses resources effectively by relying on existing programs and activities. The most successful CPTED programs include community residents, business professionals and public agencies officials, through a multidisciplinary approach. CPTED is most effective when those most affected by problems and solutions, the collaborators, participate in an ongoing dialogue to participants and stakeholders, can anticipate safety and security issues, rather than react to them. CPTED programs enlist agencies and community groups to resolve problems, rather than assume law enforcement will take on the task.

Communities and business leaders often fail to take greater advantage of CPTED because they don't understand CPTED, or how it can address crime and quality of life issues; believe CPTED conflicts with crime prevention goals; assume that CPTED will add costs to private business owners, and perceive that CPTED will create additional burdens on local government decision makers. However, CPTED programs and partnerships have successfully reduced crime in many cities.

Knoxville, Tennessee. Police, traffic engineers, public works officials, and residents collaborated on CPTED and crime-prevention training, by forming a task force to address drug trafficking and neighborhood nuisances, such as excess vehicle traffic in residential areas. The group effort resulted in street redesign, revised park schedules, and volunteer-led security survey teams.

Police officers worked with design professionals to make projects compatible with CPTED, thus reducing through traffic and drug trafficking.

Sarasota, Florida. CPTED guidelines planned to reduce crime in one neighborhood became an accepted part of the planning process. The CPTED task force of planners, law enforcement officials, agencies, and architects, organized by the city manager, recommended amendments to the zoning law for a special zoning district. CPTED became part of a successful business district revitalization project. Sarasota passed resolutions incorporating CPTED principles into all development.

Cincinnati, Ohio. A partnership of housing authority management, residents, and police officials developed a CPTED plan, consisting of community cleanups, increased maintenance, new fencing, lease enforcement, and on-site programs for parents and community youth. As a result, crime decreased 13 percent in each of three successive years after the partnership began.

Benefits

A well-crafted CPTED approach can enhance the safety goals of a community or business by using existing programs and resources to prevent crime. Benefits of CPTED within communities include:

Municipal

- Lower crime rates in neighborhoods and business areas.
- More tax revenues from safer business districts.
- Enhanced public safety in planning, development, and redevelopment projects.
- Increased use of parks and recreation facilities by residents.

Local law enforcement

- Improved community relations with residents through ongoing communication and crime prevention partnerships.
- Enhanced crime prevention training for officers.
- Increased crime prevention partnerships with residents.
- Fewer minor incidents allow more efficient community policing and coverage.

Business interests

- Lower crime rates result in reduced maintenance, repairs, insurance, and liability risks.
- More business revenues and sales tax generated.

Community residents

- Improved sense of security and quality of life.
- Fewer crimes committed in neighborhoods, fewer victimizations of residents.
- Increased interaction among residents and law enforcement to enhance relationships.

CPTED Theory, History, and Practice

Environmental design affects human behavior and influences fear of crime, opportunities for crime, and quality of life. Fear and the perception of some locations as unsafe can drive away customers, clients, employees, and residents. People form impressions of an environment based on what they hear, see, and smell, combined with personal experiences. When looking at an area, potential offenders consider familiarity of the surroundings, schedules, activities, and predictability factors.

CPTED is based on three basic principles to reduce crime: access control, surveillance, and territorial reinforcement:

Access control includes elements like doors, shrubs, fences, and gates to deny admission to a crime target and create a perception among offenders there is a risk in selecting the target. Technology and mechanical access control, including locks, bars, and alarm systems, collectively providing "target hardening," supplement natural access-control measures. Fencing around a neighborhood playground provides access control, by protecting children from wandering off and discouraging potential offenders from entering.

Surveillance utilizes design to increase visibility of a property or building by strategic location of windows, doors, corridors, paths, gates, lighting, and landscaping. Proper placement increases the likelihood individuals will observe intruders and regular users, challenge inappropriate behavior, or call the police or property owner. Natural surveillance deters crime by making the offender's behavior easily noticeable to a passing resident, employee, customer, police patrol, or private security detail.

Territorial reinforcement employs design elements such as signage, sidewalks, landscaping, and porches to distinguish between public and private areas. Users exhibit signs of ownership, sending "hands off" messages to would-be offenders. Supplementing design with regularly scheduled staff or activities, routine inspections, and maintenance enhances territorial reinforcement.

CPTED's History

Many civilizations have manipulated the natural and built environment to meet public safety needs. CPTED has evolved as a multidisciplinary area of study, developed from theories in different fields, each contributing to the links between environment and behavior. After World War II, these theories converged to form an important, widely recognized urban planning and design concept.

Within the context of CPTED, the design field professions, architecture, urban design, landscape architecture, and planning, address how land use, siting, and building design contribute to creating or reducing opportunities for crime. The social and behavioral sciences, sociology, criminology, psychology, anthropology, and geography, address how political, economic, and social conditions motivate offenders to commit crimes, and how offenders respond to environmental cues. Environmental psychology studies how people respond to their surroundings.

The first highly publicized studies of crime and the environment were conducted at the University of Chicago in the 1920s. Researchers discovered that crime patterns in Chicago were highest in the inner city and decreased in concentric circles away from the central business district. This pattern was explained with reference to "social disorganization," land use, and the city's historical development process. Since the Chicago studies, others have noted relationships between crime, growth of urban areas, and change produced by urbanization, such as crowding, homelessness, deteriorating housing stock, and traffic congestion.

In 1961, Jane Jacobs, in *The Death and Life of Great American Cities*, recounted her experiences as a resident of New York City's Greenwich Village. She observed some areas of Greenwich Village were productive and safe, while other areas only a few blocks away were nearly abandoned and frightening. The more productive neighborhoods included a mix of land uses generating round-the-clock activity; consistent block, site, and building designs; and opportunities for people to watch out for one another. These observations forever changed urban design and planning, and influenced research on crime and offenders.

Dr. C. Ray Jeffery, whose interest in crime prevention through environmental design was precipitated by Jacobs' work, called for an interdisciplinary approach to crime prevention focusing on changing the offender's behavior by changing the offender's environment. His work opened a new era in criminology, addressing the built environment and circumstances surrounding a crime incident, not just behavior.

In 1972, architect Oscar Newman published *Defensible Space: Crime Prevention Through Urban Design*. Newman worked in public housing to determine how design and social characteristics corresponded to safe and productive neighborhoods. Newman's research was based on urban planning and architectural design, with less emphasis on criminology and behavioral sciences. His work became the foundation for CPTED.

Newman identified the importance of territory and surveillance in creating safe places. When design created and defined public, semiprivate, and private spaces, residents exhibited greater indications of territoriality, deterring criminal activity by creating spaces that were defensible and defended. In the public housing study, he found crime was lowest in buildings with optimum opportunities for visibility and surveillance, based on building orientation and street location. He also found that the crime rate for buildings with minimal opportunities for visibility and surveillance was more than 100 times higher.

Defensible space concepts were refined and tested by the U.S. Department of Justice in four demonstration programs operated through the Westinghouse Electric Corporation in the mid-1970s. These included:

- A school demonstration in Broward County, Florida
- A commercial demonstration in Portland, Oregon
- Residential projects in Hartford, Connecticut, and Minneapolis, Minnesota

Research on the program, conducted by the National Institute of Justice, noted that in Hartford, traffic diversion, community policing, increased lighting, and clean-up campaigns made residents feel more in control of the neighborhood, increased interaction among neighbors, and influenced the use of neighborhood facilities.

The Westinghouse model maintained Newman's territoriality and surveillance themes and addressed the social cohesion and control issues criticized in Newman's work. Westinghouse researchers asserted residents needed to be involved in community improvement and understand how lighting and traffic pattern changes could reduce crime prevention.

CPTED and related concepts offer three key points:

- Land-use decisions affect community crime and crime-related conditions.
- Offenders work in areas and against people they know.
- Daily routines affect crime and crime risks.

Research and experience indicate land-use decisions have a direct bearing on the types of crimes committed. For example, specific types of businesses, such as adult-oriented establishments, contribute to increased crime rates in surrounding areas. In *Young v. American Mini Theaters*, the U.S. Supreme Court agreed, and found zoning is in the community interest if used to control secondary effects attributed to adult businesses, such as increased crime rates and neighborhood deterioration. Lax enforcement of land-use standards and building codes contributes to crime. A study of abandoned buildings in Newport News, Virginia, revealed burglary rates in a crime-ridden apartment complex dropped 35 percent after 100 vacant, dilapidated apartments were boarded up.

Offenders tend to commit crimes in places they know well, near home, work, school, because in these places they know those who live and work there, and who regularly visits; they understand what days of the week and times of day people will be around, are aware of the potential crime targets in the area, and know routes of quick access and egress and places of concealment.

Daily routines, combined with local rules, regulations, policies, and procedures, create or reduce opportunities for crime. For example, when large geographic areas are zoned exclusively for single-family residences, and when the people who live in these neighborhoods are away from home between 8:00 a.m. and 6:00 p.m. for work or school, no one is left to observe activity in the neighborhood, creating the perfect environment for crime. Seniors-only residential complexes or apartment buildings with many children present different crime prevention challenges and imply that those who remain home to observe activity in the community may also feel particularly vulnerable to the risk of crime.

Bringing CPTED to Communities

Understanding connections between CPTED and crime prevention, planning, and design creates an effective approach to crime problems. By gaining an understanding of the three key concepts of access control, surveillance, and territorial reinforcement, business and community leaders can move from theory to action, and address community disorders and incivilities, as well as more serious and violent crimes.

ADDRESSING CRIME WITH CPTED

CPTED programs result from problems at a site or facility, such as a street intersection, convenience store, school, park, or abandoned building. Crime may be related to the following:

Existing Land Use

- Vacant buildings or lots are taken over by juvenile gangs, drug users, or other undesirables.
- Office and commercial uses are interspersed with residential dwellings and bring outsiders through an otherwise "private" neighborhood. With so much traffic, residents no longer know each other, and homes are burglarized

Site Characteristics

- Fencing, landscaping, and inadequate lighting create opportunities to hide.
- Parking lots or garages are sited or designed without any opportunities for surveillance, making them good locations for theft or assault.

Traffic and Transit Issues

- Drug dealers establish themselves at important street intersections.
- Streets create a convenient path for through traffic.
- Bus stops serve as regional transfer points and bring outsiders to the area. Businesses complain aggressive panhandlers seeking spare change approach patrons waiting for busses. Many patrons don't return because they don't feel safe in the area.
- Parks may be busy play areas during the day, but virtually empty at night if inadequate lighting leaves residents feeling unsafe.
- In an area with a single industrial or commercial use, passersby do not notice property or other crimes committed on or near facilities, especially if they occur when facilities are not operating. With employees and business-related traffic unavailable as observers, the facility and environs are vulnerable to crime.

Demographic Changes

- Owners convert their homes into rental properties and tenants are not invested in the neighborhood. They don't know other residents, property owners, and managers, or report criminal activity visible through surveillance.
- New residents are younger, less affluent, and desire a lifestyle conflicting with more established homeowners. Elderly neighbors are afraid and stay indoors unless escorted.
- New business owners are from non-English-speaking cultures, and they are unfamiliar with security needs, safety techniques, and working with law enforcement and community groups.

Ineffective Policies

- Nonresident landlords own a high percentage of properties. They hold on to their investments but make few improvements, while deteriorating structures attract drug users to the neighborhood. The city does little to enforce building codes.

- Trash collection is scheduled infrequently, but the neighborhoods or business districts experience high turnover rates, and trash accumulates. Lack of municipal garbage collection on vacant property gives the impression that residents and property owners don't care about their neighborhood.

- Office buildings in the neighborhood are occupied only between 8:00 a.m. and 6:00 p.m., Monday through Friday, and are vandalized or burglarized on weekends.

- Warehouses are heavily oriented to truck or automobile use, rather than pedestrian traffic. Pickup and delivery are limited to a few hours a day; warehouses are burglarized and vandalized; truck drivers are assaulted.

- Convenience stores or discount retail outlets are open when other commercial establishments are not, and are the targets of late-night robbery and shoplifting.

- Speeding and traffic problems are worst when the high school lets out for the day, and most neighborhood thefts occur mid- to late afternoon.

Each of these scenarios suggests different programs and activities to change environmental conditions and reduce crime and fear. No two situations will be resolved the same way. A CPTED team must consider site characteristics and strategies. However, CPTED principles remain the basis of all efforts.

Designing an Effective Strategy

Decisions about strategies must involve all community members affected by crime. During implementation, communication should be maintained with the neighborhood, through neighborhood associations, tenant groups, community policing officers, service agencies, websites, and newsletters. (Table 3.1).

Once the list of strategies is established, the team estimates implementation costs. Many strategies do not require additional expense. Local residents and businesses may opt to cover some costs. When estimating costs and financing options, communities, business leaders, and facility managers

TABLE 3.1   Successful CPTED Strategies

1. Neighborhood festival or block party
2. Neighborhood watch program
3. Public education and advocacy programs
4. Targeted code enforcement
5. Cleanup campaign
6. Installation of upgraded target-hardening measures such as locks, fencing, alarm systems, metal detectors
7. Installation of mechanical surveillance tools such as closed circuit television
8. Community gardens
9. Landscape maintenance
10. Lighting upgrades
11. Traffic enforcement
12. Security surveys
13. Infill construction or new development
14. Property acquisition, demolition, redevelopment, and rehabilitation
15. Changes in zoning or development regulations, such as landscaping
16. New or modified traffic signal systems or changes to turning movements
17. Street closings or street privatization
18. Changes to bus routes or schedules

should consider the benefits, such as increased property values, sales tax revenues, or decreased property insurance premiums, resulting from new initiatives. When businesses and government leaders understand the return on their investment from CPTED, they are more willing to participate. Data collection during early project phases generally provides more accurate estimates.

Business leaders and facility managers applying CPTED must define roles and responsibilities at the outset of the planning process. A facility-improvement program should be the responsibility of property owners and businesses, although they cannot achieve these goals alone. Other stakeholders, who stand to gain from improved communities and increased quality of life, should be identified and kept aware of ongoing CPTED efforts. Even if they are not team members, many stakeholders and groups can provide assistance or advice throughout implementation on tactics and logistics, funding sources, and scheduling. (Table 3.2)

Evaluating the Strategy

The final element of the plan, evaluation, determines the effectiveness of CPTED strategies. Measures of success reflect how well prioritized planning goals and objectives were met. Evaluations should measure whether people feel safer, if there is less trash, fewer weeds and stray animals, and whether vandalism and graffiti have declined. For example, if the goal is to improve facility stability, evaluation might include changes in

- Residential or commercial vacancy rates
- Assessed valuation
- Property crimes
- Code violations or citations
- Building permits
- Owner occupancy

CPTED teams review how the project affected other neighborhood problems, including

- Greater neighborhood use and control of streets, parks, and other public spaces
- Less frequent or less noticeable drug or gang activity
- Lower traffic volumes and slower speeds, so children can cross the streets more safely
- Increased property maintenance, cleaning, and repairs by owners and tenants
- Better relationships and communication between owners and renters, residents and businesses, the neighborhood and government agencies

TABLE 3.2 CPTED Stakeholders and Participants

1. Planning, growth management, and/or economic development agencies
2. Design professionals: architects, engineers, landscape architects, and interior designers
3. Community residents
4. Real estate developers
5. Public works department
6. Local utility company
7. Code enforcement and licensing
8. Traffic engineering
9. Transit authority
10. Schools
11. Local law enforcement, public officials, and elected leaders
12. Chambers of commerce and merchants' associations

Establishing a CPTED Team

To achieve the full benefits of CPTED for a business or facility, decision makers should assemble a multidisciplinary team. Together with owners, managers, and employees, CPTED leaders will identify problems, analyze options, make recommendations, select solutions, and implement strategies. Ideally, team members should include representatives of local government agencies and organizations responsible for the built environment. The team should include a core of regular members, but composition may vary based on the problem, issue, or project.

Framework for Success

Incorporating CPTED into business operations can include:

1. *Know how a business operates.* Familiarity with business operations ensures CPTED will be considered in long- and short-term decisions, such as during plan review of new construction and redevelopment projects. Appropriate stakeholders should be included during decision making. In South San Francisco, California, an ordinance requires police involvement during planning for security and safety, and prohibits occupancy until the police representative signs off on the project. Community input at public hearings eliminated adult-oriented entertainment or other crime-prone businesses.

2. *Adopt laws, rules, regulations, policies, and procedures supportive of CPTED, or at least not conflicting with or contradicting the CPTED program.* Community leaders can seek interpretations of existing laws, policies, and zoning regulations consistent with CPTED. In parts of Dade County, Florida, a building code with CPTED standards was implemented for new construction. As a result, from 1975 to 1976, burglary rates for new homes fell 24 percent.

3. *Incorporate CPTED into training and professional development for law enforcement officers, planners, and public agency personnel.* Officers and government personnel can use CPTED best practices to do their jobs effectively. Baltimore, Maryland's crime control and prevention strategy incorporated CPTED training for community organizers, law enforcement officers, and agencies working with residents to mobilize neighborhoods in combating drug trafficking and other crimes.

4. *Offer CPTED educational materials to community groups and associations.* Community groups establish partnerships with government agencies and receive information about crime-related problems. Educational materials with examples of small-scale projects communicate CPTED's benefits to neighborhood associations and identify ways to solve problems. In Tucson, Arizona, during the late 1980s, the police department trained community volunteers to install crime prevention devices in homes of elderly residents. Officers worked with neighborhood watch groups on residential security surveys.

5. *Allocate necessary resources to achieve CPTED goals.* Resources need not involve cash. Examples of agency support for staff participation include incentives and allocation of staff time during plan review and CPTED projects. Ann Arbor, Michigan, assigned personnel to participate in plan review for development and redevelopment projects.

Completing a CPTED Audit

The first task for the team is auditing laws, rules, regulations, policies, and procedures governing planning, design, use and maintenance of neighborhoods and facilities, and related to CPTED principles. The audit is time-consuming but worthwhile, and will identify potential legal and institutional barriers to CPTED implementation. These documents govern how the built environment is developed. Each document should be reviewed and contradictions noted. The inventory should consider

- Comprehensive master planning, land-use plans, and development review
- Zoning, subdivision, landscape, or other ordinances

- Capital improvement plans and programs
- Building, fire, and life safety codes, and code enforcement policies
- Ordinances and policies relating to neighborhood disorder problems, such as loitering, vagrancy drinking in public, and graffiti

For each policy or process, the review should address the following:

- Agency or agencies controlling a process or policy, and enforcement powers
- Steps or early decisions in the planning process for presenting CPTED principles
- Frequency and context of plans and policy implementation and review
- Participants in review or assessment meetings
- Key people involved and contact information

Planning and CPTED

Planning and design professionals are responsible for protecting public health, safety, and welfare, by addressing building and life safety codes. Crime prevention should be considered as one of many important design criteria during preliminary project and plan review phases.

The comprehensive plan, also known as the land-use or master plan, allocates design, social, and economic resources to meet future needs. Although not a legal document in the strictest sense, the comprehensive plan illustrates future land-use options. Ideally, the comprehensive plan should address safety, crime and crime prevention, along with housing, neighborhoods, civic buildings, public institutions, recreation, and parks.

DEVELOPMENT REGULATIONS

Several types of land-use regulations are often considered during community planning and project design, including zoning, subdivision and landscape ordinances.

Zoning Ordinances

Zoning regulations are designed to provide light and air, provide security and safety from danger, prevent overcrowding, and achieve a logical pattern of land use. Often, zoning ordinances contain requirements conflicting with or limiting opportunities to apply CPTED principles of access control, surveillance, or territorial reinforcement. These might include requirements such as deep front-yard setbacks, rear lot parking, or minimum lot sizes generating low-density development. CPTED review of zoning ordinances should

- Compare zoning maps with existing land uses to see if zoning ordinances create nonconforming uses.
- Determine if variances are needed.
- Ascertain if nonconforming use language will prevent maintenance and upkeep.
- Evaluate if strict code enforcement language clearly states standards for maintenance of any CPTED application once the property is developed, and indicates how violations will be enforced.

Subdivision Ordinances

Subdivision ordinances, regulating streets, sidewalks, and open spaces, often impose requirements conflicting with basic CPTED principles. Many subdivision ordinances place a priority on unrestricted travel, especially for emergency vehicles, and require a street right-of-way wide enough for two lanes of traffic, plus street parking on each side of the street. These wide streets are perfect for "cut-through" traffic, and encourage cruising or excessive use by illegitimate or nonresidential users seeking convenient outlets from main roads.

Designers and developers often respond to concerns about cut-through traffic by creating a system of cul-de-sacs. Depending on the street length, this may make travel through the neighborhood confusing, or create isolation for residents. An alternative is street redesign to one-way streets, stoplights to slow traffic, and definition of appropriate passageways through the area.

Some communities do not require sidewalks in subdivisions, limiting pedestrian activity. Many subdivision ordinances emphasize, or require, open space. Open space will not create problems, but poorly planned open space results in unassigned territory in the subdivision, which can lead to inappropriate or criminal use by residents or outsiders. Signage, lighting, fencing, and landscaping can address this issue.

Landscape Ordinances

Landscape ordinances establish requirements for open space, installing and maintaining plant materials, if not covered under other ordinances. Landscape ordinances are designed to save or replace existing trees, provide shade, and allow for retention and absorption of storm water, or for aesthetics. They outline minimum plant dimensions, such as height, spacing, caliper, and percent coverage. Ordinances may include language governing installation of fences, walls, lighting, or other materials.

Many landscaping requirements reduce or eliminate surveillance opportunities. For example, ordinances may require solid walls or fences, berms, or dense plantings to hide parking lots, dumpsters, or other unsightly or undesired site elements. Surveillance is a factor when ordinances define minimum, but not maximum, plant sizes. At the time of installation, plant materials may allow surveillance, but quickly grow to a size that obscures clear sightlines. When maximum sizes are part of the initial design, ordinances may fail to include maintenance or enforcement provisions. Even when they exist, they are seldom enforced.

Other Development Standards

Although the above are the most common forms of land development ordinances, many types of regulations exist and must be reviewed for CPTED problems or opportunities. Performance standards take the place of zoning and subdivision requirements in some communities. They establish overall development densities and general goals, but do not place restrictions like minimum lot sizes on the developer to minimize dense cluster developments. Performance standards encourage mixed use, and may result in a mix of uses inappropriate for crime prevention purposes. Other development standards may regulate signs, parking, historic structures, or other issues impacting crime and crime prevention.

CAPITAL IMPROVEMENT PROGRAMS

Capital improvement programs include schedules and cost estimates for construction, upgrades, or maintenance of public facilities, such as schools, public buildings, streets, sidewalks, water and sewer lines, and service utilities. Proposed facility expansions may adversely affect surrounding neighborhoods by increasing traffic and use by outsiders. Expansions may require changes in transportation routes, one-way streets, street widening, intersection realignments, or changes to bus stops or bus routes to serve expanded development. Metropolitan area transportation plans offer details on proposed changes.

Other problematic facilities include parking lots and parking garages, often the scenes of robberies, thefts from cars, assaults, and vandalism. Careful consideration of CPTED will limit crime in these facilities, as well as malls, retail outlets, and apartment buildings.

CPTED education programs should provide private property owners and developers with information about crime-related liability issues. A 1996 article by the National Institute of Justice, "The Expanding Role of Crime Prevention Through Environmental Design in Premises Liability," contends that crimes occur because offenders take advantage of inadequate security or design features in a building or on a property.

Developing CPTED Goals

Reviewing rules, policies, and community experiences will assist CPTED partners in establishing goals, which may focus on:

1. *Improving neighborhood quality of life through property maintenance and code enforcement.* Laws requiring maintenance indicate people care and are around to take care of their property, facility, or neighborhood. Many communities use enforcement rules, including building and housing code enforcement and application of "public disorder" laws addressing public drunkenness; loitering; trash, weeds, litter; trespassing; and traditional criminal law enforcement. In Seattle, Washington, until a new law took effect in 1987, panhandlers prompted complaints from residents and tourists. A city ordinance was passed prohibiting sitting or lying on sidewalks in commercial districts between 7:00 a.m. and 9:00 p.m. In some downtown areas, the problem of panhandlers sitting and lying on sidewalks was eliminated.

2. *Completing neighborhood evaluations and developing neighborhood CPTED strategies.* A Knoxville, Tennessee, interagency group, working with public housing communities, determined the poor physical condition of certain areas contributed to street drug trafficking. CPTED focused on increased enforcement and targeted neighborhood action. The team surveyed areas for compliance with lighting requirements, established clearer neighborhood boundaries, trained volunteers to conduct safety inspections, and removed garbage and abandoned vehicles.

3. *Revising laws, rules, regulations, policies, and procedures that contradict or conflict with CPTED principles.* Changing local building codes can reduce delays in forcing owners to comply with laws requiring property maintenance. In New Orleans, Louisiana, community organizers worked with the county to identify problem properties and board them up while seeking changes in local laws to remove enforcement obstacles.

4. *Educating law enforcement officers, planners, and building and design professionals in CPTED principles.* In Tucson, Arizona, the police department prepared an educational CPTED presentation for community leaders, professionals, and a statewide group of architects. The presentation led to departmental involvement in training and coursework for students at the University of Arizona's College of Architecture.

5. *Educating managers, owners, and apartment complex residents in CPTED principles and applications to multifamily housing.* The Oregon state police academy led a CPTED training program on crime prevention for building managers and residents. The curriculum was a statewide model and included pilot programs.

DETERMINING RESPONSIBILITIES

Potential CPTED partners often include those with budgetary or policy authority, legislative expertise, understanding of crime prevention, and community involvement.

1. *Public Agencies.* Law enforcement officials are often chosen to lead CPTED teams due to their involvement in crime prevention and knowledge of community issues. However, some communities emphasize CPTED design elements and select planners to lead the effort. Successful CPTED programs have been led by economic development, parks and recreation, traffic engineering, or other public agencies. In some cases, the mayor or designated supervisor manages a multiagency task force.

The most appropriate group to lead the program demonstrates expertise and leadership and provides staff and resources for community needs. Success results from interdepartmental teamwork, and has less to do with who was in charge than with how the work was accomplished. Departmental team members might include representatives from the planning office, community development, the fire marshal's office, public works, traffic engineering, and law enforcement, and in some locations, an urban forester, assessor, or parks and recreation representative. In many communities, the housing and transit authorities and the school board are independent organizations and have their own law enforcement staff. Because their activities often affect adjacent neighborhoods, they should be included in discussions of problems and issues.

Resources to support CPTED efforts may be available from organizations and groups outside local government, including the following:

2. *Schools, colleges, and universities.* Educational institutions are often involved in their own crime prevention efforts to combat property crimes and crimes on school grounds. A CPTED plan may address crime on campus or opportunities for crime that institutions created in their neighborhoods. Schools invite outsiders into the community, and areas around the schools can become "hot spots" for crime. Cooperation and collaboration improve safety on campus and in the community.

Schools can contribute to CPTED efforts by encouraging security personnel to offer crime prevention education to students, staff, community residents, and businesses. Schools can offer technical assistance by recruiting faculty and staff for data collection and analysis, sampling and surveys, program evaluation, review and modification of laws or policies, design alternatives, or cost-benefit analyses.

3. *Business community.* Business owners and merchant associations have an important stake in creating safe communities. The size and nature of business interests will affect the owner's or manager's perspective on community crime issues. Small business owners who are neighborhood residents will view local crime problems differently than managers of large retail outlets or manufacturing and distribution facilities, because they are stakeholders. Hours of operation, customer volume, number of employees, and products sold will affect a business owner's perspective about crime and potential solutions. Business leaders can provide the CPTED team with information on area crime, publicize meetings to discuss proposed strategies, and provide in-kind services, such as meeting space, printing notices, and publicity.

4. *Private housing or commercial developers.* Private housing or commercial developers may be reluctant to adopt CPTED if they anticipate infringements to operational flexibility and costly changes. Many developers use security in housing and office buildings as marketing tools to boost rentals and project profitability.

The challenge is demonstrating how CPTED supports developer goals, including profit motives. The team should provide information comparing costs of crime, including lost profit, productivity, liability, and perception of the business or property within the community, with the modest investment of preventative CPTED measures, such as adjustments to location and lighting of parking lots, landscaping design, and access control through entrances and exits.

5. *Electric utilities and other companies with special expertise.* Power and electric utility companies can evaluate street lighting or site development proposals, and may establish or underwrite lighting improvement programs. Landscaping or fencing companies can estimate material costs and recommend materials to best address surveillance and maintenance.

6. *Architects and designers.* Members of the design community, including architects, landscape architects, engineers, and interior designers, have a strong interest in creating safe, livable communities, and should be an integral part of CPTED efforts. Many important design decisions are made early in planning stages, long before a public project review occurs.

7. *Legal community.* Attorneys understand how laws are interpreted and may propose changes to laws or codes. Municipal and private sector attorneys concerned about premises liability will immediately see the advantages of CPTED, because of reduced liability and reduced opportunities for victimization by crime. The costs of lawsuits to city or company finances can be significant. The detrimental impact of declining sales or tax revenues from facilities such as parking garages, downtown sports and entertainment facilities, and shopping districts not used because of fear of crime provide strong incentive for implementing CPTED.

8. *Neighborhoods.* CPTED programs should involve community residents, because of their interest in eliminating insufficient lighting, graffiti indicating gang activity, dilapidated houses abandoned by owners, or public buildings damaged by vandalism. Even in communities plagued by violent crime, residents remain concerned about quality of life, such as trash, overgrown lots, and noise nuisances. Neighborhood groups can advocate for improved lighting, maintenance, landscaping, fencing, traffic patterns, parks, and public places.

CPTED Reviews and Project Planning

Planning, design, and construction of new buildings and renovated facilities can impact community crime prevention efforts. Some localities may require a preapplication meeting before design begins, while others issue a building permit based on the site plan and do not review construction documents. Most communities require plan review for large development projects. Several phases of the design process generally occur before material is submitted for review and approval by local building department officials to ensure code compliance.

Familiarity with planning, design, and construction project phases will enable CPTED stakeholders to provide timely and valuable suggestions to building owners and the project design team, without causing schedule delays or substantially impacting project budgets. Community groups participating in CPTED reviews should understand that design recommendations made during early project phases are easier and less costly, in time and resources, to include in project design. Recommendations presented later in the design process, when most design decisions have been made, may be rejected because project budgets and schedules have been finalized. Owners may not wish to add elements or make changes resulting in delays and cost overruns, unless required by law or policy.

Project Planning, Design, and Construction Phases

Programming and planning occur at the preliminary phases of a renovation or new construction project. The project design team typically includes the architect, engineer, consultants, and the building owner. Together, they agree upon a functional and space program, with descriptions and requirements for the site, building, and interior spaces.

During the schematic design phase, the architect develops project requirements through drawings, and often models, to address site planning, building design, parking, site access points, and other design elements. CPTED participation with the project team should ideally occur during schematic design to review impact on surrounding neighborhoods, access control, surveillance, and property use policies.

After functional relationships are agreed upon during schematic design, the architect refines the design concept. The design development phase details site planning, landscaping elements, parking, and building design. The architect selects and specifies materials, finishes, colors, doors and windows, and dimensions and coordinates heating, cooling, plumbing, lighting, communications, fire protection, and building systems with the project team.

Design elements to evaluate, along with CPTED principles, might include building locations; separation of public and private activity areas; ensuring that vehicular and pedestrian routes don't conflict with one another; locations of trees, plantings, fences, walls, gates, screens, dumpsters, graphics, and signage; and lighting levels and locations. Landscaping design elements should be reviewed to minimize hiding places and maximize surveillance and observation.

When these elements are agreed upon, the architect prepares construction documents and specifications, describing how the building goes together. These documents specify building materials, finishes, and furnishings. They are used to solicit bids for construction services, and are the basis for project cost estimates. By the time construction drawings are underway, the architect has fixed room layouts, floor plans, details, dimensions, and relationships between exterior activities and interior spaces.

Specifications identify doors, windows, hardware, and locking systems; communications systems; signage and graphics; interior and exterior lighting; and finishes and details for every material or product to be installed in the building and on site. Specifications address maintenance for locks, walls, floors, and other building materials relating to breaking and entering, vandalism, graffiti, and potential long-term costs. Construction documents and specifications are distributed to contractors interested in submitting project bids.

The bidding, negotiation, and construction phases typically occur after plan review and permitting are completed. During these phases, contractors recommend material or product substitutions to reduce costs. CPTED team members trained in design can work with contractors, owners, and developers to review the desired security levels of lighting, landscaping, fencing, and locking systems. Workers may install locks or other products incorrectly or incompletely, limiting their value as security measures. Construction observation is an important responsibility for this reason.

CPTED after Occupancy

Once a construction project is completed and the building is occupied, operations, or the way a property is used and maintained, are as important to crime reduction as good design and the use of technology to control access. Operational issues affecting crime prevention include hours of activity, staffing, space assignments, property maintenance, and disciplinary codes. Through attention to CPTED principles, and collaboration among all community stakeholders seeking to enhance the quality of life, increased public safety and security can be achieved.

ACKNOWLEDGMENTS

This material was adapted, with permission, from *Designing Safer Communities: A Crime Prevention Through Environmental Design Handbook,* published by the National Crime Prevention Council.

BIBLIOGRAPHY

Jacobs, Jane, *The Death and Life of Great American Cities*, Random House, New York, 1961.

Jeffrey, C. J., *Crime Prevention Through Environmental Design*, Sage Publications, Beverly Hills, Calif., 1971.

National Crime Prevention Council, *Designing Safer Communities: A Crime Prevention Through Environmental Design Handbook*, Washington, D.C., 1997.

National Institute of Justice, *The Expanding Role of Crime Prevention Through Environmental Design in Premises Liability*, U.S. Department of Justice, Washington, D.C., 1996.

Newman, Oscar, "Defensible Space," The Macmillan Company, New York, 1972.

Zelinka, Al, and Brennan, Dean, *SafeScape: Creating Safer, More Livable Communities Through Planning and Design*, American Planning Association, Chicago, Ill., 2001.

INTERNET RESOURCES

Publications

American City & County
www.americancityandcounty.com

Campus Safety Journal
www.campusjournal.com

Governing
www.governingmagazine.com

Homeland Defense Journal
www.homelanddefensejournal.com

Planning Magazine
www.planning.org/planning

Preservation
www.PreservationOnline.org

Security Management
American Society for Industrial Security
www.securitymanagement.com

Urban Land
www.urbanland.uli.org

ORGANIZATIONS

American Architectural Foundation (AAF)
www.archfoundation.org

American Institute of Architects (AIA)
www.aia.org

American Planning Association (APA)
www.apa.org

American Society of Industrial Security (ASIS)
www.asisonline.org

American Society of Landscape Architects (ASLA)
www.asla.org

Community Associations Institute (CAI)
www.caionline.org

Congress for the New Urbanism (CNU)
www.cnu.org

Council of Educational Facilities Planners
  International (CEFPI)
www.cefpi.org

Designing Out Crime Association
www.doca.org.uk

Florida CPTED Network (FCN)
www.flcpted.org

International CPTED Association (ICPTEDA)
www.cpted.net

Local Government Commission (LGC)
www.lgc.org/center/index.html

Mayors' Institute on City Design (MICD)
www.micd.org

National Crime Prevention Council (NCPC)
www.ncpc.org

National Institute of Justice, part of the United
  States Department of Justice, Office of
  Justice Programs
http://www.ojp.usdoj.gov/nij/

National Main Street Center (NMSC)
www.mainst.org

Partners for Livable Communities (PLC)
www.livable.org

Project for Public Spaces (PPS)
www.pps.org

Security Industry Association (SIA)
www.siaonline.org

Smart Growth Network
www.smartgrowth.net

Urban Land Institute (ULI)
www.uli.org

Cities

Cincinnati, Ohio Metropolitan Housing Authority
www.cintimha.com

City of Houston, Texas
www.cityofhouston.gov

City of Sarasota, Florida
www.sarasotagov.com

Gainesville, Florida Police Department
www.gainesvillepd.org

Knoxville, Tennessee Police Department
www.knoxvillepd.org

Tempe, Arizona Police Department
http://www.tempe.gov/police

P · A · R · T · 2

PLANNING AND DESIGN

CHAPTER 4

ARENAS, SPORTS FACILITIES, CONVENTION CENTERS, PERFORMING ARTS FACILITIES: SAFETY AND SECURITY AFTER SEPTEMBER 11, 2001

Russ Simons
Principal, HOK Sport + Venue + Event
Kansas City, Missouri

Gerald Anderson, AIA
Senior Principal, HOK Sport + Venue + Event
Salt Lake City, Utah

International Association of Assembly Managers
Safety and Security Task Force

*The answer to safety and security is to be willing to spend the
appropriate amount to produce the desired outcome.*
> DONNIE DUNCAN
> *Associate Commissioner,*
> *Football Operations,*
> *Big 12 Conference*

*September 11, 2001 began a new era for public assembly
facility management.*
> TIM HICKMAN, CFE (CERTIFIED FACILITY EXECUTIVE)
> *Manager, University of*
> *Missouri Hearnes Center*

From the Super Bowl to college basketball, from major industry trade shows to pop music concerts, facility managers, building owners, and event planners are tackling a new era of heightened threats to public safety with defensive planning and tactical operations. Large public assembly venues, including arenas, stadiums, ballparks, convention centers, and performing arts facilities are implementing multidisciplinary strategies designed to mitigate acts of terrorism and violence.

The 1993 World Trade Center bombing in New York and the 1995 destruction of the Alfred P. Murrah Federal Building in Oklahoma City minimally affected public assembly facility operations. Many facility owners and operators considered these events as one-time occurrences, rather than ongoing threats to facilities and patrons.

We had a plan for emergency response and evacuation, but not one for terrorism–yet.

SCOTT WILLIAMS
*General Manager, Delta Center
in Salt Lake City, Utah*

The September 11, 2001 attacks in New York, Washington, and Pennsylvania raised the stakes, as international terrorism became a global concern. In response, facility owners, venue operators, architects, and engineers are incorporating security design, technology, and operational policies and procedures into every major public assembly project, with the goal of enhancing user safety and creating less attractive terrorism targets.

Public assembly facility managers classify venues meeting the following criteria as potential targets:

• Symbolic and economic community value

• Highly noticeable and photogenic

• Containing a high concentration of population

Mitigating potential threats requires planning and preparation by evaluating and implementing the following basic strategies:

• Use visible, external security such as cameras or foot or vehicular patrols.

• Install building and technology systems to minimize facility exposure.

• Check people and packages entering a facility.

• Familiarize facility managers and security personnel with all aspects of facility operations.

• Prepare for a lockdown, so the general public and any unauthorized individuals cannot gain access to unauthorized areas.

• Badge all employees and subcontract workers for visual identification.

• Familiarize employees with their overall building responsibilities.

• Emphasize employees' responsibility to be aware of the activities around them.

Before September 11, public assembly facility security remained in the background, striving to be transparent, invisible to the public. Public assembly security protocols were internal, rather than external, and initiatives were patron-driven. Controlling what the public brought into a facility depended on the nature of the event. If an event had a history of problems, or if the attendees might present a greater risk, operators tailored security responses to the circumstances. Staffing levels for police and peer group security depended on previous behavior in the marketplace, or research on how similar crowds acted at previous shows.

Upgraded security at some heavy metal and urban rap shows illustrates the necessary measured response when enhanced security protocols are implemented. These responses typically include hand wanding, pat-downs, and bag searches, with the goal of eliminating weapons from a potentially volatile environment, and preventing drug and alcohol contraband from entering the facility. In areas where significant threats exist due to geography or reoccurring natural hazards, facilities are more sensitive to external threats and prepare operations accordingly.

For example, in cold, northern climates, where significant snowfall could influence attendance and discourage fans from going to events, facility managers allocate appropriate assets by mobilizing extra employees to keep sidewalks, entrances, and exits clear and de-iced. In California, where significant seismic activity can occur at any time, facilities are vigilant in maintaining emergency evacuation response and training protocols.

After September 11, the priorities shifted as facility managers focused on customer expectations, assessed security conditions, and minimized the desirability of public assembly facilities as potential terrorism targets. The public needed reassurance that public assembly facilities were addressing security, and large gatherings at these venues were safe to attend. Event producers, performers, and sport participants were fearful and cancelled events and games. Many facility managers sensed the potential threats were too immense to comprehend.

Fighting terrorism is like being a goalkeeper. You can make a
hundred brilliant saves but the only shot that people remember
is the one that gets past you.

PAUL WILKINSON
British scholar, author on terrorism,
Daily Telegraph (London, Sept. 1, 1992)

THE FACILITY MANAGERS' RESPONSE TO SEPTEMBER 11

The response to these initial conditions was quick and decisive. Public assembly facility managers convened with public safety representatives and sought input from federal resources, including the Federal Bureau of Investigation (FBI), Department of Defense, Bureau of Alcohol, Tobacco, Firearms and Explosives (ATF), and United States Secret Service (USSS).

Utilizing the resources of local, state, and federal agencies, public assembly facility managers developed an initial response, while moving toward long-term safety and security standards, with the following measures:

- Securing facilities from the outside in, with limited or no access to parking or vehicular movement along the facility's perimeter
- Searching all purses, packages, and attendee baggage before entry into the facility
- Maintaining similar standards for all facility employees and the press
- Searching all attendees at entertainment, sporting, and high profile events by pat-down or hand-held electronic metal detectors (Figs. 4.1 and 4.2)
- Confirming and screening all facility deliveries and vehicles with access to the facility
- Prohibiting deliveries on the day of events
- Screening last-minute deliveries offsite before allowing them into the facility

Operational policies and procedures set the standard for existing facilities' safety and security programs, and provided the foundation for new security design criteria.

DESIGN RESPONSE TO INSURANCE ISSUES

The events of September 11 also left sports facilities, convention centers, and performing arts center owners and managers in uncharted territory when insurance rates soon rose at astronomical rates. For example, insurance premiums for the Giants Stadium, Continental Airlines Arena, and other New Jersey Sports and Exhibition Authority's holdings, just across the river from lower Manhattan and considered part of the New York City metropolitan region, increased 343 percent to $3.2 million in 2002, compared to $722,000 paid in 2000.

Insurers reacted favorably to physical "hardening" of sports, entertainment, convention, and performing arts facilities. Most, if not all, public assembly facilities added transportation barriers and checkpoints to prevent vehicular bombs, adjusted security operations, and implemented capital design programs to protect buildings and assets.

Architectural and Site Planning

Facility design should be adaptable to evolving threats, security technology, and changing operational protocols. Sports, entertainment, convention, and performing arts center architects and designers can significantly reduce facility insurance coverage premiums through security measures, such as:

FIGURE 4.1   Super Bowl XXXVII, San Diego, California, 2003. Pat-down at the entrance. Venue entries are a combination of temporary facilities and equipment operated by a mix of event staff, private security, and law enforcement personnel. (*Architect and photo credit: HOK Sport + Venue + Event.*)

FIGURE 4.2   Super Bowl XXXVII, San Diego, California, 2003. Security is an intricate part of entering each sporting event. (*Architect and photo credit: HOK Sport + Venue + Event.*)

FIGURE 4.3   Mechanical control system at Gaylord Entertainment Center, Nashville, Tennessee. The mechanical control systems must respond to a variety of circumstances. In one case, it is better to shut off the building's mechanical systems to avoid intrusion from an outside agent. In another situation, managing the interior pressure and airflow may prevent the spread of an agent within the facility. (*Architect and photo credit: HOK Sport + Venue + Event.*)

- Ensuring perimeter security and screening of all vehicles entering the site
- Providing adequate public access and queuing areas
- Monitoring loading dock access
- Routing underground building utilities entering the building away from loading docks and entrances, in case of an explosion

Mechanical Engineering Systems

- Locating air intake vents well above grade on exterior walls to prevent introduction of chemical or biological materials into air handling systems.
- Integrating exterior protection of fresh air intakes to accent facility design.
- Specifying proper controls for heating, ventilation, and air conditioning systems for appropriate emergency response (Fig. 4.3).

Mechanical control systems must be able to respond to various circumstances, such as shutting off the building's mechanical systems to avoid introduction of chemical or biological agents in the air-handling systems, or managing interior pressure and airflow to prevent chemical or biological agents from spreading within the facility.

Life Safety Codes

As in all design components related to fire protection, public health, and life safety, applicable local, state, and national codes, and standards must be reviewed for updated egress and life safety system requirements. September 11 prompted many local and national studies of building systems, construction methods, and egress requirements.

Technology

Incorporating technology into a facility's comprehensive security program is essential to management and operations. Closed circuit television (CCTV) cameras with digital storage, access control, motion detectors, magnetometers, and biometric sensors are among the most commonly used technology devices within large public assembly facilities.

Designers must form partnerships and alliances with risk carriers to deliver new and renovated facilities meeting expectations of building owners and the insurance industry. As a direct benefit of meeting owners' and insurers' expectations, designers will also address the needs and expectations of employees, the public, and event participants. Developing a comprehensive security program, integrating design, technology, and operational policies and procedures will effectively achieve these goals.

INTERNATIONAL ASSOCIATION OF ASSEMBLY MANAGERS SETS PROTOCOLS

Immediately following the September 11 terrorist attacks on the United States, the International Association of Assembly Managers (IAAM) formed the Safety and Security Task Force (SSTF), to conduct research, assess, and develop safety and security protocols for public assembly facilities.

The Task Force developed a *SSTF Best Practices Planning Guide* for safety and security at sports, convention, and performing arts venues. The guide consists of documents for use in assessing facility risk factors and determining terrorist threat levels, including a checklist to formulate safety and security plans at public venues for any event or activity. Venue management should adopt a planning process that will determine threat levels, assess risk factors, and complete a vulnerability analysis.

DETERMINING THREAT LEVELS

The IAAM Safety and Security Task Force recommends public assembly facilities establish contingency plans, based on threat levels. Most venues have emergency plans, event plans, and other planning procedures to establish and implement safety and security practices. Even in cases without terrorist threats, public assembly facilities may face other serious threats, such as crowd behavior, natural disasters, and civil unrest. Risk factors must be evaluated for each event, regardless of the program. A list of common risk factors can be used for determining safety and security plans for events.

The SSTF recommends a four-tiered system for establishing threat levels at venues. The following information provides an explanation of the general issues and illustrates the corresponding relationships between the Department of Homeland Security five-tier Governmental Alert System and venue threat levels.

Level No. 4, Security Measures (High Degree of Security Risks)

Level No. 4 is the highest level of security measures and may involve the United States Secret Service (USSS), FBI, other national or international law enforcement, and public safety agencies controlling the event security. For national security purposes, Level No. 4 requires strict measures severely limiting access to the facility perimeter before and during the event. Each employee, contractor, and patron is screened for weapons and other prohibited items through magnetometer checkpoints.

Level No. 4 Criteria

- The event is considered a "special event" under the United States Homeland Security Act.
- The United States Secret Service is required to protect a participant or certain event attendees.
- The event requires coordination and participation by national, regional, state and local law enforcement, and public safety officials.
- Local and state law enforcement officials cannot carry weapons into the secure perimeter.
- The event is most likely open to the public.
- The event is a highly public event with thousands of patrons and may include participants or patrons from other countries.
- The event otherwise presents a severe or high degree of security risks.

Level No. 3, Security Measures (Elevated Degree of Security Risks)

Level No. 3 is the second highest level of security measures and may involve the Secret Service, FBI, and other national or international law enforcement and public safety agencies on a limited basis or for specific security concerns. Level No. 3 requires strict security measures severely limiting access to all or part of the facility before and during the event. The facility or event manager controls the remaining areas of the facility. Each patron (and possibly contractors and employees) is screened for weapons and other prohibited items through magnetometer checkpoints.

Level No. 3 Criteria

- The event requires coordination and participation by national, regional, state and local law enforcement, and public safety officials.
- The event is most likely open to the public.
- The event may be televised nationally or regionally, and will most likely attract government officials as patrons and speakers.
- The event is a highly public event with thousands of patrons and may include participants or patrons from other countries.

- The event may attract patrons that carry weapons or abuse alcohol or drugs.
- Law enforcement assessed the event as having a high degree of security risks.

Level No. 2, Security Measures (Guarded Degree of Security Risk)

Level No. 2 is the third highest level of security measures and may involve regional, state and local law enforcement, and public safety agencies. Level No. 2 requires moderate security measures that may limit access to the facility before and during the event. The facility or event manager controls facility security. Each patron is screened or patted down for bottles, cans, and other prohibited items through entry checkpoints.

Level No. 2 Criteria

- The event may require coordination with regional, state and local law enforcement, and public safety officials.
- The event is televised nationally or regionally and may attract government officials as patrons and speakers.
- The event is a highly public event, but does not generally include foreign participants or patrons.
- The event may attract patrons abusing alcohol or drugs.
- The event has not been identified by law enforcement as having any particular threat outside the customary or ordinary event (sporting, theatrical, musical, or convention) occurring in an area of the country.
- Law enforcement may have assessed the event as having a moderate degree of security risks.

Level No. 1, Security Measures (Low Security Risk)

Level No. 1 is the minimum amount of security measures for an event. This event does not require the higher levels of security planning or security measures. An analysis of the event, including the number of attendees, location, television coverage, if any, and invited guests, does not present any primary concerns outside normal security factors after September 11, 2001. All events not classified in the other levels fall into this level.

Level No. 1 Criteria

- The event is a regional or local event, based on the number of attendees, nature of the event, and invited guests, and presents a minimum security risk.
- The event is not televised or is only televised locally.
- The event does not include government officials.
- The event otherwise presents only a minimum degree of security risks.

RISK ASSESSMENT FACTORS AND VULNERABILITY ANALYSIS

Every civic, assembly, and institutional facility should create a comprehensive security program. Developing a vulnerability analysis is the first step to assess the probability and impact of potential risks through a systematic evaluation process.

Many public facilities and agencies typically create a security planning committee, charged with coordinating policies and procedures, chaired by a responsible person who is an effective communicator. The security planning team should identify various emergencies and plan on response scenarios for each situation.

VULNERABILITY ANALYSIS CHART

A vulnerability analysis chart assigns probabilities, estimates impact, and assesses resources, using a numerical rating system. The Federal Emergency Management Agency's (FEMA) vulnerability analysis chart is a model for evaluating a facility's risks and vulnerabilities. The ratings are subjective, but are good indicators of where attention is required in addressing complex issues and establishing priorities. This information is adapted from FEMA's *Guide for Business and Industry* (Table 4.1).

Potential emergencies. In the first column of the vulnerability analysis chart, list all emergencies potentially affecting a facility, including those identified by the local emergency management office. Consider emergencies occurring within the facility and in the community.

Geographic. Impact on location to the facility, including proximity to flood plains, seismic faults, and dams, companies producing, storing, using, or transporting hazardous materials; major transportation routes and airports; and nuclear power plants.

Technological. Impact from a process or system failure: fire, explosion, hazardous materials incident; failure from safety systems; telecommunications; computer systems; power; heating/cooling systems; emergency notification systems.

Human error in the workplace. Emergencies can be caused by employee error, poor safety practices, and lack of emergency drills and preparation. Human error is the largest cause of workplace emergencies and results from poor training, poor maintenance, carelessness, misconduct, substance abuse, and fatigue.

Design and construction. Emergencies may result from facility design and construction, safety features, building systems, such as construction materials, methods, and building systems; haz-

TABLE 4.1 Vulnerability Analysis Chart

Type of emergency	Key indicators					
	Probability of occurrence *Rate 1–10* 10 is highest degree of probability	**Potential human impact (death or injury)** *Rate 1–10* 10 is highest degree of severity	**Potential property impact** *Rate 1–5* 5 is highest degree of severity	**Potential business impact** *Rate 1–5* 5 is highest degree of severity	**Internal and external resources** *Rate 1–5* 1 is highest degree of preparedness	**Total**
Fire						
Severe weather						
Hazardous material spill						
Transportation accident						
Earthquake						
Tornado						
Terrorism						
Other						

Source: Adapted from FEMA's *Guide for Business and Industry.*

ardous processes or byproducts; combustible storage areas; equipment layout and location; lighting; and evacuation routes and exits.

Proximity of shelter areas. Analyze each potential emergency from beginning to end and prepare emergency response scenarios for each. Consider what could happen in case of the following: prohibited access to the facility, electric power outage, communication lines down, ruptured gas mains, water damage, smoke damage, structural damage, air or water contamination, explosion, truck or vehicular bomb, building or roof collapse, trapped persons, or chemical release.

Estimate probability. In the probability column, rate the likelihood of each emergency's occurrence. This is a subjective consideration. Use a scale of 1 to 10, with 1 the lowest probability, and 10 the highest.

Assess the potential human impact. Analyze the potential human impact of each emergency, with the possibility of death or injury. Public assembly facilities, filled with people during events, carry extreme risks. Assign a rating in the Human Impact column of the Vulnerability Analysis Chart. Use a 1 to 10 scale, with 1 as the lowest impact, and 10 the highest.

Assess the potential property impact. Consider the potential property for losses and damages. Assign a rating in the Property Impact column, 1 being the lowest impact, and 5 the highest. Consider costs to replace, set up temporary replacement, or repair facilities.

Assess the potential business impact. Consider the potential loss of market share. Assign a rating in the Business Impact column, with 1 as the lowest impact, and 5 the highest. Assess the impact of business interruption, employees unable to report to work, customers unable to reach the facility, company in violation of contractual agreements, imposition of fines and penalties or legal costs, interruption of critical supplies or product distribution.

Assess the internal and external resources. Assess available resources and ability to respond. Assign a score to internal resources and external resources; lower scores are better. Review each potential emergency from beginning to end, and each resource necessary for response. For each emergency, consider whether the needed resources and capabilities would be available; and if external resources would be able to respond to the emergency as quickly as needed, or if they will have other priority areas to serve. If the answers are yes, move on to the next assessment. If the answers are no, identify what can be done to correct the problem.

Based on the previous responses, facility managers and owners may need to develop additional emergency procedures, conduct additional training, acquire additional equipment, establish mutual aid agreements, and establish agreements with specialized contractors.

Total the scores for each emergency; lower scores are better. While ratings are subjective, the comparisons will determine planning and resource priorities for threat levels and risk factors.

Facility Design

Criteria listed in the vulnerability analysis apply to safety and security features for new facility design and renovations.

- Location and size of a prospective site are potential risk factors. The ability to create buffer zones, known as standoff distance, between vehicular traffic and the structure to minimize the effects of blast pressure, are important transparent security measures for protecting public assembly facilities. For example, high-risk federal facilities, such as courthouses and office buildings, strive to maintain 50 to 100 foot standoff distances from vehicular roadways to minimize truck bomb threats. Where deep standoff is not available in urban settings, design of exterior building skin, levels of site perimeter security, and operational policies are adjusted accordingly.

- Plazas, vestibules, entrances, lobbies, and queuing areas must be carefully planned and designed to accommodate security screening stations, technology and equipment, package and bag inspections, private screening areas as needed, space to pat down or wand attendees and accommodate protests or other civil action. Clear observation of all entrances and exits from security vantage points is essential (Figs. 4.4 and 4.5).

FIGURE 4.4   Rodeo at Reliant Stadium, Houston, Texas. Arenas, stadiums, and convention centers all host large masses of people regularly. At this rodeo event in Reliant Stadium, President George Bush and former First Lady Barbara Bush were in attendance, bringing on a higher level of event security. (*Architect and photo credit: HOK Sport + Venue + Event.*)

FIGURE 4.5   Heinz Field, Pittsburgh, Pennsylvania. Large sports stadiums must follow significant security measures, such as Heinz Field, which holds 64,440 football fans. (*Architect and photo credit: HOK Sport + Venue + Event.*)

- The size and location of doors and openings must be adaptable to emerging technologies, such as magnetometers, biometric sensors, density detectors, and x-ray machines. Research by the U.S. Public Building Service of the General Services Administration indicates newer model magnetometers are increasing in size, rather than decreasing.
- Parking, loading docks, and service elements should be located in secured areas, while still allowing facility business to occur. Building utility lines should not enter the building under or near the loading dock or other entrances.

FACILITY TYPES

Arenas, stadiums, and convention centers all host large, mass gatherings of people regularly, often including prominent government officials and celebrities, and thus are considered possible targets of terrorism and social disorder. Safety and security measures, though prevalent in most venues, are increasingly overt and extensive, but must repeatedly be reviewed and evaluated for circumstantial and situational conditions.

HOW TO PLAN EVENT SECURITY

Implementing appropriate event security requires extensive planning and preparation by a multidisciplinary team. Architects and planners specializing in the planning and operation of major events collaborate with event security directors, local law enforcement, and associated federal agencies to develop suitable security programs (Table 4.2).

Typically, security planning and approvals have been the responsibility of local law enforcement and local jurisdictions in coordination with event organizers. An example would be regularly scheduled league games and local community special events, considered to have low threat levels. In these instances, event staff works with local law enforcement to plan for appropriate security levels (Figs. 4.6 and 4.7).

NATIONAL SECURITY SPECIAL EVENT

With the creation of the Department of Homeland Security, American and international terrorist threat levels are monitored, and the security plan for special events, particularly international venues, falls under the jurisdiction of local and federal authorities. Events considered a high threat or risk level are given the designation of a National Security Special Event (NSSE). Events given an NSSE designation may include the Olympics, World Cup Soccer, and events where the President of the United States and other high-ranking dignitaries may attend, such as the Summit of the Eight, an economic world conference.

Identifying an NSSE event requires a state's local governing body to apply for the NSSE designation and receive federal approval. Criteria used to determine the security level and procedures include defining the risk and threat levels, program goals, and budget implications for labor, materials, and services.

TABLE 4.2   9/11 Lessons Learned: Event Security Levels

Security was always an important component of special events in the United States. However, the events of September 11 significantly altered planning tactics and strategies employed by facility managers and building owners.

Before September 11, the goal of event security was controlling access at the venue perimeter to protect revenue and provide event exclusivity and public safety. Events owned by leagues, such as the National Football League and Major League Baseball, put a high priority on in-house security to protect athletes and VIPs.

After September 11, planning shifted to implement stadium systems focusing more on people and object control. As a result, law enforcement agencies at the local and federal levels have assumed an increasingly important role in security planning and implementation.

FIGURE 4.6 Gates at Super Bowl XXXVII, San Diego, California, 2003. Temporary modifications at Super Bowl XXXVII included canopy covers for the magnetometers, chain link fences to establish venue perimeters, and construction fencing to create queue lines. (*Architect and photo credit: HOK Sport + Venue + Event.*)

FIGURE 4.7   Super Bowl XXXVII, San Diego, California, 2003. Queue lines at the entrance allow event security staff to maintain order and enhance crowd management. (*Architect and photo credit: HOK Sport + Venue + Event.*)

Events achieving NSSE or Level 1 status receive the most stringent security requirements (Table 4.3). While high profile events such as the Super Bowl, World Series, Final Four, and various all-star games usually do not receive an NSSE designation, planning event security based on the NSSE criteria is an appropriate way to prepare for unforeseen circumstances. As the event period nears, and if threat levels increase, NSSE requirements can be implemented quickly and effectively. After determining the event security level, design and construction of temporary modifications may be required. Design work, often subject to schedule, budgets, location, circumstances, and available space, includes several components (Table 4.4).

Screening for NSSE Events

For each event, the process and protocols for screening people and vehicles should be defined. National or local level events implement the same operations to a lesser degree, as determined by local law enforcement. NSSE designations require:

- Screening of all people by magnetometers and hand wands, searching of all bags
- Searching bumper-to-bumper and X-raying all vehicles and deliveries entering the venue
- Finally, at a time determined by the Secret Service, clearing the entire venue of staff, and searching or "sweeping" by Secret Service and local law enforcement staff
- At the conclusion of the "sweep," locking down the venue so that no one is permitted access without going through the screening process and without proper credentials or tickets

Crowd Management

At any event, security begins at the in-load and continues until the last person has left the premises. Law enforcement and private security staff are involved in monitoring the crowd (Table 4.5). The number of staff required for crowd management depends upon the event size and capacity (Fig. 4.8).

Most facilities have command and control locations inside the seating area in a high position to serve as the "eye in the sky" and monitor crowd actions. Larger-scale events may require additional space available only outside the facility. Many facilities have installed closed circuit television (CCTV) surveillance systems to monitor activities in and around the building and grounds.

TABLE 4.3   National Security Special Events or Level 1 Status Criteria

- Federal resources are allocated for this level, including financial aid, specialized equipment, and personnel.
- The U.S. Secret Service (USSS) controls security and approves all event plans.
- Most likely, USSS staff will be on site up to and throughout the NSSE event, to manage security operations.
- If an event receives lower level NSSE status, involvement by the federal government and USSS is usually determined on an event-by-event basis.

TABLE 4.4   Temporary Modifications: Design and Construction Checklist

- Identify the secure perimeter, including outer fence or structure delineating the venue boundary.
- Define buffers and set-back zones, minimum distances for people and vehicles between the secured perimeter from the building or main structure, distances between the outer fence and the internal fence or barricade line.
- Erect eight-foot high fence lines using chain link to prevent people jumping the fence line.
- Establish barricades, including concrete Jersey barriers at the base of the fence to prevent vehicles from breaching the secure perimeter.
- Install gates to control people and vehicles through screening.

TABLE 4.5   Crowd Management Duties and Responsibilities

- Parking lot arrival points
- Transportation areas
- Seating and standing areas
- Queue lines
- Gate management
- Ticket tearing
- Public information assistance
- Attending to crowd movement and control
- Ushering

FIGURE 4.8   Event staff at 2002 Major League Baseball All-Star Game, Miller Park, Milwaukee, Wisconsin. Law enforcement and private security staff are involved in monitoring the crowd. The number of staff required for crowd management depends on the event size and capacity. (*Architect and photo credit: HOK Sport + Venue + Event.*)

Final Security Details

Security planning and operations must be flexible to meet evolving public safety needs. One of the main issues facing event owners is meeting appropriate security levels within the constraints of temporary facilities and space limitations.

Adjacent parking lots are often used for security, resulting in a loss of attendee parking, which must be reconciled at off-site locations with an alternate transportation system. The increased space, facility requirements, and additional labor result in reduced facility revenues and additional costs to event organizers.

CONCLUSION

Achieving effective security at public assembly facilities is a team effort, requiring extensive advance planning and preparation. The planning process must ensure that all customer groups and service providers are integrated with event operations and security staff, law enforcement, life safety officials, facility staff, city officials, and event representatives.

Roles and responsibilities of all parties must be clearly defined, with one official identified to serve as the final authority on security and public safety issues. Finally, responsibilities for additional costs must be determined. The schedule for event planning and implementation can be a few weeks to a few years, depending on the security level required. Performing a vulnerability analysis will evaluate potential risks, threats, and emergencies the event planning team must prepare for. By addressing the many design, technology, and operational criteria, public assembly facility managers and building owners will be well positioned to ensure public safety and provide high levels of security at major events of any kind.

ACKNOWLEDGMENTS

- Erin L. Jones, Marketing Coordinator, HOK Sport + Venue + Event, Kansas City, Missouri
- Carrie Plummer, Brand Manager, HOK Sport + Venue + Event, Kansas City, Missouri
- Lisa Freedman, Event Project Manager, HOK Sport + Venue + Event, Salt Lake City, Utah
- Todd Barnes, Associate Principal, Senior Event Project Manager, HOK Sport + Venue + Event, Salt Lake City, Utah

BIBLIOGRAPHY

IAAM (International Association of Assembly Managers) Safety and Security Task Force, *Best Practices Security Planning Guide: Theaters and Performing Arts Centers*, Center for Venue Management Studies, Irving, Texas, 2003.

IAAM Safety and Security Task Force, *Best Practices Security Planning: Guide Convention Centers/Exhibit Halls*, Center for Venue Management Studies, Irving, Texas, 2002.

IAAM Safety and Security Task Force, *Best Practices Security Planning Guide: Arenas, Stadiums, Amphitheaters*, Center for Venue Management Studies, Irving, Texas, 2002.

Simons, Russ, "Charted Territory: Benchmarking through Facility Analysis," *Stadia Magazine*, July 2002.

INTERNET RESOURCES

Building Owners and Managers
 Association (BOMA)
www.boma.org

Center For Disease Control—National Institute
 for Occupation Safety and Health
www.cdc.gov/niosh/topics/emres/

Concealed Weapons Laws
http://www.packing.org/states.jsp

Crowd Management Strategies
www.crowdsafe.com

Federal Emergency Management
 Agency (FEMA)
www.fema.gov

HOK Sport + Venue + Event
www.hoksve.com

International Association of Assembly
 Managers, Inc. (IAAM)
www.iaam.org

International Facility Management
 Association (IFMA)
www.ifma.org
www.ifmaseattle.org/links.html

Publications

Auditoria Magazine
www.auditoria.tv

Facility Manager Magazine
www.iaam.org/Facility_manager/Pages/
 Facility_Issues.htm

Sports Business Journal
www.sportsbusinessjournal.com

Stadia Magazine
www.stadia.tv

Stadium and Arena Management
www.sam.uk.com

Tradeshow Week
www.tradeshoweek.com

CHAPTER 5
COMMERCIAL HIGH-RISE EGRESS SYSTEMS

Carl Galioto, FAIA
Partner and Manager of Technical Group
Skidmore Owings & Merrill
New York, New York

> *The rise of terrorism is not new but must not consume us.*
> DANIEL PATRICK MOYNIHAN (1927–2003)
> *American statesman, U.S. senator*

After the events of September 11, 2001, and the collapse of the two World Trade Center Towers in New York City, exiting, or egress, from high-rise and commercial buildings took on urgent proportions as never before. Building owners, public safety officials, architects, and engineers have since been carefully studying optimal ways to design and protect buildings to ensure complete and swift building occupant evacuation. This information has formed the basis for continued research by public and private sector groups nationwide, with the goal of developing effective strategies for high-rise building design and construction techniques.

HIGH-RISE EGRESS SYSTEM OVERVIEW

The term *high-rise building*, refers to a multistory building equipped with elevators. For most commercial office buildings, the term generally applies to all buildings above a statutory height limit, usually 75 feet tall, based on firefighting equipment and procedures. This important benchmark has valid reasons. However, substantial differences in life safety requirements and egress systems exist among buildings 75 feet tall, 750 feet tall, or even 1750 feet tall. Egress systems and fire protection systems, both active and passive, for truly high-rise buildings, require greater interdependence and redundancy.

Egress refers to the act or means of going or coming out of a building, or a path, opening, or place of exiting. The components facilitating egress are termed *means of egress*.

For architects, engineers, and designers, building exiting is considered a system, similar to a building mechanical system designed to rational and code criteria, and accounting for issues such as flow, reliability, and redundancy. Unlike a mechanical system component, building exiting is an interdisciplinary system composed of architectural, structural, mechanical, electrical, and fire protection elements, all interdependent upon each other. Design considerations involve architectural input for general flow, arrangement of elements, and selection of the enclosure assembly. Mechanical, electrical, and plumbing (MEP) considerations involve stair pressurization; smoke venting, and normal and emergency lighting. The criteria for egress system design should address:

- Creating a safe environment for egress of occupants on floors affected by a life-threatening event
- Facilitating swift building evacuation
- Allowing floor access, simultaneous or otherwise, by emergency responders and firefighters

STAIR SEPARATION

A fundamental concept of egress design is use of multiple means of egress to provide occupants with an option, in case one exit is compromised by fire, smoke, or damage. For most occupancies and building configurations, two means of egress are optimal, although this number depends on the occupancy type, population, and travel distances within the space.

Separation of exits has been a building code requirement for many years. The theory of separating exits is that by increasing the distance between two points, the likelihood that both means are affected by the same event diminishes with distance.

Some codes have had vague language, such as separating the stairs "as much as practicable." Others have language requiring a separation of one-half (or one-third for fully sprinklered buildings) of the maximum travel distance on that floor or level. The result of these requirements, employed in dense urban environments, was to group stairs closely, or even back to back, as the stair separation is measured in plan from stair door to stair door. This has also permitted the use of scissor, or interlocking, stairs that, while separated from one another by fire rating, are so interwoven as to provide a minimal degree of redundancy. Nevertheless, such arrangements may still be valid in occupancies with low populations, such as residential facilities.

The weakness in this approach assumes the danger lies only in an event on one floor and the integrity of vertical exits is not compromised. Maintaining the minimum separation could be achieved by designing fire-rated corridors extending the distance between entrances, but this does not maintain a separation between the enclosures of the vertical exits. A more conservative approach would separate the entire exit enclosure, and not only the entrance. To do so would require identifying a space as the required vertical exit zone, composed of the stair width, intermediate platform, and minimum required clearance at the landing, and measuring the separation from one zone to the other.

TYPICAL HIGH-RISE TOWER

Consider a typical New York City office tower with a floor plate of approximately 35,000 square feet (Fig. 5.1), planned and designed to consider the lessons learned from the events of September 11. The New York City Building Code states, "...the minimum distance between such doors shall be the greater of 30 feet or one-third the maximum travel distance of the floor..." The maximum travel distance on this floor is approximately 120 feet, allowing a door-to-door separation of as little as 40 feet. The stairs on the plan were arranged to increase the separation between the two elements. Project criteria were set so the stair doors would be separated by one-third of the diagonal measurement of the floor plate.

The typical design for office tower floors is a rectangular core with a perimeter ring corridor for tenants and building service personnel to access the spaces within the core. This floor plan does away with the ring corridor by including an internal central corridor within the core. The arrangement has several advantages:

- *Tenant space planning.* Without doors or circulation elements around the core, tenants are able to plan their spaces with interior rooms abutting the building core surface.
- *Building services.* Maintenance personnel can circulate from floor to floor via the service elevator and rarely need to leave the center corridor area. All mechanical, electrical, telecommunication spaces, and core toilets are accessible from the central corridor.
- *Life safety.* This plan includes a safe area, or area of refuge for building occupants.

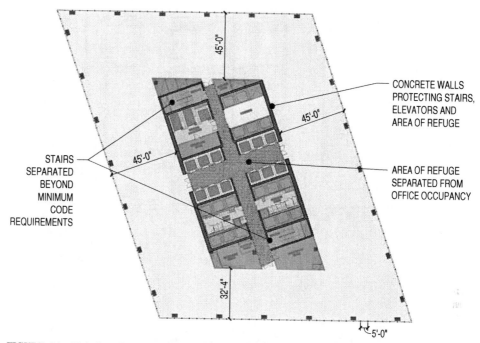

FIGURE 5.1 High-rise office tower in New York City with a floor plate of approximately 35,000 square feet. (*Architect: Skidmore Owings & Merrill.*)

The shaded cruciform shape serves as a safe area, separated from the adjoining office floor by smoke-stop doors. While it is labeled as an area of refuge, the function is to serve as a vestibule space, permitting occupants to queue up in a space protected from a possible life-threatening event as they commence building evacuation. The clotting effect of occupants at a stair door in a high-rise office tower evacuation can be developed through computer simulation (Fig. 5.2).

The term *safe area* is used in a limited number of codes. Safe area is a space used as normal circulation and access to an occupied space but that is separated from the occupied space by fire-rated construction. The most common application of this concept is a theatre lobby. An *area of refuge* is not on the normal path of access, and is a space separated from an adjoining one by fire-rated construction. There are frequently other criteria for areas of refuge, such as stair and elevator access.

Accommodating individuals in wheelchairs within fire-rated stair enclosures is generally exempted in fully sprinklered buildings. While this trade-off is certainly logical, due to improved fire suppression, a greater degree of safety for those individuals can be achieved by providing such a space. If a wheelchair does not occupy this area or landing, the larger stair landing provides emergency responders with more space and an improved working environment (Table 5.1).

Experts, such as J. J. Fruin and J. L. Pauls, have studied the movement of people in a variety of circumstances in great detail throughout the twentieth century. Despite the greater understanding achieved by such research, one consideration that has not (yet, as of this writing) been incorporated into code requirements is the stair door location and the implication for traffic flow during building evacuation. As shown in Fig. 5.3, a door is positioned so the flow of occupants into the enclosure merges with, rather than opposes, the downward movement of people.

The enclosure construction maintains the tenability of the egress system. Potential hazards include fire, impact from hose stream after a fire, and potential impact from an event outside the enclosure.

For the case study project stairway depicted in Fig. 5.3, the client directed the design team to employ a composite steel and reinforced concrete core, a conservative course of action. As the debate

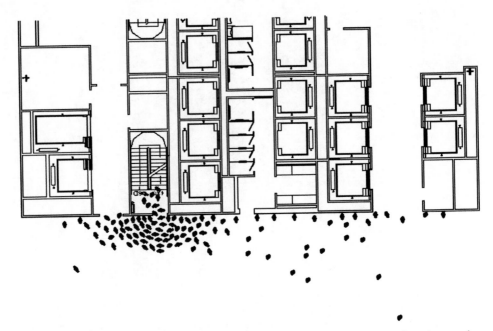

FIGURE 5.2 High-rise office tower evacuation, illustrating clotting effect of occupants at the stair tower door. (*Computer simulation drawing by Skidmore Owings & Merrill.*)

TABLE 5.1 9/11 Lessons Learned: Stair Enclosure Construction and Layout

The minimum stair width permissible by the New York City Building Code for a 35,000 square foot typical office high-rise floor plate is 56 inches. This dimension may restrict the use of two side-by-side exiting occupants and certainly restricts two-way traffic in a stair for a line of exiting occupants downward and upwardly-moving emergency responders with equipment.

The client for this project asked to accommodate the two-way movement. As a result of this request, and based on lessons learned by studying the World Trade Center Twin Towers evacuation, stairs were widened to 66 inches, allowing a better building occupant exiting flow (Fig. 5.3).

Source: Skidmore, Owings & Merrill.

over the efficacy of metal studs and gypsum drywall partitions to meet all of these criteria continues, as of this writing, no conclusions can be reached on the preferred stair enclosure system.

Another factor affecting stairway usability is visibility within the enclosure during an emergency. A stair enclosure can have multiple levels of redundancy (Fig. 5.3).

- Lighting of the stairway by normal and emergency power is required by codes, providing two levels of protection. More extreme events have proven there are occasions when the common link for such power supply could be severed, thereby requiring additional levels of protection.

- Battery-powered lighting has frequently been considered as a less desirable emergency lighting alternative due to maintenance concerns. However, a battery system that is recharged by normal power could reduce the maintenance concerns and provide a third level of redundancy.

- Lastly, in the event that all lighting fails, a relatively inexpensive option is painting handrails, stair stringers, and stair nosings with photoluminescent paint. The efficacy of this paint system when all lighting systems fail has proven to provide occupants with some guidance in using a darkened stair.

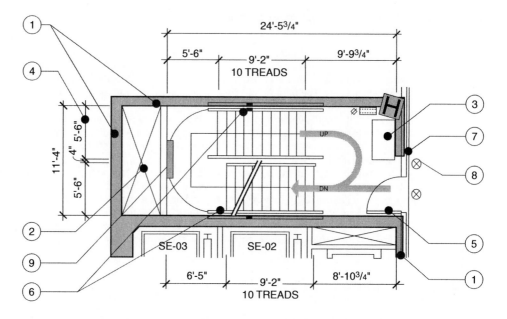

(1) 10" MIN. CAST-IN-PLACE CONCRETE SHEAR WALL SURROUNDING STAIR.

(2) STAIR PRESSURIZATION SHAFT.

(3) 30" X 48" AREA OF RESCUE ASSISTANCE.

(4) 3 UNIT STAIR WIDTH (66").

(5) "A" LABEL (2$\frac{1}{2}$ HR) DOOR AT "DOWN" SIDE OF STAIR TO FACILITATE TRAFFIC FLOW.

(6) PHOSPHORESCENT PAINT STRIPING TO IMPROVE VISIBILITY (INDICATED BY HATCHED AREA).

(7) FLOOR PROXIMITY EGRESS PATH MARKING SYSTEM AT 4" ABOVE FINISHED FLOOR.

(8) FLOOR PROXIMITY EGRESS SIGN, 18" ABOVE FINISHED FLOOR.

(9) BATTERY BACKUP AT EXIT STAIR LIGHTING.

FIGURE 5.3   Enhanced egress stairs in a high-rise commercial office tower. This stair enclosure has multiple levels of redundancy. (*Source: Skidmore, Owings & Merrill.*)

REDUNDANCY WITHIN EGRESS SYSTEMS

One of the purposes of requiring at least two means of egress from a floor is to provide a measure of redundancy within the egress system. However, the required width for stairs is based on the total occupancy of a floor and the enclosure is generally carried directly to the ground floor without additional redundancy. The purpose of bringing occupants down to the ground floor is to allow them to successfully leave the building at the exit discharge. If additional redundancy is to be introduced into the system, it should be at its most vulnerable and critical point: the exit discharge. An exit to grade that is blocked by fire, explosion, collapse, or other event would require occupants to reverse their steps back up to a point where they could cross over to the other stair enclosure and use that element to exit the building.

By introducing a "crossover floor," containing a link between the two enclosures and where the two stair enclosures from above branch off to a total of four enclosures down to grade, is one design option for providing redundancy. To provide clarity and direct the movements of the occupants, an electronic visual messaging system can be introduced at this level, informing the occupants about the optimum path to exiting. This system, controlled from the fire command center and based on preset scenarios, will modify the message in the event that any of the exit discharges are incapacitated (Fig. 5.4).

TENABILITY OF EGRESS SYSTEM

As the events of September 11 indicated, evacuating all occupants in a commercial high-rise office tower can be necessary during emergency situations. Research on building evacuation time for occupants on the 49th floor of a typical office tower to enter an exit stair can be almost seven minutes, using a baseline of three mid-rise floors (Fig. 5.5). Similarly, discharging as many as 9000 building occupants during a complete high-rise office tower evacuation can take as long as 90 minutes (Figs. 5.6 and 5.7).

VERTICAL TRANSPORTATION

As one of several essential high-rise building systems, the vertical transportation system has its own tenability as a means for emergency egress and ingress, or entering a building. The factors affecting this tenability are:

- Structural integrity of hoistway and rails, including resistance to seismic impact and fire
- Fire resistance of hoistway
- Ability of the hoistway to resist intrusion of smoke
- Resistance of elevator equipment to heat, smoke, and water
- Electrical supply to elevator equipment
- Survivability within elevator cab

CONCLUSION

If design and construction professionals are to facilitate designing future "super" high-rise towers, greater vision is required. Height limitations were overcome in the nineteenth century by the development of the elevator and steel structures. These two building components form the barriers to creating super high-rise structures of the twenty-first century and beyond.

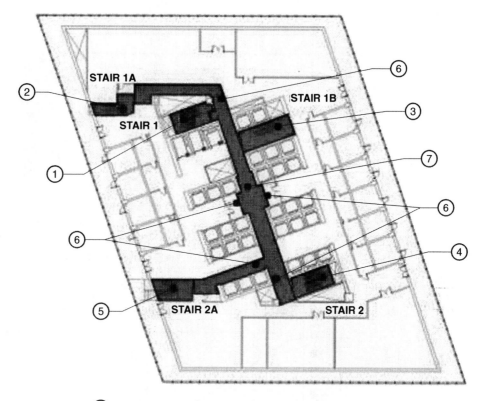

1. STAIR #1: TERMINATION OF TOWER STAIR AT TRANSFER LEVEL.

2. STAIR #1A: TO EXIT AT WASHINGTON STREET.

3. STAIR #1B : TO EXIT AT GREENWICH STREET.

4. STAIR #2: TOWER STAIR TO EXIT AT TRANSFER LEVEL (IF REQUIRED) AND GREENWICH STREET.

5. STAIR #2A: TO EXIT AT WASHINGTON STREET.

6. SMOKE STOP DOORS.

7. 2 HOUR RATED REINFORCED MASONRY VERTICAL EXIT TRANSITION PASSAGEWAY (7'-6" WIDE).

FIGURE 5.4 The floor plate of a high-rise office building with a crossover floor, containing a link between the two enclosures, where the two stair enclosures from above branch off to a total of four enclosures down to grade. (*Source: Skidmore, Owings & Merrill.*)

The strategy for occupant egress evacuation and egress, as well as emergency responder ingress, must be designed in a holistic manner, including the use of elevators, enhanced stairs, and the factors related to building tenability in emergency conditions. The evacuation of thousands of building occupants from the World Trade Center Twin Towers on September 11, 2001, provided lessons for building and life safety code experts, architects, engineers, and construction professionals. Many

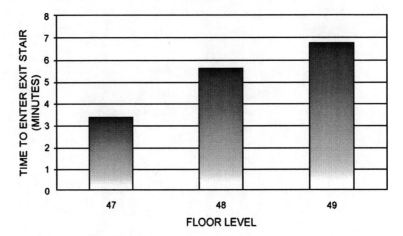

FIGURE 5.5   Time for occupants to enter exit stair during evacuation of three floors. (*Source: Skidmore, Owings & Merrill.*)

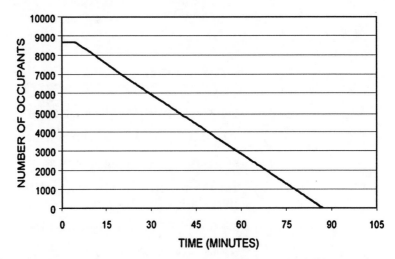

FIGURE 5.6   Number of occupants and minutes needed for a complete building tower evacuation. (*Source: Skidmore, Owings & Merrill.*)

building codes in place before September 11 regard building occupants as being safe once they reach fire-rated stairs. However, since September 11, this basic assumption has been revisited, because, as the Twin Towers incident starkly illustrated, under extreme circumstances people are not safe until they reach the ground floor.

Enhancing security within commercial high-rise office buildings, like many other building types, requires a comprehensive security plan, integrating design, technology, and operations, including internal policies and procedures. Due to the large numbers of building occupants in a typical high-rise tower,

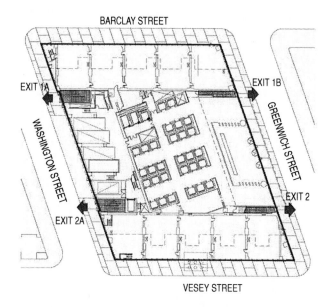

FIGURE 5.7 Ground floor plan of a commercial high-rise office tower, indicating exit discharge to grade. (*Source: Skidmore, Owings & Merrill.*)

egress systems allowing prompt evacuation are a critical issue. Building owners, code officials, and design and construction professionals can make a significant contribution to life safety design by working together to meet the many technical challenges involved with high-rise building egress systems.

BIBLIOGRAPHY

Dunlap, David W., "A Post-Sept. 11 Laboratory in High-Rise Safety," *The New York Times*, January 29, 2003.

Fruin, J. J., "Designing for Pedestrians: A Level of Service Concept," Ph.D. dissertation, Polytechnic Institute of Brooklyn, New York, 1970.

New York City Department of Buildings, "World Trade Center Building Code Task Force Findings and Recommendation," February 2003. www.nyc.gov/html/dob/pdf/wtcbctf.pdf

Pauls, J. L., "Management and Movement of Building Occupants in Emergencies," DBR Paper 78, National Research Council of Canada, Ottawa, Ontario, Canada, 1978.

Zicherman, Joseph, Editor, *Fire Safety in Tall Buildings,* The Council on Tall Buildings and Urban Habitat, Bethlehem, Pa., 1992.

INTERNET RESOURCES

Council on Tall Buildings and Urban Habitat (CTBUH)
www.ctbuh.org

National Institute of Standards and Technology (NIST)
www.nist.gov

New Zealand Fire Service, Fire Engineering: Simulating Human Behavior
www.fire.org.nz/engineer/fe_buildings/human/simulate.htm

Skidmore, Owings & Merrill
www.som.com

CHAPTER 6
COURTHOUSE SECURITY

Kenneth J. Jandura, AIA
Justice Principal, DMJM Design
Arlington, Virginia

David R. Campbell, PE
Associate Principal, DMJM Technology
Colorado Springs, Colorado

SECURING THE AMERICAN COURTHOUSE

> *Weak security improvements...are sometimes worse than doing nothing because they give a false peace of mind and convince people that safety is being addressed when it is not. Poorly designed security foils everyone...except the attacker.*
> GAVIN DE BECKER (B.1954)
> *American author and expert on violent behavior*
> *The Gift of Fear*

> *When it comes to our public buildings, we must re-inoculate ourselves with a commitment to fundamental values—to openness, to engagement, to accessibility.* DOUGLAS P. WOODLOCK
> *U.S. District Judge,*
> *Boston, Massachusetts*

Since early colonial days in American history, courthouses represented the enduring presence of government in cities and towns across the United States. As icons of American government, courthouses are targets for terrorism and crime, especially during high-profile trials, requiring high levels of security at building perimeters, exteriors, and entry points. Internal threats, stemming from family court disputes and civil cases, also pose significant security risks.

William Shakespeare said, "All power lies in the world of dreams." The power of the American justice system is based on the U.S. Constitution and the system of checks and balances among the executive, judicial, and representative branches of government. The framers of the United States Constitution had dreams for a nation built upon this solid foundation, forming the bedrock for freedom and democracy.

Balancing the need for openness and security is the major challenge for courthouse administrators, judges, planners, and designers. Courthouses provide a public forum for dispute resolution, and are environments where people express outrage at legal proceedings and outcomes. When parties in a lawsuit or case don't accept the decision of the judge or jury, they may react violently, requiring preventative security measures to minimize potential threats. At courthouses and adjacent civic buildings, security means more than installation of a visible ring of concrete planters, barriers, and curbside bollards to prevent vehicular truck bombs or terror attacks.

The early twenty-first century generation of civic architecture, especially federal courthouses, concentrates on transparent security, not readily visible to the public eye. Transparent security in civic buildings maintains a high level of design and public safety, while affirming a free and open society, promotes a legacy of quality architecture, not bunkers.

Courthouse violence is not limited to urban areas and big cities. Violence and terrorism can occur in any location, especially where prominent symbols of government are accessible to the public. Violent incidents have occurred within small jurisdictions and courthouses in California, Michigan, and Kentucky. As concern for homeland security increases, law enforcement and public safety agencies, especially in small communities and counties, should consider training for and addressing courthouse violence, including handling volatile situations before and after highly-awaited verdicts and other incidents.

Types of Courthouses

Criminal courts are mistakenly considered the most dangerous judicial venue in a courthouse. Major murder cases must ensure protection of all participants and jurors. Child custody, divorce, and family law hearings, are among the most emotionally charged, potentially violent cases heard in courtrooms. The possibility of having one's child taken away, or loss of property and money in a separation dispute can ignite uncontrollable anger and dissent, especially when court decisions seem unfair. When a person's life is severely affected by a court judgment, individuals may use violence to resolve a verdict or express frustration. For these reasons, courthouse planners and designers must consider the types of courts, nature of cases, and participants when considering security measures. Different courthouses, such as federal, state, appeal, criminal, family, civil, and state supreme courts, will each have specific programmatic and user requirements.

Security Goals

Courthouse security must maintain the integrity of the judicial system by protecting the safety of all participants during the judicial process. The three major objectives of preparing an effective security plan are to detect, deter, and detain violent behavior. A comprehensive security program should be planned proactively, rather than reactively, to control violence, based on architectural design, technology systems, and policies and procedures. Courthouse security, through architectural design and technology, is achieved through site planning, perimeter and exterior building design, and interior planning of public, private, secure, and interface areas.

Providing effective training and staffing is an integral part of a security plan. Courthouse designers must work closely with all stakeholders in the process—users, clients, and administrators—to integrate appropriate policies and procedures into the planning and design process. Operational procedures are the responsibility of those who operate and maintain courthouse facilities.

Security Planning Committee

To best address all security issues during the planning and design process, or to review existing conditions, courthouse users and owners should establish a courthouse security planning committee in the early design stages. This committee should consist of representatives from each agency housed in the structure, as well as the government entity that owns and operates the building, which may be a separate agency responsible for capital programs and consultants.

A designated committee chairperson should be responsible for coordinating efforts with the design team and developing policies and procedures prior to project completion. Critical design decisions will affect policies and procedures implemented by the security staff. Familiarity with the courthouse physical plant will allow security staff to conduct training sessions prior to move-in for new facilities, and enhance training efforts for new staff.

The committee should review and confirm how the security department and sheriff, if applicable, will staff and operate the building. Facilities are too often planned, designed, and built without owners or client agencies understanding the operational costs for providing courthouse security. Early participation in planning and design will enhance efforts to determine staffing requirements and assist government administrators when budgeting an effective security force in and around the courthouse.

SITE PLANNING

Effective site planning is the first line of defense in securing a courthouse. Site sizes, shapes, and locations vary in nature from urban to rural, flat to hilly, rectangular to geometric shapes. Several site planning considerations should be addressed during early design phases to provide security.

Access and Circulation

The primary objective of courthouse site accessibility and circulation is controlling how participants enter the site, restrict vehicular movement around the site, deter damage from moving vehicles, and safeguard all courthouse users.

Effective security plans separate various participants until they arrive in the courtroom. From the site and perimeter to the interior functional organization, separate circulation zones and entries are recommended to minimize or eliminate security breaches for public, private (judges), secure, and service areas.

Combining public and staff access, but keeping them separate from the judges and secure circulation, is acceptable if the site restricts the number of off-street access points. The primary objective of accessing the site is separating all parties. Combined circulation creates bottlenecks, placing judges or sheriffs transporting defendants at risk. Separate and distinct access points for judges and security transporting prevent the public from stalking or observing those leaving and entering the courthouse. During high-security trials, anonymity is essential for the trial participants; alternate circulation routes in and out of courthouses should be considered during planning.

Gate controls to private and secure areas of the site help restrict vehicular traffic flow. Gate control features using card readers, or smart access cards are effective ways of controlling site traffic. Smart access cards are credit card sized devices for personnel, containing integrated circuits used exclusively for identifying and authenticating individuals. The cards are used for standard personal identification, facility access, information technology network access, and system access. Video surveillance cameras can be located to observe and document individuals and vehicles entering private and restricted zones. Gates should be designed and specified based on anticipated traffic volume. Gates handling heavy volumes should be able to withstand abuse and wear resulting from continued use. A nuisance perimeter, requiring only a lift arm gate, has a short fence, or no fence at all, and is appropriate where high security is not essential, such as staff parking or restricted, but nonsecure parking areas. In other instances, a combination of lift arm gates and sliding gates may be used at a single point of access to maintain security during slow times, and sustain acceptable traffic flow rates during peak times.

The secure or judges' parking areas require a sliding gate. Perimeters include a hardened fence or at minimum, a six-foot mesh chain fence or decorative masonry wall. These secure perimeters call for a more secure access point. The sliding gate offers heightened security, but slower operation. Gates can be used in combination with card readers, intercoms, and surveillance cameras to allow access only to authorized individuals. A concealed drum barrier is another way to control access to restricted areas around the site and courthouse (Fig. 6.1).

Straight entry drives to the front of a courthouse should be avoided. A winding bend or circuitous route, along with landscaped barriers, impedes vehicles racing at a high speed toward the entry. Barrier types include landscaped boulders, bollards, fences, plantings, and low walls. Pop-up bollards allow vehicles with security clearances to access a site, while securing an off limits area from the general public. Bollards are structurally designed low piers used at pedestrian and vehicular roads to prevent and resist unauthorized traffic (Fig. 6.2).

FIGURE 6.1 Concealed drum barrier. (*DMJM Technology.*)

FIGURE 6.2 Bollards are used to restrict vehicular traffic and access. (*DMJM Technology.*)

Signage

Signage for access to and within the site must be clearly defined. Proper signage alleviates confusion over site circulation, parking, and entrance location. Carefully planned way-finding systems for users, particularly visitors, enhance the likelihood that vehicles will use designated access ways.

Signage should clearly indicate visitor and staff parking locations. Judges' parking areas should not be marked or identified, to prevent stalkers. Ideally, judges' parking areas should be separate, but if site restrictions require that judges' parking is combined with staff and public parking, unassigned numbers should be used in lieu of identifying individuals by name. Signage should clearly designate these areas as restricted parking spaces.

Surveillance

The primary role of courthouse security staff is observation and providing a visible presence in the facility. Security personnel cannot survey the entire courthouse, maintain many responsibilities, and check parking security. With appropriate surveillance equipment and security systems, these tasks are managed more effectively, and security is enhanced. All surveillance cameras should be equipped with a minimum 24-hour recording; allowing capability for recorded video as evidence should an incident occur within or outside the courthouse.

Duress

Duress, or the potential for violence, is a concern in courthouse parking areas, due to the sensitive nature of the events occurring within courthouses. Some individuals leave the courts with the intent to incite violence or vandalize public property, while others wait outside in the parking lot or garage for their intended victim to appear. With proper technology, these incidents can be stalled, suspended, or even prevented.

Duress equipment in parking lots includes emergency phones, blue strobe stations, or a combination of the two. These devices allow victims or observers of violations to quickly draw attention to and report an incident. They can readily be integrated with the surveillance system to allow security staff to identify, assess, and record incidents as they are reported.

Parking

Separation of parking areas and garages for all courthouse circulation is strongly recommended (Fig. 6.3).

Public Parking.   Parking for the public, either on grade or in a garage, must maintain a standoff distance from the courthouse. Standoff distance is governed by a threat and vulnerability assessment conducted for the project. Public parking garages should never be integrated into the construction of a courthouse but should be treated as a separate building structure.

If frequent inclement weather requires a direct connection between parking and courthouse, open or enclosed bridges and connections can be provided. Paths leading from a garage or parking lot should be consolidated to enhance direct observation of people entering and leaving the courthouse.

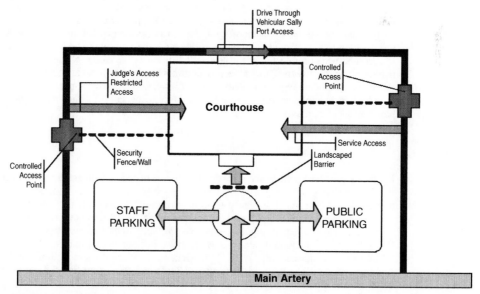

FIGURE 6.3   Schematic courthouse site plan. Relationships among entry points, security zones, and circulation patterns around the courthouse site. (*DMJM Design.*)

Violence and vandalism have often occurred within parking lots because perpetrators often know that courthouse security will not allow them to carry weapons inside. Within parking areas, use of technology, including surveillance cameras, voice activated intercoms, duress devices, and adequate lighting levels can deter violence and vandalism by careful planning and placement.

Visibility should be maximized inside and outside parking structures. Long-span construction should be utilized in parking garage design to minimize columns and other structural elements obstructing views. Locating cameras with maximum coverage will assist security personnel.

Private—Judges.   Access to judges' parking should be controlled electronically to prevent entry by unauthorized individuals. Parking spaces for judges, particularly in an open lot, should not be marked with the individual names. Numbering each parking space is the best way to maintain anonymity.

Secure—Jurors.   Parking for jurors, particularly if they are sequestered, should be separated from the general public to prevent access by the media or members of a family who may have a stake in the outcome of a trial.

Secure—Courthouse Employees.   On-grade parking for judges and staff should be protected by a six-foot-high fence or wall at minimum.

Service Deliveries.   Delivery parking should be separated both from judges and from vehicles carrying in-custody defendants. Ideally, supplies should be delivered at a remote location where they can be screened and inspected for explosives or other weapons that may be hidden inside a package. This is especially important regarding explosives, because they could potentially detonate in the remote delivery area, rather than inside the courthouse. Once inspected, government-owned vehicles can deliver supplies and packages to all government facilities. This practice is cost prohibitive in most jurisdictions, due to staffing and additional facilities required. Therefore, delivery access and loading docks should be located a minimum 50-foot distance away from entries into the judges' parking area and vehicular sally port.

Standoff Distance

Standoff distance is the setback from a protected perimeter to the structure requiring protection and is one of the most effective methods of preventing vehicular bomb threats. Increasing standoff distances between roadways and buildings reduces potential blast pressure loads on buildings during explosions.

In urban settings, where standoffs and deep setbacks are difficult to achieve, blast resistant structural systems and hardened building exteriors and materials should be used to meet security needs.

On suburban or rural sites, adequate standoff distances are easier to attain. Federal agencies recommend distances between 50 to 300 feet for courthouses, based on threat and vulnerability assessments. While state and county governments may not have standoff requirements, many local jurisdictions may look to federal design standards for guidance, especially for high-risk, high-profile buildings, and based on threat assessments.

Landscaping

Landscaping enhances the aesthetics and attractiveness of civic buildings. However, without careful planning and design, landscaping elements can be used to conceal weapons, contraband, and criminals. Tall trees and bushes should not be planted adjacent to structures, particularly near entries. Landscaping should not inhibit the ability of law enforcement and surveillance cameras to observe the structure and site.

Openness and adequate lighting enhance site surveillance capabilities around the courthouse. Bollards and pop-up bollards are effective landscaping elements to enhance courthouse site security.

Federal courthouses built by the U.S. General Services Administration (GSA) use public art, sculptors, and artisans to create attractive bollards and street furniture for public plazas at federal buildings and courthouses. Other public agencies have commissioned artists to design gates, fences, walls, and screens to combine public art and aesthetics with security requirements.

Lighting

Site lighting allows surveillance of the site at all hours and provides a comfort level for the public and employees as they walk to and from their vehicles. Continuous lighting with uniform luminance enhances performance of surveillance cameras strategically located around the site. Recommended lighting levels include 15 horizontal foot-candles for vehicular and pedestrian entrances and 5 horizontal foot-candles for perimeter and vehicular and pedestrian circulation areas. Low-level lighting around the courthouse perimeter enhances surveillance of public facilities (Fig. 6.4).

Many surveillance cameras are able to operate with minimal light, providing acceptable images. In settings where every detail must be identifiable, infrared illuminators can be added to enhance camera views, even in zero-light conditions. This technology will not replace site lighting, but should be considered for areas that for any reason cannot be lit adequately, such as a building or parking lot adjacent to a residential area.

Utilities

Utilities entering the site, such as power, water, gas and phone lines, should be protected from tampering and vandalism. Emergency generators, transformers, and cooling towers should be located in secure areas and shielded from intruders seeking to disrupt operations by cutting off main power sources. Underground vaults should be provided with locked manhole covers, and access for utility companies' service should be placed in areas where observation is unimpeded. Outdoor utility equipment should be located in private and secure zones, protected by a secure wall with surveillance cameras.

PERIMETER AND EXTERIOR PLANNING

Courthouses are symbolic icons within large and small American communities. Often located in the center of town, or on a hill, courthouses represent the power of justice and the legal system. Courthouses are also civic venues where citizens can resolve their conflicts. Balancing openness with security features must occur both at the building exterior and perimeter (Table 6.1).

Security personnel must be able to control entry points and monitor who enters the courthouse. Restricting the number of entry points saves on operational and technology costs, and provides better control.

FIGURE 6.4 Anne Arundel County Courthouse, Maryland. (*Architect: Spillis Candela DMJM, Photographer: Jeffrey Katz, CenterSpan Productions, LLC.*)

TABLE 6.1   Building Design Perimeter and Exterior Planning Considerations

- Restrict number of public entry points to a minimum of one when possible.
- Provide separate entries for off-hour operations.
- Separate entries for judges and court security transporting defendants.
- Restrict access to these points.
- Control entry by card readers, biometrics, or surveillance.
- Interlock doors at vehicular sally ports.
- Provide surveillance cameras at all access points.
- Locate service deliveries 50 feet from utility rooms and access for judges and court security.
- Locate air intake away from public areas.
- Provide nonoperable windows in public areas.
- Use appropriate glazing based on security requirements.
- Require blast-resistant design as dictated by threat and vulnerability assessment.
- Prohibit trash receptacles and mail boxes at building perimeter.
- Restrict capability of scaling exterior building.

Public entries into a courthouse should be limited, preferably to a single location. Larger jurisdictions, due to the size of the facility and traffic volumes, may require several screened entry points. Public entry should be direct from the parking area and clearly visible from the street. Architectural and landscape elements, such as bollards and barriers, should be placed at all entry points to prevent unauthorized vehicles from charging the front door and other means of egress.

Some court facilities house related agencies, such as probation and prosecuting attorneys, which typically operate after standard business hours. Separate entries, restricting the public to one area within the courthouse, should be considered in these cases. Off-hour entries can be remotely operated with an intercom and surveillance camera, so agency personnel can determine and verify scheduled clients visiting their department.

Additional access points into the courthouse should be provided for judges, service and in-custody defendants. Depending on facility policies and procedures, staff may either be screened at the front door, or enter through a controlled access point from the parking area.

Generally, judges' entries occur directly from their parking area, and are typically operated by card readers or biometric scanners. This technology, along with surveillance cameras, will provide positive identification of all individuals attempting to enter or leave the facility and will maintain recorded video data of events that can be stored and retrieved. Surveillance cameras should always be placed adjacent to entry points to allow observation.

Doors used exclusively for emergency exits should be designed for egress only, as well as monitored and alarmed to prevent unauthorized access. To allow this egress-only situation, flush hardware (doors with no pulls or levers) should be installed on the exterior of all emergency exit doors. Surveillance cameras should be placed at these locations observing the door to record individuals breaching courthouse security.

Biometric readers and card readers (Figs. 6.5 and 6.6) allow flexibility in assigning certain individuals who have authorization to enter a specific point in the courthouse. They provide the ability to quickly rescind authorized use in the event of employment termination or security alert.

Sally Ports

Vehicular sally ports provide a secure environment for transporting and delivering in-custody defendants to a courthouse, and can use a drive-through or drive-in/back-in design. If sufficient area is available, the drive-through arrangement allows an easier entry and exit sequence, particularly when additional cars, vans, and buses are waiting to deliver defendants. The design team should verify the type of vehicles used by authorities responsible for delivering in-custody defendants, such as patrol cars, minivans, or specialized buses. Vehicular width and height should be verified during programming and early design phases to ensure that clearances, doors, and bay sizes are appropriate.

FIGURE 6.5 Biometric reader. (*DMJM Technology.*)

FIGURE 6.6 Card reader. (*DMJM Technology.*)

Vehicular sally port doors and gates should be interlocked and controlled from a remote location, typically a central control station staffed with security personnel. Loop detectors, intercoms, and surveillance equipment can initiate call-ins from the vehicular sally port area. With the assistance of surveillance equipment, the security staff can review the vehicular sally port interior and exterior to insure detainees are not within the vehicular sally port. Once this is established, security personnel can allow the approaching vehicle to enter the vehicular sally port. When the vehicle clears, personnel return the sally port gate to a secure position. With the vehicle securely inside the sally port, security personnel can continue to observe and maintain movement of secured detainees from the sally port into the facility (Fig. 6.7).

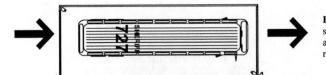

FIGURE 6.7 Drive-through vehicular sally port with recommended locations and views of surveillance cameras at exterior and interior areas. (*DMJM Design.*)

The vehicular sally port overhead door should be manufactured of heavy gauge steel, without vision panels. The vehicle sally port should be made of hardened security materials, such as solid grouted concrete masonry blocks with rebar reinforcing or a high gauge fence fabric, to prevent potential security breaches at this transition area. The gate should be a similar high gauge fence fabric with a high-security hydraulic sliding gate. Other options are enclosing the sally port and providing an overhead-coiling door, if budget allows. This is the more secure scenario and allows for concealment of activities occurring within the sally port. Sally ports should be located in areas with restricted or limited public visibility, to prevent observation of who is entering or exiting the facility.

Loading Docks

Service deliveries to loading docks must also be considered as potential threats. Loading docks should be designed to prevent service vehicles from driving under the building, and separated by a minimum of 50 feet from utility rooms and other entries, to prevent hidden explosives and package bombs from disrupting utilities. If this arrangement is impossible, loading docks and service areas should be hardened with blast-resistant design.

Air Intake Vents

Air intake vents should be placed away from public areas, and louvers should be mounted high off the ground to prevent hazardous gases or other materials from being discharged into the building system, typically 50 to 60 feet above grade. If louvers are horizontally mounted, they should be pitched to allow gas canisters to roll out of the areaway.

Windows

Windows are another instance of balancing comfort and security, especially as more buildings are designed with operable windows. Operable windows in controlled areas can weaken security levels because weapons and contraband can be hoisted illegally into a courthouse. As a rule, operable windows should be prohibited in all public areas. If courtrooms and chambers are located on the ground level, provide blast-resistant or bullet-resistant glazing.

Glazing

Various types of glazing should be considered for courthouse designers, but security glazing is in a different category.

- Standard float glass is found in many commercial or residential facilities.
- Safety glass, or tempered glass, must be provided at a distance from the finished floor to prevent injury.
- Rated glazing is typically considered security glass because of the wire mesh embedded within the glass, but this is not actually the case. Rated glazing has no threat rating, only a fire rating, and the mesh is not used to prevent access or egress, but rather to hold the assembly together in the event of increased temperatures or a direct hit from a fire hose.

Security Glazing

Security glazing is made up of a combination of polycarbonates and glass. This assembly is called a glass-clad-polycarbonate. By adjusting the thickness of the materials of these assemblies, different levels of security can be achieved.

Glazing assemblies typically do not have a fire rating, and come with different ratings, such as threat ratings, ballistic ratings, and explosive ratings. In higher end glazing, a combination of ratings is available, but each assembly serves a distinct purpose. These are all important concepts to understand when designing for security. Security glazing consists of two types: threat-resistant and bullet-resistant glazing.

Threat-resistant glazing assemblies can prevent a forced breach. In many standards, ratings are based on *forced entry*, but in this case, the word *breach* is used because glazing in a courthouse may be used to prevent ingress and egress. Threat-resistant glazing is typically designed into the perimeter courthouse security envelope, to prevent unwanted access to restricted areas or unwanted egress from holding or detainment areas.

Threat-resistant glazing assemblies vary in thickness and material makeup, but are rated under the same stringent standards to achieve a level of forced breach resistance. H.P. White Laboratories, Inc. is a commonly used industry testing agency for these glazing assemblies.

H.P. White Laboratories Inc. provides a set of standards for forced entry resistance found in, "Forced Entry and Ballistic Resistance of Structural Systems," Sd-Std-01.01, Revision G (Amended), April 30, 1993. This standard includes a table identifying three levels of forced breach: five-minute, fifteen-minute, and sixty-minute protection levels. Each level is tested under particular conditions, such as sledgehammer test, wood-splitting maul test, crowbar test, and others. These tests are timed and the effects of each assault are documented. The makeup of each level of threat breach resistance is based on testing results.

Underwriters Laboratory (UL) 752 rates bullet-resistant glazing at four different levels. Higher rating levels offer greater protection (Table 6.2).

Security glazing should be a minimum thickness of 9/16 of an inch or greater. Technology is constantly changing the performance of glazing. Designers should check with ASTM International (formerly American Society for Testing and Materials) standards and ratings and Underwriters Laboratories (UL) test results of materials to determine appropriate glazing thickness for various applications.

Blast-Resistant Design

Though blast-resistant design for courthouse exteriors is required for most federal courthouses, county and state facilities generally do not require this increased resistance. A threat and vulnerability assessment can determine whether the cost warrants this additional expense. Maintaining a standoff distance between the weapon and target building is the most cost-effective manner of protecting courthouses.

Trash Receptacles

Trash receptacles should be prohibited from courthouse perimeters because they provide a place to conceal explosives. Although wire baskets expose packages, packages and bags can still contain

TABLE 6.2   Bullet-Resistant Glazing Levels

Level	Protection from
1	Medium power small arms (9 mm)
2	High power small arms (.357 Magnum)
3	Super power small arms (.44 Magnum)
4	High power rifles (30.06 rifle)

Source: Underwriters Laboratories (UL) 752 Ballistic Specifications.

explosives. Overnight postal boxes should also be prohibited from courthouse exteriors and interiors, except by the central mailroom, where more screening and control is possible.

Finally, exterior design should prohibit individuals from scaling the side of a structure to the roof, and roof hatches should be secure to prevent entry from the roof.

INTERIOR PLANNING

Providing separate circulation patterns for the public, judges, staff, and in-custody defendants is essential to safe and efficient movement of trial participants throughout the courthouse. The courtroom then becomes the only area of interface. (See Tables 6.3 and 6.4.) The four interior areas of the courthouse are: public, private, secure, and interface zones.

When developing a user zoning and circulation system, courtroom floor plans, known as floor plates, drive the building footprint on the site. This is due to the vertical circulation system required to move all participants throughout the building and the long-span structural bays required for courtrooms (Figs. 6.8 and 6.9).

Appellate courthouses have only three interior zones, public, private, and interface, because they do not conduct trials or hearings where in-custody defendants are escorted to a courtroom.

Public Zones and Corridors

Screening of all public visitors occurs at the main courthouse entrance. Related equipment consists of a magnetometer for individual screening and an X-ray machine for package screening. To lessen the impact of a bomb explosion in the lobby, courthouse security stations should be treated, if possible, as separate building elements in the design or located away from the main building to prevent severe destruction or partial collapse of the main structure.

Public security screening points allow security staff to assess and detect problems and deter incidents from occurring. The security screening area should be designed as an integrated function of the public space, not as an afterthought. The integrated approach enhances the quality of the public lobby and indicates that security is incorporated throughout the facility design (Fig. 6.10).

TABLE 6.3   Courthouse Interior Planning: Public and Private Zones

Area	Planning considerations
Public zone	• Public screening at public entry.
	• Provide minimum 10 foot queuing from door.
	• Position screening station to optimize observation by security staff.
	• Provide security room adjacent to screening station.
	• Provide surveillance cameras at station.
	• Public corridors.
	• Provide clear and straightforward corridor system.
	• Minimum 12-foot corridors on courtroom floors.
	• Provide functional spaces to enhance security.
	• Attorney/client conference room.
	• Victim/witness waiting room.
	• Courtroom waiting.
	• Children's waiting.
	• Provide surveillance at all waiting areas.
Private zone	• Access to private zone restricted.
	• Control by card readers, smart cards, or escort.
	• Employee identification system for access.

TABLE 6.4   Courthouse Interior Planning: Secure and Interface Zones

Area	Planning considerations
Secure zone	• Access from vehicular sally port, to central holding, and temporary holding. • Environment should be hardened. • Elevators should interface with central control room. • Central control room located adjacent to vehicular sally port and central holding. • Technology: duress buttons, intercoms, card readers, surveillance cameras.
Interface zone	• Courtrooms and hearing rooms. • Sightlines. • Jury box. Location to public seating and access to jury room. • Public seating. Litigation rail. • Millwork. Ballistic resistant shield at judge's bench. • High security. Ballistic-resistant glazing at litigation rail. • Technology. Duress alarm, surveillance cameras. • Furnishings. Bolted to floor. • Arraignment. Use of video technology. • Access. Restrict and control access to private zone. • Fire release. Delay reaction to opening doors for secondary means of egress.

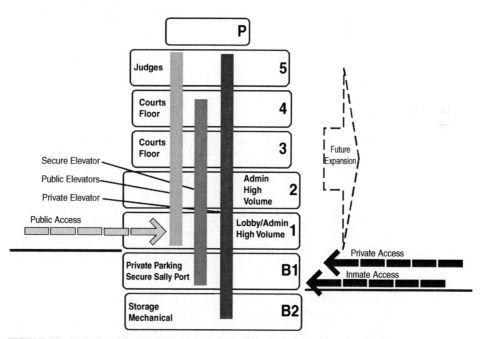

FIGURE 6.8   Vertical courthouse stacking diagram. This typical vertical arrangement shows three circulation patterns. The arrow on the left represents public circulation, the arrow on right represents in-custody defendants and judges entering the building separately. Each group travels vertically in the building through separate elevators. The only time all three circulation systems should interface is in the courtrooms on the court floors at Levels 3 and 4. (*DMJM Design.*)

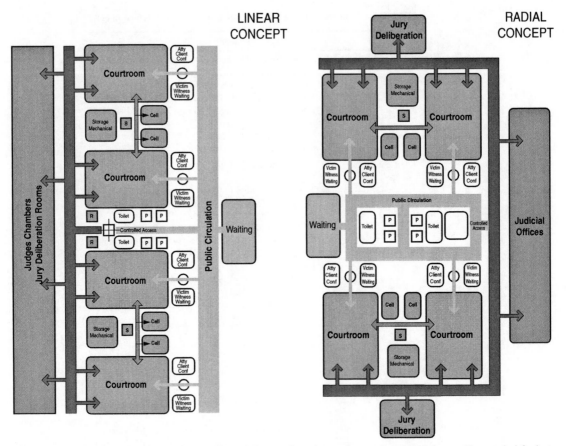

FIGURE 6.9   Courtrooms floor blocking diagram. This typical courts floor where each group, the public, judges, and in-custody defendants, moves separately to the courtroom. (*DMJM Design.*)

The entry sequence to the screening station should provide a minimum of 10 feet for queuing, or waiting, from the interior vestibule door to the screening station. This length prevents the public from waiting outside during an inclement day or when lines are long.

Screening stations should allow security personnel to observe everyone entering and leaving the courthouse. Stations should be positioned to prevent people entering the building and circumventing the station and breaching security. A physical barrier separating people entering and leaving provides an additional level of control.

The screening station layout should prevent people from circulating behind security personnel and observing staff and equipment (Fig. 6.11). Each security station area should be a minimum of 225 square feet to accommodate the queuing, magnetometer with security personnel, and x-ray equipment. The number of security stations is based on courthouse size and number of people estimated to enter on a daily basis.

The security screening station arrangement of public lobby screening is handled with magnetometer, x-ray equipment, security personnel, and queuing in front of the equipment. Security guards should have clear sightlines without obstructions to observe the public entering and exiting the building. The American with Disabilities Act (ADA) requires a side gate allowing individuals in wheelchairs to be screened by a security wand.

If staff must enter the courthouse through the main entry, access-controlled turnstiles control and check identification. Turnstiles should be equipped with card access readers to restrict access only to staff or authorized personnel.

FIGURE 6.10   Charlotte County Justice Center, Punta Gorda, Florida. Lobby security screening is integrated within the public space. (*Architect: Spillis Candela DMJM. Photographer: John Gillian.*)

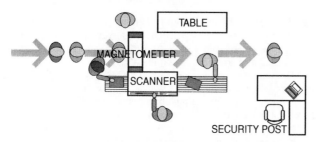

FIGURE 6.11   Security screening station. (*DMJM Design.*)

Selection of technology and design of staff access points should consider peak-hour volumes, potential waiting time, and technology activation time. Biometric readers with built-in keypads allowing turnstile access might slow line movement because user input and physical recognition are required. This technology can slow line movement if people are not familiar with the technology or forget their access code. Biometric readers, coupled with card readers to pull up an individual user profile, provide the quickest method of positive identification and access control.

Other methods, such as card readers, offer a good means of access control but no positive identification, because a card can be stolen or given away. The least desired method of access control is a keypad, which requires user input and is a slow operation. The other disadvantage of keypads is the inability to positively identify the individual attempting to access the area, as keypad numbers are easily given out and accountability is rapidly lost.

A small security room, with a minimum area of 80 square feet, should be located adjacent to the screening station. This space provides a controlled environment where security personnel can detain a suspect, rather than question and search someone in the lobby. Security staff can also store and lock items prohibited inside the courthouse, including weapons used by law enforcement officers and contraband confiscated during screening searches.

A surveillance camera should be positioned toward the screening process. Recorded videos can be used for detection and evaluation by staff, and to document that policies and procedures are fully implemented.

The public circulation system provides the main navigation system from the front door, where screening operations occur, to various departments. The pattern takes the public to the counter area of the clerk's office, the jury assembly room, attorney/client conference rooms, victim/witness waiting rooms, courtrooms/hearing rooms, public restrooms, public elevators, and reception areas for various agencies within the courthouse. The public circulation system should be clear and direct, without any bends or dead ends, to allow unobstructed observation by security personnel and surveillance cameras.

On courtroom floors, corridor widths should be 12 feet minimum, to accommodate the movement and milling of people near the courtrooms. Wide corridors allow adequate separation of individuals, particularly for those angered by a court decision and who may be prone to violence. Generous public spaces mitigate tense situations.

Separate circulation patterns, front-door screening, and technology are effective approaches to enhancing courthouse security. Essential and functional spaces should also be carefully located. For example, attorney/client conference rooms, victim/witness waiting rooms, and children's waiting areas provide a level of security by separating and isolating individuals from public areas where contact with other court participants poses security risks. These spaces provide a respite in a stressful environment where emotions run high. Providing these spaces allows security personnel to supervise individuals in more easily controlled environments.

Attorney/client conference rooms allow counselors to confer with their clients and discuss confidential matters in private. Victim/witness waiting rooms isolate individuals who are about to testify from a defendant's friends and families. Both rooms are generally located in front of a courtroom and can be used interchangeably. Without these rooms, individuals would be forced to converse with their counselors in public, where friends and family members of a defendant could listen to the conversation. This results in damaging testimony being leaked before a court appearance, or a victim or witness being placed in the traumatic situation of knowing that their testimony may harm or incriminate an individual.

Courtroom waiting areas remove people from gathering outside a courtroom while a court is in recess. They allow parties to be observed by personnel or surveillance cameras. In family court, the ability to separate spouses in volatile child custody or divorce cases, and removing the chance of physical and eye contact until all parties are seated in court, is essential.

Separate children's waiting areas are another important security feature. Although they are typically used as a short-term day care area for parents who are appearing in court, the waiting area allows staff to supervise children in family court during child custody and visitation hearings. The area prevents unauthorized removal of a child from the courthouse while the legal guardian is in court.

Public contact at the clerk's counter area and reception areas of court-related agencies like the prosecuting attorney, probation, and sheriff should provide security measures to deter violence. Each clerk station should be equipped with a duress alarm connected to the central security room and to surveillance cameras in the general area. Security glazing at the counter should be considered for staff protection. The clerk's counter area should include a separate records viewing room to allow the public to view records in a controlled environment while being supervised by the clerk's staff, to ensure records are not tampered with or destroyed. The room should be completely glazed to provide maximum visibility into the space from the clerk's area.

The reception area for court-related agencies should be securely zoned from other administrative areas of the department. Access to administrative areas should be restricted and controlled from the waiting room, either remotely operated by the receptionist, or by staff escort. Providing security glazing at the reception desk further enhances security.

Private Zone/Corridor

The private circulation zone is generally restricted to all court-related staff. Public access to this zone is controlled electronically, remotely, or by escort.

FIGURE 6.12   Ceiling mounted security camera. (*DMJM Technology.*)

On courtroom floors, private corridors are further restricted to judicial officers, selected court-related staff, escorted jurors, and court security personnel. Judicial officers should have direct access to their chamber level from the exterior entry through a restricted elevator. Controlling traffic on courtroom floor private corridors is paramount, to eliminate the potential of a mistrial should individuals come in contact with the jurors or judge during a trial.

Private and restricted elevators provide judges with a direct means of traveling from their cars to the chamber and courts floor. Elevators are controlled by card readers or biometrics programmed to restrict use to individuals or certain personnel classifications.

Security cameras should be positioned to allow surveillance from the central control room (Fig. 6.12). Corridors should be designed without bends or dead-end conditions.

Secure Zone/Corridor

The secure circulation pattern provides direct access from the vehicular sally port and central holding to the temporary holding area and courtroom. Along this route, contact with anyone within the public and private zones should be prohibited.

In-custody defendants are transported from central holding through a dedicated elevator, controlled and operated by court security. Additional equipment, such as duress buttons, intercoms, card readers, and surveillance cameras, can be installed in the elevator cab and lobbies for enhanced observation. Surveillance should be provided all along this path of circulation and at each control point to and from other zones, to ensure a secure separation between the secure, public, and private zones.

Construction materials for this zone should be durable, and hardened to prevent escape and abuse. Corridors are generally concrete masonry units with plaster and steel ceilings, and elevators are fabricated from stainless floor, wall, and ceiling construction. Elevators should be manufactured with a secure compartment when several defendants are escorted. This compartment allows the separation between the court security officer and the defendants. Corridors should be arranged as straight as possible to allow supervision by court security personnel via surveillance cameras and the control room. In-custody defendants should be escorted by security personnel within the secure zone.

Central Control Room

The central control room should be located at the main access point to the secure zone from the vehicular sally port. This is the main control location where court security maintains surveillance, monitoring, control, and communication for the entire facility (Fig. 6.13). The location of the control room should allow personnel to exit without traveling through the secure corridor. All cameras, doors, intercoms, duress buttons, elevator controls, and other security equipment should be monitored and controlled from this point.

As with the rest of this zone, the central control room should be constructed from hardened walls, with security glazing and controlled access that is the most difficult to breach. The location requires staffing during all hours of facility operation, and must be maintained if systems are operated without interruption.

Holding Cells

Temporary holding cells are located between a pair of courtrooms. Security personnel place a defendant in a cell near a courtroom during a quick court recess or if the defendant acts out in court. Holding cells should be hardened and acoustically separated with vestibules and sound locks. Central holding, located near the vehicular sally port, provides an initial staging area to unload and

FIGURE 6.13 Central control room, Anne Arundel County Courthouse, Maryland. This central control room within the central holding area has clear and unobstructed sightlines of defendants being escorted to the holding cells and secure elevators. (*Architect: Spillis Candela DMJM; Photographer: Douglas Hofstedt.*)

hold defendants prior to their movement to the court floor and appearance in court. All classifications of defendants are held in this area. Holding cell planning and design should separate males and females, adults and juveniles, visually and acoustically.

Cells should be equipped with stainless steel or concrete benches, and a combination water closet and lavatory unit, similar to those found in correctional facilities. Holding cell design should allow an officer to view the entire room from the door without any blind spots. Surveillance cameras and duress buttons should be strategically placed in this area for supervision and protection. Sizes and number of cells depend on projected courtroom utilization. Typically, an arraignment court requires multiple single and group cells, since many individuals who have been arrested are brought before a judicial officer for first appearance. This arrangement allows security officers to separate defendants based on background, criminal record, and gender (Fig. 6.14).

Attorney/Defendant Interview Rooms

Attorney/defendant interview rooms are located either in the central holding area or near the courtrooms. In both instances, secure and public access must be provided where the only interface occurs in the interview room. Interview rooms are either contact (face to face) or noncontact (separate security glazing). In a contact room, a pedestrian sally port should be located at the public/attorney entry side. This sally port operates with two interlocking doors, similar to a vehicular sally port, to prevent the defendant from escaping. Surveillance cameras should be positioned within the interview rooms.

Interface Zone

The only location where all three circulation zones interact is in the courtrooms and hearing rooms. This prevents in-custody defendants from interfacing with the public, judicial officers, and jurors, prevents the public from tampering with jury decisions, and protects the media from gaining access to information in the private zones (Fig. 6.15).

COURTROOM PLANNING AND DESIGN

Traditionally, courtrooms are centers of activity within a courthouse, where people's lives and emotions are played out before the judge, jury, counselors, and the public, and where a majority of legal

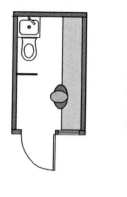
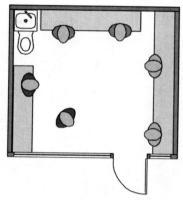

FIGURE 6.14 Single (left) and group (right) holding cells. (*DMJM Design.*)

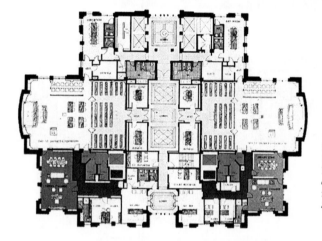

FIGURE 6.15 Albert V. Bryan United States Courthouse, Alexandria, Virginia. Plan arrangement of the three separate circulation systems and how they interface within the courtroom. (*Architect: Spillis Candela DMJM.*)

decisions are handed down. Courtrooms are also venues where individuals take their own actions if they are not satisfied with legal decisions.

At the same time, courtrooms must be places of solemnity and deliberation, sanctuaries where the spoken word of written law has a powerful impact. Just as the scales of justice balance, courtroom architecture must reflect the symmetry of balance and proportion. The openness must be balanced between the judicial system and protection. Courtroom design must reflect the importance of this space in the administration of justice (Fig. 6.16).

Sightlines

Courtrooms should avoid blind spots within the space. The judge, clerk, and court security deputy must be able to see everyone within the courtroom. The judge's bench, usually raised about three steps or 18 to 21 inches above the floor, should view the entire courtroom without any difficulty. Minimal head movement should allow the judge a clear sweeping view of the room. The courtroom security deputy is usually placed alongside the defense table where the defendant is seated. This position is generally adjacent to the door leading into the temporary holding area between a pair of courtrooms. Typical courtroom plans allow the judge a clear view of the entire room during the trial by placing the judge's bench either at the corner of the room or at the center of the room (Figs. 6.17 and 6.18).

FIGURE 6.16 Charlotte County Justice Center, Punta Gorda, Florida. Courtroom design. (*Architect: Spillis Candela DMJM. Photographer: John Gillan.*)

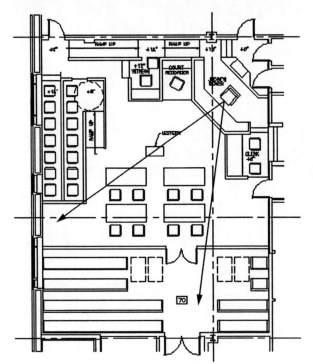

FIGURE 6.17 Courtroom design with corner judge's bench. (*DMJM Design.*)

Jury Box

Jurors render decisions regarding serious criminal or civil matters. They need to be attentive, listen, and see the arguments presented by both counsels. Jurors must be separated from the public to avoid any interference or stress that may be exerted. A minimum distance of six feet should be maintained between the end of the jury box and the public litigation rail. Access from the jury box to the jury deliberation room should be quick and direct. Jurors should not walk directly past the public area when heading towards the jury room.

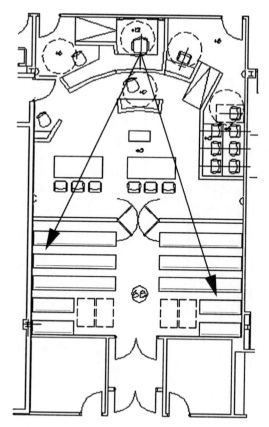

FIGURE 6.18 Courtroom design with center judge's bench. (*DMJM Design.*)

Public Seating

A public litigation rail should be placed between the litigation well and public gallery, the public seating area in a courtroom. A swinging gate should allow the public to enter the litigation well when called upon. Movement between the public gallery and litigation well should be controlled and restricted by the court security deputy and judge.

Millwork

A ballistic-resistant shield should be concealed in front of the judge's bench. This shield will protect the judge if a weapon is brought into the courtroom and aimed at the judge. The shield allows the judge to duck under the bench for protection while the court security officer restores order in the courtroom (Fig. 6.19).

High Security

In some jurisdictions, high security trials require security glazing at the spectator rail, between the litigation well and public gallery. This security glazing serves as an operable partition and is recessed into the wall when not used.

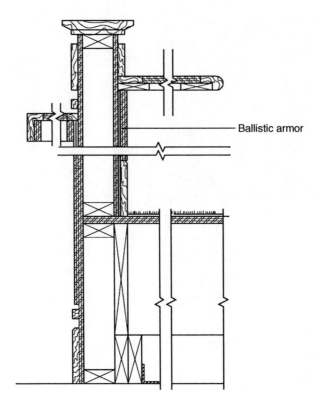

——— Ballistic armor

FIGURE 6.19 Judge's bench detail. (*DMJM Design.*)

Technology

Within the courtroom, electronic technology should be used to enhance security, such as providing a duress alarm at the judge's bench, clerk's station, and court security officer station. The duress alarm will send an audible alarm to the main security room alerting staff of an incident within the courtroom. Surveillance cameras should be strategically located to view the public gallery and litigation rail.

Video technology assesses individuals through a database and surveillance cameras. Video arraignment reduces the need to transport and escort large numbers of arrestees to court for arraignment. Cost benefits result by minimizing costs and risks of transporting defendants and reducing the need for courtroom security personnel (Fig. 6.20).

Technology provides an alternative to having all parties in the same room, a potentially difficult environment to control. Video arraignment allows the courtroom to come to the jail and the jail to come to the courtroom without physically moving participants between facilities. Through video arraignment, attorneys, defendants, and judges can all be in remote locations, tied together via multiplexed video cameras with microphones and speakers. This system saves time and money for jail staff and judges, as they can hold arraignment without traveling.

Furnishings

All courtroom furniture and fixtures should either be fixed or heavyweight to prevent use as weapons. Loose planters, chairs in the public gallery and jury box, and picture frames should be avoided.

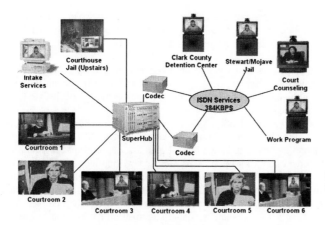

FIGURE 6.20 Video arraignment. (*DMJM Technology.*)

Arraignment

When a large group of arrestees is brought into a courtroom, a separate and secure docket box may be used to enhance security. The docket box is generally an area directly off the holding zone and recessed into the side of a courtroom where arrestees and defendants wait before appearing before the judge in the courtroom. The docket box provides a controlled means of handling a large inmate contingent within the litigation zone. In these instances, security glazing is placed in front of the docket box, with views of the courtroom proceedings.

Access

Doors leading from the courtroom into the private zone (judge's chamber and jury rooms) should be controlled to prevent public access. The doors can be controlled via card reader or biometrics. This restriction controls access when the courtroom is not used and public doors are unlocked.

Fire Release Door

In some controlled areas, access and egress must be restricted. Courthouses pose special conditions because of occupancy and code requirements. A common solution is use of time-delayed restricted egress devices, where the access control system is tied into the fire alarm system. If an alarm is activated, any restricted egress door will release and allow egress after a set period of time. This scenario is not accepted in all jurisdictions and must be reviewed and approved by local code officials.

Jury Deliberation Room

The jury room should be located within the private zone of the courthouse. Direct access should be provided from the courtroom, to avoid contact with the public, defendant, and judiciary.

CONCLUSION

An effective courthouse security plan maintains integrity of the judicial system and the judicial process by protecting participants and courthouse property. Security is further achieved by detecting, deterring, and detaining those exhibiting violent behavior within the courthouse grounds.

Three fundamental considerations are part of an effective security plan: architectural design, technology systems, and policies and procedures. Each of these facets, individually and collectively, must be considered throughout courthouse planning and design. The formation of a courthouse security committee during the initial project stages will formulate and address all the critical aspects and essential issues comprising a facility security plan. Continued participation by the committee throughout the design process will proactively prepare users, stakeholders, and security personnel for operational security requirements once the facility is completed, or when new security policies are to be reviewed and implemented at existing facilities.

Architecturally, effective site planning, secured building perimeters and exteriors, and a zoned interior circulation system allow for safe and efficient movement of the various participants around and through the site and facility. The single largest planning aspect impacting courthouse safety and security is the functional zoning into public, private, secure, and interface zones. Through effective planning and good design, all trial participants are physically separated until they meet in the courtroom. The successful implementation of this basic planning tenet is crucial to maintaining the safety and security of the facility, integrity of the proceedings, and efficient operations. At the same time, courthouse building owners, facility managers, and administrators must give careful consideration to budgeting, operational issues, and staff training for emergencies.

Technology systems complement architectural design within the courthouse security plan, and should not be the sole measure for securing a facility. Only through seamless integration of technology, architectural design, and policies and procedures will an effective security plan be realized. While sophisticated systems can be introduced, careful and thorough planning is still the first line of defense for securing the courthouse.

ACKNOWLEDGMENTS

Donald J. Dwore, FAIA, Principal, Spillis Candela DMJM Design, Coral Gables, Florida

BIBLIOGRAPHY

H.P. White Laboratories Inc., "*Forced Entry and Ballistic Resistance Of Structural Systems*, Sd-Std-01.01, Revision G (Amended)," April 30, 1993.

Jandura, Kenneth J., *The Courthouse: A Planning and Design Guide for Court Facilities*, National Center for State Courts. Coauthored lighting and acoustical design articles.

Nadel, Barbara A., "Security and Technology: 21st Century Trends." *Construction Specifier*, Construction Specifications Institute, April 2001.

INTERNET RESOURCES

American Judicature Society (AJS)
www.ajs.org

Courts Today Magazine
www.courtstoday.com

DMJM Design
www.dmjm.com

National Center for State Courts
www.ncsconline.org

CHAPTER 7

FEDERALLY OWNED OR LEASED BUILDINGS: SECURITY DESIGN

Terry L. Leach, AIA
Senior Security Specialist
DMJM System Solutions/DMJM Technology
Albuquerque, New Mexico

> *Effective security is not rocket science—it's just a mind-set.*
> PETE BRAKE, CERTIFIED PROTECTION PROFESSIONAL (CPP)
> *Lead Technical Engineer, Electronic Security Center,*
> *U.S. Army Corps of Engineers, Huntsville, Alabama*

Security design is not rocket science, but for most building owners, design professionals, and public officials, integrating the many pieces of the security puzzle remains an increasingly challenging and complex art, one that can be mastered with the proper guidance. Protecting people, buildings, and assets from risk and danger requires a sound methodology for achieving optimum security in any building type, whether publicly or privately owned.

Effective security relies on design and construction, passive and electronic systems, and operational policies and procedures put in place by building owners and managers. When integrated, the sum of the individual elements adds up to a comprehensive security system greater than any of the parts alone could provide.

Most federal government agencies have specific requirements, security methods, and systems tailored to meet their goals and missions at federal installations and facilities. These basic design requirements may be used as a guide by architects and engineers when designing facilities owned and operated by state and local governments requiring enhanced security, as well as for privately owned facilities and office buildings renting space, or hoping to rent space, to federal agencies or federal contractors requiring security clearance. The federal government has published standards and guidelines available to design and construction professionals seeking additional information.

SECURITY STANDARDS

After the April 1995 bombing of the Alfred P. Murrah Federal Office Building in Oklahoma City, the U.S. Department of Justice (USDOJ) spearheaded a major change in design philosophy of federal building projects. The USDOJ published *Vulnerability Assessment of Federal Buildings* in June 1995 to assess the vulnerabilities of their existing building inventory. Federal agencies participating in the development of the document included:

- U.S. Department of Justice
- U.S. Marshals Service

- Federal Bureau of Investigation
- U.S. General Services Administration
- U.S. Department of Defense
- U.S. Secret Service
- U.S. Department of Defense
- Social Security Administration
- Administrative Office of the U.S. Courts

SECURITY LEVELS

Because of the many differences in types of federal buildings, the document defines five levels of security based on staffing size, number of employees, use, and public access. Facilities are categorized as Levels I, II, III, IV, and V (Table 7.1). This document has become an important resource to architects, engineers, and designers during the programming process for federal building design.

Role of the U.S. General Services Administration (GSA)

GSA is responsible for providing office space for most of the federal workforce, protecting government property, and providing a safe workplace for federal employees. The Federal Protective Services (FPS), formerly a division of GSA that was moved to the Department of Homeland Security, is charged with protecting federal workers and the visiting public on federal property. The FPS is responsible for physical security and law enforcement at federal facilities. They generally provide police officers, criminal investigators, security specialists, system installers, and command and control center operators.

TABLE 7.1   Security Levels for Federal Buildings

Security level	Criteria
Level I	- 10 or fewer employees - 2500 square feet or less of office space - Low volume of public access and traffic
Level II	- 11 to 150 employees - 2500 to 80,000 square feet - Moderate volume of public access and traffic - Activities routine in nature
Level III	- 151 to 450 federal employees - 80,000 to 150,000 square feet - Moderate to high volume of public access and traffic - Tenants might include law enforcement agencies, court or related agencies and functions, and government records and archives.
Level IV	- Over 450 federal employees - More than 150,000 square feet - High volume of public access and traffic - Tenants might include high-risk law enforcement and intelligence agencies, courts, judicial offices, and highly sensitive records.
Level V	- Similar to Level IV but would include such buildings as the Pentagon or CIA headquarters. - The facility would have at least those security features as listed in Level IV.

Source: U.S. Department of Justice, *Vulnerability Assessment of Federal Buildings*, June 1995.

Interagency Security Committee (ISC)

In October 1995, the ISC was created to develop long-term construction standards for federal building security. The resulting document, *ISC Security Design Criteria For New Federal Office Buildings and Major Modernization Projects* (May 2001), is a direct result of the process and findings of the USDOJ's *Vulnerability Assessment of Federal Buildings*. Facilities falling under the ISC design criteria include:

- New construction of general-purpose office buildings
- New or lease-construction of courthouses occupied by federal employees in the United States
- Lease-constructed projects being submitted to Congress for appropriations or authorization

 Facilities not falling under the criteria include:

- Buildings under the control or jurisdiction of the Department of Defense (DOD)
- Airports
- Prisons
- Hospital/Clinics
- Border Patrol Stations
- Ports of Entry
- Unique facilities such as those buildings classified as USDOJ Level V, i.e., the Pentagon, CIA Headquarters

VULNERABILITY ASSESSMENT

Vulnerability assessment has become a critical part of the design process both in existing and new federal buildings. Although assessment is not new to the design process, the need for assessment has become better defined because of attacks on federal facilities. Various government agencies, such as the Department of State and the Internal Revenue Service, developed methodologies early on. Attacks on American embassies or those by disgruntled taxpayers on domestic facilities have been a security risk for these agencies for many years. The 1993 bombing of the World Trade Center, the 1995 Oklahoma City Murrah Building attack, and the events of September 11, 2001, confirmed that attacks can and will happen on American soil.

 Just as building codes, zoning ordinances, and the Americans with Disabilities Act (ADA) have become part of the design vocabulary, so should security design principles. Security design should be incorporated in the concept design stage of a project.

 Architects, engineers, designers, and owners should consider integrating security design into site planning and building design, just as local, state, or federal codes and life-safety issues are addressed.

 The most accepted method to determine threats, adversaries, and vulnerability to assets is to perform a vulnerability assessment. Several assessment methodologies have been developed by agencies such as the Internal Revenue Service, the Army Corps of Engineers, and Sandia National Laboratories.

 The common goal of most assessment models is ranking or prioritizing findings and determining the risk and consequences against mitigation costs.

- Threat can be actual or perceived and is intended to cause harm to persons or property including day-to-day operation of a facility.
- Vulnerability is the degree to which a building or site is susceptible to a threat.
- Consequences are the negative effects caused by an event.

 Just as every federal facility is unique, so is the approach to an assessment. If the agency doesn't have an assessment procedure, another model can be tailored to fit the needs of the user and facility.

DESIGN GUIDELINES

From a physical security standpoint, all potential problems should be stopped by perimeter security means such as fencing, barriers, guard posts, and guard patrols. The greatest potential for injury, loss of life, and destruction of property comes through the introduction of explosives or other harmful materials into or near the facility.

A balanced combination of design, technology, and operations—through manufactured and natural barriers, human observation, and electronic detection and surveillance—should be used to keep these potentially devastating materials as far away from the buildings as possible. A well designed and properly operating security system should prevent an intruder from using their most effective weapon, the element of surprise. However impossible it may be to eliminate this element entirely, the security systems designer should use all practical tools for each facility's conditions and capabilities, to give monitoring personnel the upper hand by providing an effective and reliable means of detecting and preventing terrorism and crimes committed at federal facilities.

Designers should approach federal facilities individually, as each has certain requirements, existing conditions, operational, or financial restrictions determining the kind of security upgrade or new system appropriate for a facility. Sometimes, a facility already has a substantial investment in and is satisfied with existing security systems, and adding new features is advised or necessary. In other cases, the system may have outlived its reasonable usefulness and an entirely new system should be phased in. These design and programming issues should be clarified early in the design with the contracting officer, facility manager, and other designated federal representatives. The design step most often overlooked, or not given the proper amount of emphasis, is balancing and coordinating technical product design and facility design. The existing facility physical constraints or the design and layout of new facilities should be coordinated in detail with equipment design, so that each complements and effectively supports the other.

Design professionals and consultants should use value engineering to save on operational and capital costs during all project stages. Incorporating existing security systems, equipment, or infrastructure into design of new systems should be considered wherever practical. After initial interviews with designated facility representatives, design professionals should perform a field survey of all existing security equipment and signal lines that could be included in the new system. A report to the government, with recommendations identifying those items still in good operating condition, should indicate which should be included in any new systems.

Planning and Design

Many factors must be considered during site selection, planning, and design of a new facility. Basic site considerations include the facility's location with respect to:

- Other buildings
- Terrain features
- Traffic flow
- Location of parking areas
- Nearby fire fighting, law enforcement, and other emergency public services

Facility exterior layout considerations include:

- Common risk functions
- Access design
- Barrier protection
- Exterior barriers, such as fences, trees, or hedges, can create effective obstacles to casual trespassers

• Vehicle barriers are important elements in mitigating the risks of vehicle attacks. If perimeter fencing is not sufficient to prevent a vehicle from penetrating the grounds and crashing into a building, some other means, such as steep earth berms, bollards, or strategically placed concrete benches and planters, should be considered.

The checklists for minimum security design levels provide an overview of important factors to consider for new construction and renovation and ongoing operations of existing facilities (Tables 7.2 and 7.3).

SECURITY DESIGN ELEMENTS

Local agency Facility Security Officers should be consulted for guidance on specific issues when questions arise during planning and design phases, especially regarding several important security design elements (Table 7.4).

TABLE 7.2   Site Planning and Design Checklist for Minimum Security Design Levels

1. Eliminate hiding places near the facility.
2. Provide an unobstructed view around the facility.
3. Site the facility within view of other occupied facilities on the installation.
4. Locate assets stored on-site, but outside of facility, within view of occupied rooms in the facility.
5. Minimize the need for signage or other indications of asset locations.
6. Minimize exterior signage indicating the presence or locations of assets.
7. Provide a 150-foot minimum facility separation from installation boundaries.
8. Eliminate lines of approach perpendicular to the building.
9. Minimize vehicle access points.
10. Eliminate parking beneath facilities.
11. Locate parking as far from the facility as practical, but at least 30 feet away.
12. Illuminate building exteriors or sites where exposed assets are located.
13. Secure access to power and heating plants, gas mains, water supplies, and electrical service.
14. Locate public parking areas within views of occupied rooms or facilities.
15. Locate the facility away from natural or man-made vantage points.
16. Locate trash receptacles as far from the facility as possible, but at least 30 feet away.

TABLE 7.3   Building Security Design Checklist for Minimum Security Design Levels

1. Locate critical assets on the exterior of the building.
2. Minimize window areas.
3. Back up glass doors in foyers with solid doors or walls.
4. Do not locate windows next to doors so intruders could unlock the doors through them.
5. Secure exposed exterior ladders and fire escapes.
6. Plan buildings to conceal assets, to make access to assets difficult for intruders, and to eliminate hiding places.
7. Design circulation to provide unobstructed views of people approaching controlled areas or occupied space.
8. Arrange building interior furnishings to eliminate hiding places around asset locations.
9. Locate assets in spaces occupied 24 hours per day where possible.
10. Locate activities with large visitor populations away from protected assets where possible.
11. Locate protected assets in common areas where they are visible to more than one person.
12. Locate mailrooms on the facility perimeter

TABLE 7.4 Security Design Elements at Federal Buildings

- Entry points
- Guard services and posts
- Parking
- Employee and visitor access
- Doors
- Walls, windows, and openings
- Lighting

Entry Points

Entry points should be convenient and accessible to general traffic. Vehicles waiting to enter federal facilities should not be backed up into public roadways.

- Separate entrances to limited-access areas.
- Create pedestrian entry and control for all vehicle entry points. The design should conform to the requirements of Federal Standard 795: Uniform Federal Accessibility Standards (UFAS).
- Locate card readers, keypads, and other lock systems to provide access for disabled personnel. An accessible route should be identified to all required areas by UFAS.
- Control pedestrian entry points onto federal sites with a security post.
- Locate the main entry point into federal facilities through one lobby served by one entrance with a security post.
- Ensure that the design and locations of doors, windows, and utility openings are not weak links in the facility perimeter.
- Locate key personnel and assets away from the building perimeter whenever possible.
- Locate access to upper floors and elevators beyond the restricted-access point.
- Separate elevator shafts from the garage to the lobby and from the lobby to upper floors.

Guard Services

Design professionals should determine from the user or client agency the following:

- What guard services exist or are planned
- How many guards or officers will be required
- Where their stations are
- Space needs for offices, lockers, toilets, showers, staff rooms, and other required support areas
- Special equipment needs

Parking

Parking areas pose potential hazards to federal office buildings and should be carefully analyzed.

- Design appropriate separation between parking areas and occupied buildings.
- Minimize possible damage due to vehicle bombs by ensuring perimeter government parking lots and parking inside or beneath federal buildings are controlled, through restricted parking policies, vehicle identification, or other procedures.

- Ensure that future leases provide controlled perimeter, street, and adjacent parking in close proximity to the building.
- Protect personnel and property in the parking areas and walkways. Consult with the Physical Security Specialist to determine requirements for parking area intrusion detection, video surveillance, and security lighting.

Employee and Visitor Access

Monitoring and screening of all those entering a federal facility is an important ground floor or public entry function at federal facilities.

- Locate public access functions on the ground floor with a minimal number of access points into secure spaces.
- Screen visitors with x-ray and magnetometer equipment, as recommended in Level IV buildings or other mitigating circumstances, such as high-crime areas.
- Locate screening functions either at the main building entrance(s) or the public entrance(s) into secure spaces.
- Use x-ray machines to screen incoming mail and packages.
- Provide adequate clearances for walk-through metal detectors and x-ray screening devices, including queuing space and waiting areas.
- Consult with the Physical Security Specialist and risk and threat assessments findings for specific requirements.
- Prepare procedures to screen employees and visitors entering federal facilities, based on directions from the Federal Protective Service, federal law enforcement agencies, building security committees, or specific site threats.
- Provide adequate screening devices to accommodate the typical number of persons entering or exiting during peak access times.

Doors

- Provide metal or metal-clad exterior doors and frames on all exterior exits.
- Use interior hinges, or hinges with nonremovable or tamper-resistant pins.
- Provide high-security locks for doors leading into secure and restricted areas.
- Minimize the number of entrances into secure and restricted areas.
- Provide metal-clad doors and frames between mailrooms and interior of facility.
- Provide intrusion detection on exterior doors and accessible perimeter windows.

Walls, Windows, and Openings

- Provide sound barriers where required.
- Provide blast mitigation, in the form of 4-mil-fragment retention film, to the inside face of exterior window glass.
- Minimize, eliminate, secure, or protect openings larger than 96 square inches.
- Control interior and exterior roof access.
- Monitor with access control system.
- Slab-to-slab wall construction should be provided between government space and that of other tenants or common areas in multitenant buildings, and include an approved intrusion detection system.

SECURITY LIGHTING

The primary function of site lighting is to provide a secure environment for the facility during hours of darkness. The lighting should work to discourage intruders and maximize visibility for surveillance by cameras and guards. All exterior lighting should be considered and evaluated in the site lighting design package.

Site lighting includes all lighting on building(s) exterior walls, and extends outward to the perimeter walls, fences, site entrances, and exits. This includes, but is not limited to:

- Security lighting
- Circulation lighting
- Lighting adjacent to a perimeter fence
- Building mounted lighting
- All associated controls and circuiting

An effective lighting installation supports site surveillance by direct security force observation and through closed circuit television (CCTV) cameras. Site lighting should optimize surveillance and alarm assessment conditions, and facilitate routine vehicular patrols.

The following guidelines are necessary for the proper design of all site lighting, whether for domestic federal buildings, embassies, or other facilities located outside the United States:

- Feed all site lighting that is part of the security system from the "essential" section of the utility bus.
- Ensure that security perimeter lighting reaches full illumination within 90 seconds in the event of a power failure. This includes time to power the emergency generator.
- Factor energy performance of lamps and light fixtures into all design decisions throughout the project.
- Design the entire lighting system to be capable of being turned off and on during emergency situations.
- Verify availability of replacement light fixtures and lamps to be procured in the host country, prior to specification, as applicable.
- Minimize the variety of lighting fixtures and lamps.

All light sources, light fixtures, and ballasts specified by the lighting consultant should meet the requirements of the Department of Energy's Master Specifications Section 16500, Energy Efficient Lighting for Existing Federal Facilities, May 1998.

Lighting designers should be familiar with the information and criteria in the latest edition of the *IES (Illuminating Engineering Society) Handbook,* especially the following chapters:

- Chapter 10, "Quality of Light"
- Chapter 21, "Exterior Lighting"
- Chapter 29, "Emergency, Safety, and Security Lighting"

Light Sources

- Select full spectrum light sources to reflect all colors effectively.
- Improve night visibility by ensuring contrast of objects in the field of vision, and using full spectrum light sources that discriminate between colors.
- Use high intensity discharge (HID) lamps, the most commonly used sources, for greatest efficiency.
- Consider fluorescent and induction lamps for greater efficiency.

Lamp Selection

- Use high-color rendering sources where detailed inspection, color discrimination, or object appearance is critical.
- Blend site perimeter lighting with the lighting for adjacent areas.
- Select color temperatures to enhance buildings, landscape, and people's appearance.
- Provide 2700 to 3500 K sources at building entrances lighting.
- Provide 3500 to 4100 K for landscape accent lighting.

RECOMMENDED LIGHTING SOURCES

Designers should be familiar with various types of lighting sources, lamps, ballasts, fixtures, and performances when specifying lighting for security applications.

Metal Halide Lamps

- Provide quartz restrike lamps when metal halide lamps are part of the security system.
- Use standard metal halide lamps for circulation lighting, area lighting, wall, and facade lighting.
- Consider Pulse Start lamps for longer life higher efficacy, shorter restrike time and better color rendering.
- Use low-wattage PAR metal halide lamps for accent lighting and landscape lighting.
- Use low-wattage metal halide lamps for building entrances.
- Consider electronic ballasts for longer life, higher efficacy, shorter restrike time, and better color rendering.

High Pressure Sodium Lamps

- Use standard high-pressure sodium (HPS) lamps where efficacy and lamp life are of prime importance and color rendition is not critical.
- Consider color corrected HPS lamps, but note that they have reduced efficacy and lamp life.
- Use dual arc tube HPS lamps for instant restrike or 40,000-hour life.
- Use HPS lamps for area lighting, circulation lighting, and facade lighting (where building materials are warm colors).
- Do not use HPS lamps for accent lighting, landscape lighting, or building entrances.

Fluorescent Lamps:

- Use compact fluorescent as an alternative to low wattage HID sources, except in climates where temperatures drop below negative 18 degrees Celsius.
- Use compact fluorescent for accent lighting, landscape lighting, low-level circulation lighting, and building entrances.
- Use linear, fluorescent as an alternative to low wattage HID sources, except in climates where temperatures drop below negative 18 degrees Celsius.
- Use fluorescents where broad washes of diffuse light are required, such as lighting for walls, signage, building entrances, and broad landscape areas.

Ballasts

- Remember that sources requiring ballasts are only as reliable and energy efficient as the ballasts that power them.
- Provide Pulse Start ballasts for all metal halide systems where available for higher efficacy, longer lamp life, better color uniformity, and faster warm up and restrike time. Consider electronic ballast for low-wattage, metal halide systems.
- Provide ballasts with a "turn-off" function, protecting the entire system when lamps reach end of life.
- Provide ballasts with the appropriate starting and operating temperatures for fluorescent sources.
- Provide ballasts with thermal protection.
- Provide proper ventilation and heat dissipation for ballasts.
- Provide weatherproof housing in exterior applications where ballasts are remote.
- Provide ballasts with quick disconnects.

Light Fixtures

Selection of decorative fixtures supporting representational areas should be based on style, scale, and visual presence after dark.

- Provide fixtures complying with all local and national codes.
- Consider the project budget before selecting fixtures.
- Consider life cycle costs as well as initial fixture costs.
- Specify carefully engineered fixtures for enhanced durability and ease of maintenance.
- Provide vandal resistant housings, lenses, and hardware where fixtures are accessible or prone to vandalism.
- Provide fixtures designed to withstand harsh environments in coastal and desert climates.
- Mount all poles on a concrete foundation with a minimum of four anchor bolts.
- Ensure that the top of the foundation is a minimum of 2 inches above grade.

Maintenance

- Consider maintenance concerns and limitations before specifying site lighting.
- Provide self-retaining hardware for all parts of luminaires that are loosened or disassembled for maintenance.
- Provide fixtures in locations where they can be maintained.
- Ensure that adjustable fixtures can be relamped without adjustment.
- Lock or permanently mark fixtures aimed to ensure proper alignment after servicing.
- Provide a wiring diagram on each fixture.
- Limit the variety of fixture and lamp types to facilitate maintenance. UV stabilized acrylic or glass should be used for diffusers and lenses.
- Select lighting equipment construction appropriate for the specific climate.
- Use aluminum fixtures and poles.
- Use composite fixtures and concrete or fiberglass poles in coastal climates. Steel is not recommended.

- Provide stainless steel hardware.
- Ensure that steel mounting brackets are galvanized.

Optical Control

- Consider light beam distribution to eliminate direct glare, reflected glare, and veiling luminance from the fixture and/or its reflected image.
- Avoid fixtures with refractor optics.
- Ensure that site lighting is responsive to community needs.
- Identify potential light trespass issues before the lighting design is developed. Specify fixtures accepting additional shielding.
- Ensure that peak candlepower for floodlighting directed toward the property perimeter does not exceed 65 degrees above the vertical plane.
- Reduce light pollution with fixtures controlling the light source.
- Minimize stray light by projecting building lighting upward.
- Specify emergency lighting systems at higher threat facilities. This should be a manually controlled, instant-on supplementary system. The intent is reducing visibility of the intruders by using direct glare and increasing visibility of guards with increased light levels.

Fixture Performance

- Ensure that fixture reflectors distribute light uniformly and precisely.
- Ensure that light distribution has no hot or dark spots.
- Maximize luminaire efficiency with reflectors.
- Provide the most efficient beam distribution pattern for the specific task and location.

LIGHTING SYSTEMS

Appropriate lighting design and installation can significantly enhance or detract from real and perceived security levels at a site or building.

Uniformity

- Provide uniform levels of light on horizontal and vertical surfaces throughout the entire secured area under surveillance.
- Consider that uniformity reduces the eye's adaptation process and reduces the quantity of light required to see effectively.

Obstructions

- Consider the use of objects for obstructing light patterns.
- Use obstructions such as trees, projection, or relief on building facades or parked vehicles.
- Consider that although objects add visual interest, and psychological stimulation, they can produce heavy shadows.

- Reduce heavy shadows by lighting obstructed areas with more than one fixture and from more than one direction.

Surface Reflectance

- Use light colored surfaces to produce reflected light.
- Maximize use of light colored building materials on building facades, perimeter walls, and concrete walks and drives.

Luminaire Mounting Heights

- Tall poles or high mounting heights will reduce the number of fixtures needed to uniformly light an area. However, maintenance of tall poles should be considered.
- Local ordinance, accessibility, capability of service equipment, and the spatial relationship between the luminaires and the landscape can restrict mounting heights.

Luminaire Locations

- Locate light fixtures carefully, especially regarding their relationship to each other, site elements, CCTV cameras, and patrol routes.
- Reduce potential for intruders to climb pole-mounted, wall-mounted, and building-mounted fixtures.
- Avoid pole and fixture locations on or close to walls and buildings.

LIGHTING CONTROLS

Manual and automated controls and a level of redundancy should be carefully considered for security lighting in various areas of a building or site, depending on critical nature or occupancy.

Types of Control

All site lighting should have central manual control. Lighting should be automated, either with photocell or time clocks, and be capable of interfacing with security systems for automatic control from the security monitoring room.

Flexibility Characteristics

In specific areas, different lighting schemes may be required. Control intent should be developed in conjunction with the lighting design. These areas include private gardens, guard stations, and exterior gathering spaces.

Circuiting Requirements

Security lighting system components should be fed from the essential section of the electrical utility or from the automatically starting standby generator. Site lighting system branch circuits should be arranged so that no single circuit failure would cause any two adjacent lighting fixtures to fail. An exception would be decorative lighting not part of the security system.

BLAST PROTECTION CRITERIA

The intent of blast protection criteria is to reduce the potential for widespread catastrophic structural damage and resulting injury to people. The applicable criteria for federal facilities are provided in the *Interagency Security Committee (ISC) Security Criteria for New Federal Office Buildings and Major Modernization Projects*, May 28, 2001, known as the ISC Security Design Criteria. This document, adopted by GSA on May 30, 2001, is a benchmark development containing security criteria applied to all new federal buildings, renovations, additions, and major modernization projects.

Blast protection criteria are based on the risk and protection levels determined during the risk assessment. The criteria define the performance and degree of protection provided by the structural systems and components. There are three basic approaches to blast protection; the best response is a combination of the following:

1. Blast loads can be reduced, primarily by increasing standoff distances.
2. A facility can be strengthened.
3. Higher levels of risk can be accepted.

PROTECTION LEVELS

In accordance with the ISC Security Design Criteria, an entire building structure or portions of the structure are to be assigned a protection level according to the facility-specific risk assessment. Definitions of damage to the structure and exterior wall systems from the bomb threat apply to each protection level (Table 7.5).

PROGRESSIVE COLLAPSE

Progressive collapse occurs when a structural member or component causes the collapse of another, in a domino effect. Progressive design is based on the notion that an explosion, blast, or other event

TABLE 7.5   Security Design Protection Levels

Protection level	Characteristics
Low and medium/ low level protection	• Major damage. • The facility or protected space will sustain a high level of damage without progressive collapse. Casualties will occur and assets will be damaged. • Building components, including structural members, will require replacement, or the building may be completely unrepairable, requiring demolition and replacement.
Medium level protection	• Moderate damage, repairable. • The facility or protected space will sustain a significant degree of damage, but the structure should be reusable. • Some casualties may occur and assets may be damaged. • Building elements other than major structural members may require replacement.
Higher level protection	• Minor damage, repairable. • The facility or protected space may globally sustain minor damage, with some local significant damage possible. • Occupants may incur some injury. • Assets may receive minor damage.

Source: ISC Security Design Criteria.

may cause a partial collapse of the structure. New facilities with defined threats should be designed with a reasonable probability that, if local damage occurs, the entire structure will not collapse or be damaged to an extent disproportionate to the original cause of the damage.

The following information is based on the Department of Defense Interim Antiterrorism/Force Protection Construction Standards, Guidance on Structural Requirements, March 5, 2001.

Designs facilitating or that are vulnerable to progressive collapse should be avoided. At minimum, all new facilities should be designed for the loss of a column for one floor above grade at the building perimeter without progressive collapse. This design and analysis requirement for progressive collapse is not part of a blast analysis, but is intended to ensure adequate redundant load paths in the structure should damage occur. Designers may apply static and dynamic methods of analysis to meet this requirement. Ultimate load capacities may be assumed in the analyses.

In the event of an internal explosion in an uncontrolled public ground floor area, the design should prevent progressive collapse due to the loss of one primary column, or the designer should show that the proposed design precludes such a loss. If columns are sized, reinforced, or protected so that the threat charge will not cause the column to be critically damaged, then progressive collapse calculations are not required for the internal event. For design purposes, assume there is no additional standoff from the column beyond what is permitted by the design.

As an example, if an explosive event causes the local failure of one column and major collapse within one structural bay, a design mitigating progressive collapse would preclude the additional loss of primary structural members beyond this localized damage zone, such as the loss of additional columns, and main girders. This does not preclude the additional loss of secondary structural or nonstructural elements outside the initial zone of localized damage, provided the loss of such members is acceptable for that performance level and the loss does not precipitate the onset of progressive collapse.

Structural Member Response Limits

The design intent of blast resistance is generally to avoid collapse while accepting some permanent damage of structural components. For medium levels of protection, permanent damage is accepted for the primary structural system including load-bearing walls, columns, beams, shear walls, and diaphragms; as well as secondary structural members such as girts, purlins, wall panels, and roof decking. High levels of protection generally require an elastic response of the primary structural system to the blast loads, but allow for permanent damage short of collapse, for secondary structural components.

WINDOWS AND GLAZING

GSA performance standards are specified for glazing under various protection levels. The performance standards describe the response of glazing to blast loads, as *performance condition.*

Low and Low/Medium Levels of Protection

Facilities with Low and Low/Medium Levels of Protection typically are designed to GSA performance conditions 5 and 4 respectively. These windows do not require design for specific blast pressure loads. Rather, the designer is encouraged to use glazing materials and designs that minimize the potential risks (Table 7.6).

Medium and High Levels of Protection

Facilities with medium levels of protection are typically assigned GSA performance level 3b, while facilities with high levels of protection are generally assigned GSA performance level 3a. GSA

TABLE 7.6   Low and Low/Medium Levels of Protection: Glazing Systems

Applicable to GSA conditions 5 and 4

Protection Element	Performance Criteria
Preferred glazing systems	• Thermally tempered heat strengthened or annealed glass with a security film installed on the interior surface and attached to the frame • Laminated thermally tempered, laminated heat strengthened, or laminated annealed glass • Blast curtains
Acceptable glazing systems	• Thermally tempered glass • Thermally tempered, heat strengthened or annealed glass with film installed on the interior surface (edge to edge, wet glazed, or daylight installations are acceptable)
Unacceptable glazing systems	• Untreated monolithic annealed or heat strengthened glass • Wire glass
Window film	• The minimum thickness of window film that should be considered is 4 mil. In a blast environment, glazing can induce loads three or more times that of conventional loads onto the frames, a consideration when using anti-shatter security film.
Window frames	• Windows frames should be designed so they do not fail prior to the glazing under lateral load. Anchorage should be stronger than the window frame, and the supporting wall should be stronger than the anchorage. • Window frame design strength and associated anchorage is related to the breaking strength of the glazing. Thermally tempered glass is roughly four times as strong as annealed, and heat strengthened glass is roughly twice as strong as annealed.

Source: General Services Administration.

performance levels 1 and 2 are typically used only on very high security facilities where glazing failure cannot be tolerated. Special, blast-resistant glazing systems are utilized to achieve GSA performance levels 1 and 2.

Window systems design, including glazing, frames, and anchorage to supporting walls, on the exterior facade should be balanced to mitigate the hazardous effects of flying glazing following an explosive event. The walls, anchorage, and window framing should fully support the capacity of the glazing material selected (Table 7.7).

Designers may use a combination of methods, such as government produced and sponsored computer programs (e.g., WINLAC, GLASTOP, SAFEVU, HAZL, WINDAS, and BLASTOP) coupled with test data and recognized dynamic structural analysis techniques to show that glazing either survives the specified threats or the postdamage performance of the glazing protects the occupants in accordance with the required GSA performance level. When using such methods, designers may consider a breakage probability no higher than 750 breaks per 1000 when calculating loads to frames and anchorage.

All glazing hazard reduction products for these protection levels require product-specific test results and engineering analyses performed by qualified independent agents demonstrating the performance of the product under the specified blast loads, and stating that it meets or exceeds the minimum performance required. A government-provided database indicating the performance of a wide variety of products can be made available to designers.

PERIMETER ENTRY CONTROL

A secure perimeter is the first layer of defense for a building, especially at higher risk facilities. Entry control design, such as vehicle barriers, barrier arm systems, guard stations, and fencing, are important perimeter elements.

TABLE 7.7   **Medium and High Levels of Protection: Glazing Systems**

Generally applicable to GSA conditions 3aA, 3b, 2, 1

Protection Element	Performance Criteria
Preferred glazing systems	• Thermally tempered glass with a security film installed on the interior surface and attached to the frame. • Laminated thermally tempered, laminated heat strengthened, or laminated annealed glass. • Blast curtains.
Acceptable glazing systems	• Monolithic thermally tempered glass with or without film if the pane is designed to withstand the full design threat.
Unacceptable glazing systems	• Untreated monolithic annealed or heat strengthened glass. • Wire glass.
Window fenestration:	• The total fenestration openings are not limited; however, a maximum of 40% per structural bay is a preferred design goal.
Window frames	• The frame system should develop the full capacity of the chosen glazing and provide the required level of protection without failure. This can be shown through design calculations or approved testing methods.
Anchorage	• The anchorage should remain attached to the walls of the facility during an explosive event without failure. Capacity of the anchorage system can be shown through design calculations or approved tests demonstrating that failure of the proposed anchorage will not occur and the required performance level is provided.
Window film	• In general, thicker antishatter security films provide higher levels of hazard mitigation than thinner films. Testing has shown that a minimum of a 7-mil-thick film, or specially manufactured 4-mil-thick film, is the minimum to provide hazard mitigation from blast. The minimum film thickness to be considered is 4 mil.

Source: General Services Administration.

Vehicle Barriers

Vehicle barriers, such as traffic arms, assist vehicle entrance guards in controlling traffic. The purpose of vehicle barriers is to keep explosive-laden vehicles from getting close to buildings and causing damage.

Barriers must meet performance standards and be verified through empirical testing and field deployment. The Department of State and other government agencies have certified certain manufacturers and models of vehicle barriers for use at government facilities. Designers should determine what models of barriers are certified and obtain government approval of concept and barrier type before beginning design. Barriers that are not certified may be considered if sufficient detailed (and verifiable) crash testing results data can be provided on a product. Designers may provide antiram vehicle barriers if a risk or threat assessment determines that such barriers are warranted.

Vehicle barrier design involves several engineering disciplines and requires careful planning. Design considerations include:

• Location, lighting, traffic signals, and warning signage.

• Clear visibility to motorists during day- and nighttime conditions. Since these barriers block roadways, motorists must be able to see them at a distance.

• Anchoring details, especially when barriers are to be installed on paved streets with utility easements on each side.

• Intended function and expected threat. Vehicle threats will be defined as part of a typical facility risk assessment.

As a minimum, a certified K4/L2 rating should be provided. This equates to the barrier having the ability to stop a 15,000-pound vehicle traveling at a speed no greater than 30 mph and upon hitting the barrier will penetrate no greater than 20 feet. Ideally, larger building setbacks are preferred whenever possible to avoid potential damage from vehicular threats.

For threat levels predicting heavier vehicles or speeds greater than 30 mph, additional protection will be required. Generally, fixed and transportable drop arm barrier systems are preferred. Requirements from specifications available from manufacturers are summarized below.

Fixed Drop Arm Barrier System

Barrier should consist of an above grade assembly containing a rigid crash beam hinged at one end. The beam should be raised and lowered hydraulically and should be capable of being raised or lowered in 12 seconds or less for a standard clear opening of 187 inches (4.75 m) as measured inside to inside of the bollard supports. Barrier direction should be instantly reversible at any point in its cycle from the control station. Height of barrier crash beam centerline should be nominally 34 inches (0.86 m) above finished grade.

A remote control station should be supplied to control the barrier operation. The raise and lower function of the barrier should have a key lockable main switch. Buttons clearly delineated for raise and lower will be provided. An annunciator panel should be provided to indicate status of barrier and will be provided with an audible alarm to indicate barrier having been left in the raised position for longer than a user-definable time period. Status indicators, which are driven by barrier limit switches, should be provided on annunciator panel to indicate fully raised and fully lowered.

Portable Drop Arm Barrier System

Barrier should have same ratings and features of the fixed drop arm barrier system described above with several differences.

Barrier should be modular in construction and configured for deployment and, as needed, relocation. No excavation or subsurface preparation should be required. Drop arm should be mounted on counterweights consisting of a permanent steel housing filled (locally at the installation site) with concrete. Raising and lowering should be automatic with a hydraulic power unit or manually with the weight of the drop arm being balanced to allow pass-through rates suitable for inspection and identification stations.

Guard Stations

Federal facilities with employee and visitor parking have one or more vehicle entry points staffed by a uniformed guard to check for valid identification badges and to direct visitors.

- Provide at least one continuously staffed vehicle entry control point.
- Provide an all-weather, heated, and air conditioned guardhouse, equipped with control and power wiring for the operation of vehicle gates and barriers.
- Consult with the Physical Security Specialist to determine whether bullet-resistant construction of the guardhouse is required, as well as protection against vehicles striking the guardhouse is warranted.
- Ensure that the guardhouse meets all federal accessibility standards.
- Ensure that the guardhouse is adequately anchored on the basis of the maximum probable wind load for the region.

- Protect the structure from vehicular ramming by installing concrete barriers at the nonsecure side of the guardhouse.

Fencing

- Provide a minimum of an 8-foot-high barrier along the property perimeter.
- Consider attractive masonry walls, decorative metal fencing, or vinyl covered chain link fence along property lines adjoining active public roads as alternatives to chain link fencing.

- Ensure that barrier type selection meets approval by the appropriate government agency.
- Ensure that where chain link fencing is provided, tension wires are not be used in lieu of bottom rails.
- Provide a maximum of 5-centimeters separation between fabric skirt bottom and the ground.
- Provide grounding when required by national or local codes.

ENTRY CONTROL AT BUILDING INTERIORS

Federal facilities should be designed with a single controlled main entry point, a security post, and entry control systems. Key design elements include:

- Provide adequate queuing and waiting spaces for visitors receiving temporary badges, waiting for escorts, and personnel passing through screening devices.
- Eliminate visual contact between visitors in the waiting area and government employees.
- Provide exterior glazing with protective film or blast resistive glazing installed in the waiting and queuing areas.
- Monitor and control doors leading from the entry to more secure areas by an electronic entry control system (EECS).

Metal Detectors

Federal facilities feature walk through metal detectors at each public entrance. Key design elements include:

- Provide equipment suitable for connection to alarm monitoring and control by the intrusion detection system (IDS) and EECS local processors, and able to function as a sensor or detector subsystem.
- Design to be incorporated into an EECS entry booth. When incorporated as a subsystem of an entry booth, connected to the entry booth local processor subsystem.
- Design for continuous operation.
- Use an active pulsed or continuous wave induction type detection field.
- Create a field detection pattern with no holes or gaps from top to bottom and across the passage area. Provide 100 percent Faraday shielding of the sensor coil.
- Incorporate measures to minimize false alarms from external sources. A synchronization module should be provided to allow simultaneous operation of multiple metal detection subsystems, with no degradation of sensitivity or function, when separated by 5 feet (1.5 m) or more.
- Ensure that equipment does not adversely affect magnetic storage media.
- Ensure that metal detectors are sized to fit inside the entry control booth. Freestanding metal detectors should not exceed 40 inches (1.0 m) deep by 50 inches (1.3 m) wide by 90 inches (2.3 m) high.
- Provide local audible and visual alarm annunciation. All alarms generated by the metal detector should be immediately communicated to and annunciated at the EECS central processor.
- Provide a continuously adjustable sensitivity control allowing controls to detect 3.5 ounces (100 grams) of ferrous or nonferrous metal placed anywhere on or in an individual's body.

X-Ray Machines

Many federal buildings require x-ray package search systems for detection and identification of materials and material densities. The article surveillance/x-ray device furnished should feature the following characteristics:

- Provide equipment suitable for connection to alarm monitoring and control by the EECS local processors and able to function as a sensor/detector subsystem.
- Provide adjustable contrast and a surface area threshold setting.
- Incorporate a long-term image storage system to document subsystem operations.
- Meet a minimum throughput rate of 600 packages per hour and should be designed for continuous operation.
- Meet the requirements of CFR 21 Part 1020, Section 1020.40.
- Provide local audible alarm annunciation and automatic threat alert based upon an adjustable contrast and a surface area threshold setting. All alarms generated by the article surveillance/x-ray device should be immediately communicated to and annunciated at the EECS central processor(s).
- Capable of inspecting packages and other articles up to 15 inches (380 mm) tall by 24 inches (610 mm) wide and 60 inches (1.5 m) long. Output from the x-ray tube should be able to penetrate steel up to 1/8 inch (3.2 mm) thick.
- Include dual lead-lined curtains at the entrance and exit to the conveyer system package-scanning region. The radiation exposure to operator for each package inspection should be not more than 0.2 milliroentgens.
- Ensure that equipment does not adversely affect magnetic storage media when passing through the device.
- Include a display system using a standard 525-line television monitor to present x-ray data to the article surveillance/x-ray device operator.
- Design and configure equipment to provide at least 64 gray scale shades or at least 64 distinct colors.
- Provide image enhancement, zoom, pan, split screen, and freeze-frame capabilities.
- Provide a conveyer system with foot switch controls. The conveyer should be reversible and suitable for intermittent operation with a minimum speed range of 0 to 35 feet per minute (0 to 0.178 meters per second).
- Ensure capability to detect and identify the full range of ferrous and nonferrous metals, plastics, plastic explosive compounds, drugs, and other contraband as required. The resolution of this device, including its display, should be sufficient to identify a 30 AWG solid copper wire.

Entry Control Booths

Secure areas requiring extra protection should be provided with entry control booths. Entry booths should feature the following design characteristics:

- Remain integral parts of the physical structure of the boundary for the area or facility to which access is being controlled.
- Ensure that in case of power failure, the entry booth automatically locks the high-security side door's electric strike or other facility interface release device and automatically opens the low-security side door's electric strike or other facility interface release device.
- Design and configure for direct connection to the EECS central processor; include a local processor subsystem.
- Provide enclosed structures suitable for occupancy by one person and incorporating: a personnel passage area, equipment bay, a low-security entry and exit door, and a high-security entry and exit door.
- Configure with paired card readers on the high-security entry and exit door and low-security entry and exit door; key release switch outside the low-security door; and a glass break emergency release switch. Both doors to the entry booth should be secured.
- Design to allow passage requests to be initiated from only one door at a time. The user should enter the booth by presenting a valid credential card to the card reader or keypad identification

code data to the keypad device, regardless of direction of travel. An unsuccessful attempt to enter the booth should generate an access denial alarm.

- Incorporate a personnel identity verification device, and the person should be granted egress from the booth after successful personnel identity verification. If the user fails the personnel identity verification test, the entry booth should confine the user and generate an access control alarm. The local processor subsystem should compare all data presented to the entry booth EECS terminal devices with its local reference database file contents, and grant the user's passage request if all data is valid.

- Provide capability of confining a user if a tamper alarm is generated by any of the equipment associated with the subject entry booth while a user is inside. Operating the glass break emergency release switch should command the entry door electric strike or other type of facility interface release to the fully open position, or state, with a delay after the egress door has been confirmed secured. Once inside the entry booth and prior to initiation of the personnel identity verification test, the user may exit through the door through which he or she entered.

SECURITY CONTROL CENTER

The intrusion detection system, electronic entry control system, and closed circuit televisions system should be continuously monitored in a secure location. The security control center is a dedicated room for security systems monitoring.

Programmatic and space requirements for the security control center include:

- Restroom facilities, either directly in the monitoring room or adjacent to the room.
- Supervisor area.
- Lockers.
- Lounge or break room for the guard force and console operators.
- Waiting area for visitors.
- A minimum of a two-person console to house IDS/EECS system monitors, radio equipment, CCTV monitors, and all associated security system control equipment. The console should meet all ergonomic and ADA standards as required by the government.
- An equipment space to house servers, hubs, switches, power supplies, and all necessary security equipment being monitored in the security console.
- Enough lockable EIA standard 19-inch cabinets to house all equipment with room for expansion.
- Dedicated HVAC systems, with grounding connection to the building counterpoise, cable tray, plywood on each wall, lighting intensity of 50 foot candles at 3 feet above the finished floor, and off-white vinyl composite tile floor.
- Overhead lighting system controlled by dimmers when using incandescent lighting.
- Room perimeter walls insulated with sound-batt material.
- Electronic entry control system enabled to control doors leading into the security monitoring room.
- Steel desk console, as specified in EIA 310 C.
- All equipment, with the exception of the printers, mounted in the console and equipment racks.
- A locking cabinet approximately 1.8 meters (6 feet) high, 1 m (3 feet) wide, and 610 mm (2 feet) deep with three adjustable shelves, and two storage racks for storage of disks, tapes, printouts, printer paper, ribbons, manuals, and other documentation.
- Equipment with battery backed (UPS) and generator power backup. All electrical and electronic equipment in the console, including the central processor and its ancillary equipment, should be powered from an UPS. The UPS should provide 4 hours battery backup in the event of primary power failure. Batteries should be sealed non-outgassing type.

ELECTRONIC SECURITY

The electronic security system should be totally integrated. This can be achieved by using a security management system, allowing all subsystems to communicate with each other (Table 7.8). The system integrator should be responsible for installation, testing, and training of the entire security system. A dedicated security staff should monitor security systems from a secure, control room.

Each of the subsystems should be functionally integrated with one another and should be monitored and controlled from a centralized security control center (SCC) within the building. The SCC should be continuously staffed and operating 24 hours per day, 7 days per week. From this location, system administration and monitoring of building alarms, access control points, CCTV monitors, and recording equipment will occur. All security system head-end and processing equipment should be located within equipment racks and consoles in the SCC.

The security management system should act as the integration controller for the entire security system. All security system components should be interfaced with the security management system for control of all displays, maps, automatic video routing, recorder activation, and preprogrammed instructions to security officers. An event generated by one subsystem should be capable of causing a preset action on one or more of the other systems interfaced with the SMS. If a perimeter door is forced open from the outside, the following should occur:

- A descriptive alarm message should be displayed at a security officer's security management systems workstation(s).

- A map should be called up on the same workstation showing the type and exact location of alarm.

- A preprogrammed set of response instructions should be displayed in front of the operator, showing the correct response to the situation.

- A video camera should be automatically displayed on a designated television monitor for live surveillance of the situation.

- A real-time digital video recorder should be activated to record the event.

All of these actions should occur without the need for any intervention by a security officer. Following these events, the operator will be required to acknowledge the alarm condition and enter a response detailing the exact actions taken.

Systems should be modular and distributed to allow for future expansion. Vertical communications within the building for data and video should be carried over a dedicated fiber optic backbone in order to allow for multiprotocol switching and modular expandability. Horizontal communications within the building should be transmitted over conventional copper wiring run within a partial conduit system (utilizing accessible plenum for open wire pulls). All communications outside of the building should be over outside-plant fiber optic cable to accommodate longer distances and provide electrical isolation for the head-end. Access control, alarm monitoring, intercom communications, and CCTV signals should be multiplexed and transmitted over the respective cabling to distributed riser locations and then on to the head-end in the SCC for processing, recording, and archiving.

All equipment should require distributed low-voltage power. Power supplies and step-down transformers should be centrally located and fed by the building UPS and emergency generator power circuits to ensure extended operation in the event of primary power loss. System equipment and

TABLE 7.8 Integrated Security System Components

- Security management system (SMS)
- Intrusion detection system (IDS)
- Access control system (ACS)
- Closed circuit television system (CCTV)
- Video imaging and identification system (VIIS)
- Communications (intercom) system (CS)

communications should be tamper resistant. All enclosures located in public or accessible areas should be equipped with locks and tamperproof switches that will report alarms to the SMS. All wiring between alarm monitoring devices, access control mechanisms, data gathering panels, client workstations, and the file server should be fully supervised (Fig. 7.1).

SECURITY MANAGEMENT SYSTEM

The security management system (SMS) should be a client and server based, software-driven system designed specifically for security applications and running on Microsoft NT/2000 or a similar operating system. The system should be capable of monitoring and controlling alarm points and access control points through the use of distributive processed, intelligent, electronic local processors. Alarm point and card reader access control messages should be collected by the local processors, multiplexed, and transmitted back to the SMS file server and select client workstations. All information should be permanently stored in the SMS database until systematically archived and should be readily available for review by management through database and report generation.

Communications between the local processors and the file server should be carried over redundant paths. 10BaseT Ethernet should be the primary communications protocol, with a RS-485 data loop as backup. The SMS should be capable of interface with other security and building subsystems. This interface should have the capability to include auxiliary monitoring of alarm points from fire alarm, life safety, elevator, lighting, and HVAC systems, and total integration with the VIIS and the CCTV system. This interoperability should provide a streamlined means of monitoring and managing a number of different systems, thereby reducing staff and operating costs. Aside from serving as the primary means of interface for security subsystems, the main function of the SMS should be to monitor and control all alarms and access control card readers.

ELECTRONIC ACCESS SYSTEMS

Electronic access control for the facility should be accomplished through passive proximity radio frequency cards and card readers. Proximity access control is advised in areas requiring high security (Table 7.9).

Highly sensitive areas, such as the emergency operations center, and rooms housing system head ends, should be controlled by access control devices inherently more secure than stand-alone proximity card readers, such as reader and keypad units or biometric devices. The intent is to identify the access card based on its unique code, and verify that the person holding the card is who they say they are. A unique personal identification number (PIN) or biometric profile should facilitate this requirement.

Card reader-controlled doors should be equipped with electromechanical locksets or electric strikes. These locksets, except where required by code to be fail-safe, will be fail-secure in operation. Fail-secure locksets are electronically unlocked rather than electronically locked and thereby enable extended use of the card reader controlled doors in the event of an emergency, a fire alarm, or power outage.

INTRUSION DETECTION SYSTEM

The intrusion detection system should be a subsystem to the security management system. An intrusion alarm should indicate the location, portal, and device via the SMS software. In the event of an alarm, the SMS will display a graphic plan of the building and site indicating the alarm location (Fig. 7.2).

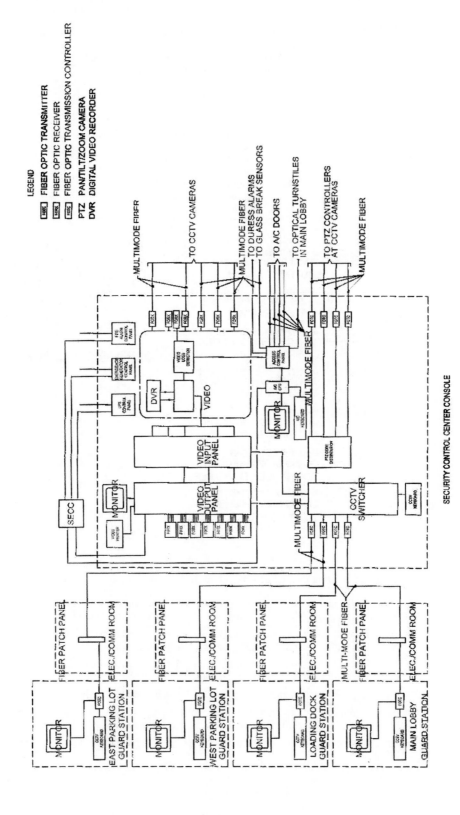

FIGURE 7.1 Typical electronic security control center block diagram. (*Source: DMJM.*)

TABLE 7.9 High Security Areas Typically Requiring Proximity Access Control

1. Site entry guard station
2. Perimeter building entrances
3. Secure corridors
4. Emergency operations center (EOC)
5. Watch command room
6. Communications center
7. Equipment closets
8. Electrical and mechanical closets
9. Radio equipment rooms
10. UPS and generator rooms

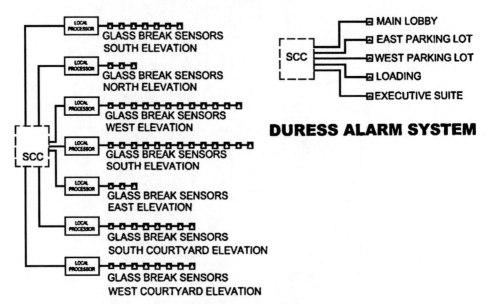

FIGURE 7.2 Typical intrusion detection block diagram. (*Source: DMJM.*)

Alarm monitoring by the SMS should occur through a variety of devices, such as:

- Concealed magnetic door position switches, used to monitor the secure status of a variety of doors within the facility, including all perimeter and card reader controlled-doors.

- Tamper switches, located on all security electronics enclosures. Duress and holdup buttons may be located within receptionist desks and at security checkpoints.

- Video motion detection, used mainly in the after-hours mode of operation to sense changes in video and alert the security console operator.

- Elevator duress and emergency stop buttons, located within each elevator cab.

- Exit alarm units at emergency exit doors, to monitor the associated door position and provide a local siren to deter use of the door, which, by code, should remain unlocked at all times.

- Door management alarm units, at doors that should not be held open past a predetermined period of time.

- Intrusion detection motion sensors, especially at interior specialty spaces.
- Glass break detectors, at grade-level interior spaces with windows to the exterior.

Video Imaging and Identification System (VIIS)

Employees should wear photo identification badges at all times while on site and within federal buildings. These ID badges should be combined with the employees' access control cards.

Following initial cardholder data input into the SMS, the cardholder's photograph should be captured by the SMS; their image will be stored as part of their cardholder database record, and then printed onto their access card.

Utilizing identification badge creation software, security staff should be able to custom design ID badge formats for different types of employees, contractors, and visitors. ID badges should contain the employee's name, ID number, employee status, photograph, and other pertinent information, including their signature. The system should allow custom logo or other unique graphics to be imported into the system and used to produce standard badge graphic templates. The system should allow special watermarks and holographs to be incorporated into the design to increase security and tamper-resistance. A return address and prepaid postage guarantee should be printed on the reverse side of all ID badges to help ensure return if lost.

The VIIS should print the custom-designed badge format directly onto the proximity access card through dye-sublimation direct-to-PVC type printing. The ID badge and access card should be the same size and thickness as a standard credit card.

Unscheduled visitors to the site will be required to check in at the site entry guard station and building front desk, where they will receive a visitor's pass. The pass will indicate their name, the person (required escort), department or user group they are visiting, and the date of pass validity. The pass will automatically expire after 24 hours by changing colors in such a way that is immediately apparent through casual observation.

Visitors to the site who have been preidentified may have visitor's passes preprinted by security staff in order to streamline processing upon arrival. When a user group is hosting a meeting with non-employees, the person responsible for meeting scheduling and coordination should provide an attendees list to security in advance. The list will be submitted via electronic mail directly to the VIIS and SMS for processing and bulk printing of passes. Security staff would coordinate all preregistration efforts.

Closed Circuit Television (CCTV)

The CCTV system should be a high-resolution (S-VHS quality; 400 TVL minimum) all color system. The system should be microprocessor controlled, which will allow assignment of any camera or sequence of cameras to any monitor within the system through user programming (Fig. 7.3).

The CCTV system should be composed of distributed CCTV cameras, digital video recorders, video motion detectors, keyboard controllers, television monitors, and a central matrix switcher. The matrix switcher should control all of the system components, provide the software interface with the SMS, and allow for camera-to-monitor assignment. Video recording should be provided in two modes, real-time and historical recording.

Real-Time Event Recording

The CCTV system should interface with the SMS to provide automatic camera selection and real-time recording of alarm events. Cameras viewing alarms generated by the SMS will automatically display and record for the alarm event duration. This alarm event recording should be real-time and high-resolution, and will be autonomous from the time-lapse recording system.

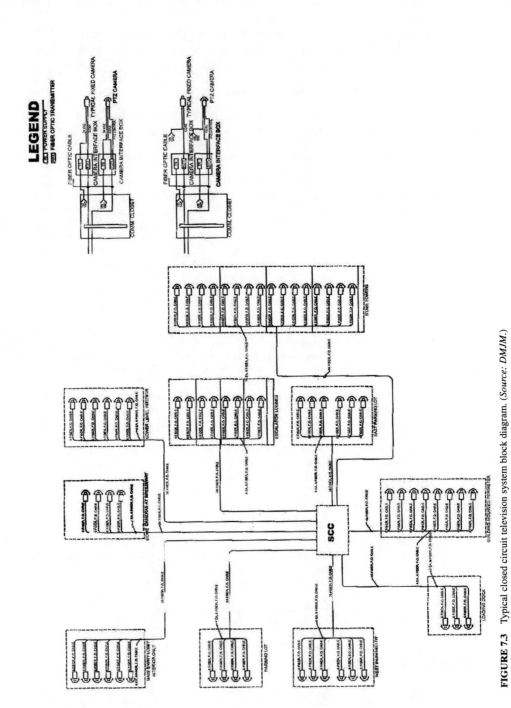

FIGURE 7.3 Typical closed circuit television system block diagram. (*Source: DMJM.*)

Historical Recording

Each camera in the system should be continuously recorded in time-lapse mode 24 hours per day. Each camera view recorded in time-lapse mode should be encoded with information to identify the camera view and the time and date it was recorded. This system will allow for the individual view of any recorded camera as well as a combined display of four, eight, or sixteen of the recorded cameras simultaneously during playback. Recorded CCTV video should be archived for a thirty-day period. Following this period of time, the oldest digital audiotapes (DATs) should be recycled, overwriting the oldest information first.

The interface with the SMS should also provide for supervision of CCTV multiplexing and recording equipment. If, for any reason, continuous time-lapse recording stops, the SMS should annunciate the alarm condition on the system workstation, and the console operator should take the appropriate actions.

Operators staffing the security control center should be able to view various parts of the site and facilities through CCTV monitors that will sequence live video camera views. The SCC console operator should be able to manually halt these views independent of each other as required for extended and more detailed views of certain cameras.

COMMUNICATIONS SYSTEM

The communications system should be composed of dedicated, hardwired intercom assistance stations, emergency assistance stations and desktop master stations. All communications between substations and master stations, and between master stations, should be dedicated and supervised for security purposes. The communications system should be interfaced with the SMS and CCTV system to allow for automatic CCTV camera selection, viewing, and recording.

Incoming intercom calls should cause adjacent cameras to be automatically displayed on a dedicated monitor within the SCC so that the console operator may see who they are speaking with and assess the situation visually. For example, if an employee forgets their access card, they would be able to call the SCC via the intercom substation located adjacent to the perimeter card reader and speak with the SCC operator. The SCC operator should be able to observe the person and compare the CCTV monitor display, in live video, with the employee's photograph, a SMS database image stored as part of the cardholder's record. After determining the person is who they say they are, the SCC operator should be capable of remotely releasing the card-reader-controlled door.

The intercom system should be a direct-select system allowing the SCC operator to answer incoming and originate outgoing calls by the touch of a button at the master station. Two-way communications should be via speakerphone or handset. Substations and emergency assistance stations should be hands-free and ADA compliant, with one button "push-to-talk" functions.

Emergency assistance stations should be located in the parking areas to provide communications and assistance to employees and visitors. The emergency assistance stations should be freestanding stanchion units, or those on vertical poles, incorporating an intercom substation, signage, and a strobe. The strobe would be activated whenever a call is initiated.

CONCLUSION

These detailed and highly tested federal security design standards provide a clear methodology for increased facility security, by addressing design, technology, and operations. This information can be applied to state and local government facilities requiring higher protection levels or to public agencies upgrading security design and construction guidelines. They provide a baseline standard for private sector facilities seeking to rent space to government agencies or federal contractors requiring high security clearances. By applying these standards to new and existing facilities, design and construction professionals, building owners, and public officials will be better prepared to secure and protect their people, property, and assets from threats and potential security breaches.

BIBLIOGRAPHY

Department of Defense, *Interim Antiterrorism/Force Protection Construction Standards, Guidance on Structural Requirements,* March 5, 2001.

General Services Administration, Public Building Service, *GSA/PBS Facilities Standards* (www.gsa.gov).

Interagency Security Committee, *ISC Security Design Criteria for New Federal Office Buildings and Major Modernization Projects,* Federal Standard 795, Uniform Federal Accessibility Standards, May 2001.

Internal Revenue Service, IR Manual MT, *Physical Security Handbook.*

Internal Revenue Service, *IRS Physical Security Standards Manual* (www.irs.gov).

Office of Foreign Buildings Operations, U.S. Department of State, *Standard Delivery System, Design Guidelines & Specifications.*

U.S. Army, Army TM 5-853-1, vol. 1, *Security Engineering Project Development.*

U.S. Army, Army TM 5-853-2, vol. 2.

U.S. Army, Army TM 5-853-3, vol. 3, *Security Engineering Final Design.*

U.S. Army, Army TM 5-853-4, vol. 4, *Security Engineering Electronic Security Systems.*

U.S. Army Corps of Engineers, *Guide Specification (CEGS) for Military Construction,* Sections 16725, 16751, and 16752.

U.S. Department of Justice, *Vulnerability Assessment of Federal Facilities,* June 1995.

INTERNET RESOURCES

American Society of Industrial Security (ASIS)
www.asisonline.org

DMJM
www.dmjm.com

International Code Council (ICC)
www.iccsafe.org

National Institute of Standards and Technology (NIST)
www.nist.gov

Underwriters Laboratories (UL)
www.ul.com

STANDARDS

The following standards should be considered in the design of the electronic security system infrastructure.

American National Standards Institute (ANSI):
    ANSI C2 (1993); *National Electrical Safety Code.*

Code of Federal Regulations (CFR):
    CFR 47 Part 15; *Radio Frequency Devices.*

Electronics Industries Association (EIA):
    EIA 170 (1957); *Electrical Performance Standards-Monochrome Television Studio Facilities.*
    EIA 232-E (1991); *Interface Between Data Terminal Equipment and Data Circuit-Terminating Equipment Employing Serial Binary Data Interchange.*
    EIA 310-C (1977; R 1982); *Racks, Panels, and Associated Equipment.*
    EIA 330 (1968); *Electrical Standards for Closed Circuit Television Camera 525/60 Interlaced 2:1.*
    EIA 375-A (1974); *Electrical Performance Standards-Direct View Monochrome Closed Circuit Television Monitors 525/60 Interlaced 2:1.*

Institute of Electrical and Electronics Engineers (IEEE):
   IEEE C62.41 (1991); *Surge Voltages in Low-Voltage AC Power Circuits.*
   IEEE Std 142 (1991); *IEEE Recommended Practice for Grounding of Industrial and Commercial Power Systems.*
   IES (Illuminating Engineering Society) Handbook:
      Chapter 10, "Quality of Light."
      Chapter 21, "Exterior Lighting."
      Chapter 29, "Emergency, Safety and Security Lighting."

National Electrical Manufactures Association (NEMA):
   NEMA 250 (1991); Enclosures for Electrical Equipment (1000 Volts Maximum).

National Fire Protection Association (NFPA):
   NFPA 70 (1996); National Electrical Code.

Underwriters Laboratories (UL) (www.ul.com):
   UL 6 (1981; Rev thru Dec 1992); *Rigid Metal Conduit.*
   UL 294 (1994; Rev thru May 1995); *UL Standard For Safety Access Control System Units, 4th ed.*
   UL 1410 (1986; Rev thru Jun 1996); *Television Receivers and High Voltage Video Products.*

CHAPTER 8
HEALTH CARE SECURITY

Thomas M. Jung, R.A.
Director, Bureau of Architectural & Engineering Facilities
Planning, Division of Health Facilities Planning
New York State Department of Health
Troy, New York

Better be despised for too anxious apprehensions, than ruined
by too confident security.   EDMUND BURKE (1729–1797)
              British orator, philosopher, and politician

From small rural community hospitals to large urban teaching medical centers, health care facilities are charged with providing medical treatment within safe environments for patients, staff, and visitors. Along with essential community roles as health providers, medical center personnel and facilities may be called upon as "first responders" to disasters, mass casualties, or life-threatening situations on a moment's notice. Ongoing operations, peak performance, life safety, and survival are among the primary security planning goals.

Security and safety issues have always been a major concern in health care facilities. Natural disasters, from blizzards and heat waves to earthquakes, tornadoes, and hurricanes, can result in scores of injured victims and rescuers requiring immediate treatment converging upon an emergency room within a relatively short period of time, with little advance warning.

The events of September 11, 2001 raised new issues relating to security and health care facilities, with terrorism, violence, and biochemical warfare among the most pressing concerns. Greater global interaction and routine intercontinental travel can facilitate the spread of major outbreaks of emerging infectious diseases, such as Severe Acute Respiratory Syndrome (SARS) and various new, unusual, and exotic flu strains. As threats and risks continue, the intensity of response and treatment increase, placing renewed emphasis on emergency preparation and facility planning.

Like other public and private institutions serving important community functions, health care facilities must develop security plans, based on vulnerabilities, risks, and threats. Integrating design, technology, and operational policies is the best way to achieve these goals. Each facility must address local, regional, and statewide issues and site-specific criteria (Table 8.1).

Hospitals and nursing homes operate 24 hours a day, seven days a week (24/7). These building types face security concerns unique to their mission, location, and patient populations. Within facilities, various departments require enhanced security or access control to maintain ongoing operations and minimize risks.

ACUTE CARE HOSPITALS

Acute care hospitals and medical centers, providing the most extensive and highest level of care serving communities, cities, and regions, are the first line of response to major disasters (Table 8.2 and Fig. 8.1). Several security issues drive facility planning and design priorities, especially regarding emergency

TABLE 8.1   Factors Impacting Health Care Facility Security Plans

- Geographic location
- Program philosophy
- Services provided
- Population characteristics
- Threat level
- Traditional security threats, including: infant abduction, crime prevention, workplace violence, narcotic storage, protecting dementia patients

TABLE 8.2   Lessons Learned from September 11, 2001

The events of September 11, 2001, in Washington D.C. and New York City serve as a vivid reminder to health care providers about the urgent need for emergency preparedness, training, and drills. The New York University (NYU) Downtown Hospital, located a few blocks from the World Trade Center site, received the first wave of initial victims, injured rescue workers, and those seeking refuge (Fig. 8.1). The facility is close to the site known as ground zero, and was affected by debris, dust fallout, loss of utilities, and security restrictions.

The emergency response, operational decisions, and experiences of the NYU Downtown Hospital will be referred to frequently as a case study for lessons learned by health care facilities and medical personnel affected by and responding to a major terrorist attack. See other boxed tables for lessons learned from 9/11.

FIGURE 8.1   View toward World Trade Center from NYU Downtown Hospital on September 11, 2001. (*Courtesy of NYU Downtown Hospital.*)

preparedness and maintaining ongoing operations (Table 8.3). With so many variables, every hospital security plan should include procedures in the event the hospital becomes a terrorist target. Facilities may be potential targets for threats because they may

- Provide essential functions within a free society
- Command stature as prestigious institutions
- Serve as historic or local landmarks and community icons
- Have owners, operators, high profile patients, physicians, or other associated international and corporate ties or affiliations with certain nationalities, ethnic backgrounds, or religions

NURSING HOMES

As the population lives longer, nursing home residents are older, more physically fragile, and likely to have dementia-related illnesses. Coupled with growing reimbursement constraints and difficulties in hiring and maintaining appropriately trained staff, nursing homes nationwide face economic and quality of care pressures.

Nursing home security design challenges must balance safety with resident rights and dignity. Secure nursing homes consider the disorientation and potential elopement of dementia residents, crime, and workplace violence, while creating pleasant, residential environments (Table 8.4). Important considerations include the following:

- Lounges, dining, and staff support areas must be provided for resident convenience.
- Staff supervision and observation should be effective, but not restrictive or oppressive.
- Staffing shortages and resident needs often result in facilities using alarm and locking features to contain residents and alert staff.

Staff hiring and retention standards must consider employee backgrounds, morale, and working conditions. Programs appropriate to functional and health needs of nursing home residents are under constant scrutiny from family members, surveillance groups, and oversight agencies.

TABLE 8.3   Acute Care Hospital Security Concerns

- Providing ongoing, uninterrupted acute care services to patients and the community
- Preventing violence and crime within and around the facility campus
- Ensuring operational and structural capabilities can respond to patient care requirements
- Preparing to treat mass casualties within a short time frame
- Accepting emergency room injuries ranging from trauma to biological, chemical, or radiological contamination

TABLE 8.4   Nursing Home Programmatic Elements and Security Issues

- Containing infection control
- Preventing resident abuse
- Averting dementia-related wandering behavior resulting in disastrous elopement
- Balancing safety with resident rights and dignity
- Hiring and retaining qualified staff
- Delivering programs meeting needs of residents and oversight entities

Emergency Response Roles

Nursing home security is often internally focused. Unlike acute care hospitals, nursing homes are less likely to be targets, less visible, and not on the first line of disaster response and emergency treatment. However, nursing homes can play a supporting role in community emergency response and must be involved in the planning process. Nursing homes require:

- Continued facility operations
- Operational procedures ensuring patient and staff safety

    In emergencies, they can:

- Assist area hospital emergency response
- Provide additional space to decant noncritical patients
- Increase local or regional response capacity

THREAT ASSESSMENT

Health care facility and institutional managers must assess potential threats and vulnerability before developing a security plan. Threat assessments should be completed by a multidisciplinary team of experts designated by the facility leadership or administration, and chaired by someone with time, ability, and skills to do the job. The team should include administrators, facility managers, in-house and consulting security personnel, local law enforcement, business interests, and design professionals, both in-house and consultants as required.

Health care facility staff must plan for mass casualties from large-scale infectious disease outbreaks or weapons of mass destruction (WMD). Identifying threats begins with a regional evaluation in coordination with community and business leaders and government officials. In large metropolitan areas with concentrations of people and potential targets, a region could encompass several cities or states.

REGIONAL PERSPECTIVE

First responding facilities may be overwhelmed with casualties, contamination, or damages, rendering them ineffective resources. Victims fleeing a disaster may travel significant distances before seeking care (Table 8.5). Health care administrators should consider the following regional issues:

- Accommodating an overflow or diversion of victims from other hospitals.
- Identifying potential targets in the immediate community.
- Assessing the impact of major cities or concentrations of population as potential terrorist targets.

TABLE 8.5 9/11 Lessons Learned: Regional Disaster Response

After the September 11, 2001 terrorist attacks in New York City, many of the ambulatory injured escaped Manhattan and traveled across the Hudson River to New Jersey, or to their communities on Long Island, to the east, or Westchester County, to the north. These people eventually sought medical care at their local hospitals, far from the scene of the attacks. At least 97 hospitals treated victims of the attack, as far away as in Canada.

All hospitals within the region of an attack or disaster should be prepared to treat the injured, and remain in communication with law enforcement agencies to determine additional needs and resources.

High visibility targets include:

- Major business, health, and social institutions
- Government centers
- Military installations
- Industrial sites
- Power generating plants

Regional Health Care Resources

Every health facility is a valuable regional resource for a coordinated response to support acute care hospitals, based on capability and specialized services, including:

- Community hospitals.
- Nursing homes, with specialized or subacute services, may be available for an overflow of non-critical victims or displaced hospital patients.
- Outpatient or satellite clinics affiliated with hospital networks.

Regional Planning

Even before the events of September 11, 2001, many U.S. communities had begun planning in response to increasing terrorism threats. Community planning efforts must include representatives from every level of government, from the local municipality to the state. As the authority having jurisdiction over health care licensure and surveillance, the local and state level health agencies will likely lead this effort. Regional disaster planning addresses:

- Internal and facility-specific disasters
- Disasters impacting entire regions
- Overall threat assessments affecting a wide geographic area
- Individual and cooperative health care facility responsibilities

In many regions, professional associations have been established to represent the interests of health care facilities, and can serve as a liaison between facilities and government agencies. Including these groups in regional disaster planning ensures efficient communication and concurrence on disaster planning issues among health care facilities.

Hospital Emergency Response Data System (HERDS)

A regional perspective and effective communication among health care institutions will encourage collaboration. The State of New York Health Department (DOH) mandates a regional planning effort, with all county and municipal governments participating. The DOH has also developed and implemented the Hospital Emergency Response Data System (HERDS), a computerized system combining geographic information systems and a comprehensive interactive database, linking all hospitals with principal planning and response agencies. This statewide disaster planning database is constantly updated. The HERDS provides a real time inventory, by facility, of disaster response requirements, including

- Available beds
- Emergency department activity
- Life support equipment
- Medical supplies

- Pharmaceuticals
- Contact list of those with designated roles in the event of a disaster
- Means of reporting and tracking all types and levels of incidents

FACILITY PERSPECTIVE

Health care facility administrators create a disaster response committee or team to develop policies and procedures to be followed by all personnel in the event of a disaster. A widely accepted protocol, known as the incident command system (ICS), is applicable to regional and facility planning. The ICS is based on five major activities and generally defines

- Staff roles
- Lines of authority, chain of command, and communication
- Operational responses to incidents or events

Health care facilities and public agencies should utilize the ICS to create a common framework, including:

- Clarifying mutual understanding and common terminology
- Delineating span of control
- Defining organizational structure
- Identifying personnel accountability
- Establishing unified command
- Creating incident action plans

In addition to designated health care facility staff, alternates must be designated to manage each component should primary staff be unavailable or require relief. Under the direction of command, authorized individuals and support staff should develop a detailed emergency response plan. The plan must be communicated and circulated among staff, and be subject to routine training and drills to ensure effectiveness.

Preparation and readiness are essential to response. The Homeland Security Advisory System is a means to disseminate information regarding the risk of terrorist acts to federal, state, and local authorities and to the American people, through five color-coded levels (Table 8.6).

In New York State, the green and blue tiers are combined into one emergency planning and preparation level. Facilities have developed readiness levels for the remaining tiers, consistent with the federal Homeland Security Advisory System status, directing some of the following activities:

- Implementing the emergency response plan by the ICS
- Communicating with staff and outside planning partners
- Monitoring of information and system status
- Activating security protocols

Under this system, an event would immediately initiate a sequence of actions and communications, by those in designated roles (Table 8.7):

1. *Incident central command center.* The central command center must function 24/7, and should include:

- Communication lines, furniture, and equipment planned for long-term, continuous use by emergency personnel

TABLE 8.6   Department of Homeland Security Advisory System

Color	Level	Threat condition
Red	Severe	Severe risk of terrorist attack
Orange	High	High risk of terrorist attack
Yellow	Elevated	Significant risk of terrorist attack
Blue	Guarded	General risk of terrorist attack
Green	Low	Low risk of terrorist attack

Source: U.S. Department of Homeland Security.

TABLE 8.7   Incident Command System (ICS) Elements

1. Incident command center
2. Staff education and training
3. Disaster planning protocols
4. Communications
5. Affiliations and partnerships
6. Record keeping, data collection, and tracking patients

- Communications, building services, electrical power, and ventilation designed for 24/7 operations, with emergency backup power in case of failure
- Secure location, close to the emergency department, since that area will likely be the hub of the initial response to an incident

2. *Staff education and training.* Facility personnel should be educated about the disaster response plan and their collective and individual responsibilities.

- Training should be ongoing, to ensure that new employees receive proper information.
- All employees should have access to routine refresher courses.
- Training should address preparedness for staff families at home. Hospital staff will be better prepared to focus on their job responsibilities if they have a level of confidence that their families are safe and prepared at home.

3. *Disaster planning protocols.* Each facility should have a detailed plan for initiating protocols in response to every type of incident or event.

- The response must be appropriate to the first symptoms, and be capable of increasing or decreasing accordingly, as the situation develops.
- Similar to "code" systems utilized for fires, criminal activity, system failures, and other emergencies, security and communication systems must be in place to alert hospital security forces and medical staff, and initiate planned elements of the ICS.

4. *Communications.* Planning protocols and coordinating effective communications with off-duty staff, emergency resources, and public agencies is essential well in advance of an event.

- Establishing lines of communication between health care facilities, law enforcement and federal, state, and local government agencies will enhance operations, relief, and resupply efforts.
- Identifying emergency contacts for major utility and service providers, security, and law enforcement will ensure rapid reporting and response.
- Creating a directory or listing with important contact numbers of key people and agencies, and distributing it to designated personnel will assist staff in acting quickly.

Redundant communication systems will ensure uninterrupted contact among all ICS components and outside agencies. Alternate communication methods include:

- Satellite phones
- Ham radio
- Two-way radios—they must be compatible throughout a facility, area, and region
- Couriers and runners

Communication between hospitals and the public, media, and local community is recommended. Sharing the existence and general elements of readiness, without revealing confidential details, reduces confusion and panic in the event of a disaster. Public anxiety and concern is allayed with awareness that local institutions are preparing and implementing disaster plans (Tables 8.8 and 8.9).

5. *Affiliations and partnerships.* Since the 1990s, the number of affiliations, partnerships, and mergers among facilities within the health care environment has grown. Health care systems offer several advantages for community and regional health care disaster response, including shared:

- Medical and support services (Table 8.10 and Fig. 8.2)
- Backup staff
- Supplies

TABLE 8.8   9/11 Lessons Learned: Compatible Communications Technology and Equipment

After the World Trade Center attacks, cellular communications and telephone lines in Lower Manhattan and the New York City area were interrupted and unreliable for quite some time. The lack of communication and news on the rescue effort progress was equally disturbing and counterproductive. Police and Fire Department radios were not compatible, preventing them from sharing information.

Communications technology and equipment must be tested, reliable, and compatible within and among public agencies, facilities, cities, areas, and regions.

TABLE 8.9   9/11 Lessons Learned: Maintain Communications with Rescue Services and Security Checkpoints

After the World Trade Center attacks, police and National Guard troops at security checkpoints delayed delivery of vital fuel for the NYU Downtown Hospital's emergency generators because they were hesitant to allow tanker trucks to enter the ground zero vicinity. Off-duty staff recalled to duty had difficulty in clearing the same checkpoints.

Communications among law enforcement personnel and health facilities must be maintained on reliable, secure equipment and lines.

TABLE 8.10   9/11 Lessons Learned: Managing Volunteers and Credentialed Professionals

The number of volunteers coming forward to offer help after a major incident can be overwhelming. Immediately after the World Trade Center attacks, many unaffiliated medical and nursing personnel converged upon NYU Downtown Hospital to volunteer their services. Without any way of verifying their credentials, volunteers required oversight by known and qualified medical and nursing staff. A database of credentialed staff should be maintained by public and private entities within a facility and health care system on a regional basis, and through professional organizations. The Medical Society of the State of New York and the New York State Nurses Association developed databases of credentialed professionals and volunteers, providing access to instant identification and background confirmation.

FIGURE 8.2 Ambulances at NYU Downtown Hospital Emergency Department on September 11, 2001. (*Courtesy of NYU Downtown Hospital.*)

TABLE 8.11 **9/11 Lessons Learned: Records, Patient Tracking, and Preparing for Mass Casualties and Injuries**

The number of victims treated at NYU Downtown Hospital due to the World Trade Center attacks quickly depleted the paper tags utilized for triage.

Metropolitan hospitals must anticipate a large patient influx at once, types of emergency supplies to be required, and plan for storage and access on demand.

- Medical equipment
- Operational coordination

6. *Record keeping and patient tracking.* Record keeping and tracking of those who are treated within a facility are essential to emergency planning and patient care follow-up, and may help avert subsequent lawsuits. Systems must be capable of:

- Recording and tracking all victims to ensure accountability
- Maintaining proper medical records
- Identifying names and subsequent locations of all patients receiving treatment (Table 8.11)

VULNERABILITY

A vulnerability analysis, performed by in-house personnel and professional security consultants, identifies potential local and regional threats and impact to facilities. Each hospital and facility must determine the most appropriate mitigation measures for a range of potential hazards. For example, health care facilities in North and South Carolina have found that gravel roof ballast can become deadly projectiles, due to hurricane-force winds, and therefore must select roofing systems accordingly, to mitigate potential problems.

Planning and design to address potential threats is most efficient and cost effective during new construction, when design elements and technology can be integrated with proposed operations. However, most health care security design will involve retrofitting, which is generally more costly, because compromises must be made. Owners and designers must prioritize and balance security needs, financing, and operations, especially when phased completion is involved.

Planning Team

All aspects of health care facility operations must be evaluated in accordance with the threat assessment. To address security design needs, the facility leadership should create a multidisciplinary planning team, including but not limited to the following:

- Hospital administration
- Medical and nursing staff
- Facility managers
- In-house personnel involved with operations, security, and finance
- Architects and engineers, in-house and outside consultants
- Security consultants as needed to advise on threats, technology, and operational protocols

Site and Perimeter Security

Site security in and around the facility is important before, during, and after an incident. Public roadways and access points should be secured for control and traffic segregation. Planning issues include:

- Monitor vehicular and public access to mission-critical areas, such as the central power plant, emergency department, and surgical suites, through visual and electronic surveillance.
- Design and route access roadways away from main hospital emergency areas.
- Isolate critical areas by bollards, berms, and physical barriers.
- Ensure that site access and control allows emergency vehicles, facility support, and medical staff to be quickly screened and admitted to the facility.
- Provide treatment space and facilities for walk-ins and other casualties to be screened and admitted in a timely manner.
- Accommodate concerned family members looking for information about a loved one. Provide a waiting area with a room or area for private consultations.
- Determine extent and access of press and media representatives. Security planning should consider how the facility will handle media relations in an emergency, and designate an area to handle media personnel and vehicles.
- Ensure that parking areas and pedestrian circulation paths are well lit and under visual surveillance by the public and facility staff.
- Protect building utilities and services and provide emergency backup.
- Secure emergency generators and fuel supply from tampering.
- Provide portable generators and mechanical support equipment, with connections conveniently located.
- Plan for the role of mobile facilities to augment health care services, including designated docking locations and access to support utilities and services.
- Locate fuel tanks and bulk and liquid oxygen storage in areas safe from tampering, unauthorized access, and potential threats.
- In earthquake prone regions, storage tanks must be structurally secure and sufficiently isolated to facilitate continued operation during and after an earthquake.

BUILDING SYSTEMS

Every access point to the building is a potential security breach. Hardening of building systems, blast and bullet resistant glazing, and protective design structural framing may be necessary at certain hospital areas, such as the emergency department, surgical suite, and major public zones.

HVAC

Heating, ventilation, and air conditioning (HVAC) intakes and returns must be located to minimize contamination by outside agents entering the mechanical systems.

- Central system fresh-air intakes should be located above grade at a sufficient height to prevent contamination and tampering.
- The immediate area around the intake should be secured with barriers to prevent unauthorized access.
- Adequate separation between exhaust outlets and fresh air intakes, in keeping with applicable building codes and regulations, must be maintained.
- Return-air components should be secured against tampering and unauthorized access.

Emergency Systems

Emergency generators should be located away from vulnerable areas (Table 8.12).

- Locate generators above the highest expected water level, especially in regions subject to flooding or storm surges.
- Prevent unauthorized access.
- Allow convenient maintenance, upgrade, and replacement.
- Plan for long-term operation of emergency systems.

Compartmentalization

Physical isolation of building and HVAC systems can maintain health care facility operations if the security or physical integrity of the facility is breached. Compartmentalization will isolate and minimize compromising conditions.

- Separating the emergency department (ED), physically and environmentally, enables the rest of the facility to remain operational if the ED is contaminated.
- Planning for progressive building failure must consider the location and functional relationships between essential patient care facility components and support functions.

PLANNING AND DESIGN

Balancing the need for security and openness is an ongoing challenge for all public buildings. Health care facility design has a responsibility for creating an environment of care to enhance a positive experience within the facility, and protecting patients, staff, and visitors from violence and crime.

These concerns are not mutually exclusive. Health care facilities focus on treatment and healing; a bunker mentality or aesthetic can be perceived as counterproductive. Security measures should be "transparent" where possible, not visible to the public eye, to promote the image of health care facilities as welcoming, healing institutions.

TABLE 8.12   9/11 Lessons Learned: Maintaining Operation of Emergency Power

NYU Downtown Hospital ran rooftop emergency generators continuously for several days after the World Trade Center attacks. The generators had to be constantly cleaned of dust and debris. Gauges and indicators were physically monitored on a 24-hour basis, to ensure early warning of any pending problems.

Emergency generator locations should allow routine monitoring and protection from damage, whether underground or on rooftops.

Location and Circulation

Minimizing exits and entries limits unauthorized access and allows the option of a lock-down in an emergency. Providing adequate security and staff supervision reduces opportunities for crime and terrorism directed at and within the facility. Other considerations include:

- Clearly delineate public and patient care areas, for easy access.
- Provide good sight lines and observation.
- Encourage staff to monitor the care environment and ensure that visitors are authorized.
- Utilize way-finding strategies and signage to enable patients and visitors to understand where they are and how to locate other areas within the facility.

Certain facility areas, not appropriate for unauthorized or public access, should be less obvious to the public, and positioned for staff access only.

- Pharmacies, with narcotic and drug storage, are generally located in support space zones, away from public areas.
- Nuclear medicine departments, particularly "hot labs," where radiological materials are stored and handled, are also ideally located away from public circulation. Although weapons-grade material is not common within health care facilities, risks may exist as a result of inappropriate handling or theft of these materials, regardless of intent. In addition to standard requirements for shielding and handling, the department location should not be identified by signage or be readily accessible to the public.

Public circulation routes should be logical and well marked, especially to elevators, the admissions department, coffee and gift shops, and public functions. Clear circulation addresses the need for an environment of care and security concerns, allowing a clear distinction between public circulation, staff, and support zones, and facilitating identification of unauthorized persons in secure areas.

Critical Program Elements

Traditional hospital design and planning is based upon standards of health care for routine diagnostic and treatment protocols:

- Emergency departments (ED) are configured for ambulance access directly to the treatment area, and walk-in patients are met by reception and triage functions.
- Radiology is typically adjacent to the ED to facilitate imaging for emergency diagnosis and treatment.
- Operating rooms (ORs) are also convenient to the ED for emergency surgery
- Critical care units, the intensive care unit (ICU), and cardiac care unit (CCU), must be accessible to the ED and ORs for postsurgical recovery or direct admission from the ED.

Security planning concerns require a new level of spatial relationships, isolation capability, and access control. The facility's disaster response requires clinical elements and building services to remain operational, including structural systems, service utilities, and support access.

EMERGENCY DEPARTMENT RESPONSE TO TERRORISM

According to a July 2003 news report published in *The New York Times,* a 2001 planning exercise involving simulated release of smallpox virus showed that crucial public health decisions had to be made in the early stages of bioterrorist attacks. Governments at all levels have spent and will continue to allocate billions of dollars for first responders, consisting of police officers, firefighters, ambulance and hospital workers, and National Guard units to improve emergency training for chemical, biological, and nuclear attacks.

As the first line of response to an infectious disease outbreak, terrorist event, or bioterror attack, hospital emergency departments, routinely delivering trauma care, must be prepared to accept victims of unforeseen disasters. Hospital planning, design, and operations must factor in the emergency training and needs of all those involved in first response, and how to best accommodate large numbers of victims coming into a hospital at high rates within a short time.

- Highly trained emergency department staff providing medical care must be protected from personal threat, including contamination and infection, to ensure they remain effective and alert caregivers.

- Security personnel are a constant presence in most emergency departments, especially in urban areas or where a heightened risk of violence and crime exists. Security stations should be located for continuous observation of the main walk-in entrance, registration and triage area, and the main public waiting area.

- The expanded roles of security personnel during bioterror attacks should be planned and part of emergency drills.

The emergency department must be designed to accommodate layers of public access on a 24-hour basis, with a definitive, defensible separation of public waiting and intake areas from the treatment spaces, limited access, and lockable doors. Although separating waiting, intake, and treatment areas is often a basic planning consideration, this issue becomes even more important during a major disaster or event, when a crowded emergency room could contain many agitated patients and family members, many requiring care, and others accompanying and seeking to advocate for them.

Circulation and connections between the ED and back-of-house functions should not be overlooked for security purposes. The complexity of hospital planning often results in corridor placement resulting in potential public access from the rear of the department, adjacent to radiology and nursing units. The emergency department must be capable of complete isolation, requiring all access points to be secured and monitored.

Disaster Planning

Planning for an infectious disease outbreak or casualties from a significant intentional disaster is the most complex and difficult scenario for any incident command system. The extent of mass casualties can vary by community, region, and type of disaster. The basic design parameters of emergency departments remain constant:

- Enable the public to identify and access the ED by nonambulance transports seeking aid.

- Provide sufficient treatment spaces and support areas for triage and clinical services, commensurate with the overall hospital size and program configuration.

- Locate the department convenient to basic support functions in the main hospital, including radiology, the surgery suite, and intensive care units.

Decontamination

The stark twenty-first century reality is that health care facilities must consider the prospect of for mass decontamination in the wake of a terrible disaster. Numerous chemical, biological, and radiological (CBR) agents could be used for terrorism. However, the general decontamination process is essentially similar for all agents.

Decontamination is a major component of any ED disaster plan. Some decontamination of victims is likely to be done by rescue personnel at a disaster site. Hospitals must be prepared to address on-site decontamination, particularly for mass casualties and walk-ins.

Chemical, Biological, and Radiological (CBR) Agents

CBR agents used in a terrorist attack may be delivered in the form of a gas, liquid, or particulate matter associated with an explosive device. Any resulting contamination of victims will either be internal, by being inhaled, ingested, or absorbed through wounds to the skin, or external. Clinical protocols will identify the best means of dealing with internal contamination, including flushing of wounds. External contamination involves victims with loose particles, materials, or substances on their body or clothing, presenting some contamination risk to rescue and medical personnel.

Radiological agent exposure, or irradiation, occurs when victims are exposed to a source of radiation. Exposure does not ordinarily render a victim radioactive or contaminated, nor do they typically pose a radiation risk to others.

Emergency departments are required to include decontamination facilities by applicable codes and regulations, consistent with threat assessments. Decontamination areas are typically near the ambulance entry. Clothing must be removed, as most contaminants are concentrated on clothing, and showering with tempered water is immediately required. One or two decontamination areas are generally provided.

The prospect of decontaminating many victims of terrorism or a disaster at once may require public hospitals to carefully review the adequacy, scope, and design of existing decontamination facilities, and prepare for treating large numbers of victims in a relatively short time.

DECONTAMINATION FACILITY DESIGN

Permanent decontamination facilities may not be feasible at all hospitals, unless conveniently located space is available, flexible, and alternative use of the space can be arranged.

Temporary, portable, and collapsible structures for decontamination, stored in limited space until needed, are an alternative solution to permanent construction. Ancillary support structures, such as canopies protecting ambulance bays or parking garages, can also be used for a planned emergency decontamination conversion, by adding portable sidewall enclosures (Table 8.13).

TABLE 8.13   Decontamination Facility Planning Issues

Planning issue	Planning criteria
Site issues	• Locate decontamination facilities near, but not in front of, the ambulance entrance. • Minimize impact of decontamination facilities to ongoing hospital functions. • Avoid contaminating the hospital and uninvolved personnel. • Plan for a location on the hospital campus or grounds well in advance of emergencies.
Space planning issues	• Arrange a sequential flow of patients from ambulance transport to undressing, decontamination, drying, and access to the emergency room. • Maintain patient privacy and dignity at all times. • Accommodate patients on stretchers, wheelchairs, and those who are ambulatory.
Mechanical and plumbing issues	• Provide climate-controlled heating and cooling, water service, and appropriate means of storing decontaminated runoff. • Configure hose bibs to provide tempered water. • Consider the impact of water temperature. Water too warm can cause skin pores to open, admitting more of the agent. The effects of some agents can facilitate hypothermia in victims if water is too cold. • Avoid high-pressure hoses, to prevent damage to potentially compromised skin, and to reduce the likelihood of driving agents further into skin.

Hot and Cold Zones

Decontamination areas must be zoned into at least two clearly marked areas.

- The "hot" zone is the decontamination area limited only to the victims, medical staff, and rescue personnel wearing personal protection equipment (PPE).
- The "cold" zone is where the victims are transferred immediately after decontamination for triage. Treatment can also occur in this zone, depending upon the size and location of the decontamination area. The cold zone must be upwind and uphill from the hot zone.

Seal Adjacent Openings

To prevent further airborne contamination within the hospital, openings on the exterior hospital or facility walls, adjacent to the decontamination area must be sealed, including:

- Window, atrium, and skylight openings
- Access and exit doors
- Air intakes and vents, for HVAC and hospital equipment.

INFECTION CONTROL

Infection control, in response to an infectious disease outbreak or terrorist attack, is difficult to plan for. Tuberculosis, various flu strains, SARS, or other disease can strike a community with little warning, and people will converge on emergency waiting rooms for treatment. Infection control concerns extend to the victims and their families, coworkers, those accompanying victims, hospital staff, and their families. Unconfirmed cases must be treated very carefully.

The first victims and those accompanying them to the emergency room could be unaware of the cause and effect of their illness, as was often the case during the anthrax outbreaks in September 2001. The outset of a biological attack or infectious disease outbreak may not be immediately obvious to victims or medical staff.

Syndrome Surveillance Protocols

Hospital disaster plans must include syndrome surveillance protocols in the emergency department and the diagnostic laboratory.

- Mandatory training of treatment and laboratory staff in the symptoms of expected and known infectious diseases, and chemical or biological agents that might be utilized in a terrorist attack will ensure that the first victims seeking aid will serve as an essential data element.
- Sharing this information among the ED, diagnostic lab, other health care providers, and local health and government agencies in accordance with jointly planned reporting activities, will alert the health care system of an infectious disease or CBR agent, before large numbers of victims are affected and begin seeking care.
- Surveillance activity should be an essential, ongoing element of any regional or facility incident command system and disaster plan.
- Outreach can be a component of surveillance for those times when voluntary quarantine can benefit from education and awareness of infection control measures at home.

Special measures are required to reduce the contact and airborne infection transmission among family members, those accompanying patients, and uninfected patients waiting for care. Transmission of infectious agents is likely to occur by airborne droplet nuclei, droplet spread, or physical contact. Several options for public waiting areas and triage areas exist (Table 8.14).

TABLE 8.14   Techniques for Reducing Airborne Transmission of Infectious Agents

1. Small groupings, physical separation, and visibility in public waiting areas
2. Airborne infection isolation and ventilation in the treatment area
3. Air-handling systems in treatment areas
4. Isolation rooms with negative pressure
5. Personal protective equipment
6. Disposal and disinfection of contaminated materials
7. Surge capacity and flexibility of spaces

Waiting Areas

Waiting areas segregated into small groups of seating are increasingly viewed as an environment of care benefit. These configurations reduce anxiety for patients and those accompanying them. During stressful times, people tend to sit away from others if seating options are available.

- Small groupings reduce physical proximity among people and the potential for contact or droplet spread transmission.
- Transparent and half-height partitions are another option.
- Physical separation must be carefully considered to ensure that reception, control areas, and security personnel have unobstructed visibility of the entire waiting area.

Airborne Infection Isolation and Ventilation

Designing waiting areas as airborne infection isolation rooms may be impractical, but ventilation details must move beyond the standards of comfort, and address potential infectious disease transmission.

- A higher number of unidirectional diffusers replacing the standard supply diffusers, in combination with low-level exhaust, could provide equivalent comfort with a lower degree of mixing with such laminar-like airflow. These configurations are likely to require more total air changes to maintain comfortable conditions on a routine basis.
- Enclosed entry vestibules can maintain desired air movement.
- The waiting area should be under negative pressure with respect to adjacent spaces.
- All air should be exhausted directly outdoors or subjected to limited recirculation within the ED, with no recirculation to other areas of the hospital.
- Public toilet rooms serving the emergency waiting area should be readily accessible, without traversing other areas of the hospital, and routinely maintained, to ensure that hand washing is always available.

Air Handling Systems in Treatment Areas

Treatment areas require special attention to reduce the risk of transmitting highly infectious diseases or biological agents. Mechanical and HVAC systems are costly to reconfigure and maintain, but design must be consistent with the level of care and response anticipated by threat assessments and facility needs.

Dual systems are an option, consisting of one system for routine operations, and a second for infection control provisions for a lockdown scenario. Infectious disease outbreaks or chemical and biological incidents may not always be immediately obvious however, rendering a dual or switchable system ineffective at the critical outset of the event.

Generally in hospitals, air moves from clean and sterile areas to soiled and less sterile areas. Positive pressure is used in clean areas and negative pressure in soiled areas. Maintaining these relationships within the emergency department is prudent. However, the entire emergency department HVAC system should be isolated, without any air recirculation to other hospital areas. Typically, ED air is returned to an air-handling unit for reconditioning and reuse for the ED and other areas connected to that unit.

- Some codes do not require, and limited funds typically do not support, a separate ED HVAC system, which could be an important element in infection control design.
- A separate unit or system should be capable of operating with 100 percent outside air.
- Staff should be trained to switch the unit to 100 percent outside air under the appropriate conditions. In this mode, the exhaust should be equipped with necessary filters.
- The entire emergency department should be under negative pressure, with respect to adjacent areas.
- Exhaust discharge vents must be located away from fresh air intakes
- As in airborne infection isolation rooms, recirculating room units required to increase air exchange rates should be equipped with HEPA filtration or other filters deemed effective.

Isolation Rooms

When dealing with infectious diseases and biological agents, airborne infection isolation treatment rooms are required within the emergency department. The programmed number of rooms depends on the facility threat assessment, and level and degree of response anticipated. Isolation rooms should be single occupancy, to treat known victims, and to isolate unconfirmed patients showing symptoms of a known biological agent.

For many hospitals, the cost of building and maintaining several airborne infection isolation rooms in the ED may be financially prohibitive or physically not feasible. Alternatively, an inventory and census of all available airborne infection isolation rooms should be maintained throughout the hospital. This would increase the capacity for housing known or suspected patients elsewhere in the facility, provided appropriate transport and observation protocols are followed.

In addition to isolation and treatment of known victims of an infectious disease or biological agent, consideration should include those who have not yet been identified and diagnosed. Space for testing and observation of family members, and those accompanying known victims, should be provided in areas near the waiting room, but isolated from the treatment area.

Personal Protective Equipment

Personal protective equipment (PPE) must be available for all emergency department personnel. This equipment must be available for varying levels of protection, from masks and lab coats, to body suits and hazmat (hazardous material) gear. Training and drills in the appropriate use of equipment is essential to ensure that staff are familiar with the use and limitations of all personal protective equipment. Medical personnel should not experience the limitations of PPE for the first time during an emergency. Equipment providing the highest level of protection provides such a significant protective barrier between the caregiver and the patient that the provision of "hands on" nursing care becomes almost impossible.

Disposal and Disinfection of Contaminated Materials

Adequate planning and provisions must be made for the disposal or disinfection of contaminated materials, including:

- Victims' clothing.
- Runoff from the decontamination showers.

- Personal protective equipment worn by staff.
- Disposable medical supplies used in treatment.
- Durable medical equipment, including stethoscopes, blood pressure cuffs, and monitoring and diagnostic equipment, should either remain in the room with the patient for the duration of stay or treatment, or be meticulously cleaned and disinfected in accordance with the hospital's infection control procedures.

Surge Capacity and Flexibility of Spaces

Worst-case scenarios could result in huge numbers of people needing emergency treatment and assistance resulting from a terror attack or disaster. The need for emergency services and follow-up medical care to address what is known as "surge capacity" must be considered by public health officials, facility administrators, and health care design professionals. Even the most comprehensive disaster planning may not effectively avert contamination of the emergency department, excessive casualties, or conditions eventually limiting, eliminating, or overwhelming full emergency department capabilities. Generic spaces that may be converted for treatment of uncontaminated victims can include:

- Conference rooms.
- Waiting areas.
- Lounges.
- Large open spaces allowing for treatment and staff circulation (Figure 8.3).
- In these areas, handwashing options may include disposable alcohol based products.

Depending upon the CBR agent involved, grouping patients requiring similar treatment together according to exposure may be a viable option. Design for contingency treatment spaces should:

- Provide the capability for negative pressure and direct exhaust, even if achieved with portable equipment.
- Consider the location of portable fans in converted spaces, the direction of exhaust, and potential for exposure.
- Be located near existing patient care areas, for convenient access to required services.
- Avoid locations in public areas.

FIGURE 8.3   NYU Downtown Hospital cafeteria converted for emergency care on September 11, 2001. (*Courtesy of NYU Downtown Hospital.*)

PATIENT CARE NURSING UNITS

Nursing units for acutely ill patients ranging in age from neonates to the elderly have unique planning and security design concerns. In the event of a major disaster, nursing units must be considered as backup space for post-emergency care and to accommodate surge capacity for large numbers of victims. Existing patients may require relocation or discharge to other units or facilities.

Nurseries and Maternity Units

Infant abduction is a major threat and security concern within maternity wards and neonatal units. Nursery planning and design typically includes intervening workrooms and staff locations arranged to control and observe all unit access points.

Electronic security systems, with door monitoring and locking arrangements, are generally used, but staff control of all access points is the primary line of defense. Infant security extends beyond the nursery to the postpartum unit. The movement toward "rooming in" and single-bedded rooms results in a less secure environment than the nursery, which is under constant supervision. Postpartum nursing units should be arranged to minimize through traffic, and to take advantage of the same staff control functions serving the nurseries.

Medical/Surgical Units

Medical/surgical (M/S) nursing units for acute patient care typically feature nursing stations located at the entrance to the unit, or within clear, direct sightlines of the unit access doors, to allow observation control of visitors, patients, and staff.

The complement of airborne infection isolation rooms will likely be the most valuable nursing unit resource in the event of an infectious disease outbreak or bioterrorism attack. The number of isolation rooms provided within a unit and facility-wide is often consistent with the facility's functional program and infection control risk assessment.

If high casualty numbers overwhelm emergency room infection-control capabilities, infection control resources on medical/surgical units will serve as a vital backup option for confirmed and unconfirmed cases. Although the first-instance issue of capacity is more a planning than design issue, the need for additional surge capacity is an important element of the incident command system.

Additional surge capacity for patients not requiring infection-control isolation rooms may also be achieved with adequately sized and located ancillary spaces within nursing units.

- Lounges or conference rooms within the unit could be converted for temporary patient care areas.
- Availability of support services and equipment, like hand washing and oxygen, are essential for these areas. (Table 8.15)

TABLE 8.15   9/11 Lessons Learned: Maintain Available Supply of Portable Oxygen Tanks and Medical Supplies

During NYU Downtown Hospital's response to the World Trade Center attacks, the supply of medical equipment, portable oxygen tanks in the emergency department, and paper goods used to treat victims was very low. Portable equipment, such as oxygen, suction, and diagnostic radiology equipment, should be identified and available. Although all hospitals maintain a supply of portable oxygen tanks, reliance upon a central system typically limits this inventory.

The incident command system must identify a means of storing and securing portable oxygen tanks and other medical supplies and equipment commensurate with the threat assessment.

Hospitals are generally considering the growing consumer and medical support for all, or a vast majority of, single-bedded rooms on M/S nursing units. This configuration could facilitate the accommodation of patients and victims of infectious disease or biological agents, especially if a number of rooms or nursing units were equipped for immediate emergency conversion to airborne infection isolation rooms with standby exhaust fans, equipped with HEPA or other appropriate filtration.

Intensive Care Units

Intensive care unit (ICU) design accommodates most typical security concerns. The nature of patients care warrants high staff-to-patient ratios, and the units are highly restricted to limit unauthorized access. Similar to medical/surgical units, intensive care units provide infection-control capabilities consistent with the facility functional program and infection-control risk assessment. The use of ICUs for enhanced infection control and surge capacity must be considered by the incident command system during planning stages.

HOSPITAL INFRASTRUCTURE

Building and mechanical systems play an important role in isolating departments, zones, or areas within a hospital, especially during a disaster or bioterror attack.

Mechanical Systems

Effectively designed hospital HVAC systems can reduce the spread of infectious diseases and biochemical agents, and are vital to achieving a facility's clinical goals. Planning for infectious disease treatment or a bioterrorism outbreak may involve modifying or compromising systems originally designed to maintain continued operations. Engineers must be involved with every aspect of planning, and participate in developing the incident command system, which guides the facility's disaster response. HVAC systems are a primary source of protection, and a potential source of compromise.

When part of an automated building or energy management system, HVAC system controls are valuable for assessing vulnerability and designing facility system upgrades. In addition to the goals of upgrading filters and reducing leakage, the potential exists for designing a system facilitating desired pressure relationships and airflow management, in response to a specific disaster. Where appropriate, the original design intent of clinical and design performance could be maintained.

The importance of automated and computerized building and energy management systems found in modern structures lies in the capability of automatically increasing or decreasing system parameters throughout the entire building, by zones or floors, depending upon heating and cooling loads, outside temperatures, and even time of day. These systems could be valuable, because of their automated control features, for designers planning disaster scenarios. The ventilation characteristics of specific zones of the facility could be programmed for an automatic response.

For example, if the ER waiting room becomes contaminated, the facility could have a system whereby pushing a single button makes the whole room "negative pressure" with respect to the balance of the ER, isolating the HVAC system within the ER from the rest of the hospital, and going to full exhaust. This rapid automated response would take the place of recognizing a problem, locating HVAC plans, determining the fans serving certain areas, and sending maintenance personnel to each fan for inspection, shut down, or action as required.

Fire Protection and HVAC

Fire protection, alarm, and life safety systems are important HVAC components, and include engineered smoke removal systems and HVAC supply and exhaust fan shutdowns. If an area or department within a health care facility is compromised or contaminated, HVAC system adjustments may be useful, especially in corridors and means of egress. For instance, pressurized stairwells to keep exit paths free from smoke infiltration can also protect stairwells from contamination. Other issues include:

- Upgrading filters in emergency rooms and treatment spaces can improve HVAC performance.
- Filter efficiencies should be designed to anticipate contamination.
- Existing air-handling units should be evaluated for increased static pressure and power requirements resulting from enhanced filtering.
- If maintaining enhanced filtering results in excessive energy costs, standby fans equipped with enhanced filters are an alternative.
- When reviewing filter efficiencies and upgrades, consider system controls and clinical and environmental performance criteria.
- Facility and engineering staff must also review duct performance, use of nonducted plenums, and the structural capacity of filter racks to ensure a stable and airtight platform.
- Engineers familiar with health care facility requirements and security needs should be involved in system planning and design.

Maintaining Indoor Air Quality

Designing a tight building envelope meets energy conservation criteria and protects the interior environment from dust, outside particulate matter, and contamination (Table 8.16).

ELECTRICAL SERVICE

Continuous availability of electrical power is essential to health care facility operations, medical equipment, fire and life safety systems, lighting, communications, and HVAC components. Emergency circuits should be reviewed for the potential of shutting down nonessential loads and utilizing spare capacity to operate equipment not ordinarily on emergency power.

Cogeneration Power Systems and Emergency Power

In response to rising energy costs and concern over maintaining facility operations through natural disasters, the benefits of cogeneration power systems are of growing interest to health care facilities. These systems use alternate fuel sources to power electrical generators, in sufficient quantities to meet most, if not all, of a facility's electrical needs. Cogeneration systems often provide:

- Energy savings
- Increased efficiency
- Continued availability of electrical service, even during interruption of the electrical power grid, due to a natural or intentional disaster.

During a disaster, health care facilities must have continued fuel to operate electrical generators and remain functional. Health care facilities concerned about service interruptions should have contingency plans in place for fuel delivery, including backup fuel for cogeneration plants.

All facilities are required to have an alternate power source of sufficient capacity to operate circuits intended for short-term outages. The incident command system must include protocols for maintaining emergency generators and fuel supply for longer durations, and augmenting equipment with portable or backup generators, for expected servicing and repairs associated with long-term operation. Emergency transfer circuits should be designed for auxiliary hookups. Contingency plans for emergency

TABLE 8.16 9/11 Lessons Learned: Filtering Recirculated Air to Isolate Interiors from Outside Contamination

---

Immediately after the attacks on the World Trade Center, NYU Downtown Hospital, located a few blocks from ground zero, was inundated with dust and debris from the fallen structures, prompting a complete shutdown of the HVAC system to isolate the interior environment. Maintaining interior comfort and clinical performance standards, while limiting or eliminating outside air, was a major challenge for the facility.

If recirculated air is adequately filtered, health care services should be able to continue operations, subject to the buildup of carbon dioxide, which should be monitored. Fresh air changes mandated by codes and regulations may pose problems for providing a barrier to outside contamination. Engineering design and HVAC disaster response should examine viable solutions to extreme conditions of outdoor dust and debris.

---

power should address building areas requiring isolation or conversion to other uses for handling patient surge capacity.

Large Scale Blackouts: Planning for Emergency Power

The value of planning for operations under emergency power was made clear on August 14, 2003, when a problem with the national distribution system resulted in the largest interruption of power in U.S. history. Affecting more than 50 million people across 9300 square miles in six northeastern states and parts of Canada, the blackout lasted from one hour in some areas to 48 hours in others, causing billions of dollars of lost revenue. A heightened level of preparedness, due to previous efforts addressing anticipated Y2K problems and the aftermath of September 11, 2001, resulted in a health care system better prepared to confront an extended lack of power (Table 8.17).

WATER SERVICE

A reliable domestic water source is another essential building system within health care facilities. Potable water and sanitary and infection control are heavily dependant upon a safe and dependable water supply. Protecting the water source is usually the responsibility of the local community or state-level authorities. However, individual health care facilities can take steps to protect their in-house water supply.

Facilities routinely address the potential for bacteria and opportunistic waterborne pathogens to enter domestic hot water systems. Outside or preservice connection contamination of the water supply may be out of the control of the hospital, and internal contamination by intent is difficult. Mitigation procedures, such as the following, may be useful:

- Constant recirculation
- Increasing the temperature of hot water supply tanks
- Hyperchlorination
- Ozone injection
- Copper-silver ionization
- Ultraviolet light

Wastewater drain configurations are subject to various requirements, such as indirect drains for food service preparation initiated by public health concerns and flushing drains in cystoscopy procedure rooms for infection-control concerns.

Diagnostic or treatment areas subject to contamination due to treatment of victims of a chemical or biological attack, especially in the emergency department, must have a dedicated or closed drainage system with portable or isolated collecting vessels. The size of these tanks should be designed within the parameters of the facility threat assessment.

TABLE 8.17   Lessons Learned from the Blackout of August 14, 2003: Planning for Adequate Emergency Power

During the blackout of August 2003, some minor problems occurred within health care facilities, primarily due to inadequate fuel for generators and equipment breakdowns. However, the increased attention paid to disaster planning minimized the impact of the blackout at affected hospitals and nursing homes in New York.

Need for upgrades. Despite adequate testing of emergency generators and equipment, the extended duration of the blackout provided evidence to some health care facilities that their systems require major upgrades and repair, which may not be readily apparent during typical limited-time operation testing.

Extended need for emergency power. Routine testing (monthly per NFPA 99) of the emergency generator, under load, may NOT be an accurate indicator of the emergency power system's capability for running under load in an actual emergency for an extended period of time. An engineering evaluation should be undertaken periodically to ensure that all emergency power system components are maintained, replaced, and upgraded on a scheduled basis.

Technology. Advances in technology have increased the reliance on electricity in health care. Testing and maintenance of emergency power systems are routine tasks, but evaluating the emergency power system capacity may not be, resulting in an inability to run life support systems and equipment for an extended time from emergency generators. Facilities should evaluate emergency power systems to ensure adequate sizing for current, peak, and anticipated future demands.

Fuel levels. Facilities routinely testing emergency generators must ensure that at least a minimum level of fuel is always available.

Regional impact. Health care facilities routinely plan for power outages, but the blackout of August 14, 2003, affected all facilities in a region simultaneously. This presented challenges to vendors delivering fuel for emergency generators, and reduced options for available regional surge capacity, since all facilities were affected.

Communications. Health care facilities are more reliant on information technology systems, particularly after September 11, 2001, when the need for constant communication and data-sharing between facilities and government agencies was essential. All health care facilities should review emergency power system configurations, to ensure that critical data sharing and emergency circuits support communication systems.

An Extreme Cautionary Note.   Connecting wastewater drains from hospital areas treating victims of a chemical biological attack to a public or municipal water system is clearly not advised, as this action could result in water supply contamination.

Waste disposal continuation through sewer lines is another security concern. Ejection pump failures or broken or blocked main sewer lines can quickly result in conditions contrary to sterile and infection control protocols. If not already on circuits, related equipment should be capable of being switched to emergency power. Access to main sewer system components should be hardened against unauthorized access to prevent tampering.

Maintenance and housekeeping support functions must be maintained during an emergency. Repair and reinforcement of building elements; repair of equipment; and cleaning, disinfection, and decontamination of treatment areas are ongoing activities to be administered throughout the duration of a disaster.

GENERAL FACILITY ISSUES

Several general concerns relating to contamination, planning, and security apply to all health care facilities reviewing threat assessments and disaster planning.

Contamination Prevention

Homeland security and public safety agencies demand that the potential threat, risks, and impact of chemical and biological attacks are well understood by law enforcement, health care facilities, and first responders. Preparedness requires planning, communicating, and educating medical personnel, facility managers, policy makers, and designers about the need for contamination prevention. Health care personnel in emergency departments, the first responders in a disaster, and clinical and support personnel must be aware of how to prevent contamination in a room or area and how to administer proper decontamination procedures.

- Wherever diagnosis or treatment of confirmed and suspected cases of contaminated patients occurs, appropriate handling, cleaning, and treatment procedures must ensure that all staff remain safe and contamination is contained.

- All disposable medical equipment and medical waste products must be appropriately discarded. Materials must be treated according to appropriate standards as regulated medical waste. Planning and design standards often require identifying dedicated areas for what could be large amounts of medical waste. Protocols must ensure all medical waste is packaged and properly identified.

- All treatment rooms and spaces used to care for victims must be decontaminated in accordance with standard protocols. Selection and specification of finishes and materials in treatment areas should be able to withstand decontamination and cleaning procedures, methods, and substances.

Clinical Laboratories

Clinical laboratories within health care facilities are essential to surveillance, early detection, and timely treatment of an infectious disease or a chemical or biological agent. Planning and design of clinical laboratories must include:

- Appropriate biosafety equipment for testing and containment to protect staff handling specimens.
- Strict protocols for specimen packaging and transport, to ensure safety of transport staff and others between the specimen source location and the laboratory.

Victims

If transport of confirmed or suspected victims of an infectious disease or a chemical or biological outbreak is required within the hospital, proper transportation precautions are needed. Those responsible for planning, design, and operations should identify transport routes between certain departments, such as the emergency department, surgery, radiology, autopsy, morgue, patient care units, and other spaces potentially designated for surge capacity, and minimize travel distance and public spaces traversed during transport.

Mortuary

Major natural disasters or terrorist acts can potentially generate many fatalities. Accordingly, mortuary and autopsy services must be reviewed to ensure that proper treatment and storage of corpses is available. If infectious disease or CBR agents are involved, staff must be equipped with appropriate personal protection equipment and follow established infection control and contamination prevention protocols. The incident command system must define procedures for the handling, tracking, identification, and storage of corpses confirmed, or suspected, of contamination. Similar protocols must be developed for mortuary release to ensure proper handling after leaving the hospital.

PLANNING FOR SURGE CAPACITY

Surge capacity for patient overflow should be accommodated within the facility before considering locations outside the hospital. This emergency planning is similar to a phasing plan developed for complex renovation and construction projects, complete with decanting and relocation of existing functions to other temporarily converted space. Initially, during the first phased moves, activities should create a clean and protected environment within the health care facility, and provide the most efficient locations for surge and displaced functions.

In the event of mass casualties, adequate postemergency care nursing units must be available to create additional emergency department treatment spaces. Alternative spaces, such as conference rooms, cafeterias, or other large communal areas should be planned and designed to serve as interim nursing units. These temporary locations could be used to cohort, or group together, disaster victims or existing hospital patients with similar syndromes, whose conditions allow temporary treatment areas.

Temporary or converted spaces adjacent to the emergency department can augment treatment areas during peak periods when more treatment and holding areas are needed (Fig. 8.4). Clinical and engineering staff must confirm that designated surge and cohort locations are equipped with adequate HVAC, plumbing, and waste disposal services to facilitate medical care and infection-control procedures.

Not all victims of a natural or intentional disaster require emergency or trauma care. Planners, designers, and health care administrators should identify areas of the facility available for nonemergency treatment, such as outpatient clinics, medical office buildings, and other spaces connected or adjacent to the hospital. Urgent first aid services, inoculations, and antidote distribution could occur in these areas without overwhelming the emergency department. Use of off-site, freestanding clinics for nonemergency care is another treatment space option. Other off-site alternatives, where necessary, may include the conversion of nearby school gymnasiums or auditoriums for surge capacity in triage, treatment, or isolation.

Mobile Units

Coordination with other health care organizations, state and federal agencies, or even the military, as possible resources, may result in the need to accommodate various mobile and transportable treatment and diagnosis medical units. Site planning and design should consider interior hospital spaces, functional adjacency, and exterior on-site locations for transportation of the unit, parking, and utility connections.

On-Site Disaster Mobile Services Most hospital disaster and emergency planning is based on bringing patients to the hospital, where services are available. However, delivering services to patients on-site at a disaster location can also occur through mobile service units provided by the

FIGURE 8.4 NYU Downtown Hospital overflow treatment in cafeteria on September 11, 2001. (*Courtesy of NYU Downtown Hospital.*)

hospital and staffed with medical personnel. Reliable communication technology must be in place between the mobile units and the hospital. Information from the disaster site will enable hospital personnel to anticipate and prepare appropriate medical services needed to treat victims.

Incident command systems should review building occupancies and functions near the hospital that could be directly affected by a disaster and might require hospital support and assistance (Table 8.18).

Recovery Time

The impact on services, operations, and utilities resulting from a major disaster can extend for weeks, months, or years, well beyond the time when some areas or regions have returned to normal conditions (Table 8.19).

SECURITY CONTROL

All health care facilities have dedicated security resources for crime prevention. The incident command system must outline the role of security forces and address collaboration with local law enforcement during a major natural or intentional disaster. The hospital's role as an important community resource can be lost if security is compromised. Security measures include:

- Maintain a minimum number of access points into the facility; keep other entries locked to prevent unauthorized access.
- Utilize security checkpoints to ensure secure transport and arrival of victims, admittance of authorized personnel, supply, and equipment delivery.
- Develop security protocols for loading docks and service access points.
- Create policies requiring appropriate vendor identification.
- Implement use of identification badges for staff and approved visitors to enable swift identification of unauthorized individuals by security and facility staff.

TABLE 8.18   9/11 Lessons Learned: Ascertain Presence of Special Needs Populations near a Disaster Scene

A high-rise residence for the elderly is located across the street from the NYU Downtown Hospital. With the loss of utilities after the World Trade Center attacks, lack of electrical power and elevator service in the building was a hardship for residents seeking to leave or secure food, supplies, and medications. Hospital staff provided meals and primary medical care to this dependent population for a significant period of time.

Health care facilities should know their neighbors in the community and work with outreach groups to be able to assist them when necessary.

TABLE 8.19   Prepare for Extended Postdisaster Recovery Time

The duration of emergency operations and postdisaster recovery time may exceed contingency plans or expectations. Long after September 11, New York City area hospitals provided mental health services to survivors and rescue workers, especially for post-traumatic stress syndrome and continuing physical disabilities. Respiratory problems were an ongoing problem for many New York City rescue personnel.

Even after treating disaster victims, a high level of readiness and ongoing services may need to be maintained, to care for rescue personnel injured in the response and recovery efforts. Staffing plans and replenishing supplies and equipment must consider an extended response.

- Control on-site circulation by security forces.
- Establish control points before entering the hospital campus.
- Monitor the hospital grounds.
- Anticipate and plan appropriate locations on the site or campus for staging, decontamination, helicopter transport, and other emergency functions.
- Limit hospital ground access to authorized personnel, ambulances, patient transport vehicles, and equipment and supply delivery vehicles.

ADDRESSING STATUS OF VICTIMS AND MISSING PERSONS

Family members of victims and missing persons will likely arrive at the hospital searching for information. Security forces should plan for a large number of concerned, distraught, and potentially angry individuals seeking word on the status of loved ones. Depending upon the nature of the disaster, the hospital may also be viewed as a safe haven, because of emergency power and the level of activity. Facilities should consider the possibility of people seeking refuge, in addition to victims and those accompanying them. Hospitals can address victim status with the following steps:

- Designate a large area, such as the main lobby, auditorium, or other space capable of being secured from the rest of the hospital, as the place to provide victim information.
- Clearly identify the space for easy way-finding and to direct crowds.
- Equip the space with a communication system capable of accessing information in the emergency department.
- Install digital cameras in the emergency room, with capability to transmit images to where victim information is to be provided. Victims treated after decontamination may be without personal identification or personal effects. Digital photographs of victims could be transmitted for identification to those waiting in the central information area.
- Prepare and train staff on procedures for dealing with the status of victims and missing persons. Ensure that at least one staff member working with victims in the ED and in the public area is familiar with the digital imaging technology used to transmit and receive images of victims.

Ancillary Public Areas

The hospital should allocate space for ancillary support services, such as blood donation and refreshment stations for rescue and medical personnel, typically required during and after a major disaster. These areas can involve the general public and volunteers during emergency response.

Media Briefing Area

Members of the media must also be accommodated to inform the public about the status of the disaster, rescue, and recovery efforts. An area for press briefings, status reports, and information updates should be established, preferably away from the emergency department and medical treatment areas. A single spokesperson or department should be designated as the media point of contact.

Administrators should develop a media policy well in advance of any disaster and share the procedures with all hospital personnel, to ensure that the institution speaks with one voice and conveys accurate information. Parking areas for media trucks and vehicles should be designated, to ensure that they do not impede emergency vehicular traffic.

CONCLUSION

*All that is necessary for the triumph of evil is that good men
do nothing.*   EDMUND BURKE (1729–1797)
British orator, philosopher, and politician

As the world learned from the events of September 11, 2001, the human spirit and capacity of
first responders to help those in need knows no bounds. The events of September 11 added new
dimensions and challenges for health care facilities serving communities of all sizes, demographics,
and populations. The prospect of a terrorist act, natural disaster, or biochemical attack upon a building,
city, region, or simultaneous sites within the United States, or against American interests and citizens
abroad, has forced the health care community and public policy makers to assess services, capabilities,
preparedness, and flexibility of operations as never before.

The examples highlighted at NYU Downtown Hospital after the events of September 11 clearly
illustrate that lessons previously unimaginable can be learned from even the most horrific events.
These unique benchmark experiences have been shared to inform and illuminate health care planners, designers, administrators and medical personnel as they develop and refine disaster planning
policies and procedures.

Balancing public policy needs and limited resources against ongoing medical service delivery,
and real and potential threats, risks, and worst case scenarios is the fundamental challenge facing the
twenty-first century health care industry, and the many owners, operators, facility managers, and
administrators.

Every local, state, and federal government agency understands that emergency preparedness requires
adequate funds and resources to cover costs related to personnel, equipment, and training. However,
obtaining these funds and resources, for allocation to local health care facilities, remains another ongoing
challenge. Regardless of debates about homeland security funding, logistics, and public policy, health care
facilities are still responsible for maintaining a high level of emergency and disaster preparedness.

The most vital information health care facilities require for security design is based upon local,
regional, and state level disaster planning efforts and threat assessments. The federal Office of
Homeland Security coordinates with corresponding state-level public safety agencies in each of the
50 states. Among their many roles in homeland security, these agencies are charged to protect, defend,
respond, inform, support, and coordinate related local, regional, and state level activities. Based on
information available from law enforcement agencies, security personnel, industry organizations,
and other institutions, health care facilities of every size and location must develop disaster plans, or
more specifically, an incident command system (ICS), outlining necessary policies and procedures
for emergency preparedness in the event of a major disaster or terrorist attack.

*We are at the very beginning of time for the human race. It is
not unreasonable that we grapple with problems. But there
are tens of thousands of years in the future. Our responsibility
is to do what we can, learn what we can, improve the solutions, and pass them on.*
RICHARD FEYNMAN (1918–1988)
U.S. educator and physicist

Comprehensive security planning integrates the best health care design practices, technology, and
carefully considered policies and emergency procedures. Since the 1990s, the health care arena has
encouraged creating a renewed culture of patient safety, and an environment of care, through advanced
technology, design, and operations. Innovations, such as computerized charting, patient-oriented
design, procedures aimed at reducing medical errors, ongoing community outreach, and patient education, have all contributed to the expanded role of health facilities in the twenty-first century.
Federal OSHA standards for activities and functions performed by hospital personnel contribute to
work environment safety.

However, investing in costly new, dedicated, and specialized facilities to meet twenty-first century security needs is not always necessary or feasible. Administrators and policy makers are faced with the difficult task of balancing budgets, and weighing use of limited resources against assessing the risks and probability of potential threats.

Many health care facilities will be able to enhance existing disaster planning and preparedness options by revisiting the ways spaces are planned, programmed, designed, located, staffed, and operated. Planning flexible use of space, always a fundamental health care design tenet, takes on new meaning when the prospect of treating mass casualties from a bioterrorism attack in a main lobby, cafeteria, or conference room is put forward by hospital administrators and public safety officials. Health care owners and operators must be prepared to prioritize phased implementation and budgeting for security upgrades, and coordinate these efforts with facility strategic plans and capital program improvements. Within this context, the health care community must address the following:

- Provide health care services integral to a facility's primary mission, whether regional acute care, community health, nursing home care, or other specialized function.

- Prepare a flexible response to extreme conditions stemming from a disaster or terrorist attack.

- Outline options for providing services in the event of loss of power, services, utilities, or space due to terrorism, crime, disaster, or contamination.

- Revisit use of major spaces for treating a surge in patient population after a disaster.

- Protect the building systems, facility infrastructure, and emergency backup supplies that maintain ongoing hospital operations.

- Minimize service disruption, potential loss of life, and the inevitable chaos ensuing during and after a power outage.

- Increase the inherent ability to accept advances in health care equipment, technology, clinical programs, and patient care initiatives.

- Present a safe, friendly, attractive, and efficient environment for healing to patients, visitors, and the public.

- Continue to remain vigilant about traditional security issues, including infant abduction, crime prevention, workplace violence, narcotic storage, and protecting dementia patients.

- Provide a safe and pleasant workplace for management, medical, and support personnel.

- Communicate the facility's preparedness and value to the community, through being a good neighbor, public outreach, and patient education services all year round, not only during disasters and times of need.

Ongoing dialogue with the health care facility's state licensing authority and local building construction officials ensures that variances from strict regulatory requirements are based on common understanding and concurrence. These "authorities having jurisdiction" (AHJ) have extensive experience and are knowledgeable about disaster preparations. Issues such as flexible land use and zoning, and compromises in operations and programs, must become an early part of planning discussions with each AHJ, to maximize disaster planning effectiveness.

The human capacity to fight back will always astonish doctors and philosophers. It seems, indeed, that there are no circumstances so bad and no obstacles so big that man cannot conquer them.
JEAN TETREAU (1683–1728)
Canadian author

The twenty-first century security risks and threats facing civilized society are daunting. The stakes are high, and the challenges are great, but they are by no means insurmountable.

ACKNOWLEDGMENTS

- Mary Ellen Hennessy, Emergency Preparedness Planner, Hospital Bioterrorism Preparedness Program, Office of Health Systems Management, New York State Department of Health, Troy, New York
- Michael Rawlings, Director of Engineering & Project Executive, New York University Downtown Hospital, New York, New York

GLOSSARY

authorities having jurisdiction (AHJ)   Regulatory agencies, at all levels of government, responsible for the approval, certification, and surveillance of services, facilities, and operations. Compliance is determined via established laws and regulations.

Airborne infection isolation room   Single occupancy rooms where environmental details are controlled to minimize the transmission of infectious agents normally spread through droplet nuclei associated with coughing and inhalation.

chemical, biological, radiological (CBR)   The types of threats likely to be identified as part of bioterrorism.

emergency department (ED)   A department within an acute care hospital providing diagnosis and treatment of unscheduled medical emergencies. Services available in EDs vary at each hospital, from treatment of minor medical problems, known as fast track, to high-level trauma care. EDs provide emergency services and staffing on a 24-hour basis to patients who independently seek care, and those transported by ambulance.

Hospital Emergency Response Data System (HERDS)   This interactive database, established by the New York State Department of Health, is a mandatory element of emergency planning for all hospitals in New York. There are a number of established data elements, including the availability of beds, medical supplies, personnel, and an assessment of immediate care needs that are routinely updated to reflect conditions in real time.

incident command system (ICS)   A management tool establishing a standardized method of response to any occurrence requiring action. The ICS provides coordinated planning and implementation among the many individuals and agencies who may be involved in an emergency response, and addresses potentially overlapping terminology, equipment, responsibilities, and procedures required from all involved parties. An ICS must be sufficiently comprehensive and flexible to allow an orderly transition through each stage of one or more events.

infection-control risk assessment   A multidisciplinary organizational process focusing on reducing infection risks. Coordinates knowledge from experts in infectious disease and infection control, facility design, engineering, and ventilation, construction, epidemiology, and safety.

BIBLIOGRAPHY

American Institute of Architects, The Facilities Guidelines Institute, *Guidelines for Design and Construction of Hospital and Health Care Facilities,* Washington, D.C., 2001.

Department of Health and Human Services, Centers for Disease Control and Prevention, National Institute for Occupational Safety and Health, *Guidance for Protecting Building Environments from Airborne Chemical, Biological, or Radiological Attacks,* U.S. GPO, Washington, D.C., May 2002.

Johnston, David, "Report Calls U.S. Agencies Understaffed for Bioterror," *The New York Times,* July 6, 2003.

Sidell, M.D., Frederick R., Patrick III, William C., Dashiell, Thomas R. *Jane's Chem-Bio Handbook,* Jane's Information Group, Alexandria, Va., April 2000.

INTERNET RESOURCES

American Association of Homes and Services
for the Aging (AAHSA)
www.aahsa.org

American College of Healthcare Architects
(ACHA)
www.healtharchitects.org

American Institute of Architects (AIA)
Academy of Architecture for Health (AAH)
www.aia.org; www.aia.org/aah

American Society for Healthcare Engineering
(ASHE)
www.ashe.org

Best Practices Magazine
www.aahsa.org

Centers for Disease Control and Prevention
(CDC)
www.cdc.gov

GNYHA Emergency Preparedness Resource
Center
www.gnyha.org/eprc/

Healthcare Construction & Operation
www.healthcarefacility.net

Health Facilities Management
www.hfmmagazine.com

Hospital Connect
www.hospitalconnect.com

Hospitals & Health Networks, Health Forum
www.hhnmag.com

Modern Healthcare
www.modernhealthcare.com

National Association of County and City
Health Officials (NACCHO)
www.naccho.org

National Institute for Occupational Safety and
Health (NIOSH)
www.cdc.gov/NIOSH/homepage.HTML

New York State Department of Health
Hospital Bioterrorism Preparedness
Program
www.health.state.ny.us/nysdoh/bt/bt.htm

New York State Office of Public Security
Homeland/Public Security Links – state,
federal and private sector
www.state.ny.us/security/links.html

U.S. Department of Homeland Security
www.dhs.gov

Washington Hospital Center – ER One
www.er1.org

CHAPTER 9
HISTORIC PRESERVATION GUIDANCE FOR SECURITY DESIGN

Sharon C. Park, FAIA
Chief, Technical Preservation Services
Heritage Preservation Services
National Center for Cultural Resources
National Park Service, U.S. Department of the Interior
Washington, D.C.

Caroline R. Alderson
Program Manager, Center for Historic Buildings
Office of the Chief Architect, Public Buildings Service
U.S. General Services Administration
Washington, D.C.

The new security constraints on Federal building are opportunities for enriching architecture. Once you understand the limitations, they should be cause for invention and analysis that allows you to push beyond your preconceptions. The security issues should allow you to invent a vocabulary that not only solves the problem but also creates an appropriate architectural image.   CHARLES GWATHMEY, FAIA (B. 1938)
Architect of the U.S. Mission to the United Nations in New York City, from Vision & Voice—Design Excellence in Federal Architecture: Building a Legacy

The September 11, 2001 destruction of the World Trade Center and portions of the Pentagon, a registered National Historic Landmark, heightened awareness about the vulnerability of America's cultural icons and heritage properties. Tempering these concerns, however, is an increased ambivalence about the effects of security measures on the quality of American life and the urban environment. Fortunately, replacement of expedient, temporary installations with more permanent architectural solutions is now creating an opportunity for design professionals to take a more imaginative approach to security retrofit for historic buildings and sites.

Although the pace of the response may be unusual, the challenge of accommodating new requirements without sacrificing historic materials and design cohesiveness is nothing new. Preservation is an established design specialty in which consensus exists that historic buildings require—and merit—a specialized approach. Established preservation standards and guidelines are a sound starting point for planning security improvements at historic properties (Table 9.1). Methods developed to prevent and manage natural disasters at heritage sites are also relevant. Security retrofit considers operational issues first and tailors design to the unique site characteristics.

Successful approaches to security design, along with model solutions developed for a variety of public properties, have been achieved at historic buildings across the United States. The overall approach centers on five principles emerging from collaborative discussions among government agencies, preservation institutions, and practitioners (Table 9.2).

TABLE 9.1   Principles of Security Design for Historic Buildings

1. Protecting the national heritage is in the public interest.
2. Maintaining accurate information on historic resources is fundamental to preserving them.
3. Maintaining the values of an open and democratic culture is possible through good planning and design.
4. Balancing public safety and preservation requires thoughtful integration of technology and operations.
5. Collaborating among many partners on a project team is key to successfully protecting people, historic structures, and settings.

TABLE 9.2   Principles for Development of Security Measures for Historic Places

1. **Heritage protection is in the public interest.**
   Protection of human life is paramount. Protection of heritage values is necessary to preserve the American way of life. An affirmative message should be conveyed that planners and public officials responsible for public safety and security should respect and consider heritage values. "Safety" and "security" should not be used as a patent excuse or pretext for poor planning, insensitivity to heritage values, and failure to consider alternatives if they are feasible in safeguarding the public at historic places.

2. **Balancing public safety and heritage protection is an evolving field.**
   Balanced solutions should be based upon appropriate risk assessment. Security and disaster preparedness are based upon understanding effects on people and facilities. When making decisions, we should emphasize commonsense measures and consider changes in technology, professional practice, and other relevant factors.

3. **Accurate information about heritage resources is fundamental to effective preparedness plans.**
   Complete survey information and resource documentation needs to be stressed in order to improve preparedness and response for a natural or man-made disaster. Redundancy of key records and documentation should be considered for major facilities. Systematic means for factoring risk assessment into decisions on inventory and documentation priorities at the regional, state, or local level need to be developed.

4. **Historic resource values should be preserved in remediation actions.**
   Disaster preparedness and security measures in or adjacent to historic areas, including appropriate hazard mitigation and "force protection," need to be planned and executed in as sensitive and design-conscious a manner as possible. Physical modifications, including fencing, bollards, and other landscape elements, should be compatible with significant historic features to the maximum extent feasible. Inappropriate temporary or interim installations for security and related purposes should not be permitted to become permanent fixtures of the property or its surroundings.

5. **Consultation with others during planning and implementation is necessary and important.**
   Disaster preparedness and security measures need to be planned in consultation with emergency organizations and other concerned parties, not executed in a vacuum. Determinations need to be made about how much information can be made public, and how much can be shared with other public officials and review authorities. Release of such information should err on the side of sharing as long as that release would not jeopardize public safety or national security. An appropriate balance needs to be struck among timeliness, security, and allowing for a reasonable public process.

Source: The Advisory Council on Historic Preservation and The Federal Preservation Institute, National Center for Preservation Technology and Training, National Park Service.

DESIGN STANDARDS FOR HISTORIC BUILDINGS

Under the National Historic Preservation Act of 1966, the Secretary of the Interior was charged with developing *Standards for the Treatment of Historic Properties*. These standards were issued in 1977 and are to be used to evaluate the effects of federal undertakings on historic properties and to qualify rehabilitation projects for preservation tax credits and federal grants. Many state and local governments, nonprofit organizations, and private institutions subsequently adopted these standards as well. The best-known standards are the Secretary of the Interior's *Standards for Rehabilitation* (Table 9.3).

While these include ten specific standards, the intent is for all work on historic buildings to be undertaken in a manner that protects historic materials, respects historic character, and is sensitive to the scale, form, detailing and other visual qualities of the historic resource.

The National Park Service has a number of publications and internet-based resources providing clear, consistent guidance to owners, developers and federal agency managers planning alterations to historic buildings. Owners can identify the period of significance of their facilities and evaluate the building's historic character-defining elements to receive the highest level of preservation (Table 9.4). Character-defining elements should be

- Kept in sound condition through cyclical maintenance
- Repaired when damaged
- If not repairable, then replaced in a fashion matching the visual qualities of the historic element

When considering upgrades to historic buildings for security purposes, the same methodology should be followed so that security modifications do not result in damage to these character-defining elements.

TABLE 9.3   **Secretary of the Interior's Standards for Rehabilitation**

Rehabilitation is defined as the act or process of making possible a compatible use for a property through repair, alterations, and additions while preserving those portions or features conveying historical, cultural, or architectural values.

Standards for Rehabilitation
1. A property will be used as it was historically, or be given a new use requiring minimal change to its distinctive materials, features, spaces, and spatial relationships.
2. The historic character of a property will be retained and preserved. The removal of distinctive materials or alterations of features, spaces, and spatial relationships that characterize a property will be avoided.
3. Each property will be recognized as a physical record of its time, place, and use. Changes that created a false sense of historical development, such as adding conjectural features or elements from other historic properties, will not be undertaken.
4. Changes to a property that have acquired historic significance in their own right will be retained and preserved.
5. Distinctive materials, features, finishes, and construction techniques or examples of craftsmanship characterizing a property will be preserved.
6. Deteriorated historic features will be repaired rather than replaced. Where the severity of deterioration requires replacement of a distinctive feature, the new feature will match the old in design, color, texture, and, where possible, materials. Replacement of missing features will be substantiated by documentary and physical evidence.
7. Chemical or physical treatments, if appropriate, will be undertaken using the gentlest means possible. Treatments causing damage to historic materials will not be used.
8. Archeological resources will be protected and preserved in place. If such resources must be disturbed, mitigation measures will be undertaken.
9. New additions, exterior alterations, or related new construction will not destroy historic materials, features, and spatial relationships characterizing the property. The new work will be differentiated from the old and will be compatible with the historic materials, features, size, scale and proportion, and massing to protect the integrity of the property and its environment.
10. New additions and adjacent or related new construction will be undertaken in such a manner that, if removed in the future, the essential form and integrity of the historic property and its environment would be unimpaired.

TABLE 9.4   Character Defining Elements for Historic Buildings

Element	Characteristics
1. Building setting and landscape	Grounds and natural habitats
2. Building exterior	Architectural materials and design; roofing configuration, materials, and details; entrances and windows; special features such as porches, dormers, cupolas, balconies
3. Building interiors	Public spaces such as entrance lobbies, grand stairs, elevator lobbies, circulation corridors, large auditoriums or meeting spaces, offices.
4. Decorative elements	Depending on finish quality, highly articulated materials, mosaic tiles, painted frescoes, marbles, hand-crafted finishes; vernacular expressions of plaster and trim work. Each resource must be evaluated to ensure protection of unique spaces, finishes, and features.

SECURITY DESIGN STANDARDS

After the bombing of the Alfred P. Murrah Federal Building in 1995, the federal government began taking steps to protect public building perimeters against truck or car bombs. The Department of Justice issued new security requirements mandating exterior surveillance cameras, visitor screening, and vehicle barriers for most federal facilities. Concrete Jersey barriers and concrete planters were quickly installed at prominent Federal buildings in city centers. Projects involving costly measures such as structural reinforcement, window modification to prevent injury by shattered glass, and replacement of temporary vehicle barriers with permanent architectural installations, will continue for some time.

Security Design Guidelines were developed by the Interagency Security Committee (ISC), of which the General Services Administration (GSA), the Department of Defense, the Department of Justice, the National Park Service, the Federal Protective Service (now the Department of Homeland Security), and the National Capital Planning Commission (NCPC), among others, are members. These guidelines establish specific performance criteria in a variety of areas for construction or rehabilitation of facilities housing federal employees.

For example, security standards require establishing minimum building setbacks for new construction, since blast impact decreases dramatically with distance, and hardening of building walls by incorporating blast-resistant windows, where minimum setback requirements cannot be met. The specific standards are not published for security reasons, but the principles behind them are reflected in the security-enhancing methods discussed here and illustrated in the federal project case studies. A consortium of government agencies and organizations concerned with preservation, design, and urban planning has also emerged to develop design guidance on appropriate approaches for ensuring public safety while maintaining open cities and vibrant public spaces. A number of states and municipalities are adopting similar standards.

While some buildings, such as state capitols and institutions, can meet the recommended setbacks, known as *standoff distances,* of 50 feet for medium risk occupancies, or 100 feet, for higher risk occupancies, most historic properties cannot meet these requirements. The goal is to add features that increase the safety of building occupants and the public without sacrificing historic integrity or creating a climate of fear in spaces meant to be inviting and open.

The checklist "Historic Preservation Guidance for Security Modifications" examines security retrofit within the framework of principles articulated in the Secretary of the Interior's standards (Table 9.5).

PLANNING FOR PROTECTION

Many institutions and museums have natural disaster plans in place that can be expanded to include protection against damage from direct attack or from collateral damage by fire and water. Disaster planning requires

- Establishing levels of risk and priorities for protection
- Developing emergency response procedures
- Implementing protective measures

Measures for protecting building occupants from blast damage include

- Siting new buildings to allow for appropriate standoff distances
- Designing or reinforcing structural systems to prevent progressive collapse
- Designing or modifying windows to reduce flying debris, especially shattered glass
- Creating secured screening areas
- Limiting airborne contaminant infiltration through ventilating systems
- Developing and regularly testing mass notification systems

Historic properties may not fit the standard approach for upgrading as recommended for other existing structures. Security protection planning for historic properties begins with specific steps taken by project architects and building administrators to evaluate the significance of the resource and then to provide a reasonable level of protection consistent with the Department of the Interior's Standards for Rehabilitation (Table 9.6).

Documentation

Detailed documentation is critical to accurate reconstruction, should portions of a property be destroyed. Existing sources of documentation, such as the *Historic American Building Survey*, the *National Register of Historic Places* and local archives, should be consulted to determine if documentation

TABLE 9.5   Historic Preservation Guidance for Security Modifications Checklist

1. Understand the architectural design of the historic building and landscape.
2. Refrain from making changes damaging to the significant historic materials or unduly altering the historic character of the building and setting.
3. Document historic buildings and settings with adequate photographs, drawings and descriptive narratives to provide a basis for accurate reconstruction or repair, should the property be damaged.
4. Investigate all means of providing security through electronic and administrative procedures before pursuing physical intervention that would compromise the historic character of the building or setting.
5. Use perimeter security measures, such as setback distances and appropriately designed planters and bollards to provide protection without impeding vistas, landscape, and pedestrian enjoyment or traffic flow in historic surroundings.
6. Avoid unnecessary architectural compromises by accurately assessing direct risks and indirect risks of collateral damage from high-risk sites nearby prior to undertaking physical changes beyond those required for safe exiting.
7. Concentrate on protection from flying debris.
8. Design historic building reinforcement to be inconspicuous and reversible to the greatest extent possible.
9. Design new measures to be additive to the historic building features, rather than subtractive, so that the historic materials may remain in place and there may be a distinction between original historic elements and new features.
10. For federal projects, understand the Interagency Security Committee (ISC) concepts and standards and work with expert security engineers and preservation specialists to identify appropriate, performance-based design solutions.
11. For nonfederal projects, use local historic district guidelines, preservation administrators, and technical experts to assist in the development of emergency response measures and security improvement plans.
12. Develop a plan for quick response stabilization in the event of major building damage by having a design and consulting team in place that is familiar with the historic resource.

TABLE 9.6 Evaluating and Protecting Historic Resources

Task	Action
1. Documentation	Identify the building's significant history, construction documents, and artistic contents; secure building records.
2. Risk assessment	Identify risk zones, analyze setting and neighboring site.
3. Preliminary planning	Develop operational and physical changes to protect life-safety.
4. Long-term planning	Implement emergency plans and community coordination; develop postdisaster contacts.
5. Design for physical alterations	Respect the historic resource and its contents.
6. Implement security measures	Refine design as necessary to preserve historic character, while addressing security needs.
7. Assessment	Test and refine new protection technologies.
8. Cyclical maintenance	Keep building and site in sound condition.

exists. *Historic American Building Survey* standards provide useful guidance for recording and documenting historic structures. The *National Register of Historic Places* and historical archives often have detailed information on the significance of individual resources.

A *Historic Structures Report* outlining a property's history and evolution is also a valuable document for any historic building and is generally developed as part of a rehabilitation or restoration plan (Table 9.7). Architects, architectural historians, and preservation specialists can provide these services. Depending on the resource, recording methods might include

- Measured architectural drawings
- Large format photography
- Field research, historic photographs, permit records, other original documents
- Written historical reports, descriptive narratives

Documentation and inventory of artwork, antiques, significant interior features or furnishings, and other artifacts of a building or site are also important. Many museums have extensively documented their collections, and many corporations have documented art objects through insurance policies.

While original works of art are generally not reproduced after loss, many damaged pieces can be repaired. Master artisans can restore murals, mosaics, or decorative features to their former appearance. Without good photographic evidence, color studies, or material descriptions, accurately restoring these items may be difficult or impossible. The artifact inventory is imperative for recovering items lost as a result of theft or disappearance during emergency removal.

OPERATIONAL IMPROVEMENTS

Operational improvements are important elements to any security plan and can reduce the need for more costly or invasive physical changes. Policies and procedures should be in place for emergencies and as part of a disaster-planning program. Many of these items are not specific to historic buildings,

TABLE 9.7 9/11 Lessons Learned: Document Historic Buildings and Store Copies Off-Site

After the events of September 11, 2001, several important landmark buildings were extensively documented using photolaser scanning, which an experienced team can usually accomplish within one week. Even buildings not of landmark status should be documented photographically with as much detail as possible for potential replacement of all or parts of the damaged building or artwork.

Documents should be updated periodically and a copy kept off-site, along with other copies of drawings and photographs.

TABLE 9.8   Operational Checklist for Security Preparedness

1. Conduct regular evacuation drills for employees.
2. Plan for employee notification during an emergency and continued communication afterward.
3. Familiarize the local fire department with the site and any special considerations, such as museum collections needing removal in an emergency.
4. Separate public and private zones of the building with simple shatter-resistant glass walls that do not obstruct views of the significant historic spaces.
5. Assess existing features that might be useful during an emergency, such as existing fire shutters to protect windows from nearby flames or shutting off air intake systems if there is smoke or gas present outside.
6. Designate staff members to perform prescribed tasks in an emergency.
7. Equip staff with emergency kits, including flashlights and smoke masks for evacuation, and plastic bags to cover computers quickly for protection from dust and smoke.
8. Establish a facility engineer's checklist program for shutting off systems, water and utilities as maintenance staff exit the property and for identifying which systems need to remain in operation until the entire building is evacuated.
9. Prepare a post-disaster plan with appropriate team members, such as insurance agents, contractors, and building suppliers, to plan for future remediation and repairs.

but are critical to ensuring the protection of buildings and their contents. Coordination with local and regional plans for evacuation and infrastructure improvements is also beneficial (Table 9.8).

For historic buildings, there is a great advantage in placing administrative controls in a central location. Central control rooms enable monitoring of building systems to pinpoint security and fire breaches and broadcast instructions through public address systems. However, high-performance fire detection and suppression equipment depends on sophisticated technology requiring appropriate maintenance and backup energy systems.

Local building and life safety codes should be consulted before making any improvements, as a request for performance-based compliance or use of equivalencies developed to accommodate historic buildings may be necessary. Battery or generator powered backup lighting systems for stairs and egress routes can be supplemented with appropriate outdoor security lighting, motion detection, and fluorescent paint or strips on the edges of nonornamental exit stair treads and exit paths to light the way for a short period of time should all the lighting go out. Battery packs can often be recessed into walls for a flush installation, leaving only lamps exposed. In elaborate buildings, backup generators can be installed to supply power to selected fixtures.

Routine maintenance is the key to long-term preservation. Building owners should routinely perform annual inspections of all building components and pay attention to projecting elements or features over exit routes that could come dislodged as a result of a blast force. As has been proven in earthquake zones, buildings maintained in sound physical condition fare better than weaker buildings. All parapets should be anchored; coping stones should be set firmly; projecting features, such as window heads, door surrounds, cornices, and overhangs, should be checked for loose mortar, deterioration, and weak connections, and repaired promptly.

A facility management study should be made of the building to study how air intake moves through a building and whether any natural historic features can be used advantageously for protection during fires or other potential life-threatening safety situations (Table 9.9).

POSTDISASTER PLANNING

Building owners should develop a plan identifying contacts for coordinating with local law enforcement and response teams, including those who will assess damage after an incident and those who will repair the building. This contact list should be kept in duplicate or triplicate at one or more off-site locations.

Although security upgrade efforts tend to focus on physical changes, the value of administrative measures should not be underestimated. Lives can be saved by nonphysical actions such as evacuation and postdisaster planning. Preplanning for postdisaster recovery can give a building priority with

TABLE 9.9   Lessons Learned from 9/11: Tall, Open Spaces can Serve as Smoke Evacuation Chambers

Tall open spaces can contribute to a building's continued habitability in some emergencies. When New York City's historic Tweed Courthouse was completely renovated in the late 1990s, the historic rotunda was designated as a smoke evacuation chamber. This was useful on September 11, 2001, as smoke engulfed Lower Manhattan, following the collapse of the nearby World Trade Center towers. The design features of the rotunda and the fire shutters maintained building indoor air quality during evacuation.

Mechanical vents should be closed to stop smoke from coming inside when heating and ventilating systems are shut down during evacuation. Practice drills with the maintenance staff should include sequenced shut downs of building systems and utilities.

contractors and better prospects with permitting officials for timely return to functionality. Agencies and institutions may benefit from retaining emergency service contractors on indefinite quantity contracts to minimize administrative delay initiating recovery efforts. After the Loma Prieta, California earthquake of 1989, building owners prepared with recovery plans and established relationships with repair contractors were more likely to receive approval to retain and repair their buildings and avoid mandatory demolition for public safety.

PLANNING PHYSICAL CHANGES

Security-related modifications to historic structures fall into four major categories, each contributing to enhanced building safety (Table 9.10).

OFF-SITE

At high-risk sites where meeting minimum standoff distances or major modification of the building envelope is not possible, traffic modifications may offer the only alternative for eliminating risks associated with moving and stationary vehicles (Fig. 9.1). Coordination with municipal planning offices concerning proposed traffic changes should address any effects site infrastructure changes, such as lighting, may have on adjoining public areas.

SITE

The most common physical security changes to building exteriors are surveillance cameras and exterior lighting.

Surveillance Cameras and Lighting

Exterior cameras reinforce physical perimeter barriers, alarm systems, and other security infrastructure by allowing activity around the building to be continuously monitored from a single remote location. Cameras are either fixed or movable and are generally placed to allow as wide a viewing plane as possible.

Where additional lighting is necessary for cameras to detect movement, light fixtures and sources should be selected and tested with on-site mockups to avoid inappropriately altering the character of the property by introducing unsympathetic lighting color or glare. Design goals include minimizing the visibility of surveillance camera equipment and avoiding damage to historic materials (Table 9.11).

TABLE 9.10   Security Performance Elements for Historic Building Modifications

Condition	Performance element
1. Off-site (public right-of-way)	Traffic patterns, parking, curbs, and sidewalk features, such as vehicle barriers
2. Site	Surveillance cameras, lighting, guard houses, vehicle barriers, perimeter fencing, bollards, and grade modifications
3. Building exterior	Shatter-resistant window treatments and structural reinforcement
4. Building interior	Safe exiting and fire suppression, lobby screening stations, circulation control, interior surveillance, and ballistic protection

FIGURE 9.1   Historic properties often cannot meet setback requirements. Limiting street access using sympathetically designed concrete barricades is one solution for medium- or high-risk tenants in buildings located close to sidewalks. (*Source: Chad Randl, National Park Service.*)

TABLE 9.11   Minimizing Visibility of Surveillance Camera Technology

1. Anchor into masonry joints, flat painted wood, and other repairable surfaces—never into masonry units, moldings, or other surfaces not easily repaired.
2. Specify brackets and fastenings of stainless steel or other materials that will not produce rust stains.
3. Install cameras as high above grade as possible.
4. Locate cameras on nearby roofs or support buildings, where feasible.
5. Camouflage camera housings and supporting brackets by painting to match adjoining materials.
6. Locate cameras so as to minimize visibility from the front of the building, from public rights of way, and from public areas of the building.
7. Specify the smallest camera components needed to satisfy functional requirements.
8. Where appropriate, use separate component systems allowing all parts except camera lenses to be concealed.
9. Mount cameras on sympathetically designed freestanding poles as an alternative to mounting on visible areas of the building façade.

Security engineers for government agencies, large institutions, and other entities involved in volume procurement of security equipment often prefer camera assemblies in which both lens and moving components for remote operation are contained in a globe-like protective housing. The globes protect equipment from the weather and simplify installation, at the cost of increased conspicuousness. Separate component systems may be more troublesome to install and maintain, but are generally less conspicuous because all but the lens and attached portion of the pan-tilt device can be placed out of view. There are a variety of ways to reduce the visual and physical impact of both types of camera systems:

• Damage to historic facade materials can be avoided by mounting cameras in masonry joints on the rear side of parapet walls, on the underside of overhang framing members, on adjoining building rooftops, or on existing or specially designed poles or other freestanding elements.

- Pole and off-site mounting offer the advantages of a wider field of vision and eliminate potential damage to historic materials.
- Poles can be designed, painted, or patinated (chemically treated to create a deep bronze statuary finish), to blend into the streetscape along with lamp standards and other street furniture.

A model pole developed for monumental Federal buildings in Washington, D.C., by the General Services Administration, in coordination with the National Capital Planning Commission and Commission on Fine Arts, features a slender gooseneck profile, statuary finish, and contoured base suggesting turn of the century lamp standards. Globe housings are offered in a range of sizes, so the smallest diameter housing should be specified. Colored portions of the housing should match the pole. Shorter, functionally designed poles can sometimes be made less obvious by their placement along fences, screened by plantings, and amidst other perimeter features (Fig. 9.2).

Guard Houses

Increased exterior screening for parking areas and loading docks has increased demand for exterior gatehouses and guardhouses. New gatehouses should be planned as discreet new site elements, subservient to the historic resource, sympathetic in design but not presented as part of the historic construction (Fig. 9.3). Prefabricated structures are rarely sympathetic with historic buildings and should be

FIGURE 9.2 Exterior surveillance camera mounted on a post contoured to blend with nearby streetlights eliminates the need to penetrate or visually alter the facade. The camera's globe housing and post have been patinated to read as single assembly. (*Source: General Services Administration.*)

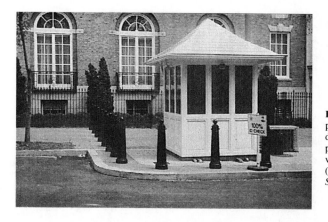

FIGURE 9.3 The small scale and simple design of this guard station does not detract from the historic building it is protecting. Deep foundation bollards provide antiram protection to the guardhouse. (*Source: Chad Randl, National Park Service.*)

used only where not visible from public rights of way or in view of principal facades. Like all historic buildings additions, guardhouses and gatehouses should be

- Located on secondary elevations or to the side of front elevations
- Small in size relative to the main building
- Compatible with existing materials but differentiated as new construction

Vehicle Barriers

Successfully integrating vehicle barriers into historic properties requires tailoring the barrier design to the architectural character and conditions of each site. Prior to planning perimeter security changes, character-defining features and qualities of the site should be identified to establish appropriate design parameters for any site changes. At properties not considered high risk, especially those featuring designed landscapes or simple entrances within view of the public right of way, serious consideration should be given to the necessity of vehicle barriers. Smaller, low occupancy properties may be served adequately by plantings and low features configured to discourage entrance to a property in other than the designated walkways and roadways.

For federal offices and other properties requiring vehicle barriers, there are many ways to secure buildings against vehicular intrusion without resorting to fortresslike Jersey barriers or off-the-shelf concrete planters. Potentially seamless landscape solutions such as new *berms* or landscaped *plinths* raising the grade of the property above that of the roadway may not be in keeping with the historic character of every property. They might be the best alternative, however, where architectural barriers would appear too formal or utilitarian *bollards* too industrial. A traditional solution that does not strictly meet ISC engineering standards but does present a deterrent is to plant a row of trees spaced closely enough to block vehicle access (Fig. 9.4).

Where such additions are appropriate for the site, landscape amenities can be engineered to protect building occupants against vehicular impact (Fig. 9.5).

Sympathetic architectural solutions include traditionally detailed cast iron bollards installed along public rights-of-way adjoining the White House and portions of Pennsylvania Avenue, in Washington, D.C. Tapered shafts, fluting, and finials mitigate the bulkiness and hard contemporary geometry that concrete barriers and planters typically introduce. These bollards are also appropriate for nineteenth century row houses and other properties where cast iron street furniture may have been used in the past.

Similarly sympathetic, somewhat simplified, retractable elements will be installed in places where flexibility in traffic control is needed. For locations such as Pennsylvania Avenue and ceremonial parade routes, these technologies are an excellent solution for providing security on a daily basis with provision for vehicle access during public events. All site interventions should be designed to be reversible and leave the character defining qualities of the property intact (Figs. 9.6 and 9.7).

FIGURE 9.4 Palm trees supplement other barriers and provide relief from the desert sun in this building's otherwise spartan plaza. (*Source: General Services Administration.*)

FIGURE 9.5 Artfully designed benches, fountains, and other landscape amenities can be engineered to serve as structural barriers. (*Source: General Services Administration. Landscape design by Martha Schwartz.*)

FIGURE 9.6 Temporary road barricades are being replaced with retractable bollards designed to be compatible with nearby historic buildings while providing flexibility in traffic control. (*Source: Chad Randl, National Park Service.*)

A hybrid landscaped-architectural solution that may offer the best of both worlds for barriers rimming monumental properties is a structural garden wall barrier prototype developed by the General Services Administration. The garden wall concept combines a variety of structural and nonstructural elements integrated discretely into landscape design. This approach avoids the staid repetitive appearance of using one feature only.

In 2001, GSA commissioned Cox, Graae+Spack (formerly KressCox Associates PC) to develop a master plan and conceptual design for integrating security enhancements, landscape design, and urban planning into the outdoor spaces of the Federal Triangle in Washington D.C. Their sophisticated urban design approach proposed introducing sculpture, a water element, traffic calming features, and perimeter garden walls as public amenities intended to make the complex safe and inviting to pedestrians (Fig. 9.8).

The vehicle barrier system proposed for the two grand avenues defining the Federal Triangle incorporates structural iron railings, low stone pillars, raised planter boxes, and seating into a garden wall designed to visually strengthen the pedestrian right of way. The perimeter security structure is concealed within the wall of the raised planter box facing the street, while the inner wall of the planter is set in at selected locations to accommodate street furniture, such as benches and bus shelters. Openings between planter boxes permit pedestrian circulation at building entrances and street corners, where integrally designed bollards block vehicle access. The net effect is to more clearly define the pedestrian right of way by creating a formal street edge and comfortable sense of path enclosure mitigating the width of street (Table 9.12).

FIGURE 9.7 Proposed retractable bollards will allow vehicular access on Pennsylvania Avenue for parades and other occasions. (*Source: Michael Van Valkenburgh Associates, courtesy of the National Capital Planning Commission.*)

FIGURE 9.8 Simulated view of garden wall barrier system illustrates how architecturally integrated antiram planter barricades, railings, pillars, and nonstructural seating can be attractively designed as street furniture. (*Source: Cox, Graae+Spack, courtesy of the General Services Administration.*)

GSA commissioned van Dijk Westlake Reed Leskosky in 2002 to further develop the garden wall perimeter security concept through development of construction drawings, specifications, and construction cost estimates. The prototype design applies the Cox, Graae + Spack (formerly KressCox) garden wall model to a specific, center city, public building site presenting a variety of street conditions and site-specific engineering requirements. These streetscape variations serve as the basis for creating a template "kit of parts" for adapting the multiple-element garden wall concept to a variety of architectural contexts (Table 9.13).

The principal pilot study building is an imposing, early twentieth century Beaux Arts courthouse faced in limestone (Fig. 9.9). An alternative "kit of parts" was developed for buildings of different styles and eras. The two pilot variants were a nineteenth century Romanesque building constructed of red brick and a boldly contoured 1960s modernistic building constructed of concrete (Figs. 9.12 to 9.14 and Table 9.14).

Streetscape conditions may call for combining perimeter security elements in different ways on each side of the building. The site and adjoining urban contexts are first analyzed to establish distinct perimeter security zones dictating appropriate types of perimeter security elements (Table 9.15). With

TABLE 9.12   General Design Parameters for Barrier Systems

- Conceal the protection.
- Retain pedestrian access, requiring permeability.
- Integrate security design and urban design.
- Incorporate streetscape elements, such as trees and light standards, only as nonstructural components of the barrier design.
- Incorporate a variety of security elements, rather than relying on a single type of element, such as bollards.
- Combine elements for the best aesthetic effect and public benefit appropriate to the street, site, location, and urban design.
- Ensure that all elements are designed and tested to resist site-specific vehicular threats.

TABLE 9.13   Design Parameters for Passive Security Elements

Security Element	Design parameter
1. Bollards with deep-set continuous foundations	• Minimum 8-inch outside diameter • 1/2-inch-thick steel filled with concrete • Foundations in soil if possible, tied at maximum spacing with 4-foot clearance
2. Antiram knee walls with foundations	• Minimum 3-foot height • 18-inch-thick reinforced concrete • Openings no greater than 4-foot clear
3. Planters with foundations	• 3 feet above grade • 12 inches below grade or to frost line, whichever is deeper • 12-inch-thick outer wall, 6-inch-thick inner wall • Minimum 3-foot overall width
4. Surface-mounted planters	• Minimum 1-inch indent in slab • Any shape or design • Engineer to vehicle speed and weight
5. Seating with foundations	• Seat set higher than axle of wheel
6. Bodies of water	• Pools, fountains, or water features • Flush body with antifriction surface, slope, and/or depth sufficient to impede vehicle motion • Raised pool with parapet or other impact-engineered features, generally higher than axle of wheel

FIGURE 9.9 Perimeter security design pilot building, illustrating a range of streetscape conditions typical at monumental civic buildings located in historic city centers. (*Source: van Dijk Westlake Reed Leskosky, courtesy of the General Services Administration.*)

TABLE 9.14   Generic Palette of Perimeter Barrier Elements

Perimeter barrier elements	Characteristics
1. Monumental bench of stone or concrete	• Structural features designed to complement the building façade
2. Monumental bollard of stone or concrete	• Masonry clad, detailed to blend with architecture, combined with structural benches to form an element group, serving as transition between benches and ornamental metal bollards
3. Monumental planter of stone or concrete	• Masonry faced, formally articulated to blend with principal facade and ceremonial area
4. Monumental screen wall of stone or concrete	• Barrier visually screening utilitarian streetscape amenities, integrated with design of other monumental elements of the articulated garden wall, such as benches, planters, bollards
5. Ornamental bollard of cast bronze	• Detailing derived from areaway posts
6. Ornamental railing of cast bronze	• Detailing derived from historic grilles
7. Basic steel bollard	• Simplified geometry for secondary facades where a more economical approach is appropriate
8. Retractable bollard	• For vehicle access to garage and one-way exit roads

a palette of perimeter barrier elements and streetscape conditions identified, prototypical elements can be adapted to specific sites (Figures 9.10 and 9.11 and Table 9.16).

Figures 9.12 through 9.15 illustrate the security element design vocabulary tailored to a nineteenth century brick building and a mid-twentieth century modernist building constructed of concrete.

BUILDING EXTERIORS

Building exteriors should be kept in excellent physical condition. Architectural elements should remain in sound condition and well attached, to prevent flying debris, falling materials, and potential injuries in case of an unforeseen event. Annual inspections, or routine observation after heavy rain,

TABLE 9.15 **Streetscape Conditions and Perimeter Security Elements**

Site context	Perimeter security elements
1. Permeable	• Fixed bollards of mixed styles allow maximum pedestrian access at principal entrances • Retractable bollards where vehicular access required
2. Partially enclosed	• Seating and public amenities are incorporated near public spaces • Used where pedestrian activity is high but does not require the openness of a principal entrance
3. Enclosed	• Articulated wall combining solid wall treatment and railings • Used where pedestrian access is not required or desired
4. Setback	• Building distance from curb allows incorporation of substantial plantings
5. Visually compromised	• Screen walls provide visual and physical barrier relating architecturally to other garden wall elements • Used to establish a cohesive frontage in areas adjoining utilitarian street amenities, such as bus shelters, newspaper vending machines, and trash receptacles

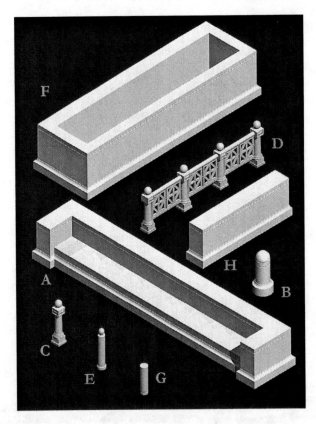

FIGURE 9.10 By relying on a variety of security elements, rather than a single element type, such as bollards, the perimeter barrier "kit of parts" provides flexibility to respond to a range of urban design conditions, combining elements for the best aesthetic effect and public benefit. (*Source: van Dijk Westlake Reed Leskosky, courtesy of the General Services Administration.*)

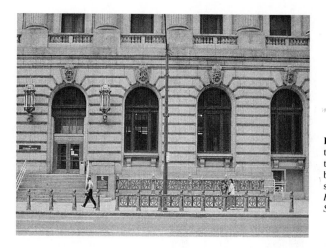

FIGURE 9.11 Simulated view, perimeter security garden wall system tailored to the permeable pedestrian setting of the building's principal entrance. (rendered simulation) (*Source: van Dijk Westlake Reed Leskosky, courtesy of the General Services Administration.*)

TABLE 9.16   Design Parameters for Site Adapting Prototype Security Elements

Site condition	Design parameters
1. Landscaping design	• Drainage, hardscape, wetland, climate, maintenance and operations, local guidelines or standards.
2. Plant material selection	• Hardiness, sun exposure, disease resistance; tolerance for salt, soil compaction, and pollution. • Site visibility, for safety purposes. • Planting program should include year round use of planters, rotating plants for seasonal interest.
3. Concealed conditions	• Site circulation, utilities, and other potentially concealed conditions to be determined in coordination with facilities staff or other experts familiar with the building.
4. Historic features	• Taking cues from, not necessarily replicating, historic features, details, proportions, scale, and materials in new security features.
5. Perimeter site conditions	• Relating perimeter elements to building massing, rhythm, and features.

FIGURE 9.12 Perimeter security pilot variant—nineteenth century brick building. (*Source: van Dijk Westlake Reed Leskosky, courtesy of the General Services Administration.*)

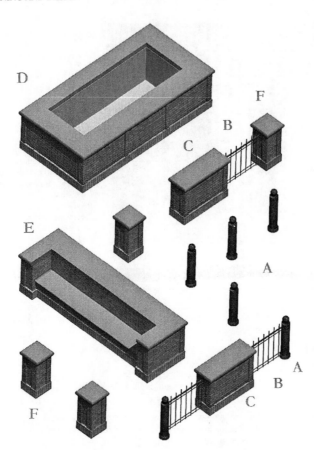

FIGURE 9.13 Perimeter security elements adapted for nineteenth century brick building. The palette of security elements created for this building type includes stone-capped brick pillars and structural benches articulated with inset panels and ornamental iron railings. (*Source: van Dijk Westlake Reed Leskosky, courtesy of the General Services Administration.*)

FIGURE 9.14 Perimeter security pilot variant, 1960s modernist building. (*Source: van Dijk Westlake Reed Leskosky, courtesy of the General Services Administration.*)

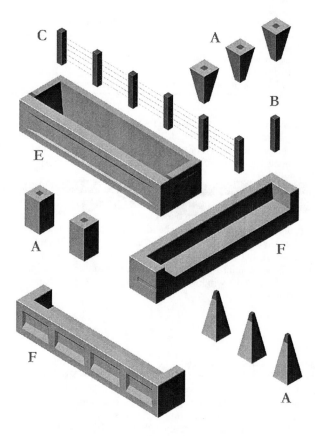

FIGURE 9.15 Perimeter security elements adapted for a modernist building. The security elements for this building type are fabricated in bicolored cast architectural concrete with stainless steel accents. Benches embellished with recessed panels, articulated joints, and pyramid shaped bollards respond to the building's clean, formal geometry. (*Source: van Dijk Westlake Reed Leskosky, courtesy of the General Services Administration.*)

snow, winds, or severe weather changes, are advised to ensure architectural elements remain securely fastened and do not sustain seasonal damage. Items to inspect include

- Roofing units, such as slates, should be securely anchored.
- Projecting elements, such as porticos and areas over exit routes, should be securely attached.
- Attached elements, such as lighting fixtures, shutters, and surveillance cameras, should be checked periodically to ensure they are firmly bolted and secured.

WINDOWS

Windows and grand entrance doorways are important character-defining elements of a building. When upgrading or replacing windows and glazed doors in historic structures, designers should examine ways to maintain historic materials and design and minimize potential risks to occupants from flying glass.

Identifying potential threats is the first step to protecting a facility. A risk assessment should indicate the need to provide protection against the hazards of glass fragmentation. The threat identification, along with an analysis of the site layout, existing perimeter protection, security operational procedures, and types and locations of existing windows provides the required data from which prudent retrofit options may be developed. Window treatment options to protect building occupants from flying glass should be considered as part of the exterior and interior assessment (Table 9.17). For large public

TABLE 9.17   **Options for Minimizing Potential Risks from Flying Glass**

1. Applied film
2. Laminated blast-resistant glass
3. Blast curtains
4. Interior blast-resistant storm windows or replacement windows

buildings, window frames and sashes are often constructed of steel, bronze or heavy mahogany. For smaller historic buildings, they are generally made of locally available woods or residentially scaled steel sash. Glass may be either small paned or large in size, hand blown or manufactured. Unless they have been upgraded, windows generally are not dual glazed, although some have storm panels, either external or internal to the sash.

Every effort should be made to keep historic frames and sashes in place with a modification of the glazing by adding films, interior storms, or using reinforced laminated glass. Historic wooden, small paned windows may be difficult to protect from blast damage, and reinforcing the small panes may not be cost effective. Often, the best option is protecting building occupants with internal blast-resistant storm windows or blast curtains. Both solutions are considered among the most effective window upgrades.

Replacement ballistic-resistant windows weigh more than the carrying capacity of most existing structures. Unless there is substantial interior reinforcement, installing these specialty windows is sometimes not feasible. Many of the window units weigh over 1000 pounds and are not detailed to match historic configurations.

Window Films

As part of a risk assessment study done at the outset of a renovation or retrofit project, the vulnerability of the building to the hazards of glass fragmentation needs to be examined. Factors contributing to the risk of injury by glass fragments include narrow building setbacks, proximity to other high profile buildings or public places, and unprotected glazing in windows, walls, or doors. For some buildings, applying shatter-resistant film to window glazing is the least costly and least intrusive option for reducing risk of injury from flying glass as a result of high wind or a blast condition. However, only film systems designed to be mechanically attached to the window frame offer protection against entire sash units becoming airborne, at potentially fatal velocity. These systems require robust frames, capable of reinforcing the sash connection to the frame and, if necessary, upgrading the window frame anchorage to the masonry walls. For frame buildings, which may not fare well in a blast, protecting occupants from flying glass may be the only result that can reasonably be achieved.

Caution should be used in applying any material directly to antique glass, as the performance over time has not been well tested. Film may not properly adhere to irregular glass surfaces and differential thermal movement between film and glass could cause stress cracking.

Four basic methods are typically used to attach film to window systems, for protection against glass fragmentation (Table 9.18).

Each retrofit alternative has advantages and disadvantages. In designing any system for the protection against flying glass hazards, designers must analyze the effects of the retrofit beyond the glass. The condition and effects on the glass, window frame, and surrounding support structures must be considered in the design.

Replacement Glazing

Alternatively, storm panels of safety glass, acrylic, or synthetic clear glazing can be added to existing window systems. Polycarbonate panels may be appropriate as a low-cost retrofit solution for windows containing period glazing.

Replacing glass with a shatter-resistant laminated glass or specialty dual glazing may change the profile of period muntins, the strips of wood or metal separating and holding panes of glass in a window.

TABLE 9.18   Methods for Attaching Film to Window Systems

Method	Description
1. Daylight attachment	• Film is applied only to the vision opening. • Daylight films provide the minimum glass fragment hazard reduction. • At greater levels of force, the glass and window with the frame can be propelled in one large piece, posing a greater hazard than the risk of injury by glass fragments.
2. Edge-to-edge attachment	• Applied beyond the vision opening to the edge of the glass. • Edge-to-edge application may provide additional safety benefit by exercising the strength of the film membrane in frames with deep glazing pockets. • Requires removal of the glass from the window.
3. Wet-glazed attachment	• Either daylight or edge-to-edge film is installed with a silicone bead along the edge of the frame to bond film to the sash. • Requires higher quality control measures to ensure proper installation.
4. Mechanical attachment systems	• Aluminum batten bars are screwed to the window frame to hold the film after the window breaks. • Best protection among film systems against glass fragmentation and detachment of sash from window opening

Before selecting this option, the impact of any change should be evaluated. Often delicately detailed, divided-light window sashes are important building components. Wider muntins to hold new, heavier glazing may not be appropriate.

Larger, simpler sashes may accept replacement glazing and improve thermal performance without substantially changing the window profiles and detailing. Fanlights and sidelights to exterior historic doors can be similarly retrofitted for improved blast resistance, but as these features are at eye level, the integration of films, new glazing, or panels should be carefully detailed. Overhead skylights or decorated stained glass should also be reinforced with some measure of protective film or secured glazing to protect persons below.

Blast Curtains and Blast Shades

Reversible high performance alternatives for securing glass, sash, and frames include

- Structural blast curtains
- Blast shades
- Laminated interior storm windows

Blast curtains and shades generally serve as stand-alone blast protection, but may be used in conjunction with window film, where the possibility exists that curtains will be left open. This technology, suitable for a variety of commercial, civic, and residential properties, is commonly used in the United Kingdom, Israel, Ireland, and South Africa, and has effectively limited blast damage and injuries from flying glass.

Blast curtains are made from high performance, tightly woven materials, such as polyester, KEVLAR®, or carbon fiber. The curtains are designed to protect building occupants by catching exploding glass shards and debris. Excess material concealed in a pocket at the window sill gives way and expands during an explosion or other disaster to contain the volume of shards.

Blast shades work like roll-down window shades anchored at both ends. An advantage of the shades is that they can be detailed to leave the exterior appearance of arched or otherwise contoured windows intact at little or no extra expense. A principal disadvantage of the shades is the extent to which the heavy metal weave reduces daylight.

Blast curtain performance and amount of light transmission varies by material and manufacturer. These curtains are part of a growing industry of high performance security products (Figs. 9.16 and 9.17).

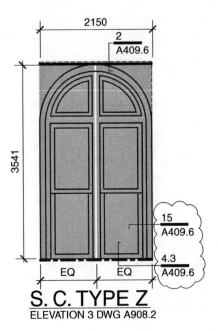

2150

2
A409.6

3541

15
A409.6

4.3
A409.6

EQ   EQ

S. C. TYPE Z
ELEVATION 3 DWG A908.2

FIGURE 9.16 Blast shade elevation detail. Blast-resistant shades provide protection against glass fragments and sash detachment without disturbing original arched windows or altering the exterior appearance of the building. (*R.M. Kliment and Frances Halsband Architects, Wank Adams Slavin Associates, and Armor Holdings, Inc., courtesy of the General Services Administration.*)

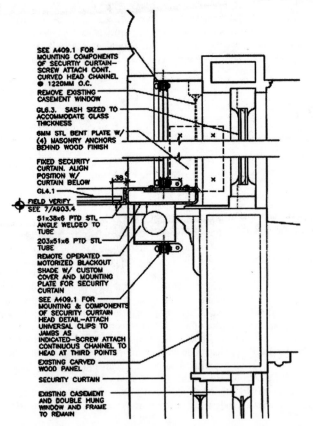

SEE A409.1 FOR
MOUNTING COMPONENTS
OF SECURTIY CURTAIN—
SCREW ATTACH CONT.
CURVED HEAD CHANNEL
@ 1220MM O.C.

REMOVE EXISTING
CASEMENT WINDOW

GL6.3. SASH SIZED TO
ACCOMODATE GLASS
THICKNESS

6MM STL BENT PLATE W/
(4) MASONRY ANCHORS
BEHIND WOOD FINISH

FIXED SECURITY
CURTAIN. ALIGN
POSITION W/
CURTAIN BELOW

GL4.1

FIELD VERIFY
SEE 7/A903.4

51x38x6 PTD STL
ANGLE WELDED TO
TUBE

203x51x6 PTD STL
TUBE

REMOTE OPERATED
MOTORIZED BLACKOUT
SHADE W/ CUSTOM
COVER AND MOUNTING
PLATE FOR SECURITY
CURTAIN

SEE A409.1 FOR
MOUNTING & COMPONENTS
OF SECURITY CURTAIN
HEAD DETAIL—ATTACH
UNIVERSAL CLIPS TO
JAMBS AS
INDICATED—SCREW ATTACH
CONTINUOUS CHANNEL TO
HEAD AT THIRD POINTS

EXISTING CARVED
WOOD PANEL

SECURITY CURTAIN

EXISTING CASEMENT
AND DOUBLE HUNG
WINDOW AND FRAME
TO REMAIN

38

FIGURE 9.17 Blast curtain section. Blast-resistant shades anchored at the window head and sill protect occupants by catching exploding glass shards. (*R.M. Kliment and Frances Halsband Architects, Wank Adams Slavin Associates, and Armor Holdings, Inc., courtesy of the General Services Administration.*)

Laminated Glass Storm Windows

Among the most discrete high-performance alternatives are laminated glass storm windows. Storm windows also offer the energy saving advantage of reducing heat loss and gain. The demountable units are structurally anchored to the frame, relying on a flexible connection and cable between sash and subframe to absorb, rather than resist impact, much as a tree bends with the wind, then returns to its normal position (Figs. 9.18 and 9.19). These specialty storm windows are available as operable or fixed windows. One product incorporates interior miniblinds for exceptional energy efficiency (Figs. 9.20 and 9.21).

Large, fixed glass expanses common in newer buildings and multileaf doors not actively used can be secured using steel cables anchored into the building structure. Patented systems address a variety of facade configurations and are visible at close range, but are not noticeable from exterior grade level view.

BUILDING INTERIORS

Historic interiors often contain carefully designed lobbies and public areas. Elaborate materials and decorative features, such as marbles, mosaics, paneling, and murals, tend to be concentrated at entrances, public circulation spaces, and auditoriums. These spaces should be treated in a manner that preserves the gracious and open feeling of the original design intent and protects decorative elements, to every extent possible, from damage or insensitive alteration.

Photographic documentation can provide details should damaged areas need repair in the future. Any new designs to be incorporated into major public spaces should, to the extent possible, eliminate the intrusive appearance of bulky or awkward security scanning devices.

New products are constantly entering the market to enhance interior and exterior building security. Basic surveillance and monitoring systems may eventually be supplanted with "smart building" technologies seamlessly incorporated into new buildings. Numerous security surveillance systems are available for museum and corporate research facilities to monitor the personnel movement in a building

FIGURE 9.18   Interior view of blast-resistant storm windows. They are designed to contain flying debris, preserve the historic character of building exteriors and interiors, admit daylight, offer energy savings and, with operable product options, allow fresh air inside the building. (*Source: Oldcastle-Arpal, Inc., courtesy of the General Services Administration.*)

FIGURE 9.19 Exterior view illustrates that the appearance of the restored sash is unaffected by storm window assembly on the inside of the opening. Original window frames built into the masonry are securely attached and require no reinforcement. (*Source: Oldcastle-Arpal, Inc., courtesy of the General Services Administration.*)

and on a campus. Separate, freestanding screening facilities located at the edge of a property can screen visitors and admit employees with appropriate electronic badges, eliminating the need to modify ceremonial entrances.

Interior Wall Treatments

Proprietary lining systems are available that impart shatter-resistance to existing interior walls to protect building occupants from flying debris. Wall liners are also used to catch shattering glass in blast curtains. However, the heavy weight generally requires extensive support and armature. To be fully effective, blast curtains must remain in a closed position. Shatter-resistant storm panels are more appropriate for interior window openings.

Wall Liners

This ceramic-based material knits smaller construction units together as a membrane. Injury to employees occupying renovated areas of the Pentagon was greatly reduced by a proprietary lining that had been installed under the new wall surfaces (Table 9.19).

Wall liners are effective for extensive rehabilitation in secondary areas with nonornamental surfaces, but may not be practical for small remodeling projects. They are not appropriate for use on ornamental finishes or in significant spaces, such as historic lobbies.

FIGURE 9.20 General view of demountable blast-resistant storm windows with built-in blinds offering convenient control of daylight and exceptional energy efficiency. (*Source: Chad Randl, National Park Service.*)

FIGURE 9.21 Detail view of demountable blast-resistant storm windows with built-in blinds to control daylight. (*Source: Chad Randl, National Park Service.*)

Protection of interior spaces and building structure against a bomb carried into a lobby does not depend on installing blast-resistant enclosures within the lobby, but rather on reinforcing the walls and structure as necessary to prevent undermining the building's structural integrity. Such structural modifications should always be on the rear, or less significant face of the wall, typically within office space. If, as part of a major rehabilitation, wall linings are used where paneling is also present, the paneling should be reinstalled over the new lining materials (Table 9.19).

TABLE 9.19   Lessons Learned from 9/11: Blast-Resistant Windows, Shades, and Wall Liners Reduce Glass Fragmentation Casualties

> Injury to employees occupying renovated areas of the Pentagon was greatly reduced by blast-resistant windows and a proprietary fabric lining that had been installed under the new wall surfaces to prevent fragmentation. Reinforced columns remained in place and office walls hardened in the renovations completed prior to September 11, 2001—including areas immediately adjoining the area of impact—held for 35 minutes prior to collapsing, allowing employees time to vacate the building. Collapsing ceilings and fixtures caused most injuries.

LOBBY SCREENING AND CIRCULATION CONTROL

The Federal Government's P100 Facility Standards specifically call for principal public entrances to remain as such, with the intent of maintaining a gracious entry experience. Rather than relegate visitors to below grade security processing areas, ceremonial lobbies can be thoughtfully modified to provide appropriate protection for building occupants, while continuing to serve their intended function.

Security Desks

One positive result of the increased focus on security design is a growing trend toward architectonic treatment of desks as built-in furniture. Increasingly, image-conscious government offices and institutions are aware of the impact security design, good and bad, has on visitors' first impressions of an organization. Architecturally integrated desks, fabricated in finishes of comparable quality to original lobby finishes, visually elevate the security function, encouraging point of contact individuals to serve a concierge role.

The Main Archives Building on the National Mall in Washington, D.C., reminiscent of the Roman Pantheon, illustrates a monumental approach to architecturally integrated circulation control. The semicircular contours and axial placement of the guard desk within the space reinforce the monumental symmetry of the entrance lobby. Attention to detail, color, texture, and linear elements of new features, such as the generous base molding on the desk, maintain visual continuity with the adjoining stone walls (Fig. 9.22).

Desks and security-related enclosures should be designed to conceal computer monitors and other equipment, without substantially increasing the bulkiness of the enclosure. Enclosures should provide

FIGURE 9.22   Semicircular contours and axial placement of the guard desk reinforce the monumental symmetry of this classically inspired entrance lobby. (*Source: National Archives Administration.*)

ample tolerances for removal and replacement of equipment. Desks can be designed and fabricated to accommodate dual orientation and to serve as wayfinding aids.

Security Screening

Architecturally integrating sizable security screening equipment is more challenging. Custom enclosures are an option, but the cost and bulk of architecturally concealing metal detectors, x-ray machines, and circulation control devices, such as turnstiles, in casework is often not feasible. Advancing technology can rapidly render equipment obsolete, thus discouraging investments in elaborate housings and custom enclosures, especially for items, such as magnetometers, likely to be replaced by smaller compact models or larger high performance products.

A better approach, where spatial configuration permits, is locating security-processing functions in ancillary space (Fig. 9.23). Rather than bypass ceremonial entrance lobbies, as interstate exchanges bypass town centers, entrance lobbies can provide gracious queuing space or receiving areas for visitors, after security screening is complete. Design goals should include

- Creating effective security and an inviting first impression
- Providing ample security control, queuing space, and appropriate amenities
- Using quality materials and detailing reflecting the building's noteworthy historic qualities
- Encouraging visitors to enjoy the entrance experience intended by the building's original architects

A second approach is creating transparent barriers, using specialized glazing for doors or partitions, at spatial junctures to provide physical separation with minimal visual impact. For example, at a notable modernist courthouse, butt-jointed laminated glass partitions aligned with the grid of the exterior glass wall discreetly separate the entrance and adjoining elevator lobby, preventing visitors from circumventing security processing to access elevators (Figs. 9.24 to 9.26).

A third approach is an interior expression of the garden wall vehicle barrier concept, combining visitor screening and public amenities. Thoughtfully clustered amenities create a subtle physical separation within a welcoming environment. Various furnishings may be designed to serve as lobby circulation barriers (Table 9.20).

Like the ancillary space approach, this alternative avoids truncating historic lobbies and allows building occupants and visitors to enjoy the originally intended entry experience.

To avoid the appearance of a walled enclosure, furniture groupings should be of nonuniform height and well below eye level to allow open views of the lobby. Where the lobby configuration permits, circulation containment should allow visitors to step into an open queuing area, even if passage into the larger lobby area is restricted. Designers should avoid introducing narrow passageways or chute-like enclosures, even glazed enclosures, directly at the entrance door. Ballistic protection for security screening personnel should be incorporated into screening stations, rather than being used to create a visitor containment chamber (Fig. 9.27).

Combining a variety of elements is recommended over using fewer elements, or a single element, to contain circulation. Combining elements of different heights, depths, and types focuses visitor attention on the amenities rather than the containment function. Like the garden wall barrier ensemble, this concept can be implemented attractively on a large scale by developing a kit of standard amenities adapted with different architectural vocabularies to serve a variety of building styles and types (Fig. 9.28).

CONCLUSION

Protecting historic resources depends equally on operational planning and well-designed change. Planning for extensive security modifications should always begin with a comprehensive risk assessment to arrive at a reasoned approach to physical intervention. Operational and technical improvements should be explored first, to ensure against compromises to the historic character that might be avoided.

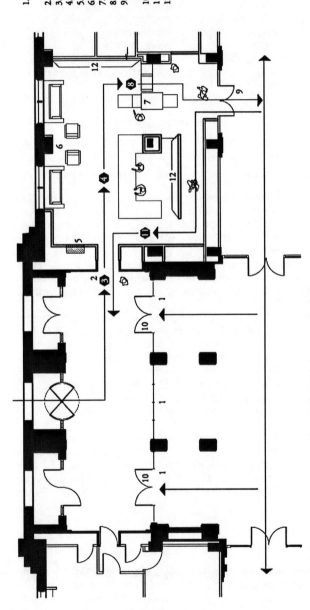

1. Replicated Historic Grill With Electronically Controlled Exists
2. Entrance to Welcome Center
3. Guard / ID Check
4. Visitor / Parent Sign-In
5. ATM
6. Visitor / Parent Waiting Area
7. Line Scanner Stations
8. Magnetometer
9. Controlled Entrance from Welcome Center to Building
10. Exit Points From Building
11. Visitor / Parent Sign-out
12. GSA Information/Display

FIGURE 9.23 Historic vestibule walls or new glass walls can provide separation between entrance screening and principal lobby space. Locating security screening in ancillary space eliminates the need to clutter ceremonial lobbies with screening equipment. (*Source: Gensler Architects, courtesy of the General Services Administration.*)

FIGURE 9.24 Contextually designed glass wall controls circulation by separating elevators from entrance lobby screening. (*Source: General Services Administration.*)

FIGURE 9.25 The butt-jointed glass panels of the glazed security wall have been thoughtfully aligned with the grid of the building's exterior steel and glass wall. (*Source: General Services Administration.*)

FIGURE 9.26   Detail of exterior glass wall in public lobby providing a design vocabulary for the new security wall. (*Source: General Services Administration.*)

TABLE 9.20   Public Amenities Serving as Lobby Circulation Barriers

- Conciergelike security desks
- Way-finding kiosks
- Benches
- Interpretive displays connected by ornamental grilles or low transparent enclosures

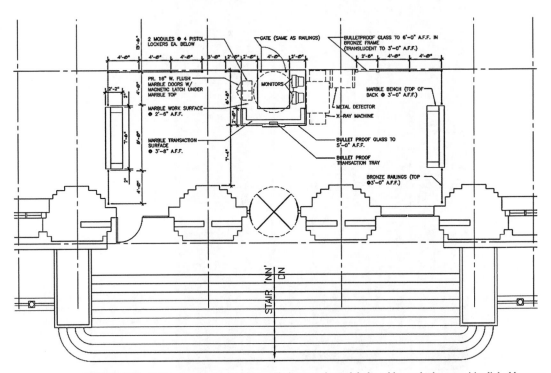

FIGURE 9.27   Lobby plan showing architecturally integrated guard desks, tables, and other amenities linked by ornamental grilles to provide circulation control for courthouses and other security-sensitive occupants. (*Source: van Dijk Westlake Reed Leskosky, courtesy of the General Services Administration.*)

FIGURE 9.28 Furniture groupings separate lobby queuing for security screening from general circulation and maintain unobstructed views of the ceremonial entrance lobby. (*Source: van Dijk Westlake Reed Leskosky, courtesy of the General Services Administration.*)

Architectural modifications should be as reversible as possible and designed contextually, to respect the character-defining qualities of the historic building and site.

Emergency planning, including contingency plans for stabilization and repair with contact lists of consultants and suppliers, can make the critical difference in a building's recovery prospects following a disaster. Established relationships with contractors increase the chances that a building will get prompt attention after an emergency from a firm familiar with the facility. As part of the contingency plan, alternate locations for employee workspace, records, and other building contents should be explored and the adequacy of current insurance coverage assessed.

Readily available design documentation is also important. Copies of archival building records and other visual documents essential to rebuilding should be maintained off-site. Arrangements should be made to develop additional documentation when existing records are incomplete.

With forethought and a skilled, multidisciplinary project team, increased security requirements can be met without compromising the graciousness of important public spaces or fragile beauty of irreplaceable heritage buildings and sites. One promising sign is the quality of architecturally integrated solutions replacing the temporary barriers installed in the aftermath of the Oklahoma City and World Trade Center attacks. Federal design studies and pilot programs have demonstrated the merits of combining innovative urban planning ideas with security design for public places. By seizing opportunities, while improving site security, to create new and welcoming public amenities, building owners, architects, engineers, and planners are making significant contributions to the built environment and increased public safety.

New products are constantly emerging in the marketplace to enhance the quality and appearance of interior and exterior building security. Basic surveillance and monitoring systems may eventually be supplanted with "smart building" technologies, seamlessly incorporated into new construction and renovated facilities. In this environment of raised public expectations and market competition, design professionals can raise the common standard by fueling market demand for greater variety and quality in product choices for retrofitting historic buildings.

With informed, imaginative design, appropriate use of technology, and sensible operational planning, increased safety needs can be met while preserving the unique qualities of historic buildings and sites for future generations.

ACKNOWLEDGMENTS

The authors wish to thank the design firms, creative minds, and technical experts who contributed to the model design solutions illustrated in this chapter:

- Paul Westlake, FAIA, principal, and project designers Amy Dibner, AIA, and Nick Doichev, AIA of van Dijk Westlake Reed Leskosky, authors of the study extensively drawn from in the chapter's guidance on integrating landscape, architecture, and urban design in perimeter barrier systems, including the perimeter security "kit of parts" and prototype lobby screening enclosure

- Neil Dean, landscape architect, Sasaki Associates, Inc.
- Lorraine Lin, blast expert, Hinman Consulting Engineers
- Larry Prickett, structural consultant, Barber & Hoffman, for their contributions to the perimeter security prototype
- Bill Spack, AIA, Cox Graae+Spack (formerly KressCox Associates), creator of the Federal Triangle garden wall concept
- Project team BTA Architects, Design Consultant; Rhodeside & Harwell, Inc., Landscape Architect; A Morton Thomas, Civil Engineering; and Hinman Consulting, Security Consultant
- Suman Sorg, FAIA, Eric Cook, RA and T. David Bell, AIA of Sorg and Associates, PC; for coordinating the ground-breaking study and charrette to generate architecturally integrated solutions for Federal Triangle security
- Michael Van Valkenburgh Associates, designers of the National Capital Planning Commission vision for security in public spaces surrounding the White House

The authors are also grateful to the following for sharing their technical expertise on window and wall retrofit and reinforcement technology:

- Moty Emek of Oldcastle-Arpal, LLC
- Ken White of Armor Holdings, Inc.
- Peter James of CLS Cintec

The concepts for integrating historic preservation policy and standards with the upgrading of historic buildings for security purposes began just after September 11, 2001 with the formation of the National Park Service sponsored conference "Our Public Safety and Historic Places; Balancing Public Safety and the Protection of Historic Places and Collections." Envisioned by the leadership of the NPS Associate Director for Cultural Resources, thanks are extended to

- Fran P. Mainella, Director of the National Park Service
- Katherine H. Stevenson, then Associate Director for Cultural Resources
- deTeel Patterson Tiller, Deputy Associate Director for Cultural Resources
- John Robbins, Assistant Director, Cultural Resources
- Constance Werner Ramirez, NPS National Preservation Institute

For further work and support on the topic, thanks are extended to NPS staff, including

- H. Bryan Mitchell, Chief, Heritage Preservation Services
- David W. Look, AIA, NPS Pacific Great Basin Support Office
- Michael Auer and Chad Randl, Technical Preservation Services staff
- Claire S. Mastroberardino, and National Conference of State Historic Preservation Officers staff, who contributed invaluable time, technical knowledge, and support

The vision behind the model solutions began with a committed group of federal design and preservation professionals determined to maintain inviting, attractive, and safe public spaces through imaginative and resourceful problem solving. Contributing GSA staff include

- Bayard Whitmore, Project Manager for the perimeter barrier prototype, historical architect with the Center for Historic Buildings
- Pamela Wilczynski, Midwest Region Project Manager

- Regina Nally, Midwest Regional Historic Preservation Officer
- Philip Wagner, National Capital Region (NCR) Project Manager for GSA's 1997 Federal Triangle security master plan
- Susan Sylvester, NCR Project Manager, and Donna Twinam, NCR, for the *Culture and Commerce* study
- Andrea Mones-O'Hara, NCR Regional Historic Preservation Officer, for initiating the two Triangle studies and the championing architecturally integrated security design
- Thomas Grooms, Program Manager for Federal Design Initiatives, for putting together the Triangle charrette team
- GSA Security Engineers, Bruce Hall and Steven Smith, Program Manager for GSA's Glass Fragmentation program, Office of the Chief Architect

The perimeter barrier prototype study was sponsored by GSA's Center for Historic Buildings and would not have been possible without the support of

- Edward A. Feiner, FAIA, Chief Architect, Public Buildings Service, GSA
- Rolando Rivas-Camp, AIA, Director, Center for Historic Buildings

National Capital Planning Commission project team members for the National Capital Urban Design and Security Plan include

- Elizabeth Miller, Project Officer
- William Dowd, Director, Office of Plans Review
- George Toop, Urban Designer
- Paul Jutton, Graphic Designer
- Edel Perez, Jeffrey Hinkle, Eugene Keller, and Kenneth Walton, Community Planners
- Nancy Witherell, Historic Preservation Specialist
- Marybeth Murphy, writer/editor

Other important contributors include

- Thomas Walton, Ph.D, Associate Dean, Catholic University School of Architecture and Planning, writer/editor of the Triangle charrette report
- Ron Anzalone of the Advisory Council on Historic Preservation

The views and opinions expressed in this chapter are those of the authors and do not necessarily reflect the policies of all agencies within the federal government.

GLOSSARY

bollard An upright structural element typically made of concrete or steel, serving as a traffic barrier. Security bollards have deeply set foundations and are designed to resist ramming impacts.

berm A low-lying slope or ledge in a narrow band intended to shield an area or create a barrier.

historic structures report A comprehensive preservation planning document outlining a property's history, evolution, original appearance, and current condition with guidelines for restoration and repair, often prepared as part of a rehabilitation or restoration project.

photolaser scanning A digitized point cloud process for recording three-dimensional surfaces. This process is advantageous for sculptural objects or large decorative elements, where two-dimensional traditional photographs would not show depth or reveal in surfaces. This is a computerized method of recording, requiring sophisticated software, technicians, and equipment.

plinth The continuous base of a wall or the blocks on which a column or vertical element rests.

standoff distance A recommended setback from the public right of way; 50 feet for most public buildings. High-risk occupancies require a 100 foot setback.

BIBLIOGRAPHY

General Services Administration, *Culture and Commerce: Bridging the Federal Triangle,* prepared by KressCox Associates (Cox, Graae+Spack), December 2000. Concept design for public space activation surrounding the Ronald Reagan Building and International Trade Center, Washington, D.C. Includes a master plan and conceptual design for integrating security enhancements, landscape, and urban planning into the outdoor spaces of the Federal Triangle.

General Services Administration, *Perimeter Security for Historic Buildings: Technical Pilot,* prepared by van Dijk Westlake Reed Leskosky, 2003.

General Services Administration, *Urban Design Guidelines for Physical Perimeter and Entrance Security: An Overlay to the Master Plan for the Federal Triangle,* prepared by Sorg and Associates, PC, 1998. Includes draft GSA security criteria, urban design parameters, general design principals, a master plan and conceptual design for integrating security enhancements, landscape design, and urban planning into the outdoor spaces of the Federal Triangle in Washington, D.C.

General Services Administration, *Vision & Voice—Design Excellence in Federal Architecture: Building a Legacy,* Center for Design Excellence and the Arts, Office of the Chief Architect, December 2002. Reflections of great American architects and Design Excellence program founders on the 40th anniversary of the Guiding Principals for Federal Architecture.

National Capital Planning Commission, *The National Capital Urban Design and Security Plan,* prepared by Michael Van Valkenburgh Associates, 2003.

National Park Service, *CRM Bulletin,* (Cultural Resource Management Bulletin), Washington, D.C. vol. 24, no. 8. Cultural Resources Protection and Emergency Planning, 2002, and Vol. 23 No. 6. Disaster Planning, 2001. Both periodical issues contain articles dealing with protecting cultural resources during various disasters. Bibliography available. http://crm.cr.nps.gov/issueindex.cfm

National Park Service, U.S. Department of the Interior, *The Secretary of the Interior's Standards for Rehabilitation & Illustrated Guidelines for Rehabilitating Historic Buildings,* reprinted in 1997. This richly illustrated book contains case studies and how-to examples for historic property rehabilitation. Available from the Government Printing Office in printed format (GPO stock Number 024-005-01091, $13.00), and on the Web: http://www2.cr.nps.gov/tps/standguide/rehab/

Nelson, Carl L, *Protecting the Past from Natural Disasters,* National Trust for Historic Preservation, Washington, D.C., 1991. Covers all types of natural disasters, with good bibliography.

Spennemann, Dirk H. R., and David W. Look, eds., *Disaster Management Programs for Historic Sites,* U.S. National Park Service, Western Chapter of the Association for Preservation Technology, San Francisco, Calif. and the Johnstone Centre, Charles Sturt University, Albury, Australia, 1998. Includes proceedings of the 1997 San Francisco symposium of the same name; articles on protecting historic sites after a disaster and protection planning.

STANDARDS

The following are standards for design and documentation:

Facility Standards for the Public Buildings Service, General Services Administration 2003.
www.gsa.gov/p100

Historic American Building Survey
http://www.cr.nps.gov/habshaer/pubs/guide.htm

National Register of Historic Places
http://www.cr.nps.gov/nr/listing.htm

Secretary of the Interior's Standards for the Treatment of Historic Properties
http://www2.cr.nps.gov/tps/standguide/index.htm

TECHNICAL INFORMATION

GSA Historic Preservation Technical
Procedures
A searchable database of information on the
maintenance and repair of historic materials
organized using the Construction Specifications
Institute (CSI) format. Under the search feature,
enter Historic Preservation Technical
Procedures for specific materials entries.
http://www.gsa.gov/Portal/home.jsp

NPS Preservation Briefs
Over 40 technical bulletins are available from
the Government Printing Office
http://www2.cr.nps.gov/tps/briefs/presbhom.htm

Whole Building Design Guide:
A searchable Web site dedicated to the systematic
planning of whole buildings, including security
upgrades to existing buildings and new construction. Provides a single portal for access
to government standards and design guides,
technical resources and product information.
http://www.wbdg.org

INTERNET RESOURCES

Armor Holdings, Inc
Manufacturer of blast resistant curtains to
prevent damage and injury by glass
fragmentation and window detachment
www.protecharmored.com/systems/blastshield

Association for Preservation Technology
www.apti.org

CLC Cintec, Inc.
Manufacturer of a steel and epoxy-grout structural
reinforcement system for exterior walls and
openings to prevent structural failure caused
by a seismic or blast stress.
www.cintec.com

GlassLock
Anchored window film system manufactured by
Western Glass Restraint Systems, Inc.
www.glasslock.com

KEVLAR® A lightweight, strong, flexible fiber
made by Dupont can be used as a shatter
resistant wall lining.
www.kevlar.com

National Park Service
www.nps.gov

National Trust for Historic Preservation
www.nationaltrust.org

Oldcastle-Arpal, Inc.
Manufacturer of Arpal operable laminated glass
windows, storm windows, and Blast-Tec cable
reinforcement system for large windows and
glass expanses.
www.oldcastlearpal.com

Safetydrape
Blast-resistant fabric curtains available in a
wide range of custom colors for decorative
and institutional applications
www.safetydrape.com

Thermolite, Inc.
Manufacturer of blast resistant, laminated glass
storm window with built in mini-blinds for
sunlight control.
http://www.thermolite.com

3M Manufacturing
Manufactures window films for safety and
security. There are a number of films,
adhesives and methods of integrating
these products.
www.3m.com/US/index

U.S. General Services Administration
Public Buildings Service
www.gsa.gov

CHAPTER 10
HOSPITALITY FACILITY SECURITY

Bradley D. Schulz, AIA
Principal, KGA Architecture
Las Vegas, Nevada

*Adversity is merely an obstacle; those who are wise
simply walk through it.*   ERIC STRIFE

Hospitality properties, encompassing hotels, motels, casinos, conference centers, and resorts, are designed to be open and welcoming to guests, visitors, and the public. For these same reasons, they are vulnerable to crime, terrorism, and violence. With large volumes of transient travelers arriving by car, taxicab, public transportation, and on foot, many with luggage and packages, hospitality venues must be thorough in developing comprehensive security plans to remain safe and pleasant places to stay. The challenge to owners, facility managers, and designers is balancing transparent and visible security measures to make visitors and guests feel comfortable and safe.

In order for a design team to plan and design effective solutions for new or renovated hospitality facilities, all project team members must understand the potential threats, policies, functions, and security concerns. The primary security concerns in hospitality design are to protect the security of guests and employees; the facility; and at gaming properties, known as casinos, the gaming license. These factors must be considered during facility design and security planning. Concentration on any one aspect of security, to the exclusion of the others, could leave the facility vulnerable.

THREAT ASSESSMENT

After September 11, 2001, terrorism is the overwhelming concern among hospitality property owners and managers. Threat and vulnerability assessments assist in identifying potential problems and appropriate security solutions, through design, technology, and operational policies and procedures.

Terrorist acts are difficult to predict, but the hierarchy of targets is readily identifiable. For example, government buildings and landmarks symbolizing American democracy are considered targets. Similarly, higher-profile facilities, such as a large gaming property or a major city convention hotel, are potentially more vulnerable than a motel in a quiet rural area. Location, ownership, and the potential of major disruption are all factors to be considered during the threat assessment and vulnerability analysis.

Location

In real estate, the three most important factors are "location, location, location." The same concept applies when assessing hospitality property security threats. Key factors include the city location, as some American and international cities are considered more at risk than others; where in the city the property is located; proximity to other structures or monuments; and proximity to transportation facilities.

Ownership

Property ownership, whether individual or corporate, should be reviewed during a threat assessment. Nationality, race, or religious background of an individual owner can pose security risks. For corporate owners, affiliations and international relationships should be reviewed, as they may increase threat and risk levels.

Type of Threat

Potential threats to a hospitality facility can be by explosive device or fire. In addition, these facilities are susceptible to biological threats, such as airborne hazards, contaminated water systems, and tainted food supply. Guests and employees are exposed to theft and personal injury. Personnel should be familiar with policies and procedures to be followed when any of these threats occur. Policies and procedures should change based on national threat levels. More severe restrictions are required at higher levels than at lower levels.

Facility design and location of new and existing properties will determine appropriate security protection measures. These factors leave a facility vulnerable to threats, which could be from an individual, group, vehicle, or direct attack by military weapons (Table 10.1 and Figs. 10.1 to 10.3).

OPERATIONAL ISSUES

Security in hospitality facilities relies on how owners and facility managers operate their facilities, and the policies and procedures in place for guests, employees, consultants, and vendors.

TABLE 10.1 Hospitality Facility Security Concerns

Building type	Characteristics and security concern
Downtown properties	• Extend to city sidewalks. • Vulnerable to vehicular impact or truck bomb parked on a street.
Large resort and gaming properties	• Facility is generally open to the public. • Vulnerable due to multiple entry points and openness. • Flow, collection, and storage of money.
Entry Porte Cocheres	• Roofed structures extending from the building entrance over an adjacent driveway sheltering those getting in or out of vehicles. • Vulnerable to bomb blast. (A taxicab loaded with explosives could pull into a porte cochere without much scrutiny.)
Service and delivery areas	• Used around the clock. • Many larger facilities have construction and renovation projects going on almost continuously. • Heavy vendor traffic.
Convention facilities	• Have exhibits coming from all parts of the world. • Large numbers of people in a single location.
Garages	• Less visible and harder to protect.

FIGURE 10.1   Photo of urban hotel. (*Source: KGA Architecture.*)

Industrial Intelligence

Large properties conduct their own intelligence, with sophisticated security forces and highly trained personnel to analyze current world affairs and update threat assessments through global intelligence networks. This, along with continuous training, keeps their security force up-to-date with the latest in intelligence and technology. Smaller properties rely on alerts broadcast from law enforcement and intelligence services. They may use outsourced agencies or in-house security forces, based on threat assessments tailored for each location.

Workforce Issues

Physical protection of hotel properties, regardless of size and location, begins with sound hiring practices. All facilities are vulnerable to employee activities. Background checks for all employees, regardless of their job descriptions, should be conducted. Many facilities also require suppliers, or any contracted company with access to a facility, to perform background checks on their employees (Table 10.2).

GENERAL SECURITY DESIGN ISSUES

Large and small properties must carefully address several design elements and operational issues to maximize security for guests and employees.

Parking Garages

Garages should be designed with space at entrances to allow for inspection of vehicles without causing traffic to back up. Surveillance cameras should be positioned to cover public and employee parking areas. Emergency call boxes should be provided. Bike patrols are used in large garages at major properties.

FIGURE 10.2   Photo of large gaming facility. (*Source: KGA Architecture.*)

FIGURE 10.3   Photo of porte cochere at major hotel (*Source: KGA Architecture.*)

TABLE 10.2   9/11 Lessons Learned: Employee Background Checks

> After September 11, 2001, background checks, once considered a minor issue, are increasingly required for many workplaces, as any employee could be a link to terrorism or theft. Large gaming properties have a workforce of several thousand people, with a 15 percent annual turnover rate or greater. At these properties, background checks are routinely required for all employees, tied through several law enforcement agencies. Screening usually extends a minimum of five years, while checks on key employees often go back ten years. Thorough background checks can also reduce employee pilferage and theft from guests.

Loading Docks

Loading docks should be designed to allow for observation of all trucks entering the dock area. The preferred way to monitor a dock area is to provide a security checkpoint at the entrance to the dock before any trucks enter.

Entries

Hospitality properties have many entrances for the public, employees, and services. Entry porte cocheres should not be built under occupied floors, because floors above a porte cochere would be unprotected from a car or truck bomb. Public entry doors should be arranged to allow direct visual or camera views. All doors into the property other than these public entries should be locked. Fire exits should be monitored so that alarms sound if opened; hardware should prevent access from the outside. Employee and vendor access should be through designated doors monitored by security personnel and cameras. Vendors should be registered by the facility, and issued photo identification. No one, other than employees, should be allowed access to back house areas unless escorted.

Lobby areas

Lobby design should provide space for personnel to screen and monitor those who enter a hotel, especially during evening hours. In addition to cameras, many large urban hotels ask guests to show room keys to enter the facility or room tower, a function impacting lobby design and the number of public entries.

Surveillance

Large properties install cameras in sensitive locations and at entrances, with pan, tilt, and zoom capabilities, for maximum surveillance. Gaming properties often install several hundred cameras, each connected to a tape machine or digital recording devices. Smaller properties may have only a few cameras, but each is important in maintaining video records of events, especially if later analysis is required after an incident. Training of personnel is the key to sound security

Employee and Workforce Issues

Hotels and larger gaming properties should be designed to segregate employees, depending on job descriptions. All employees would have access to certain areas, such as the employee dining room, but they would not have access to the entire facility. Segregation limits the number of people with access to all areas. Food and beverage employees should have access to kitchen and storage areas only. Casino workers should have access to the casino only. Cage (cashier) workers on the casino floor should access money areas only.

At larger facilities, segregation means employees see fewer faces and recognize people who belong in an area. Seeing unfamiliar faces should raise concern. Policies should require employees to report seeing unfamiliar personnel in staff areas.

Money Areas

The flow, collection, and storage of money drives many planning and design decisions, circulation routes, and building materials. Access to money handling routes should be minimized to as few employees as possible. All point of sale positions should be under video surveillance, with automatic camera activation when the register or point of sale device is used.

All sales transactions should be recorded and available for review at a later date if necessary. Employees who are aware that their actions are being watched and recorded will be less likely to steal, especially in high volume bar areas. "Instant-on" emergency lighting should be provided at all point of sale locations. If power goes off, there should never be a time of total darkness, even the 10 to 15 seconds for power from emergency generators to restart. "Instant-on" fixtures must be on battery backup systems.

Biological Hazards

Airborne hazards can result from small amounts of toxic agents and can cause a major incident. Mechanical systems should be designed with filters and detectors that can shut off systems when necessary. This is not cost effective for smaller properties, but risk factors based on size, location, and functions, must be considered. Outside air vents to mechanical systems should be carefully located to minimize access by intruders.

Biological agents in water systems are not easily detected, but water can be controlled and shut off once a hazard is identified. Tainted food can cause a large-scale problem, and might be traced from the food distributor or potentially from the kitchen staff. A tainted food delivery would not be easily or immediately detected. Thus, ongoing in-house intelligence efforts and employee background checks are important.

Emergency Power

Hospitality facilities have a high need for many areas to be lit in the event of a power outage. Areas with need for high security, gaming areas, and points of sale, should be protected with standby power. The amount of time a facility needs to run on standby and emergency power depends on historical data regarding power outages, weather conditions, and threat perception. The length of time a generator runs is solely dependent on the amount of fuel stored. The sizing of the fuel tank should take into consideration the availability of diesel fuel in normal and emergency situations.

Backup battery power systems or uninterrupted power systems (UPS) should be provided for all electronic systems, including gaming tracking, points of sale, phones, and key surveillance locations. Due to the functions and nature of activities occurring in hotels and gaming facilities, backup requirements are all in addition to code-required life safety emergency power.

Command Centers

Large gaming properties typically include central command centers, independent from code-required fire command centers. As the nerve center of the facility, these operational hubs are located deep within the property, away from exterior walls, which can more readily be breached. Rooms are constructed as bunkers, surrounded by large amounts of reinforced concrete.

Independent air supply, water, and power sources are provided, along with several days of food storage, supplies, and sleeping areas if necessary. Separate phone and data lines, including satellite communication, are installed to allow monitoring all aspects of the facility from the command center, and to direct operations from the command center in the event of an attack. Monitoring can also be done remotely in an offsite location. This redundancy allows for more flexibility, but also leaves the facility vulnerable to external hacking, or unauthorized access to computer and other vital building systems.

SPECIFIC SECURITY DESIGN ISSUES

Various hospitality facilities have unique security concerns, based on operational, site, and design factors.

Hotels and Resorts

The extent of security measures implemented to protect guests and employees is a decision made by property owners, who may weigh the costs of potential lawsuits against the costs of protection. Guests must be secure in public areas and private areas, such as guest room corridors, which should be monitored by video surveillance. Guest room towers should be accessible only by showing or activating a room key in the elevator.

Doors in emergency stair shafts should be locked, preventing access from the stair back into the corridor. This is subject to review by local code enforcement authorities. Guests must be protected in parking lots and pool areas, especially from local trespassers, through a combination of cameras and security personnel.

Downtown Properties

Due to the lack of area around the facility, downtown properties must incorporate hardening of facades and structural systems to distribute loads if one or more columns are weakened or destroyed by bomb blast, enabling the structure to remain standing while occupants evacuate.

Large Resort Properties

Large resort properties usually have room towers surrounded by low-rise areas that can potentially shield high-rise towers from a truck bomb. These properties are more vulnerable due to the amount of area involved, multiple entry points, and general openness of the facility.

Gaming Properties

Gaming properties must have a license to operate, and meet requirements to ensure the license is not jeopardized. Effective security results from integrating design, technology, and operations with policies and carefully screened personnel who handle money.

Slot, or gaming, machines are secured by locking devices.   When the machines are opened for coin collection or maintenance, at least two employees must be in the immediate area. Chips at table games are secured under glass when the game is not in use. Several cameras view each hand played at table games, including the dealer's. Cash placed on the table is exchanged for chips. The cash is pushed through a slot in the table and dropped into a lock box. These boxes are collected periodically and replaced by empty boxes.

The lock boxes containing cash are taken from the floor to "count" rooms, where money is counted. Boxes are loaded on a cart, pulled by an electric "mule." The cart is escorted by at least two guards, and is followed by video surveillance along the route. The entrance to the "cage," or main cashier area, should include a security checkpoint. Movement of cash in these areas should occur at different times on different days. Predictability makes money more vulnerable to theft.

The money room should be accessed through a vestibule known as a man trap, which functions similar to a sally port. A man trap is a small room or hall with a door at each end. Each door has an electric strike that can be opened by either a keypad or by switch within the vault area. Only one door can be opened at a time. If the first door is open, the second door cannot be unlocked. Only when the first door is locked behind the money cart can the second door be opened (Fig. 10.4). After going through the man trap, the cart is taken to either hard or soft count areas. The hard count is for coins; the soft count is for counting currency, or bills.

Vaults should be provided for storage of coins and currency, built with masonry walls and solid ceilings. Count rooms may be of stud construction, with a wire mesh between the drywall and the studs. Access to the money room from outside the facility should occur only through the back of house or service areas, and even then, by a short and direct circulation route, separated from other back-of-house functions.

Armored vehicles should be allowed to enter the facility via a sally port, which functions like a man trap. The vehicle enters the facility, and the exterior door closes before the lock on the interior door is released. Identities of the vehicle and officers are verified by camera before the inner door is opened. The vehicle can then be loaded or unloaded within the protected sally port.

Facial Recognition Technology. Video surveillance and trained security personnel are the best ways to identify those trying to cheat the games or steal from guests. Theft from gaming devices can be accomplished through use of devices to fool the machine or by using counterfeit coins or currency. This is usually detected by direct visual means or by unusual payout patterns from the machine. Payouts outside the norm are scrutinized and machines checked. Theft from other patrons is usually accomplished by slight of hand or distraction. Most gaming properties employ people, who, at one time, made their living as cheats. These "reformed" cheats are well suited to detect other cheats.

The biometric facial recognition technology used to identify terrorists is also used to detect known gaming cheats, although they are relatively few in number within the gaming industry. This technology works best when combined with continued surveillance. Suspected cheats are detected first by trained personnel. Once a person has reason to be under surveillance, they are continually tracked on camera, with full facial shots, so that images can be analyzed by computer to see if they match anyone in a database of known cheats. However, those trained in this field often recognize a cheat before the computer makes a match.

LITIGATION ISSUES

Ensuring that properties are safe from crime and personal injury is important for all building owners. Many individuals and groups perceive hospitality facilities as easy litigation targets. Fraudulent

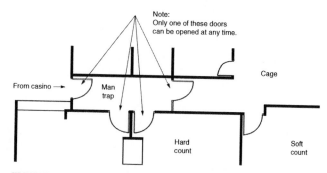

FIGURE 10.4 Schematic diagram of a mantrap. (*Source: KGA Architecture.*)

TABLE 10.3   Minimizing Slip and Fall Hazards in Hospitality Facilities

1. Single-step conditions invite falls and should be avoided.
2. Flooring materials should not be overly slick or uneven.
3. Flooring materials on stairs or steps should provide good footing.
4. Doors requiring large amounts of force to open can lead to injury.
5. Handrails and guardrails should be designed for ease of use, especially for the handicapped, and not in a way that would confuse the guests and visitors.
6. Too often in hotels, materials are selected for looks and style, instead of function. Good design combines aesthetics and functional needs.

"slip and fall" claims, involving doors, escalators, wet floors, and other situations, are a frequent occurrence, especially at gaming properties. Good design, ongoing surveillance, and well-trained employees are the best ways to address this issue and reduce claims. Several effective design strategies can minimize slip and fall hazards (Table 10.3).

CONCLUSION

Hospitality security is a complex issue that must address people, property, and, in some cases, large amounts of cash. To keep facilities open and welcoming environments for numerous guests, suppliers, and visitors, security must be more transparent, not visible to the public eye, than in many other public building types.

Securing hotels, resorts, and gaming facilities from most threats depends on a careful integration of design, trained personnel, and appropriate technology. Until the public is willing to live with more fortified facilities, owners in the hotel and hospitality industry will determine the limits and costs for how secure individual facilities need to be.

INTERNET RESOURCES

American Hotel and Lodging Association
www.ahla.com

Hotels Magazine
www.hotelsmag.com

KGA Architecture
www.kga-architects.com

Lodging Magazine
www.lodgingmagazine.com

CHAPTER 11

MULTIFAMILY HOUSING: SECURITY CHECKLIST FOR BUILDING OWNERS AND REAL ESTATE PROFESSIONALS

James W. Harris

Former Vice President, Property Management
National Multi Housing Council/National Apartment Association
Joint Legislative Program
Washington, D.C.

*There is no good reason why we should fear the future, but
there is every reason why we should face it seriously, neither
hiding from ourselves the gravity of the problems before us,
nor fearing to approach these problems with the unbending,
unflinching purpose to solve them aright.*
                                THEODORE ROOSEVELT (1858–1919)
                            Inaugural Address, 6th U.S. president 1905

Building owners, real estate professionals, and apartment management executives reviewed and adjusted their property operating procedures and security features after September 11, 2001. New York City apartments in Lower Manhattan, adjacent to the World Trade Center, were not the only properties affected by the attacks that day. Subsequent warnings from the Federal Bureau of Investigation (May 2002) and the Department of Homeland Security (February 2003) identifying apartments as possible soft targets, or even staging grounds, for terrorist attacks made security a higher priority for all apartment properties.

   This chapter provides a series of optional checklists of specific operating considerations found in management guidance issued by the National Multi Housing Council/National Apartment Association Joint Legislative Program (NMHC/NAA JLP). These operating considerations are an optional resource only and do not constitute a standard of care for industry operations—owners and firms may accept, reject, or improve on individual considerations listed here at their discretion (Tables 11.1 to 11.8).

TABLE 11.1   Operating Considerations for Management of Multifamily Housing Properties

1. Internal reporting
2. Resident communications
3. Unit inspections
4. Contractors and employees
5. Resident applicant verification
6. Cooperation with law enforcement
7. Community security measures

Source: NMHC/NAA JLP.

TABLE 11.2   Internal Reporting Checklist

1. Share public information about terrorism-related developments affecting apartments with all on-site management and instruct them to make all employees aware of the information.
2. Advise all employees and contractors to be vigilant and aware of any suspicious behavior with respect to property, residents, and prospective residents.
3. Report any suspicious activity to the local FBI field office. Ask to speak to the representative with the Joint Terrorism Task Force. A list of those offices can be found at www.fbi.gov.
4. To better understand nuclear, chemical, and biological risks and response, property management executives and staff may want to browse the Department of Homeland Security's public preparedness web site at www.ready.gov/get_informed.html.

Source: NMHC/NAA JLP.

TABLE 11.3   Resident Communications Checklist

1. Encourage residents who believe they have witnessed something suspicious to contact the FBI field offices first, but also to notify you as well.
2. Send a letter or e-mail message to residents and/or put a message in the community newsletter or on the community Web site from management, in the event of major news coverage of terrorism related to apartments.
3. Encourage resident-to-resident communications through resident social and information events, and crime safety awareness programs.
4. Per FBI guidance, be aware of student residents who do not appear to leave the property to attend classes.
5. Take steps to address concerns of residents who complain about being subjected to harassing behavior by other residents and guests on the basis of various protected classes under the Fair Housing Act. The Department of Housing and Urban Development (HUD) addressed this issue in guidance provided in January, 2003, as follows:

> *Landlords and property managers are working to keep their buildings safe, but at the same time they are responsible for making sure their efforts do not infringe on the fair housing rights of current or potential residents...While landlords must be responsive to complaints from tenants, they should be careful to take action against residents only on the basis of legitimate property management concerns. Landlords should consider whether a complaint may actually be motivated by race, religion, or national origin.*

> "Rights and Responsibilities of Landlords and Residents in Preventing Housing Discrimination Based on Race, Religion, or National Origin in the Wake of the Events of September 11, 2001," January 6, 2003, www.hud.gov/offices/fheo/library/sept11.cfm. State laws also may treat repeated harassment as a hate crime.

Source: NMHC/NAA JLP.

TABLE 11.4   Unit Inspections Checklist

1. Inspect occupied units, where permitted under local law, providing notice where appropriate under the lease and/or local law.
2. Inspect all vacant units regularly to make sure they are vacant and secured.
3. During inspections of common areas and property grounds, look for suspicious or prohibited materials or unauthorized occupants. The FBI has told real estate owners to be on the lookout for items that can be used for pipe bombs, such as gunpowder, PVC or metal piping, nails, and dismantled kitchen timers. Firearms or ammunition and industrial-grade chemicals may also require closer inspection.
4. Expand daily property-wide tours to include a viewing of all building perimeters to inspect for any suspicious materials or evidence of any invasive undertakings on the building exteriors.

Source: NMHC/NAA JLP.

TABLE 11.5   Contractors and Employees Checklist

1. Review work performed by contractors on a regular basis, perhaps daily. In particular, contractor work in nonpublic areas should be closely inspected.
2. Require that contractors both screen employees for prior criminal history and bond employees.
3. Consider reviewing existing contractor and employee verification procedures for compliance with applicable law—including background checks, background check authorization forms, and compliance with applicable noncitizen work eligibility laws—and ensure that appropriate documentation is on file.

Source: NMHC/NAA JLP.

TABLE 11.6   Resident Applicant Verification Checklist

1. Require each adult occupant to complete an application.
2. Verify the identification prospective residents provide when leasing an apartment. Criminal background search firms and similar service providers offer these services. Law enforcement representatives have emphasized that a signed lease can provide proof of occupancy for residents for other circumstances, such as obtaining a driver's license and other official documents.
3. Require original documents to prove identity. Some law enforcement representatives have cautioned about the possibility of applicant fraud where duplicate documents are presented with rental housing applications. Note, however, that state privacy laws may prohibit an owner from requiring a Social Security number as a condition of the application process. Applicants may choose to provide valid, unexpired, alternative identification to the Social Security number from work visas, passports, and other sources.
4. Review existing applicant files for Social Security numbers, work visas, and other identification numbers provided by applicants for possible fraud, such as shared identification numbers by two or more people and/or mismatch between identification number and other applicant information.
5. Know that it is not a violation of the Fair Housing Act to ask applicants to document their citizenship or immigration status during the screening process, as noted by HUD in its January 2003 guidance. (For federally assisted properties, know that HUD regulations define what kind of documents are considered acceptable evidence of citizenship or eligible immigration status and outline the process for collecting and verifying such documents.) Above all, be sure to apply citizenship documentation procedures uniformly.
6. Verify provided visa and work history information for accuracy, subject to fair housing laws. Individuals with expired visas may be awaiting additional clearance from the U.S. Citizenship and Immigration Services (http://uscis.gov/graphics/index.htm) (formerly the Immigration and Naturalization Service) and thus may be in the country legally, notwithstanding an expired visa.
7. Verify prior addresses provided by the applicant for conformity with available credit and criminal and reference check information.

TABLE 11.6   Resident Applicant Verification Checklist (*Continued*)

8. Request residents to explain any gaps in prior addresses of record. Management may then verify such explanations through criminal history and background checks.
9. Undertake individual applicant checks on each individual resident applicant participating in a corporate or national guarantor or corporate tenant program.
10. Note any one individual or group renting multiple apartments at the same time.
11. Firms renting to students may choose to require regularly updated evidence of school registration, subject to applicable fair housing laws and/or state or local student protections.
12. Review applicant, resident, and property coinvestor names (and, if available, company name and business information) against Specially Designated Nationals and Blocked Persons List from the Department of Treasury's Office of Foreign Assets Control (OFAC). The list is updated regularly and can be found at www.treasury.gov/offices/enforcement/ofac/sdn/index.html. Some background search firms include this list in their search files.

Source: NMHC/NAA JLP.

TABLE 11.7   Cooperation with Law Enforcement Checklist

1. Maintain open lines of communication with local law enforcement.
2. Review security operating procedures in light of Department of Homeland Security recommended operating procedures appropriate to the applicable Homeland Security Advisory System threat level. Additional information is available at www.dhs.gov.
3. Be cooperative with law enforcement, but respect resident privacy as well. Consider requesting a subpoena or warrant before releasing nonpublic information about a resident to law enforcement.
4. If law enforcement asks management to undertake a file audit of transactions with specific characteristics (e.g., paying the entire lease term up front in cash or residents breaking a lease and leaving early under suspicious circumstances without a forwarding address), then, before cooperating, be sure that any audit conforms with the Fair Housing Act and resident privacy laws. For maximum liability protection, provide such information only under a subpoena or magistrate's order.
5. Understand the protections and obligations created by the USA PATRIOT Act (Pub. L. 107-56). The Act provides important protections to property owners cooperating with law enforcement in terrorism investigations. Section 215 of the act authorizes FBI representatives to obtain "tangible things," including books, records, papers, and other documents, for international terrorism and covert intelligence activity investigations. This section provides immunity from liability for property management who, in good faith, produce documents or other tangible information pursuant to such an order. The FBI must first obtain a magistrate's order in order to exercise its authority under this section. Section 215 could apply to resident and/or employee records. Importantly, under the section, owners and managers may not disclose "to any other person (other than those persons necessary to produce the tangible things under this section) that the FBI has sought or obtained tangible things under this section."

Source: NMHC/NAA JLP.

Section 225 of the Act amends the Foreign Intelligence Surveillance Act (FISA) to provide immunity to apartment owners and other "landlords" who assist law enforcement in FISA-authorized activities. The Act states that no court will accept jurisdiction over a cause of action filed against "any provider of a wire or electronic communication service, landlord, custodian, or other person" that supplies information, facilities, or technical assistance in accordance with a court order or request for emergency assistance authorized under the Act. This broad and important provision allows owners to comply with law enforcement requests for assistance under FISA without risking exposure to lawsuits.

TABLE 11.8 Community Security Measures Checklist

1. Keep nonpublic areas—especially equipment areas, shops, and storage areas—off-limits to all but identified employees and those allowed for specified business purposes with those employees.
2. Manage key and lock control at unit turnover closely. Keep access codes, locks, and keys under tight control, with access limited to identified employees. Report loss of keys, access cards, and codes.
3. Require photo identification when a resident requests a lockout key.
4. Enforce stated "no solicitors" policies.
5. Inventory industrial-grade chemical supplies and materials in each storage area on a regular basis.
6. Review property parking lots for unattended or unauthorized vehicles.
7. Review package delivery procedures and ensure that unclaimed packages are disposed of in a timely fashion. Some firms now require residents to advise the leasing office in advance of a package delivery or management will refuse delivery of the package.
8. Review existing company site emergency recovery plans and recovery programs to ensure that information is understood by site staff and up-to-date. The Department of Homeland Security's public information Web site encourages "individuals and families, schools, daycare providers, workplaces, neighborhoods, and apartment buildings [to] all have site-specific emergency plans." Details on building emergency plans, with special contingencies for high-rise buildings, and family emergency plans can be found at www.ready.gov.

Source: NMHC/NAA JLP.

CONCLUSION

Since September 11, 2001, real estate operators face a new level of public and customer interest in their security features, plans, and procedures. Voluntary operational considerations will undoubtedly evolve over time. While real estate operators can never guarantee security against acts of terrorism, customer and public attention to operators' security programs can be expected to evolve in response to any additional terrorism-related developments.

BIBLIOGRAPHY

Ryan, D.J., "Fair Housing: September 11: What Now?" *Perspective Magazine,* California Apartment Association, Jan./Feb. 2002.

INTERNET RESOURCES

Federal Bureau of Investigation
www.fbi.gov

Department of Homeland Security—Advisory
system threat level
www.dhs.gov

Department of Homeland Security—Public
preparedness
www.ready.gov/get_informed.html

Department of Homeland Security's Bureau of
Citizenship and Immigration Services (BCIS)
www.immigration.gov (formerly the
Immigration and Naturalization Service)

Department of Housing and Urban
Development (HUD)
"Rights and Responsibilities of Landlords and
Residents in Preventing Housing
Discrimination Based on Race, Religion, or
National Origin in the Wake of the Events of
September 11, 2001," January 6, 2003.
www.hud.gov/offices/fheo/library/sept11.cfm.

Department of Treasury
Office of Foreign Assets Control (OFAC)
Specially Designated Nationals and Blocked
  Persons List.
www.treasury.gov/offices/enforcement/ofac/
  sdn/index.html.

National Multi Housing Council
www.nmhc.org

Materials on property management
  and anti-terrorism
www.nmhc.org/Content/BrowseContent.cfm?
  IssueID=318

Publications

Apartment Finance Today
www.housingfinance.com

Multifamily Executive
www.multifamilyexecutive.com

Multifamily Trends
www.urbanland.uli.org

Multihousing News
www.multihousingnews.com

CHAPTER 12
HOME AND BUSINESS SECURITY, DISASTER PLANNING, RESPONSE, AND RECOVERY

Barbara A. Nadel, FAIA
Principal, Barbara Nadel Architect
Forest Hills, New York

*There are two big forces at work, external and internal. We have
very little control over external forces such as tornadoes, earthquakes, floods, disasters, illness and pain. What really matters is
the internal force. How do I respond to those disasters?*

LEO BUSCAGLIA (1925–1998)
U.S. author and educator

Residential and commercial buildings share the common need to protect occupants, assets, and
ongoing operations. Safe cities and streets instill civic pride and enhance the quality of life for those
at home, school, and work. Maintaining secure homes and communities ensures personal safety
and peace of mind.

History has shown that acts of terrorism, crime, violence, natural and human-error disasters,
and unpredictable emergencies can indelibly change physical, economic, and emotional landscapes around the world. In an increasingly global society, disasters often have ramifications far
beyond their immediate point of impact, through disrupted lives and livelihoods, and nations sending disaster response teams. Governments inevitably shoulder most of the response and recovery
costs, in human and financial resources. However, the ability of individuals, households, businesses, organizations, and communities to plan for and respond to disasters efficiently and
rebound quickly can mitigate personal and economic losses. Mitigation activities can prevent an
emergency, reduce damaging effects of unavoidable crisis situations, and result in orderly service
restoration.

This chapter provides an overview of home and business security issues, including crime prevention, natural disasters, disaster response efforts, and emergency management techniques (Table
12.1). Many of the checklists and design guidelines may be applied to either home or business and
to various types of disasters and emergencies. Readers seeking further information on specific areas
are directed to the Resources section at the end of this chapter.

TABLE 12.1   Home and Business Security, Disaster Planning, Response, and Recovery

Home and business security	Disaster response efforts
1. Deterring burglaries	11. Assembling a disaster response team
2. Crime prevention through environmental design (CPTED)	12. Volunteering services in emergencies
3. Safe rooms	13. Using indemnification language in contracts and agreements
4. Terrorism	
5. Chemical-biological hazards	Emergency management
6. Preparing for a power outage	14. Planning for business emergencies, response, and recovery
Natural disasters	15. Assessing insurance coverage
7. Floods and tsunamis	16. Preparing for crisis management and public relations after an emergency
8. Hurricanes	
9. Tornadoes and high winds	
10. Wildfires	

HOME AND BUSINESS SECURITY: SHARED CONCERNS

A comprehensive approach to home and business security integrates design, technology, and operations. Individuals and organizations concerned about personal safety must be aware of options, solutions, costs, and local applicable building codes before embarking on new construction or security upgrades. Security planning requires building owners and occupants to address potential vulnerabilities and risks.

- Identify assets to be protected.
- List potential threats, such as crime, terrorism, natural disasters, and hazards.
- Assess existing vulnerabilities that may not adequately protect occupants and assets.
- Prioritize strategies to address threats and vulnerabilities.
- Implement a plan of action integrating design, technology, ongoing operations, and emergency procedures.
- Update disaster plans and practice emergency drills regularly.

DETERRING BURGLARIES

Single-family homes are easy targets for crime, especially when occupants are away. Each year one out of every 20 homes will be burglarized, but 90 percent of these crimes can be prevented with preparation and planning. While there is no guaranteed way to prevent or protect homes and businesses from break-ins, preventive steps can be taken to increase security. If a break-in requires over four to five minutes, burglars are likely to move on (Table 12.2).

Intruders are deterred by time and light. Securing a home begins at the property line, well before the front door. Keeping trees, shrubs, and vegetation low and trimmed allows patrolling law enforcement and neighbors to observe suspicious activities. Before leaving for the day or an extended trip, home owners and tenants should review home and property to avoid the signs that burglars use to recognize unoccupied facilities:

- House and property are totally dark at night.
- Valuables are visible through the windows.
- Mail and newspapers are piled up.
- Lights are on 24 hours a day.
- Grass is overgrown or snow is unshoveled.

TABLE 12.2 Home Security Checklist

1. Add a security alarm system.
2. Install quality locks on doors, windows, and skylights.
3. Install solid and wood or metal doors and windows, of consistent construction quality and weight around the exterior. Don't install a heavy front door and lock set and lightweight back and side doors with weak locks.
4. Ensure that security bars installed on windows can be opened from the inside in the bedrooms for escape in the event of a fire.
5. Install dead bolts in all exterior doors. Secure jamb strikes with screws drilled deep into the jamb.
6. Remove overgrown trees and shrubs that provide access to second-story windows; remove shrubs from the side of the house where intruders can hide.
7. Keep all entrances and windows clear to allow observation from the street.
8. Install good lighting levels, automatic solar timers, and motion-activated lights to turn on as someone approaches to discourage intruders; locate them high enough to prevent tampering.
9. Store photos and videos of all rooms and articles in each room off-site.
10. Update insurance policies to reflect personal needs in the event of a loss or disaster.

Source: Terrance J. Brown, FAIA.

CRIME PREVENTION THROUGH ENVIRONMENTAL DESIGN

Crime prevention through environmental design (CPTED) was developed during the 1970s to prevent crimes from occurring in housing projects by using design and "eyes on the street" to increase direct community observation of neighborhood activities. CPTED supports creating tiered, or layered, defense systems; providing rings of security around a site; and building through design. The rings of defense start at the property line, known as the outer site perimeter, and continue toward interior private spaces. Access control systems, surveillance, and territorial reinforcement are crime-reducing design approaches. Fortifying, or hardening, each ring of defense creates greater obstacles for intruders to overcome when attempting to break into a home.

Gates and fences define property boundaries and can be passive or active, with electrical, pulsed, or fiber optic systems (Tables 27.1 and 27.2). Closed circuit television (CCTV) and small cameras with night vision capabilities, discreetly hidden in shrubbery or prominently placed over entries to let visitors know they are being watched, can provide constant surveillance. Alarm systems and motion detectors are additional options, depending on security needs and budgets.

Strengthening the exterior building envelope (including penetration of pipes, ducts, and vents) and building systems (such as materials, walls, doors, locks, windows, and skylights) is the next step in a layered defense. Heavy-duty doors, lock sets, and windows should be carefully evaluated and consistently installed throughout the building envelope. The quality of construction materials and methods should maintain the same security levels around the building envelope, otherwise weak spots can be discovered and breached.

Burglary-resistant and bullet-resistant laminated glass windows might also be considered in certain circumstances. Applicable building codes and industry standards should be carefully reviewed before specifying walls, roofing, and glazing in regions prone to earthquakes, high winds, and hurricanes (Table 29.1).

The building footprint, or outer wall configuration of a structure, should not have indented niches and corners where intruders can hide and not be seen from the street or the house, especially near building entrances. Straight exterior walls, without hiding places, enhance visibility. Clear sight lines for unobstructed observation between the property line and the building, with adequate exterior lighting levels, low shrubs, and landscaping, allow good surveillance.

Control panels and street-level connections to utilities and building systems, such as electrical, water, sewer, gas, and telephone lines, should be clearly visible from the building or street, and locked securely to prevent unauthorized tampering and vandalism. Ideally, controls and panels should be located inside, rather than outside, buildings. Eliminating opportunities for vandals to cut power and telephone services or tamper with the water supply should be reviewed for homes, businesses, and at-risk facilities, such as government or religious buildings. When hurricanes, tornadoes, or other natural disasters are a threat, indoor control panel locations are preferable so that people do not have to venture outdoors to turn off services.

Roofs, skylights, and other interior access points should be monitored and fully secured to prevent intruders from unauthorized entry. This is true especially for multistory buildings with rooftop mechanical equipment rooms, access to ventilation systems, and air intake ducts, to prevent unauthorized infiltration of chemical or biological agents into building systems.

SAFE ROOMS

Within homes and other buildings, rooms or areas may be designated as safe rooms to protect people or property. Depending on threats, building type, and context, safe rooms may be designed to protect against:

- Intrusion and forced entry
- Theft of valuable assets
- Chemical and biological attack
- Ballistic assault
- Fire and smoke
- Explosives and blast
- Tornadoes, wind storms, and hurricanes

If safety from intruders is a concern, the first line of defense should be securing the site perimeter, at the property line, to prevent unauthorized entry to the property without permission, such as through the use of fences, gates, walls, and landscaping. Territorial reinforcement of the inner site perimeter, or the area between the property line and the building, and hardening the building envelope should follow. Unless these elements are addressed, a safe room within a site or building that may be easily breached will likely not be as effective or safe as intended. Once the site perimeter and building envelope are breached, other than in hostage situations, a safe room is generally designed for use of up to a few hours.

Safe rooms should not be confused with a high-security vault and may not necessarily be resistant to every possible type of attack. Designers and homeowners should identify the circumstances they wish to protect against before adding or constructing safe rooms, whether by fortifying existing rooms, building new ones, or installing prefabricated units.

Many prefabricated safe rooms are on the market, designed to resist specific threats. Prefabricated safe rooms are available in various materials to provide ballistic and forced entry attack protection, with equipment and amenity options. Materials of any prefabricated safe room should be tested as a finished assembly against recognized industry-testing standards, and should meet applicable local building codes. Door and wall seams and window casings must be tested to eliminate weak points that may be vulnerable to ballistic attack, forced entry, and chemical or gas penetration. Specifications should address performance compliance with industry protocols from recognized organizations such as Underwriters Laboratories and from the U.S. Department of State, which builds and operates American embassies and federal buildings outside the United States.

Safe rooms for tornado and hurricane protection, known as in-residence shelters, have different design criteria and standards than those for intrusion and forced entry, because of the need to resist high wind velocities. The Federal Emergency Management Agency (FEMA) has studied the effects of tornadoes and hurricanes and developed design guides for architects, engineers, building officials, and potential shelter owners. The Wind Science and Engineering Research Center at Texas Tech University is another resource for information, floor plans, and details regarding wind-resistant shelters.

FEMA encourages communities to do a risk assessment and determine needs for a community shelter, especially in high-risk tornado and hurricane-prone areas. Wind velocities from these storms can reach 200 to 250 miles per hour (mph); therefore, any large shelter should be designed to withstand high velocities and hold a significant number of occupants.

TERRORISM

Terrorist acts often cause senseless loss of life and seek to threaten the democratic ideals of freedom and liberty, typically represented by American icons, landmarks, and facilities. Local law enforcement agencies are the best sources of information for heightened security levels, especially about specific or general threats. As with other emergencies and natural disasters, everyone—individuals at home, work, school, and in any public venue—should remain aware of what to look for, how to prepare, and what to do in the face of a crisis (Table 12.3).

CHEMICAL-BIOLOGICAL HAZARDS

Chemical and biological hazardous materials may be introduced into the environment after an accident or a terrorist act, especially in public places where large gatherings of people are anticipated (Table 12.4). For new buildings and retrofits, locations of air intake vents should be carefully evaluated. Building air intake vents should not be located at grade level or at readily accessible rooftop locations to prevent introduction of chemical and biological agents into building ventilation systems. Minimum heights for air vent locations are generally recommended at several stories above grade, and may be addressed in applicable building codes, federal design and construction guidelines, or other industry building standards.

PREPARING FOR A POWER OUTAGE

In August 2003, a power outage, or blackout, affected the northeastern United States and parts of Canada. Since most homes, businesses, and institutions were not fully prepared to be without power for an extended time in the middle of the summer, the event prompted every household and

TABLE 12.3   Terrorism Disaster Response Checklist

1. Know that terrorists seek visible targets where they can avoid detection before or after an attack, such as international airports, large cities, major international events, resorts, and high-profile landmarks.
2. Learn about the different types of terrorist weapons including explosives, kidnappings, hijackings, arson, shootings, and chemical and biological substances.
3. Prepare to deal with a terrorist incident by adapting many of the same disaster response techniques used to prepare for other crises and emergencies.
4. Be alert and aware of the surrounding area. The nature of terrorism suggests there may be little or no warning.
5. Take precautions when traveling. Be aware of conspicuous or unusual behavior.
6. Learn where emergency exits and stairs are located. Think ahead about evacuating a building, subway, or congested public area quickly.
7. Notice immediate surroundings. Be aware of heavy or breakable objects that could move, fall, or break in an explosion.

Source: FEMA.

TABLE 12.4 Chemical-Biological Agents: Disaster Response Facts

Chemical agents

1. Chemical agents are poisonous gases, liquids, or solids that have toxic effects on people, animals, or plants. Most chemical agents cause serious injuries or death.
2. Severity of injuries depends on the type and amount of the chemical agent used and the duration of exposure.
3. Were a chemical agent attack to occur, authorities would instruct citizens to seek shelter where they are and seal the premises, or evacuate immediately.
4. Exposure to chemical agents can be fatal.
5. Leaving the shelter to rescue or assist victims can be a deadly decision.
6. There is no assistance that the untrained can offer that would likely be of any value to victims of chemical agents.

Biological agents

1. Biological agents are organisms or toxins that have illness-producing effects on people, livestock, and crops.
2. Biological agents cannot necessarily be detected and may take time to grow and cause a disease; it may be almost impossible to know if a biological attack has occurred.
3. If government officials become aware of a biological attack through an informant or warning by terrorists, they would most likely instruct citizens to seek shelter where they are and seal the premises, or evacuate immediately.
4. A person affected by a biological agent requires immediate attention by professional medical personnel.
5. Some agents are contagious; victims may need to be quarantined.
6. Some medical facilities may not receive victims for fear of contaminating the hospital population.

Source: FEMA.

organization to take stock of their ability to withstand a subsequent outage of 48 hours or longer. Unlike occasional weather-related brownouts lasting only a few hours in limited areas, the scale of this blackout, over entire regions, states, and provinces, created additional challenges for institutions, transportation networks, and power-dependent businesses unable to rely on regional backup systems.

The blackout served as a reminder that human and mechanical errors, not only terrorism and natural disasters, can cause widespread disruption to daily routines in an increasingly technological society. Households and businesses should create and review emergency plans, procedures, and supplies to be able to handle a power outage or other crisis with minimal inconvenience (Tables 12.5 and 12.6).

NATURAL DISASTERS

Floods, tsunamis, hurricanes, tornadoes, high winds, and wildfires are among the most destructive natural disasters. (Earthquakes, for the purposes of this analysis, are not included, because of the specific needs of seismic design.) Federal, state, and local government agencies provide most disaster recovery relief funds, but insurance companies and not-for-profit organizations, such as the Red Cross, contribute substantially to disaster response and recovery efforts. Where funding is limited, home and business owners must often cover their own repair and damage costs. Understanding potential threats, developing disaster plans, and designing buildings according to local building codes, best practices, and established industry standards will mitigate potential damage, recovery, and rebuilding costs, especially where codes do not cover every situation.

TABLE 12.5   Lessons Learned from the August 2003 Blackout: Emergency Preparedness

On August 14, 2003, a widespread power outage affected over 50 million people across 9,300 square miles in six northeastern states and parts of Canada. Many residences, from urban high rises with elevators to suburban communities and rural areas, were without power for two days. New York State hospitals and nursing homes discovered that routine testing of emergency power generators generally anticipated an outage of only a few hours, not a day or more, especially when power is out in an entire state or region, prompting re-evaluation of procedures.

Phones. To maintain phone service, keep at least one hard-wired, corded, or landline phone plugged directly into the telephone jack, not into another device. Unlike cordless phones, hard-wired or corded phones can work without electricity. The phone company supplies the power needed to operate phones through the phone lines. If power is lost, phone calls can be made or received. Cell phones may not work during power outages. Phone service may be interrupted on cellular or ground lines, or lines may be overloaded.

Design. Nonslip floor surfaces, rugs, and floor coverings prevent falling in the dark or in dimly lit areas. For older residents, textures can differentiate one area from other and can be located before a stair landing or curb to warn of a change in floor level.

Supplies. Homes and businesses should be prepared for unexpected power outages of 24 to 48 hours, or longer, and be stocked with necessary supplies in the event of such an emergency, including flashlights, portable radios, batteries, bottled water, oil lamps, glass-enclosed candles, and nonperishable food.

TABLE 12.6   Power Outage Planning Checklist for Businesses

1. Assess how loss of power, surges, and voltage fluctuation might affect critical equipment and electronic records, including during nights and weekends.
2. Develop shutdown procedures for internal technology and other critical operations.
3. Assess redundant emergency power resources, including on-site emergency generators and back-up energy storage systems.
4. Review facility issues, including site security, evacuation, and safety procedures, and personnel issues, such as employees being stranded.
5. Identify critical functions that can be transferred to other companies or facilities.
6. Explore sharing arrangements with noncompeting businesses and colleagues.
7. Determine how an unplanned interruption of business operations might affect contractual obligations to meet schedules, and whether contract adjustment provisions are in place.
8. Create a system to communicate with staff and clients if power is interrupted or lost for an extended length of time.
9. Coordinate planned activities with local law enforcement and other emergency services.
10. Test the strategies developed through regular drills with all personnel.

Source: Victor O. Schinnerer & Company, Inc.

FLOODS AND TSUNAMIS

On the northern plains, nature is less an enemy than a sparring partner, trading rounds in a grudge bout that never ends.
JOHN MCCORMICK
Journalist, former Chicago bureau chief,
Newsweek magazine, 1997

Floods rank second to fires as the most common and widespread natural disaster. They can rapidly inundate buildings and devastate entire communities over several hours or days, while months and years may be needed to recover from the damage. Spring rains, thunderstorms, hurricanes, tsunamis, and winter snow thaws can cause flooding in cities, rural farm communities, and low-lying coastal areas (Fig. 12.1). Floods cannot be prevented, but preparation can minimize flood damage to essential services, save homes, businesses, and millions of dollars in personal losses, insurance costs, and government aid (Table 12.7).

FIGURE 12.1 Flooded house in Kansas, 2001. (*Source: Charles Harper, FAIA.*)

TABLE 12.7 Lessons Learned from the Great Plains 1997: Flood Emergency Action Procedures

In 1997, rising tides from winter blizzards and spring floods inundated the Red River and Minnesota River valleys. The rivers kept rising, setting new flood records for the "Flood of the Century," and devastated small, rural communities in Minnesota, North Dakota, and South Dakota, with meager financial and labor resources. In North Dakota, flooding caused power outages; disrupted water, sewage, and electrical services; blocked transportation routes; and caused evacuation of over 50,000 people. Protecting potable water supplies and sanitary systems was easier for communities with existing disaster plans.

During recovery, the Midwest Assistance Program (MAP) prepared a Flood Emergency Action Procedures (FEAP) manual, outlining tasks for flood preparation, during fall of the previous year. Criteria include floodwater origins, community infrastructure, and permanent flood protection programs. The FEAP should be updated regularly to reflect infrastructure improvements, flood protection, equipment, emergency contacts, hazardous materials, and evacuation plans.

Sources: Rural Voices Magazine; Midwest Assistance Program.

The National Flood Insurance Program defines a flood as a temporary condition of partial or complete inundation of two or more acres of normally dry land or two or more properties from overflow of inland or tidal waters, unusual and rapid accumulation or runoff of surface waters from any source, or a mudflow. Floods can cause collapse or subsidence of land along a lake shore or body of water as a result of erosion, undermining caused by waves, or water currents, exceeding anticipated cyclical levels.

Tsunamis are a series of giant waves, traveling up to 450 mph, caused by an underwater disturbance or an earthquake, occurring in coastal regions of the Pacific Ocean. Earthquakes, volcanic eruptions, landslides, ground rumblings, or rapid changes in coastal waters are warning signs that tsunamis may be imminent. Ten large tsunamis have killed 4000 people since 1990. Predicting and sending tsunami warnings can save lives but remains challenging.

Floods and tsunamis are caused by different natural occurrences, but both can leave buildings flooded, uninhabitable, and structurally damaged. Similar disaster response measures are called for after these events (Table 12.8).

There are two forms of flood damage: rising water filling a structure, but the force of the water does not cause damage, and moving water, generating a force causing structural damage. If as much as one inch of floodwater enters a structure, disaster response should be implemented immediately to minimize

TABLE 12.8   Flood and Tsunami Disaster Response Checklist

Before a flood or tsunami:
- Know how and when to turn off gas, electricity, and water if evacuation is necessary.
- Fill bathtubs, sinks, and plastic bottles with clean water.
- Bring outdoor lawn furniture, grills, and trash cans inside or tie down securely.

During a flood or tsunami:
- Don't drive through flooded areas. More people drown in cars than anywhere else.
- Don't walk in flooded areas. Six inches of moving water can knock a person over.
- Avoid contact with downed power lines and electrical wires. Electrocution is a major source of deaths in floods. Electric current passes easily through water.
- Watch for animals, especially snakes, seeking shelter after floods.

After a flood or tsunami:
- Before entering a building, look for structural damage, electrical shorts, and hot wires.
- Keep power and utilities turned off in damaged homes until inspection. Do not step in water to get to the fuse box or circuit breaker.
- Use flashlights when entering buildings, not matches, cigarette lighters, or flames, since gas may be trapped inside.
- Open windows and doors to help dry out the building.
- Shovel mud while still moist so walls and floors can dry.
- Floodwaters pick up sewage and chemicals from roads, farms, and factories. If a home is flooded, protect personal health by cleaning up right away.
- Boil water for drinking and food preparation vigorously for five minutes before using.
- Use caution: steps and floors are slippery with mud, debris, nails, and broken glass.

Source: FEMA.

damage. Buildings should not be occupied until conditions are inspected and surveyed by an architect, engineer, or local building official. Time is the main factor in determining the extent of flood damage. Many construction materials may be reused if water does not remain standing in a building longer than two to three hours. After that time, gypsum wallboard and insulation become damaged beyond repair.

FLOODWATER DISASTER RECOVERY: DETAILED CHECKLIST

See Table 12.9:

1. *Wild animals.* Animals living in creeks and river bottoms displaced by rising waters will seek high ground for shelter. Inspect closets, cabinets, and attics for animals and snakes upon reentering a home or building.

2. *Carpets and rugs.* Remove carpeting and rugs immediately. Place outdoors to allow air circulation to dry carpets thoroughly. Pads may be destroyed during carpet removal.

3. *Wood flooring.* Swelling from floods can force wood flooring to buckle. Generally, wood floors should be removed and replaced after a flood. For pier and beam construction, the floor and subflooring can be removed by cutting the floor along the interior wall plate line and replacing both after the structure dries.

4. *Interior walls.* For buildings with wood studs and gypsum board walls, one or two hours of flood exposure will not cause significant damage, but longer exposure will be damaging. Wallboard will powder and mildew, causing odors and an unacceptable paint base. Remove gypsum board from at least 12 inches above the high water line to the floor below. Remove insulation, if any, from the wall, as it will not be reusable. Allow framing to dry thoroughly before applying new gypsum wallboard.

TABLE 12.9   Floodwater Disaster Response and Recovery Inspection Checklist

1. Wild animals	8. Electrical systems
2. Carpets and rugs	9. Gas system
3. Wood flooring	10. Appliances
4. Interior walls	11. Exterior walls
5. Floor covering	12. Mildew and mold
6. Doors and cabinets	13. Repainting
7. Ceilings	14. Hiring a contractor

Source: Charles Harper, FAIA.

5. *Floor covering.* Floor covering other than carpet, such as clay tile, weathers floods well. Vinyl, vinyl asbestos, and vinyl composition tile may curl at the edges and adhesives may not keep tiles secured to the floor. Removal and replacement may be necessary.

   WARNING: All materials containing 1 percent or more asbestos fibers are required by law to be removed and disposed of in accordance with the Environmental Protection Agency (EPA), OSHA, and applicable state laws. Skilled persons should be employed to accomplish this. Failure to do so may result in large fines and cleanup costs.

6. *Doors and cabinets.* Plywood and particleboard doors swell and delaminate with time. Swelling won't appear until several days after waters recede and plywood layers on doors peel apart. Wood panel doors are not usually affected and may be used after drying.

7. *Ceilings.* Floodwaters may not reach ceilings, but extreme humidity may cause swelling above gypsum board and ceilings to loosen from framing. Check by pressing upward on the ceiling: if a nail head appears on the surface, damage exists. Renailing and refinishing may be needed, and replacement may be necessary. Check attic insulation when this occurs, as it may be moist and not allow the gypsum board to dry, causing mildew. If insulation is rockwool or cellulose, replacement is required.

8. *Electrical systems.* Check electrical systems thoroughly, especially if floodwaters rose above the wall or floor outlets. Silt can collect in these openings and cause short circuits. Check light fixtures for water.

9. *Gas system.* Water can collect in gas lines, causing the pilot to burn improperly and possibly go out. Gas can escape if there is a faulty valve or thermocouple.

10. *Appliances.* Most appliances have electric motors mounted very low to the floor, so even a small amount of water can cause damage to the motors and bearings. Do not use these until qualified technicians check motor controls and other elements.

11. *Exterior walls.* Many homes are constructed of brick veneer with water-resistant sheathing, which will not be damaged if weep holes are free. To ensure that water can escape and the wall cavity can dry, remove a brick at the base every four feet. If done properly, mortar can be cut around a brick and the brick saved for replacement. In extreme cases, bricks at the top of the wall may need to be removed.

12. *Mildew and mold.* Both grow well with high humidity and warm air. Do not use heating systems to dry materials; this accelerates mildew and mold growth. Natural drying is the best defense, with floor fans, open doors, and windows. Keep spaces well ventilated for several days until materials dry. For extensive soaking, test materials with a moisture meter. Common household bleach rids structures of mildew and mold.

13. *Repainting.* Areas that appear sound and reusable may still have stains, which will bleed through new coats of paint if preventive steps aren't taken. Cover the stain with white shellac, paint materials, a stain cover, or primer. Thoroughly dry all surfaces before painting or the paint will blister and peel.

14. *Hiring a contractor.* Flood victims making repairs should know the contractor, check and verify local references, and should not advance money before work begins.

HURRICANES

Preparation through education is less costly than learning through tragedy.

MAX MAYFIELD
*Director, National Hurricane Center,
Coral Gables, Florida*

A hurricane is a severe tropical storm, forming in the southern Atlantic Ocean, Caribbean Sea, Gulf of Mexico, or eastern Pacific Ocean. Under the right conditions, hurricanes produce violent winds, torrential waves, and floods that result in millions of dollars in property damage, insurance costs, and lost business days. During the Atlantic hurricane season, from June to November, every coastal state is vulnerable to storm damage. According to the National Hurricane Center, the value of insured property in hurricane-prone areas along the U.S. coastline in 2002 was about $2 trillion. As development increases along coastal areas in these states, more homes and businesses are at risk from severe windstorm damage.

Hurricane winds are at least 74 miles per hour. The Saffir-Simpson Hurricane Scale measures intensity, pressure, wind speeds, storm surge, and damage, in five categories, with Level 5 as the highest and most destructive storm (Table 12.10). These factors may be helpful as design and building code guidelines for hurricane-prone or coastal areas.

On average, there are six Atlantic Ocean hurricanes annually; over a three-year period, approximately five hurricanes strike the U.S. coastline, from Maine to Texas. When hurricanes reach landfall, heavy rains, strong winds, and huge waves can damage buildings, trees, and cars. Dangerous heavy waves, called storm surges, are the major reason to avoid the ocean during a hurricane. Flying glass from broken windows, failed roofing systems, and damaged building elements are among the most severe problems during and after a major hurricane.

Hurricane Andrew

In 1992, Hurricane Andrew devastated parts of South Florida, causing $15.5 billion in insured losses, estimated damage in the United States of $25 billion, with indirect and other costs exceeding $40 billion (Fig. 12.2). As insurance costs rise, insurers often seek to reduce their potential losses from

TABLE 12.10   **Saffir-Simpson Hurricane Classification Scale**

Category	Wind speed (mph)	Storm surge (ft)	Damage	Typical damage
1	74–95	4–5	Light	Some damage to shrubs and trees, signs. Some coastal road flooding and minor pier damage.
2	96–110	6–8	Moderate	Some damage to roofing, doors, windows. Considerable damage to shrubs, trees, signs and piers. Coastal and low-lying escape routes flood 2–4 hours before hurricane center arrival.
3	111–130	9–12	Extensive	Structural damage to homes and buildings. Large trees blown over. Escape routes flood 3–5 hours before hurricane center arrival.
4	131–155	13–18	Extreme	Roofs and walls torn off houses; trees blown down; extensive damage to doors and windows.
5	Over 155 mph	Over 18	Catastrophic	Complete roof or total building failure. Small buildings blown away. Severe damage.

Source: National Weather Service, NOAA.

FIGURE 12.2 Catastrophic damage from Hurricane Andrew; Homestead, Florida; August 1992. (*Photographer: Charles Harper, FAIA.*)

TABLE 12.11   Hurricane Disaster Planning Checklist

1. Assess building vulnerability to storm surge, flooding, and high winds.
2. Check local building codes for hurricane glass requirements
3. Install storm shutters or 5/8-inch plywood on all windows.
4. Inspect homes for local building code compliance.
5. Install straps or clips to secure roof joists to framing.
6. Construct a wind shelter or safe room to provide a high degree of protection for remaining in the house.
7. Trim trees and remove weak branches around buildings.
8. Secure all outdoor equipment.
9. Prepare for power outages and loss of elevator service in high-rise buildings.
10. On June 1, hurricane season onset, check supplies, replace batteries, use food stocks on a rotating basis. Store several days' supply of food. Plan three days per person.

Sources: NOAA, Terrance J. Brown, FAIA.

severe wind and hailstorms by requiring policyholders to bear a greater share of repair and disaster recovery costs. After Hurricane Andrew, the design and construction industry and Florida building code officials developed hurricane-resistant glazing systems and enhanced performance criteria to prevent such widespread, catastrophic losses and devastation from recurring, especially in areas to be rebuilt (Tables 29.10 through 29.12).

Building owners and landlords can mitigate building damage, costs, and inconvenience by alerting tenants of storm warnings. They can encourage tenants to plan ahead for supplies and necessities, and prepare for a temporary loss of building services, such as lack of functional elevators should a power outage occur. This could affect the elderly, the disabled, and delivery schedules. (Table 12.11).

TORNADOES AND HIGH WINDS

The United States and Canada are the most tornado-prone areas in the world. Tornadoes have occurred in every one of the lower 48 states and in most of the populated Canadian provinces in nearly every month of the year over the last 150 years. Anyone living in these locations may be struck at any time.

CHARLES HARPER, FAIA
U.S. architect and disaster response specialist

Tornadoes are violently rotating columns of air extending from thunderstorms to the ground. The most violent tornadoes reach wind speeds of over 250 mph and cause tremendous destruction in their paths, which can range from over a mile wide and 50 miles long. On average, 800 tornadoes are reported annually in the United States, resulting in 80 deaths and 1500 injuries (Fig. 12.3).

Tornadoes occur throughout the world, and most often in the Great Plains, between the Rocky Mountains and the Appalachians, during spring and summer. Tornado Alley refers to the area of the United States in which tornadoes are most frequent, encompassing lowland areas of the Mississippi, Ohio, and lower Missouri River valleys.

Thunderstorms develop in warm, humid air, producing hail, strong winds, and tornadoes. During the winter and early spring, tornadoes may result from strong, frontal systems forming in the central United States, moving east. Occasionally, tornadoes occur with hurricanes and tropical storms making landfall, or as part of severe thunderstorms. They are most common to the right and ahead of the storm center path as it reaches land. Signs of an oncoming tornado include a dark, greenish sky; wall cloud; large hail; and loud roar. Tornadoes can appear transparent until dust and debris are picked up, or as a funnel extending partially to the ground, with debris below the funnel. Some tornadoes are clearly visible; others can be obscured by rain or low-hanging clouds, and can develop rapidly without warning.

The F-scale is the most widely recognized tornado and high-wind classification rating method used by weather agencies. Developed by T. Theodore Fujita in 1971, the scale relates the degree of damage to the wind intensity (Table 12.12). Different winds may cause the same damage, due to variables at each location, including how well built a structure is, wind duration, and battering by flying debris. F-5 tornadoes are the most severe and cause catastrophic damage, leveling entire buildings and communities in their paths (Fig. 12.4).

Violent winds and flying debris slamming into buildings cause most tornado-related structural damage and result in deaths and injuries. Building occupants should leave windows closed, and immediately go to an in-residence shelter or other safe place. Homes, businesses, schools, and health care and public institutions should have disaster plans in place for protecting building occupants, especially the mentally or physically disabled, the young, elderly, and those with language barriers (Table 12.13).

Build for a Tornado: Design and Construction Issues

Wind-resistant design and construction methods should be applied to buildings in tornado-prone areas. Connections are crucial, starting with how the ground floor of the structure connects to the ground, and whether or not a basement exists. Basements can be good shelters in a windstorm but can be very dangerous if not constructed properly. Structures should have as many walls and columns in basements as are feasible and affordable. This will prevent the upper portion of the building from collapsing into the basement and potentially crushing occupants seeking refuge.

FIGURE 12.3 Tornado destruction; Wichita Falls, Texas; April 1979. (*Photographer: Charles Harper, FAIA.*)

TABLE 12.12   Tornado Damage F-Scale

Scale	Wind estimate (MPH)* and damage extent		Typical damage
F0	<73	Light	Some damage to chimneys; branches broken off trees; shallow-rooted trees pushed over; signs damaged.
F1	73–112	Moderate	Peels surface off roofs; mobile homes overturned from foundations, moving autos blown off roads.
F2	113–157	Considerable	Roofs torn off frame houses; mobile homes demolished; boxcars overturned; large trees snapped or uprooted; light-object missiles generated; cars lifted off ground.
F3	158–206	Severe	Roofs and some walls torn off well-constructed houses; trains overturned; most trees in forest uprooted; heavy cars lifted off the ground and thrown.
F4	207–260	Devastating	Well-constructed houses leveled; structures with weak foundations blown away some distance; cars thrown and large missiles generated.
F5	261–318	Incredible	Strong frame houses leveled off foundations and swept away; automobile-sized missiles fly through the air in excess of 100 meters (109 yards); trees debarked; incredible phenomena will occur.

*Important Note about F-Scale Winds: Do not use F-scale winds literally. Wind speed numbers are guesses and have never been scientifically verified. Different wind speeds may cause similar-looking damage in different buildings. Without a thorough engineering analysis of tornado damage in any event, actual wind speeds needed to cause that damage are unknown.
Source: Storm Prediction Center, NOAA.

FIGURE 12.4   Debris field after a tornado in Hoisington, Kansas, April 2001. (*Source: Charles Harper, FAIA.*)

Tornado and High Wind Design Criteria Checklist[*]

1. *Anchors.* A house should be well anchored to the ground, such as through concrete slab on grade. Pier and beam floor systems should be connected with metal ties to large corkscrews, extending well below grade.

2. *Wall-to-foundation connection.* Some building codes require steel bolts to the concrete foundation. These should never exceed 48-inch spacing and should be carefully embedded in the foundation. Plywood sheathing or chipboard should be required and installed according to local codes, with a minimum of 8d nails at 8 inches on center.

---

[*]Source: Charles Harper, FAIA.

TABLE 12.13   Tornado Disaster Planning Checklist

1. Create a disaster plan and have frequent drills.
2. Designate a tornado shelter. Basements or interior rooms and halls on the lowest floor and away from windows are advised; get under a sturdy piece of furniture.
3. Review prototype design and construction methods for in-residence shelters.
4. Avoid assemblies in large rooms if severe weather is anticipated. Gymnasiums, cafeterias, and auditoriums offer no protection from tornado-strength winds.
5. Move building occupants to interior rooms or corridors on lowest level, and assume tornado protection position: crouch on floor, head down, hands over back of neck.
6. Inspect and correct potential hazards, e.g., items that move, fall, break, and catch fire.
7. Learn when and how to turn off water, gas, and electricity if the facility is damaged.
8. Keep supplies to meet needs for at least three days, and disaster supply kit in the car.
9. Keep important documents in a waterproof container.
10. Replace stored batteries, water, and food every six months.

Sources: NOAA, FEMA.

3. *Building corners.* Foam, gypsum board, and insulating sheathing will not reinforce walls or keep out flying projectiles during a tornado or hurricane. Plywood or chipboard sheathing will reinforce walls properly and protect against wind-driven missiles.

4. *Roofing.* The top wood plate joining walls to the roof structure is an important connection. Many homes are built with prefabricated wood joists spanning the entire structure, but connections for a rafter roofing system should also be reviewed.

5. *Use hurricane clips.* Not many codes require hurricane clips, which are small metal straps installed on each bearing location of the roof structure, but all should. These clips are a low-cost insurance policy to keep the roof in place.

6. *Connection plates.* Many prefabricated wood trusses have large gang nail joint connections. While the plates may be enough to withstand building code loads, they will not always hold the joist together in a tornado. Get the best connection plates that the wood joist fabricator can use.

7. *Roof deck.* Many codes allow a 1/4-inch-thick plywood roof deck, but it should be thicker to withstand the missiles of a storm. A 3/8-inch thickness is preferable and 1/2 inch is better. The spacing of the wood trusses may be increased with thicker decks.

8. *Windows.* Windows should be small, with fewer openings on a building's west and south sides. Install sturdy storm windows, to reduce window breakage. Consider a storm sheltering wall when large glass openings are used. Avoid overhangs wider than 24 inches.

9. *Chimneys and fireplaces.* A well-braced chimney will stand in a storm, but if not correctly constructed and tied together, will fall into the structure, damaging the building and potentially killing occupants. Fireplaces should have good dampers and front fire screens. Avoid the fireplace in a windstorm.

10. *Garage doors.* Garage doors are very likely to fail and allow wind into the house. Most commercially manufactured doors will not withstand windstorms but can be reinforced on-site. Side rails should be securely fastened, with large screws into the garage door jambs.

11. *Mobile homes.* Mobile homes cannot be made tornado-resistant and should be evacuated.

12. *In-house, or in-residence, shelters.* These shelters should be in every home. People get injured trying to reach outside shelters. In-house shelters are simple to build in a closet, bathroom, or other space. The Texas Tech Wind Institute has developed several prototypes.

In-Residence Tornado Shelters

An in-residence shelter is a small interior room, such as a closet, bathroom, or study that has been strengthened to resist effects of wind pressures, atmospheric pressure change, and impact from tornado-generated windborne debris. They are recommended for homes without a basement and are preferable to outdoor cellars. Four common types of construction are as follows:

1. Reinforced concrete masonry walls with cast-in-place reinforced concrete roof slab
2. Reinforced masonry cavity walls with cast-in-place reinforced concrete roof slab
3. Cast-in-place reinforced concrete walls and roof slab
4. Wood stud walls infilled with concrete

Prototype in-residence shelters, developed by the Institute for Disaster Research (IDR) at Texas Tech University, are designed to give near absolute occupant protection from 99 percent of all recorded tornadoes, resist wind speeds of 260 mph, resist an end-on impact of a 2- by 4-inch timber 15-foot-long, traveling at 120 mph and are vented to equalize the atmospheric pressure change. When properly constructed, the shelter provides safety that is readily accessible from anywhere within the house. The area can be used for other purposes when not needed as a tornado shelter.

Shelter construction costs range between $800 and $1500 (in 2003 dollars), depending on size and construction parameters. Shelters can be built using conventional building techniques and readily available building materials. Prototype plans are for 8- by 8-foot shelters. They can be made smaller, but should not be enlarged without assistance from an engineer or architect trained in wind-resistant design. (*Disclaimer:* Although in-resident tornado shelters provide 99 percent protection from all recorded tornadoes, neither the Institute for Disaster Research at Texas Tech University nor any person acting on their behalf can assume any liability with respect to the use of, or for damages resulting from the use of, this information.)

WILDFIRES

To learn to read is to light a fire; every syllable that is spelled out is a spark.

VICTOR HUGO (1802–1885)
French author

Wildfires ravage entire communities, forests, and landscapes in a very short time, especially when the right combination of dry weather, arid terrain, and high winds are present. The May 2000 Cerro Grande, New Mexico, fire and the October 2003 southern California fires were the worst in each state's history, causing billions of dollars in damage and destroying homes, buildings, and businesses (Tables 12.14 and 12.15 and Fig. 12.5).

TABLE 12.14   Lessons Learned from the 2000 Cerro Grande, New Mexico, Fires

On May 5, 2000, the Cerro Grande, New Mexico, fire, an approved fire at Bandelier National Monument, raged out of control. Due to increasingly high winds, contained spot fires soon became wildfires, moving from the Santa Fe National Forest to the Los Alamos Canyon on May 7. Burning embers blew over a mile in every direction, toward Los Alamos and White Rock, NM. Over 18,000 residents were evacuated. By May 10, the fire burned 18,000 acres, destroying 235 homes, and damaging many other structures (Fig. 12.6).

Los Alamos residents returned to their homes after being displaced for over a week. The community required substantial cleanup and rehabilitation, provided by a team of volunteers and government agencies. A multidisciplinary Burned Area Emergency Rehabilitation (BAER) team assisted the community to assess damage, implement rehabilitation plans, and reduce natural resource damage. Home and business owners learned the importance of emergency planning, disaster response, and fire-resistant design.

Source: U.S. Dept. of Energy, Office of Environmental Management.

TABLE 12.15   Lessons Learned from the 2003 California Wildfires

In late October 2003, several wildfires engulfed Southern California, before being contained in early November 2003, costing over $2 billion in damages. The Cedar Fire, covering 281,000 acres outside San Diego, population 1.2 million, was the single largest California fire in history, destroying 2200 homes. The wildfires burned 750,000 acres, contained by over 14,000 firefighters. Over 105,000 people evacuated their homes, 22 were killed, 3600 homes were destroyed and over 740,000 acres of brush and forests burned. Mudslides were a disaster recovery concern, because the fires burned away trees and vegetation that kept soil in place on hillsides. Recovery workers reseeded soil, dug flood control trenches, and brought in sandbags.

Architects, homeowners, building officials, and insurers in damaged areas must be familiar with building and fire codes, design criteria, and fire-resistant materials when rebuilding, renovating, and retrofitting structures. The scale and duration of the wildfires emphasized the need for evacuation, disaster, and recovery planning for home and businesses.

Sources: FEMA, Associated Press.

FIGURE 12.5   House with melted plastic siding, 200 feet from the Los Alamos forest fire, May 2000. (*Photographer: Charles Harper, FAIA.*)

FIGURE 12.6   Burned wood frame two-story apartment house with masonry chimney standing; Los Alamos, NM, forest fire; May 2000. (*Photographer: Charles Harper, FAIA.*)

Wildfire disaster response and recovery relies on volunteers, the design and construction industry, insurance companies, and government agencies to rebuild homes and restore community services. In New Mexico, after the 2000 Cerro Grande fires, volunteer architects assisted with disaster response, building assessments, and reconstruction activities. Protecting structures and landscapes through informed site planning and fire-resistant design and construction methods will minimize loss of life, property damage, and disaster recovery costs.

FIRE-RESISTANT PLANNING AND DESIGN

Planned communities in southern California, where lack of rain contributes to potential fires, have incorporated several techniques to mitigate wildfire damage. No home or subdivision can be made fireproof, but many fire-resistant design approaches have proved to be effective.

Site Design and Vegetation

1. Plan wide streets to accommodate fire trucks.
2. Create defensible space, or fuel break, with driveways, gravel walks, or lawns between habitable structures and oncoming wildfires, allowing firefighters to defend buildings.
3. Apply oversized house address numbers for easy identification by firefighters.
4. Clear vegetation in front of each house, from 30 to 200 feet, for firefighting equipment.
5. Plant drought-resistant, fire-retardant vegetation.
6. Create a safety zone to separate structures from combustible plants.
7. Avoid highly flammable eucalyptus trees, pine, and sumac.
8. Keep landscaping moist, surrounding vegetation irrigated, and brush cleared.
9. Prune all branches around residences to 8 to 10 feet high. Keep trees adjacent to buildings free of dead or dying wood and moss.
10. Establish swimming pools and patios as safety zones. Equip swimming pools with valves to enable firefighters to use the water.
11. Install electrical lines underground. Keep tree and shrub limbs trimmed to avoid contact with wires.

Building Materials and Maintenance

1. Use low-maintenance, fire-resistant materials: tile, stucco, metal siding, brick, concrete block, rock, steel, copper roofs, metal skin, travertine floors, and plaster walls. Stone walls can act as heat shields and deflect flames.
2. Avoid cladding roof materials, including wooden shakes and shingles.
3. Avoid exterior wood walls and vinyl siding, which burn easily.
4. Use only thick, tempered safety glass in large windows and sliding glass doors.
5. Protect windows with aluminum windscreens and steel fire shutters.
6. Use handrails of glass, metal, or wire.
7. Prevent sparks from entering by covering vents with wire mesh no larger than 1/8 inch.
8. Use spark arrestors in chimneys. Keep chimney and storage areas clean.
9. Make trellises of nonflammable metal.
10. Clean leaves and pine needles out of rain gutters regularly. If they catch fire, the house may burn.
11. Store combustible or flammable materials in approved metal safety containers and keep them away from homes.

Water Supply

1. Provide ready access to water supplies.
2. Add shallow rooftop pools of standing water for firefighting.
3. Install sprinklers, water storage tanks, and automated pumps with their own generators.
4. Maintain irrigation systems, hoses, and generators regularly.

Life Safety

1. Maintain at least two ground level doors as safety exits in homes.
2. Provide at least two means of egress (door or window) from each room.
3. Install smoke detectors on every level of the home and near sleeping areas.

DISASTER RESPONSE EFFORTS

After a disaster or emergency, volunteers often come forward offering to help in rescue, recovery, and building assessments. Public agencies and local law enforcement are generally charged with directing disaster response programs and allocating resources and equipment to the scene. Professional organizations can serve as a point of contact for public officials seeking assistance and as coordinators for disaster response team volunteers.

Design professionals volunteering their services should receive training from coordinating agencies and organizations to be aware of what to look for during site inspections and proper ways to complete forms. Potential liability issues should be addressed at the outset of all disaster response efforts.

DISASTER RESPONSE TEAM

After a major tornado, the former governor of Oklahoma wrote to the American Institute of Architects (AIA) Eastern Oklahoma Chapter requesting volunteer professional services to assist tornado victims. The following examples reflect information and typical worksheets used by disaster response teams, led by Charles Harper, FAIA.

Clothing to Wear

- Heavy-duty pants, socks, and shoes with high tops or boots with thick soles
- Long-sleeved shirt or jacket
- Hard hat

Supplies to Bring

- Flashlight
- Three-copy report form
- Drinking water or canteen, if required
- Pocket knife
- Ballpoint pen
- Ten-foot tape measure
- Cellular phone (if not available, use handheld CB radio and get local frequencies)
- Local telephone numbers

When Entering Damaged Structures

- Watch for low-hanging items and holes in the floor. Large concentrations of fiberglass insulation may be present and pose a threat.
- Determine if electricity is connected and if the wires are hot.

- Smell for natural gas leaks.
- Remember not to smoke on the site or in the area.
- Have the owner or owner's representative present at all times, and ensure no one rummages through the damaged structure or moves debris.

Damage Assessment

If a structure has been damaged from high winds, or windstorms resulting from tornadoes and hurricanes, disaster response team members should look for damage and note abnormal conditions (Tables 12.16 and 12.17).

Architects, engineers, and other volunteers who perform damage assessments after a disaster should receive training on what to look for, and how to complete assessment forms to ensure a level of consistency for those who subsequently use the information. A damage assessment worksheet should be simple to fill out in the field, may be printed in triplicate, and could be loaded into a handheld electronic device for ease of use (Table 12.18).

PROVIDING VOLUNTEER SERVICES IN EMERGENCIES

During emergencies and disasters, design professionals volunteer their services to assist protecting public health and safety, and to provide immediate services aiding in recovery. With such volunteer efforts, or with any immediate response effort involving a limited scope of services during the aftermath of an emergency, potential liability exists.

TABLE 12.16 Damage Assessment Inspection Checklist for Wood Frame Structures Damaged by Tornadoes and Hurricanes

---

Wood frame structures: exterior
  1. Fence support broken at the ground or blown over.
  2. Landscape damage, largest size broken limb or trunk to check against F- scale.
  3. Roof blown off or displaced (check wall-roof connection; sometimes it is not evident).
  4. Broken windows will indicate wind forces entered the building.
  5. Brick blown off walls or in place.
  6. Chimney and roof vent condition, which may cause carbon monoxide poisoning if used in damaged condition.
  7. Aboveground utility services connected or off.

Wood frame structures: interior
  8. Check what happened to occupants if they were in the structure during the storm.
  9. Always look ahead and keep the exterior in sight.
 10. Do not touch exposed electrical wires or lights.
 11. Check wall-roof connections. Look for evidence of separation.
 12. Check for diagonal fracture of wall surfaces, if rigid like gypsum board.
 13. Watch for spilled liquid in and near kitchens, bathrooms, and garages. Very dangerous!
 14. Look for loose structural items that might collapse. Always assume they will.
 15. Check stability of interior walls.
 16. Check conditions of any basements, cellars, and outbuildings.

Report preparation
 17. Prepare report with owner or occupant.
 18. Turn in report to local office.

Other structures
All of the above plus specific checklists for the structure.

Source: Charles Harper, FAIA.

TABLE 12.17 Damage Assessment Inspection Checklist for Steel and Concrete Structures Damaged by Tornadoes and Hurricanes*

Steel frame or load-bearing walls
 1. Bent frame.
 2. Broken welds on beams and trusses and at connections.
 3. Reverse-loaded steel beams and trusses.
 4. Racking of the frame.
 5. Wind bracing broken, bent.
 6. Glass breakage.
 7. In high-rise buildings, watch for frame twisting, offsets.

Concrete frame and slab
 8. Gouges from columns and floor surfaces from impacts.
 9. Cracks running parallel with reinforcing steel.
10. Splitting out of the reinforcing bars.
11. Column-slab junctures and conditions. Watch for concrete spalling (chipping and flaking).
12. Look for previous water damage and spalling.
13. Concrete structures perform well in windstorms. Veneers, glass, and other materials not directly fastened to the concrete structure will usually be blown off.

Report preparation
14. Prepare report with owner or occupant.
15. Turn in report to local office.

Note: See checklist for wood frame structures for additional items.
Source: Charles Harper, FAIA.

Many states do not have volunteer protection acts that afford the immunity of the state to licensed professionals who provide services during an emergency situation, such as a flood, hurricane, or other disaster. While a state governor may decide to use the police powers of that state to provide immunity to volunteer design professionals, such actions are rarely taken in support of professionals providing emergency services.

Although there may be no specific immunity, a framework for limiting risk is provided by the general rule that professionals who perform voluntary or emergency services must do so in accordance with the same care and diligence as other design professionals who provide similar services under the same conditions.

In evaluating components of the built environment following a disaster, the design professional's risk can be reduced by qualifying any stated determination in a way that clearly identifies the determination as being made from information available at a specific time and representing a professional opinion. No reasonable professional would provide an absolute statement of structural integrity, habitability, and conformance to water quality standards or safety. The standard of care expected of a design professional would be less in such an emergency situation than would be normally.

Some professional liability policies may cover an insured firm in a volunteer capacity in the same way the firm would be covered when providing services for a fee. If a firm authorizes its employees to donate their professional services during an emergency, the firm should first verify if their liability coverage will stand behind their professional contributions. Each firm should check its professional liability coverage regarding disaster assessment and volunteer situations.

A state government may choose to provide the immunity of that state to design professionals who respond to the request of a government official to an emergency situation. A state agency, or even a private party, may opt to defend and indemnify design professionals for any claims, costs, losses, or damages incurred by design professionals for all but their gross negligence if the immunity of a volunteer protection statute, commonly known as the Good Samaritan law is not available. Design professionals should refer to examples of language addressing this form of legal protection as part of a rational risk management program, and review their liability insurance policy before providing services.

TABLE 12.18 Damage Assessment Worksheet

Applicant's Name: _____ Home Phone: _____
Business Phone: _____ Cell: _____
Address: _____ Market Value: _____
  Rent:_____Age of Building:_____
Owner's Name: _____ Temporary Phone: _____
Temporary Address
Appointment: _____ Extent of Damage: _____
  _____Severe _____Moderate _____Minor
Financial Status: _____ Existing Capital
Contacts: _____ SBA   HUD   Other
Insurance Company, Amount: _____

NOTE: APPLICANT PLEASE DO NOT WRITE BELOW THIS LINE

CONSTRUCTION TYPE	Approximate size _____sq. ft.	Roofing:
_____ Wood-Frame	_____ Brick Veneer	_____ Wood Shingles
_____ Concrete Block	_____ Wood Joists	_____ Asphalt Shingles
_____ Masonry	_____ Steel Joists	_____ Built-Up
_____ Siding	_____ Asbestos	_____ Other
_____ Wood	_____ Stucco	

EXTENT OF DAMAGE   No. of sq. ft. affected
Structural-Type   Floor
Exterior Walls   Partitioning
Roof   Doors
Garage

INTERIORS   BUILDING SYSTEMS
Storm Doors
Windows   Electrical
Storm Windows   Plumbing
Ceiling   Mechanical

SURVEY REMARKS   DATE PREPARED:
Surveyor: _____   Date Received: _____
Architect: _____   Architect's Remarks

Source: Charles Harper, FAIA.

INDEMNIFICATION LANGUAGE WHEN PROVIDING LIMITED PROFESSIONAL SERVICES DURING AN EMERGENCY

The following are contractual provisions that the CNA/Schinnerer program of professional liability insurance has recommended for use when providing services to private clients for a fee (Table 12.19) and when acting as a volunteer (Table 12.20) during the aftermath of an emergency. Such provisions limit the risk of the design professional, and should be considered as additions to the written contract used by the design professional or, at a minimum, as an agreement attached to a letter outlining the limited scope of services provided by the design professional. If at all possible, in addition to the risk allocation provision, some form of agreement with the client should clearly spell out the scope of services and the limits of the ability of the design professional based on the conditions encountered. Design professionals are cautioned to seek specific recommendations from legal counsel as to their risk and appropriate contract language to minimize that risk. The general provisions in Tables 12.19 and 12.20 are provided to address the basic concerns of design professionals.

TABLE 12.19   Indemnification Language for Design Professionals Providing Services in an Emergency Situation: Version A (to Be Used when Providing Services for a Fee)

In response to the declared natural disaster associated with the (NAME AND DATE OF DISASTER), (NAME OF A/E FIRM) has agreed, at the specific request of (NAME OF CLIENT), to conduct a visual observation of certain projects/facilities for structural integrity or non-structural elements affecting health and safety. Further, based upon such limited observation (NAME OF A/E FIRM) will render a professional opinion as to the integrity of the project/facility for its normal use and/or occupancy.

In return for (NAME OF A/E FIRM) providing evaluation services during a declared disaster or local emergency, (NAME OF CLIENT) agrees that neither (NAME OF A/E FIRM), nor its consultants, agents or employees shall be jointly, severally or individually liable to the (NAME OF CLIENT) in excess of the compensation to be paid pursuant to this Agreement. In addition, (NAME OF CLIENT) agrees to indemnify, defend and hold (NAME OF A/E FIRM), its consultants, agents or employees, harmless from and against any and all claims, defense costs, including attorneys' fees and dispute resolution costs, damages and other liabilities, actual or alleged, arising out of, or in any way be connected with, (NAME OF A/E FIRM)'s providing professional services, regardless of how or under what circumstances or by what cause such injuries or damages are sustained provided, however, that this indemnification shall not apply in the event of a willful act or omission by (NAME OF A/E FIRM) constituting gross negligence.

Note: Version A to be used when providing services for a fee to a private client. Similar language may be possible with public entities, although negotiating an indemnification provision with a public client may be problematic.

Source: Victor O. Schinnerer & Company, Inc.

TABLE 12.20   Indemnification Language for Design Professionals Providing Services in an Emergency Situation: Version B (to Be Used when Providing Services on a Voluntary Basis)

In response to the declared natural disaster associated with the (NAME AND DATE OF DISASTER), (NAME OF A/E FIRM) has agreed, at the specific request of (NAME OF CLIENT), to conduct a voluntary visual observation of certain projects/facilities for structural integrity or non-structural elements affecting health and safety. Further, based upon such limited observation (NAME OF A/E FIRM) will render a professional opinion as to the integrity of the project/facility for its normal use and/or occupancy.

In return for (NAME OF A/E FIRM) providing evaluation services during a declared disaster or local emergency on a voluntary basis (NAME OF CLIENT) agrees that neither (NAME OF A/E FIRM), or its consultants, agents or employees shall be jointly, severally or individually liable to the (NAME OF CLIENT). In addition, (NAME OF CLIENT) agrees to indemnify, defend and hold (NAME OF A/E FIRM), its consultants, agents or employees, harmless from and against any and all claims, defense costs, including attorneys' fees and dispute resolution costs, damages and other liabilities, actual or alleged, arising out of, or in any way be connected with, (NAME OF A/E FIRM)'s providing professional services, regardless of how or under what circumstances or by what cause such injuries or damages are sustained provided, however, that this indemnification shall not apply in the event of a willful act or omission by (NAME OF A/E FIRM) constituting gross negligence.

Note: Version B to be used when providing services on a voluntary basis. A public client may not be able to legally limit liability or provide an indemnification without a special authority being granted.

Source: Victor O. Schinnerer & Company, Inc.

EMERGENCY MANAGEMENT

Emergency management is the process of preparing for, responding to, and recovering from an emergency situation or disaster. Not every emergency situation is a disaster; every organization does not need to react the same way. An inconvenience to a large national company may destroy operations of a smaller organization. A forced vacation for a sole practitioner could obliterate the records and the reputation of a corporation.

BUSINESS SECURITY: EMERGENCY PLANNING, RESPONSE, AND RECOVERY

Disasters and emergencies cannot be prevented but planning ahead can minimize disruptions, physical or environmental damage, deaths and injuries to employees, clients, and the public. Contingency planning enables an organization to fulfill its responsibility to protect employees, serve the community, and safeguard the environment. Primary considerations include:

- The ability of the work site to cease to exist for one day or permanently without jeopardizing the organization's viability
- How the organization would survive the financial disaster created by loss of work in progress, equipment, records, or employees
- How the organization would respond immediately and continually to recreate the business and meet client needs

An emergency management program enables organizations to quickly resume operations. Steps should include the following:

- *Establish a planning team.* Designate an individual or group charged with developing the emergency management plan. Emergency planning is a high-level activity and should involve top management.
- *Analyze capabilities and hazards.* Risk management requires analysis of the probability of an unfavorable outcome and creating a response to avoid or manage risk. Current capabilities and potential hazards should be reviewed, through a vulnerability analysis.
- *Conduct a vulnerability analysis.* Determine an organization's capabilities for handling emergencies. This effort assesses facility vulnerability by exploring the possibility and potential impact of each emergency. The analysis assigns probabilities, estimates impact, and assesses resources to guide the planning process (Table 12.21).

Most emergency situations are within a facility; others may involve an entire community. Meeting with government agencies, community groups, and utility companies to ask about potential emergency response plans and available resources will assist an organization in analyzing strategies and developing a plan of action. For example, if the organization's building is permanently destroyed, determine the immediate priorities and what must be recreated in order to continue. Emergency management plans focus on long-range details that may need significant time, multidisciplinary input, and resources to identify (Table 12.22).

TABLE 12.21   Vulnerability Analysis: Impact Assessment Checklist

1. Consider what could happen as a result of prohibited access to the facility, the loss of electric power, or the failure of communications systems.
2. Analyze the potential impact of each emergency, e.g., the possibility of death or injury.
3. Consider potential property losses and damages.
4. Assess the business impact, work disruption, potential loss of clients, and customers.
5. Determine the extent of potential interruption on daily business activities.
6. Assess the inability of employees to report to work.
7. Identify impact of inadequate client communication capabilities.
8. Determine potential violation of contractual agreements.
9. Estimate the extent of potential imposition of fines and penalties or legal costs.
10. Evaluate interruption of collaboration with key consultants and suppliers.

Source: Victor O. Schinnerer & Company, Inc.

TABLE 12.22   Emergency Management Plan Checklist

1. Develop emergency evacuation plans.
2. Plan for an alternative work site during emergencies.
3. Establish procedures specifying circumstances when a facility will close, who decides, how the decision is communicated, and if employees will be paid.
4. Develop plans for alternative electricity, water, gas, and other public utilities.
5. Identify a public relations spokesperson with responsibilities and authority that is carefully and thoroughly defined.
6. Require individuals with key responsibilities to keep copies of the emergency plan at their homes in the event of an emergency.
7. Establish a procedure to update the plan annually.
8. Determine if there are local industry-specific groups to offer support, such as professional societies, trade associations, or business alliance groups.
9. Create and maintain a list of emergency contact phone numbers for key employees, building services, local law enforcement, and public officials.
10. Communicate emergency policies and procedures to employees.

Source: Victor O. Schinnerer & Company, Inc.

Administration and Record Keeping

An organization must maintain complete records and plans to ensure an efficient emergency response and recovery. Certain records may also be required by regulation or insurance carriers, and may prove to be invaluable if legal action occurs after an incident. Managers should:

- Document drills, exercises, and their critiques
- Maintain complete telephone logs and records of events
- Keep a record of injuries and follow-up actions
- Document incident investigations and recovery operations

Direction and Control

The system for managing resources, analyzing information, notifying affected parties, and making decisions is called direction and control. Procedures must be established to designate a person or group to assume command and assess the situation. Decisions can range from activating emergency resources to ordering an evacuation. An organization should establish procedures for employees to report an internal emergency so that immediate action can be taken. A leader must be present to oversee all incident response activities and declare the incident over.

Life Safety

Protecting the health, safety, and welfare of building occupants is the first priority in an emergency. Evacuation planning should establish a clear chain of command. Identify personnel with the authority to order an evacuation and designate personnel to assist others. Evacuation procedures should include a system of accounting for all personnel. Situations could result from a highly localized problem, such as a fire or explosion, to a communitywide evacuation, such as a bomb threat or release of hazardous materials.

Confusion can lead to unnecessary and dangerous search-and-rescue operations. Facility managers should establish a method of accounting for nonemployees, such as visitors, suppliers, customers, and clients. Some facilities develop emergency escape routes, procedures for employees responsible for critical operations during an evacuation, and medical duties for assigned employees.

Property and Records Protection

Protecting facilities, equipment, and vital records is necessary to restoring operations once an emergency has occurred. Few organizations understand the importance of establishing an alternative work site, a hot site, where back-up equipment, software, communications systems, and records are ready for use. Mutual aid agreements, coordinated through professional societies or trade associations, allow an organization displaced by an emergency to continue operations.

In any organization, the most critical items are business records. Storing copies of critical information, such as accounts receivable, client and customer information, or outstanding billings in a safe and secure off-site location will avert a total loss. Maintaining daily backups of records and work in progress, and back-up equipment necessary to continue operations at a location other than the primary work site, will rapidly restore operations (Table 12.23).

Recovery and Restoration

Business resumption relates to an organization's ability to earn revenues. Keeping people employed and the organization operational enables a business to meet contractual commitments and satisfy customers and clients. Service interruptions, loss of facilities, or the absence of professional and technical staff can challenge an organization's viability, particularly for professional service firms and other business entities that rely heavily on employee intellectual capital (Table 12.24).

In some recovery situations, management continuity may be an issue, because not every key person will be readily available or physically at the facility or replacement site after an emergency. Corporations will need to consult legal counsel regarding laws and corporate bylaws governing management continuity. Employee support is important during recovery. Management might consider services to be provided, or allow employees to regain productivity while preserving family relationships.

ASSESSING INSURANCE COVERAGE

Homeowners, tenants, and businesses often discover they are not properly insured only after they have suffered a loss. Lack of appropriate coverage can be financially devastating, especially as insurance

TABLE 12.23 Lessons Learned from September 11, 2001: Records Protection

> After the events of September 11, 2001, businesses, organizations, and residents in Lower Manhattan were forced to evacuate their premises and relocate to other sites, for weeks and months before being allowed to reenter their buildings. Many businesses, including design and construction organizations and residences, lost all records, drawings, and files, and had to find alternative ways to recreate information, through clients, customers, and consultants, if back-up systems were destroyed or did not exist. Off-site back-up systems of records and data will expedite business continuity after an emergency or disaster.

TABLE 12.24 Disaster Recovery and Restoration Checklist

1. Make contractual arrangements with vendors for post-emergency services.
2. Plan for records preservation, equipment repair or replacement, and immediate communication systems restoration.
3. Determine critical operation and plan to bring critical systems back online.
4. Review management continuity policies and procedures.
5. Establish recovery decision-making chain of command.
6. Evaluate property and business continuity policies and claims with insurance carrier.

Source: Victor O. Schinnerer & Company, Inc.

companies place increased burdens on policyholders. The key to staying afloat after a disaster is advance planning and preparation. Creating a continuity plan and assessing the important factors relating to appropriate insurance coverage is the first step to ensuring a swift disaster recovery phase (Table 12.25).

DISASTER RESPONSE: CRISIS MANAGEMENT and PUBLIC RELATIONS

During any emergency, the first response requires quick, decisive action. Whether the situation concerns a building, local emergency, or regional disaster, professionals, business owners, and public officials should review, prepare, and become familiar with the basic elements of public relations and effective communications with the media, before disaster strikes. Professional service firms, public agencies, and nonprofit organizations should include media relations as another disaster planning criteria. The following information is directed toward design professionals, but the fundamentals of preparation, research, communication, honesty, and control may be applied to many organizations dealing with the media in a crisis situation.

Technical Expertise

Design professionals may be challenged by the media to show how their design may have caused or exacerbated a crisis, or may be confronted with leading questions to elicit a technical analysis and a technical response. In some instances, design professionals have been characterized by the media as focused on efficiency or building appearance, and not on the health, safety, and welfare of the public. Professionals can provide expertise and serve as authoritative sources of information for potentially confusing technical issues. Preparing for events should include collecting and ascertaining facts, before taking action or speaking to the media.

Communication with the public can enhance public image during emergencies. During crisis situations, the media may contact organizations and individuals seeking comment, because of their expertise. Familiarity with crisis response skills is important for effective communication.

TABLE 12.25   Disaster Recovery: Key Factors for Assessing Insurance Coverage

1. Property values
2. Policy coverage for perils or cause of loss
3. Deductibles
4. Policy actions and requirements in the event of a loss
5. Records and documentation to be required by insurance company
6. Safe location of records where they can be obtained after an emergency
7. Extent of coverage for loss due to interruption of power
8. Coverage availability for on- and off-premises power interruption
9. Coverage for lost income in the event of business interruption
10. Adequacy of overall insurance coverage
11. Duration of insurance coverage
12. Duration of coverage for lost income if a business is closed by a civil authority
13. Extent of coverage for reduced income due to clients not immediately returning once the business reopens
14. Impact of the business emergency management program affecting insurance rates
15. Business interruption insurance
16. Extra expense coverage for the temporary relocation and extended indemnity to allow extra time to restore revenue to predisaster levels

Source: Victor O. Schinnerer & Company, Inc.

Preparation

One of the major challenges of crisis management public relations is providing the media with information consistent with the facts. Professionals should avoid hysteria by analyzing and synthesizing facts and developing meaningful, accurate information. In a technically complex situation, the media may not know who or what to believe and could report inaccurate information. Most reporters, under deadline to write a story, rely on experts to provide background. The more people who speak to the press, the greater likelihood there is for conflicting or inaccurate stories.

- Develop an action plan to handle all types of crises that could occur. Whether the situation is a problem with a project that has received public attention or is a major catastrophe, if a crisis strikes, the organization will be ready.
- Designate a media point of contact in-house or a public relations consultant, to coordinate inquiries and interviews when dealing with a crisis. This person will field media inquiries, arrange press conferences and interviews with key people, prepare and coordinate release of updates and fact-checked information. This person will not necessarily be the organization's spokesperson, but should coordinate statements of the spokesperson.
- Identify a representative to speak to the media and be the public face of the organization. This spokesperson should be able to handle complex, detailed information, announce the organization's position, articulate an overview of what is being done to remedy the situation, and express concern for those affected. The organization's spokesperson should be able to hold up under extreme pressure, look confident, and express concern.

Research and Dissemination

It is impossible to answer news media questions about a crisis situation in an accurate, informative, and positive fashion without knowing as many of the facts as possible. There may be pressure to respond without direct knowledge of the facts.

- Gather information available about the crisis and prepare written statements.
- Do not speculate about the incident or an emergency.
- Do not permit unauthorized personnel, including staff, consultants, or those on the job site, to release information.
- Direct staff to forward all inquiries to the media point of contact.
- Establish procedures for ascertaining that information to be released to the media is complete, accurate, and approved for public release.
- Encourage accurate reporting by preparing a statement or fact sheet with important information. Documenting information increases the likelihood that the public and the media will better understand and report the facts (Table 12.26).

TABLE 12.26   Media Fact Sheet and Public Statement Checklist

1. Provide date, name, and contact data for the primary media point of contact, or organizational spokesperson.
2. Discuss the problem.
3. Describe what can be done.
4. Show concern for those affected.
5. Describe specific efforts and the next steps the organization will be making to solve the problem.

Source: Victor O. Schinnerer & Company, Inc.

Communication

Get information to the media as quickly as possible, since the longer an organization waits, the greater chance there is for inaccurate information to be disseminated. Make a point of updating the media as new information becomes available. This precludes reporters from doing their own investigation and analyses. Establishing relationships with local or beat reporters is helpful before a crisis occurs, so they will know who can provide timely, reliable information.

Honesty

Never provide misleading information to the news media. That is the fastest way of developing a negative public image. Do not give any information to the news media that has not been fact-checked or that cannot be confirmed. Rumors or speculation do not represent a professional opinion. Do not try to hide information to protect the organization's reputation. Do not cover up the facts or place blame for an incident. If reporters learn of such an effort, they will question subsequent materials and information from the organization.

Control

If a crisis occurs at a specific location, such as a project or building site, ensure that the organization has trained staff on location to answer questions and keep reporters from interfering with any objective investigation. If a media point of contact has not yet been designated, alert staff at the office to handle media inquiries by reading from a fact sheet and taking messages for the organization's official representative. By controlling the form and delivery of information, the likelihood and damage of misinformation can be minimized.

In any crisis situation, the media is an organization's most important link to the public. By developing and maintaining positive relations with the local print and broadcast media outlets in an area, an organization can exhibit professionalism and convey expertise by communicating vital public information in an emergency or crisis situation.

ACKNOWLEDGMENTS

Disaster planning, response, and recovery:

- Charles F. Harper, FAIA, Principal, Harper Perkins Architects, Wichita Falls, Texas
- Terrance J. Brown, FAIA, CDT Senior Architect, ASCG Inc., Albuquerque, New Mexico

Professional liability, risk management, emergency response: Information was adapted, with permission, from materials prepared by Victor O. Schinnerer & Company, Inc.

- Frank D. Musica, Esq., Risk Management Attorney, Victor O. Schinnerer & Company, Inc., Chevy Chase, Maryland
- Paul V. Riccardi, Publications Specialist, Victor O. Schinnerer & Company, Inc., Chevy Chase, Maryland

BIBLIOGRAPHY

Broder, John M., "With California Blazes Out or Down, Firefighters are Sent Home," *The New York Times,* Nov. 2, 2003.

Geer, Ira (Ed.), *Glossary of Weather and Climate,* The American Meteorology Society, Dec. 1996.

Giovannini, Joseph, "Fighting Fire with Steel, Pools and Plaster," *The New York Times,* Oct. 30, 2003.

Harper, Charles, FAIA, "Design and Construction Can Help Rural Homes Avoid Wind Damage," *Rural Voices,* Housing Assistance Council, Fall 2000, pp. 5–7 www.ruralhome.org/pubs/ruralvoices/VoicesFall2000.pdf

Insurance Information Institute, *Hurricane and Windstorm Deductibles,* June 2002.

Liepold, Paula, "Lessons for Rural Infrastructure from the Flood of the Century," *Rural Voices,* The Housing Assistance Council, Fall 2000, vol. 5, no. 4, pp.10–11.

Murphy, Dean, "In California's Inferno, an Oasis of Fire Safety Planning Stands Out," *The New York Times,* Nov. 2, 2003.

National Severe Storms Laboratory, National Weather Service, NOAA, *Tornadoes: Nature's Most Violent Storms,* May 12, 1998, updated March 13, 2002.

Prudential Property and Casualty Insurance Company, *Your Guide to a Secure Home,* Holmdel, N.J., 2000.

Robinson, Sherry, "Damage Isn't All Visible: State AIA members Are Volunteering in Los Alamos," *Albuquerque Tribune,* May 29, 2000.

Spagat, Elliot, "Largest California Wildfire Contained," *The State* (Associated Press), Nov. 4, 2003.

U.S. Department of Energy, Department of Environmental Management. *New Mexico's Cerro Grande Fire Rehabilitation.,* Dec. 5, 2000.

Victor O. Schinnerer & Company, Inc., *Schinnerer's Guidelines for Improving Practice,* Chevy Chase, Md.

- *Assessing Insurance Coverage for Disaster Recovery,* Sept./Oct. 2001.
- *Emergency Planning, Response and Recovery,* Sept./Oct. 2001.
- *Indemnification Language When Providing Limited Professional Services in an Emergency Situation,* Sept./Oct. 2001.
- *Preparing for a Power Outage,* Sept./Oct. 2001 and May/June 2001.
- *Providing Services in an Emergency Situation,* Sept./Oct. 2001.
- *Responding to a Crisis as a Professional,* Sept./Oct. 2001.

INTERNET RESOURCES

Disaster Assistance Team Program
"Guidelines for Disaster Response and
  Recovery Programs"
American Institute of Architects, 1999
www.aia.org/security/DisasterAssistanceHandbook.pdf

Federal Emergency Management Agency (FEMA)
www.fema.gov

Disaster Communities
www.fema.gov/tabs_disaster.shtm

National Oceanic and Atmospheric
  Administration (NOAA)
www.noaa.gov

National Severe Storms Laboratory
www.nssl.noaa.gov

National Weather Service
www.nws.noaa.gov

Bioterrorism

U.S. Department of Health and Human Services
Centers for Disease Control and Prevention
www.bt.cdc.gov

Disaster Planning and Response

Federal Disaster Management
www.disasterhelp.gov

Institute for Disaster Research, Wind Science
  and Engineering Research Center
Texas Tech University, Lubbock, Tex.
www.wind.ttu.edu/idr.asp

Fires

Firewise, *Tips around Your Home: Design and Maintenance, Construction, Landscaping* www.firewise.org.

U.S. Fire Administration
Department of Homeland Security, FEMA
www.usfa.fema.gov

Floods

FEMA, *Homeowner's Guide to Retrofitting: Six Ways to Protect Your House from Flooding* www.fema.gov/hazards/hurricanes/rfit.shtm

Hurricanes

National Hurricane Center
Tropical Prediction Center, NOAA
www.nhc.noaa.gov

FEMA, *Surviving the Storm: A Guide for Hurricane Preparedness* www.fema.gov/hazards/hurricanes/ survivingthestorm.shtm

Insurance

Insurance Information Institute
www.iii.org

Victor O. Schinnerer & Company, Inc.
www.schinnerer.com

Safe Rooms

National Performance Criteria for Tornado Shelters www.fema.gov/hazards/tornadoes/npc_ts.shtm

FEMA, *Safe Rooms for Tornadoes* www.fema.gov/mit/saferoom/

- FEMA, *Taking Shelter from the Storm: Building a Safe Room Inside Your House*, FEMA 320, August 1999.
- FEMA, *Design and Construction Guidance or Community Shelters*, FEMA 361, July 2000.

National Storm Shelter Association
www.nssa.cc

Wind Science and Engineering Research Center
Texas Tech University
www.wind.ttu.edu

In-residence tornado shelters
www.wind.ttu.edu/inshelter/inshelte.asp

In-residence shelter plans and details by TTU and Harper Perkins Architects
www.harperperkins.com/shelter.htm

Tornadoes

National Weather Service, Storm Prediction Center www.spc.noaa.gov

Tornado Information—NOAA
http://w3.noaa.gov/tornadoes.html

CHAPTER 13

INDUSTRIAL FACILITIES AND OFFICE BUILDINGS: SAFETY, SECURITY, SITE SELECTION, AND WORKPLACE VIOLENCE

Barbara A. Nadel, FAIA
Principal, Barbara Nadel Architect
Forest Hills, New York

Randomness and lack of warning are the attributes of human violence we fear most, but you know that human violence is rarely random and rarely without warning.
> GAVIN DE BECKER (b. 1954)
> *Author, The Gift of Fear*
> *U.S. expert on violent behavior*

From automotive manufacturers and window assembly plants, to computer companies and halls of government, security requirements at industrial and civic facilities are major concerns. Industrial espionage, workplace violence, theft, and acts of terrorism, regardless of their origin, are the twenty-first century realities all businesses and employers must address.

Security planning and design are important factors when evaluating sites for new facilities, retrofitting, or moving into existing facilities. A comprehensive security plan will enable industrial facility managers to reduce potential liability exposure, without always installing costly technology equipment. Integrating security policies and procedures into ongoing operations results in a safer workplace for management, employees, visitors, and members of the surrounding community (Fig. 13.1).

SITE SELECTION ISSUES

As soon as the decision is made to review properties for site selection, whether for new construction or an existing building location, building owners can begin assembling information to help them during the identification, evaluation, and analysis process.

Crime statistical data reports, organized by census tract, provide useful information about an area, such as crimes against people and property, homicides, rapes, assaults, auto theft, and burglary. These reports are useful when considering the nature of the potential workforce, including the ratio of males to females, whether operations will be primarily conducted on a nine-to-five basis or around the clock, and the types of public and private transportation to be used by most potential employees in the vicinity.

FIGURE 13.1 Intel Computer Chip Manufacturing Plant, Rio Rancho, New Mexico. (*Pen and ink drawing: Terrance J. Brown, FAIA.*)

TABLE 13.1 Environmental Design Elements for Industrial Facilities

- Carefully placed and maintained landscaping to maximize observation from the street
- Appropriate lighting levels
- Clear and unobstructed sight lines
- Building setbacks from the street
- Large trees planted where they can stop cars from battering a building
- Limited vehicular access in certain areas
- Low-rise concrete barriers, or bollards, in front of entries and high-security zones
- Designated parking zones for visitors, staff, and service vehicles

Crime prevention through environmental design (CPTED) is a planning concept based on access control, surveillance, and territorial reinforcement. Workplace safety can be improved by implementing CPTED principles, by layering security levels inward from site perimeters to building interiors. Physical site characteristics, such as soft boundaries and transition zones, through creation of low height berms and gently graded slopes, can delineate public and private areas without fencing (Table 13.1).

Liability Concerns

Land use adjacencies may be a prime factor during the site selection and review process. Industrial facility owners seeking to maintain a low profile would not be likely to locate a plant next to a site drawing high traffic, visitors, and the public. In an effort to increase their tax base by luring new business to local cities and counties, municipalities occasionally offer financial packages, tax breaks, and other incentives from neighborhood revitalization programs. Industrial owners must carefully evaluate the terms of any shared development costs and specifications. Municipalities may seek use of parks and green space on an industrial site for public recreation. Such activity could present liability problems if someone got hurt on the grounds of an industrial site. Owners may wish to seek an official release from liability and damages if they agree to allow the public to use privately owned property.

The beauty or advantage of an area drawing people in could turn out to be something else entirely, and become an attractive nuisance. For example, employee ball fields on a privately owned site are a concern when seeking to avoid litigation. Owners should find ways to discourage local residents from using the fields, unless an agreement is struck with the local municipality regarding liability.

Perimeter Security

Perimeter fencing defines and protects the site, by keeping people out as well as keeping goods and assets inside. Local zoning ordinances may require variances to exceed design or height requirements. Fencing, walls, gates, and enclosures should be selected on the desired level of security, visibility, and image, as well as the character of the surrounding environment (Fig. 13.2).

Lighting

The most significant deterrent to criminal activity is lighting. Good lighting levels, at surface parking lots, parking garages, and all property access points, is essential for employee safety. Lighting levels should enable observation in a parking lot and enable an employee to look around and feel more comfortable.

In parking areas, the ground, not surrounding buildings, should be illuminated. Criminals do not want a situation where they can be easily identified. The Illuminating Engineering Society of North America provides industry standards for lighting levels in most facilities.

Physical Plants

Site landscaping creates a first impression about a property, company, or agency and can enhance or detract from security and image. Perimeter security should not include hiding places in the natural environment or exterior walls of the building envelope. Regularly trimmed trees and low shrubbery will allow good sight lines and visibility opportunities for pedestrians and vehicular security or police patrols. Property owners should coordinate with local law enforcement to ascertain if they will patrol private property regularly or if contracted private security companies are necessary to monitor large sites.

Parking Garages and Lots

Building and property owners can enhance employee safety by reviewing parking lot locations and circulation routes between parking and workplace areas. Good lighting, communications devices, such as intercoms and phones, and the ability to see others in the garage should be provided. A single vehicular access and egress point will minimize the likelihood of vandalism, theft, or muggings. Perimeter fencing at surface lots may be warranted in neighborhoods where these measures may not be sufficient.

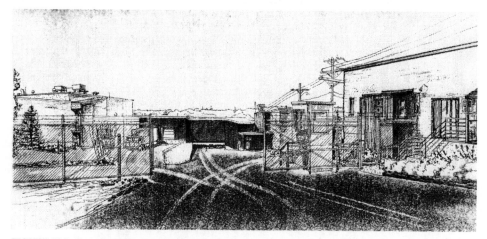

FIGURE 13.2 Factories and industrial plants maintain perimeter security to safeguard assets and limit access to public utility lines. (*Pen and ink drawing: Francis J. Sheridan, AIA.*)

Helical parking garages with ramps and without flat floors are inadvisable, as they create blind spots that cannot be viewed across a single level. Optimal visibility is achieved when an entire parking level can be seen from the middle of one level. For existing parking garages, security can be increased by the following responses:

- Performing a lighting survey to ensure that levels are at acceptable standards
- Upgrading routine maintenance procedures
- Repainting to increase reflective surfaces
- Adding a guard at the entrance
- Installing duress communication systems, such as intercoms, panic buttons, and closed circuit television (CCTV)
- Controlling access in and out of the garage
- Preventing intruders from climbing over a fence into one level from another

Facility Operations

Building owners and facility managers determine motion policies for visitors, staff, and service personnel with their sites and each building. Once access is permitted, a visitor or employee may be free to circulate on the campus or may be given an escort or pass.

Buildings may be secured individually, requiring identification at each exterior entrance, even within designated interior areas for additional access. Entry security often includes a card-swipe system to open doors, turnstiles allowing access to one person at a time, or a metal detector to screen for weapons and contraband.

CONSISTENT POLICIES

Unless all employees, including management, administrators, support personnel, and visitors are required to follow security screening and operational procedures, opportunities for security breaches will exist (Table 13.2). Research and development laboratories or highly sensitive facilities often use CCTV and other electronic recording devices to identify those in each area. Collectively, security responses monitor workplace access, products, and employees. For example, at a high-tech computer chip company, based on a security review and threat assessment, measures might include installing metal detectors to x-ray parcels going in and out of the facility, CCTV, and internal inventory controls. The need to control inventory, prevent theft, and contain hazardous material spills, whether intentional or by accident, are ongoing concerns at industrial plants (Fig. 13.3).

Intellectual property is also a valuable asset. Business, industry, and government agencies often closely guard formulas, patents, manufacturing information, finances, competitive strategic plans, client lists, and other proprietary data subject to espionage and pilferage. These assets must be protected from theft, damage, and illegal access, including by computer "hacking," or unauthorized entry to electronic computer data. At automotive and pharmaceutical plants, for example, a single building may have different security levels at different times of the day. Free movement may occur during business hours, but after hours, access may be limited in some areas, such as accounting, engineering, and research. Engineering and maintenance personnel may require total access to all facility areas, but assembly workers may be restricted to manufacturing floors and buildings.

For many industrial facilities, maintaining ongoing operations is critical to goods, services, and production, especially when these functions rely on public utilities such as power, gas, and telephone lines. To ensure industrial facility security and workplace safety, three criteria must be met:

- Protect people and assets
- Continue operations
- Prevent litigation

TABLE 13.2   Lessons Learned from 9/11: Security Screening Policies

After September 11, 2001, various forms of security screening, including sign-in sheets, requests for visitor photo identification, employee ID smart cards, and metal detectors, were installed in most New York City government and high-rise buildings.

In July 2003, a New York City councilman brought a visitor to City Hall. Despite the high security and law enforcement presence, the visitor entered City Hall carrying a concealed gun because by prior agreement, elected officials and guests were exempt from going through metal detectors. Shortly after arrival, the visitor used his concealed handgun to kill the councilman. A police officer in the council chamber immediately shot and killed the visitor. Until the facts were determined and terrorism ruled out, Manhattan mass transit networks were closed, causing great disruption. The policy was changed, requiring everyone entering City Hall to go through metal detectors, with the goal of preventing future incidents.

Tragically, we live in a world where we have to balance security with people's rights to come and go. We don't want to shut down people's right to visit City Hall or to come and express themselves.

NEW YORK CITY MAYOR, MICHAEL R. BLOOMBERG
July 23, 2003

FIGURE 13.3 Industrial worker in protective gear. (*Pen and ink drawing: Stanley Stark, AIA.*)

Building owners should also:

- Review utility feed locations, lines, and point of entry to the site and buildings (Fig. 13.4).
- Ensure that critical utilities are protected from vandalism.
- Secure transformer valves, chemicals, and gas canisters from the surrounding neighborhood.
- Discourage the public and children from entering and playing in open fields and areas where hazardous materials are stored.

Terrorists, competitors, criminals and disgruntled employees may attempt to damage or interrupt utility services and operations. For some industrial facilities, failure to maintain utility lines and continuous feeds for production schedules could result in a severe loss of inventory or data, and necessitate retooling and reprogramming. Dual feeds and emergency back-up generators, remotely located from each other, may be worth the long-term investment to protect production and ensure uninterrupted power service in the event of a natural disaster, attack, or outage.

On-site water retention areas are considered attractive nuisances, especially if they contain harmful chemicals and toxic substances. These areas should be clearly marked and enclosed or screened, to deter intruders, prevent potential accidents, and minimize liability.

ESTABLISHING POLICIES

Training programs for employees and security personnel are essential at industrial facilities, regardless of whether owners use an in-house security team or outsourced security services. Well-designed training programs describe company expectations toward security procedures, site access protocol, and emergency situations. Employee awareness training can educate workers about:

- Proper use of technology, such as access cards and biometric scanners

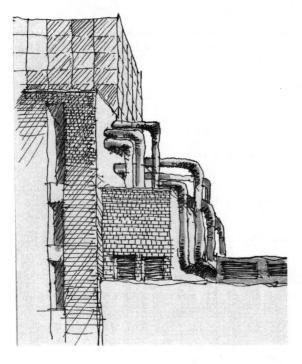

FIGURE 13.4 Industrial research facility, New York, New York. Exposed utility feeds into a building should be monitored, with limited access, to avoid vandalism. Urban research facilities must have sufficient emergency generator capacity to maintain operations for extended periods of time in the event of a blackout or power outage. (*Pen and ink drawing: Stanley Stark, AIA.*)

- Policies about allowing visitors into secure areas without proper identification
- Identifying and requiring a point of contact to report an unusual or emergency situation

For example, if an individual without identification is observed within a site, employees should know whom to call, and the person taking the call should be familiar with follow-up procedures, documentation, and investigation of the situation.

Large companies and industrial facilities with many employees and high turnover run the risk of dealing with personal problems spilling into the workplace. Human resources personnel, as well as security officers, should be aware of employee concerns, danger signs, and precautionary measures available if the need arises.

A comprehensive security plan anticipating threats and scenarios can recommend measures to address potential problems, and reassure employees about their safety. An example would be a female employee at a large industrial company employing hundreds or thousands of people, who obtains a court order against her ex-husband, preventing him from contacting her. The man succeeds in entering the secure area of her workplace several times, making the woman's co-workers nervous. Due to the high employee turnover, personnel were not familiar with rules about allowing access to nonemployees. Recommendations would include:

- Monitoring all entries by security officers
- Assigning a single visitor entrance, with sign-in and sign-out procedures
- Directing CCTV cameras to carefully monitor entries and other facility areas
- Informing employees about whom to call when an unauthorized or unidentified individual is observed on the grounds or in the building
- Training those receiving the calls on how to respond immediately and prepare proper documentation about various situations, which may be needed at a later date

DISASTER PLANNING

After the September 11, 2001 attacks, many commercial and industrial building owners revisited or created business continuity plans, disaster recovery plans, and terrorist response plans, in preparation for restoring normalcy to business operations after a disaster or security breach (Table 13.3).

Disaster Recovery Plans

Regardless of the type of workplace operation, disaster recovery plans allow businesses to rebound quickly from unforeseen events (Table 13.4). In some cases, the planning process, tasks,

TABLE 13.3   **Lessons Learned From 9/11 and the August 2003 Blackout: Disaster Planning and Review of Egress Systems.**

Within an hour after the airplanes slammed into the World Trade Center on September 11, 2001, thousands of people had evacuated the buildings through stairways because the elevators were not functioning. Subway service in New York City was suspended, forcing workers to find alternative ways to get home, many by walking to other parts of New York City to their homes or to find transportation.

On August 14, 2003, shortly after 4 p.m., E.T., a widespread blackout affected six states in the Northeast and parts of Canada, trapping many people in elevators and high floors of urban high-rises. Building occupants walked down long flights of stairs to evacuate buildings and found alternative ways to get home because the subway was not working. Many buildings were dark and exit paths were not always apparent, especially when emergency power did not cover all building zones. Some areas were without power for as long as 48 hours, and New York City subway service did not resume until the weekend, requiring the Mayor to declare August 15, 2003, a "snow day" so workers would stay home.

Employers and facility managers should review all life safety codes to ensure that emergency generators can function for extended lengths of time and building egress systems are functional. They should make plans to contact employees if the workplace is closed for any reason. Workers should keep an emergency kit at their desk, workspace, or in their cars, including a flashlight in case power goes out, and a comfortable pair of walking shoes in case public transportation is not readily available or roads are closed.

TABLE 13.4   **Developing a Disaster Recovery Plan**

Item	Tasks
Create a recovery team.	• Appoint a real estate disaster recovery team, task force, or committee. • Designate a leader or chair. Participants should include those in technology, real estate, facilities, personnel, and law. • Replicate the team in each corporate office or region nationally and globally. • Establish centralized or corporate-wide standards to be modified as necessary by satellite locations.
Establish procedures for the recovery process.	• Create a matrix of tasks and personnel to identify who will be responsible for various items during recovery. • Involve personnel responsible for finance, health and liability insurance, disability, and reconstruction in the planning process.
Identify and prioritize goals and objectives.	• Determine the most important tasks to do immediately, within a few days, a week, or months, such as restoring data and voice communications, computer operations, power and utilities, site cleanup, and lease negotiations. • Establish project management teams to determine who will be responsible for leading and ensuring completion of each activity.
Create a schedule.	• Outline the critical path and estimated time needed for each phase of the recovery process. • Coordinate simultaneous activities such as those performed by human resources, operations, facilities management, and finance.

and management skills necessary for disaster recovery are similar to those needed during emergency response.

Public and private organizations are vulnerable to terrorism, violence, and disasters. Continuity and disaster recovery plans are essential for business to remain in operation and function as safe workplaces. Contingency plans should be reviewed periodically, from a facilities and financial perspective, to ensure that all information is accurate and up-to-date.

Contact data for managers, employees, vendors, local law enforcement, media, public officials, community leaders, and software maintenance agreements should be confirmed, updated and stored in a safe place, off-site from the premises, and distributed to key people. Ongoing training and review of plans allow recovery teams to be familiar with their responsibilities. It is never too late to develop contingency operation plans to prepare for a disaster.

WORKPLACE VIOLENCE

On July 8, 2003, an assembly-line worker shot and killed five workers and wounded nine at an aircraft parts plant in Meridian, Mississippi—America's deadliest plant shooting in two and a half years. This incident, and others, raised public awareness about the threats of workplace violence, and prompted facility managers, and security directors to examine policies and implement security measures (Table 13.5).

WORKPLACE THREATS

The International Facility Management Association (IFMA) Corporate Facility Monitor conducted a survey among its members about workplace violence and security in January 2001. The survey found that over 88 percent of respondents rated security as a high priority. Industrial employers are concerned about threats from downsizing, layoffs, outsourcing, restructuring, striking workers, and replacing permanent workers with temporaries.

TABLE 13.5 Notable Incidents of Workplace Shootings, 1995 to 2003

Incident	Location	Date
1. New York City councilman shot in City Hall.	New York, New York	July 23, 2003
2. Assembly-line worker shoots and kills five people, wounds nine at Lockheed Martin aircraft parts plant.	Meridian, Mississippi	July 8, 2003
3. Software tester fatally shoots seven people at Edgewater Technology.	Wakefield, Massachusetts	December 26, 2000
4. Five people shot by fired employee at car wash.	Dallas, Texas	March 20, 2000
5. Copier repairman fatally shoots seven people at Xerox	Honolulu, Hawaii	November 2, 1999
6. Trucker kills three coworkers	Pelham, Alabama	August 5, 1999
7. Day trader kills nine people at two offices	Atlanta, Georgia	July 29, 1999
8. Lottery accountant kills four lottery executives	Newington, Connecticut	March 6, 1998
9. Fired employee kills four former coworkers at maintenance plant	Orange, California	December 18, 1997
10. Fired assembly-line worker kills four at parts plant	Aiken, South Carolina	September 15, 1997
11. Firefighter kills four superiors at firehouse.	Jackson, Mississippi	April 24, 1996
12. Former employee shoots five at refinery inspection station	Corpus Christi, Texas	April 3, 1995
13. City electrician shoots four supervisors at technical center.	Los Angeles	July 19, 1995

Source: USA Today, May 2002.

Table 13.6   Typical Workplace Threats

1. Major thefts
2. Verbal threats among employees
3. Threatening phone calls
4. Destruction and vandalism of company property
5. Verbal threats from employees to management
6. Bomb threats
7. Fights
8. Domestic violence at work
9. Weapons brought to work
10. Sexual assault
11. Hostage situations
12. Actual or attempted bombings
13. Actual or attempted murders

Source: International Facility Management Association, *Corporate Facility Monitor Survey,* January 2001.

Survey respondents reported a variety of threat types (Table 13.6). Based on the IFMA survey, workforce size directly impacts the volume of incidents reported, resulting in larger companies implementing more security measures. Facilities that are open to the public are more likely to have greater security in place than other properties. Among the most prevalent precautions were controlled building access, security guards at building entries, security patrols, and closed circuit television.

CONCLUSION

Industrial facilities and office buildings have specific security requirements, based on size, function, number of employees, site, and location. Threat assessments and security surveys identify vulnerabilities and assets, and are effective when combined with a comprehensive security plan to balance design, technology, and operations. Workplace safety can be enhanced by:

- Identifying real and potential threats to people, buildings, and assets.
- Knowing what situations make employees vulnerable.
- Watching the competition. Remain alert to the security measures competitors in the same region or industry are providing. Facilities with fewer opportunities for breaches will be subject to fewer risks.
- Evaluating the site perimeter and building envelope to prevent security threats from affecting the property. In the long run, well-designed facilities are more cost effective, especially if 24 hours-a-day/7 days-a-week security patrols can be avoided.
- Applying security in layers, based on the CPTED principles, at the site perimeter, building exterior, vestibules, lobbies, and loading docks. Defensible layers should create a consistent security ring. If one entry is staffed with a guard to monitor deliveries, all other building entries should be observed or be subject to restricted access. Different means can be used to ensure the same results.
- Preparing and regularly updating disaster recovery and business continuity plans.

Greater security at industrial facilities and office buildings will result in a safer workplace, better staff morale, cost-effective operations, good community relations, and potentially reduced risk and liability.

BIBLIOGRAPHY

Armour, Stephanie, "Employers Fight Violence, Many Taking New Steps to Keep Workers Safe," *USA Today,* May 9, 2002.

International Facility Management Association, Corporate Facility Monitor, *Workplace Violence and Security Survey,* January 2001.

Nadel, Barbara A., "Safe & Secure: Lock Out Crime at Properties with a Comprehensive Security Program," *Commercial Investment Real Estate,* May/June 2001.

Nadel, Barbara A., *Building Security through Environmental Design: Developers, Building Owners, and Tenants Can Protect People and Assets by Planning Ahead,* National Association of Industrial and Office Properties, Northern Virginia Chapter, Herndon, Va., May 2002.

Tomlinson, Asha, "Re-evaluating Your Workplace: Is It Safe and Secure?" *Canadian HR Reporter,* February 25, 2002.

INTERNET RESOURCES

American Society of Industrial
Security (ASIS)
www.asisonline.org

Area Development Magazine
www.area-development.com

Canadian HR Reporter—Journal of Human
Resource Management
www.hrreporter.com

CCIM Institute
www.ccim.com

Commercial Investment Real Estate Magazine
www.ccim.com/magazine

Illuminating Engineering Society of North
America (IESNA)
www.iesna.org

International Facilities Management
Association (IFMA)
www.ifma.org

National Association of Industrial and Office
Properties (NAIOP)
www.naiop.org

Security Management
www.securitymanagement.com

Today's Facility Manager
www.TodaysFacilityManager.com

CHAPTER 14
LOBBY SECURITY DESIGN: FIRST IMPRESSIONS

Casey L. Jones
Director, First Impressions Program
Office of the Chief Architect
Public Buildings Service
U.S. General Services Administration
Washington, D.C.

Openness in Federal architecture is a symbol of inestimable value. Our government is not distant. It is a government of the people. And our public buildings must say they are about people and our democratic values.

STEPHEN BREYER (B.1938)
U.S. Supreme Court Justice

Prior to the terrorist attacks of September 11, 2001, concern about internal building security was often limited to specific building types. Airports, courthouses, and banks had systems in place to protect building occupants and assets against various threats. Libraries and retailers installed preventative security measures to reduce and eliminate theft, while schools, religious facilities, health clinics, and industrial workplaces, to name a few, have frequently had to address unique threats related to building occupants and functions.

However, since September 11, 2001, lobby screening has become standard policy for many public and private sector facilities. In the United States, many building owners have implemented changes in operational procedures, design, and technology to address potential threats, especially for iconic American landmarks and other highly vulnerable targets.

Lobbies of federal properties are gateways to governmental and judicial services. They shape visitor perception of the federal government. Integrating good design and security checkpoints in federal building lobbies conveys professionalism and assures visitors their personal safety and welfare is a primary concern (Fig. 14.1).

Based on the wisdom, research, and experience of the U.S. Marshals Service (USMS), the Federal Protective Service (FPS), and the Public Buildings Service (PBS) of the U.S. General Services Administration (GSA), information has been made available, along with case studies, for use by project and building managers, the design community, and security personnel as they design, construct, and maintain security screening stations in federal lobbies nationwide.

Using the research, experience, and case studies generated by the federal government, as presented here, state and local agencies, private sector landlords, and developers charged with protecting high-risk buildings have access to a significant body of information necessary to secure their facilities and protect the public.

FIGURE 14.1 Lobby rendering. (*Photo: R.M.Kliment & Frances Halsband Architects.*)

FIRST IMPRESSIONS

Although security screening stations have been installed in federal courthouses since the mid-1980s, screening stations in many federal office buildings were hastily pieced together to provide added security after the 1995 Oklahoma City bombing and the September 11, 2001 terrorist attacks. To quickly accommodate the need for furniture and equipment, the FPS and the USMS, working with local building security committees, assembled screening stations by procuring security equipment and using available "excessed" furniture. The equipment and furniture in these facilities were often haphazardly arranged to fit within a variety of vestibules and lobby configurations. While the effort provided needed building security, the collection of large equipment and mismatched furniture often resulted in a chaotic appearance.

The General Services Administration instituted the First Impressions program in 1998 to ensure that all federal facilities presented a good first impression to those entering the building, conveying an aura of professionalism, conscientiousness, and capability, while improving security effectiveness. The program challenges designers to balance architecture and security in federal lobbies.

BUILDING DESIGN STANDARDS

Federal building security is evaluated on a case-by-case basis by the FPS and USMS. The overall responsibility for security on federal property belongs to the FPS. The U.S. Marshal Service has the primary role in courthouses. These agencies work with either the court security committee in the case of courthouses, or the building security committee in the case of multitenant buildings, to create a security policy for the property. These evaluations are based upon the building's security risk classification, as determined by the U.S. Department of Justice Vulnerability Assessment of Federal Facilities.

On federal projects, it is strongly recommended that every designer and project manager consult either the USMS or the FPS, depending upon the type of federal building being renovated or constructed, at the earliest possible project stage, to properly address the building's specific security needs.

ENTRANCES

Where security is an issue, buildings should generally be provided with a single, public entrance. For U.S. courthouses, this is a strict requirement. Security stations must be positioned to provide security officers with clear views of the building entrance from their posts. Designers must provide adequate room for visitors queuing in front of the security screening station. Minimum dimensions apply, but actual dimensions of this space must be carefully coordinated with the volume of traffic expected in the building (Fig. 14.2).

Separation of Entrance and Exit Paths

Separation of the entrance and exit paths is critical to prevent the passing of items between screened and not-yet-screened visitors. If positioned properly, the station can act as a natural separator of these paths. Vertical organization must be considered regarding this separation. For example, an atrium space allowing not-yet-screened visitors to drop or pass items to screened visitors would be unacceptable.

Adequate Queuing Space

On the entrance side of the station, designers must provide adequate space for queuing. The space should allow visitors to stand in line comfortably, while maintaining the security officers' views of the entrance area. The amount of space provided must be adequate for the expected number of visitors to the building. Similarly, if elevators are on the secure side of the screening station, adequate space must

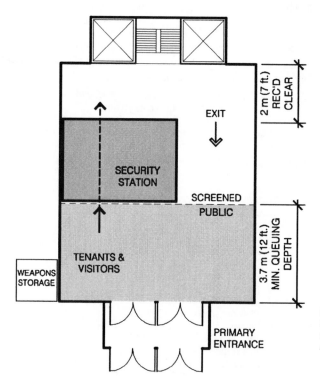

FIGURE 14.2 Lobby diagram illustrating separation of entry and exit paths. (*Photo: R.M.Kliment & Frances Halsband Architects.*)

be provided for queuing, so as not to impede security guard movement. If this space is not available, GSA recommends designers provide a rear partition to clearly demarcate the security station zone.

When a building receives a high volume of traffic, or when a lower threat level permits, a supplemental screening system should be considered to handle tenant traffic. In these cases, tenants are typically prescreened by a security agent and provided with a building identification card, to be checked upon entering. Employees with identification may forego metal detectors and x-ray machines when entering.

FREE ZONE

A free zone is interior space located between the exterior plaza and secure portions of the interior. This space, integral to federal building planning, provides a public environment without cumbersome restrictions. The size of a free zone can vary from a generously scaled room to a small vestibule, and might contain a building directory, concierge, information kiosk, or public seating. The free zone can be a space within the principal building volume, or a space separate from the building.

In addition to the impact a free zone may have on public perception of a federal building, the free zone satisfies several functional requirements. Functional needs vary greatly by building type, but may include

- Access to government forms, such as IRS tax returns or other informational brochures
- Interaction with government printing facilities
- Access to computer stations to gather information about federal government services

Design of the exterior plaza, free zone, and secure lobby should be seen as opportunities to support building security requirements.

- A free zone should be sized to allow comfortable visitor queuing prior to screening.
- A plaza should be sized appropriately to accommodate programmed activities.
- The secure lobby should be large enough to accommodate high traffic volumes to and from elevator banks, stairs, waiting areas, and information facilities.
- Plaza space outside of a building is an extension of the free zone, and for many projects, may be the only place for public interaction prior to building security.

Many free zone functions may be incorporated into plaza design. The plaza, free zone, and secure lobby must meet project requirements and restrictions. These areas should be sized and designed to accommodate street furniture, graphics, signage, and other site-specific design elements (Tables 14.1 to 14.3 and Fig. 14.3).

TABLE 14.1   Plaza Design Elements

1. Art
2. Landscape
3. Information kiosk
4. Food cart
5. Honor boxes
6. Places to sit
7. Places to eat
8. Places to smoke
9. Phones
10. Bicycle racks
11. Bus shelter
12. Events: farmers' market, craft fair, music festival

Source: U.S. GSA.

TABLE 14.2   Free Zone Design Elements

1. Art
2. Building directory
3. Information kiosk
4. Concierge and sign-in desk
5. Post Office
6. Food café
7. Seal and flags
8. President's portrait
9. Charter of Freedom
10. IRS forms
11. Government printing
12. Retail
13. Places to sit
14. Computers
15. ATMs

Source: U.S. GSA.

TABLE 14.3   Secure Lobby Design Elements

1. Art
2. Food café
3. Newsstand
4. Fed kids, child care center
5. Telephones
6. Business center
7. Computers
8. Federal Credit Union ATMs
9. Find Our Children
10. HUD Next Door
11. Stamp vending
12. Hassle-free kiosk

Source: U.S. GSA.

SCREENING STATIONS

Security screening stations should be located to provide an unobstructed view of the lobby and entrance area.

Location

An unimpeded view of the entrance allows monitoring of those who have not yet been screened. Depending on the lobby configuration, clear views may eliminate the need for an additional security officer to monitor the entrance, resulting in an operational cost savings. In the majority of installations, locating the security screening station directly between the entrance and the interior lobby is the simplest and most effective layout. The need for directional signage is minimized. Security stations should be positioned so the entry and exit paths are clearly separated. The security station can act as a natural barrier (Fig. 14.4).

In buildings with significant threat levels, the entrance area should be kept separate from the principal building volume. In this arrangement, potential threats from persons not yet screened by security

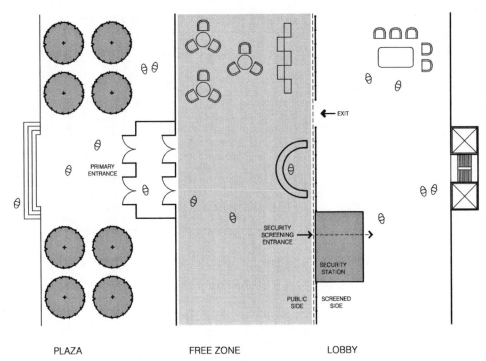

PLAZA   FREE ZONE   LOBBY

FIGURE 14.3 Schematic diagram of plaza, free zone, and secure lobby. (*Photo: R.M.Kliment & Frances Halsband Architects.*)

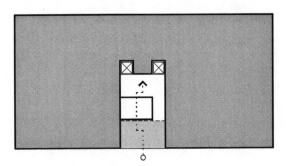

FIGURE 14.4 Diagram of simple security station location. (*Photo: R.M.Kliment & Frances Halsband Architects.*)

personnel are reduced because they are not beneath the building's principal structural frame. This approach might also be used in retrofitting existing buildings with limited interior space (Fig. 14.5).

In settings where building tenants do not require screening each time they enter the building, a separate entrance must be provided (Fig. 14.6). This entrance should be clearly separated from the building exit path. Optical scanners can be used to detect anyone trying to breach security by entering through the exit, against traffic.

In certain situations, locating the security screening station directly adjacent to the lobby may be advantageous, such as in a small, existing lobby, or a lobby with historical significance. Special consideration should be given to directing visitors out of the main space and through the security station. As with all security stations, security personnel must still have a clear view of the building entrance (Fig. 14.7).

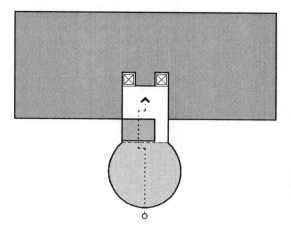

FIGURE 14.5 Diagram of free zone separated from principle building volume. (*Photo: R.M. Kliment & Frances Halsband Architects.*)

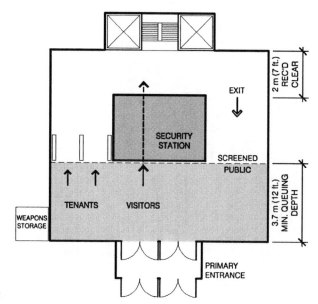

FIGURE 14.6 Lobby diagram illustrating separate entrances for visitors and tenants. (*Photo: R.M.Kliment & Frances Halsband Architects.*)

STATION ARRANGEMENT AND OPERATIONS

The typical security screening station arrangement utilizes the services of two security officers.

- The primary function of the officer positioned within a protected security station is to observe the x-ray scanner and the monitor.
- The other officer is positioned on the secure side of the metal detector and monitors visitors as the equipment screens them.

This arrangement facilitates placement of items loaded onto the x-ray scanner front conveyor belt. The visitor places bags or other items requiring scanning on the x-ray scanner conveyor belt and

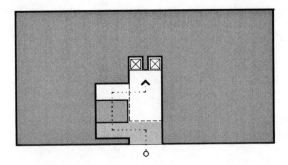

FIGURE 14.7 Diagram of security screening station adjacent to lobby. (*Photo: R.M.Kliment & Frances Halsband Architects.*)

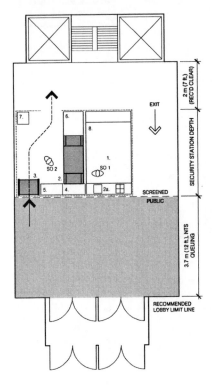

FIGURE 14.8 Diagram of security screening station layout. (*Photo: R.M.Kliment & Frances Halsband Architects.*)

places metal personal items (coins, pens, rings) in the tray, which is then passed through the x-ray scanner. The visitor then passes through the metal detector, while being observed by the security officer. The security officer pulls scanned items requiring further investigation from the rear conveyor belt to a baggage search table.

Any security station should be designed so that both security officers can access these areas from either side of the station. Entrance and exit paths should be clearly separated. The layout should be simple and allow for efficient staffing of the security station and good traffic flow (Fig. 14.8).

Because of the weight of the ballistic material forming the enclosure, the development of any security station must involve appropriate structural analysis of the floor below and should be coordinated with any additional requirements from the responsible security agency. The final design must include a complete supporting structural frame whose connections provide structural continuity, and which may require anchorage or additional members.

EQUIPMENT

Federal facilities, like airports, are equipped with metal detectors and x-ray machines in the lobby to screen individuals entering the building.

Metal Detectors

For walk-through metal detectors federal agencies require the following:

- All metal detectors must be ADA-compliant, with the inner width dimension clearing at least 32 inches.
- Decorative millwork or panels around the metal detectors must allow for quick and easy removal of the whole unit for routine maintenance.
- The enclosures must also allow for reasonable increase in the dimensions of replacement equipment.
- The enclosures around the walk-through metal detector can have metal trim, but cannot consist wholly of metal sheets as they interfere with the machine's signal.
- Walk-through metal detectors should not be placed too close to the moving metal parts of other building equipment, such as metal doors.

See Figs. 14.9 to 14.11.

FIGURE 14.9 Typical metal detector, front view. (*Source: CEIA-USA.*)

X-Ray Machines

For x-ray machines, federal agencies require the following:

- All decorative millwork or panels around the x-ray must allow for quick and easy removal of the whole unit for routine maintenance.
- The enclosures must also allow for reasonable increases in dimensions of replacement equipment. Unlike most evolving technology, newer generation X-ray machines are often larger than older models. Enclosures should be designed to accommodate larger, newer equipment.
- Intake and discharge areas should be clean and unobstructed, with adequate room to review the contents of scanned materials, as necessary.
- Intake counters should allow disabled people to deposit their personal items on the conveyor belt for scanning.

See Figs. 14.12 to 14.14.

Secure Area

The secure area starts immediately after visitors have passed through the security station. To maintain the secure zone, the area should be designed so unscreened

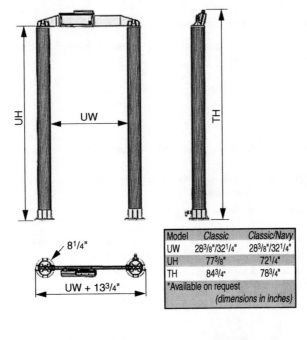

Model	Classic	Classic/Navy
UW	28³/₈"/32¹/₄"	28³/₈"/32¹/₄"
UH	77³/₈"	72¹/₄"
TH	84³/₄"	78³/₄"
*Available on request		
	(dimensions in inches)	

FIGURE 14.10   Typical metal detector, details. (*Source: CEIA-USA.*)

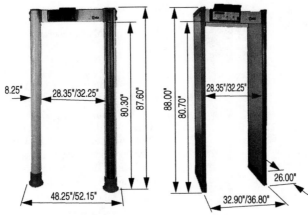

FIGURE 14.11   Typical metal detectors, with clearances. (*Source: CEIA-USA.*)

visitors may not come in contact with screened individuals, preventing anything from being handed off from one area to next. The security station should be located so there is sufficient secure space for people to queue in front of elevators, reorient, and redirect themselves. Exits from the secure area back into the lobby should be positioned so security officers can easily supervise them.

CASE STUDIES

The following case studies examine the layout and positioning of the security screening stations in various federal buildings. Each study provides an overview of how spaces are arranged, and is not

FIGURE 14.12   Typical x-ray scanner and related equipment. (*Source: Heimann Systems.*)

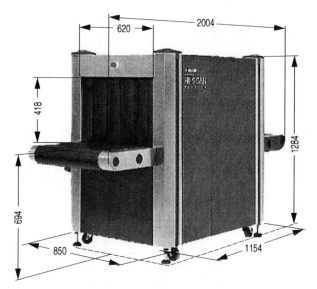

FIGURE 14.13   Typical x-ray scanner, with dimensions. (*Source: Heimann Systems.*)

intended as a critique of the building design. At federal properties, many factors impact decisions regarding planning and design of security systems, including, most importantly, the vulnerability assessment by the presiding federal security agency.

These examples are suited to a specific context and may not meet the needs of other projects. General comments regarding the architectural planning of each case study are followed by the highlights of each security screening station design. The security assessment of each case study focuses solely on the positive attributes of the screening station. Descriptions of potential vulnerabilities are not included.

Boston, Massachusetts: John Joseph Moakley U.S. Courthouse (Architect: Pei Cobb Freed & Partners)

The entrance hall of the John Joseph Moakley U.S. Courthouse is sized to receive large numbers of visitors. The scale and open arrangement of the lobby's free zone provides a welcoming

FIGURE 14.14   Typical x-ray scanner attachments. (*Source: Heimann Systems.*)

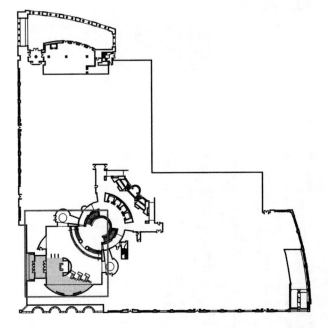

FIGURE 14.15   John Joseph Moakley U.S. Courthouse, Boston, Mass. Building plan. (*Architect: Pei Cobb Fried & Partners; photo: GSA.*)

public space. Passive supervision of the space is provided through a centrally located concierge desk. Three security stations are provided to one side of the concierge desk facing the entrance. The stations are staggered to accommodate queues of varying length within the lobby. Tenants and employees with appropriate identification are granted separate, controlled access through optical scanning stations. Exiting is provided directly adjacent to the employee entrance (Figs. 14.15 to 14.19).

Security stations are clad in millwork, detailed with flat panels that reveal joints, complementing the building's modern aesthetic. Keyboards and monitors for the x-ray machine are contained within millwork enclosures, which are elegant, but may pose maintenance issues. The discharge and baggage-search tables are designed as a single surface. Magnetometers are handsomely fitted out with wood casework, creating framed gateways. Following security screening, visitors ascend a short flight of steps through a large rotunda to the elevator lobby.

- The exit and entrance paths are clearly separated.
- The discharge end of the x-ray machines provides good baggage search and retrieval space.

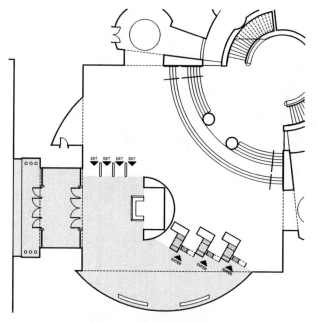

FIGURE 14.16 John Joseph Moakley U.S. Courthouse, Boston, Mass. Lobby plan. (*Architect: Pei Cobb Fried & Partners; photo: GSA.*)

FIGURE 14.17 John Joseph Moakley U.S. Courthouse, Boston, Mass. Lobby screening station approach. The free zone is large enough to provide sufficient indoor queuing space during peak times. (*Architect: Pei Cobb Fried & Partners; photo: GSA.*)

FIGURE 14.18 John Joseph Moakley U.S. Courthouse, Boston, Mass. Exit from lobby. The wall screening the concierge desk serves to separate the exit from the entrance creating two distinct zones in the lobby. (*Architect: Pei Cobb Fried & Partners; photo: GSA.*)

FIGURE 14.19 John Joseph Moakley U.S. Courthouse, Boston, Mass. Lobby screening station from secure side. Custom cabinetry surrounding the security equipment presents a well-organized face to visitors. Ample inspection surfaces provide security officers space to fully search suspicious items. (*Architect: Pei Cobb Fried & Partners; photo: GSA.*)

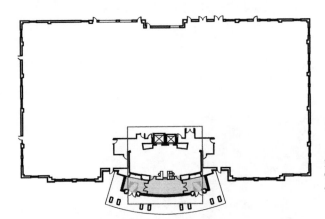

FIGURE 14.20   U.S. Courthouse, Covington, Ky. Building plan. (*Architect: Sherman-Carter-Barnhart; photo: GSA.*)

Covington, Kentucky: U.S. Federal Courthouse (Architect: Sherman-Carter-Barnhart)

At the entrance to the U.S. Courthouse in Covington, Kentucky, a double height porch directs visitors into a large vestibule, then on to a small free zone. The vestibule and free zone lie outside the main structure of the building. Visitors passing through the security checkpoint cross the building's threshold. The metal detector is the symbolic portal into the courthouse and is clad in a stone-like material. The x-ray machine flanks the metal detector on the right, with the guard station to the left. Exits are provided on the outside ends of the security station. The elevator lobby is directly behind the security station, allowing visitors to orient themselves as they enter.

- The screening station is located in close proximity to the entrance.
- The enclosure height allows security officers direct supervision of the free zone and building lobby.

See Figs. 14.20 to 14.24.

Denver, Colorado: Byron G. Rogers Federal Building [Architect: Gensler (renovation)]

The Denver Federal Building contains an appropriately scaled security station for a federal office building. The security checkpoint is located between an open, light-filled lobby functioning as a

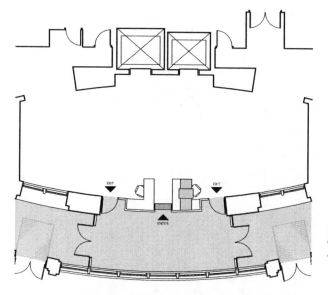

FIGURE 14.21 U.S. Courthouse, Covington, Ky. Lobby plan. (*Architect: Sherman-Carter-Barnhart; photo: GSA.*)

FIGURE 14.22 U.S. Courthouse, Covington, Ky. Lobby. The double height lobby creates a feeling of openness despite the presence of a security screening station. (*Architect: Sherman-Carter-Barnhart; photo: Walt Roycraft.*)

FIGURE 14.23 U.S. Courthouse, Covington, Ky. Building entrance. The security screening station is detailed to be compatible with the overall design of the space. (*Architect: Sherman-Carter-Barnhart; photo: Walt Roycraft.*)

FIGURE 14.24 U.S. Courthouse, Covington, Ky. Mezzanine view of lobby. (*Architect: Sherman-Carter-Barnhart; photo: Walt Roycraft.*)

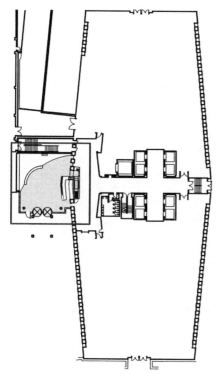

FIGURE 14.25   Byron G. Rogers Federal Building, Denver, Colo. Building plan. (*Architect: Gensler; photo: GSA.*)

free zone and informal meeting place, and the elevator lobby at the core of the office building. The guard station is a long, low countertop, designed to encourage interaction with visitors seeking information. The building directory, incorporated into the desk, is another welcoming feature. The guard station is centrally located, between streams of incoming and outgoing traffic. The central location allows guards to monitor incoming and outgoing visitors, and to interact with visitors on the secured and unsecured sides of the lobby (Figs. 14.25 to 14.28).

Metal detectors are minimal design elements, vertical wands with no crossbars overhead. The x-ray machine is incorporated into the desk design, minimizing the impact on the space. The low desk allows visitors to see into the space they are entering, maximizes penetration of natural light, and maintains views out to the landscaped plaza adjacent to the lobby.

- The location of the security station provides adequate queuing space.
- The security station design fits seamlessly into the overall space.
- Security officers have clear sightlines of visitors entering the building.

Gulfport, Mississippi: U.S. Courthouse (Architect: R.M.Kliment & Frances Halsband Architects/Canizaro Cawthon Davis)

The building entrance for the U.S. Courthouse in Gulfport, Mississippi is conceived of as a series of layers. On the exterior, a large gateway marks the entrance. The public vestibule, immediately behind the gateway, funnels visitors into the building's compact free zone. A continuous metal scrim, stretching the full length of the lobby, shields the free zone from the security station. Set at an angle to the space, the scrim directs visitors into the screening station.

The decorative metal scrim is the work of artist Michele Oka Doner, selected through GSA's Art-in-Architecture Program to work with the project designers. Behind the scrim, the security station is located between streams of incoming and outgoing traffic. The curvilinear form of the gateway allows queuing space for incoming traffic, and channels visitors to the entrance. An opening in the scrim frames a series of freestanding metal detectors. The remainder of the screening equipment is hidden behind the scrim. The x-ray machine and guard's desk are enclosed in cabinetry, unifying their appearance.

- The screening station is located in close proximity to the entrance.
- The scrim shields equipment from casual observation from the side and rear.
- The exit and entrance are clearly separated.

See Figs. 14.29 to 14.32.

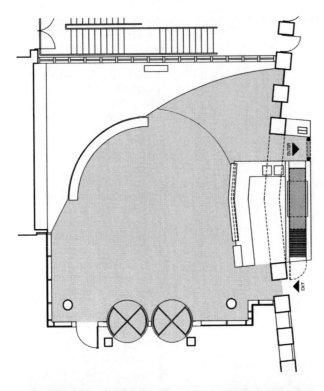

FIGURE 14.26 Byron G. Rogers Federal Building, Denver, Colo. Lobby plan. (*Architect: Gensler; photo: GSA.*)

FIGURE 14.27 Byron G. Rogers Federal Building, Denver, Colo. Lobby screening station approach. The information desk and metal detectors are carefully designed to fit neatly within the lobby's column grid. (*Architect: Gensler; photo: GSA.*)

Islip, New York: Alfonse M. D'Amato U.S. Courthouse and Federal Building (Architect: Richard Meier & Partners/The Spector Group)

The U.S. Courthouse and Federal Building in Islip, New York is one of the largest courthouses in the country, with appropriately grand interior and exterior public spaces. The distinctive formal element of the courthouse is a public lobby, visible from afar. This iconic structure is a welcoming public space, a free zone scaled for public events (Figs. 14.33 to 14.36).

FIGURE 14.28 Byron G. Rogers Federal Building, Denver, Colo. Lobby screening station from secure side. Security and concierge functions are neatly contained behind a low counter, creating a pleasing focal point from both secure and nonsecure sides. (*Architect: Gensler; photo: GSA.*)

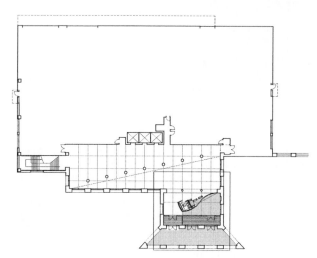

FIGURE 14.29 U.S. Courthouse, Gulfport, Miss. Building plan. (*Architect: R.M.Kliment & Frances Halsband Architects/ Canizaro Cawthon Davis; photo: GSA.*)

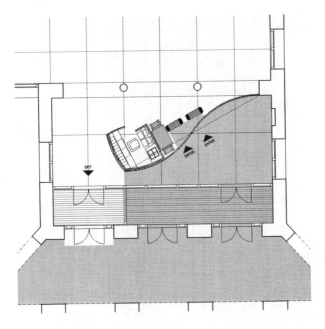

FIGURE 14.30 U.S. Courthouse, Gulfport, Miss. Lobby plan. (*Architect: R.M.Kliment & Frances Halsband Architects/ Canizaro Cawthon Davis; photo: GSA.*)

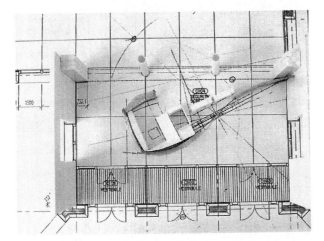

FIGURE 14.31 U.S. Courthouse, Gulfport, Miss. Model of proposed security screening station. (*Architect: R.M. Kliment & Frances Halsband Architects/ Canizaro Cawthon Davis; photo: R.M. Kliment & Frances Halsband Architects.*)

Security stations are located in a narrowed connection between the lobby and the courthouse building. The guard station is an enclosed workspace, with windows overlooking the lobby, and secured areas beyond. Metal detectors and x-ray machines are directly adjacent to the enclosure, visible from the guard station. An enclosed area with a second x-ray machine provides a protected space for extended security checks. Exiting traffic is routed to the far side of the security checkpoint. The guard station location provides easy access for visitors requesting information before they enter the secure zone. The layout maintains an open, welcoming atmosphere, while providing secure space for the guards.

- The entrance and exit paths are well defined.
- The enclosures allow easy maintenance of security equipment, while providing guards with a protected vantage point.
- The screening station is positioned outside of the building footprint.

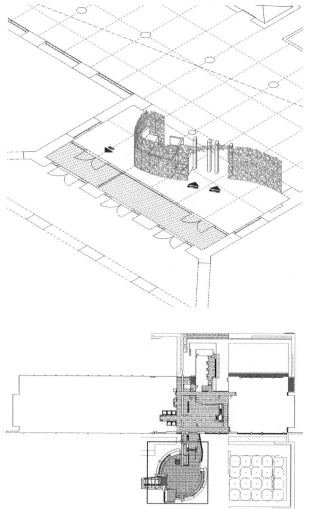

FIGURE 14.32 U.S. Courthouse, Gulfport, Miss. Axonometric drawing of proposed screen separating security from the entrance's free zone. (*Architect: R.M. Kliment & Frances Halsband Architects/ Canizaro Cawthon Davis; drawing: R.M. Kliment & Frances Halsband Architects.*)

FIGURE 14.33 Alfonse M. D'Amato U.S. Federal Courthouse, Islip, N.Y. Building plan. (*Architect: Richard Meier & Partners, Architects/The Spector Group; photo: GSA.*)

Las Vegas, Nevada: Lloyd D. George U.S. Courthouse (Architect: Cannon Design/Harry Campbell Associates)

The Lloyd D. George U.S. Courthouse is a fine example of a building that welcomes the public. The design provides an inviting outside plaza, partially shaded by a canopy. The building entrance is through a rectangular volume at the base of a generous rotunda protruding into the plaza. The rotunda serves as the public lobby of the building and provides easy access to the elevator lobby behind. In exchange for a smaller free zone, a generous plaza and public lobby are provided. The security station is contained within the entrance volume at the base of the rotunda. The security equipment and guard station have a simple linear layout.

- The screening station is located within the rotunda, outside the main building footprint.
- Security officers have good sightlines to the entrance.
- The entrance and exit paths are clearly separated.

See Figs. 14.37 to 14.40.

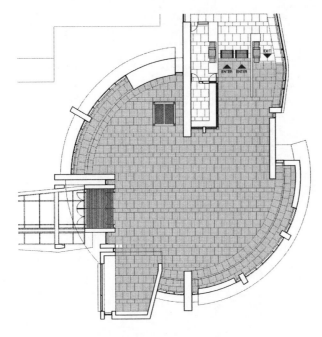

FIGURE 14.34 Alfonse M. D'Amato U.S. Federal Courthouse, Islip, N.Y. Lobby plan. (*Architect: Richard Meier & Partners, Architects/The Spector Group; photo: GSA.*)

FIGURE 14.35 Alfonse M. D'Amato U.S. Courthouse, Islip, N.Y. View down to entrance. Light from the rotunda's skylight animates the volume's pristine, white walls. Balconies overlooking the building entrance provide a vantage point for passive supervision of those entering and exiting the courthouse. (*Architect: Richard Meier & Partners, Architects/ The Spector Group; photograph courtesy of Richard Meier & Partners, Architects.*)

Newark, New Jersey: Peter Rodino Jr. Federal Building [Architect: Gensler (renovation)]

At the Peter Rodino Jr. Federal Building, new security stations are seamlessly integrated within the original entrance area. Screening stations are located along the sides of the entry corridor, creating an unobstructed exit in the center of the lobby. The security is shielded from the rest of the lobby by near full-height wing walls constructed of wood and translucent glass. These walls mask activity behind them, creating a clean, streamlined lobby. While there is no free zone, the lobby beyond is generously scaled. The scheme utilizes one-way automatic sliding doors to control the flow of traffic at the exit.

- Security stations have a minimal impact on the lobby.

FIGURE 14.36 Alfonse M. D'Amato U.S. Courthouse, Islip, NY, View up to oculus. Visitors pass through the building's soaring rotunda before passing through a security checkpoint. The geometric skylight floods the lobby with natural light, creating a welcoming space in which people may orient themselves. (*Architect: Richard Meier & Partners, Architects/ The Spector Group; photograph courtesy of Richard Meier & Partners, Architects.*)

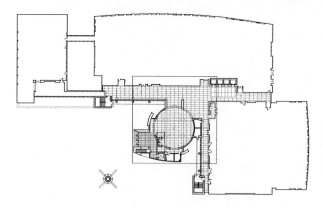

FIGURE 14.37 Lloyd D. George U.S. Courthouse, Las Vegas, Nev. Building plan. (*Architect: Cannon Design/Harry Campbell Associates; photo: GSA.*)

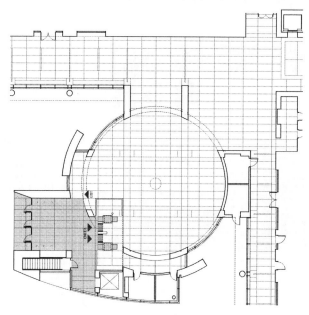

FIGURE 14.38 Lloyd D. George U.S. Courthouse, Las Vegas, Nev. Lobby plan. (*Architect: Cannon Design/Harry Campbell Associates; photo: GSA.*)

FIGURE 14.39 Lloyd D. George U.S. Courthouse, Las Vegas, Nev. View to security. The light filled public lobby is entered through a single, secure entry. Visitors arriving at the building quickly pass through the screening stations and emerge into the daylight-filled lobby. (*Architect: Cannon Design/Harry Campbell Associates; photo: © Peter Aaron/ESTO.*)

FIGURE 14.40 Lloyd D. George U.S. Courthouse, Las Vegas, Nev. View up into oculus. A three-story rotunda delivers an abundance of natural light into the lobby, creating a welcoming environment on the secure side of the entrance. (*Architect: Cannon Design/Harry Campbell Associates; photo: © Peter Aaron/ESTO.*)

- The entrance and exit paths are clearly defined.
- The stations provide ballistic protection for the security officers.

See Figs. 14.41 to 14.44.

Pittsburgh, Pennsylvania: William S. Moorhead Federal Building [Architect: Gensler (renovation)]

At the William S. Moorhead Federal Building in Pittsburgh, the entire security screening process occurs outside the building lobby. Visitors approaching the building are directed to a security screening space adjacent to the lobby. The security station's symmetrical arrangement uses a single x-ray machine and two metal detectors, one on each side. The equipment is shielded by a partition serving as the guard station and providing a surface for organizing signage. Visitors exit the building from the main lobby.

- The entrance and exit paths are clearly separated.
- The stations are located with ample queuing space and keep the lobby clear of screening equipment.

See Figs. 14.45 to 14.48.

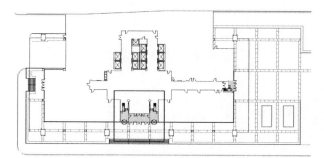

FIGURE 14.41 Peter Rodino Jr. Federal Building, Newark, N.J. Building plan. (*Architect: Gensler; photo: GSA.*)

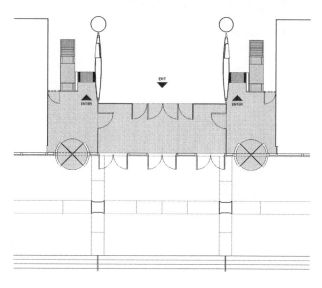

FIGURE 14.42 Peter Rodino Jr. Federal Building, Newark, N.J. Newark, N.J. Lobby plan. (*Architect: Gensler; photo: GSA.*)

FIGURE 14.43 Peter Rodino Jr. Federal Building, Newark, N.J. Newark, N.J. Shielded from the lobby, the clutter of the screening station disappears from view. (*Architect: Gensler; photo: GSA.*)

FIGURE 14.44 Peter Rodino Jr. Federal Building, Newark, N.J. Newark, N.J. The exit from the building is unimpeded by the screening station. (*Architect: Gensler; photo: GSA.*)

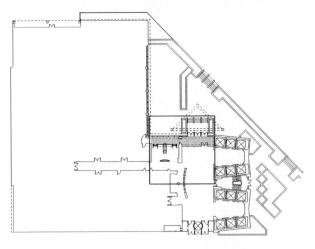

FIGURE 14.45 William S. Moorhead Federal Building, Pittsburgh, Pa. Building plan. (*Architect: Gensler; photo: GSA.*)

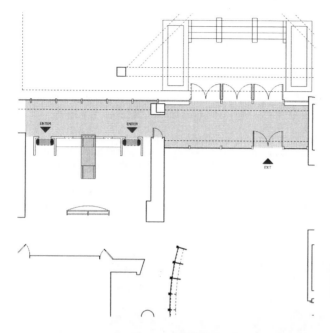

FIGURE 14.46 William S. Moorhead Federal Building, Pittsburgh, Pa. Lobby plan. (*Architect: Gensler; photo: GSA.*)

FIGURE 14.47 William S. Moorhead Federal Building, Pittsburgh, Pa. Locating the screening station adjacent to the lobby allowed the designer sufficient space to clearly layout the station. (*Architect: Gensler; photo: GSA.*)

St. Louis, Missouri: Thomas F. Eagleton U.S. Courthouse (Architect: Hellmuth, Obata + Kassabaum, Inc.)

The main rotunda of the Thomas F. Eagleton U.S. Courthouse serves as the building's free zone. The security screening stations are located directly opposite the building entrance, at the back of the vast oval space. Security is contained within an architectural pavilion, featuring the same neoclassical detailing found throughout the building. The exit path is on either side of the security station, providing modest separation between the two routes. This station also features a raised floor within the guard station, an option often requested by the FPS and USMS.

- The raised floor within the station gives the security officer a physical advantage and a clearer sightline to the entrance.
- The rotunda provides ample space for visitor queuing.

See Figs. 14.49 to 14.52.

Tampa, Florida: Sam M. Gibbons U.S. Courthouse (Architect: Hellmuth, Obata + Kassabaum, Inc.)

The Sam M. Gibbons U.S. Courthouse offers a generous free zone integrated into a large exterior pergola. The security station is centrally located opposite the building entrance. The security partition finishes and detailing are consistent with the lobby design and neatly disguise the security equipment and guard station behind.

Two entrances each lead to metal detectors and x-ray scanners on either side of the partition. Exiting occurs adjacent to these entrances, visually separated by building piers. From the rear, the

FIGURE 14.48   William S. Moorhead Federal Building, Pittsburgh, Pa. The lobby is unobstructed by security equipment, allowing visitors sufficient space to properly orient themselves once they are in the building. (*Architect: Gensler; photo: GSA.*)

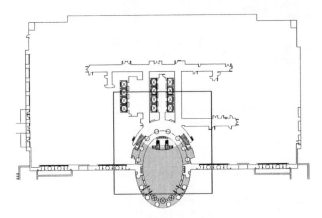

FIGURE 14.49   Thomas F. Eagleton U.S. Courthouse, St. Louis, Mo. Building plan. (*Architect: Hellmuth Obata + Kassabaum, Inc.; photo: GSA.*)

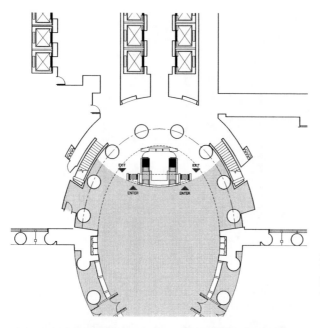

FIGURE 14.50 Thomas F. Eagleton U.S. Courthouse, St. Louis, Mo. Lobby plan. (*Architect: Hellmuth Obata + Kassabaum, Inc.; photo: GSA.*)

FIGURE 14.51 Thomas F. Eagleton U.S. Courthouse, St. Louis, Mo. Entry into the courthouse is open and gracious. Visitors proceed through security at the back of the lobby. (*Architect: Hellmuth Obata + Kassabaum, Inc.; photo: Timothy Hursley.*)

FIGURE 14.52 Thomas F. Eagleton U.S. Courthouse, St. Louis, Mo. Security is well integrated into the lobby. The security station presents a well-organized face to visitors. (*Architect: Hellmuth Obata + Kassabaum, Inc.; photo: Timothy Hursley.*)

stations are concealed, so the appearance on the interior is slightly cluttered, requiring rope lines to direct traffic away from the back of the station.

- The independent left and right screening posts allow the possibility of easily switching screening operations to the opposite side, should either the walk-through metal detector or x-ray machine malfunction.
- The design allows easy maintenance of the metal detector and x-ray machine

See Figs. 14.53 to 14.56.

CONCLUSION

Federal building lobbies are the first line of defense against terrorism and violence directed at the government, federal employees, and the public. At the same time, they are also the first impression visitors have of the federal government. Through careful analysis and planning, facility managers, building owners, and designers in the public and private sectors and at all levels of government can take steps to improve building lobbies and enhance the safety and security of the general public. These case studies and lessons learned illustrate that thoughtful design solutions can accomplish these two seemingly disparate goals.

ACKNOWLEDGMENTS

- Frances Halsband, FAIA, Principal, R.M.Kliment & Frances Halsband Architects, New York, New York
- Yetsuh Frank, RA, Project Architect, R.M.Kliment & Frances Halsband Architects, New York, New York
- Alan Camp, Former Director, First Impressions Program, and Regional Chief Architect, Rocky Mountain Region, GSA, Denver, Colorado.
- Caroline Alderson, Program Manager, Center for Historic Buildings, GSA Office of the Chief Architect, Washington, D.C.

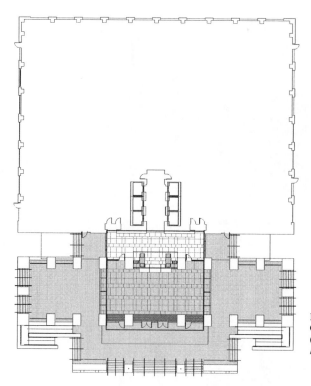

FIGURE 14.53 Sam M. Gibbons U.S. Courthouse, Tampa, Fla. Building plan. (*Architect: Hellmuth Obata + Kassabaum, Inc.; photo: GSA.*)

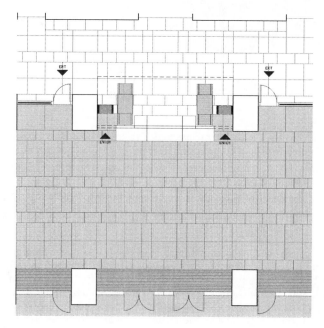

FIGURE 14.54 Sam M. Gibbons U.S. Courthouse, Tampa, Fla. Lobby plan. (*Architect: Hellmuth Obata + Kassabaum, Inc.; photo: GSA.*)

FIGURE 14.55 Sam M. Gibbons U.S. Courthouse, Tampa, Fla. Lobby screening station approach. Designed to be as unobtrusive as possible, the security station sits discretely at the back of the lobby. (*Architect: Hellmuth Obata + Kassabaum, Inc.; photo: GSA.*)

FIGURE 14.56 Sam M. Gibbons U.S. Courthouse, Tampa, Fla. Lobby screening station from secure side. (*Architect: Hellmuth Obata + Kassabaum, Inc.; photo: GSA.*)

- Leslie Shepherd, Director, Center for Architecture, Engineering and Urban Design, Office of the Chief Architect, Public Buildings Service, U.S. General Services Administration, Washington, D.C.
- Edward A. Feiner, FAIA, Chief Architect, Public Buildings Service, U.S. General Services Administration, Washington, D.C.
- David Hubbuch, Chief, Office of Judicial Security Systems, U.S. Marshals Service, Washington, D.C.
- Wendell Shingler, Director, Federal Protective Service, U.S. Department of Homeland Security, Washington, D.C.

This material is adapted with permission from *The Design Notebook for Federal Building Lobby Security,* published by the U.S. General Services Administration and the U.S. Marshals Service, 2003. *Note:* The Federal Protective Service (FPS) was moved to the Department of Homeland Security after publication of *The Design Notebook for Federal Building Lobby Security.*

The concept for this chapter arose from design studies of lobby renovations for the First Impressions Program. *The Design Notebook for Federal Building Lobby Security* (the U.S. General Services Administration and the U.S. Marshals Service, 2003) was developed by R.M.Kliment &

Frances Halsband Architects, under contract to GSA. Research, site visits, and design charrettes were organized over one year together with the following groups:

- General Services Administration
- Public Buildings Service
- Office of the Chief Architect
- Federal Protective Service
- First Impressions Program
- U.S. Marshals Service
- Office of Judicial Security Systems
- Administrative Office of the U.S. Courts
- Robert Silman Associates, Structural Engineers
- Gensler
- Lehman-Smith & McLeish
- Heimann Systems

Case Study Architects

- Boston, Mass., Pei Cobb Freed & Partners
- Covington, Ky., Sherman-Carter-Barnhart
- Denver, Colo., Gensler (renovation)
- Gulfport, Miss., R.M.Kliment & Frances Halsband Architects/Canizaro Cawthon Davis
- Islip, N.Y., Richard Meier & Partners/The Spector Group
- Las Vegas, Nev., Cannon Design/Harry Campbell Associates
- Newark, N.J., Gensler (renovation)
- Pittsburgh, Pa., Gensler (renovation)
- St. Louis, Mo., Hellmuth, Obata + Kassabaum, Inc.
- Tampa, Fla., Hellmuth, Obata + Kassabaum, Inc.

BIBLIOGRAPHY: SUMMARIES OF GOVERNMENT GUIDELINES AND STANDARDS

Administrative Office of the Courts, *U.S. Courts Design Guide*, 1997. This guide focuses on functional program requirements, departmental and interdepartmental adjacency relationships, finish materials, and performance criteria for environmental systems, including heating, cooling, and lighting. It also addresses acoustic, security, telecommunications, and audio/visual design requirements.

Department of Justice, *Vulnerability Assessment of Federal Facilities*, 1999. A survey of existing security conditions at federal buildings, and conclusions and recommendations for minimum security standards.

Interagency Security Committee, *Interagency Security Committee: Security Design Criteria*, 1998. Physical security design and construction criteria and standards for federal buildings developed to ensure that security becomes an integral part of the planning, design, and construction of new federal office buildings and major modernization projects. Considers security criteria in all building systems and elements.

U.S. General Services Administration, *GSA Facilities Standards for the Public Building Service*, P100, March 2003. Establishes design standards for new buildings, major and minor alterations, and work in historic structures for the Public Buildings Service. Portions of relevance to lobby design include Chap. 8: "Security Design," and Chap. 9: "Design Standards for U.S. Courts Facilities."

U.S. General Services Administration and the U.S. Marshals Service, *The Design Notebook for Federal Building Lobby Security,* 2003.

U.S. Marshals Service, *USMS Key Elements: Court Security Officer Lobby Screening Stations,* 2000. A detailed list of the elements required by USMS for all court security screening stations. Outlines these requirements within five elements: location, layout, weapons storage, weapons storage area, and power source.

U.S. Marshals Service, *USMS Requirements and Specifications for Special Purpose & Support Space Manual,* vol. 3, 2001. Provides finish criteria for USMS functional program requirements, spatial relationships, electronic/physical security, plus hardware standards.

INTERNET RESOURCES

First Impressions program and First Impressions Signage Guidelines
http://hydra.gsa.gov/pbs/firstimpressions

U.S. General Services Administration
Go to Public Building Service, then Design & Construction.
www.gsa.gov

U.S. Marshals Service, U.S. Department of Justice
www.usdoj.gov/marshals

CONSTRUCTION STANDARDS

The following standards should be considered for all federal projects:

- All ballistic resistant materials must meet UL Standard 752, Level III.
- Outlets on a dedicated 15-amp, 120-volt AC circuit must be included for monitor of computer equipment. Power outlets must be tied to an emergency backup system.
- X-ray and walk through metal detectors require 20-amp, 120-volt AC dedicated electrical outlets linked to an emergency backup system. Outlets may be flush mounted within the flooring, but must be within close proximity to the machines.
- Lobby lighting systems should ensure that the entire screening station is illuminated with emergency lighting during power outages.

CHAPTER 15
MUSEUM AND CULTURAL FACILITY SECURITY

Arthur Rosenblatt, FAIA
Principal, RKK&G Museum and Cultural Facilities Consultants, Inc.
New York, New York

Art is the signature of civilization.

BEVERLY SILLS

Since the 1980s, museum design has increased dramatically, as the public in the United States and overseas became intensely aware and interested in viewing art and cultural heritage artifacts. Modest-sized communities and major urban centers take great pride in their museums and cultural institutions, whether for displaying art, exploring the sciences, expressing a strong local birthright, remembering historical events, or serving as a plant and animal habitat. The upsurge in museum construction resulted in renovations, additions, and retrofits of existing, often historic properties for security, climate and lighting, as well as new buildings to hold expanding collections (Fig. 15.1).

The twenty-first century museum serves as more than a place to view art. Cultural institutions have become high-volume tourist destinations, places to have a quick or leisurely meal, purchase reproductions and gifts, enjoy multimedia shows and film screenings, and attend elegant receptions. With so many activities and programmatic functions occurring within a museum, security of art, artifacts and assets, and public safety in the event of an emergency, are paramount concerns for architects, building owners, museum professionals, facility managers, and arts administrators charged with daily operations.

As is the case with every building type, architectural planning and design addresses life safety and egress issues surrounding the museum building and site perimeter, based on local codes, conditions, and best practices. Development of a security master plan, using the same vulnerability and risk criteria applicable to all building types, will assist building owners in identifying threats and appropriate solutions.

Each museum and cultural facility is unique. However, all cultural institutions, regardless of size, from museums, galleries, and performance venues to monuments and historic sites, face security problems. Cultural arts facilities need protection from theft, intrusion, fire, vandalism, terrorism, and other disasters. The most effective security program combines elements of design, technology, and operations, based on a thorough, multidisciplinary analysis. Architects, planners, building owners, museum professionals, and arts administrators should be familiar with the fundamental requirements and standards to be met in providing cultural facilities with appropriate and adequate protection.

FIGURE 15.1 Kimbell Art Museum, Fort Worth, Tex. (*Architect: Louis I. Kahn, FAIA; pen and ink drawing: Terrance J. Brown, FAIA.*)

SECURITY ASSESSMENT SURVEY

An effective security program for a cultural facility should consider various types of threats (Table 15.1). The museum or cultural facility should initiate a comprehensive assessment survey to determine and evaluate security conditions of every area, including the site perimeter, building envelope, and exhibit and storage spaces.

THREAT ANALYSIS

Concurrent with the security survey, the institution should initiate a threat analysis to evaluate possible dangers and vulnerabilities, along with potential programs and solutions to mitigate risk (Table 15.2).

ELECTRONIC BUILDING PROTECTION

Alarms detect change, but do not interpret or deduce the cause of the change. Alarms are only effective when they work properly and generate a prompt response (Table 15.3). There are also forms of electronic building protection that are not alarms. These include electromagnetic lock exit and card reader entry and closed circuit television (CCTV). CCTV is a form of electronic building monitoring, but is not an alarm.

DETECTORS

Detectors do not, by themselves, protect anything. They detect a specific activity and report the event. Museums and cultural facilities also use combinations of proximity or capacitance sensors, requiring highly trained technicians for installation and maintenance, with portable systems for special events. Twelve types of detectors commonly used in cultural facilities include the following:

Simple Magnetic Contact Switch or Contact Sensor.   The movement of two elements in a magnetic field actuates a reed-type or mechanical switch. These are often installed on doors and windows. There are surface-mounted and hidden or flush-mounted versions, as well as versions for roll-up doors.

- In low-security cases, they are used to detect the opening and closing of office doors, windows, and closets.

- They are placed on doors in exhibit cases or in cabinets, where the switch is inside the case or cabinet.

TABLE 15.1   Potential Threats to Cultural Facilities

General threat	Specific threats
Natural hazards	• Floods, tornadoes, hurricanes, snow loads on roof • Lightning • High winds or storms of great magnitude • Smoke and fire • Mold and mildew
Building hazards	• Loss of air conditioning, heating, and air circulation • Loss of electrical power • Loss of emergency response mechanisms • Structural collapse • Explosion • Any combination of these
Criminal activity	• Robbery or theft by either staff or public • Deliberate destruction of property and collections • Trespassing • Vandalism and graffiti • Purposeful civil disturbance • Bomb or related threat • Terrorist attack • Personal behavior, including illegal use of drugs, alcohol, weapons, and sex crimes

TABLE 15.2   Typical Museum or Cultural Institution Threat Analysis Considerations

- Minor fire
- Major fire
- Minor collection theft
- Major collection theft
- Flood from rains
- Armed robbery
- Roof leak
- Pipe burst or flooding
- Power loss

TABLE 15.3   Four Basic Elements of an Alarm System

1. Sensors detecting a disturbance and starting a message
2. Communications system to send the message
3. Annunciator to deliver a report to the responsible authority
4. Human response to the alarm

Balanced Magnetic Contact Switch.   The separation of two biased magnets actuates a switch. The maintenance of the magnetic field to a simple magnetic contact switch keeps that switch from operating. Any change in the magnetic field around the switch sounds an alarm.

- Perimeter doors and windows
- High-security openings
- Roll-up doors

Microswitch and Plunger Switch.   A mechanical pressing or releasing of a lever or plunger physically moves a small electric switch. This is often used to detect the movement of objects where there is room for only one of the two parts of a device or in hard-to-reach areas, such as in a vitrine, which is a glass showcase or cabinet often used for displaying fine wares or specimens.

- A tamper switch for electrical boxes, terminal cabinets, or other security mechanisms
- To detect the lifting of a vitrine or exhibit case
- To detect the lifting of an object on display
- To detect the opening or closing of doors and windows

Foil Tape.   A silver- or gold-colored tape mounted on smooth glass about 4 inches, or 10 centimeters, from the edge contains two electrical conductors. A small electric current is maintained in the foil to ensure that no break occurs in the supporting glass. When the foil breaks, usually through the breaking of the glass, the electrical circuit breaks, and an alarm sounds. Foil tape is an inexpensive and reliable system, used widely in basic security.

- On windows to detect breaking glass

Glass Window "Bug."   A round disc, about 1 inch in diameter and ¼ inch thick is glued to window glass 4 inches in from the corner. When glass breaks there is a change or difference in electrical current, and the alarm is sounded.

- Installed on perimeter windows and on display vitrines

Audio Discriminator or Audio Glass Break Detector.   This device completes an electrical circuit when it detects the unique sound frequencies of breaking glass or splintering wood.

- Perimeter windows, glass towers, or other large expanses of glass

Vibrators.   A spring-loaded, mechanically operated electric switch turns on or off when the surface where it rests moves or vibrates, causing the two pieces of metal to touch and complete a circuit. The switch reacts in a few microseconds and contains a latching relay to hold the equipment in an alarm condition.

- Window breakage detection, sometimes referred to as a "window bug"
- Mounted on exhibit case vitrine to detect smashing of vitrine
- Used on walls to detect forcible entry into a room by breaking through a wall

Shock or Impact Sensors.   A model vibrator balances a gold- or silver-plated ball or ring on the tips of two wires inside a small metal box. When the sensor detects vibration, the ball or ring bounces off the wire, turning off the circuit and sending an alarm to an annunciator.

- Glass break detection
- Used on walls to detect forcible entry
- Mounted on fence posts to detect people climbing fences

Lacing. Lacing is a very fine wire woven into a wall or on a wall surface. The wire carries a small electric current, and an alarm sounds when the wire breaks, detecting an attempt to penetrate the wall.

- Used on walls, floors, and ceilings of secure rooms and vaults
- May be used across the face of large ducts or other openings entering into security-sensitive areas

Pressure-Sensitive Mats. A rubber mat embedded with pairs of metal strip electric conductors. When a person or object applies a minimum of pressure to the top of the mat, the two metal strips touch to complete an electric circuit and send an alarm.

- Inexpensive and easy to install, used for "traps" in hallways, steps, and doorways
- Can detect an object or work of art being removed when the object weighs at least 10 pounds

Motion Detectors. Four common types of motion detectors include ultrasonic, microwave, infrared, and passive infrared. Motion detectors are mechanisms that call attention to movement through an area (Table 15.4). Each of the mechanisms requires two pairs of wires—one to supply electrical current to the mechanism and one to activate the alarm. The energy fields created are weak and not harmful to people or objects.

- Notes movement in an area, thus detecting someone staying behind when the museum or cultural facility closes
- May be placed in a vitrine or display case to detect movement

Photoelectric Beams. A light mechanism sends a narrow light beam to a receiving mechanism, which measures the light intensity. When the light beam breaks, especially momentarily, the detector measures the difference of light received and an alarm sounds. This mechanism can also use mirrors to create special beam configurations.

- Detects movement across the edges of exhibition platforms
- Detects movement across an area or exhibition gallery

Museums and cultural facilities also use combinations of proximity or capacitance sensors, requiring highly trained technicians for installation and maintenance, with portable systems for special events.

TABLE 15.4 **Types of Motion Detectors**

Type	Characteristics
Ultrasonic	- The ultrasonic detector sends an energy wave into a directed area at a frequency just above the level of human hearing. - The equipment evaluates the frequency of the same wave when it returns after bouncing off objects in the area. - If any moving object changes the speed of the reflected wave, the equipment detects the frequency difference and activates the alarm.
Microwave	- The microwave motion detector uses the Doppler effect to detect wave frequency differences at a much higher frequency than is used with either ultrasonic or infrared detectors.
Infrared	- The infrared detector uses the Doppler effect at a frequency lower than with microwave motion detectors. - Each of the Doppler mechanisms requires a sending unit and a receiving unit.
Passive infrared	- The passive infrared motion detector does not send out energy waves. It evaluates the normal amount of infrared energy in the directed area. - When someone with infrared energy, such as with body heat, enters the directed area, the equipment detects the difference of infrared energy and alarms.

OPERATIONS

Daily operations, procedures, and alert personnel are important to maintaining security. Like many other facilities and building types, museums and cultural institutions should establish a security control center operating 24 hours and 7 days a week for alarm annunciation and management, monitoring building systems, CCTV, and as an emergency response center for guards and personnel. All personnel should be familiar with security policies, evacuation procedures, and what to do and who to contact in the event of an emergency.

CONCLUSION

Museums and cultural facilities must develop security and protection programs according to their unique requirements. No single security program is right for every institution. By combining good design, appropriate technology, and sound operational policies and procedures, cultural facilities of all types will be well prepared to protect people, art, artifacts, and assets under the most challenging circumstances.

BIBLIOGRAPHY

Bernard, Robert, *Intrusions Detection Systems,* Butterworth, Boston, 1988.

Fennelly, Lawrence, *Museum, Archive and Library Security,* Butterworth, Boston, 1983.

International Committee on Museum Security, *Museum Security and Protection,* Routledge Inc., London, 1993.

Rosenblatt, Arthur, *Building Type Basics for Museums,* Wiley, Hoboken, N.J., 2001.

INTERNET RESOURCES

RKKG Museum and Cultural Facilities Consultants, Inc.
www.rkkg.com

CHAPTER 16
PERIMETER SECURITY: THE AESTHETICS OF PROTECTION

Deborah Bershad
Executive Director, Art Commission of the City of New York
New York, New York

Jean Parker Phifer, AIA
Former President, Art Commission of the City of New York
Thomas Phifer & Partners
New York, New York

> *Art is the demonstration that the ordinary is extraordinary.*
> AMEDEE OZENFANT (1886–1966)
> *French painter, Foundations of Modern Art*

Since 1898, the Art Commission of the City of New York has served as the design review agency for the City of New York. The commission reviews all works of art, architecture, landscape architecture, and street furniture on city-owned land in New York City for their aesthetic appropriateness. Part of the commission's mandate to ensure a high quality of design for public buildings and spaces is to make the pragmatic elements of security as attractive as possible. As perimeter security develops into an essential program goal in the design of all public buildings and facilities, this focus on aesthetics has become increasingly important.

DESIGNING FOR SECURITY

The Art Commission has been concerned about the aesthetics of security for many years and encourages design review agencies across the country to address these issues. In fact, research for the publication, *Designing for Security: Using Art and Design to Improve Security/ Guidelines from the Art Commission of the City of New York,* was first initiated in 1997, in partnership with the Design Trust for Public Space. At that time, the commission had noted and wished to address a rise in the application of perimeter barriers and other security elements that was occurring in response to vandalism and other crime. After September 11, 2001, the need for appropriate, thoughtfully designed perimeter security in urban spaces became more apparent (Table 16.1).

TABLE 16.1   9/11 Lessons Learned: Integrating Urban Design, Public Art, and Streetscape Elements for Perimeter Security

Since September 11, 2001, the imposition of barriers and perimeter security elements in public spaces has increasingly led to the degradation of the public realm. Cumulatively, perimeter barriers can overwhelm attractive or imposing structures, and turn pleasant streetscapes or plazas into grim and oppressive spaces. Although most security consultants advise building owners to install a continuous ring of bollards or barriers around the perimeter of their properties, as close as possible to the curb, the Art Commission of the City of New York encourages designers to use these items within a varied but integrated system of streetscape elements. Interspersing bollards with planters, benches, or street trees, where clearances allow, deemphasizes the security function of the barriers and mitigates the unattractive repetition of identical elements.

The Art Commission applauds the report, *The National Capital Urban Design and Security Plan* (October 2002), issued by the National Capital Planning Commission, which addresses the integration of security elements with good urban design. The Art Commission works constantly with other city agencies, most notably the Department of Transportation and the Department of City Planning, to reach a balance between an attractive streetscape and a secure facility.

DESIGN QUALITY

For many years, the Art Commission has promoted the combination of aesthetic sensibility and security elements in a variety of ways, including improving the quality of materials used, such as, stone, rather than concrete, addressing issues of scale and style, so that items relate to the context within which they are placed, and requiring superior fabrication of barrier elements. This approach has improved the general quality of installations and raised the standards of city agencies and designers with whom the commission works.

However, one of the most successful methods of enhancing security with design has been the integration of public art into the design and construction process. By having artists design elements such as fencing, window grilles, and lockable gates, these items are transformed into aesthetically pleasing forms that improve, rather than degrade, the quality of the urban environment.

Percent for Art Program

Experience indicates that the most successful applications of this approach occur when artists are involved early on in the facility design process, and have the opportunity to work as part of a team with the architect and other design professionals. For New York City, this means encouraging cooperation between city agencies and the Percent for Art program of the Department of Cultural Affairs.

The Percent for Art law was enacted in 1982, requiring that one percent of the budget for city-owned capital construction projects be spent on artwork. The selection of artists for each installation of public art is made by means of panels, including arts professionals, members of the project team, and members of the community. The early involvement of an artist can bring an open and creative approach to design that can make a substantial difference in the quality of the final product. Several of the projects listed below were conceived as part of the Percent for Art program.

CASE STUDIES

The following examples of well-designed perimeter security elements have been excerpted from *Designing for Security*. These examples, found throughout the City of New York, illustrate how the creative design of security elements can enhance the perception of safety, while enriching the public realm (Table 16.2).

TABLE 16.2   Examples of Perimeter Security Design Elements and Public Art in New York City

Design element	Building type	Building shown	NYC borough
Walls	Aquarium	New York Aquarium	Brooklyn
Fence	Public school	PS 234	Manhattan
Gate	Nature center	Blue Heron Park Nature Center	Staten Island
Gate	Subway stations	Gates at turnstile areas	Citywide
Gate	Museum	The Studio Museum in Harlem	Manhattan
Fence	High school	Townsend Harris High School	Queens

Source: Art Commission of the City of New York.

Walls

The New York Aquarium: First Symphony of the Sea

Boardwalk and West 8th Street, Coney Island, Brooklyn, New York

Artist: Toshio Sasaki

Architect: Goldstone and Hinz

Security issues: Controlling perimeter access, deterring graffiti and vandalism

At the New York Aquarium, the sculptural relief on the long sea wall has effectively eliminated graffiti as a maintenance problem (Figs. 16.1 and 16.2).

With the installation of a new Sea Cliffs exhibit at the Aquarium, a 332-foot-long wall was to be constructed along the boardwalk in Coney Island. Using sea imagery and motion, Sasaki created a concrete wall with terrazzo and ceramic tiles that enlivens the boardwalk and appropriately evokes the marine environment.

Four tons of concrete rise ten feet above the boardwalk and face the ocean to form the sculpture wall. The wall was cast in 26 sections in custom designed molds. Relief elements, such as eggshell and fin shapes, were made from terrazzo and ceramic tiles and attached to the wall after fabrication. Unlike the rest of the boardwalk, the wall has not been marred by graffiti.

Fences

Public School 234: Dreaming of Far Away Places: The Ships Come to Washington Market

300 Greenwich Street, Tribeca, Manhattan, New York, New York

Artist: Donna Dennis

Architect: Richard Dattner Architect

Security issues: Controlling perimeter access, deterring graffiti and vandalism

At P.S. 234, the delightful silhouette of ships and maps has elevated a common security fence to an imaginative and inspiring display of public art for children (Fig. 16.3).

Located in a landmark neighborhood, P.S. 234 is a focal point of the community. A new fence was needed to control access to school grounds, and was commissioned by the Board of Education through the Percent for Art Program. The fence encloses the yard with a procession of silhouetted ships, recalling the history of Washington Market and its growth through the city's shipping industry. The fence is safe for children, and gaps between the ground and all solid imagery on the fence allow views from one side of the fence to the other.

The 224-foot fence consists of 14 steel panels of grade ASTM A36 set into arches and piers designed by the architect. Composed of layered flame- and saw-cut steel plates on steel bars, the fence was fabricated based on the artist's full-scale templates.

FIGURE 16.1 First Symphony of the Sea. The New York Aquarium, Coney Island, Brooklyn, New York. (*Artist: Toshio Sasaki; architect: Goldstone and Hinz.*)

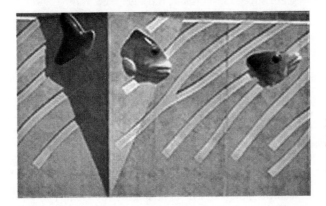

FIGURE 16.2 First Symphony of the Sea, detail. The New York Aquarium, Coney Island, Brooklyn, New York. (*Artist: Toshio Sasaki; architect: Goldstone and Hinz.*)

FIGURE 16.3 Dreaming of Far Away Places: The Ships Come to Washington Market. Public School 234, Tribeca in Manhattan, New York City. (*Artist: Donna Dennis; architect: Richard Dattner Architect.*)

Gates

Blue Heron Park Nature Center: Decorative Cattail and Heron Gate

Staten Island, N.Y.

Designed by New York City Department of Parks and Recreation

Security issues: park and center building security, deterring graffiti and vandalism

The entry gate at Blue Heron Park Nature Center was designed to incorporate natural forms relating to the function and educational focus of the center (Fig. 16.4).

The Blue Heron Park Nature Center is located in a remote wooded section of Staten Island. Before construction of the new facility, there had been attempts to crash an existing gate with a vehicle, and it was decided that a strong gate was needed to keep out vehicles when the center was closed. The Department of Parks and Recreation personnel designed the gates, using the heron theme.

Gate panels are 11 feet wide by 3 feet, 6 inches high, made of hand-forged steel. The panels are painted a very dark, black-green. Steel posts support the weight of the gates so they swing easily. The gates were manufactured by Green Mountain Gate Company, which had designed security gates for the White House, embassies, and other secure facilities.

FIGURE 16.4 Decorative Cattail and Heron Gate. Blue Heron Park Nature Center, Staten Island, N.Y.. (*Designed by New York City Department of Parks and Recreation.*)

FIGURE 16.5 The Wave, Metropolitan Transportation Authority, Arts for Transit program throughout the New York City subway system stations. (*Artist: Valerie Jaudon.*)

FIGURE 16.6 Long Division, Metropolitan Transportation Authority, Arts for Transit program throughout the New York City subway system stations. (*Artist: Laura Bradley.*)

FIGURE 16.7 Medallion, Metropolitan Transportation Authority, Arts for Transit program throughout the New York City subway system stations. (*Artist: Laura Bradley.*)

Gates

Metropolitan Transportation Authority, Arts for Transit Program: The Wave, Long Division, and Medallion

At stations throughout the New York City subway system.

Artist: Valerie Jaudon, *The Wave*

Artist: Laura Bradley, *Long Division* and *Medallion*

Security issues: Fare evasion, passenger security, improving visibility

The Wave, Long Division, and Medallion railings installed throughout the New York City Subway system enliven what would otherwise be hostile barriers to prevent fare evasion (Figs. 16.5 to 16.7).

As part of the Metropolitan Transportation Authority's capital rebuilding plan, Arts for Transit was established in 1985 to oversee all performing and visual arts initiatives, including the Permanent Art program. The MTA realized that at subway station turnstile entrances, people jumping turnstiles to evade fare payments had become a growing problem. A method of separating paid and unpaid customers was needed, and the Arts for Transit program commissioned these elegant gates that function as physical barriers, yet avoid creating a hostile environment. Enhancing the customers' sense of security is the visibility through the barriers, which allows customers to see where they are headed and what is behind them.

Gates

The Studio Museum in Harlem: Entrance Gates

West 125th Street, Manhattan, New York, New York

Artist: Rogers Marvel Architects

Security issues: Perimeter security

At the Studio Museum, old-fashioned corrugated metal security gates were replaced with elegant translucent glass gates, which swing entirely open to reveal the courtyard inside, and when closed, glow with light from within (Fig. 16.8).

The transformation of a vacant lot into a sculpture court required a new entry for the museum that would ensure security while creating a lively presence on the street. The design uses translucent panels of durable Reglit glass. The broad gate can be swung open during operating hours so that the sculpture court is visible, inviting passersby to enter the museum, and then the sculpture court. The Reglit panels of the façade glow at night, replacing existing roll-down metal security gates.

FIGURE 16.8   Entrance Gates, The Studio Museum in Harlem, New York City. (*Artist: Rogers Marvel Architects.*)

Fence

Townsend Harris High School: Pangea Fence

149th Street and Melbourne Avenue, Queens College campus, Flushing, Queens, New York

Board of Education and Percent for Art program

Artist: Fred Wilson

Architect: HOK

Security issues: controlling perimeter access, deterring graffiti and vandalism

The only fence against the world is a thorough knowledge of it.

JOHN LOCKE (1632-1704)
British philosopher,
Some Thoughts Concerning Education

At the Townsend Harris High School, the artist used the perimeter fence to playfully manipulate our concepts of how the world is organized (Fig. 16.9).

The policy of the Board of Education and the School Construction Authority is to surround the property of all New York City schools with a perimeter fence to control access and deter graffiti and vandalism. Through the Percent for Art program, artist Fred Wilson was commissioned to create a fence for this new high school, located in a residential area of Queens, the most diverse county in the United States, where over 130 languages are spoken.

Pangea, the title of the fence, means "all earth" in Greek, and refers to a hypothetical super-continent that included all the land masses of the earth before the Triassic Period, 200 million years ago. The world images painted on the steel fence and gate are silhouetted in black, with the spokes representing latitude lines. The continents are varying scales and are arranged according to the artist's design. The arrangements are metaphors for ideas about various countries' relationships and positions of importance in the world, and some of the continents are inverted. Wilson's design is a commentary on the arbitrariness of the standard orientation of world maps, suggesting that while nature creates continents, human beings create borders.

FIGURE 16.9 Pangea Fence, Townsend Harris High School, Queens College, Flushing, Queens, New York. (*NYC Board of Education and Percent for Art program; artist: Fred Wilson; architect: HOK.*)

ACKNOWLEDGMENTS

Material in this chapter has been adapted, with permission, from *Designing for Security: Using Art and Design to Improve Security Guidelines from the Art Commission of the City of New York,* Art Commission of the City of New York and the Design Trust for Public Space, 2002. The publication is available from the Art Commission at www.nyc.gov/artcommission.

BIBLIOGRAPHY

Kelling, George L., Catherine M. Coles, and James Q. Wilson, *Fixing Broken Windows: Restoring Order and Reducing Crime in our Communities,* Free Press, New York, 1998. The authors' prescriptions are based on research showing that reduction of minor infractions in neighborhoods reduces more serious types of crime.

National Capital Planning Commission, *The National Capital Urban Design and Security Plan,* Washington, D.C., October 2002. Available at www.ncpc.gov.

Russell, James S., Elizabeth Kennedy, Meredith Kelly, and Deborah Bershad (ed.), *Designing for Security: Using Art and Design to Improve Security/Guidelines from the Art Commission of the City of New York,* Art Commission of the City of New York, March 2002.

Wilson, James Q., and George L. Kelling, "Broken Windows," *The Atlantic Monthly,* March 1982, pp. 29–38. The original exposition of the broken windows crime reduction theory, explored in greater detail in Kelling et al., *"Fixing Broken Windows,"* cited above.

INTERNET RESOURCES

Art Commission of the City of New York
www.nyc.gov/artcommission

City of New York
www.nyc.gov

Design Trust for Public Space
www.designtrust.org

Justice Information Center of the National
  Criminal Justice Resource Service
www.ncjrs.org

National Capitol Planning Commission
www.ncpc.gov

National Crime Prevention Council
www.ncpc.org

The Planning Center
www.planningcenter.com

CHAPTER 17
RELIGIOUS INSTITUTIONS AND COMMUNITY CENTERS

Anti-Defamation League
New York, New York

*If I am not for myself who will be for me? And if I'm for
myself alone, what am I? And if not now, when?*
          HILLEL (FIRST CENTURY B.C TO FIRST CENTURY A.D.)
                              Talmudic sage and teacher
                              Ethics of the Fathers

Regardless of affiliation, religious and community institutions are integral parts of neighborhoods, metropolitan areas, and the fabric of an open, free, democratic society. They provide many services to people of all ages and backgrounds, and are stabilizing influences in large and small communities, operating over long hours, seven days a week.

Religious institutions and related community centers must be designed to be open and welcoming, yet secure. Unlike other civic facilities, public attractions, and sites, security measures in religious institutions may be viewed as an affront to the spiritual nature of the community. Providing physical security for religious institutions must balance safety with openness (Fig. 17.1).

Transparent security, not visible to the public eye, can achieve these goals through careful planning, operational policies, good design, and prudent use of technology. Proven planning strategies, such as crime prevention through environmental design (CPTED), are effective, often low cost, highly collaborative methods of first defense for institutional facility design. Building relationships with local law enforcement agencies will enhance crime prevention efforts, and establish networks well before a disaster or in the event of an emergency.

The Anti-Defamation League (ADL) has long been at the forefront of providing information to Jewish institutions for coping with the heightened, frequent, global security concerns facing this community. While ADL does not, and would never presume, to have detailed knowledge of the needs of other religious communities, ADL believes all religious institutions, and related community centers, will benefit from preventative, proactive information, based on extensive research and experience.

SECURITY PHILOSOPHY

Because of the open nature of most religious, also known as communal, institutions and the range of constituents, employees, and visitors using them, designing secure facilities must include their selected user participation in, and in some cases, goading and guiding toward, an overall security plan. Without an integrated plan, even the most well-designed facility will be unable to thwart and fully recover from a security breach. A sound institutional security plan equally reflects management and operational issues as well as technology and design.

FIGURE 17.1   Beth Shalom Synagogue, Elkins Park, Pa., completed 1954. (*Architect: Frank Lloyd Wright; pen and ink drawing: Terrance J. Brown, FAIA.*)

Staff, leaders, and community members must be motivated and educated to understand the need to create and implement a security plan. Religious institutions may see advantages of implementing a security plan, after comparing the cost savings of addressing security during initial planning and design phases of new construction or renovation against the costs of retrofitting existing facilities.

CREATING A SECURITY PLAN

Creating a security plan is essential to understanding necessary facility design considerations. A sound security plan integrates design, technology, and operations, comprised of policies and procedures. Preparing the security plan, installing hardware, and hiring additional staff are only the beginning, not the end of the process. All leaders, employees, and constituents must be aware of the plan, and agree to practice procedures, review requirements, and implement key items. Regular training and review of the security plan are critical to an institution's security. Creating a secure environment is a three-step process, consisting of

- Assessment
- Planning
- Implementation

Institutions are strongly advised to consult with local law enforcement agencies or retain a professional security firm for assistance in threat assessment.

Assessment

Potential Threats.   Identify potential threats specific to the institution:

- What does the news report about the current national and international climate?
- What do the local police indicate about the local climate?
- What does the ADL Regional Office say about extremist and anti-Semitic activity in the area?
- Is there something about the building or the staff that would attract a terrorist attack, such as high-profile programs, high-profile members, or an extremely visible building?

- Is the institution at risk from collateral damage from an attack on a high-risk neighbor, such as political offices, controversial international and domestic corporate offices, or family planning clinics?
- Is the institution at risk from employees or other "insiders"?
- Is it too easy to find the institution? The question of directional signs on public streets is one only the institution can answer; ADL takes no position on this difficult question.

Identify Targets for Protection. Identify what the institution needs to protect, including people, property, and data, and what makes those things vulnerable. Different strategies exist for protecting children, adults, property, and data. Planning must account for all strategies. Sometimes these areas are related; for example, theft of a computer containing membership lists and payment information can greatly damage an institution's reputation and member safety.

Relationships with Law Enforcement. Developing a working relationship with local law enforcement agencies is important at all stages of security planning. Local police departments may have a crime prevention officer who will perform an on-site inspection and review the security plan. This outreach provides useful information, and builds relationships with local law enforcement before an incident occurs.

Planning

Risk Reduction. Identify the most appropriate and affordable, measures to reduce risk, and recognize that risk can never be completely eliminated. The most appropriate initial steps may be as simple as replacing and rekeying locks to control those with keys to the building.

Command, Control, and Communications. In any emergency event, lines of command, control, and communications are essential.

- Identify a decision maker who will have the authority to act.
- Ensure that decisions can be effectively communicated to those who need to know them.
- Plan contingencies in case a designated decision maker is unavailable during an emergency, whether out sick, on vacation, at lunch, or away from the office for a meeting.
- Ascertain immediately who is in charge at any given point.
- Develop a succession list or chain of command in the event of an absence, even a temporary one.
- Create a simple, user-friendly form to document threats coming to the institution, whether by phone, mail, or other means, containing checklist items identifying the threat and person making the threat, so staff can readily fill out and identify characteristics for law enforcement should an investigation be needed. Women's health clinics and at-risk facilities use this approach to document ongoing threats.

Explosives Planning

- Create and maintain a bomb search plan and emergency evacuation plan.
- Contact and include the local bomb squad in early discussions. They will explain the steps a facility is responsible for during a bomb emergency, including searching, and when they will respond. Many bomb squads will not come to a site until a suspicious item has been discovered. As many bomb squads do not allow individual organizations to contact them, communication with the bomb squad may need to go through the local police department. This is yet another reason to develop a relationship with the local police department.
- Identify ways to notify and, if necessary, evacuate everyone in the facility during an emergency.
- Designate a meeting point to ensure that everyone is safe.

Varied Use Plans. Create plans addressing varied building uses. School days and high-traffic events, such as the High Holidays, receptions, weddings, community meetings, and days when the facility is not used create different security circumstances.

Business Recovery. Review business recovery plans, strategies, and all insurance policies. Business recovery plans may include off-site data storage, vendor and membership lists, and plans for emergency corporate governance policies.

Available Resources. Work with security specialists, the police, emergency services, and the Anti-Defamation League regional office.

Implementation

Accountability: The Security Manager

- Designate a staff member as security manager, accountable for implementing, reviewing, and constantly updating the security plan.
- Make sure that everyone is trained to implement the plan, especially those who will be on the front lines and those who know the building best, the maintenance personnel.
- Ensure that the security manager is a responsible, organized senior staff member, who will have enough time to fulfill security responsibilities, especially when first assuming the position. Often, the security manager has no security experience and may have a significant learning curve and time commitment. This person is responsible for continued training and updating the plan.

Training Is Critical. Conduct communal and staff training, drills, role playing, and regular refresher exercises. Drills and role-playing ensure that the plan is workable, up-to-date, and fresh in people's minds.

Implementation. Constantly reassess and update the plan.

Build Relationships. At every stage of security planning, build relationships with the local emergency services.

- Get to know local law enforcement, and get them to know the institution, *before* there is a problem.
- Invite local police officers to use the gym, to join members for a weekly Sabbath service, holiday festivals, celebrations, special events, community meetings, or just to visit the building and become familiarized with the premises, personnel, and standard operations.

PHYSICAL SECURITY

Unlike most civic facilities that must be open and available to the public, religious institutions are de facto privately owned and operated. Physical security starts with a basic premise: those who do not belong on the institution's property should be excluded from the institution. This occurs in three, often interrelated, ways:

- When those who do not belong are identified, stopped, and denied admission by a person.
- When those who do not belong are denied admission by a physical device, such as by a locked door.
- When those who do not belong are denied admission because they decide that the institution is too difficult to enter, and thus, they do not even try.

There are ten critical concerns relating to excluding those who do not belong in religious institutions (Table 17.1).

TABLE 17.1 Ten Considerations for Religious Institution Security

1. Access control
2. Key control and locks
3. Protective devices/alarms
4. Windows and doors
5. Fencing
6. Lighting
7. Explosive devices
8. Weapons of mass destruction
9. Suicide bombers
10. General target hardening

Access Control

Access control means that when the facility is open, no visitor, delivery, service person, or unknown individual is able to enter the facility without being directly or indirectly observed and approved. This may be accomplished by

- *Security desk.* Establish a security desk in the main lobby of each building with an open-access or open door policy. A sign-in/out logbook supervised by an employee who validates identification *prior* to allowing visitors to proceed into the building is highly advisable.

- *Monitor entrances.* Ideally, an institution should have a single entrance only, monitored by a staff person and equipped with an intercom system for communicating with anyone who comes to the door. External barriers may also be considered. An open door policy does not mean every door needs to be left open and unlocked.

- *Check credentials.* Before allowing individuals to enter institution property, check that their identification papers or other credentials, including membership cards, are valid. Police and most utility employees carry identification cards and other documents.
  - Employees cannot always tell the difference between valid and forged documentation and credentials. Police and most utility employees carry such identification, but staff may not be able to accurately distinguish real and fake IDs.
  - A uniform or equipment may readily be purchased, enabling an intruder to pretend that they have a legitimate reason to enter the facility.
  - It is worth a few moments to contact the person's company or organization to determine the legitimacy of the person requesting admittance. Never be embarrassed to ask for more identification or to ask a person to wait until his/her identity is checked. Any individual who becomes agitated or angry at such a request should be considered of questionable legitimacy.

- *Visitors.* At no time should visitors be allowed to roam freely through the property unescorted or without being observed. This is especially true for individuals who expect to work on the most sensitive systems such as burglar alarms, fire alarms, communication systems, or computers. Special diligence should be applied to those individuals when they visit the institution. For larger institutions, certain areas should be considered off-limits to all but authorized personnel.
  - Community centers for youth and seniors, facilities with gymnasiums, and other institutions, desire to maintain open and free access. Allowing visitors free access to the facility does not mean they should be allowed to go anywhere, such as to restricted areas or office spaces. Visitors should perceive that institution personnel observe their presence and actions.

- *Stay-behinds.* End-of-day locking procedures should include a visual examination of all areas of the institution to prevent "stay-behind" burglars.

- *Photo identification.* All employees should have identification cards, to immediately identify non-employees, and settle identity questions.

- All employees should be provided with and wear photo identification cards. Photo IDs enable individuals to immediately identify those who work in an institution and understand that they are part of their organization's security program.
- Photo identification should not be issued without accompanying education about their care, procedures to follow if they are lost, and the manner in which employees should approach unknown individuals.
- Using ID cards requires care. Cards should have clear photographs, along with the employees' names. Each institution must decide if their name should be placed on the card.
- Employees should be instructed to wear their cards prominently while in the building and, for their own safety, kept from view when away from the building. There is no reason why any person on the street or on a train should be able to identify who someone is and where he or she works.
- Lost cards should be reported immediately.

Key Control and Locks

A key-control policy is essential to a sound security program. Failure to track those who have keys to specific locks at all times defeats the purpose of a security system.

Key Control.   Institutions should bear in mind that disgruntled former employees or volunteers might subsequently break into the building. Establishing a central key control location for master keys, entry to which is controlled by management, will address this issue.

- *Registry.* A central key control registry should be established for all keys and combinations. Employees and leadership should be required to sign for keys upon issuance and receipt. Key return should be part of ending service and exit interviews, if applicable.
- *Issuance.* Supervisory approval should be required for issuance of all keys and locks. Spare keys and locks should be kept in a centrally located cabinet, locked under the supervision of a designated employee. Master keys should be issued to a restricted number of employees and should be checked at least twice each year.
- *Rekeying.* When key control is lost, rekeying an institution's locks may be worthwhile.
- *Combination locks and codes.* Where combination locks and coded locks are used, combinations and codes should be changed at least every six months, or when employees or leadership leave service. The combination should also be kept under strict management control.
- *Special keys.* It is good policy to use locks with keys that cannot be duplicated on the outside without special key blanks.
- *Key card ceaders.* Key card readers, while expensive, make key control and locking more effective and nearly automatic. Large institutions, or those with valuable assets, may find key cards worth the investment because they can track and print out who comes and goes into specific rooms at any time.

Locks.   Durable locks are essential to building and operational security. A professional locksmith should be consulted for religious and institutional facilities. While the suggestions offered in this section are detailed, every institution has unique local circumstances to be addressed. The following is intended as a starting point for discussions with an experienced locksmith who can assess an institution's circumstances and provide specific recommendations. Door locks should be chosen and installed to provide appropriate security levels for each location.

- Locks with single cylinders and interior thumb turns, installed on doors with glass panels, should be placed more than 36 inches away from the nearest glass panel.
- Dead-bolt locks are the most reliable and should seat at least an inch into the doorframe or lock-bolt receiver.

- Padlocks should be of high-grade material designed to withstand abuse and tampering.
- At all times, the door-locking system must meet applicable life safety and fire codes, to allow emergency exiting without impediment.

Exterior Lock Considerations

- *Exterior locks.* All exterior door lock cylinders should be protected with metal guard plates or armored rings to prevent cylinder removal. The guard plates should be secured with round-head carriage bolts. Some highly pick-resistant cylinders have a guard plate assembly built around them.
- *Automatic closers.* Doors that have air, hydraulic, or spring returns should be periodically tested to ensure that doors return to the fully closed or locked position.
- *Selection and specification.* All exterior locks should meet several criteria during selection and specification (Table 17.2).
- *Lock management.* The institution's security manager should be responsible for the following:
  - Regularly inspect and report all defective and damaged locks; repair quickly.
  - Establish a chain of responsibility for all locks at doors and windows; ensure that locks to be locked are indeed locked, and report all failures to do so.
  - Ensure that keys are not left unattended.
  - Recommend installation of additional locks where necessary.
  - Add the locking key control program as part of the periodic security audit.
- *Survey all lock locations.* In addition to exterior locations into the facility, locks are present on interior doors, windows, offices, filing cabinets, and storage closets.

Armed Intruders. The local police department has likely considered this issue and should be involved in crime prevention discussions. The only thing worse than facing an armed intruder is facing one without preparing a response to the situation (Table 17.3).

Protective Devices, Alarms, and Technology

Selection, specification, and installation of protective devices and security technology require professional advice. Begin by contacting local law enforcement and requesting help from the crime prevention, crime resistance, or burglary prevention officers who are specially trained and can offer expert guidance. Keep in mind that law enforcement officers are not selling a product or system.

Protective Devices.   Protective devices, including intrusion detectors, fire detection systems, alarm systems, and cameras slaved to a closed-circuit TV (CCTV) system, are an important, and costly, part of institutional security. CCTV coverage allows surveillance of exterior exits and interior corridors by a trained security officer at the central control console. However, even the most sophisticated and costly devices are limited by human factors.

TABLE 17.2   Exterior Locks: Selection and Specification Considerations

1. Lock cylinders should be highly pick-resistant.
2. Dead-bolt locks should have a minimum bolt extension of one full inch.
3. Drop-bolt locks should be installed with the proper strike: wood frame, angle strike, metal frame, and flat strike.
4. All exterior door-lock cylinders should be protected with metal guard plates or armored rings to prevent cylinder removal. The guard plate should be secured with round-head carriage bolts. Some highly pick-resistant cylinders have a guard plate assembly built around them.
5. The jamb must be sufficiently strong, as a strong lock entering a weak jamb will fail.
6. At all times, the door-locking system must meet applicable life, safety, and fire codes, to allow emergency exiting without impediment.

TABLE 17.3   Armed Intruders: Protective Measures and Emergency Procedures

1. Communicate with staff to direct a lockdown or to lead people to evacuation routes away from the area occupied by the gunman.
2. As discussed in dealing with explosive threats, quickly establishing the three "Cs": command, control, and communications is critical here.
3. Fire alarms should not be activated as they cause panic and may lead people to move directly into the path of the intruder.
4. Find a way to contact the local police department that does not require returning to an area of danger.
5. Maintain a cell phone in the facility at all times.
6. When speaking with a police dispatcher, speak calmly and quietly, informing the dispatcher of the danger facing the institution. If shots are being fired, it is critical to inform the dispatcher there is an "active shooter" on the premises and immediate intervention is required.
7. Lockdown may be preferable to evacuation. During a lockdown, students and faculty should be directed to lock their room doors and windows and move away from windows and other glass. Institutions may wish to develop a method of signaling officials where a room contains locked-down persons. This may be as simple as placing green or red paper in a window, the former to indicating there are people inside who are well, the latter that emergency attention is required.
8. This is yet another opportunity to state the importance of establishing relationships with law enforcement before an incident occurs.
9. Establish a procedure for employees to communicate with and inform leadership or management that they are safe. One option is to designate a muster, or meeting point, though this may not be practical in light of the panic following an armed intrusion.
10. Other possibilities include using cell phones to contact a nearby institution, known to the staff, which can take names of staff calling in. At the same time, keep an off-site staff list, including home and cell phone numbers of all personnel.

Technology Selection.   Many types of technology systems are available on the market for institutional applications. Selecting the appropriate system can be a challenge to the layperson. Institutional facility managers, members of the institution's building committee, licensed architects and engineers, as well as reputable, and ideally, certified, security consultants can assist with selecting appropriate technology and protective devices. Ultimately, the facility manager or administrator must understand how to use and maintain the system and be sure that any technology performs the necessary tasks to secure the premises.

CCTV.   CCTV systems will be marginally effective if they are not properly maintained and monitored, or if those tasked with monitoring cameras are overworked, poorly trained, tired, or distracted. Most institutions are unlikely to have resources for continual monitoring. An alternative is a videotape or digital system. Video surveillance will fail when not properly used, or when no one is assigned to check, review, and change the tapes. Digital systems can store images on a computer console, rather than on racks of videocassettes, and can call up specific views and times on a computer screen when programmed.

Surveillance Cameras.   Surveillance cameras should be placed at the institution's entrances, as a deterrent to potential intruders. Cameras can document criminal acts occurring on the property, which can later be used to identify and prosecute perpetrators. Although first costs are often expensive, in the long run, cameras are economical when compared to the costs of potential losses (Table 17.4).

Alarms.   Alarm systems, like locks, require professional guidance. Alarm systems are designed to protect an institution from intrusion, and can materially benefit facility security. The size, location, and type of institution will determine the type of system required (Table 17.5). Alarm systems consist of three components:

- Sensor, which detects an intruder
- Control, which receives information from the sensor
- Annunciator, which visibly or audibly alerts someone of the intrusion

TABLE 17.4 Surveillance Cameras: Selection and Specification Considerations

1. Use wide-angle lenses to survey entrances.
2. Use cameras with infrared illumination to enhance nighttime video.
3. Couple the camera with a time-lapse recorder for permanent recording.
4. Make sure the camera has a time and date recorder.
5. Compare the cost of color versus black and white, digital versus video.
6. Save video film for a minimum of 72 hours.
7. Replace video film at least every six months.
8. Investigate digital capabilities.

TABLE 17.5 Alarm Systems: Selection and Specification Considerations

1. Ensure that all alarm systems have emergency backup power sources.
2. Conceal the alarm control box and limit access to it.
3. Choose the system that best fits the need of the establishment.
4. Select a system with an electronic circuit delay of 30 seconds.
5. Ensure that the alarm can be heard throughout the property.
6. Contract with a central alarm monitoring company to monitor the alarm system.
7. Protect all wiring components and sirens from tampering.
8. Make sure that the alarm comes with a "test" option.
9. Test the alarm system regularly to maintain effectiveness.
10. Apply alarm-warning stickers in windows, entrances, and exits.
11. Ensure that the alarm system meets local legal and code requirements.
12. Determine if the city or town prohibits directly dialing to police.
13. Educate staff and leadership about using the equipment and how the monitoring company will handle all alarms, including false alarms.
14. Consider adding panic buttons to the alarm system, to allow the alarm to be triggered from locations other than the main alarm panel. Consider panic button placement in key offices used during off hours, and in locations where intruders may first be confronted, such as in reception areas.

The sophistication and coverage provided depends on the system.

- Special features might include emergency panic buttons and robbery signal circuits.
- Motion detectors or automatic sensors responding to sound or movement are excellent protective devices, used alone or in conjunction with the institution's lighting system. These detectors and sensors are economical and can be used inside or outside the building.
- Two effective, inexpensive solutions are alarms using magnetic contacts and trip wires. Alarms with motion, sound, or light detectors are more expensive, but are generally more dependable. The cost invested in a dependable alarm system is generally less than the cost of damages caused by an intruder to the institution.

Windows and Doors

When renovating, upgrading, or modifying existing facilities, or designing new facilities, a licensed architect and engineer should be consulted to design and specify appropriate, code-compliant windows, doors, screens, gates, skylights, and building construction materials, and to ensure that facility design meets applicable local life safety, building, and fire codes.

Doors.   All exterior doors, main building doors, and lobby doors leading to common corridors should meet several important criteria (Table 17.6).

TABLE 17.6   Exterior, Main Building, and Lobby Doors: Selection and Specification Considerations

1. Solid core, wood, or metal are acceptable, depending on code requirements.
2. Glass door panels or side panels should be reinforced with metal or steel mesh, or else replaced with shatterproof glass.
3. Where there is an alarm system, glass breaker sensors that detect glass breakage should be installed close to glass doors or windows.
4. Doorframes should be sturdy and appropriate for the door type. Weak frames should be replaced or rebuilt.
5. Exterior door locks should conform to guidelines found in the section on locks.
6. Interior or office doors should be equipped with heavy-duty, mortised latch sets with dead-bolt capability. Rim-mounted, deadbolt, or drop-bolt locks can be installed to increase security of important offices or rooms.
7. Doors with external or exposed hinges may be vulnerable to pin removal. The hinge pin should be made non-removable by spot welding or other means, or the hinges should be pinned to prevent separation.
8. Doors to utility closets should be equipped with dead bolts and kept locked at all times. Such closets, if unsecured, can become hiding places for "stay-behind" criminals or explosive devices.
9. All exterior doors without glass vision panels should be equipped with wide-angle viewers, or peepholes, mounted at a height accessible to tall and short individuals.
10. Interior doors should have two-way visibility at stairways and corridors. There should be a clear view of room interiors from the doorway.
11. Access to offices, kitchens, electrical, mechanical rooms, and storage rooms must be limited to appropriate staff and locked when not in use.

TABLE 17.7   Fire Doors: Selection and Specification Considerations

1. Fire doors must conform to all local fire and building codes and should have an Underwriters Laboratory (UL) rating.
2. Fire doors should be secured with approved latching or locking hardware, such as a panic bar with a spring latch or safety lock.
3. If a fire door has a solid core, the interior material must be fire resistant.
4. An adjustable spring or air return will ensure that the door is always closed.
5. As with all doors, sensor devices connecting to a sound device or system announce their opening.
6. All doors or gates not observed, either directly or remotely, should be secured.
7. Placing height marks next to exit doors will allow employees to estimate height of suspicious persons.

Fire Doors.   Fire doors are those leading to and from a means of egress in a building, such as a stairway or exit to the outside (Table 17.7).

Windows.   Windows should provide light, ventilation, and visibility, but not easy access for intruders.

• Glass block can be used to seal a window, allowing a continued light source while providing increased security, although visibility and ventilation will be diminished. Local building codes should be consulted regarding placing glass block in rated corridors, egress paths, or building occupancies to ensure conformance to applicable fire ratings.

• Gates and expanded steel screens, while often unattractive, provide a high degree of security. Local building codes and fire safety regulations should be consulted prior to all such installations to avoid costly violations.

• Skylights, roof access, ventilators, and large door transoms can provide easy access to intruders unless properly protected. If permanent sealing is not possible, steel bars or screens of expanded metal may be required, if permitted by fire codes.

• *A critical note on glass:* Flying glass can be as dangerous in an explosion as the actual explosion. Consider replacing traditional glass with safety or shatter-resistant glass, or using a clear protective film to secure the glass to the frame.

Fencing

Fences make an intruder's entry more difficult and give the appearance of a secure institution. When considering any protective element, institutional building owners, administrators, and facility managers should consult local building and zoning codes regarding installation of fences, prior to planning, design, and construction.

In keeping with the planning principles of crime prevention through environmental design (CPTED), uses of fencing, natural site features, and perimeter site lighting are relatively low cost, low-tech opportunities to reduce problems and enhance security (Table 17.8).

Protective Lighting

Adequate lighting is a cost-effective line of defense in preventing crime. As with all other aspects of design and construction, institutional building owners and facility managers should consult with a security professional, licensed architect, engineer, or lighting consultant to determine locations and the best type of lighting for each institutional site (Table 17.9).

TABLE 17.8   Fencing: Selection and Specification Considerations

1. All physical barriers added to a religious institution should be compatible with the aesthetics of the neighborhood or surrounding environment. Institutions should make every effort to avoid alienating neighbors who may serve as part of a neighborhood watch and provide additional "eyes and ears" to the overall security program.
2. Open ornamental fences, unlike walls, do not block visibility, are less susceptible to graffiti, and are more difficult to climb.
3. Fences should be at least six feet high. Institutions should take advantage of any small incline or hillock along which to build the fencing.
4. Fences should be designed to prevent a person from reaching in with their hand or a wire to open the fence gate from the outside.
5. If a panic bar is required on the inside of a fence gate, a solid metal or plastic shield should be used to prevent a person on the outside from opening the gate.
6. Walls should be constructed where there is a need for privacy and noise control.
7. Fence lines should be kept free of trash and debris. Clear away trees and vines that might aid a climber. Weeds and shrubs along fence lines, sides of buildings, or near entrance points could hide criminal activities.
8. Keep shrubs low, less than 36 inches, or clear them away completely. Cut back vines attached to buildings to prevent determined intruders from gaining access to upper windows or unprotected roof access.
9. Creating an impenetrable physical barrier unprotected by personnel is difficult. Even when protected by personnel, people grow fatigued, inattentive, bored, and make mistakes.

TABLE 17.9   Protective Lighting: Selection and Specification Considerations

1. Interior and exterior lighting can be provided without being intrusive to neighbors.
2. All entrances and fences should be well lit.
3. For outside lighting, the rule of thumb is to create light equal to full daylight.
4. Light should be directed downward, away from the building or area to be protected and away from security personnel patrolling the facility.
5. Where fencing is used, lighting should be inside and above the fencing to illuminate as much of the fence as possible.
6. Lighting must be consistent to reduce contrast between shadows and illuminated areas. Lighting levels should be uniform on walkways, entrances, exits, and in parking areas.
7. Perimeter lights should be installed so the cones of illumination overlap, eliminating areas of total darkness if any lamp fails to light.
8. Lighting fixtures should be vandal-resistant. Repair and replace defective or worn-out bulbs immediately.
9. Prevent trees or bushes from blocking lighting fixtures.
10. Timers and automatic photoelectric cells protect against human error, and ensure operation during inclement weather, even when the building is unoccupied.

Explosive Threat Planning

The best way to secure an institution from explosives is to prepare a physical security plan. Institutions must take all responsible steps to prevent the introduction of an explosive into the environment. The first step in creating an explosive threat response plan (ETRP) is preparing a physical security plan to prevent the planting of any device. Since no physical security plan is foolproof, even the most secure institution should have an ETRP (Table 17.10).

An ETRP requires an understanding of precisely how local law enforcement will respond to explosive threats. In some areas, the police, or explosive unit, will not respond to such a threat until a device is discovered. In other areas, the police, or the explosive unit may respond to a called-in credible threat, but will not search a facility without a staff member present. This information is absolutely critical to planning, and underscores the need to build relationships with local law enforcement well before a problem arises.

Car and Truck Bombs. Without extensive physical alterations and an extensive security program, defending against truck and car bombs is very difficult. Nevertheless, well-planned physical security precautions implemented by an institution represent an improvement over doing nothing at all.

Car and truck bomb prevention is a matter of physical security first, and search and evacuation second. The key defenses are excluding potentially dangerous vehicles from the institution, and, if they are admitted to the grounds, keeping them far enough away to prevent damage.

The institution may consider adding physical barriers, such as concrete Jersey barriers, between the street and the facility. In an urban environment where on-street parking is close to the facility, consider requesting no-parking designations from the local police department.

Ideally, all vehicles entering the facility's grounds should be scrutinized before being admitted. While less than ideal, scrutinizing vehicles once they are on the grounds or parked is still significantly better than doing nothing.

Car and truck bombs might be identified by the outward appearance of the vehicle, behavior of the driver, and other suspicious indicators (Table 17.11). None of these items are indicators of potential violence, and many are consistent with innocent behavior. However, they are clues to observe and consider for truck bomb security (Table 17.12).

TABLE 17.10 Ten Tips on Explosive-Specific Physical Security

1. Offices and desks should be kept locked, especially those unused and unoccupied. Utility and janitorial closets should remain locked at all times, as should access to boiler rooms, mailrooms, computer areas, switchboards, and elevator control rooms.
2. Identify and secure potential hiding spaces for explosives. A device does not have to be large to cause severe physical and psychological damage.
3. Trash receptacles, especially dumpsters, should be kept locked, inaccessible to outsiders, and far away from buildings. The areas around these items should remain free of debris.
4. Cars and trucks should be required to maintain a safe, 50- to 100-foot setback from the facility. If no parking setback is possible, consider allowing only properly identified vehicles owned by staff or leadership to park closest to the building. When planning new facilities, create as deep a setback, known as standoff distance, as possible.
5. Consider using blast-resistant walls and shatterproof, blast-resistant windows to block the effects of a blast.
6. Shrubs and other plants and trees should be trimmed, so they will not provide a hiding space for explosives and those carrying them.
7. Employees should be encouraged to maintain tidy work areas so that they or their coworkers will notice if something is out of place.
8. Flying glass is a grave source of danger in the event of a blast. Consider minimizing glass panes, and coating with shatter-resistant film.
9. More than one exit may be damaged in a sufficiently large blast. Plan for several alternative emergency escape routes. Practice evacuation drills with building occupants.
10. Examine the local area to identify risks from neighboring institutions and potential targets. Jewish institutions, political offices, international government facilities, medical facilities where abortion services are provided, global corporations, and corporate offices are possible targets.

TABLE 17.11   Car and Truck Bombs: Suspicious Signs to Look for

1. The vehicle's driver does not enter the facility, but rather runs or walks away.
2. The car or truck appears to be sitting very low on its springs, indicating great weight.
3. The car or truck is parked illegally or too close to the building. The facility should restrict parking closest to the building.
4. Older cars and trucks, and rental vehicles, are more likely to be used in a car bombing. Be wary of any type of vehicle appearing to have been abandoned, such as an expired or missing inspection sticker, registration, or license plate.

TABLE 17.12   Incremental Steps for Truck Bomb Security

1. Restrict parking closest to building, by eliminating parking or limiting parking to staff and key lay-leader vehicles. Institutions may choose to issue a windshield identification sticker to determine who belongs and who needs further scrutiny.
2. Train staff and security personnel to be aware of types and appearance of vehicles used in these incidents.
3. Use barriers, gates, and fences to prevent access to the facility by nonauthorized persons.
4. Cars and trucks should be required to maintain at least a 50- to 100-foot setback from the facility. If no parking setback is possible, consider allowing only properly identified vehicles owned by staff or leadership to park closest to the building.
5. Consider using blast resistant walls and shatterproof, blast-resistant windows to block the effects of a blast.

A Brief Look at Weapons of Mass Destruction (WMD)

The following general information, adapted from a fact sheet developed by the Federal Bureau of Investigation (FBI), is intended to enhance knowledge and ability to recognize potential WMD-related threats or incidents. Other government sources, such as the Federal Emergency Management Agency (FEMA) can provide additional detailed information about how to respond to a WMD incident.

Of Critical Importance. WMDs are extremely hard to manufacture and difficult to deliver effectively. Most so-called weapons of mass destruction will have a limited effectiveness range. Thus, risk from WMDs is likely to be minimal. However, those concerned with public safety and security should understand WMDs and be able to prevent and react to their use.

Chemical, biological, and radiological material can be dispersed in the air, drinking water, or on surfaces of physical contact. Dispersion methods could include placing an open container in a heavily-used area, using conventional garden and commercial spray devices, or detonating an improvised explosive device to disseminate chemical, biological, or radiological material.

Chemical incidents are characterized by the rapid onset of medical symptoms, in minutes to hours, and easily observed signatures, such as colored residue, dead foliage, pungent odor, and dead insect and animal life. In the case of a biological or radiological incident, characteristic symptoms may take days to weeks to appear. In all cases, being alert to a variety of factors could assist law enforcement and emergency responders in evaluating potential threats (Tables 17.13 to 17.15).

Suicide Bombers

Considering the possibility of suicide bombers is perhaps the most worrisome security issue any institution, organization, or governmental agency must consider. As international events in the Middle East have indicated, there are no easy answers or solutions to this threat.

Role-Playing. Members of the security committee, board of directors, and "front line" personnel, such as greeters, ushers, hired security guards, their managers, and others, should role-play as a team to prepare for possible threat scenarios and responses. To do this, determine whether any member of

TABLE 17.13 Potential Indicators of Weapons of Mass Destruction (WMD) Threats or Incidents

1. Unusual packages or containers, especially those found in unlikely or sensitive locations, such as near HVAC (heating, ventilation, air conditioning), air-intake systems, rooftops, stairwells, or building entrances.
2. Unusual powders, liquids, droplets, mists, or clouds, especially those found near air-intake vents and HVAC systems.
3. Indications of tampering in targeted areas and equipment, such as locked ventilation and HVAC systems; stocks of food and water supplies.
4. Reports of suspicious person(s) or activities, especially those involving sensitive locations within or around a building.
5. Surveillance of targeted areas by unknown individuals, including but not limited to hotels, entertainment venues, subway systems, aircraft, water sources, office buildings, apartment buildings.
6. Theft of chemical products and equipment.
7. Dead animals, birds, fish, or insects.
8. Unexplained or unusual odors. Smells may range from fruity and flowery to sharp and pungent, garlic and horseradish, bitter almonds, peach kernels, and newly mown grass or hay. Of course, some of these smells have innocent explanations.
9. Unusual and unscheduled spraying or discovery of spray devices or bottles.

TABLE 17.14 Weapons of Mass Destruction: Protective Measures

1. Maintain a heightened sense of awareness.
2. Place increased emphasis on the security of immediate surroundings.
3. Conduct periodic inspections of building facilities and HVAC systems for potential indicators and irregularities.
4. Review emergency operations, evacuation plans, and procedures for all locations, building tenants, and organizations to ensure that plans are up-to-date.
5. Promptly report suspicious activities to appropriate law enforcement authorities.

TABLE 17.15 Emergency Procedures for Weapons of Mass Destruction When Potential Threat Is Identified and Confirmed

1. Maintain a safe distance and evacuate the area. If outside, move to upwind location; if inside, keep outside doors and windows closed.
2. Call local 911 for law enforcement and public safety personnel, after reaching safe area.
3. Do not handle or disturb suspicious objects.
4. Remove possibly contaminated external clothing, including hats, shoes, and gloves.
5. Follow emergency operations plans and instructions from emergency response personnel.
6. *Note*: To prevent spreading contamination and to ensure appropriate decontamination and medical treatment, after moving to safety, do not leave until instructed to do so by law enforcement.

the institution has experience in this field. Otherwise, a small group should develop scenarios involving the approach of a suicide bomber, his/her attempt to gain entrance, and the possibility that he/she may actually gain entrance to the facility. Alter the nature of the scenarios and carefully analyze lessons learned.

For instance, if role-playing leads someone to try to engage the suspicious person in conversation while someone else dials 911, the players need to determine

● Who will dial 911 or contact emergency personnel
● Who will make the decisions
● What is said to the potential attacker, to try to engage him or her

Possible Indicators of a Suicide Bomber. Suspicious people may often be identified by their behavior. No one behavior proves that someone is planning to carry out an attack, and many of the following

TABLE 17.16   Behavioral Factors to Consider for a Suicide Bomber

1. Nervousness, nervous glancing, or other signs of mental discomfort, being ill at ease. This may include sweating, "tunnel vision," or staring forward inappropriately, repeated inappropriate prayer, especially outside the facility, or muttering.
2. Repeated entrances and exits from the building or facility.
3. Inappropriate, oversized, loose-fitting clothes, such as a heavy overcoat on a warm day.
4. Keeping hands in pockets or cupping hands, as if holding a triggering device.
5. Constantly favoring one side or one area of the body as if wearing something unusual or uncomfortable, such as a holster, a bomb belt, or vest. Pay attention to a person constantly adjusting waistbands, ankles, or other clothing. Projected angles under clothing may indicate a firearm, especially at the waist or the ankle. Suicide bombers have been known to repeatedly pat themselves to verify their bomb vest or belt is still attached.
6. Carrying packages.
7. Security personnel should be told, when possible, to observe people as they exit their cars; by watching how they adjust clothing and how they approach the building, looking for signs that a person might be carrying a weapon.

behavioral indicators are consistent with innocent behavior. While no list could ever be complete, several factors can assess whether someone poses such a threat (Table 17.16). Many of these, especially the last items, are often consistent with innocent explanations.

Be Observant and Notice the Details.   After the rash of suicide bombings in their communities, Israelis became aware that some suicide bombers shaved off beards prior to committing their acts, leaving unusual facial tan lines. In Israel, the majority of bombers have been males, ages 18 to 27. Some also anointed themselves with scented oil, which may be another obvious clue to someone in their vicinity.

Responding to a Perceived Threat.   While no one factor is a certain indicator of a problem, once a problem is identified, ushers and security personnel have three options:

- Do nothing.
- Investigate and decide whether to take emergency steps.
- Immediately take emergency steps.

This is a decision only an institution's personnel can make in light of the circumstances, their personal comfort level, and safety considerations. They must, at all times, be aware of the threat to worshipers, students, or others if the individual who is the focus of concern gains access into the facility.

- If they choose to investigate, one technique is for security personnel to greet the person in a friendly fashion, asking, "Can I be of assistance?" Evasive or unusual answers may trigger emergency procedures. Security personnel may excuse themselves and initiate security procedures, perhaps by using a predetermined code word with colleagues.
- If there is credible reason to believe an individual poses a threat, every attempt should be made to deny access into the facility.
- If a call is made to 911, ensure that the dispatcher understands the emergency nature of the call and the need for a law enforcement response without sirens. Off-duty officers are generally armed and are aware of security procedures.
- If suspicions remain, and even if the person leaves immediately, call the police.

General Target Hardening

Visible security devices and technology, such as lighting, fences, CCTV, and alarms, make a facility look less inviting to a potential attacker. Target hardening is based on the premise that the more

TABLE 17.17   Five Examples of Target Hardening

1. Signs indicating the presence of an alarm system
2. Visible security patrols and vehicles
3. Well-maintained perimeter fencing and lighting
4. The general appearance of a well-maintained facility
5. Regular presence of local law enforcement on or near the grounds

TABLE 17.18   Preparing for Disaster Recovery

1. Maintain off-site, current backups of critical data, vendor lists, employee, constituent and donor contact lists, and other mission-critical information. This may entail someone taking a disk home with them, but if the disk or data is lost, information may get into the wrong hands. Backup security is vital.
2. Conduct an insurance review to ensure that insurance is adequate to cover all institutional needs. Keep insurance records with backup information.
3. Explore legal aspects of recovery with the institution's attorney, including discussions as to whether someone has the authority or can be designated with legal authority to take emergency steps on behalf of the institution.
4. Plan for relocating students, patients, campers, seniors, and staff ahead of time before disaster strikes.
5. Inventory everything that would cause the institution to cease operations if destroyed.
6. Review all existing service agreements and whether they include adequate postdisaster service provisions and recovery assistance.

uninviting an institution is to an attacker, the less likely the attack. Institutions should not reveal detailed security measures, but should provide clear evidence of security features to prevent an attack (Table 17.17).

Disaster Recovery.   Disaster recovery is part of postincident work. Recovery is easier if preparation is done beforehand (Table 17.18).

CONCLUSION

Religious facilities and related community centers must remain open and welcoming to their members, and occasionally, to the public, while remaining alert and prepared for any type of emergency or threat. Building relationships with local law enforcement agencies will enhance crime prevention efforts and establish critical networks well before a disaster or in the event of an emergency.

As long as terrorist attacks remain potential threats to the public and religious institutions, more defensive, proactive precautions are required. Balancing the need for transparent security, not visible to the eye, through operations and design, with clear evidence of safety precautions and technology, is the major challenge facing all religious institutions and civic facilities considered designated targets. Knowledge of how to best achieve this delicate balance within each religious institution is the first step to ensuring personal safety and security for all who believe in democracy and a free society.

ACKNOWLEDGMENTS

- Abraham H. Foxman, National Director, The Anti-Defamation League, New York, New York
- Steven C. Sheinberg, Coordinator, Security Awareness Programs, Special Assistant to the National Director, The Anti-Defamation League, New York, New York

- Morris S. Casuto, Regional Director, The Anti-Defamation League, San Diego, California
- Myrna Shinbaum, Director, Media Relations and Public Information, The Anti-Defamation League, New York, New York

This chapter is adapted from *Keeping Your Jewish Institution Safe* (www.adl.org/security), © 2003 Anti-Defamation League, and is used with permission.

INTERNET RESOURCES

Anti-Defamation League
www.adl.org
www.adl.org/security
www.adl.org/learn (threat information)

Faith & Form: Journal of the Interfaith Forum on Religion, Art and Architecture (IFRAA)
www.faithnform.com

Federal Bureau of Investigation
www.fbi.gov

Federal Emergency Management Agency
www.fema.gov

CHAPTER 18
RESEARCH FACILITIES: SECURITY PLANNING

Regis Gaughan, PE
Managing Partner, HLW International LLP
New York, New York

Joseph Calabrese, PE
Former Principal, HLW International LLP
New York, New York

Stanley Stark, AIA
Managing Partner, HLW International LLP
New York, New York

*Research is the art of seeing what everyone else has seen, and
doing what no one else has done.* ANONYMOUS

Facility safety and security planning have long influenced planning, design, and operation of research facilities. The sensitive and confidential nature of research operations and the need to control access to potentially hazardous functions and materials have a powerful impact on research facility planning and design. As a result, security and life safety system design are vital elements to successful research facility performance.

Since the terrorist attacks of September 11, 2001, and the subsequent incidents related to anthrax, the federal government and the scientific and technical communities have proposed or adopted heightened security measures to counteract terrorism. This includes the PATRIOT/USA Act, P.L. 107-56, signed by President Bush on October 26, 2001. The Public Health Security and Bioterrorism Preparedness and Response Act of 2002 provides regulatory oversight for the use and possession of specific pathogens or toxins as defined by the Department of Health and Human Services and the U.S. Department of Agriculture.

Developing a comprehensive security plan and integrating the plan into the research facility design process are essential tasks for the design team, building owners, and facility managers. The security plan has two key elements:

- Site and architectural features
- Standard or emergency operating procedures (SEOPs)

The design team must understand the relationship between design features and operating procedures and how they influence one another. This process works best as an integral part of the front-end planning and conceptual design phase, with contributions from all vested stakeholders. A security consultant may be helpful in facilitating the planning process (Fig. 18.1).

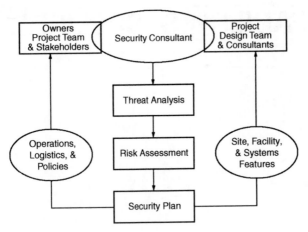

FIGURE 18.1   The design team. (*Source: HLW International LLP.*)

RESOURCES

One of the most comprehensive guidelines for security planning is published in the Centers for Disease Control and Prevention (CDC)/National Institutes of Health (NIH), Biosafety in Microbiological and Biomedical Laboratories (BMBL), the 4th edition. Appendix F of the CDC/NIH BMBL is intended to assist research facilities in meeting the regulatory mandate of 42 Code of Federal Regulation (CFR) 73, established specifically for those laboratories using selected biohazard agents under the biosafety levels (BSL) 2, 3, or 4 as described in Sections II and III of the BMBL. Biosafety levels (BSL) define the level of containment required for each category of biohazard agent used in the lab. BSL-4 represents the most stringent and highest level of containment. Although all research facilities are not under the jurisdiction of CDC/NIH, the BMBL provides an excellent guideline for security planning as it relates to biological safety and risk.

SECURITY PLANNING

The prerequisite to an effective security plan is a risk assessment, based on a threat analysis and vulnerability assessment of the facility, assets, and operations (Table 18.1).

Research and development facilities are at a higher risk for industrial and economic espionage and malicious vandalism. Rapid advances in technology have made laboratories prime targets for outsiders and foreign governments to attempt to acquire intellectual properties by various methods, bypassing the enormous costs of research and development.

Controversy over various types of research and the use of animals for experimental purposes have led activist groups to take action against facilities, primarily to disrupt research. Research facilities

TABLE 18.1   Threat Analysis Identifies and Evaluates Threats Based on Several Factors

Threat analysis evaluation criteria
• Internal and external threats
• Threat magnitude and likelihood
• Downside potential of each threat event
• Disruption of services
• Potential to affect life and safety

face a dual security task: keeping threats out, while containing potential hazards and risks, and keeping proprietary information inside the premises.

The vulnerability assessment determines the likelihood of success for each threat. The risk assessment is a decision process tool to identify and prioritize the security plan (Table 18.2).

Many security elements influence facility design. From a global perspective, some large corporate, government, and institutional research entities have security master plans encompassing all their enterprise campuses and site locations.

SITE AND FACILITY LOCATION

The basic tenet of security design is creating a hierarchy of layered access control for the site and facility. The layering concept creates a filtering effect, where different or increasingly restrictive levels of access control can be employed. Different configurations may be used, depending on the nature of the site on which the facility is located.

Research facilities are located in a wide variety of environments and site types. These differ in setting—urban, suburban, and rural—and by the size and type of organization, such as private corporation, university, government, or institution. In general, the following apply:

- Large pharmaceutical companies are likely to be a closed campus.
- Medical schools and academic facilities are likely to be an open campus.

Designing a facility for a green field site, typically an undeveloped, large, suburban plot of land has significantly different factors than designing a facility as part of an existing, developed campus. The green field site selection process should include criteria related to implementing a security program (Table 18.3).

TABLE 18.2 Security Plan Elements for Research Facilities

- Access control for the site and buildings
- Security policy for personnel, visitors, and contractors
- Information technology and computer system security
- Policy for normal and off-hour operations
- Security and safety training
- Emergency response plans based on scenarios defined or hypothesized by the threat analysis
- Redundancy for critical utilities and support systems related to life and operational safety
- Tracking and monitoring critical materials and select biological agents from receipt to discharge
- Reporting policy for incidents, injuries, and breaches
- Central monitoring and control center
- Enforceable policies that can be monitored, relating to secure handling of critical information

TABLE 18.3   Research Facility Site Selection Criteria for a Green Field

- Proximity to major roadways and traffic control
- Opportunity to create a natural raised berm, trench, or physical barrier
- Setback of the lab building from the site perimeter
- Parking setback from the lab building
- Separation of pedestrian, auto, and truck flow patterns
- Access control points for personnel, visitors, deliveries, and contractors
- Location and protection of critical site utilities
- Storage and disposal of hazardous waste

The security plan for a new facility must be coordinated with the overall campus security master plan, with attention to the following:

- The capacity of existing security and safety systems infrastructure to absorb the new building
- Technology compatibility between new and existing systems
- Extending existing protocols, policies, and staffing to include the new building

TIERED ACCESS CONTROL SYSTEM

The access control system hierarchy falls into three broad categories:

- Site perimeter
- Building envelope
- Facility interior

Each layer functions as a filter or control point to govern and monitor access. The location and space requirements necessary to accomplish controlled access are critical to success. Integrating these features is most effective when they are considered as part of the planning and programming phase and they are related to the staff and operational flows within the facility.

SITE PERIMETER

The initial step in configuring a controlled access plan is to analyze the facility site perimeter as the first layer in the hierarchy (Fig. 18.2). A perimeter barrier and containment system should be considered, along with perimeter monitoring systems, including closed-circuit TV (CCTV) surveillance for site boundary and access points. Perimeter barriers include

- Raised berms, trenches, trees, fences, and concrete barriers.
- Gated access or guard stations for pedestrian and vehicular traffic.
- Serpentine road sections leading to access points. These roads and other devices like speed bumps are employed to reduce vehicle speed.

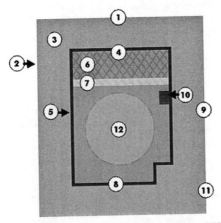

Key to Site Perimeter Diagram

1. Main entry site
2. Site perimeter
3. Buffer zone
4. Building entry
5. Building envelope
6. Public spaces (lobby, reception, restrooms)
7. Barrier between public and private sector
8. Back door/nonpublic access
9. Service entrance
10. Loading dock/mail room/deliveries
11. Employee site entrance
12. Interior layers

FIGURE 18.2   Site perimeter diagram. (*Source: HLW International LLP.*)

The site circulation system connects the perimeter with the buildings and should be integrated with the planning and design process. The following traffic and circulation needs will directly influence the security status of the facility:

- Vehicular traffic for personnel and designated parking areas
- Pedestrian traffic related to off-site transportation
- Designated and segregated visitor vehicular sign-in, checkpoint, and parking
- Designated site entry checkpoint for deliveries and contractors
- Special designated and protected front door drop-off, pick-up points

The use of a perimeter barrier system must balance the need to control site access with the desired architectural feel of the site or campus. The perimeter system should create a sense of awareness and security, while avoiding the adverse affects of confinement.

Access points from public thoroughfares can be designed with staffed guard stations to control or restrict public access. In the absence of staffed security stations, gated entry points designed with card access and intercom systems will allow identity verification and two-way communication with security personnel. A closed-circuit televised monitoring system will provide site surveillance for real-time monitoring and digital documentation at a central monitoring and control center. Multiple, or satellite, control centers may be appropriate if the risk assessment determined the need for redundancy. Balancing operational and staffing costs with technology and potential risks of one central control center are issues that building owners must address in determining whether satellite command centers are needed. Increasingly, most major research sites employ central guardhouses where visitors park, check in, and either take a shuttle bus to their destination or are escorted.

In urban research buildings, the site perimeter and the building exterior wall are often the same element. Unlike suburban sites, no spatial separation exists between the external urban environment and the controlled activities within, except for the exterior wall (Fig. 18.3).

SECURITY CONTROL CENTER

The security control center (SCC) is the hub of security systems monitoring and security communications (Fig. 18.4). In suburban research campuses, the SCC is generally within a guardhouse or a major facility. In urban buildings and campuses, the SCC is generally on the ground floor of a major facility near a main lobby. The SCC should monitor all site and campus security activities including all campus buildings with a building control center (BCC). Security monitoring may be combined with monitoring safety systems for the campus. This needs to be coordinated during planning for both entities for operations procedures and facility design considerations. The SCC is staffed as a 24-hour-a-day/7-day-a-week (24/7) operation, to monitor critical functions (Table 18.4).

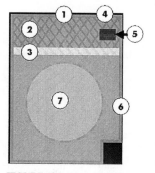

Key to Site Perimeter Diagram for an Urban Building:

1. Main building entry
2. Public spaces
3. Barrier between public and private sector
4. Services/delivery entry
5. Mailroom
6. Building envelope
7. Interior layers

FIGURE 18.3 Site perimeter diagram for an urban building. (*Source: HLW International LLP.*)

FIGURE 18.4   Security control center. (*Source: Corbis.*)

TABLE 18.4   Critical Functions Monitored by the Security Control Center

1. Central monitors and digital recording equipment for all site and building CCTV surveillance systems
2. All site access stations, staffed and unstaffed
3. Security and safety alarm central monitoring and communications
4. Vehicular activity
5. Command center for site security patrol
6. Control point for all critical equipment, such as sample storage freezers, and critical environmental control parameters, such as vivarium room temperature
7. Control point for fire alarm and life safety systems

One of the planning issues for the SCC is to determine under what normal and adverse conditions the SCC needs to be operative. The SCC may need to remain in operation under severe circumstances or in case of a security incident. These circumstances must be defined as part of the security plan and related to the threat analysis. The degree of severity under which the control center needs to remain in operation and for how long defines how "hardened" or protected the center needs to be. Levels of hardening define some of the following features:

- Structural integrity and requirements to withstand defined events
- Mechanical and electrical system requirements and redundancy
- Standby fuel requirements for backup systems
- Communications and IT requirements
- Staffing requirements and special training

The size and location of the SCC and satellite control centers are part of the security planning process. This is most effective when accomplished during the project planning and programming phase.

BUILDING ENVELOPE

After the site perimeter and connective roadways, the building envelope is the next security layer to be addressed. For urban buildings, the building envelope is the site perimeter. Similar to other high-risk, high-occupancy building types, research and development facilities may require a level of hardening consistent with the level of risk. The level of risk is defined during the security planning process, specifically during risk assessment. The building structure should be adequate to protect against the determined level of threat.

Glazing systems and external building skin elements should be evaluated consistent with the need to resist a specific category of threat, for example, blast protection. The strategic location and hardening of the following elements should be considered for new and renovated laboratories, both in suburban as well as urban settings (Table 18.5).

The building envelope is the major line of defense for facilities located on an open campus or for stand-alone buildings. Building envelope monitoring can be provided by a CCTV system with strategically located cameras. Camera locations should focus on the following:

- All entry doors and truck docks
- Wall sections with windows close to grade
- Utility or grade-mounted equipment
- Entry plazas or courtyards
- Roof and wall configurations that could be scaleable by intruders

Exposed system elements such as cameras and physical barriers such as bollards can create a visual deterrent and sense of higher security and could become part of a design vocabulary conveying a sense of awareness and vigilance. Staffed security locations and the CCTV locations should report to the SCC.

Strategic goals should include limiting the number of entry points, consistent with code safety, such as the following:

- Building entry points include the main entrance and secondary entrances for pedestrian traffic, truck docks, and delivery entrances.
- Pedestrian access control includes research personnel, visitors, and nonresearch support and facility staff.

The main entrance is normally the location of the main security desk that monitors incoming personnel, oversees visitor registration, checks badges, issues access cards, photo identification, and other security procedures used at the facility. If metal detectors are to be used, or bags are to be searched, to ensure that intellectual property or equipment is not leaving the premises, an area must be planned and designed to accommodate these functions.

A visitor reception and holding area may be appropriate to accommodate a sign-in procedure, showing photo identification, and receiving an escort for all designated areas. Limiting the nature of visits to the laboratory proper is another way of maintaining visitor control. Sales or vendor meetings, for example, could be held in small, secured conference areas adjacent to the reception area, outside the secured lab area. The visitors' entrance is usually coordinated with a designated visitors' parking zone.

TABLE 18.5   Checklist of Top 10 Facility Elements to Be Hardened

1. Site utilities, such as power, gas, water, waste, and their building access points.
2. Central utility plant (CUP) equipment, including boilers, chillers, cooling towers. and standby power generation.
3. Outdoor air intakes, located beyond the reach of the public or visitors.
4. Mechanical and electrical equipment rooms, enclosures, and areaways.
5. Mailrooms, which are a major entry portal for much of the outside world, should be segregated from other facilities.
6. Loading docks.
7. Chemical and hazardous waste storage.
8. Tank farms and other outdoor areas where either incoming chemicals or outgoing waste are stored in bulk are vulnerable. They need to be isolated and protected from general traffic.
9. Front door entry and pick-up and drop-off zones.
10. Central and satellite control centers, as well as externally located satellite antenna arrays, need to be protected.

Research personnel and support staff may be able to enter through several controlled access points, primarily as a convenience related to parking proximity. These access points may be either staffed or controlled by a security technology system selected by building owners. The security plan may require that both entry and exiting be controlled, monitored, and video recorded.

OVERVIEW OF MAJOR SECURITY SYSTEM TECHNOLOGIES

Advances in security system technology include applications for wired and wireless system features, miniaturization of system components, and biometrics (Table 18.6 and Fig. 18.5). These systems are often combined to increase effectiveness. For example, a card access swipe system, combined with a biometric scanner, may help prevent unauthorized pedestrian tailgating, which occurs when a person follows another person into an area without providing authorized identification.

BUILDING INTERIOR ACCESS AND SECURITY SYSTEM TECHNOLOGIES

For research to be productive, the facility should create a pleasant working environment that fosters collaborative intellectual pursuits and a strong sense of identity, where researchers can interact informally in laboratories, offices, and classroom settings. These design goals often conflict with creating a safe environment, while balancing security and openness.

The programming phase of the design process articulates the research program into space requirements, space adjacencies, and the desired interaction between and among the research and support staff. The resultant blocking, stacking, and adjacency diagrams are the first step in planning the hierarchy of secured areas within the facility. Security levels for each space depend on function, location, and those who should have access to the space.

Research facilities often include spaces that are not laboratories or laboratory support spaces. Access to these spaces is part of security planning, including the following:

- Cafeteria and dining facilities
- Auditoriums and large conference areas
- Administration and other nonlaboratory office functions

The secured laboratory areas of the facility may also have a security hierarchy. This hierarchy may relate to the specific type of research being conducted; how risky the activity is, such as biosafety level 2, 3, or 4; or how confidential the research is. The secured area of the laboratories may be referred to as the controlled access laboratory area (CALA). The level of security may be referred to as CALA

TABLE 18.6   Most Common Security Technology Applications in Research Laboratories

- Closed-circuit TV (CCTV) and digital recording
- Keypad door access
- Magnetic swipe access cards and readers
- Door hardware and contact systems
- Smart cards containing microprocessors and memory chips
- Biometric identification scanning devices for iris and retinal scanning; fingerprint, hand, or face geometry scans; and voice pattern identification
- Optical turnstiles for high-traffic areas
- Infrared and motion-detection systems

FIGURE 18.5 Security technology applications: optical turnstile, CCTV surveillance camera, card reader, and biometric hand scanner. (*Source: HLW International, LLP.*)

1, CALA 2, etc., as a means to establish access clearance for increasing levels of security. Once inside the secured sector of the building, access throughout the facility should be validated via a card access system and monitored via the CCTV system. This would provide an audit trail of all individuals, a visual and electronic record of their activities, and prohibit access to unauthorized areas.

Optical turnstiles are just one of several effective means of controlling the transition point between public spaces and secured areas of the building. A valid access card should be required to allow entry into the secured zone. If an unauthorized entry is attempted, an alarm should alert security personnel, and a strategically located CCTV camera should record an image of the intruder.

All personnel and visitors leaving the lab facility should likewise be identified and cleared for exit, to ensure the person leaving is the same person who came in. Authorized facility personnel should be required to present their access card at the controlled access point to validate their exit. Visitors should be required to follow sign-out exit procedures.

Building elevators should be provided with card readers, to control access within the facility. This could be accomplished by three methods:

1. Install a card reader adjacent to the *hall call button* (up and down arrow buttons outside the cab). In secure mode, pressing either the up or down arrow button will do nothing until a valid code or card is presented to the card reader. The user will then have a period of time, usually 10 seconds, to press one of the buttons. Once the cab arrives, the user enters and selects the floor he or she wishes to go to. This option provides the lowest level of security, but is also the least expensive form of elevator control.

2. Install a card reader in the elevator cab. During night mode, a user enters the elevator cab, enters a valid code or presents a valid card to the reader, then has a period of time to press the floor he or she wishes to access. Each user is assigned to a control zone that defines which floor(s) he or she is authorized to access, and when.

3. Install a reader in the elevator cab. During night mode, a user enters the elevator cab, enters a valid code or presents a valid card to the card reader, and the floor button is automatically selected, as defined by the user's control zone. This should be employed when the user has access to only one floor; otherwise multiple floor buttons would be selected.

If users have a requirement to access multiple floors, a modified version of this option would be installing a reader in the elevator cab, so that the user could enter his or her access code followed by the floor number he or she wishes to access. If authorized, the specific floor requested would be automatically selected.

Card readers and CCTV cameras should be strategically located throughout each floor. The level of protection should be consistent with the security level of the protected area. CCTV camera locations may include the following:

- Elevator lobbies
- Stairwell doors and corridors
- Lab access points

Biometric readers, which verify individual characteristics such as fingerprints, hand geometry, or retinal images, are well suited to laboratory facilities. The readers should be located at entries to high-security areas, such as containment labs, which deal with biohazards.

Once registered at the entry location, access would be restricted by the individual's access card. Without proper registration at the entry location, the individual's card would not be valid beyond that point. To further restrict and monitor access to high-security areas, revolving doors controlled by a card access device or biometric reader could be used.

Providing card readers on the opposite side of the portal is a way to monitor egress. A portal is a small access area with two doors, each with controlled access, similar to a sally port. Once access is obtained through the first door, the second door will not open until the first door is secured and the second door access control has been approved. By implementing this option, the card access system could be used to count occupants and allow arming of an intrusion system when the last person leaves. When the intrusion system goes into alarm, the security office could be advised of the event.

Along with card access and CCTV systems, an intrusion detection system (IDS) may be incorporated into the design. This system monitors the status of alarm devices installed at all controlled access points and reports an alarm to the building control center and to the security control center. Door contacts and motion detectors should be installed at all secure locations, to activate an alarm if an unauthorized entry is attempted. Door contacts are low-voltage contacts, installed as opposed contact surfaces on the door and doorframe, and monitor whether the door is opened or closed by sensing if the low-voltage circuit is open or closed. Door contacts installed on portals provided with a card reader could be switched off for a predetermined period, if a valid card is presented for access. If the door is left ajar after the authorized entry or exit, a similar alarm would be reported to the BCC and SCC. Upon activation of a door contact or area motion detector, the event should also be recorded on the CCTV system and brought up on a monitor at the SCC.

SECURITY AND CONTROL OF BUILDING SYSTEMS

Several important factors contribute to building system security and control, encompassing design, technology, and operational elements to be addressed by the design team and the building owner. The mechanical, electrical, and life safety systems are among the most important safety components of a research and development facility. Mechanical and electrical equipment rooms (MERs) and penthouses contain equipment necessary to safely operate a research facility. Access to these areas should be controlled.

Personnel Screening

The greatest potential security threat to any facility or operation is among the people who work there. Security and personnel screening are important operational functions that must be carefully considered by facility owners and managers when determining who will maintain and operate building systems and engineering equipment.

- *In-house.* If in-house facility management staff will be used, personnel or human resources must be responsible for thorough background checks and security clearances.
- *Outsourced.* If operations of building systems and engineering equipment are to be outsourced, special attention should be given in selecting reliable companies that thoroughly screen their employees.

Mechanical and Electrical Equipment Room Access

Two major concerns must be considered when planning access to the MER:

- Intentional or malicious disruption of system equipment operation that could create an unsafe condition within the research area
- The potential for harmful substances to be introduced into the building's air supply system from within the equipment room

Air intakes should be carefully located and visually monitored to prevent introduction of bio-chemical or biological agents in a building mechanical system. Card access should be considered for MERs, along with a CCTV surveillance system. Special air-handling features, such as filters, air monitoring for hazardous agents, and isolation dampers can be incorporated into the system design. These systems must be planned carefully, by reviewing facility needs.

ASHRAE: LESSONS LEARNED FROM SEPTEMBER 11, 2001

In January 2002, the American Society of Heating Refrigeration and Air Conditioning Engineers (ASHRAE) Presidential Study Group issued a report on *Risk Management Guidance for Health and Safety under Extraordinary Incidents*, in response to the terrorist events of September 11, 2001, and the subsequent events related to anthrax exposure (Table 18.7).

Designing special features into the HVAC system for laboratories needs to be thought out very carefully. As of 2003, air monitors and sensors are not available for all possible airborne threats such as chemical, biological, and radiological. Air filters are being developed to handle most of the categories of airborne contaminants. Isolation dampers are available; however, these need to be controlled and sequenced into operation, in accordance with a well-conceived emergency system control mode.

HVAC Systems

Supply air and exhaust air systems are designed to provide a safe and comfortable environment. General lab ventilation rates are designed in accordance with standards established by OSHA, ASHRAE standard 62-189, local and state codes, and standards and guidelines issued by owners.

TABLE 18.7   Lessons Learned from September 11, 2001: Airborne Contamination of Building Systems

Since the Study Group began its work on November 12, 2001, many articles have been reviewed and the personal experiences of the members have been discussed through telephone conference calls, three scheduled meetings, and e-mail communications. From these deliberations several lessons have been learned from the catastrophic events of September 11th and the subsequent contamination of spaces and sickness and deaths attributed to the distribution of anthrax via the postal system. These lessons focused on methods of protection from intentional attacks, but are also related to accidental and naturally occurring, extraordinary incidences. Lessons that apply to all buildings being considered in the scope of this study include:

1. Buildings in the U.S. have important safety factors that have proven effective against some threats because of the quality of the standards of care practiced in the U.S., the enforcement of building codes and standards during design and construction, and because of the legal liability of designers, constructors, and owners of these buildings.

2. If protection against aerosol attacks launched from a source exterior to a building is to be accomplished, then the openings into the building that could allow airborne aerosols to enter must be capable of timely closure, located sufficiently remote from any launch site, or equipped with adequate filtration.

3. If protection against aerosol attacks launched from a source interior to a building is to be accomplished, then the space in which the aerosol is released or present must be capable of timely isolation by the closure of all openings communicating with other spaces.

4. Sensors, monitors, and other means of forewarning are not presently available or are not reliable for many contaminants. Therefore, strategies other than feedback control are relied upon today.

5. It is unlikely that areas of refuge are economically viable in many buildings. Therefore, a practical and commercially viable application of HVAC technology is the enhancement of building egress paths and the isolation of significant contamination to selected building volumes.

6. Enhanced filtration is a desirable, but not a sufficient, control strategy to reduce occupant risk to an airborne contaminant. A comprehensive strategy is needed which includes enhanced filtration coupled with pressurization of the building interior relative to the outdoors; this, in turn, requires improved air tightness.

Source: Excerpt from *Risk Management Guidance for Health and Safety under Extraordinary Incidents*, ASHRAE, January 2002.

Research activities that are potentially harmful to scientists are generally conducted in special enclosures, such as fume hoods or biosafety cabinets. Devices measuring critical functions, such as fume hood face velocity, monitor these special containment enclosures. If the operation of such a device falls outside the acceptable range, an audible alarm sounds to warn the occupants and a signal is sent to the building management system.

For those areas where flammable vapors are a concern, concentrations can be monitored by a lower explosion limit (LEL) detection system. Once detected, any abnormalities would be reported to the building control center for appropriate action and to the building management system so that selected mechanical systems would be indexed to operate (Fig. 18.6).

Where flammable or explosive chemicals or gases are present within the facility, the electrical distribution system must also be properly engineered to eliminate any potential ignition sources. The engineering systems for these spaces must be designed in accordance with hazard classifications defined in the International Building Code (IBC) and the National Electric Code (NEC).

To prevent the transmission of airborne infectious agents to adjacent areas by biohazards or chemicals resulting from a particular process, room pressure differentials must be properly maintained and monitored. Containment or barrier areas utilizing either positive (barrier spaces) or negative (containment areas) pressure relationships are key elements of a properly designed system. Pressure differential between adjacent spaces is required to be monitored by a pressure sensor, which would signal an alarm and activate related mechanical systems to readjust the differential or implement the appropriate safety action and alert the occupants of the occurrence.

Electrical Systems

To further protect the occupants and facility, a number of electrical system design elements should be integrated into building infrastructures.

An emergency generator plant is required to provide power to life safety and mission critical systems—that is, those systems vital to the facility's mission and purpose, in the event of failure of the utility power source. As a minimum, it is required that several essential loads be connected to the generator (Table 18.8).

The emergency distribution plant should be strategically located and separated from the normal power system via two-hour fire-rated construction. Diverse routing should be considered for normal and emergency electrical feeders with emergency feeders routed within fire-rated construction or be of fire-rated mineral insulated (MI cable) construction. To prevent failure of the plant, the system should be designed with N+1 redundancy, or 100 percent backup capacity, to maintain system integrity in the event of failure of a single component.

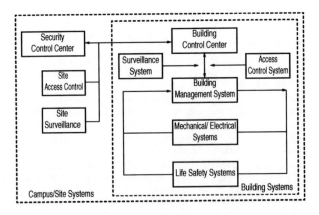

FIGURE 18.6 Diagram of systems architecture illustrating the functional relationship between building control systems, management systems, building control center, and security control center. (*Source: HLW International LLP.*)

TABLE 18.8   Essential Generator Loads in Research Facilities

Life safety functions	Mission critical functions
Exit and emergency lighting	• Security building management systems (BMS) and related monitoring systems
Fire alarm and communication systems	• Functional lighting
Elevators	• Refrigerators, freezers, and environmental rooms
Fire pump and related components	• Select mechanical equipment
Smoke control systems	• Uninterruptible power system (UPS) serving voice/data networks.
Hazardous area exhaust systems	

Redundancy and Backup Systems

Defining the level of redundancy for mechanical and electrical systems is an important part of facility planning. Mechanical and electrical systems and major equipment fall into a hierarchy of components (Table 18.9).

In determining the need for redundancy, two concepts generally emerge:

• For site utilities, the benefit of having dual service entrances remote from each other may be appropriate.

• For major equipment in the CUP or in the building shell and core, the need for N+1 redundancy may be required.

N+1 redundancy is the number of pieces of equipment required for peak load conditions, plus one additional equipment setup as a standby unit. In addition to the installation of a properly engineered emergency generator, several electrical design features should be considered (Table 18.10).

TABLE 18.9   Hierarchy of Mechanical and Electrical Systems for Redundancy and Backup Systems

1. Site utilities, including power, water, gas, and sanitary
2. Central utility plants (CUP), including standby power generation, central chillers and cooling towers for cooling, and central boilers for heating
3. Building shell and core infrastructure, which includes air-handling units for supply air, exhaust air fans, building transformers, and special water systems, such as pure water for laboratory use
4. Laboratory fit-out systems, or the systems available at lab benches

TABLE 18.10   Electrical Design Considerations for Redundancy and Backup Systems

• Emergency generators
• Upgraded stairwell and egress illumination levels
• The use of emergency battery packs in stairwell and egress lighting fixtures to provide illumination in the event of failure or disruption of the individual circuit serving the space
• Low-level exit signs and/or directional aisle lighting so the exits and egress routes can be easily located during a smoke condition
• The use of fire-rated cabling for emergency communication and similar life safety and evacuation systems
• Enhanced voice evacuation and communication system to supplement code-required systems
• Integration of all building control, security, and automation systems

Building Management System

Individual laboratory, security, and safety systems can be fully integrated into a centralized building management system, providing maximum safety, decreased operating costs through energy management, high reliability, and system flexibility. Integrating laboratory controls, security, and safety devices with the building management system offers some important benefits. They facilitate monitoring the status of each system from a central location and enable the archiving of critical operating and alarm data. The benefits of integration improve facility management, expanding the scope and utility of the building management system (Table 18.11).

TABLE 18.11   10 Benefits of Integrating Building Management Systems

1. Comprehensive monitoring and diagnosis of all systems performance
2. Ability to track and monitor energy usage
3. Early identification of system malfunctions
4. Immediate identification of safety alarms, allowing prompt emergency response and action
5. Ability to generate printed reports related to alarm monitoring, safety analysis, and energy management
6. Ability to control emergency response systems from a central location
7. Audio and visual assessment of alarm conditions by providing two-way communication and CCTV capability between the command center and alarm location
8. Ability to quickly scan and search incoming and outgoing personnel and packages
9. Ability to communicate quickly and comprehensively with law enforcement and first responders
10. Ability to maintain on-line tutorials and policy guidance for how security personnel should relate to staff

CONCLUSION

> *Any intelligent fool can make things bigger, more complex,*
> *and more violent. It takes a touch of genius—and a lot of*
> *courage—to move in the opposite direction.*
>   ALBERT EINSTEIN (1879–1955)
>   *U.S. (German-born) physicist*

In an era of heightened risks and threats, research and development facilities are particularly susceptible and, as a result, increasingly sensitive to the issues of operational and facility security. Security planning ranks high on the research facility design agenda.

Security planning involves systems and components, operational procedures, attitudes, and mindsets. This pervasive theme must be integrated with other factors, such as function, openness, and collaboration, which collectively make research facilities successful. Incorporating effective security planning requires the collaborative efforts of all facility stakeholders—owners, the research community, operating staff, architects, engineers, and construction team members—to achieve desired levels of excellence within each aspect of project execution.

ACKNOWLEDGMENTS

- Leevi Kiil, FAIA, Chairman and CEO, HLW International LLP, New York, New York
- Vicki Lewko, Account Manager, CarryOn Communications, Inc., New York, New York
- Natalie Schellenberg, Marketing Coordinator, HLW International LLP, New York, New York

BIBLIOGRAPHY

American Society of Heating Refrigeration and Air Conditioning Engineers (ASHRAE), Presidential Study Group, *Risk Management Guidance for Health and Safety under Extraordinary Incidents,* January 2002.

Centers for Disease Control and Prevention (CDC)/National Institutes of Health (NIH), *Biosafety in Microbiological and Biomedical Laboratories (BMBL),* 4th ed., App. F. The CDC/NIH BMBL is intended to assist research facilities in meeting the regulatory mandate of 42 Code of Federal Regulation (CFR) 73, established specifically for those laboratories using selected biohazard agents under the biosafety levels (BSL) 2, 3, or 4 as described in Sections II and III of the BMBL.

INTERNET RESOURCES

American Chemistry Council (ACC)
www.americanchemistry.com

American Society of Heating, Refrigeration and Air-Conditioning Engineers (ASHRAE)
www.ashrae.org

American Society for Industrial Security (ASIS)
www.asisonline.org

American Society for Testing and Materials (ASTM)
www.astm.org

Centers for Disease Control and Prevention (CDC)
www.cdc.gov

Chlorine Institute (CI)
www.cl2.com

HLW International LLP
www.hlw.com

Illuminating Engineering Society of North America (IESNA)
www.iesna.org

Institute of Electrical and Electronics Engineers (IEEE)
www.ieee.org

International Code Council (ICC)
www.iccsafe.org

National Institutes of Health (NIH)
www.nih.gov

CHAPTER 19

RETAIL SECURITY DESIGN

Jeffrey J. Gunning, AIA
Vice President, RTKL Associates, Inc
Dallas, Texas

Lance K. Josal, AIA
Senior Vice President,
RTKL Associates, Inc
Dallas, Texas

Architecture is inescapably a political art and it reports faithfully for ages to come what the political values of a particular age were. Surely ours must be openness and fearlessness in the face of those who hide in the darkness.
                    DANIEL PATRICK MOYNIHAN (1927–2003)
                         U.S. senator from New York
                              November 27, 2001

terrorism   *The unlawful use or threatened use of force or violence by a person or an organized group against people or property with the intention of intimidating or coercing societies or governments, often for ideological or political reasons.*
                    The American Heritage Dictionary of the
                         English Language, 4th ed.

The September 11, 2001 attacks against civilian targets on American soil prompted a swift response from the retail marketplace. Retail owners, operators, and developers expanded security requirements beyond ongoing concerns about inventory shrinkage, to the prospects of bombs and biohazard threats (Fig. 19.1).

Retail destinations must remain open and hospitable, while maintaining a real and perceived sense of security. Customers and employees must be comfortable within these environments, without feeling they are vulnerable to property crimes, violence, or terrorism.

Large public gathering places such as malls and "big box" retail centers, are vulnerable to terrorist threats. For those seeking attention by inflicting massive collateral damage, few targets are more visible, or poignant, than a mall filled with holiday shoppers. These issues are relatively new to American retailers. However, property owners, managers, and security directors in politically unstable areas of Europe and the Middle East, such as Northern Ireland and Israel, have dealt with these conditions for decades.

Retail owners, managers, and consumers must be alert and think proactively, without overreacting. Understanding the nature of threats and developing appropriate responses will enhance security in the retail environment. The challenge for retail security planners is creating welcoming environments for

FIGURE 19.1 Security design in a retail environment emphasizes freedom of movement for legitimate users, while impeding illegitimate activities. (*Photo: RTKL Associates, Inc.*)

customers, while deterring terrorism and criminal activities. The retail industry cannot afford to lose customers who turn to the exclusive use of catalogs and the Internet because they fear for their lives at the regional mall.

SECURITY CONCERNS IN THE RETAIL REALM

Retail center owners in the United States have always been aware of criminal threats to their employees, customers, records, and inventory. As retailers and center managers examine options for securing operations, they realize that the majority of threats will remain more traditional property crime or personal crime, rather than terrorism (Table 19.1).

TABLE 19.1   Traditional versus Emerging Security Concerns in Retail Environments

Traditional security concerns	Emerging security concerns
Personal: • Assault or attack on one person by another • Robbery: pickpocketing, purse snatching, and theft of individual property Property: • Theft: unauthorized removal of merchandise from premises • Vandalism: destruction and removal of furniture, décor, or merchandise • Mild violence: collateral damage from fights and more serious criminal activities	Personal: • Life and limb: serious threats to personal health and safety from large-scale events, armed raids, bombings, and biocontamination Property: • Catastrophe: weather, warfare, and accidents • Terrorism: politically motivated, military-style assaults on civilian targets, including shootings, bombings, and contamination • Mass violence: shootings, bombings, and other large-scale events, not necessarily politically motivated

After September 11, 2001, traditional security concerns for retail facility owners and managers expanded to include violent threats for the purposes of intimidation and disruption.

Traditional and emerging security concerns pose a challenge to retail facility stakeholders, including owners, managers, individual store tenants, vendors, delivery services, employees, and customers. Retail security plans must consider all these constituencies, because each group is susceptible to different threats, which vary by building type and facility needs, and change over time.

RETAIL BUILDING TYPES

Retail centers range from urban galleries to enclosed, regional malls, each with unique physical conditions and vulnerabilities (Table 19.2).

RISKS AND VULNERABILITIES

All retail facilities are vulnerable to criminal and terrorist threats. Designers and retail center owners should be aware of building systems and spaces that are most vulnerable to potential threats (Table 19.3).

VULNERABILITIES

Each type of retail facility faces various security challenges and risks, depending on location, site planning, building design, tenants, owners, and often the involvement of communities and neighborhood groups in local business districts.

Urban

The clustered arrangement of a galleria retail center increases the concentration of stores and customers in a smaller space. The likelihood of large gatherings of people in galleries creates a higher need for control through observation, operations, and technology.

TABLE 19.2   Retail Building Types

Building type	Characteristics
Urban	• *Galleria*. A clustered group of shops; may be arranged around a courtyard or passageway, or stacked vertically within a small lot • *Main street*. The classic linear progression of shops along a central shopping boulevard
Suburban	• *Strip centers*. Smaller format stores fronted by parking • *"Big box" retailers*. Large-footprint stores, either stand-alone or grouped together and fronted by large parking areas
Regional	• *Enclosed malls*. The traditional arrangement, anchored by department stores and surrounded by parking • *Main street, town center, hybrid developments*. New regional retail centers echoing traditional urban central business districts; may include open air and enclosed elements, and a series of streets augmented by mall-style parking lots

TABLE 19.3   Risks and Vulnerabilities in Retail Environments

Primary vulnerabilities	Characteristics
Air-handling systems	• Prime entry point for toxic materials, including chemical and biological agents • Disabled ventilation systems may trap commercial fumes in the building
Street frontage	• Common point of entry for ballistic and other violent threats • Potential for drive-by criminal or terrorist activities
Parking lots	• Pose numerous opportunities for vehicular threat and personal assault • Difficult to secure, especially against pedestrians and small vehicles like motorcycles
Consumer entrances	• Difficult to screen those entering and exiting • Easy ingress and egress for legitimate shoppers, employees, and illegitimate users
Service entries	• Often concealed from general sight • Must allow access by large vehicles, with potential for massive ballistic threat
Outdoor assembly	• Waiting lines, amphitheatres, and public plazas • Provide large-scale gathering places, difficult to patrol and secure

Secondary vulnerabilities	Characteristics
Interior public assembly areas	• Interior courts • food courts • cinemas • restaurants

The more linear main street configuration, found in many vibrant downtowns, has different vulnerabilities due to individual store ownership or tenant mix. Unlike an enclosed center, most main street centers lack a single authority, such as mall security personnel, responsible for the safety of the business district. Intertenant communication can be diminished or nonexistent in a traditional neighborhood streetscape, reducing opportunities to coordinate preventative measures and threat responses.

Some urban and neighborhood shopping areas have established dues-paying merchants associations or business improvement districts, to provide enhanced security, communications about common concerns, and trash collection, to supplement available public services (Table 19.4).

TABLE 19.4 **Urban and Main Street Security Design Issues**

- Multiple access points, unlike controlled egress points in enclosed retail facilities
- Unmonitored activities of public streets
- Drive-by accessibility
- Decentralized servicing, both curbside and rear dock loading

TABLE 19.5 **Suburban Shopping Strip and Big Box Center Security Concerns**

- Individual store ownership and operation
- Multiple entrances
- Low level of intertenant communication
- Low level of curbside monitoring
- Decentralized service, usually at back, out of view
- Drive-by accessibility
- Expanse of unmonitored parking

Suburban

Suburban strip centers and big box centers share some of the same security concerns as urban shopping boulevards due to their openness and linearity (Table 19.5).

Stand-alone retailers are at risk because they lack opportunities for surveillance and observation from neighboring storeowners and employees. Strip center owners and stand-alone retailers often lack the resources for private security patrols and guards, unlike regional centers, where more tenants can share security costs.

Regional

Enclosed malls are easier to secure than urban and suburban venues. Owners and national retailers are able to spend more on security, but malls face other potential security problems (Table 19.6). Enclosed spaces

- Create places for large groups to congregate

- Provide a good shield for terrorists

- Represent a compelling target for those seeking attention-grabbing mass casualties

CRIME PREVENTION THROUGH ENVIRONMENTAL DESIGN

Crime prevention through environmental design (CPTED) is a proven planning concept used for many building types, and is especially appropriate for retail centers. Through citizen participation and collaboration with local law enforcement, CPTED has become a widely accepted strategy, based on the premise that better surveillance reduces opportunities for crime and improves the quality of life. CPTED enhances safety and the perception of safety in public spaces through planning and design (Table 19.7). Effective design approaches using CPTED in high-density environments include

- Placement and type of building security features

- Wayfinding, with clear graphics and signage, important in retail environments

TABLE 19.6 Vulnerabilities Creating Opportunities for Crime at Mall Parking Lots and Garages

- Infrequent security patrols
- Low lighting levels
- Layouts enabling hiding, ambush, and vehicular bombs
- Compromised entrance access and visibility
- Service entries with large access doors permitting vehicles to enter the building
- Moderate curbside monitoring
- Partially hidden service areas

TABLE 19.7 How CPTED Can Enhance Safety in Public Spaces and Retail Environments

Element	Task
Design	• Planning • Space programming • Facility design • Technology
Management and operations	• Staff training • Official policies and procedures • Maintenance
Activity	• Events encouraging an active, lively building or business district

- Escape and building evacuation routes
- Design elements minimizing stress, confusion, and fear of crime

Situational crime reduction incorporates technology and environmental impediments to crime, based on the principle of least effort. Terrorists and criminals will avoid places where they encounter difficulty in carrying out their intentions. In commercial environments and shopping centers, anti-crime measures should allow business to proceed uninterrupted, and staff and customers to go about their activities.

CPTED distinguishes between legitimate users, the store and mall employees, and customers; potential offenders, criminals, and terrorists; and observers who can watch and respond to threats, including security staff, courtesy personnel, and facility managers, to create a safe, secure, and functional environment.

RETAIL SECURITY DESIGN AND MANAGEMENT STRATEGIES

Retail centers, malls, and multitenant facilities share similar security concerns. The most cost-efficient and effective way to incorporate security design and technology is during the planning and design phases of new construction or renovation work, rather than during the retrofitting of existing facilities.

Preventing terrorist attacks in retail centers focuses on two CPTED strategies: design and management. Activity generation is effective against smaller scale crimes, personal attacks, and petty theft.

Design

From planning to final fit-out, design of a secure retail facility should

- Encourage natural surveillance
- Eliminate obscure hiding places
- Maintain access control
- Create territoriality

All programmatic elements of a retail facility, site, entrances, interiors, service areas, building systems, and wayfinding, should be considered as part of the security planning process.

Site Planning and Landscaping

Site planning and design can significantly enhance security by applying CPTED principles. Retail facilities depend on dramatic design features, ornamental plantings, sculptural elements, and decorative signage to create appealing and commercially viable environments. However, these elements often conflict with security planning objectives (Figs. 19.2 and 19.3).

Low lighting levels in a space, even if designed to create a dramatic experience, can have a direct effect on customer comfort. Designers, owners, managers, and security consultants should collectively consider how to strike a balance between welcoming graphics and landscaping elements and pragmatic security practices. In retail design, perhaps more than with any other building type, compromises between best business practices and best security approaches must be weighed (Table 19.8).

ENTRANCES

The best-designed mall entrances are warm, inviting, and welcoming front doors. In an image-conscious and experience-driven industry, retail facility owners must balance security at building

FIGURE 19.2 Bollards can be used, as long as they're not obtrusive. (*Photo: RTKL Associates, Inc.*)

FIGURE 19.3   Retail centers can establish a no-drive zone between entrances and roadways to provide standoff in the event of a blast. (*Photo: RTKL Associates, Inc.*)

TABLE 19.8   Site Planning Checklist for Retail Facilities

Design element	Criteria
Visibility	• Create and maintain clear sightlines from all building entrances to the street. • Maintain visibility around parking lots and other surrounding parcels. • Discourage potential hiding places, such as tall shrubs, large trees, maintenance sheds, and structures that block views.
Proactive obstacles	• Bollards and berms prohibit vehicles from getting too close to the building. • Security gates can slow access to parking areas. • Shrubs will impede pedestrian access to nonpublic areas.
Lighting	Lighting levels should be consistent and adequate: • At public entrances • In parking lots • In rear loading zones
Parking facilities	With large surface areas distributed over multiple levels, low lighting and intricate layouts, enclosed parking facilities present security challenges because they: • Are open to the public • Contain ample hiding places • Inhibit light distribution • Include blind spots at elevators and stair lobbies, which cannot be observed except with CCTV

entrances with an awareness of the architectural implications for the building and experiential implications for consumers (Fig. 19.4 and Tables 19.9, and 19.10). Parking facilities can enhance security by integrating design, technology, and operations.

Service Access Control

Service entrances are vulnerable facility access points. Retail center security officers and facility managers must determine who belongs in this area and who doesn't, and respond appropriately. Design and technology measures can reduce the risks of criminal and terrorist activities, theft, ballistics, and personal violence (Tables 19.11 and 19.12).

FIGURE 19.4 Well-designed entrances provide clear sightlines and natural visibility, such as with outdoor café tables, to curtail criminal activity, while addressing potential vehicular threats via bollards. (*Photo: RTKL Associates, Inc.*)

TABLE 19.9   **Strategies to Increase Security of Parking Garages**

1. Elevators and glazed stair lobbies open to parking areas, located on perimeters
2. Adequate, uniform, and glare-free lighting
3. Durable, tamperproof, low-maintenance fixtures
4. Finishes encouraging brighter space, such as white-stained concrete walls
5. Maximized open space, minimized dead-ends, nooks, and crannies
6. Controlled access for pedestrians and small vehicles
7. Clear and legible graphics, signage, and wayfinding systems
8. Technology, such as CCTV
9. Operations, such as unscheduled security patrols

TABLE 19.10   **Mall Entrance Security Design Strategies**

1. Install barriers, bollards, and berms to be nonintrusive.
2. Maintain accessibility for the disabled.
3. Use landscape features allowing pedestrian movement and vehicular access.
4. Keep plants and hedges trimmed to maintain sightlines and minimize shadows.
5. Provide access control at all points, including skylights, skyways, and service entrances.
6. Understand that customers tend to exit where they entered, creating hazardous bottlenecks.
7. Provide courtesy patrols serving as greeters and casual surveillance teams.
8. Monitor traffic in and out of the mall building via greeters posted at entrances.
9. Maintain unobstructed sightlines from building to street.
10. Create transparency into building from street.
11. Provide less coverage for terrorist events inside the facility.
12. Use a central control center to monitor security and technology throughout the facility.
13. Employ technology such as CCTV monitoring, alarm annunciation, vehicle barriers, and automatic building and site lighting controls.

TABLE 19.11   Security Design Elements for Retail Service Entries

Design element	Criteria
Gates and headache bars	• Control access to loading and service areas. • Prevent entry by unsolicited vehicles. • Stall exit of perpetrators.
Closed circuit television (CCTV)	• Track customers from a parking lot entry point to a store interior and back out again. • Assess and record incidents in remote areas. • Reduce staff and operational budgets. • Track intruders and provide post-incident analysis. • Provide a visual deterrent to criminals when cameras are visible. • Allow viewing of web-connected CCTV at central control monitors or remotely.

TABLE 19.12   Technology Applications and Operational Roles in Retail Facilities

Element	Application
Technology	• X-ray of palettes, vehicles, and packages • Metal detector • Hand wand • Mirrored hand trolley to screen vehicular undercarriage for threatening devices • Electronic explosive sensing devices, used at airports, such as sprinkler heads distributed throughout a retail center and reporting to a central surveillance station • Access control • Electric locks • Magnetic contacts • Card readers • Combination locks
Operations	• Staffing and direct control • Staff training and drills for emergency procedures • Policies and procedures

BUILDING SYSTEMS

Electrical, mechanical, fire, safety, and communications building systems should be regularly tested and maintained to prevent failure or sabotage (Table 19.13).

WAYFINDING

Wayfinding is critical in retail environments, where volumes of people flow into the space constantly, and need to know locations of stores, restrooms, food courts, and exits to parking areas and the street.

TABLE 19.13 Building Systems Security Design Strategies

1. Protect outdoor air intakes and return air grilles.
2. Locate air intake vents well above ground level, to prevent contamination of HVAC system with chemically or biologically hazardous materials.
3. Prevent public access to maintenance areas and roofs.
4. Isolate loading docks and storage areas from public spaces for containment in the event of a biological or chemical attack.
5. Restrict access to building information and plans.
6. Train staff to respond quickly and appropriately to systems failure or tampering.
7. Provide backup power and utility systems, including uninterrupted power supply (UPS) systems, where appropriate.
8. Install water treatment systems.
9. Install communications systems and computer facilities including N+1 or N+ 2 redundancies, as appropriate.

Wayfinding systems are part of a graphically compelling signage package, and contribute to the environmental ambiance and comfort level of shoppers. Graphics and signage should include

- Clearly marked building evacuation routes
- Locations of safe havens
- Exits leading to the outdoors

MANAGEMENT AND OPERATIONS

American shopping center owners and managers can look for guidance to those in countries where retail venues have historically been terrorist targets. In Israel, where suicide bombers and explosive threats have often occurred in public gathering places, mall customers are rigorously screened before entering the premises. Staff members are highly trained because security hinges on their abilities to communicate effectively, move quickly, and respond to incidents.

Security staffing levels should be sufficient to defend against threats and respond to heightened security levels. Building owners and tenants must determine whether in-house security personnel or outsourced companies provide the most cost-effective and efficient services, together with technology, to save operational costs. Ongoing communications with local authorities, neighbors, and nearby retail facilities will alert others to potential problems.

Techniques used for years in high-risk, high-crime neighborhood shopping areas are increasingly used in urban and suburban American retail centers to combat terrorist threats and increased security alerts.

Management

Security is everyone's responsibility. Facility staff and employees should be trained to recognize, assess, and report potential threats. Establishing and following policies and procedures will enhance security operations (Table 19.14).

Tenant Participation

Facility managers and center security personnel are charged with establishing and maintaining retail facility security parameters. Individual retail tenants, working together with other tenants, are responsible for their own security and security of neighboring tenants (Table 19.15).

TABLE 19.14   Policies and Procedures Checklist to Increase Retail Security

1. Deploy appropriate number of security staff.
2. Train and equip security staff to respond effectively.
3. Develop security policies and procedures and distribute to staff, visitors, and service and maintenance personnel.
4. Ensure that staff is visible enough to be effective, yet unobtrusive.
5. Create a rapid response team with knowledge of emergency procedures.
6. Ensure that roving patrols spend minimal time in one place and most of their time traveling between points.
7. Increase emergency response time through adequate, facility-wide staffing deployment, more frequent patrols, and technology.
8. Verify that staff and service personnel have valid identification.
9. Train staff on use of emergency call buttons.
10. Educate staff about security protocol and jurisdictions of security officers.
11. Confirm and inform staff that security officer responsibilities are limited to legal property boundary of the facility hiring them.
12. Inform staff of procedures when an off-site threat occurs on a public street or adjacent property, including any required documentation.
13. Instruct security officers to alert local law enforcement and rely on them to respond.
14. Provide security personnel with emergency contact information for local law enforcement, facility managers, tenants, and building owners.
15. Build relationships with local law enforcement and community leaders before an incident occurs.

TABLE 19.15   How Retail Tenants Can Increase Security

- Train staff to be observant and vigilant about community concerns
- Create communications networks among tenants
- Develop a self-policing community
- Learn about CPTED, crime prevention, and awareness
- Recognize and report suspicious behavior
- Curb potential problems through collaborative problem solving
- Build relationships with local law enforcement
- Work with neighborhood watch groups, merchant associations, and local civic organizations concerned with quality of life.

CONCLUSION

Security challenges the fundamental business values within the aesthetically-oriented, service-minded retail industry. The keys to successful retail security design are:

- Creating an open, welcoming, and appealing environment for customers, employees, and inventory
- Protecting shoppers and retail personnel
- Balancing visible and transparent security

Retail owners, facility managers, and designers must understand the risks and threats they will invariably encounter, and prepare to respond with design, technological, and operational solutions. In an era of heightened awareness, the retail industry depends on effective use of these elements to boost long-term profitability and security.

ACKNOWLEDGMENTS

- Harold L. Adams, FAIA, RIBA, JIA, Chairman Emeritus, RTKL Associates, Inc., Baltimore, Maryland
- Charles R. Greenland Jr., AIA, CSI, CCS, CCCA, Baltimore, Maryland
- Keith Kellner, Graphic Design, RTKL, Associates, Inc., Baltimore, Maryland
- Matthew S. Klinzing, Associate AIA, Baltimore, Maryland
- Lily Thayer, Public Relations Manager, RTKL, Associates, Inc., Baltimore, Maryland
- David V. Thompson, AIA, Vice President, RTKL, Associates, Inc., Baltimore, Maryland
- Robert P. Wingard, AIA, Baltimore, Maryland

GLOSSARY

big box retailer   A large-footprint store, either freestanding or grouped together with others of similar size, and fronted by large parking areas.

CPTED   Crime prevention through environmental design is a planning concept to improve public safety by designing physical environments to influence human behavior in a positive way.

enclosed mall   A grouping of stores under one roof, typically anchored by large department stores, and surrounded by parking.

environmental design   Wayfinding systems, signage, ornamental and thematic graphics, logos and identity programs, and tenant criteria within a space.

galleria   A retail facility consisting of a clustered group of shops.

illegitimate users   Individuals entering a retail establishment with the intention of committing property or personal crime.

legitimate users   Patrons and staff of a retail facility.

main street   A linear progression of retail establishments along a central shopping boulevard.

operations   The day-to-day activities of guards, employees, visitors, and deliveries within a facility. Includes hours of operation, delivery routines, building and ground maintenance, vetting of vehicles, and package inspection.

situational crime reduction   The prevention of criminal activities by eliminating opportunities to commit crime.

strip center   A group of stores, typically smaller than big box retailers, arranged laterally in an unenclosed configuration fronted by parking.

technology or technical security   Types of hardware and software to deter, detect, and respond to threats. Includes alarms, sensors, readers, cameras, access cards, and monitoring devices.

terrorism   The unlawful or threatened use of force or violence by a person or an organized group against people or property with the intention of intimidating or coercing societies or governments, often for ideological or political reasons.

vehicle barrier   A device or element designed for traffic control; must be designed for the weight and speed parameters of the threat vehicle; may be passive or active.

BIBLIOGRAPHY

Cooper, Desiree. "How architects can create a sense of safety, from the Renaissance Center to the neighborhoods." *Detroit Metro Times*, 28 July 1997. www.metrotimes.com/news/stories/cul/17/40/design.html

Davis, Stephania H. "Bridgeport, Connecticut—Area Shoppers Pay More Attention to Mall Security." *Connecticut Post* (Bridgeport, Conn.), February 23, 2003.

DePass, Dee. "Scenting Trouble; Local Landmarks Are on Guard against Terrorism." *Star Tribune* (Minneapolis, Minn.), March 29, 2003, business sec., p. 1D.

"Freedom Without Fortresses? Shaping the New Secure Environment." *Idea Lab,* issue 1, RTKL, Spring 2002.

Gallagher, Patricia E., et al. "Building Security Through Design: Protective Environments in an Open Society," *Designing for Security, Conference Proceedings,* American Institute of Architects, New York, 2002

Geason, Susan, and Paul R. Wilson, "Preventing Retail Crime," Australian Institute of Criminology, Canberra, Australia, 1992. www.aic.gov.au/publications/crimprev/retail/

Jacobs, Jane, *The Death and Life of Great American Cities,* Random House, New York, 1961.

Jeffrey, Dr. C. J., *Crime Prevention Through Environmental Design,* Sage Publications, Beverly Hills, Calif., 1971.

McAndrew, Mike, "Vigilance Urged for Mall Security; Skaneateles Man, Former FBI Agent, Addresses Conference on Safety Concerns." *The Post-Standard* (Syracuse, N.Y.), March 31, 2003, local sec., p. B2.

Nadel, Barbara A., "Safety through Strategy," *Retail Traffic* (formerly *Shopping Center World*), January 2000. Http://shoppingcenterworld.com/ar/retail_security_safety_strategy/index.htm

National Institute of Justice, *The Expanding Role of Crime Prevention Through Environmental Design in Premises Liability,* Washington, D.C., 1996.

Newman, Oscar, *Defensible Space,* Macmillan, New York, 1972. www.defensiblespace.com.

Ritter, Ian, "Open-Air Security: Shopping Center Safety Isn't Just a Mall Issue." *Shopping Centers Today,* March 2003, p. 15A.

Smith, Mary S., "Crime Prevention Through Environmental Design in Parking Facilities." *National Institute of Justice Research in Brief,* April 1996.

INTERNET RESOURCES

International Council of Shopping Centers (ICSC)
www.icsc.org

Retail Traffic Magazine (Formerly *Shopping Center World*)
www.retailtrafficmag.com

RTKL Associates, Inc.
www.rtkl.com

CHAPTER 20
SCHOOL SECURITY: DESIGNING SAFE LEARNING ENVIRONMENTS

Thomas Blurock, AIA

Principal, Thomas Blurock Architects
Costa Mesa, California

*If we are to reach real peace in this world, we shall have to
begin with the children.*

MAHATMA GANDHI (1869–1948)
Indian nonviolent civil rights leader

The April 20, 1999, shootings at Columbine High School in Littleton, Colorado, in which two students shot and killed 12 students, 1 teacher, and wounded 23, were a national wake-up call about the need for creating safe learning environments for students, teachers, administrators, and visitors. Sensational news stories about child abductions, gang and workplace violence, guns in schools, and teenage street crime have raised public awareness about the need for creating safe schools and safe streets. National and local terrorism alerts have prompted school administrators to develop emergency plans and procedures to enhance security and be ready to handle any situation that might arise (Table 20.1).

Schools are places where students should feel safe within a calm and protective sanctuary for learning. The physical environment should provide transparent security, invisible to the public eye, but with carefully designed measures in place. The best way to achieve a safe educational environment is through a comprehensive security plan, encompassing design, technology, policies, and procedures.

Designers and administrators can create safer, more nurturing environments by

- Understanding the factors relating to school size
- Maximizing the role of design in enhancing security
- Developing a threat analysis and risk assessment for each facility

This information, prepared for all building types where security is a concern, will assist in identifying appropriate responses and solutions tailored to each community, school district, and building. At the same time, school safety officials are responsible for developing emergency procedures, including contact information if an evacuation is necessary, and informing parents about school security programs.

ESTABLISH POLICIES

School administrators and safety officials can prevent or minimize tragedies in their schools by establishing policies and procedures to be followed under different situations (Table 20.2).

TABLE 20.1 Lessons Learned from Columbine High School Shootings

The 1999 Columbine High School shootings, and six other fatal school shootings between 1997 and 1999, provided the American public with deadly benchmarks questioning school safety and security. Educational professionals consider this violent incident to be an isolated case of psychological dysfunction. Adolescent behavior may be erratic and unpredictable. Problems build up slowly, making detection more difficult. Often, the violent or sudden actions of disturbed young people surprise those around them. Early intervention by parents, teachers, and peers can prevent similar tragedies from happening.

TABLE 20.2 School Security Policies Checklist

Element	Item
District policies	1. Establish protocols for investigating potential threats.
	2. Create district-wide written policies requiring each school to have an emergency plan.
	3. Establish district-wide written policies related to building security.
	4. Require each school to have building-specific security procedures.
	5. Establish district wide policies requiring a security review for construction and renovation projects.
	6. For remodeling an existing school, review or create an emergency plan.
	7. For remodeling an existing school, review or create written school-specific security procedures.
	8. Ensure insurance policies and premiums for premises and liability are in place, with copies maintained off-site.
School policies	1. Implement an action plan covering various scenarios, including student and workplace violence, natural disasters, terrorism, hostage taking, and hazardous materials.
	2. Prepare written security procedures and an emergency plan.
	3. Distribute security procedures and emergency plan to staff.
	4. Stage drills as needed with students, teachers, administrators, and others as needed.
	5. Create procedures for documenting incidents in a written follow-up report.
	6. Establish a contact list of officials, parents and agencies to call in emergencies.
	7. Maintain liaisons with local law enforcement and community leaders.
	8. Inform parents and community leaders about emergency plans, security policies, and procedures.
	9. Review emergency procedures with students to maintain preparedness.
	10. Ask everyone to be alert to unusual behavior, suspicious persons, packages or vehicles on or near school grounds, and establish central reporting procedures for such instances.

Source: Wyoming State Legislature, School Finance Office; National Clearinghouse for Educational Facilities.

Students, parents, teachers, and administrators can be better prepared for emergencies, acts of violence, and natural disasters when schools establish and distribute emergency plans and building security procedures. Many public and nonprofit institutions have detailed policies, plans, and reporting forms to document threats, violent incidents, and emergencies that can be readily adapted by school administrators and teachers. The National Clearinghouse for Educational Facilities (http://edfacilities.org/rl/) offers an excellent resource list of information relating to disaster preparedness for schools and safety and security, including strategies developed by states and cities.

In some instances, potential civil liberties or liability issues may be involved. For these reasons, legal counsel should be consulted during development of security policies. Issues to be covered include

- Take all threats seriously; report them to administration and local law enforcement if necessary.
- Create and publish a policies and procedure manual and distribute it to all staff.
- Develop standard forms and policies for threat investigation, punishment, and documentation of all incidents.

- Schedule practice drills for all school personnel to prepare for emergency procedures in the event of violence, natural disasters, terrorism, hostage taking, perimeter breaches, irate parents, bomb threats, hazardous materials, and other scenarios.

SMALL SCHOOLS ENHANCE SECURITY

Studies indicate that learning is directly related to the size of the school community, with smaller schools providing more learning opportunities and greater security. When student communities are smaller, interaction improves, students become familiar and take responsibility for each other, the learning atmosphere is enhanced, and security is better.

Adult and student contact is another essential factor for enhancing security. Some experts claim the Columbine shootings, and other high-profile violent incidents, were the result of alienation among troubled teens living in safe, low-crime communities. School culture, student body size, and community interaction may play a larger role in these incidents than school planning and design.

Studies and statistics confirm this observation. A study by the U.S. Department of Education, "Violence and Discipline Problems in U.S. Public Schools: 1996–1997," compared small schools, consisting of 300 students or less, with big schools, consisting of 1000 students or more (Table 20.3).

Small schools are generally defined by enrollments of 500 students or less. Research indicates smaller schools are better learning environments than larger schools. For older children, school size is more critical in their development, especially between grades 7 through 12. High schools and middle schools of 500 students or less generally produce significantly better test results than larger schools.

Nevertheless, national construction trends, in response to demographics, indicate that larger high schools of 1000 to 2000 students or more are being built more often than smaller schools. In an era of tight public budgets, school officials opt for larger schools because they offer economies of scale, more academic and student body diversity, and stronger athletic programs. Finding sites for new schools within existing communities is often problematic, resulting in expansion of existing facilities.

Creating Small Schools within Large Schools

Within large urban centers, smaller neighborhoods provide residents with a sense of community by breaking down the scale and pace of city life. Similarly, creating smaller, autonomous learning communities within larger schools enhances learning and security, such as the following:

- Small groups of 100 to 500 students within schools of 1000 students and more are effective.
- Separate administrative functions in small group schools, such as counseling or subadministration, aid autonomy.
- Exclusive teacher areas, such as lounges and workrooms, create a sense of community.
- Independent administration and teacher areas enhance autonomy and effectiveness.

TABLE 20.3 **Statistical Comparison between Bigger and Smaller Schools**

Bigger schools (1000 students or more)	Smaller schools (500 students or less)
• 825% more violent crime • 270% more vandalism • 378% more theft and larceny • 394% more fights and attacks • 3200% more robberies • 1000% more weapons incidents	• Dropout rates were significantly lower. • Student achievement was significantly higher. • More students advanced to higher education.

Source: U.S. Department of Education, "Violence and Discipline Problems in U.S. Public Schools: 1996–1997."

SECURITY STRATEGIES

School administrators should assess the threats facing their facilities and review appropriate active and passive design, technology, and operational responses. Security solutions should be developed for each school and community to suit unique conditions.

Crime Prevention through Environmental Design

The goal of crime prevention through environmental design (CPTED) is to prevent crime through designing a physical environment that positively influences human behavior. People who use the areas regularly perceive them as safe and would-be criminals see the areas as highly risky places to commit crimes.

Applying CPTED principles will enhance school and neighborhood security. Visibility, clear sight lines, good lighting, surveillance, and natural barriers, such as landscaping and low shrubs, can enhance safety without creating bunkers and fortresses. Technology, such as alarms, surveillance cameras, and metal detectors, are other tools to augment CPTED strategies.

Best Practices

The following guidelines represent best practices and strategies for school security, for use when evaluating existing facilities or planning new buildings. Coordination of design, technology, and policy-driven security efforts should be a collaborative effort among school administrators, public officials, local law enforcement, and design professionals (Table 20.4).

Perimeter Control.   Perimeter control is paramount for good school security, especially in urban communities. In an era of increased liability for school districts, many more schools have closed campuses, where students are not allowed to leave the campus during school hours.

Buildings as Campus Perimeter.   This often occurs in colder climates, where all activities occur in a single building, which also serves as an entry barrier. In temperate climates, where outdoor activity allows multiple structures and exterior circulation, buildings may be sited to define an effective secure perimeter.

Building Penetrations and Openings.   Building openings, such as windows and doors, are among the most vulnerable elements protecting a perimeter, and should be designed for appropriate security levels. Architectural details and hardened materials for high-security levels, such as metal doors and frames and concrete block, may seem oppressive in areas where they are not required.

- Openings above eye level allow light or air to enter, and are less vulnerable to being breached.
- Use of translucent panels or impact-resistant materials allow light to enter while restricting interior visibility.

TABLE 20.4   CPTED Strategies and Design Elements for School Security

1. Perimeter control
2. Buildings as campus perimeter
3. Building penetrations and openings
4. Distinguishing building exits from entrances
5. Fencing and barriers
6. Roof configuration
7. Sight lines to maximize perimeter surveillance
8. Multiple perimeters for multiple functions

- Decorative metal gratings on windows reduce a fortresslike appearance.

Distinguishing Building Exits from Entrances.   Fire exits and doors not used for building entries should be visually neutral so as not to attract attention as entries.

- Do not use hardware on door exteriors.
- Paint openings in noncontrasting colors so they blend into the façade.
- Install door alarm doors on the inside.

Fencing and Barriers.   Intermediate fencing and barriers between buildings and around open spaces are some of the most overlooked elements of perimeter security. As with other elements, a well-designed perimeter is a good example of transparent security, not noticeable to the public.

- Avoid elements that can be scaled vertically. Fencing should have vertical, rather than horizontal, design elements to discourage climbing.
- Architectural elements should not create hiding places.
- Perimeter walls and fencing should be high enough to discourage climbing and have elements on top to prevent intruders.

Roof Configuration.   Rooftops are commonly used by intruders to enter buildings.

- Ensure that roof configuration does not provide opportunities for breaching school perimeter.
- Ensure that rooftop access doors, skylights, vents, and other penetrations are locked.
- When roofing contractors repair the roof, have a school representative ensure that heavy materials cannot fall off the roof into occupied areas. Have them lock appropriate access ways at the end of the workday. Prepare procedures to monitor contractor workers present in and around existing school buildings.

Sight Lines Maximize Perimeter Surveillance.   It is safer for everyone if the area around the school is clearly visible to all.

- Site elements should be designed to promote maximum visibility, clear sight lines, and observation of the school premises and nearby roads, streets, buildings, and wooded areas.
- Minimize or eliminate hiding places, nooks, corners, and other screened areas where intruders can lurk.

Multiple Perimeters for Multiple Functions.   Schools have multiple functions and security demands. After-hours activities and weekend use of playfields are critical community functions but complicate security needs.

- Functions such as gymnasiums, multipurpose rooms, libraries, auditoriums, and swimming pools should have separate entries.
- After-hours activity areas, playfields, and common spaces should have a separate perimeter to keep other parts of the school secure.
- Alarms should be zoned for after-hours activities.

SITE PLANNING

Attention to design and maintenance of school grounds and property is the first line of defense for enhancing security. Fencing, playfields, surveillance, and landscaping are among the important design elements to be addressed (Table 20.5 and Fig. 20.1).

TABLE 20.5   School Security Site Planning Checklist

Element	Item
Fencing	1. Provide fencing at school grounds and play areas. 2. Maintain fencing height to keep intruders out. 3. Install locked gates. 4. Ensure all areas of school building and grounds visible and accessible to cruising local law enforcement vehicles and emergency vehicles.
Play areas	1. Allow visual surveillance of play areas and equipment from a single vantage point. 2. Install tamperproof fasteners on play area equipment. 3. Separate play areas for kindergarten and pre-kindergarten children. 4. Extend protective surfaces around playground equipment to at least six feet. 5. Space structures over 30 inches high at least nine feet apart.
Surveillance	1. Allow open sight lines for building layout and landscaping. 2. Place remote and high-risk areas under camera surveillance. 3. Design athletic fields for single point surveillance.
Landscaping	1. Plant trees away from buildings to prevent access to the roof and upper floors. 2. Ensure location and height of landscaped elements allow clear observation and surveillance. 3. Ensure trees are set back from intersections to allow sight lines for traffic, including buses. 4. Design exterior covered walkways, walls, and landscaped elements to prevent rooftop and upper level access, allow good illumination of areas, and clear sight lines.

Source: Wyoming State Legislature, School Finance Office; National Clearinghouse for Educational Facilities.

FIGURE 20.1 Good visibility enhances security. Oak Grove Elementary School, Alpine, California. *(Architect: Thomas Blurock Architects; photographer: Milroy/ McAleer.)*

Playfield Fencing

Careful thought should be given to playfield zones, as defined by fencing and other barriers.

- Perimeter fencing at property lines and adjacent to public streets should be at least 12 feet high, to prevent trespassing and to keep balls and other equipment inside.

- Playfields should be zoned with low fencing and other barriers to aid supervision and protect specialized fields.

- Playfield fencing should generally be open, to allow good visibility.

Playfield Design

Many incidents occur during nonsupervised play, such as recess and after-school activities. As playfields become more congested, the problem is exacerbated. Playfields also serve as joint community facilities, prompting other security needs (Fig. 20.2).

Supervision

Most incidents of violence, fighting, hazing, and other problems occur in corners or in unsupervised areas.

- One person located on the playfield should be able to observe all activity.
- Secondary supervision from the office or other inside space should enhance supervision, not be the primary supervision.
- If parts of the playfield are not visible to the primary outside supervisor, they should be fenced off.

VEHICULAR CIRCULATION AND TRAFFIC ELEMENTS

The vehicular entry and primary vehicular circulation for nonschool personnel should be clearly defined, with signage and graphics, especially during periods of peak congestion (Table 20.6).

Emergency Vehicle Routes

Schools should have a plan for emergency vehicle access, such as fire trucks, ambulances, and police cars. Since incidents and injuries often occur at times of peak congestion, emergency routes should be separated and kept clear and open at all times.

Bus Drop-Off Zones

Bus traffic should be separated from other vehicular traffic as much as possible. Bus drivers can be directed to where to park for bus drop-off, away from the most heavily used vehicular routes. Bus drop-off otherwise has similar characteristics to parent drop-off zones.

FIGURE 20.2 Playfields are a primary source of school incidents. Good visibility enhances security. Oak Grove Elementary School, Alpine, California. *(Architect: Thomas Blurock Architects; photographer: Milroy/McAleer.)*

TABLE 20.6 School Security Traffic Planning Checklist

Element	Item
Parking	1. Ensure parking areas are clearly visible from the main administrative area.
	2. Design parking lots to prevent speeding by avoiding long straight runs.
	3. Install speed bumps to slow traffic.
	4. Raise sidewalks to separate pedestrians in parking zones.
	5. Separate student parking areas from other parking.
Circulation	1. Minimize number of school building entrances and exits.
	2. Eliminate congestion with simple and direct traffic flow.
	3. Designate separate visitor parking areas.
	4. Separate car and bus traffic.
	5. Eliminate hazardous entrances off main thoroughfares.
	6. Ensure fire lanes are wide enough for fire trucks and EMS vehicles, and kept clear at all times.
Bus loading zones	1. Restrict bus loading zones to buses only.
	2. Park buses in a single row.
	3. Ensure buses can turn or park without backing up.
	4. Provide covered areas and bus shelters for students waiting for buses.
Parent drop-off and pick-up zones	1. Clearly define drop-off and pick-up zones.
	2. Ensure students do not have to cross roads or vehicular traffic to reach these zones.

Source: Wyoming State Legislature, School Finance Office; National Clearinghouse for Educational Facilities.

Parent Drop-Off Zones

Parent drop-off zones are some of the most difficult site design problems in schools. Morning drop-off is quick, with parents leaving their children and moving on. In contrast, afternoon drop-off is slow, with parents waiting for children to emerge from school or the grounds. These two functions inevitably happen in the same space. The following criteria may not always be achievable because of site area required but represent good practice.

- Long curb lengths are the ideal drop-off configuration, with minimum for 10 to 20 cars; more is preferable.
- One-way traffic is best.
- Locate drop-off on the right-hand side of the car.
- Drop-off areas should be supervised from one strategic location.
- Create benches for waiting along the drop-off zone.
- Separate drop-off zone from visitor and other parking areas.
- Create a clear path of travel from the site entry to the site exit.
- Avoid stacking of cars spilling off into the street.

SCHOOL BUILDING AND GROUNDS

Security planning extends from site and property lines to building exteriors and interior spaces. Every design element, from lighting and signage, to exterior construction materials and building systems, contributes to overall security. Architects, engineers, and facility managers should remain alert to the impact that design and specifications and subsequent maintenance of materials and systems will have on all building occupants (Table 20.7).

TABLE 20.7   School Building Security Checklist

Element	Item
Building exterior	1. Provide graffiti-repellant exterior wall finishes, to allow repeated cleanings.
	2. Create one clearly marked, visible visitors' entrance.
	3. Provide exterior courtyards that can be supervised by one person.
Security systems	1. Install remotely monitored, central alarm systems.
	2. Ensure key areas are protected by the alarm system, including the main office, computer areas, cafeteria, gymnasium, shops, labs, and others as needed.
	3. Install two-way communications between areas such as classrooms and main office areas; portable classrooms and the main office; large group areas and the office.
Lighting	1. Ensure school perimeter is well lit with appropriate fixtures that will not disrupt nearby residential areas.
	2. Provide sufficient lighting with marginal coverage in case a light goes out.
	3. Specify accessible light fixture lenses made of unbreakable material.
	4. Provide additional lighting at entries and possible points of intrusion.
	5. Locate switches, controls, and electrical panels in restricted access areas, protected from tampering.
Signage	1. Install signs declaring school grounds as drug-free and gun-free zones.
	2. Install signs indicating the penalty for trespassing.
	3. Provide welcome signs directing visitors to check in at the main office.
	4. Use interior signage to direct visitors to the main office and other public spaces.
	5. Create signage that encourages way finding that is consistent throughout the building.
Outbuildings	1. Locate outbuildings, sheds, and portable classrooms on the site to allow clear sight lines and visibility.
	2. Provide portable classrooms with securely fastened panels to enclose grade-level crawl spaces.

Source: Wyoming State Legislature, School Finance Office; National Clearinghouse for Educational Facilities.

School Entrances

The main school entry provides orientation for the entire facility and should be carefully planned.

- The main building or complex entry should be visible from the street and main vehicular access to the school.

- Secondary entry points should be designed to appear as secondary entry points, not main entries.

- The entry should have multiple points of surveillance to key areas, such as parent drop-off, parking, waiting zones, school entry, and administration.

- The main school entry should be at least 20 feet minimum width, to prevent congestion and crowding.

Graffiti Control

Graffiti is an ongoing problem in and around schools, especially in urban areas. When people cannot get access to walls, graffiti is reduced. Graffiti symbols can also represent gang activity and designated gang turf in a neighborhood.

If gang-related graffiti is an ongoing problem, schools should notify local law enforcement. Increasingly, many local police departments have a gang-tracking database, utilizing graffiti examples and body tattoos as identification and crime-fighting tools across neighborhoods and cities. Planning and design strategies can reduce and potentially eliminate graffiti (Table 20.8).

TABLE 20.8   Tactics to Deter Graffiti in and around Schools

- Plant tough landscape, such as thorny shrubs against buildings and site walls, or climbing vines, to effectively deter graffiti.
- Install fencing at least six feet from walls to discourage vandalism and graffiti.
- Clean up graffiti as soon as it appears. When culprits are caught, involve them in clean-up operations, and notify local law enforcement if the problem is pervasive.

Site Lighting

Providing well-lit areas is one of several effective solutions for enhancing security:

- Bright site lighting in areas of high ambient light, such as cities with street lighting, is one of the most effective security devices available. Site lighting should make the building perimeter, the main entry, and parking areas visible to adjacent streets and be brighter than the surrounding ambient light. For sustainability, light the ground, not the sky.
- Low or no site lighting should be used where surrounding ambient light is low. In rural or undeveloped areas, visibility is enhanced when there is little light in a school building complex. In theory, an intruder would need a light source to operate.
- Motion-activated lighting aids security and helps reduce electricity use.

Portable Classrooms: Special Problems

Portable classrooms are a fact of life on many school campuses, due to overcrowded facilities. Because they are often hastily installed, they can be haphazardly sited, disrupting well-planned campuses with a negative effect on security, outdoor play areas, parking, entries, and other campus functions. Many portable classrooms are low-density, nonfire-rated stand-alone buildings, and create spaces that become hiding places and obstacles to otherwise well-planned campuses.

- When site planning with portables, maintain established sight lines.
- Fence spaces between portables to avoid creating hiding places.
- Review door placement to ensure good visibility at circulation areas.

SCHOOL PROGRAMMING, PLANNING, AND DESIGN

During the early programming and planning phases of new construction, renovation, or addition projects, the design team, along with the client and users, should review all operational and design decisions, to ensure they will result in safe and secure environments for students, teachers, staff, and visitors (Table 20.9).

Design of several essential school building interior spaces and areas can significantly enhance personal safety of all building occupants (Table 20.10).

Circulation Systems

Movement through school corridors can cause problems when students bump into each other, become disoriented, or anxious. There are times of day when all students are moving at once, creating

TABLE 20.9 School Security Programming, Planning, and Design Checklist

Element	Item
Circulation	1. Provide clear sight lines to minimize the number of staff positions needed to observe hallways and common spaces. 2. Ensure that each room has a minimum of one window to be used for emergency rescue or escape. 3. Ensure that entrance lobby is visible from main office area. 4. Provide main hallways at least 10 feet wide for elementary and middle schools and 12 feet wide for high schools. 5. Recess doors opening into corridors. 6. Provide daylight sources in locker rooms and laboratories to allow egress during power outages. 7. Provide corridor doors with vision panels, mounted so the bottom height of the glass allows an adult to see into the room. 8. Provide electronic surveillance in enclosed stairways. 9. Design elevators for limited access, in accordance with handicapped standards, and install electronic monitors. 10. Ensure that cafeteria layout enhances efficient circulation flow.
Space planning	1. Allow unused areas to be closed during after-school activities. 2. Ensure that locker rooms are visible from the gym teacher's office. 3. Provide basketball courts with minimum six-foot safety borders 4. Install locked storage areas and cabinets in nurse's office. 5. Design well-spaced library stacks no higher than four feet, to allow clear visibility to all areas.
Materials	1. Install shatterproof mirrors in toilet rooms and dance classrooms. 2. Install hard-surface ceilings in toilet rooms and locker areas, not lay-in acoustical ceiling tiles, to eliminate potential hiding places for contraband.
Ventilation	1. Locate kilns in separate rooms, not storage areas, with code-compliant exhaust and ventilation. 2. Store hazardous materials and equipment in well-ventilated areas with a two-hour fire separation wall.
Toilet rooms	1. Ensure that toilet partitions and equipment are sturdy and securely attached. 2. Locate rest rooms close to interior spaces and away from exterior doors. 3. Protect light switches for toilet rooms and corridors from tampering.

Source: Wyoming State Legislature, School Finance Office; National Clearinghouse for Educational Facilities.

the potential for congestion and conflict. Stairs are the means of vertical circulation in schools. Elevators are for staff use and handicapped students, not the general population.

- The internal layout of the school, the floor plan, must be "legible," enabling those in the space to "read" and orient themselves at all times. Large floor plans are challenging because sprawling schools can be perceived as disorienting mazes, especially for new students.

- Avoid bottlenecks at major hallway intersections. Sharp changes in direction, narrow corridor widths, and other circulation changes impede pedestrian flow.

- Hallways should be at least 10 feet wide, and more in heavily used areas.

- Columns and other circulation obstructions should be carefully placed so as not to impede traffic flow.

- When stairs are narrower than the circulation systems feeding them, ensure they are highly visible and allow queuing areas to prevent bottlenecks at either end.

TABLE 20.10 School Security: Key Program Elements

1. Circulation throughout the school building
2. Hallways
3. Administration areas
4. Common areas
5. Lockers
6. Classroom security
7. Toilet rooms
8. Locker rooms

FIGURE 20.3 Visibility from classrooms to hallways enhances surveillance and allows supervised use of these often dismal and dangerous spaces. Pueblo Elementary School, Pomona, California. *(Architect: Thomas Blurock Architects; photographer: Milroy/McAleer.)*

Hallways and Circulation: Multiple Points of Supervision

Getting around between class, recess, and other activities represents the largest unsupervised time in most schools. Long hallways are difficult to supervise (Fig. 20.3).

- Installing hallway glazing is one of the least used and most effective hallway supervision strategies. Visibility into and from classrooms enhances hallway observation and allows use of supervised corridors. Glazing between adjacent classroom spaces is also effective.
- Door alcoves should keep door swings out of the line of traffic, but should not compromise visibility in corners and hiding places.

- Avoid blind spots, corners, niches, nooks, and crannies off corridors.
- Where weather and circumstances allow single-loaded circulation and balconies, provide supervision from adjacent spaces.
- When using upper-level balconies for circulation, full-height screens, or attractively woven fencing, rather than railings, can prevent students from throwing items on students below or even jumping.

Administration Areas: School Nerve Centers

As the school command center, the administration area should control a maximum number of important functions. The location, design, and configuration of administrative areas are critical to monitoring school activities and emergency response.

- The administrative area is the front door to the school and should be welcoming, while allowing monitoring of the comings and goings of the students, teachers, and visitors. All those entering the school should be observable by those in the administrative area.
- The administrative reception area should be designed to enhance observation capability. The reception area should be located near the school front door and continuously staffed during school operating hours.
- Staff in the administrative area should be able to observe parent drop-off areas, visitor parking, and bus drop-off zones to the maximum degree possible.
- The principal's office should be adjacent to the reception area; staff in the principal's office should be able to hear what goes on in the reception area and view activity areas.
- Provide a supervised time-out area within the administration area to isolate students with discipline or anger problems.

Common Areas: Maximize Surveillance

Common areas such as cafeterias, locker areas, and other places where students gather informally between classes are points of concern. Social interactions occur in unsupervised free-time areas; thus observation capability is important.

- Common areas should be designed with clear visibility so one staff member can supervise an entire area.
- All large areas within the school, even if they are not specifically designed to be, are considered common spaces.
- Provide ample places to sit and gather. Sitting areas can be articulated with benches, walls, tables, and other formal or informal site furniture. Gathering areas should be designed to allow good supervision.
- Students should not always feel they are under surveillance. Except in the most extreme circumstances, supervision should be of a passive, or transparent, nature.
- Corners, nooks, and crannies off main hallways and corridors and other potential hiding places create supervision problems and should be carefully avoided during design.
- Circulation through common areas should clearly and directly indicate how to enter, leave, and move through spaces, even the most informal areas. Carefully trace movement through spaces to avoid bottlenecks.

Lockers or No Lockers: No Easy Answer

Personal lockers, once deemed essential in secondary schools, are becoming increasingly questionable items. Lockers can be hiding places for drugs, weapons, or other contraband, and are therefore used less frequently, especially in urban schools. However, as schools get more impersonal, providing personal space for students is important. The practical problem of what to do with books, coats, supplies, and other gear a student uses during the day remains unsolved. Many parents fear children carrying heavy backpacks are susceptible to unnecessary risk of theft and back problems. There is no consensus or universal solution. If lockers are used, special care should be taken.

- Clustering lockers together may hinder observation.
- Hallway lockers in open areas are easier to supervise.

Classroom Security

Although classroom interiors and other enclosed teaching spaces are generally safer than unsupervised hallways, security concerns remain. Most student activity occurs in classrooms, equipment and computers are vulnerable to theft, and many incidents happen in classrooms, despite the presence of a teacher.

- Classroom security is enhanced with visibility from adjacent spaces such as hallways and other teaching spaces. Glazing between spaces increases surveillance, facilitates team teaching, and sharing of resources.
- Adequate lockable storage in classrooms prevents theft. Equipment lists should guide storage planning, closet sizes, and locations.
- Classroom computers are potential targets for theft. Computer-securing devices are commercially available.
- Each classroom and teaching space should have emergency communication available to the administration office.
- Motion-activated sensors for classroom lighting save energy and detect intruders.

Toilet Rooms: Privacy and Security

Because of inherent unsupervised privacy issues, many surreptitious activities from smoking to drug use occur in toilet rooms. Audible surveillance is often the only possible means of observation.

- Use open privacy locks for entry so activity can be heard from the adjacent spaces. Doors offer sound protection for illicit activity.
- Lock bathrooms during class times.
- Do not use hung ceilings with lay-in ceiling tiles, as they provide hiding places for illegal substances and contraband.

Locker Rooms: Multiple Hazards

Because lockers are used around periods of physical activity, many injuries and incidents occur in locker rooms. Visual supervision is important but is often complicated because locker rooms are crowded and filled with equipment.

- Maintain sight lines to all activities.
- Provide maximum visibility from coach and teacher areas into the locker room. Raising the floor level of the office area improves sight lines.
- Maximize placement of lockers on outside walls. Freestanding lockers should be no higher than eye level.
- Shower areas should be well supervised and as spacious as possible.

CONCLUSION

Students of all ages, from prekindergarten to college, are in school to learn about the world around them. Learning is enhanced when schools generate a feeling of safety and well-being through invisible security so they don't look like fortresses.

Creating safe learning environments in schools is an ongoing challenge for teachers, administrators, parents, architects, and landscape designers. With judicious use of planning criteria, design elements, and operational strategies available to the school design team, a high level of transparent security and greater personal safety can be achieved in any learning environment.

BIBLIOGRAPHY

Green, Mary W., *The Appropriate and Effective Use of Security Technologies in U.S. Schools; A Guide for Schools and Law Enforcement Agencies,* Sandia National Laboratories, Sept. 1999, NCJ 178265. U.S. Dept. of Justice, National Institute of Justice, U.S. Dept. of Education Safe and Drug Free Schools Program, the U.S. Dept. of Energy, Sandia Laboratories. www.ncjrs.org/school/home.html

U.S. Department of Education, *Violence and Discipline Problems in U.S. Public Schools: 1996–1997.*

Wyoming State Legislature, School Finance Office, Cheyenne, Wyo. *Safety and Security Checklist for Wyoming Schools,* National Clearinghouse for Educational Facilities, 2001.

INTERNET RESOURCES

American Institute of Architects (AIA)
Committee on Architecture for Education
www.aia.org or www.aia.org/cae

American School & University
www.asumag.com

Campus Safety Journal
www.campusjournal.com

Council of Educational Facilities Planners
  International (CEFPI)
www.cefpi.org

National Clearinghouse for Educational
  Facilities (NCEF)
NCEF Safety and Security Design for Schools
www.edfacilities.org/rl/safety_security.cfm

National Institute of Justice
http://www.ojp.usdoj.gov/nij

NCEF Resource lists
http://edfacilities.org/rl/

School Construction News
www.schoolconstructionnews.com

Thomas Blurock Architects
www.tblurock.com

U.S. Department of Education
National Clearinghouse for Educational
  Facilities at the National Institute of
  Building Sciences
www.edfacilities.org

U.S. Department of Justice, Office of
  Justice Programs
http://www.ojp.usdoj.gov

CHAPTER 21
WOMEN'S HEALTH CENTERS: WORKPLACE SAFETY AND SECURITY

Barbara A. Nadel, FAIA
Principal, Barbara Nadel Architect
Forest Hills, New York

*You gain strength, courage and confidence by every experi-
ence in which you really stop to look fear in the face. You are
able to say to yourself, "I have lived through this horror. I can
take the next thing that comes along." You must do the thing
you think you cannot do.*

ELEANOR ROOSEVELT (1884–1962)
U.S. diplomat and reformer

*Be prepared, before an emergency occurs. No matter what the
crisis: think before you act, then act swiftly to minimize your
exposure to danger.*

PLANNED PARENTHOOD GOLDEN GATE
Security Reference Guide

Women's health centers must seek a balance between security and accessibility. Those who work,
volunteer, or are affiliated with women's health centers, and their families, have faced violent threats
and personal safety risks, in the workplace and at home. Patients and their significant others, en route
to receive care and leaving clinics, have been targeted for harassment and injury.

Health care facility design should create a safe, inviting place to receive care and a pleasant environment in which to work. Transparent security measures, invisible to the public eye, are advantageous in a clinic setting, by avoiding a fortresslike appearance. In some locations, visible security
measures are appropriate. Design elements, such as bullet-resistant wall materials; technology
devices, such as emergency alarm systems; and strictly enforced policies and emergency procedures
strengthen facility security for patients and staff.

The illustrations in this chapter of the two San Francisco clinics show how integrating good
design and security can create attractive and safe health environments and workplaces. The series of
detailed checklists, policies, and procedures, developed by Planned Parenthood Golden Gate, can
assist staff in tracking and documenting any kind of threat. These strategies and checklists may be
readily adapted to many workplaces, regardless of business, industry, and building type.

VIOLENT INCIDENTS

Violence, in the form of arson, bioterrorism, firebombs, and vandalism, has been a fact of life for women's health centers since the early 1970s in the United States. Between 1998 and 2000, over 80 letters threatening anthrax contamination were sent to American clinics in 16 states. Anthrax spores are potentially fatal bacteria if inhaled into the lungs. All the letters were proved to be hoaxes, but succeeded in scaring people, making them fearful to come to work and created undue stress among hundreds of people and their families nationwide.

Shortly after the September 11 attacks in New York City and Washington, D.C., anthrax letters appeared in offices of public officials and the news media in New York, Washington, and other cities. Several letters contained the harmful substance, whereas others were hoaxes. In October 2001, women's clinics in 13 states received over 150 letters marked "Time sensitive security information enclosed," with return addresses from law enforcement groups, mailed from a total of five states. Inside were a death threat letter and a powdery substance. Several letters were found to be hoaxes.

Many clinics, especially in California, where the threatening incident rate has historically been higher than in other states, have reported threats, vandalism, assaults, blockades, and related crimes. Clinic personnel are frequently stalked, harassed, threatened, and targeted at their homes, offices, and other places away from clinics and medical offices.

Between 1994 and 1998, in Canada and New York, five doctors were shot through a glass window or door at their homes. In each case, the shooter used a rifle and shot through the rear of the doctors' homes at dusk or in the evening. In October 1998, Dr. Barnett Slepian was shot and murdered in his Amherst, New York, home outside Buffalo. His killer was sentenced in 2003.

As a result of these ongoing threats to personal and workplace safety, nonprofit organizations, such as Planned Parenthood, have developed security design strategies and procedures for their staff, volunteers, patients, and providers to follow. Many of the design and operational strategies apply to any workplace or religious institution subjected to ongoing threats. In addition to facility design and technology in and around clinic facilities, developing security policies and emergency procedures is essential to clinic operations. These policies include staff training on handling incoming mail and suspicious packages, ensuring facility access, and documenting all threats in written reports to be shared with law enforcement agencies as needed.

THREATS AGAINST WOMEN'S HEALTH CENTERS, PATIENTS, AND STAFF

Women's health centers, and those affiliated with them in any way, have historically been subjected to numerous types of threats (Table 21.1).

TABLE 21.1 Ten Threat Types against Women's Health Centers, Patients, and Staff

1. Murders and attempted murders of physicians and providers, by snipers, inside and outside clinics, and at their homes
2. Bomb threats, firebombing, and arson
3. Invasion, assault and battery, vandalism, and burglary
4. Stalking of physicians and staff, at the facility and at home
5. Harassing phone calls
6. Death threats
7. Hate mail, anthrax letters, and acid
8. Blockading access to clinic entries
9. Protesters and picketers in front of facilities, mostly men, videotaping women who enter
10. Web sites that post names, photos, office and home addresses of health care providers, judges, legislators, and their spouses and children that may incite violence

The Federal Clinic Access Act

The federal Freedom to Access Clinic Entrances Act, known as the Access Act, the FACE Act, or FACEA, passed by the U.S. Congress in May 1994, is designed to prohibit clinic violence by providing legal grounds for prosecuting those who threaten clinics and other facilities.

The law was written to protect reproductive health service facilities, their staff, and patients, from workplace violence, threats, assaults, vandalism, and blockades. Provisions of the law make it illegal to use "force, threat of force, or physical obstruction" to intentionally injure, intimidate, interfere with, or attempt these actions against someone engaged in or providing or receiving reproductive health services. The law established criminal and civil penalties for these actions, including prison time and substantial fines.

The FACE Act offers the same protection to prochoice and prolife crisis pregnancy centers, abortion clinics, physicians' offices, and reproductive health clinics. It also assures that people can worship where they wish without harassment, at churches, synagogues, mosques, temples, and other religious facilities.

SITE PLANNING AND SELECTION

Many women's centers are located in convenient neighborhood areas, malls, small medical buildings, shared space with other health care tenants, or on busy streets in residential communities. Freestanding buildings, owned by the organization or health care provider, are preferred, because eviction is not an issue when potential problems arise.

Clinic Access

Federal agencies recommend building setbacks, or standoff distances, to prevent vehicular bombs from getting too close to courthouses and other government facilities. Similarly, building setbacks for women's health centers enhances security by providing more opportunities to control access for patients and staff. The FACE Act does not specify minimum street setbacks, but some judges have noted setback or buffer zone requirements when issuing injunctions against protesters, depending on the site. If setbacks are not possible, consideration must be given to accessing and controlling the entrance.

DESIGN ISSUES

Careful attention to site design, building materials, and interior planning can enhance the safety of patients and staff, while maintaining a pleasant and well-designed environment.

Site Issues

- Provide clear, unobstructed sight lines to parking areas and staff entrances from within the facility
- Ensure visibility and observation to the surrounding outdoor site and perimeter, and within the facility (Fig. 21.1).

Parking

- Secure parking areas, whether garages or surface lots, with a gate, electronically monitored, and provide direct access to the facility
- Separate pedestrian and vehicular entrances for staff and the public
- Provide staff leaving at night with an escort to their cars or to public transportation

FIGURE 21.1   Eastmont Mall Planned Parenthood Clinic, Oakland, California. Clinic entry from Eastmont Mall. Security features include obscured glass for privacy, while allowing natural light transmission, and buzzer doors. *(Architect: Fougeron Architecture; photographer: Fougeron Architecture.)*

FIGURE 21.2   Eastmont Mall Planned Parenthood Clinic, Oakland, California. Window between waiting room and corridor. Security features include bulletproof glass and bulletproof wall material. *(Architect: Fougeron Architecture; photographer: Richard Barnes.)*

Entry, Waiting, and Registration Area

- Create the first layer of defense within the building at the reception and registration area (Figs. 21.2 and 21.3).
- Audio and closed-circuit television (CCTV) monitoring at reception and entrances allow visitors to be screened before receiving permission to enter.

FIGURE 21.3 Eddy Street Planned Parenthood Clinic, Oakland, California. Clinic reception window. Security features include bulletproof glass, bulletproof wall material, and buzzer doors. *(Architect: Fougeron Architecture; photographer: Fougeron Architecture.)*

FIGURE 21.4 Eastmont Mall Planned Parenthood Clinic, Oakland, California. Clinic waiting room and reception window. Security features include bulletproof glass, buzzer doors, and air gap between bulletproof wall to avoid intercom use. *(Architect: Fougeron Architecture; photographer: Richard Barnes.)*

- Prevent visitors from getting beyond the entry vestibule to the waiting area without being buzzed in. Even though most clinics insist on scheduled appointments, many offer scheduled open hours for drop-in clients, including existing and new patients, who are unknown to the facility (Figs. 21.4 and 21.5).

- Consider creating at least two different areas, including a vestibule, where visitors are screened and buzzed in to the waiting area.

- Provide bullet-resistant vision panels and window enclosures to protect the reception areas and bullet-resistant exterior windows (Fig. 21.6).

FIGURE 21.5   Eastmont Mall Planned Parenthood Clinic, Oakland, California. Clinic waiting room. Security features include bulletproof glass, buzzer doors, armored doors and walls, and keypad entry. *(Architect: Fougeron Architecture; photographer: Richard Barnes.)*

FIGURE 21.6   Eastmont Mall Planned Parenthood Clinic, Oakland, California. Reception area. Security features include bulletproof glass, buzzer doors, and bullet-proof wall material. *(Architect: Fougeron Architecture; photographer: Richard Barnes.)*

Interiors and Technology

- Provide bullet-resistant walls, as needed, throughout the facility interiors.
- Install panic or call buttons in all exam rooms, connected to the main desk, where someone can call 911 if necessary in the event of an emergency.
- Use colors, lighting, materials, finishes, and furnishings to create pleasant and inviting spaces for patients, visitors, and staff.
- Install closed-circuit television with split and zoom digital capabilities and tape storage for at least a week, in areas considered to be security risks.

POLICIES AND PROCEDURES

Facility managers and executive directors of all building types play a vital role in ensuring the safety and security of staff and visitors. They are responsible for developing, communicating, and distributing policies and procedures to all personnel. These policies should cover every likely threat and possible scenario that may occur at or near their facility, or be directed toward staff members and patients, including at the homes of health care providers.

Conducting a threat analysis and vulnerability assessment, with the assistance of local law enforcement or a security consultant, is an effective way to ensure that appropriate security strategies are developed in response to ongoing, potential, and most likely threats. To achieve optimum preparedness, facility managers can implement a series of basic, proactive operational procedures to protect the safety of all occupants and users of the building (Table 21.2). A series of checklists can familiarize staff about potential problems they may encounter and prepare them for the best ways to address likely threats (Table 21.3).

TABLE 21.2 **Policies and Procedures for Facility Managers**

1. Maintain written documentation of all threats and violent events (Tables 21.5 and 21.11).
2. Identify local, state, and national emergency hotline telephone numbers for reporting suspicious substances, and include them in policy and procedures manuals (Tables 21.6 and 21.7).
3. Provide information, training, and emergency drills to enhance staff response to emergencies under pressure (Tables 21.8 to 21.10 and 21.12 to 21.18).
4. Coordinate and communicate with federal and local law enforcement agencies, public officials, district attorneys, and community groups to inform them when problems arise.
5. Educate local law enforcement about clinic needs, concerns, and potential threats.
6. Ensure that the facility administrator or receptionist has a point of contact with local law enforcement to call in an emergency.
7. Remove all personal information and names of staff from official Web sites and outdoor signage.
8. Create a reference guide with important emergency procedures and contact phone numbers.

TABLE 21.3 **Security Reference Guide and Checklists for Women's Health Centers**

1. Safety and security procedures
2. Security incident report form
3. Site emergency telephone numbers
4. Important phone numbers
5. Butyric acid attack
6. Biohazard threat
7. Bomb threats
8. Bomb threat report form
9. E-mail threats
10. Fire
11. Hostile clients
12. Protesters
13. Robbery and armed intruder
14. Stalking and following
15. Suspicious packages and mail

Source: All checklists courtesy of Planned Parenthood Golden Gate, San Francisco, California.

SECURITY REFERENCE GUIDE

Planned Parenthood Golden Gate, in San Francisco, California, published an attractively designed and illustrated, easy-to-use, spiral-bound reference guide. This desk reference contains an array of check-lists, forms for documenting threats for law enforcement records, emergency contact information, daily protocols, and security procedures to be implemented during emergencies. Such information may be readily adapted for any building type or facility (Tables 21.4 to 21.18).

TABLE 21.4   Safety and Security Procedures Checklist

1. At work, wear employee ID badge at all times.
2. Be aware of your surroundings, and report suspicious people, objects, and packages.
3. Remain calm and act in a professional manner during an emergency.
4. Write incidents or events down as soon as possible using forms provided by the employer (Table 21.7).
5. Follow procedures for entry, exit, and securing facility.
6. Report all emergency situations to Clinic Manager immediately.
7. When in doubt, call the designated Security Manager, and keep phone and pager numbers handy (Tables 21.6 and 21.7).

Source: Checklist courtesy of Planned Parenthood Golden Gate, San Francisco, California.

TABLE 21.5   Security Incident Report Form

SECURITY INCIDENT REPORT FORM

Date: _____

Time of incident: _____   Clinic location: _____

TYPE OF INCIDENT (circle)

Arson	Burglary	Suspicious Package
Assault and/or Battery	Death Threats	Stalking
Bioterrorism (anthrax threat)	Hate Mail/Harassing Phone Calls	Trespassing
Blockade	Internet/Email Threat	Vandalism
Bomb Threat	Invasion	Other:

BRIEFLY DESCRIBE INCIDENT:

Your Name _____   Phone Number _____

Please complete this form within <u>one</u> day of the incident and forward to the Security Manager

Investigative Follow-up:

Completed by:

TABLE 21.6   Site Emergency Telephone Numbers

Facility Name _____

Address _____

Telephone Number _____

List the locations of the following:

Emergency Phone List _____

Staff Home Phone Numbers _____

Manual Fire Alarms _____

Fire Extinguishers _____

Evacuation Routes _____

Evacuation Meeting Areas _____

Emergency procedures for your location:

TABLE 21.7   Important Phone Numbers Form

Emergency 911

Local police (nonemergency number) _____

Alarm Company _____

Fire Department _____

Postal Inspector _____

Facilities Manager

Office _____

Cellular _____

Security Manager

Office _____

Cellular _____

Pager _____

Center Manager or Director

Office _____

Cellular _____

Other important numbers and contacts:

_____

_____

TABLE 21.8   Butyric Acid Attacks Checklist

Butyric acid has powerful smell, like rotten eggs.
If you come in contact with this odor, the following steps should be taken:

1. Notify the person in charge.
2. Call the local police who will notify the Hazardous Material Team. If necessary, call the 24-hour emergency response hazardous materials clean-up company (check with Security Manager or Facilities Manager).
3. Evacuate the building immediately.
4. Wait for the police and follow their instructions.
5. Call the Security Manager.
6. Document the incident on the Security Incident Report (Table 21.5).

Source: Checklist courtesy of Planned Parenthood Golden Gate, San Francisco, California.

TABLE 21.9   Biohazard Threat Checklist

If a letter is received claiming to contain anthrax or an unknown powdery substance, the following steps should be taken:

1. Remain calm. There is a very low risk of disease transmission, but still be cautious.
2. Move people away from the immediate area.
3. Close the envelope and place it in a plastic or paper bag.
4. Immediately wash your hands and arms thoroughly with soap and water if you handled the package.
5. Notify the on-site manager or person in charge.
6. Call 911.
7. Call the local, state, or national emergency hotline numbers designated for reporting suspicious substances. These numbers should be identified before an incident occurs and published in policy and procedures manuals.
8. Call the Security Manager.

Source: Checklist courtesy of Planned Parenthood Golden Gate, San Francisco, California.

TABLE 21.10   Bomb Threats Checklist

In the event of a telephone bomb threat:

1. Do not panic. Stay calm and alert.
2. Keep the caller on the line as long as possible by asking questions on the Bomb Threat Report Form (Table 21.11).
3. Attempt to get someone else to listen to the call.
4. Immediately report the incident to the person in charge.
5. Complete the Telephone Bomb Threat Checklist.
6. When caller hangs up, notify the local police department.
7. Conduct security sweep and if necessary evacuate the building using appropriate procedures.
8. Wait for police and follow their instructions.
9. Complete Security Incident Report (Table 21.5) and send to the Security Manager.

Source: Checklist courtesy of Planned Parenthood Golden Gate, San Francisco, California.

TABLE 21.11   Bomb Threat Report Form

Questions To Ask Caller:

1. When is the bomb going to explode? _____

2. Where is the bomb right now?_____

3. What does the bomb look like? _____

4. What kind of bomb is it?_____

5. What will cause the bomb to explode?_____

6. Did you place the bomb?_____

7. Why? _____

8. What is your address?_____

9. What is your name? _____

Exact Wording of Bomb Threat:

_____

_____

Sex of caller   Age   Race

Telephone number at which call is received   Length of call

Time call received   Date call received

Caller's Voice (Circle)

Calm	Soft	Stutter	Excited
Laughter	Rasp	Rapid	Normal
Nasal	Angry	Loud	Lisp
Slow	Crying	Deep	Distinct
Slurred	Ragged	Disguised	Accent
Whispered	Deep breathing	Clearing throat	Cracking voice

Familiar (If voice is familiar, who did it sound like?)

_____

Background Sounds (Circle)

Street noise	House noises	Factory machinery	Office machinery
Animal noises	Long distance	PA system	Music
Voices	Motor	Booth	Pots and pans
Clear	Static	Local	

Other (please specify)

_____

_____

Bomb Threat Language (Circle)

Well spoken (educated)	Incoherent	Foul
Taped	Irrational	Message read by threat maker

Remarks

_____

Your name _____   Position _____

Phone number _____   Date checklist completed _____

Source: Checklist courtesy of Planned Parenthood Golden Gate, San Francisco, California.

TABLE 21.12   E-Mail Threats Checklist

If you receive an e-mail threat, the following steps should be taken:

1. Immediately notify and forward a copy of the e-mail to the Information Technology (IT) Department and to the Security Manager.
2. Save the e-mail. DO NOT delete it.

Source: Checklist courtesy of Planned Parenthood Golden Gate, San Francisco, California.

TABLE 21.13   Fire Checklist

In case of fire, the first person at the scene will:

1. Alert staff, patients, and visitors.
2. Pull lever in fire alarm box.
3. Call 911.
4. Evacuate everyone in immediate danger from fire area.
5. If possible, confine the fire by using extinguisher and closing all doors and windows.

If trapped in a room during a fire:

1. Place cloth material under the door to prevent smoke from entering.
2. Retreat and close as many doors as possible between you and the fire.
3. Be prepared to signal for help from a window.
4. If caught in smoke, drop to your hands and knees and crawl.
5. If clothes catch fire: stop, drop, and roll.

To use a fire extinguisher, remember P.A.S.S:

P Pull the safety pin. Twist first to break plastic tie, then pull.
A Aim at the base of the fire.
S Squeeze the trigger hands together.
S Sweep water from side to side across the base of the fire.

Even if you are able to contain the fire, call the Fire Department to report the incident. Ask the Fire Department to come check for any residual risk (i.e., electrical problems).

Source: Checklist courtesy of Planned Parenthood Golden Gate, San Francisco, California.

TABLE 21.14   Hostile Clients Checklist

If you have to deal with an irate or angry person, you should:

1. Assume an open posture and do not hide your hands.
2. Maintain eye contact.
3. Whenever possible, get the person seated because this is a less hostile position.
4. Keep your voice a little below your normal volume.
5. Acknowledge hostile person's anger and irritation.
6. Avoid ultimatums, threats, and intimidations.
7. Inform supervisor and document the incident on the Security Incident Report (Table 21.5).

Source: Checklist courtesy of Planned Parenthood Golden Gate, San Francisco, California.

TABLE 21.15   Protesters Checklist

Nonviolent/nonintrusive

1. Avoid speaking with protesters.
2. Remain calm and nonconfrontational.
3. Avoid physical contact with protesters.
4. Avoid calling a fellow staff member by name in the presence of a protester.
5. Do not confront protesters at any time.
6. Inform Clinic Manager or Supervisor at once.

Steps for Clinic Manager or staff member in charge:

1. Observe activity and count number of protesters involved.
2. Call the Security Manager.
3. Call the local police for extra patrol if necessary.
4. Complete the Security Incident Report (Table 21.5) and forward to the Security Manager.

Nonviolent, nonintrusive protesters will usually gather on the sidewalk in front of the facility or at the driveway entrance to the property. These protesters are legally expressing their opinions. They may consist of prayer groups, people holding antichoice signs, "sidewalk counselors," or persons handing out antichoice literature. They are not allowed to block entrances to the clinic.

Protesting is legal but can lead to unlawful activities that include:

1. Trespassing onto the clinic's private property
2. Obstructing access to the building
3. Harassing, intimidating, or following clients and staff
4. Creating disturbances that prevent clinic personnel from continuing their work
5. Violating the FACE Act (Freedom of Access to Clinic Entrances Act)
6. Violating a civil injunction or court order

Protesters/violent/intrusive—if a person enters the clinic with a threat of violence:

1. Get out of harm's way.
2. Alert other staff members and patients. Move patients to another predetermined location.
3. Call 911.
4. Do not confront the invader.
5. Remain in safe area until police arrive.
6. Call the Security Manager.

Source: Checklist courtesy of Planned Parenthood Golden Gate, San Francisco, California.

TABLE 21.16   Robbery and Armed Intruder Checklist

In the event of a robbery:

1. Remain calm and follow the intruder's directions.
2. Be alert. Note the suspect's description.
3. Call 911. (Use Panic Button, if available.)
4. Notify supervisor in charge.
5. Follow the instructions from the police responding to the scene.
6. Document the incident on the Security Incident Report (Table 21.5).

In the event of an armed intruder:

1. Immediately get out of harm's way.
2. Lock yourself in a designated safe room or safely exit the building.
3. Alert others in the building as appropriate and when it is safe to do so.
4. Call 911. (Use Panic Button, if available.)
5. Stay in locked room until help arrives.
6. Document everything you can remember about the intruder.

Source: Checklist courtesy of Planned Parenthood Golden Gate, San Francisco, California.

TABLE 21.17   Stalking and Following Checklist

If you are being followed or stalked while walking:

1. Never confront the person following you.
2. Walk quietly to a well-lit, populated safe area, and call the police.
3. If confronted or attacked, attempt to escape and run to the nearest well-lit, populated safe area.

If you are being followed or stalked while driving:

1. Make four successive right turns and observe through your rear view mirror.
2. If the vehicle is still following, attempt to drive to the nearest police station.
3. If you have a cell phone, call 911 and follow instructions.
4. Memorize the license plate and vehicle description.
5. Never stop your vehicle and confront the driver.
6. Never drive home when being followed.
7. Always keep your gas tank at least half a tank full.

Source: Checklist courtesy of Planned Parenthood Golden Gate, San Francisco, California.

TABLE 21.18   Suspicious Packages and Mail Checklist

When handling mail, there are a few ways to identify a suspicious package or letter:

1. Excessive or no postage.
2. Inaccurate or misspelled names and addresses.
3. Lack of return address or return address and postmark are from different areas.
4. Noticeable messiness or discoloration, unusual odors, lopsided or unprofessional wrapping.
5. Drawing, unusual statements, poor typing, or handwritten address.
6. Statements such as "Open by Addressee Only," "Special Delivery," or "Personal and Confidential."
7. Restrictive markings.
8. Addressed to title only (President).
9. Wrong name with title.
10. Rigid or bulky.
11. Badly typed or written.
12. Fictitious, unfamiliar, or no return address.
13. Protruding wires.

What to do:

1. Trust your instincts. If the package doesn't "feel" right, do not handle it.
2. Isolate the package.
3. Notify supervisor in charge.
4. Notify the police and follow evacuation procedures if necessary.

What not to do:

1. Do not shake a suspicious article.
2. Do not open a suspicious article.
3. Do not place a suspicious article in a confined space such as a cabinet or desk drawer.
4. Call or page the Security Manager as soon as the event stabilizes and the police arrive.
5. Notify supervisor in charge.
6. Notify the police and follow evacuation procedures if necessary.

Source: Checklist courtesy of Planned Parenthood Golden Gate, San Francisco, California.

CONCLUSION

Women's health centers provide patient care to women from all segments of society. Historically, these facilities have received many types of threats directed toward their premises, patients, providers and staff, especially when entering and exiting the centers. The 1994 Freedom of Access to Clinic Entrances Act has reduced, but not eliminated, threats and violence against those who provide or seek reproductive health services, and offers protection from harassment at health centers and places of worship. The law established civil and criminal penalties, including prison time and substantial fines.

Nonprofit organizations have developed security strategies and procedures applicable to women's health facilities and other workplaces. Preparation and personnel training, along with good design and technology, can prevent threats from escalating into fatal incidents.

ACKNOWLEDGMENTS

- Anne Fougeron, AIA, Fougeron Architecture, San Francisco, California
- Dian J. Harrison, MSW, President and CEO, Planned Parenthood Golden Gate, San Francisco, California
- Annabelle Ison, graphic designer for the *Security Reference Guide*, Ison Design, San Francisco, California
- Elizabeth Kubany, Kubany Communications, Maplewood, New Jersey
- Anne Tipp Tierney, Fougeron Architecture, San Francisco, California
- Therese Wilson, Vice President, External Affairs, Planned Parenthood Golden Gate, San Francisco, California
- The International Archive of Women in Architecture, Virginia Tech, Blacksburg, Virginia, for the 2003 IAWA Milka Bliznakov Prize Commendation.

The checklists and forms in this chapter were adapted, with permission, from the *Security Reference Guide*, published by Planned Parenthood Golden Gate, San Francisco, California.

BIBLIOGRAPHY

McCullough, Marie, "Anthrax Letters to Clinics Hoaxes, Early Tests Show," *Philadelphia Inquirer,* Oct. 17, 2001.
Planned Parenthood Golden Gate, *Security Reference Guide,* San Francisco, Calif., 2002.

INTERNET RESOURCES

FACE statute language
www.usdoj.gov/crt/split/facestat.htm

International Archive of Women in Architecture (IAWA)
http://spec.lib.vt.edu/iawa/

Planned Parenthood Federation of America, Inc.
www.plannedparenthood.org

Planned Parenthood Golden Gate
www.ppgg.org

U.S. Department of Justice, Civil Rights Division
Access to Reproductive Health Clinics and Places of Religious Worship, or the FACE Act
www.usdoj.gov/crt/split/face.htm

P·A·R·T · 3

ENGINEERING

CHAPTER 22
PROTECTIVE DESIGN OF STRUCTURES

Richard L. Tomasetti, PE
Co-Chairman, The Thornton-Tomasetti Group
New York, New York

John Abruzzo, PE
Vice President, LZA Technology
The Thornton-Tomasetti Group
New York, New York

Human history becomes more and more a race between education and catastrophe.

H.G. WELLS (1866-1946)
English author and historian,
Outline of History

History is rife with violent incidents directed toward people, buildings, and property. The events of September 11, 2001, and others during the late twentieth century directed toward Americans at home and abroad underscored the need for the design and construction community to reach even higher in the quest for advanced engineering techniques to save lives during a terrorist attack or disaster.

From benchmark events such as the 1983 attack on the American embassy in Beirut, the 1993 bombing of the World Trade Center, and the 1995 bombing of the Alfred P. Murrah Federal Building in Oklahoma City, to subsequent attacks on public and private American facilities, embassies and installations overseas, building performance and the ability of a structure to withstand blast have become two of the more important issues that engineers, architects, and building owners must address.

Engineering research after each terrorist event resulted in technological advances and evolving best practices designed to save lives, allow swift and complete building evacuation, and increase life safety. The events in Oklahoma City prompted an industry-wide examination of progressive collapse, reduction of the impact of flying glass, and minimization of damage to neighboring buildings during and after an event or disaster.

Much of the testing and evaluation of building systems and construction materials generated after the Oklahoma City bombing was produced for the federal government, initially under the auspices of the U.S. Department of Justice (USDOJ), with the participation of several federal agencies. In June 1995, USDOJ published *Vulnerability Assessment of Federal Buildings,* assessing the existing building inventory at the time. In October 1995, the Interagency Security Committee (ISC) was formed to create long-term design and construction standards for federal building security. The document, *ISC Security Design Criteria for New Federal Office Buildings and Major Modernization Projects,* issued in May 2001, was based on the USDOJ's earlier findings.

Although the security design criteria apply to federal facilities, the standards and mitigation strategies are applicable to state, local, and private sector buildings housing government agencies, government contractors, tenants requiring improved security levels, and owners seeking a greater degree of safety for their tenants and properties. With these standards, building owners, working with design and construction professionals, can develop a comprehensive security plan for a building or site. The security plan:

- Addresses risks, threats, design, operations, and technology requirements
- Identifies low probability, high risk threats to the building, known as abnormal loads
- Establishes the required structural performance

Transparent Security

Integrating design, operations, and technology into the security plan is the most effective way to achieve transparent security, invisible to the public eye. Sound structural systems and protective design principles are essential elements of maintaining transparent security and enhancing the built environment.

- Design encompasses planning, programming, design, and construction of physical protective barriers, such as walls, screens, floors, roofs, and standoff or the distance between the target and the blast threat.
- Operational security includes policies and procedures within a facility or organization. Operations address every aspect of emergency and disaster planning, and the role of personnel to ensure the safety of people and property.
- Technology is an integral part of security planning, and it works best when integrated early in project development with design and operational policies to achieve operational and capital savings. Selection of appropriate detectors, sensors, surveillance cameras, and other technology is ultimately a decision made by building owners, often based on the advice of security consultants or in-house experts.

PROTECTIVE DESIGN OF STRUCTURES

Protective design of buildings is accomplished by integrating into the architectural and engineering building design program various means of mitigating threats, such as biological, chemical, and radiological attack, and force protection from blast, fire, ballistic attack, and illegal entry.

Protective design of structures deals with the mitigation of force protection threats or abnormal loads acting on building structural framing and exterior walls. Protection is generally achieved through a combination of standoff, redundancy, and hardening.

- *Standoff*, in suburban settings, can be measured in hundreds of feet from public streets. Standoff of 350 feet or more is recommended for suburban sites, but is impractical in urban settings. However, even a few feet can make a substantial difference in terms of damage to the structure. Therefore, standoff in urban settings is no less critical to protective design of the structure.
- *Redundant systems* provide a means of surviving the unanticipated. Redundant structural systems are necessary for preventing progressive collapse.
- *Hardening* and energy absorptive shields can be used to enhance critical structural elements, walls, stairwells, loading docks, and windows where standoff alone is insufficient to reduce the threat to tolerable levels.

While each of these three strategies can be effective as protective measures, project constraints usually demand a combination of these three measures to provide a solution. For instance, in most urban environments, it is not practical to even consider a standoff of 350 feet. In urban centers, standoff of even 20 feet can have appreciable cost. Therefore, hardening and redundancy need to be incorporated into the design process to accommodate the effects of abnormal loads.

ABNORMAL LOADS

Abnormal loads on buildings may be caused by vehicular impact, blast loads from accidental or purposeful explosions, or local failure due to fire. Once the threat is defined, the structure must perform to a level consistent with established performance criteria, such as preventing structural collapse of part or all of the building.

Protection against abnormal loads incurs cost. To maximize the benefit of protection expense, the first step is determining where protection is needed. This is based on the assets housed in a building and the structural capabilities required for asset protection.

For example, if assets are housed within a building in a hardened, underground space, commonly known as a bunker, they may not be vulnerable to failure of a structural member supporting the building entrance canopy. Hardening the entrance canopy to provide additional protection will not achieve the security design goal of asset protection.

However, the asset may not be protected if a street level blast destroys a column supporting the building above, precipitating building collapse and destroying the bunker. In this case, increasing building resistance against collapse may be the most efficient means of increasing the protection level for the bunker and assets. The bunker is indirectly vulnerable to the failure of a street level column, but not the failure of the canopy support.

Identifying vulnerabilities requires establishing performance limits of critical and noncritical elements. Performance limits discern a failed member from a functional member, or a failed system from a functional system. In the example, the failure of a street level column can affect the performance of the bunker.

Risk assessment addresses the likelihood of potential threats and the structural vulnerability of a building. For example, the owner of a mid-rise building leasing space to a tenant threatened by a domestic organization with a history of using pipe bombs as a weapon of choice could decide to minimize the risk of severe structural damage or collapse. If a determination is made that severe structural damage will not occur from a pipe bomb, the risk of threat may be high, but the structural vulnerability to the potential threat is low. Operational security measures, such as increased security personnel, installation of surveillance cameras, and enhanced police presence may be sufficient deterrents to potential threats. Adding security film over windows or installing laminated glass may provide increased protection by reducing the risk of hazard from breakage of street-level glazing.

Determining likely threats against a building or site depends on the assets to be protected, the assets of adjacent facilities, and the profile of those likely to carry out potential threats (Table 22.1). Of the 199 international attacks reported by the U.S. Department of State in the 2002 report *Patterns of Global Terrorism 2002,* almost 70 percent were bombings, and 50 percent of the targets were businesses.

If a building is across the street from a target of organizations known to detonate vehicular bombs, the security solution for a pipe bomb threat may be inadequate. Vehicular bombs pose a greater threat to buildings because structural systems are more vulnerable to collapse from a car bomb than a pipe bomb, and the extent of glass damage increases significantly beyond the street level.

PROGRESSIVE COLLAPSE

Evaluating building performance against abnormal loads should consider the local impact of the threat and the consequences to adjacent structures and sites in the vicinity. For example, a bomb detonated on the street may affect the near column with a tremendous blast load. This single column member

TABLE 22.1 Description of Terrorist Organizations

Organization	Description
CONUS groups (continental U.S.)	• Ethnic and white supremacy groups • Generally threats are less severe than OCONUS terrorists • Objectives include death, destruction, and publicity
OCONUS groups (outside continental U.S.)	• Better organized and equipped than CONUS groups • Attacks are more severe and more frequent than CONUS groups
Paramilitary OCONUS groups	• Predominately ethnically or religiously based • Military capabilities, frequently state sponsored • Military and improvised weapons • Most serious attacks including suicide attacks • Predominately ethnically or religiously based

Source: Adapted from *Structural Design for Physical Security*, ASCE, 1999.)

must then be assessed or analyzed for the expected level of damage. If the column is expected to fail, the consequences should be considered for the surrounding structure and adjacent structures. At minimum, progressive collapse or more precisely, disproportionate collapse, of the structure should be prevented.

According to *Minimum Design Loads for Buildings and Other Structures,* SEI/ASCE 7-02:

> Progressive collapse is defined as the spread of an initial local failure from element to element eventually resulting in the collapse of an entire structure or a disproportionate large part of it.
>
> ... Some authors have defined resistance to progressive collapse to be the ability of a structure to accommodate, with only local failure, the notional removal of any single structural member. Aside from the possibility of further damage that uncontrolled debris from the failed member may cause, it appears prudent to consider whether the abnormal event will fail only a single member.

An example of limited local damage is containment of damage to adjacent bays and within two or three stories of a multistory structure. This damage may be the result of an explosion that damages the floors above and below the point of detonation and causes column failure. Restricting progressive collapse requires containing the damage to areas directly loaded.

Floors above should remain stable, yet may sustain damage due to loss of a column. Floor framing in bays not immediately adjacent to the affected framing should also remain stable. Lastly, lateral load systems provided to carry wind and seismic loads should not be depleted, but must have sufficient alternate load paths to remain viable systems.

Vulnerabilities identified can be mitigated. Mitigation may include hardening to increase strength, ductility enhancements to increase energy absorption, the addition of alternative or parallel systems to create redundancy, or any combination of these methods. Building vulnerabilities should be identified and performance levels assessed as part of the risk assessment and security plan.

STRUCTURAL SYSTEMS

Buildings must resist several forces:

• Vertical loads due to gravity
• Lateral loads due to wind
• Load effects due to seismic motion
• Loads due to blast and impact

Resistance is accomplished by integrating two load-carrying systems:

- Gravity load system
- Lateral load system

Gravity Load System

The gravity load system transfers or carries loads imposed by the forces of gravity. For steel or concrete-framed buildings, the load path starts on the floor slab, which carries the load to floor beams or joists. The beams or joists carry the load to the girders, which carry the load to the columns, and finally, from columns to footings, and to the ground.

Some concrete buildings consist of floor plates and columns without horizontal beams. In these cases, the columns support the floor plate, as four legs support a tabletop. In either case, each element of the gravity load system has a gravity load influence area.

Influence Area

The influence area establishes the load path hierarchy. The influence area of a member is determined by defining the total floor area that produces a load effect in the member upon the loading of that floor area. Influence areas are not restricted to a single floor, as with the case of columns or transfer girders.

The influence area is important when assessing potential for structural damage by failure of an element. Greater influence areas indicate more critical roles for the structural element. The influence area of a column can be an order of magnitude greater than for a floor beam or girder. The potential to cause substantial structural damage is much higher for failure of a column or bearing wall than for a beam or girder, although one is not always independent of the other.

For instance, beams often provide lateral restraint necessary to ensure column stability. If the beams are no longer capable of providing this restraint, a failure of the column may ensue. The hierarchy of the potential to cause structural damage follows the influence area of the element, with the highest level typically being the columns, then girders, and lastly, floor beams (Table 22.2).

TABLE 22.2   Lessons Learned from Oklahoma City: Influence Area

At the Alfred P. Murrah Building in Oklahoma City the front columns were spaced along the perimeter at 20 feet on center, and the next interior line of columns was 35 feet inward. Based upon this pattern, each perimeter column had an influence area of 1400 square feet per floor Figs. 22.1 and 22.2).

However, at the third floor, a transfer girder along the front supported every other column above. Only half the columns projected down through the third floor. The columns continuing to the ground carried the load from columns terminating at the third floor. The influence area of these columns increased twofold, from 1400 to 2800 square feet per floor as seen in the figure. If the members were ranked by importance to the gravity load system, these columns are on top of the list.

The loss of three of the lower level columns represented 6300 square feet of floor area at each floor, or 80 percent of the building's front bay.

Clearly, the collapse of a substantial part of the Alfred P. Murrah Building showed that progressive collapse must be avoided. The loss of life due to the collapse of the structure far exceeded the loss of life directly attributed to the blast. New designs should incorporate more redundancy to accommodate the loss of a perimeter column. Furthermore, lower level columns should be detailed to enhance ductility. This may require additional ties in reinforced concrete columns or increased flexural resistance of steel columns.

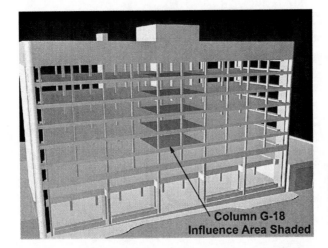

Column G-18
Influence Area Shaded

FIGURE 22.1 Influence area (shown shaded) of perimeter column G-18 of the Alfred P. Murrah Federal Building, Oklahoma City, Oklahoma. (*Source: LZA Technology.*)

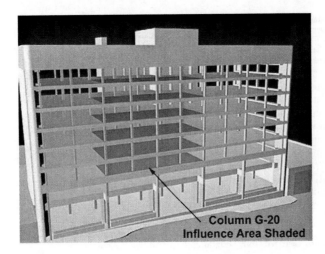

Column G-20
Influence Area Shaded

FIGURE 22.2 Influence area (shown shaded) of perimeter column G-20 of the Alfred P. Murrah Federal Building, Oklahoma City, Oklahoma. (*Source: LZA Technology.*)

Lateral Load System

The lateral load system carries horizontal load from the superstructure to the ground and provides resistance to overall and interstory lateral movement. Lateral loads are typically due to wind, but may be introduced by abnormal loads, such as a blast or impact. Resistance to interstory movement caused by lateral loads must be provided to ensure structural stability.

Structures can become unstable by buckling and collapse if they are too flexible or deform excessively due to lateral load or seismic motion. Lateral loads must be carried from floor to floor through:

- Flexural (bending) resistance of columns
- Diagonal braces spanning between floors
- Walls between floors; i.e., shear walls
- Combinations of these systems

STRUCTURAL REDUNDANCY

Structural systems must be capable of transferring load to supports or the ground. For a structure to be stable, at least one load path capable of carrying loads must exist within the structure. The load path must satisfy strength demands and static equilibrium. The structure must be restrained from moving as a rigid body or linkage. If the load path is interrupted, due to the effects of a bomb or blast, then the structure will collapse if no alternate load path is available. Redundancy in load paths allows redirection of loads to alternative load paths. This maintains structural integrity, should one load path fail.

For example, a table with three legs is stable, but should one leg be removed, the table will surely tip. Removal of one leg releases the restraint against movement of the table, causing it to become unstable. If one leg is removed from a four-legged table, the table will likely remain stable, as the other three legs continue to provide a stable load-bearing system. Alternate load paths provide redundancy.

Redundancy for gravity load systems can be tested mathematically by performing an analysis of the structure upon the removal of particular elements. An example would be removing a column from a structure. If one column can be removed and the structure remains stable, an alternate load path exists.

For modeling of federal buildings, the U.S. General Services Administration (GSA) recommends testing single-column removal of each column along the building perimeter to represent failure from blast or impact. As each column is removed, the remaining structure is tested to carry the self-weight of the constructed building, plus 25 percent of the live load. The reduction in live load is suggested since the probability of the extreme live load occurring at the time of an impact or blast is highly unlikely for most commercial office buildings.

There are structures where acceptable levels of damage are relatively low (where it is particularly important to limit the extent of damage). For example in stadiums and arenas where large masses of people are concentrated in one area for a short period of time, the main goal may be to provide clear egress from damaged to safe zones, for the most severe threat considered.

Multistory buildings can be grouped into highly redundant, moderately redundant, and non-redundant structural systems (Table 22.3).

- Highly redundant systems are those that can distribute loads in three dimensions, such as two-way moment frames, two-way truss systems, or two-way flat slab construction.

- Moderately redundant systems are those that have planar moment frames with seismic detailing, reinforced concrete frame structures with seismic detailing, structural systems that can develop catenary behavior, or reinforced masonry construction.

- Nonredundant systems are typically nonreinforced masonry structures, long-span trusses with little cross framing, light-framed steel structures with minimal lateral bracing, or lightly reinforced concrete structures with floor systems of flat plate construction. Corner bays of building floor plates are generally the most susceptible to collapse, since there is no continuity at two faces.

TABLE 22.3   Structural System Redundancy Levels for Multistory Buildings

Highly redundant	Moderately redundant	Nonredundant
Two-way steel or reinforced concrete moment frames with seismic detailing	Planar steel or reinforced concrete frames with seismic detailing	Nonreinforced masonry construction
Two-way truss systems	Structural systems that can develop catenary action	Light framed steel structures with minimal lateral bracing
Two-way flat slab construction	Reinforced masonry construction	Lightly reinforced concrete structures with flat plate construction

In practice, redundancy must be combined with standoff and hardening. Architects and engineers must understand the blast or impact loads and the behavior of structural elements to these loads if a balanced design is to be achieved.

BLAST LOADS

Blast loads are short duration loads produced by two physical occurrences (Fig. 22.3.).

- The first is the collision of the shock wave and the structure. The shock wave radiates spherically from the point of detonation at an extremely high rate of speed. A triangular load function provides a reasonable representation of the load function due to the shock wave. This overburden pressure is marked p_{so} in the figure.

- The second load is due to the air moving past the structure, similar to the pressure caused by wind. This is typically referred to as the gas pressure p_d. It is generally a longer duration load but of smaller magnitude than the load due to the shockwave.

Typical blast loads due to the shock wave vary for different threats defined by two parameters, standoff and TNT charge weight, resulting in pressure (pound per square inch, or psi), and impulse or integration of pressure and time (psi per millisecond, or psi/msec) (Table 22.4). These loads are provided as an equivalent uniform load over the height of a vertical element. The duration of the load can be computed given the pressure and impulse. For the common assumption of a triangular load function the duration is twice the impulse divided by the pressure. For example, if a 5-pound explosive is detonated 10 feet from a plate glass storefront, the glazing will be exposed to a dynamic pressure of 64 psi and an impulse of 43 psi/msec. The calculated duration is then 1.3 msec. Because members respond differently to ordinary, slow or static loads, and to quick blows, time dependent effects must be considered when evaluating structural performance for these short duration shock waves.

The time dependence is a function of the duration of the load, the flexibility of the structure or body being loaded, and the mass of that object. The time-dependent or dynamic load can be converted to an equivalent static load to compute member response. For the case of blast where the dynamic load can be considered to have an instantaneous peak and then decay linearly, the equivalent static load will be smaller for a flexible structure than for a stiff structure. In effect, the flexible structure can better "roll with the punch." Likewise, the static equivalent load will be smaller for a

FIGURE 22.3 Photograph of blast showing the shock wave front and fireball, and the pressure variation as the wave moves outward. Note the change in refracted light due to the change in air density at the shock wave front. (*Source: CHB Industries.*)

TABLE 22.4   Reflective Blast Pressure and Impulse for Various Bomb Threats

Standoff, ft)	TNT Charge weight, lb	Dynamic pressure, psi	Impulse, psi/msec
10	5	64	43
	10	120	71
	50	570	232
	150	1507	530
20	5	15	24
	10	25	39
	50	100	123
	150	307	277
	1000	1800	1200
50	5	4	10
	10	5	15
	50	12	47
	150	27	102
	1000	150	400
100	5	1.5	4.7
	10	2	7.5
	50	4	23
	150	7	48
	1000	24	180

Source: Computations based on TM5-855.

more massive structure than for a lighter structure. It takes more energy to get a massive structure to move, and movement is the source of internal forces. In general, as the period of the structure increases relative to the duration of the load, the equivalent static force decreases. Increasing the mass or increasing the flexibility results in longer building periods.

Given the typical structural properties of a storefront assembly, the approximate static equivalent load associated with the 5-pound bomb detonated at 10-foot standoff would be on the order of 7 psi. The pressure will diminish rapidly as one moves away to greater standoff distances. This peak local static pressure of 7 psi is sufficient to damage or even collapse a nonreinforced brick wall.

Most windows will fail at dynamic loads less than 2 psi. Therefore, it is probable that a non-hardened storefront will not have sufficient strength to withstand this threat. It is possible to harden a storefront for this threat by using laminated glass and frames engineered for blast load. To illustrate the effect of standoff, note that a building situated 50 feet away, perhaps across the street, would likely suffer little damage, perhaps minor glass damage.

Structural dynamics tools can evaluate how vulnerable a building will be to blast. Applying these techniques readily exposes vulnerabilities resulting from typical structural detailing and construction methods (Table 22.5).

STEEL CONSTRUCTION

When analyzing vulnerable building features, three conditions common in steel construction should be evaluated to ensure better performance. Most multistory steel buildings require columns to be spliced at every other floor since columns are generally provided in 36-foot to 45-foot lengths. The floor framing beams and girders are generally connected at the ends with connections capable of resisting the required gravity loads. These beam-to-column and beam-to-beam connections can play a role in the prevention or mitigation of progressive collapse. The taller high-rise buildings generally use built-up column sections at the base (Tables 22.6 and 22.7).

TABLE 22.5   Vulnerable Building Construction Features

Material	Area of vulnerability
Steel construction	• Column splices • Interconnectivity of components of built-up sections • Beam-to-column and beam-to-beam connections
Concrete construction	• Lack of sufficient ties and stirrups • Limited ductility • Brisance
Glass fenestration	• Brittleness of glass • Connection of frame to building • Connection of glass to frame • Limited ductility of frame

TABLE 22.6   9/11 Lessons Learned from the World Trade Center Collapse

Structural systems that are inherently redundant will perform well under duress. The two towers of the World Trade Center remained standing after the initial impact of the aircraft because their highly redundant perimeter tube structure redistributed the load around the damaged areas. The eventual collapse of the towers indicates that other assumptions regarding the interaction of fire and structure need to be considered for potential future threats.

It is generally acknowledged that steel frame buildings with fire protection will endure a building fire because the typical office environment does not provide enough fuel to sustain a fire for the duration needed to cause structural failure. The introduction of aircraft or diesel fuels changes the criteria. Means of preventing large deliveries of fuel, either from aircraft or storage within the building, must be improved. Furthermore, much of the spray-on fire protection was abraded from the steel during the aircraft impact and explosion, leaving the steel unprotected. For future terrorist threats, improved fire protection should be considered.

Hardening and increased redundancy of egress routes, emergency equipment, and emergency systems (electrical, mechanical, communication, and sprinkler) will enable a better emergency response. Typically, these systems are protected against fire by fire-rated dry wall enclosures. Hardening these enclosures to blast and impact should be considered.

TABLE 2.7   9/11 Lessons Learned from the Attack on the Pentagon

The area of the Pentagon directly impacted by the aircraft exhibited severe and extensive damage to the columns. The collapse of the floor above was significantly more limited. This has been attributed to:

• Redundancy of the reinforced concrete floor framing systems in the form of flexural continuity of the beams and girders through the columns and the ability of the exterior wall (non-load-bearing) to, in reality, carry floor load
• Short spans between columns that limit the remaining span should a column be removed
• Spiral reinforcement of the concrete columns that increase the capability of the column to carry axial load after sustaining damage due to blast and impact

Column Splices

For steel construction, the column splice location and strength of splice are critical. During a blast, the column must be capable of resisting the combined axial forces due to gravity loads above and the bending imposed by the blast loads. Most columns splice connections are located four to six feet above the floor, near the location of maximum stress within the column span. The column splice should not govern the strength of the column for combined effects of axial load and bending. Where blast loads are anticipated at particular floors, such as street level, the typical splice similar to the one shown in Fig. 22.4 may be moved to an upper level floor further from the point of detonation, or the strength of the column splice may be increased to accommodate the full flexural strength of the column.

Beam-to-Column and Beam-to-Beam Connections

Shear capacity of beam-to-column connections should be capable of resisting the shear associated with the full flexural strength of the beams. This prevents the shear connections from being the weak link, allowing a more ductile flexural failure of the beam. Aside from the shear forces, moment continuity or axial tension continuity should be considered to enhance the resistance to progressive collapse (Fig. 22.5). This continuity is critical if nonlinear geometric behavior, such as membrane

FIGURE 22.4 Photograph of a typical column splice detail. (*Source: Thornton-Tomasetti Engineers.*)

FIGURE 22.5 Photograph of typical beam-to-column connections. Detail A is a shear connection. Detail B is a moment connection providing moment and axial continuity through the column. (*Source: Thornton-Tomasetti Engineers.*)

behavior, is considered as a means of mitigating progressive collapse. Some building codes developed in environments where terrorism has been active, such as Great Britain, incorporate prescriptive requirements for axial tension continuity to mitigate progressive collapse.

Built-Up Sections

Built-up column sections are often used where columns exceed the dimensions of the rolled shapes. Traditionally, the components or elements of built-up members are interconnected, based upon local buckling criteria. Components are often interconnected with intermittent welds of minimal size. Columns built to these criteria will not achieve fully composite bending strength. To best mitigate load effects due to blast, the components should be interconnected to provide the full composite cross sectional capacity. In many cases, this capacity can be achieved with minor increases in weld material (Fig. 22.6).

CONCRETE CONSTRUCTION

Three aspects of concrete construction are often vulnerable to failure and should be carefully evaluated: shear failure, brisance, and limited ductility. Shear failure will occur when the shear force exceeds the shear strength of a member. Steel ties, stirrups, and spirals are used to reinforce concrete columns and beams, providing additional strength to supplement the relatively weak concrete shear strength.

Like the concrete shear strength, the concrete tensile strength or resistance to tension or pulling is also weak. Therefore, concrete elements are susceptible to a brisance failure from the effects of blast or impact. Furthermore, concrete is an inherently brittle material. Without steel or composite fiber reinforcement, the concrete will not sustain deformations typical of more ductile materials such as steel and iron. In general, concrete is used in construction because it is an inexpensive and readily available material with good compressive strength. Shear failure, brisance, and ductility are less dependent upon compressive strength and must be prevented from dominating the behavior.

Shear Failure

When subjected to blast loads, the columns of concrete frame buildings are susceptible to shear failure. This mode of failure is exhibited by a sliding movement parallel to a transverse crack and is generally

FIGURE 22.6 Photograph of built-up cross section. (*Source: Thornton-Tomasetti Engineers.*)

a less ductile mode of failure of concrete beams or columns. Closely spaced ties or spiral reinforcement in columns and stirrups in beams provide the traditional shear reinforcement of concrete members. For common-tie spacing, columns often lack sufficient shear strength to enable full flexural strength to be developed and a flexural failure to occur.

Shear failures should be avoided. Providing adequate shear reinforcement relative to the flexural reinforcement can prevent shear failure. Column ties can be spaced to provide sufficient shear strength to prevent a failure due to shear; however, this spacing is more stringent than the minimum column-tie spacing required by most codes. Concrete columns that are spirally reinforced or wrapped with composite fiber or steel jackets provide the best resistance to blast loads.

Shear failure in concrete members is generally nonductile. Ductility dramatically increases the energy absorption since energy is expended as an element deforms. Therefore, the more flexible but stable system will provide better blast resistance by preventing the shear failure from occurring with limited deformation and allowing a full flexural capacity to develop up to flexural failure with significantly larger deformation.

Brisance

Cement-based materials exhibit a relatively low tensile strength, often as little as 10 percent of the compression strength. When subjected to high pressures, concrete is susceptible to brisance, or the disintegration of the concrete (Table 22.8).

Limited Ductility

Reinforced concrete structures can exhibit tremendous ductility or virtually none at all. The ductility resides in the details of reinforcement. Therefore, concrete structures may be susceptible to nonductile modes of failure due to abnormal loads. Assessment of concrete structures should include a review of the details such as the arrangement of reinforcement in joints, at splices, and at anchorage points. Any improvement in detailing similar to those used in seismic design guides will enhance building performance under abnormal loads.

Enhancements

Structural system enhancements can often be provided at very little cost, but can significantly improve building performance (Table 22.9). Some of these enhancements are similar to the enhancements needed for seismic design. Improved ductility and redundancy are common threads for mitigating the effects of blast and seismic loads on structures because performance may be measured by limiting damage. Increased ductility and redundancy will limit damage. Therefore, much can be learned from seismic design of buildings; however, blast loads and seismic loads are different phenomenon that must be considered independently in the analysis and design.

TABLE 22.8   Lesson Learned from Oklahoma City: Brisance

Brisance accounted for the failure or disappearance of the column closest to the blast at the Alfred P. Murrah Federal Building in Oklahoma City. This column segment was never recovered, and is believed to have disintegrated. The dynamic blast pressures at this column were calculated to be well in excess of the compressive strength of the concrete.

Because the quantity of the explosive was large, brisance occurred even though the column was nearly 20 feet from the bomb. However, much smaller bombs can produce similar effects when placed nearer to the columns. Increased standoff, a steel jacket, or a blast shield can provide an effective means of mitigating brisance.

TABLE 22.9   **Enhancements for Protective Design in New Construction**

Material	Enhancement
Steel construction	• Increase weight of column sections at lower levels • Full moment connection splices at the lower level • Full moment capacity beam-to-column connections • Details emphasizing ductility
Concrete construction	• Spiral reinforcement or closely spaced ties in columns • Continuity of steel reinforcement • Higher concrete strength • Wraps or jackets around columns
Glass fenestration	• Laminated glass • Tempered glass • Higher glazing strength • Enhanced glass frame design

EXTERIOR WALL SYSTEMS

The glass used in windows, walls, and doors is one of the most fragile materials in building construction. Windows, walls, and doors typically consist of a frame and infill. In commercial applications, the frame is generally made of aluminum and the infill consists of a glass plate product. System performance depends on individual component performance, the interaction of components, and their connections to the supporting structure.

Glass Fenestration

Glass for building construction and fenestration is available in four forms:

• Annealed
• Heat strengthened
• Tempered
• Laminated

The most common glazing is annealed glass, followed by heat strengthened, tempered and laminated. These glazing types exhibit three distinct patterns of fracture:

• Annealed and heat strengthened glass fractures into large, sharp shards.
• Tempered glass fractures into much smaller fragments.
• Laminated glass is a composite of glass and polymer membrane or sheet interlayer. The fracture pattern of laminated glass depends upon the type of glass used as the outer layer, but whether annealed glass shards or tempered glass fragments, the glass is held fast by the interlayer (Fig. 22.7).

Window film can be applied to annealed or tempered glass as a means of retaining broken glass in the frame or in a single sheet. Preventing glass fragments from becoming airborne results in a safer environment. Anchoring window film may be achieved by various methods (Fig. 22.8).

Commercial application window frames are typically extruded aluminum products made of 6061 or 6063 aluminum. The 6063 material is often adequate for wind load resistance, but 6061 may be used if a stronger material is needed. Substituting laminated glass for annealed glass may not achieve the full benefits of laminated glass if the frame fails to hold or retain the glass. For the frame to retain

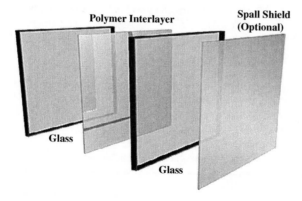

FIGURE 22.7 Structure of Laminated Glass. (*Source: LZA Technology.*)

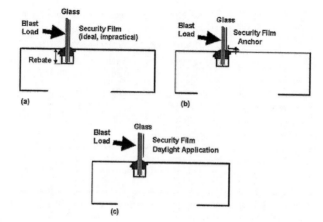

FIGURE 22.8 Anchorage of window film. (*Source: LZA Technology.*)

the glass, frame deformation should be consistent with the manner in which the glass is retained. As the unit is loaded, the frame and the glass will bend and deform. The deformation of the frame must be controlled to maintain active restraint of the glass. If the frame buckles and twists, the glass may be released. Sufficient glass area should be engaged to force the glass to shear, rather than slip through the frame. Enhancements can be provided by silicone reinforcement of the bite. The bite is the depth that the glass intrudes into the frame. Additional silicone reinforcement around the edge of the window increases the contact between the glass and the frame.

Catch Systems

An effective way of minimizing potential harm to building occupants from flying glass shards due to blast is through implementing a catch system. This mitigation technique is designed to catch glass sheets and pieces as they exit the frame. Because "daylight" window film installations hold glass together but do not necessarily hold glass in the frame, catch systems are frequently coupled with film applications.

A blast curtain catch system can be employed when window film or laminated glass is not a viable option. The curtains catch glass fragments as they enter the interior space, much as a net captures a ball or a puck in sports. Other systems incorporate cables or flexible bars to catch glass sheets held intact by film. The cable or cables are mounted inside the frame and deflect or capture an inward flying glass sheet because "daylight" window film installations hold glass together but do not necessarily hold glass in the frame.

Window Performance Criteria

GSA has developed recommendations for establishing fenestration performance levels (Table 22.10 and Fig. 22.9). Computer programs such as Wingard (available from the GSA—Office of the Chief Architect, www.oca.gsa.gov) provide predicted response of glass keyed to the GSA levels of protection or performance conditions.

TABLE 22.10   GSA-Recommended Criteria for Window Performance

Performance condition	Protection level	Hazard level	Window description
1	Safe	None	Glazing does not break. No visible damage to glazing or frame.
2	Very high	None	Glazing cracks but is retained by the frame. Dusting or very small fragments near sill or on floor acceptable
3a	High	Very low	Glazing cracks. Fragments enter space and land on floor no further than 3.3 ft from the window.
3b	High	Low	Glazing cracks. Fragments enter space and land on floor no further than 10 ft from the window
4	Medium	Medium	Glazing cracks. Fragments enter space and land on floor and impact a vertical witness panel at a distance of no more than 10 ft from the window at a height no greater than 2 ft above the floor.
5	Low	High	Glazing cracks and window system fails catastrophically. Fragments enter space impacting a vertical witness panel at a distance of no more than 10 ft from the window at a height greater than 2 ft above the floor.

Note: In conditions 2, 3a, 3b, 4, and 5, glazing fragments may be thrown to the outside of the protected space toward the detonation location.
Source: U.S. General Services Administration.

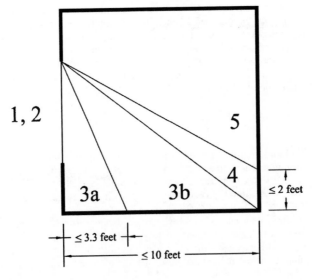

FIGURE 22.9 Schematic section of a room with a window, indicating distances, height, and GSA window performance conditions given in Table 22.10. (*Source: Adapted from U.S. General Services Administration.*)

MASONRY WALLS

Masonry construction is classified as load bearing and non-load bearing. Masonry provides a relatively high degree of protection against fire and ballistic impact. However, unless masonry is reinforced, there is little resistance to high explosives that are package-size or larger (Table 22.11).

Retrofit Improvements

Existing buildings may require upgrades or retrofits to accommodate required performance levels identified in the security plan (Table 22.12).

CONCLUSION

The lessons learned from Oklahoma City in 1995 and the events of September 11, 2001, at the World Trade Center and the Pentagon have alerted engineers and building designers to the importance of design for terrorist threats. Cost-effective protective design can be achieved through the appropriate balance of standoff, redundancy, and hardening measures. Future building designs should incorporate these concepts to improve the security of people who enter, occupy, and exit those buildings. A

TABLE 22.11   Masonry and Reinforced Concrete Walls Ranked by Protection Levels

Highest Level of Protection
1. 10-inch-thick concrete wall reinforced with #5 steel bars @12 inches on center each face
2. 12-inch-thick masonry block wall reinforced with #5 steel bars each face, each cell (based on two cells per block)
3. 12-inch-thick masonry block wall reinforced with #5 steel bars centered in each cell
4. 8-inch-thick masonry block wall reinforced with #5 steel bars centered in each cell
Lowest Level of Protection

TABLE 22.12   Retrofit Options for Protective Design

Material	Retrofit option
Steel construction	• Increase weld sizes between plates of built-up sections • Strengthen connections and splices • Strengthen members by adding steel plate reinforcement • Concrete encasement of columns • Energy absorbing blast shields around columns
Concrete construction	• Composite laminate wrap around columns • Steel jacketing of columns • Energy absorbing blast shields around columns
Glass fenestration	• Clear membranes anchored to frame • Catch systems such as cable or cloth
Masonry	• Composite laminate reinforcement • Improvement of lateral attachment to floor systems

security plan or program will help to identify the abnormal loads that should be considered in addition to the typical loads such as gravity and wind loads. The security program will also identify areas of the structure that may benefit from hardening, such as using concrete cores or hardened walls around egress stairs, hardened chases for mechanical and electrical emergency systems, and designing critical structural framing members to minimize structural damage and allow egress.

Protective design of existing building structures requires the identification of threats and the structure's vulnerability to those threats. Analysis of the structural system will identify the level of damage associated with threats on local and global scales. Retrofits may be required to reduce potential damage to a tolerable level. Maximizing the standoff, providing some local reinforcement of critical members, preventing nonductile modes of failure, and improving connections to enhance redundancy will create safer structures and better protect building occupants and property.

GLOSSARY

axial tension   Tensile forces acting along the longitudinal axis of the member.

bite   The distance that glass plate is embedded into a frame or the overlap of glass and frame.

brisance   The crushing or shattering effect of a high explosive on brittle materials.

column splice   The connection between upper and lower column segments. The splice is usually located a few feet above a typical floor level.

dead load   The weight of the structure including fixtures and partitions.

ductility   The ability of a material to stretch or deform under load prior to fracture or breaking.

fenestration   The arrangement, proportioning, and design of windows and doors in a building.

flexural   Of or relating to bending deformation of a beam or plate.

glazing   The glass surface of a glazed opening.

live load   The code-mandated variable or transient load for an occupancy.

membrane behavior   Shell or tensile fabric behavior where structures carry loads not by flexure but through tension or compression in the plane of the member. For example, an inflated balloon, a dome, or a net carries load through membrane action.

moment continuity   Detailing to provide flexural strength from beam through column to beam. For concrete structures, this entails providing steel reinforcement on the top and bottom faces of the beams through the intersecting column. For steel structures, it entails providing beam-to-column connections capable of transferring moment or bending forces.

progressive collapse   An initial local failure that spreads from element to element eventually resulting in the collapse of an entire structure or a disproportionately large part of it.

shear failure   Failure of a beam or plate by offset displacement across a cross-sectional plane that is transverse for direct shear or at 45 degrees for diagonal shear.

standoff   The distance between, or the proximity of, the target to the blast threat.

BIBLIOGRAPHY

Abruzzo, J., and Panariello, G. F., "Reduce Damage, Increase Safety," *The Military Engineer*, Society of American Military Engineers, vol. 95, n. 625, Sept.-Oct. 2003.

American Society of Civil Engineers, *Minimum Design Loads for Buildings and Other Structures*, SEI/ASCE 7-02, Reston, Va., 2003.

American Society of Civil Engineers, *Structural Design for Physical Security: State of the Practice,* Committee Report, Reston, Va., 1999.

Biggs, John M., *Introduction to Structural Dynamics,* McGraw-Hill, New York, 1964.

Bulson, P.S., *Explosive Loading of Engineering Structures,* E & FN Spon (Spon Press), London, 1997.

Smith, P.D., and Hetherington, J.G., *Blast and Ballistic Loading of Structures,* Butterworth Heinemann, Oxford, 1994.

INTERNET RESOURCES

American Concrete Institute (ACI)
www.aci-int.org

American Institute of Steel Construction (AISC)
www.aisc.org

American Society of Civil Engineers (ASCE)
www.asce.org

Blast Mitigation Action Group
http://bmag.pecp1.nwo.usace.army.mil

CHB Industries (Window Films)
http://www.chbwindowfilm.com

Civil Engineering Magazine
www.pubs.asce.org/ceonline/newce.html

Concrete International
www.concreteinternational.com

Council on Tall Buildings and Urban Habitat (CTBUH)
www.ctbuh.org

Engineering News Record
www.enr.com

Journal of Architectural Engineering
www.pubs.asce.org/journals/ae.html

Modern Steel Construction
www.aisc.org/MSCTemplate.cfm

National Institute of Building Sciences (NIBS)
www.nibs.org

National Institute of Standards and Technology (NIST)
www.nist.gov

Protective Glazing Council (PGC)
www.protectiveglazing.org

Protective Technology Center (PTC)
www.ptc.psu.edu

The Society of American Military Engineers (SAME)
www.same.org

The Thornton-Tomasetti Group Inc.
www.thettgroup.com

U.S. Department of Homeland Security (USDHS)
www.dhs.gov

U.S. General Services Administration (USGSA) Public Building Service
www.gsa.gov

CHAPTER 23
MECHANICAL, ELECTRICAL, AND FIRE PROTECTION DESIGN

Andrew Hlushko, PE
Senior Vice President, Flack + Kurtz Inc.
New York, New York

*Let every nation know, whether it wishes us well or ill, that
we shall pay any price, bear any burden, meet any hardship,
support any friend, oppose any foe, to assure the survival and
success of liberty.*

JOHN F. KENNEDY (1917–1963)
35th U.S. president

*One of the greatest discoveries a man makes, one of his great
surprises, is to find he can do what he was afraid he couldn't do.*
HENRY FORD (1863–1947)
U.S. automobile industrialist

The post-September 11th world has forced building services engineers to refocus and realign priorities
when embarking on mechanical and electrical system design. As one of the most essential, yet transparent, security elements in buildings, invisible to the public, engineering systems provide many
aspects of life safety and security. When building for life safety, mechanical and electrical systems are
successfully integrated with design, technology, and operational procedures, thus collectively providing a level of security far surpassing anything deemed necessary before September 11, 2001.

A building's mechanical and electrical systems brings its architecture to life. Mechanical and electrical systems include heating, ventilation and air conditioning (HVAC), power distribution, lighting,
fire alarm, plumbing, fire protection, and communications systems. Building occupants depend on
reliable and ongoing operation of these engineering systems.

Health care institutions, criminal justice buildings, power plants, financial institutions, and other
critical public facilities have established design criteria requiring mechanical, electrical, and plumbing
(MEP) systems to be extremely reliable.

Building owners should undertake a risk assessment and threat analysis to determine vulnerabilities
in the physical plant and identify potential solutions for security and optimal system reliability. Risk
assessments analyze probability of system availability and single points of failure and determine
mean time between failures (MTBF) and mean time to repair (MTTR). A typical criterium utilized
by financial institutions, for example, is Sigma 6, which equates to systems being available 99.9999
percent of the time (Tables 23.1 and 23.2).

The design approach for a new building, or safety assessment of an existing facility, must review the
site and overall environment. Similarly, a mechanical and electrical system design depends on unique
site and building conditions (Table 23.3).

TABLE 23.1   Checklist for Assessing Fire Risk

1. Does the building have an automatic sprinkler system?
2. Does the building have a standpipe system?
3. Does the building have an audible and visual alarm system and does it automatically notify the emergency response team?
4. Does the building have a fire or smoke detection system?
5. What is the water source for the fire protection system?
6. Does the building have a smoke management system?
7. Is the smoke management control system part of a documented and regular building maintenance program?
8. Does the building have an emergency power system? Where is its fuel source located?
9. Is emergency lighting provided so that occupants can clearly find the path of egress from the building, and what is the power source?
10. Does the building have a public address system so that building management and emergency responders can effectively communicate with building occupants?

Source: Flack + Kurtz.

TABLE 23.2   Building Risk Assessment Criteria

1. Location: urban, suburban, or rural environment
2. Prominent address
3. Ease of vehicular approach
4. Property's tenants
5. Nearest neighbors
6. Building function

TABLE 23.3   Site and Building Considerations for Mechanical and Electrical System Design

1. Property's tenants
2. Business types
3. Prominence of businesses, tenants, individuals occupying the building
4. Brand names
5. Property location
6. Proximity to significant addresses, such as government facilities

Engineering systems design and appropriate use of technology are essential to assuring the reliability, ongoing operations, and security of the building against potential hazards, including fire, earthquakes, windstorms, explosions, and biochemical attacks.

CODES AND STANDARDS

Building and life safety codes and standards provide the basis for design and construction of safe environments. These guidelines, however, cannot account for every situation. Building codes and guidelines, such as the *New York City Building Code, International Building Code* (ICC), and *National Electrical Code* (NFPA), have been developed and modified over the years addressing fire and natural disasters, from hurricanes to tornadoes. The need for enhanced security within the built environment has prompted a comprehensive review of how best to address and anticipate potential disasters resulting from terrorist acts. These disasters would include immediate and total building evacuation, introduction of biochemical hazards in ventilation systems, and the extent of sprinklers and fire protection in high-risk buildings and facilities.

The prescriptive nature of building codes cannot apply to every situation. Each building and project must address the performance of all individual components within overall building systems. The primary goals of high-performance building design are to:

- Decrease exposure to risks
- Mitigate effects of potentially catastrophic events
- Increase probability of achieving full and safe evacuation in the event of a disaster

ELECTRICAL SERVICE

The security of a building's electrical service relies on the service provider and facility location. For example, in an urban environment, the system may be arranged as a network with services to a building consisting of multiple underground feeders, multiple transformers, and may have redundancy built into the integrity and reliability of the service. Alternatively, in a suburban or rural environment, services may be transported by overhead transmission lines, which are susceptible to damage by natural disasters and more accessible for human intervention.

Emergency generators supply power to critical building and life safety systems that must maintain operations during utility power loss. Critical life safety systems include fire pumps, elevators, smoke management systems, emergency egress lighting, and fire alarm systems. Due to the life safety aspects of these systems, especially when occupants are forced to evacuate a building, emergency generators must respond when called upon to operate. System responsiveness depends on availability, design, use of appropriate technology, maintenance, and the presence of knowledgeable facility staff who are familiar with operating sophisticated building technology and systems. Redundant emergency power systems increase the likelihood that systems will be available when called upon. Ideally, redundant systems should be located remote from each other.

As an example, the emergency generator system of the World Trade Center (WTC) in New York City was located in a basement level. The system was made up of multiple generators, that relied on a remote cooling system provided through a single set of pipes. The WTC bombing in 1993 caused damage to these pipes, which resulted in the generators being inoperable. The system was highly reliable based on the prevalent criteria of the period when designed.

After September 11th and increased security concerns, design criteria were enhanced with emergency power systems (Table 23.4). For example, each generator could supply specific loads, and distribution systems could be interconnected for backup (Fig. 23.1).

Many building codes mandate periodic testing of emergency generator systems, to ensure systems remain in working order at all times. Testing also familiarizes building operating personnel with system operations and better prepares them to react quickly and correctly under the pressures of an emergency situation.

WATER SERVICES

Building occupancy is highly dependent on water source availability. Water for potable and non-potable uses, and make-up water for HVAC systems, is required under normal operating conditions. During emergency conditions, water is required for fire suppression.

TABLE 23.4   Key Elements of an Enhanced Emergency Power System

1. Redundant systems
2. Diverse locations
3. Interconnected distribution systems
4. Secure and hardened enclosures

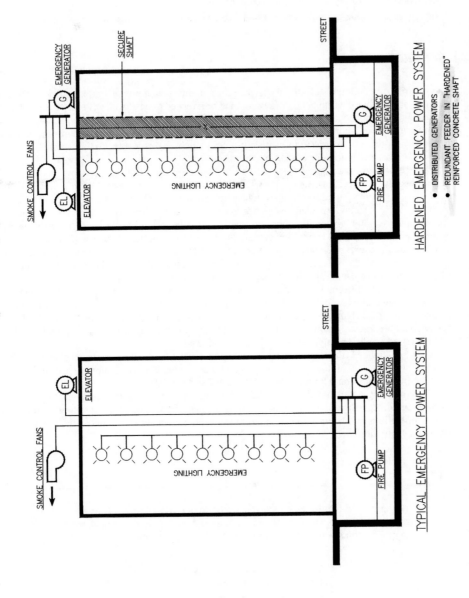

FIGURE 23.1 Improved emergency power system, indicating a typical emergency power system and hardened emergency power system. (*Source: Flack + Kurtz.*)

Water sources vary for each building and could include a municipal water supply, private water supply, or supply from a well. Reliability of the water supply should be reviewed during a facility threat analysis and risk assessment. Depending on local conditions, an on-site water storage system may be required. Hospitals, research laboratories, utility generating facilities, and other mission-critical facilities are highly dependent on water availability. In such cases, alternative water sources should be considered during facility planning and design.

Many codes require provision of redundant water services from public utility or municipal supplies. Providing redundant water sources following different routes to the facility and entering the building at different, remote locations should be considered for moderate- to high-risk buildings. Where these services combine, appropriate check valves should be installed as part of the design to protect against an internal pipe break, so as to prevent rendering both services nonoperational. Building codes or building location often require on-site water storage. The location and quantity of storage tanks, piping and valve configuration, quantity and arrangement of pumping facilities, and maintenance of these systems will impact system availability and reliability.

Fire pumps are required for facilities lacking adequate water service main pressure to reliably supply building fire suppression systems. Effective operation is essential for providing sprinkler and standpipe building services. Nonoperational fire pumps could endanger a facility and building occupants in an emergency. Providing redundant fire pumps in different locations, with independent electrical supplies and controllers, can enhance fire pump system reliability. Consideration should be given to providing one electrically operated pump and one diesel-driven pump, to offer greater diversity. Failure of the primary electric service would allow the electric pump to be supplied from the diesel emergency generator and the other pump to be driven by the internal diesel engine. Should the diesel emergency generator fail to operate, a fire pump would still be available to support the building fire suppression system.

FIRE SUPPRESSION SYSTEMS

Fire suppression systems, specifically for fully sprinklered buildings, have dramatically decreased the number of fire-related deaths over the years. Fire containment and suppression by sprinkler systems limit the spread of fire and increase evacuation time available for building occupants (Table 23.5).

Sprinkler and standpipe systems are often combined, although the extent of piping used for sprinkler systems is far greater than piping used for standpipes. Sprinkler coverage requires that vertical riser piping and branch piping extend to all areas of each building floor. Given the extent of piping, failure of a sprinkler pipe, potentially caused by pipe failure or a blast event, would render the standpipe system inoperable for fire department use, in addition to quickly exhausting the fire reserve. Dedicated, vertical standpipe systems can be more easily protected from failure than horizontal sprinkler systems. Vertical piping can be encased within hardened shafts, which can be integrated with hardened enclosures for stairwells or fire vestibules (Fig. 23.2).

TABLE 23.5   Enhanced Fire Suppression System Considerations

1. Reliability of water source
2. Redundant fire pumps
3. Types of fire pumps, e.g., electric, diesel
4. Interconnection of water services
5. Quick-acting check valves
6. Separation of sprinkler and standpipe systems
7. Location and/or vulnerability of fire-protection piping
8. Flow limiting or flow shut-off valves

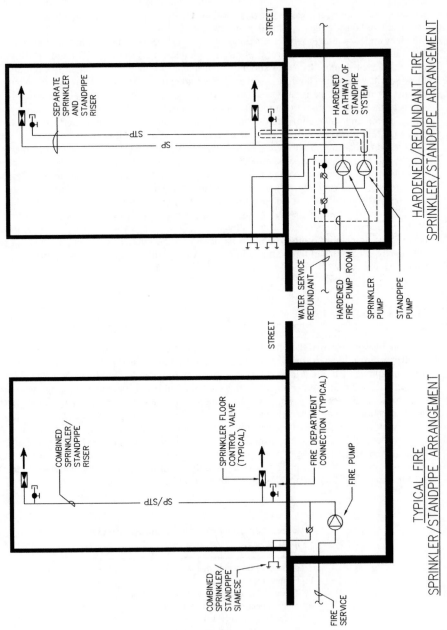

TYPICAL FIRE SPRINKLER/STANDPIPE ARRANGEMENT

HARDENED/REDUNDANT FIRE SPRINKLER/STANDPIPE ARRANGEMENT

FIGURE 23.2 Improved sprinkler and standpipe systems, indicating a typical fire sprinkler/standpipe arrangement, and a hardened/redundant fire sprinkler/standpipe arrangement. (*Source: Flack + Kurtz.*)

Sprinkler system reliability depends on water availability, with minimal opportunity for system failures in the event of a fire or emergency. Tamper and basic flow alarms identify when the system may not be prepared to deliver water when needed. The value of introducing other water flow control measures, such as automatic valves, in high-risk installations to provide flow limiting or flow shut-off valves on sprinkler systems should be assessed. These valves would limit flow or shut-off on excessive flow, such as a pipe break, thereby conserving the water supply.

FIRE ALARM SYSTEM

The detection, annunciation, and communication functions of building fire alarm systems are essential to safety and security within the built environment. Fire alarm systems can be the focal points for all information throughout a building in an emergency (Tables 23.6 and 23.7).

Fire command centers provide vital information to local fire departments responding to emergencies. The fire command center is typically located at the main building entrance, together with the central security control center. Should this area become inaccessible due to an external or internal event, information available to the emergency response team will be impacted (Table 23.8).

TABLE 23.6   Fire Alarm System Integrity Considerations

1. Fire command center located in a protected location and a redundant fire command center
2. Fire alarm system architecture provided with distributed modular intelligence
3. Cable distribution looped and isolated
4. Addressable devices to locate events and faults
5. A well-thought-out, extensive response plan
6. An explicit, comprehensive audio-visual annunciation program
7. Redundant, hardened connectivity to notification devices

TABLE 23.7   Building Systems Interfacing and Communicating with Fire Alarm Systems

1. Fire suppression systems
2. Elevator systems
3. Emergency power system
4. Security systems
5. Smoke control systems
6. Ventilation systems
7. Building automation systems.

TABLE 23.8   9/11 Lessons Learned: Building Information Cards

After the events of September 11, the New York City Department of Buildings World Trade Center Building Code Task Force recommended that all high-rise office buildings maintain a Building Information Card (BIC) listing a building's vital information.

The information would be located at the fire command center, readily accessible to the responding fire department. Categories of information to be provided include: occupancy, building statistics, elevators, stairways, communications, fire safety, water supply, utilities, temporary considerations, hazardous materials locations, ventilation, and a schematic plan for indicating locations of elevators, mechanical equipment rooms, access stairs, and standpipes (Figs. 23.3, 23.4, and 23.5).

FIRE DEPARTMENT, CITY OF NEW YORK
BUILDING INFORMATION CARD

BUILDING INFO:
Address: _____
Aka: _____
Date Constructed: _____
Office Floors:_____
Retail Floors:_____
Residential Floors:_____
Building Population: _____
Day: _____ Night:_____ Weekend: _____
Location of Disabled Persons _____

BUILDING STATISTICS:
Height: _____
Width: _____
Type of Construction: _____
Type of Fire Proofing: _____
Stories: _____
Truss Systems Locations:_____
Fire Tower: _____

ELEVATORS:
Bank Designation   Car Numbers   Floors Served
_____   _____   _____
_____   _____   _____
_____   _____   _____
Location of Freight Elevators: _____
Sky Lobby Locations: _____

STAIRWAYS:
Designation   Floors Served   Pressurized   Standpipe
_____   _____   _____   _____
_____   _____   _____   _____
_____   _____   _____   _____
Access /Convenience Stair Located Between Floors:
_____   _____   _____   _____
Roof Access Provided by Stairways:.
_____   _____   _____   _____

COMMUNICATIONS:
Repeater System: _____
Number of Radios for FDNY Use: _____
Communications for FDNY Use:_____

BUILDING FIRE SAFETY INFO:
(including Emergency Contact numbers)

Fire Safety Director: _____
  Work: ( )___-___
  Cell: ( )___-___
Building Engineer: _____
  Work: ( )___-___
  Cell: ( )___-___
Managing Agent: _____
  Work: ( )___-___
  Cell: ( )___-___

WATER SUPPLY:
Standpipe Locations: _____
S/P Isolation Valve Locations:_____
Fully Sprinklered: _____
Partially Sprinklered: Floors ___ ___ ___ ___
Fire Pump Locations: _____
Flow Restrictors on S/P? Floors _____

UTILITIES:
Fuel Oil Tank Location: ___ ___ ___ ___
Fuel Oil Tank Capacity: ___ ___ ___ ___
Natural Gas Service: _____
Emergency Generator Location: _____

TEMPORARY CONSIDERATIONS *(TO BE FILLED IN WITH ERASABLE MARKINGS)*
Examples—Construction in building, OOS systems

HAZARDOUS MATERIALS & LOCATIONS:

NAME OF PRODUCT   LOCATION
_____   _____
_____   _____
_____   _____

VENTILATION:
HVAC Zones: _____
Smoke Removal Capacity: _____

INDICATE ON BUILDING SCHEMATIC (NEXT PAGE) THE LOCATION OF FOLLOWING CRITICAL ITEMS USING THE APPROPRIATE SYMBOL

| E | ELEVATORS
| MER | MECHANICAL ROOMS
| AS | ACCESS STAIRS
| SP | STANDPIPES

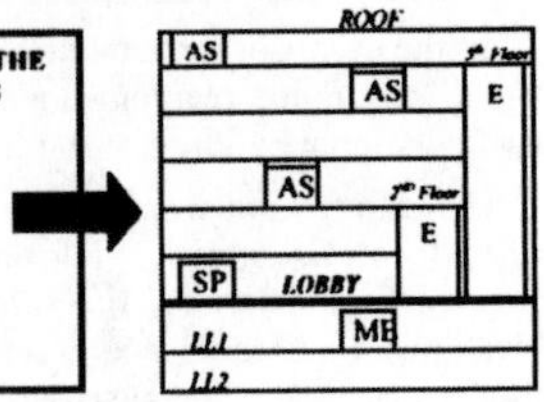

ROOF
AS
AS   E   1st Floor
AS   7th Floor
E
SP   LOBBY
111   ME
112

FDNY: August 2002

FIGURE 23.3   Proposed New York City Building Information Card. *(Source: City of New York Department of Buildings.)*

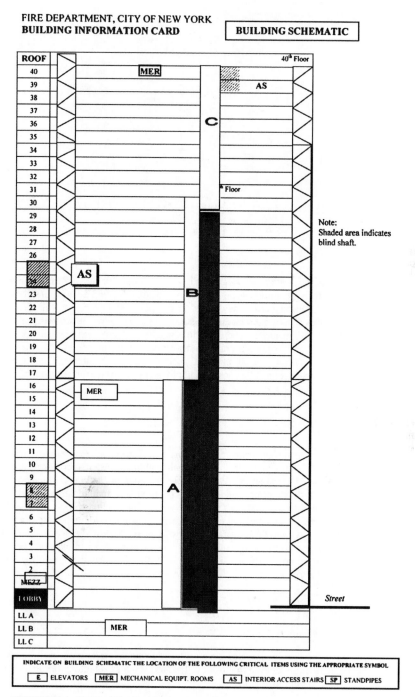

FIGURE 23.4 Proposed New York City Building Information Card, with building schematic. *(Source: City of New York Department of Buildings.)*

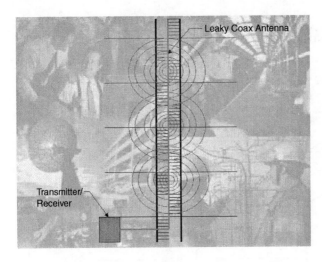

FIGURE 23.5   Maintaining wireless connectivity. *(Source: Flack + Kurtz.)*

Providing an alternate or slave fire command center in a protected area duplicating the control and monitoring features of the fire command center should be considered during the risk assessment analysis. Additional costs may be offset by operational necessity (Fig. 23.6).

Fire alarm systems are integral to emergency preparedness plans and policies developed by building owners, facility managers, and operations personnel. Continued operation of all fire alarm system components is critical to gaining a rapid understanding of overall building conditions and systems. Fire alarm system design must consider eliminating single points of failure and continued system operation. Each system component must be considered individually, as well as the integrated, overall system (Fig. 23.7).

VENTILATION SYSTEMS

Buildings are complex structures that must be able to breathe in order to make them safe and habitable for occupants. Introducing fresh air through ventilation systems provides a high level of indoor air quality. Air intake louvers are the links between the outdoors and the built environment. Ventilation system design, system component technology, operation, and maintenance are critical to ventilation system reliability and security. At the same time, ventilation systems will distribute airborne contaminants, biochemical hazards, and particles to all points throughout a building, posing serious potential health hazards.

Fresh air is introduced to the building at air intake louvers. Realistically, there is no air block or other way to prevent foreign substances from entering an air intake once access is gained. Depending on facility vulnerability and risk factors, restricting access to air intake areas may be achieved through the following:

- Ordinary lock and key
- Intruder alarms
- Security cameras

Locating louvers and air intake grilles high above grade level, where they will be relatively inaccessible to those seeking to introduce hazardous materials into building air distribution system, is the best way to minimize risk.

- The U.S. General Services Administration (GSA) guidelines require that louvers be located a minimum of 40 feet above ground level.

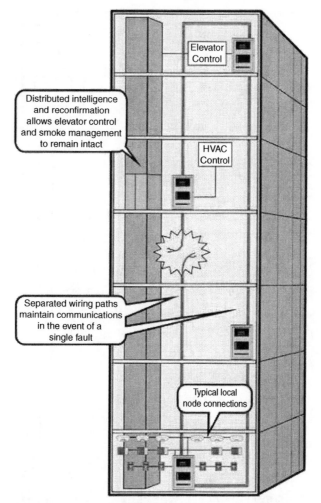

FIGURE 23.6 Improved fire alarm system with redundant risers and distributed intelligence. Preferred Style 7 (Class A) communications routing in high-rise buildings. *(Source: Flack + Kurtz.)*

- The NYC Department of Buildings World Trade Center Building Code Task Force recommends that air intakes in all new construction be located at least 20 feet above grade and away from exhaust discharges or off-street loading bays.

Careful coordination of air intake louvers and grilles is a critical issue between engineers and architects on any building type, to achieve a balance among aesthetics, security, and function (Fig. 23.8).

Mechanical equipment that conditions and distributes air throughout a building consists of various components, including filters, cooling and heating coils, fans, diffusers, and final filters. Air filters remove a percentage of particles from the air. Standard filters, used in office buildings, are typically 85 percent dispersed oil particulate (DOP) filters. In hospitals, laboratories, clean rooms, and other installations that require cleaner environments, the air filters that are generally specified are 95 percent DOP, electrostatic filters, or 99.97 percent HEPA. Air filtration for biochemical hazards could be increased with the installation of activated carbon filters and ultraviolet light systems (Fig. 23.9).

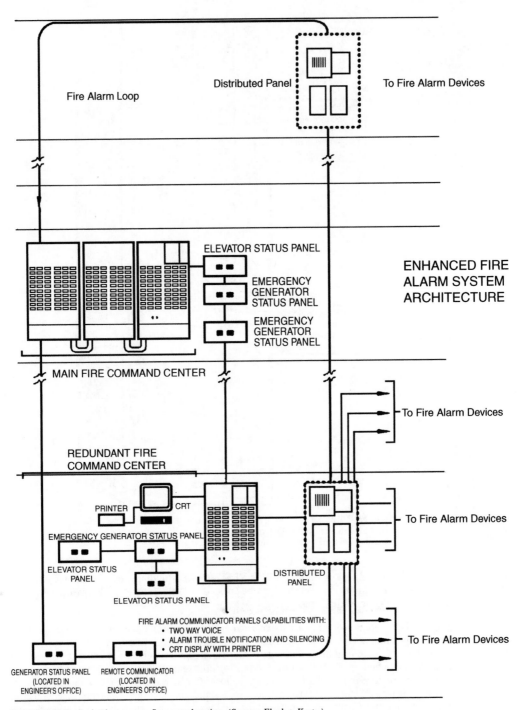

Distributed Panel

To Fire Alarm Devices

Fire Alarm Loop

ELEVATOR STATUS PANEL

EMERGENCY GENERATOR STATUS PANEL

EMERGENCY GENERATOR STATUS PANEL

ENHANCED FIRE ALARM SYSTEM ARCHITECTURE

MAIN FIRE COMMAND CENTER

To Fire Alarm Devices

REDUNDANT FIRE COMMAND CENTER

PRINTER   CRT

EMERGENCY GENERATOR STATUS PANEL

ELEVATOR STATUS PANEL

ELEVATOR STATUS PANEL

To Fire Alarm Devices

DISTRIBUTED PANEL

FIRE ALARM COMMUNICATOR PANELS CAPABILITIES WITH:
• TWO WAY VOICE
• ALARM TROUBLE NOTIFICATION AND SILENCING
• CRT DISPLAY WITH PRINTER

To Fire Alarm Devices

GENERATOR STATUS PANEL (LOCATED IN ENGINEER'S OFFICE)

REMOTE COMMUNICATOR (LOCATED IN ENGINEER'S OFFICE)

FIGURE 23.7   Redundant remote fire control station. *(Source: Flack + Kurtz.)*

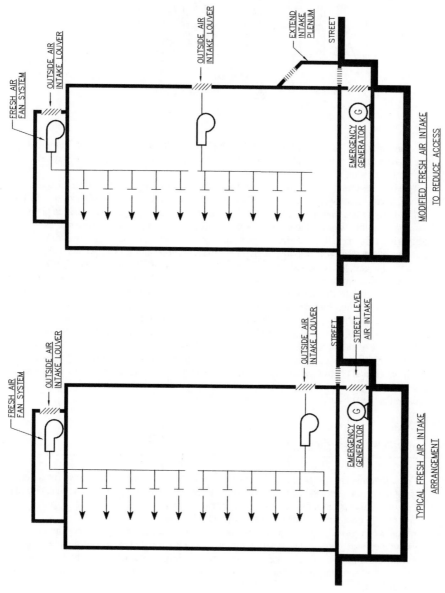

FIGURE 23.8 Improved ventilation system, illustrating a typical fresh air intake and a modified fresh air intake to reduce access. (*Source: Flack + Kurtz.*)

23.13

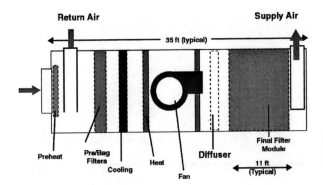

FIGURE 23.9 Chemical-biological air handling system. *(Source: Flack + Kurtz.)*

Ventilation system design utilizing high-efficiency filtration would result in increased first costs, due to the need for larger fan motors to overcome added static pressure of the system and increased operating costs.

Risk assessments can assist in identifying the most appropriate filtration. For example, the U.S. Department of State advocates cascading pressure relationships in combination with HEPA filters, and does not allow internal recirculation between spaces. Typically, there are three pressure zones: the lowest for public spaces, the second for state department work areas, and the highest for critical areas requiring clearance. This zoning helps minimize distribution of an internally released contaminant.

Because mechanical systems distribute air to all building areas, in addition to limited louver access, restricted access to primary air systems minimizes the risk of introducing chemical-biological hazards. Mechanical isolation of certain areas with dedicated HVAC systems, such as mailrooms and loading docks, will limit the likelihood of contaminants entering through these semipublic areas and infiltrating the entire building. Systems serving these spaces would have dedicated air intakes, could be provided with higher ventilation rates, and would not transfer air to other areas of the building (Table 23.9).

Sensors quick and reliable enough to automatically initiate appropriate protection modes of operation are not readily available in the marketplace. However, air-quality detection systems are a primary focus for research and development divisions of major manufacturers. Sophisticated building automation and control systems enable quick responses by building operations personnel in emergencies. Building control systems can quickly shut down other systems and isolate a facility from further contaminant exposure.

SMOKE MANAGEMENT SYSTEMS

HVAC systems are controlled by a building automation system, which allows for quick response to shutdown or for selectively controlled airflow throughout the building. When managing the migration of smoke , this system must be closely coordinated with the fire alarm system. Together, these systems can assist in containing smoke to a specific building area.

Stairwell pressurization is an integral part of a smoke management strategy. The stair pressurization system increases stairwell air pressure to prevent smoke from entering, thus maintaining a clear egress path for building evacuees. In the event of a mass building evacuation, many doors into the stairwell will be open simultaneously and maintaining positive pressure relative to adjoining spaces will be very difficult.

Introducing stairwell vestibules with associated pressurization systems would provide a buffer between egress stairwells and occupied floor areas. The vestibules, if adequately sized, could be utilized as areas of refuge assistance for those not physically able to use the stairs, thereby providing places for building occupants to await emergency evacuation assistance.

TABLE 23.9   Chemical or Biological Threat Considerations

1. Protection of air inlets
2. Recording of visitors for future notification of exposure
3. Airflow isolation of vulnerable functions, e.g., mailrooms, loading docks
4. Filtration enhancement only for extreme threats
5. Effective detection coming in the future

Building elevator shafts can function as chimneys, allowing floor-to-floor air migration. In the event of a fire, smoke from the fire floor may migrate to an adjacent higher floor. Similarly, these shafts provide a path for airborne contaminants, such as chemical or biological hazards, to spread through a building. A high-risk building may need isolated elevator lobbies with pressurization systems designed to limit or eliminate migration of smoke and contaminants into the elevator lobby. Because elevator lobbies are often substantial in size, these spaces may also function as areas of refuge for physically impaired occupants.

CONCLUSION

The security of buildings and safety of occupants continue to evolve as the dangers and threats change. The design of a building's mechanical and electrical systems is also evolving to meet these new criteria. Each event, from the World Trade Center bombing, anthrax mailings, to natural disasters, is typically followed by an evaluation of system performance by a task force.

Not all security and enhancement measures are appropriate for every building. The owner and design team must assess the potential threat to the building and the tenants and identify the most appropriate performance-based solutions. Technological advances must be closely monitored and analyzed for potential application to the building services. The design of building systems, development, and integration of new technologies into this design, and the training and preparedness of building operators and first responders, collectively provide an integrated approach to enhanced security and safety.

ACKNOWLEDGMENTS

- Norman D. Kurtz, PE, Chairman, Flack + Kurtz Inc., New York, New York
- Daniel H. Nall, FAIA, PE, Senior Vice President, Flack + Kurtz Inc., New York, New York
- Robert Sedlak, PE, Senior Vice President, Flack + Kurtz Inc., New York, New York

BIBLIOGRAPHY

Council on Tall Buildings and Urban Habitat, *Building Safety Assessment Guidebook,* Bethlehem, Pa., 2002.

Council on Tall Buildings and Urban Habitat, *Building Safety Enhancement Guidebook,* Bethlehem, Pa., 2002.

Isner, Michael S., and Thomas J. Klem, *Fire Investigation: Report World Trade Center Explosion and Fire.* National Fire Protection Association, Quincy, Mass., Feb. 26, 1993.

Kurtz, Norman D., Andrew Hlushko, and Dan Nall, "Engineering Systems and an Incremental Response to Terrorist Threat," *Building Standards,* July/Aug. 2002.

New York City Department of Buildings, *World Trade Center Building Code Task Force Findings and Recommendation,* Feb. 2003. www.nyc.gov/html/dob/pdf/wtcbctf.pdf (Building Information Card is found on pp. 42 and 43 of the pdf.)

U. S. Department of Health and Human Services, *Guidance for Protecting Building Environments from Airborne Chemical, Biological, or Radiological Attacks*, May 2002, DHHS (NIOSH) Publication No. 2002-139.

INTERNET RESOURCES

American Society of Civil Engineers (ASCE)
www.asce.org

American Society for Healthcare Engineering (ASHE)
www.ashe.org

American Society of Heating, Refrigeration and Air-Conditioning Engineers (ASHRAE)
www.ashrae.org

American Society of Mechanical Engineers (ASME)
www.asme.org

Building Standards Magazine Online
www.icbo.org/Building_Standards_Online/

Council on Tall Buildings and Urban Habitat (CTBUH)
www.ctbuh.org

Civil Engineering Magazine
www.pubs.asce.org/ceonline/newce.html

Construction Specifications Institute (CSI)
www.csinet.org

Engineering News Record
www.enr.com

Engineering Times Online
www.nspe.org/1et.asp

Flack + Kurtz Inc.
www.flackandkurtz.com

IEEE Spectrum
www.spectrum.ieee.org

Institute of Electrical and Electronics Engineers (IEEE)
www.ieee.org

International Code Council (ICC)
www.iccsafe.org

Lawrence Berkeley National Lab
www.lbl.gov

Mechanical Engineering Magazine
www.memagazine.org

National Fire Protection Association (NFPA)
www.nfpa.org

National Society of Professional Engineers (NSPE)
www.nspe.org

New York City Department of Buildings
www.nyc.gov/html/dob/

Sandia National Laboratories
www.sandia.gov

U.S. General Services Administration (USGSA)
Public Building Service
www.gsa.gov

CHAPTER 24
CHEMICAL AND BIOLOGICAL PROTECTION

Michael C. Janus, PE
Battelle Memorial Institute
Manager, Engineering Applications & Operations
Battelle Eastern Science & Technology Center
Aberdeen, Maryland

William K. Blewett
Battelle Memorial Institute
Chief Engineer, Engineering Applications & Operations
Battelle Eastern Science & Technology Center
Aberdeen, Maryland

The only thing we have to fear is fear itself —nameless, unreasoning, unjustified terror which paralyzes needed efforts to convert retreat into advance.
FRANKLIN D. ROOSEVELT (1882–1945)
32nd U.S. president
March 4, 1933, First inaugural address

The basis of optimism is sheer terror.
OSCAR WILDE (1854–1900)
Irish dramatist, novelist, & poet

Threats to buildings and infrastructure are constantly evolving. As engineers, architects, scientists, building owners, law enforcement, and public officials develop and implement protective strategies and systems to minimize risk and mitigate threats, terrorists and criminals continue to plan increasingly deadly threats once considered unthinkable in a civilized society.

Although physical threats remain the primary threat to building security, chemical and biological (CB) threats are a key consideration to building protection planning. CB terrorism includes many chemical and biological agents and toxic industrial chemicals that may be delivered to a building via air, water, food, or surfaces. Airborne threats are typically considered of greatest concern to architects, engineers, building owners, and operators.

CB terrorism is a challenging problem due to the high level of uncertainty associated with the problem and solution. A brief history of events makes threat assessments difficult to conduct and the problem difficult to define. The variety of potential CB agents with diverse properties, in addition to limited and costly protection technologies, makes the solution difficult to define.

Since the anthrax scare after September 11, 2001, chemical and biological terrorism has captured headlines in the United States and around the world, but the threat has existed for centuries (Table 24.1). Government and military entities worldwide have addressed this problem for years and developed many solutions. Unfortunately, a high level of uncertainty remains. Urban centers and population densities make buildings attractive targets. Buildings are vulnerable to CB terrorism for several reasons (Table 24.2).

The objective of this chapter is to describe the basics of CB building protection, rather than provide an in-depth discussion. This chapter covers characteristics of CB agents, basic components of a CB protection system, and how they affect building design, and describes a prototype CB building protection system.

CHEMICAL AND BIOLOGICAL THREAT OVERVIEW

The threat from CB agents is diverse and depends on properties such as the physical state of the threat agent, volatility, vapor density, and toxicity. The physical state defines how the CB agent can be disseminated, its persistence, and how it enters the body to cause harm.

Chemical agents include chemical warfare agents (CWAs) and toxic industrial chemicals (TICs). These can exist as gas, aerosol, or liquid, depending on the agent. Dissemination methods vary for each and result in different modes of ingestion into the body. An agent in the gas phase is primarily taken into the body via inhalation. Once in the lungs, the agent is rapidly absorbed by lung tissue passing into the bloodstream. If the agent is highly toxic, this mode of dissemination can be very efficient. However, in the case of TICs, which are not as toxic as CWAs, a larger mass of the agent must, in general, be released to achieve the same effect as a small quantity of CWA.

The volatility of the chemical agent determines the most efficient means of dissemination. A common industrial chemical such as chlorine exists as a gas under normal conditions. Dissemination of chlorine or other gas requires only that a valve to a pressurized cylinder be opened upwind of the target. Nerve agents such as sarin are moderately volatile and exist as liquids at normal temperatures. Sarin's volatility is similar to that of water. Agents with moderate volatility can be vaporized readily by pouring the agent onto a surface in a warm environment, by heating the agent using a hot plate, or by spraying the agent into a fine mist using a common device such as a paint sprayer. All of these methods can produce an airborne concentration that can be deadly under the right atmospheric conditions. For example, outdoors in brisk winds, an agent may have little effect, but indoors, with normal ventilation, the agent can produce severe effects. A chemical agent with vapor density greater than

TABLE 24.1   Chemical and Biological Threats through History

Threat	Time frame
• Smoke from lighted coals and sulfurs	• Peloponnesian War in 423 B.C.
• Chemical agents	• World War I, 1915–1918
• Nerve agents	• Iran-Iraq Conflicts in the 1980s
• Nerve agents	• Japanese terrorists in the 1990s
• Anthrax	• U.S. postal system in 2001

TABLE 24.2   Why Buildings Are Vulnerable to Chemical-Biological Terrorism

- Small quantities of agent can produce hazardous concentrations indoors.
- Mechanical ventilation systems can spread agents rapidly throughout a building.
- Agent can be delivered covertly from outside a building and secure surroundings through air intakes, mail, water, and other routes.
- Agents can create a residual hazard in a building and render a building uninhabitable for an indefinite period of time.

air can settle into low-lying, poorly ventilated spaces and remain for long periods of time, making decontamination efforts hazardous. Chemical agents with vapor density less than air can be rapidly dispersed and not present a long-term threat.

Chemical agents of low volatility, such as VX, can be disseminated as an aerosol that can travel much like a vapor; however, because of their low volatility, they remain as liquid droplets. Disseminated as an aerosol, these agents can enter the body through either the lungs or the skin. Once inhaled, the liquid aerosol can be rapidly absorbed into the bloodstream. Once the liquid aerosol comes in contact with the skin, it can also be absorbed into the body and reach the bloodstream. Agents of low volatility can also be placed on surfaces to act as point contact hazards.

Biological agents are most effective if released as an aerosol. Such aerosols are generally composed of a liquid buffer solution to keep the biological agent viable. Once inhaled, the biological agent is transported to the lungs where it can begin to grow or enter the bloodstream. Biological agents can also be disseminated using vectors. For example, a person could purposely infect him- or herself with a virus or bacteria and transmit the disease while in the infectious stage.

CB PROTECTION SYSTEM COMPONENTS

The design of a CB protective system is driven by the particular threat. Protective systems for buildings currently range from simplistic, low-cost protective measures such as sheltering-in-place to complex and costly integrated positive-pressure collective protection systems coupled with advanced control and early warning systems. As of this writing, recognized standards and requirements for designing and constructing a CB building protection system do not exist. Several ongoing government research and development programs are developing applicable standards and requirements (Table 24.3).

When designing for CB protection, the first objective is determining the appropriate strategy and identifying the best combination of basic elements for implementation. The building design and construction team should employ a qualified CB building protection consultant to ensure protection solutions are properly planned and implemented. Elements most relevant to the design and construction team are as follows:

- Air filtration
- Detection
- Airflow management
- Decontamination

TABLE 24.3   Basic Elements for CB Building Protection Systems

1. Advanced controls
2. Airflow management
3. Building system modifications
4. Chemical and biological detection
5. Collective protection and filtration
6. Decontamination
7. Emergency power
8. Individual protection
9. Medical assets
10. Notification
11. Physical security
12. Response plans and procedures
13. Skilled personnel
14. Training

These elements are described in the following sections, along with how integration of a CB building protection system affects the design of other building systems.

COLLECTIVE PROTECTION AND AIR FILTRATION

Air filtration is the basis for protection from airborne hazards. Against an outdoor source of hazardous materials, the level of protection achievable varies with the removal efficiency of air filters in the building. The greater the efficiency, the higher the level of protection, but only if all air entering the protected envelope passes through the filters. To ensure that all outside air is introduced through filters, the envelope must be pressurized by introducing filtered air at a rate sufficient to produce an outward flow through cracks, pores, seams, and other openings. Pressurization prevents infiltration driven by wind, buoyancy pressures, and exhaust fans. For pressurization to be achieved economically, sealing measures must be taken to reduce leakage of the envelope.

High-Efficiency Air Filters

Protection against the spectrum of chemical and biological agents requires high-efficiency filters for both aerosols and gases. This involves three different mechanisms of filtration: physical adsorption for chemicals of low vapor pressure, chemisorption for chemicals of high vapor pressure, and particulate filtration for aerosols. Adsorbers of activated, impregnated carbon are used for high-efficiency filtration of chemical agents. High-efficiency particulate air (HEPA) filters are the standard for the filtration of aerosols. A HEPA filter is always employed in series with an adsorber; however, a HEPA filter is often employed without a carbon filter if the requirement is only to remove aerosols.

The efficiency of a HEPA filter is at least 99.97 percent; that is, only 0.03 percent of particles of the most penetrating size range (about 0.3 micron) that enter the filter will exit the filter. Carbon filters have a wide range of efficiencies, but those for protection against toxic chemicals are often designed in military applications to maintain an efficiency of at least 99.999 percent throughout their intended service life. The perceived threat will determine the appropriate type and level of filtration.

Filters for Chemical Agents

A carbon adsorber removes molecules from an airstream by adsorption, trapping molecules in the micropores of carbon granules. This process works best against large molecules, that is, chemicals of low vapor pressure. As a rule of thumb, compounds having vapor pressure less than 10 mm Hg (at the temperature of the filter bed) are readily adsorbed and retained in the carbon pores. Activated carbon is an effective sorbent for removing a broad range of chemical agents because of its extensive microporosity and wide range of pore sizes. Typically, the pores in highly activated carbon have a total surface area exceeding 1200 square meters per gram. Generally, filtering chemicals of high vapor pressure requires a chemical reaction with impregnants added to the carbon. These impregnants react with the gas as it passes through the filter and forms reaction products that are innocuous or that can be retained by the filter.

The performance of filters is defined in terms of efficiency and capacity. Efficiency is the percentage of agent removed in a single pass, and capacity is the quantity of agent a filter can remove before it ceases to filter at the specified efficiency. A military-grade, high-efficiency filter with a two-inch bed of fine mesh (12 × 30) carbon can be expected to physically adsorb about 20 percent of its weight in agent, to remove about 5 to 10 percent of its weight in reactive gas, and to maintain an efficiency of at least 99.999 percent throughout its intended service life. The disadvantages of carbon filtration are as follows:

- There is no single adsorbent capable of removing all toxic chemicals.
- Carbon filter systems are relatively expensive.
- Operating and maintenance costs are relatively high.

The service life of an impregnated carbon filter is defined by the reactive gas life and physical adsorption life. Life against reactive gases is generally the shorter of the two; therefore, the replacement cycle is usually based upon the degradation in reactive gas capacity. Filter life is site-specific, however, as both capacities are affected by the environmental air quality. Physical adsorption life is reduced by adsorption of air pollutants. Capacity for reactive gases diminishes gradually over time, and with the best impregnated carbon it is typically lost within about four years of exposure to humidity in ambient air. The rate at which the impregnant degrades varies with the temperature and amount of water adsorbed by the carbon bed, and degradation begins once a filter is opened to the atmosphere. There is no simple means for determining how much capacity remains in a carbon filter. Because the service life varies with the environment in which it operates, it can be replaced according to time in service using a conservative estimate, or its remaining capacity can be measured by the use of test canisters.

Filters for Aerosols

The HEPA filter is the standard filter for high-efficiency filtration of biological agents and irritants that are either solid aerosols or liquid aerosols of low vapor pressure. The efficiency of HEPA filtration in removing 1- to 5-micron particles from an airstream is approximately 99.999 percent. Filters of less than HEPA efficiency, such as the ASHRAE 95 percent filter, provide substantially lower performance, with efficiencies of about 98 to 99 percent against the 1-micron particle, which equates to substantially lower protection factors for external filtration. Ultraviolet germicidal irradiation (UVGI) systems have been developed for killing biological agents in an airstream; however, UVGI systems do not protect against other solid or liquid aerosols. With a threat that includes these aerosols, a UVGI system would be a supplement to, rather than a replacement for, the HEPA filter. Advantages of the UVGI system are lower resistance to airflow and elimination of changing filters and handling contaminated filters.

Efficient Integration of Filters

There are two basic approaches for applying air filtration to a building. The first is external filtration, in which air is drawn from outside the envelope and discharged inside it. This provides the higher level of protection but also involves higher costs. The second is internal filtration, in which air is drawn from inside the envelope and discharged inside.

The relative levels of protection of the two approaches can be seen in terms of protection factor: the ratio of external dose (concentration integrated over time) and internal dose. External filtration systems with high-efficiency filters can yield protection factors greater than 100,000. For internal filtration, the protection factors are likely to be less than 100 and are highly variable. The protection achievable with internal filtration varies with a number of factors:

- Air-exchange rate of the enclosure
- Efficiency of the filter
- Flow rate of the filter unit
- Volume of the room or building in which the filter unit operates

Filter systems can be employed in either active or passive protective systems. Active systems are those energized upon detecting a hazard. In this type of application, the filter system remains in standby mode, usually for the purpose of reducing operating and maintenance costs. For active systems, effectiveness diminishes as response time increases. Rapid detection of hazards is therefore critical to the effectiveness of active systems. The shortcomings of detectors for chemical or biological agents with regard to response time and accurate multiple-agent detection capability may yield relatively low levels of protection for active systems.

Passive systems operate continuously and do not require a means of detection. Passive systems provide more reliable protection. Although a passive system may have higher operating and maintenance costs, its overall costs may be lower than an active system when the costs of detection equipment and automatic dampers are considered, particularly if the system is designed for a low-pressure drop across the filters.

The main cost component of operating the filter units is the electrical power required to force air through the filters. The airflow resistance of HEPA filters is typically about 1 inch, water gauge (iwg), and this resistance increases steadily as the filter loads with dust or other fine particles in service. For high-efficiency carbon filters, the pressure drop may range from about 1 to 4 iwg. Maintenance costs involve periodic filter replacement.

Filtration Units for Makeup Air (External Filtration)

Typical air-handling units filter both makeup air and recirculated air together. Although filtering recirculated air (internal filtration) is beneficial for purging and for limiting the spread of contaminants if an internal release occurs, it yields lower protection factors than external filtration. For protection against an external release, the greater benefit of high-efficiency filtration is in filtering makeup air.

The most economical approach to filtration is to employ a separate filter set for each of the two airstreams and filter only the makeup air at high efficiency. This approach maximizes protection against an external release; it requires a separate makeup air unit incorporating a fan, prefilter, HEPA filter, high-efficiency gas adsorber, and cooling and heating coils.

The challenge of integrating high-efficiency filtration systems is to minimize bypass, which typically occurs at poorly sealed filter frames and racks, leakage paths between the fan and the filters in draw-through-type air-handling units, and as infiltration through the envelope in unpressurized systems.

To prevent bypass, high-efficiency filter units are designed to have sealing racks allowing minimum bypass. These are checked upon installation to allow bypass of only 0.1 to 0.01 percent.

There are several types and models of high-efficiency air-filtration units providing a high level of protection against external hazards, including commercial and military systems. The recommended carbon for filtering a broad range of toxic chemical vapors and gases is ASZM-TEDA carbon, per military specification EA-C-1704A. Among the adsorber systems available for use with buildings—flow rates of approximately 1000 cfm and higher—are radial flow filter units using military adsorber cells and commercial V-bed filter units. Commercial HEPA filters with low-leakage housings are available from various manufacturers.

The flow rate of filtration units needed for pressurization of an envelope is determined by leakage characteristics and building size. The cost of installing a high-efficiency filtration system varies directly with the leakage rate; a higher leakage rate equals higher costs.

Leakage rates of office buildings typically vary from roughly 0.1 cfm per square foot to 2 cfm per square foot at a pressure of 0.2 iwg, depending upon the type of construction. In design, leakage rates can be estimated with building leakage data from fan-pressurization tests, as is presented in U.S. Army Corps of Engineers ETL 1110-3-498, entitled, *Design of Collective Protection Shelters to Resist Chemical, Biological and Radiological (CB) Agents*. For tight construction, as with 12-inch-thick walls of concrete, a concrete roof, and well-sealed windows, an overpressure of 0.05 iwg can be achieved with about 0.15 cfm per square foot. For construction with concrete walls and gypsum wallboard ceilings, the airflow required for 0.05-iwg pressure is approximately 0.35 cfm per square foot. For loosely constructed buildings with framed walls or prefabricated metal walls, the airflow required for 0.05 iwg is about 0.75 cfm per square foot. Airflow rates can be substantially higher in buildings that have only lay-in ceilings with unsealed roof-wall junctures.

Certain spaces are usually excluded from the envelope being protected: spaces having or requiring high rates of air exchange with the outdoors, such as mechanical rooms containing boilers or generators and receiving areas. Mechanical rooms containing air-handling units must be included within the protective envelope.

Filtration Units for Recirculated Air

Internal filtration, filtering air recirculated within the building, is the simplest application of filtration. Internal filtration, however, provides a much lower level of protection against an external release than does high-efficiency external filtration. Against an external release, protection factors are limited to about 100 or less, however, because internal filtration does not control the air exchange caused by wind and buoyancy pressures. An advantage of internal filtration, however, is in purging contaminants from a building following an internal release. It is lower in cost than filtration of makeup air. Internal filtration can be applied with both gas and aerosol filters; however, it is more practical and less costly with aerosol filtration only.

The simplest application of internal filtration involves the use of freestanding units referred to as indoor air purifiers or indoor air quality filter units. There are many of these on the market that contain filters for removing both aerosols and chemicals. These typically have high-efficiency filters for removing aerosols; however, the chemical filters are of lower efficiency. In these units, the carbon filters do not typically contain the impregnated carbon capable of removing chemicals of high vapor pressure. Manufacturers provide guidance on the size of room that a single unit will accommodate. Because these are designed mainly for filtering pollen and dust and removing odors, there are no claims or guidance as to their protective capability.

Internal filtration can also be applied by installing HEPA filters or low-efficiency carbon filters in place of standard dust filters in air-handling units. Air-handling units are not designed, however, to accommodate a large increase in airflow resistance that a HEPA filter or thin carbon filter would add. The capability of the existing air-handling unit must be examined before such installations are attempted. In typical air-handling units, dust filter slots allow relatively high bypass around the filter media, reducing overall efficiency of the HEPA filters.

CHEMICAL AND BIOLOGICAL DETECTION

Rapid identification of a chemical or biological agent involved in any hazardous material incident in or near a building is vital to protection of building occupants and effective treatment of casualties. CB detectors internal and external to the building are required to initiate active building protection systems, such as standby filtration systems. In order for active protection systems, and passive protection systems to a lesser extent, to be effective these detectors must be properly positioned, highly reliable, respond quickly, have low false alarm rates, and be integrated into an overall control and early warning system.

Past application of CB detection technology to building protection systems is somewhat limited, primarily due to detection technology limitations, lack of testing in building environments, and high costs. Many detectors have problems in a building environment primarily due to high false alarm rates and inadequate response times. These shortcomings are partially due to the fact that most CB detectors were designed for use on the military battlefield, and have not been designed or thoroughly tested for a building environment. A number of ongoing government research and development programs are improving CB detection technology. Significant improvements can be anticipated over the coming decade. The following sections overview the basics of chemical and biological detectors.

Chemical Agent Detection

The applicability of detectors for chemical warfare agents and TICs to buildings depends on detector characteristics, type, and concentration of agent to be detected, and the protective response strategy of the building. Several technologies are available for chemical detection, and some technologies are available for detection and identification of liquid droplets of chemical agents on surfaces. There are also many laboratory-based technologies for detection of toxic industrial materials in water. The quality of analytical results from the various analyzers depends upon the ability to effectively sample the environment and get the sample to the analyzer.

Analyzers designed for sensing vapors are not readily applicable for detection of low-volatility liquid contamination on surfaces or contamination in water. Also, many analyzers could have difficulty in identifying a small amount of toxic chemicals in a high background of nonhazardous environmental chemicals. For example, a chemical vapor detector may readily detect trace levels of toxic chemicals in an outdoor setting, but the same detector may not be capable of detecting the same level of agent in a crowded portion of the building. These environments contain many chemicals produced by everyday activities (such as driving an automobile and using deodorant, perfumes, and insecticides) that appear as a toxic chemical to the analyzer and may affect the reliability and sensitivity of the instrument. As technology advances, more effective and accurate detection methods will become commercially available at lower costs.

Chemical agents can be detected by several means incorporating technologies grouped into three major categories:

- Point detection
- Standoff detection
- Analytical instruments

The type of technology needed for a specific application depends on the agent type and role within the protective scheme of the building.

Point detectors can be used as warning devices to alert personnel to a toxic vapor at a specific location, such as an entry point or HVAC return. Technologies used for chemical point detection include ion mobility spectrometry (IMS), surface acoustic wave (SAW), flame photometry, and others. Point detectors may also be used following an event to determine which people have been contaminated, as in contamination triage.

Standoff detectors give advance warning of a chemical agent cloud outdoors. They typically use optical spectroscopy and can detect chemical agents at distances as great as 5 kilometers. Agent-free spectra must be used as a baseline to compare with freshly measured spectra that may contain a chemical agent. Standoff detectors are generally difficult to operate and usually require the operator to have some knowledge of spectroscopy in order to interpret results. Available standoff detectors use infrared spectroscopy with either passive or active sensing.

Analytical instruments can analyze samples as small as a few microliters or milligrams. Analytical instruments employing mass spectrometry (MS) and gas chromatography (GC) are designed to differentiate between and accurately measure the unique chemical properties of different molecules. These instruments are quite sophisticated in order to detect and differentiate subtle differences between trace amounts of different molecules. Accuracy and reliability require use of very pure reagents and very rigid protocol and operating procedures. This typically precludes their use outside a laboratory environment staffed by technically trained operators. However, some analytical instruments have been developed for field applications. Additionally, instruments do not display the measured data in a straightforward manner. Interpretation of measured data typically requires a technical background and extensive formal training.

Biological Agent Detection

The utility of biological agent detection equipment to building protection depends on detection equipment characteristics, type of agent to be detected, environment in which the sampling takes place, and skill of the operator. The quality of analytical results from the various analyzers depends upon the ability to draw samples effectively from the environment and deliver the biological agent to the analyzer.

Biological agent detectors lag far behind their chemical-detection counterparts. The September 11, 2001, terrorist attacks and the fall 2001 anthrax incidents have given significant impetus to development of biological detection technologies. As a result, there are many biological detection systems in the research and early development stages, and a small number of biological detectors are commercially available. However, because of the complexity and transient nature of the biological agents, these devices still have limited utility. They respond to only a small number of agents, give excessive false negative or positive results, and are generally high in cost.

Caution is strongly advised when considering purchase of any device claiming to detect biological agents and toxins. The main reason for limited availability of biological detection equipment is that biological agents are much more complex systems of molecules compared to chemical agents.

This complexity makes them much more difficult to identify. For example, ionization/ion mobility spectrometry, an excellent system for collection, detection, and identification of chemical agents, is not currently capable of detecting or discriminating biological agents. Another reason for the limited availability of biological detection equipment is that detecting biological agents requires extremely high sensitivity because of the very low dose needed to cause infection and spread the disease. It also requires a high degree of selectivity because of the large and diverse biological background in the environment.

The need for high-efficiency collection, concentration of the sample, high selectivity, and high sensitivity results in very complex detection systems consisting of various subunits. Each subunit performs a specific collection, detection, and signal transduction task. As a result, a biological agent detection system applies sampling, probe (detection), and signal-transducer technologies.

Sampling involves manual or mechanical sample collection (cyclones, virtual impactors, and bubblers/impingers). Probe (detection) technology deals with how the assay or detection device recognizes the particular target biological agent and includes those based on nucleic acids, antibody/antigen binding, and ligand/receptor interactions. Some detection devices use nucleic acid–based techniques, which are based on the precise genetic base sequences of a particular agent. Other detection devices use immunoassay techniques, which mimic the human body's creation of antibodies to ward off a disease attack. Detection techniques could also be based on the principle that every cell has a specific surface protein (ligand) that binds other specific molecules. Signal transducer technology deals with how the assay or detection device communicates the activity of the probe to the observer by using electrochemical, piezoelectric, colorimetric, and optical signals.

Methods based on physical properties and separation, such as mass spectrometry, fall into the category of hybrid technologies with no clear division of probe and transducer functions. Mass spectrometry, which ionizes molecules and breaks them into characteristic fragments, each with specific mass spectrum, has been successfully used in chemical detection and identification. It is also being used for biological detection. Other techniques include the standard culture, or a combination of two or more techniques.

Various technologies using common principles are grouped into a class of techniques: nucleic acid–based, antibody-based, ligand-based, optical, biosensor-based, hybrid techniques, and standard culture.

Commercially available biological detection systems or those in research and development fall into two general types: long-range monitoring (standoff) and point-detection (at the site of a suspected release). The principal differences between the point-detectors and standoff detectors are size, weight, portability, and logistical support requirements.

AIRFLOW MANAGEMENT

The technology for automatic, real-time detection of agents in air defines the performance of active systems for protection. Airflow management is an active strategy of protection requiring detection. It involves preventing infiltration of outside air, purging, or containing contamination by pressurizing or depressurizing specific zones of a building. Efficient airflow management may require both architectural and mechanical modifications.

Sheltering-in-place is the simplest application of airflow management. Normal sheltering-in-place does not involve substantial filtration; therefore, it is effective for only limited periods of time. This limitation exists because even a tightly constructed building does not prevent the exchange of air between indoors and outdoors. As air is exchanged, even at a small rate, the protection provided diminishes over time. The effectiveness of this measure is limited by the capability to detect a hazardous condition and initiate the protective actions—shutting down fans and closing doors, dampers, and windows. Sheltering-in-place can be initiated with real-time automatic detection or human observations. Higher protection factors in the range are possible only if the protective actions are completed before the hazardous plume reaches the building. For office buildings, rapid response requires:

- A single switch or HVAC control system to rapidly deactivate all fans and close all dampers from a single location

- A mass notification system to inform building occupants to close all doors and windows
- Plans, procedures, familiarization training for sheltering-in-place, to include turning on purge fans once the outdoor hazard has dissipated

Protection by sheltering-in-place requires two distinct actions to be taken to alter the air exchange rate of a building.

- First, reduce the air exchange rate before the airborne hazard reaches the building. This is done by closing all windows and doors and turning off air conditioners, combustion heaters, and fans that induce indoor-outdoor air exchange.
- Second, increasing the indoor-outdoor air exchange rate as soon as the hazard has passed. This is done by opening all windows and doors and turning on all fans to ventilate the building. This step is necessary for purging the airborne contaminants that have entered the building while the external hazard was present.

SAFE ROOMS

A single room in a building can be selected as a safe room for sheltering-in-place (Table 24.4).

There is no substantial advantage in a room on the higher floors of a low-rise building. A location should not be selected based on height above ground level if it increases the time for building occupants to reach the shelter in an emergency. Although an interior room is preferable, one with windows can be used if the windows seal well when closed. Modifications can prepare a safe room or a building to provide greater and more reliable protection for sheltering-in-place (Table 24.5).

Sealing

Measures for tightening the envelope include sealing all penetrations for pipes, conduit, ducts, and cables using caulk, foam sealants, duct seal, or weather stripping. Most leakage occurs through the top of the envelope, particularly where suspended lay-in ceilings are used without a hard ceiling, or without a well-sealed roof-wall juncture above the lay-in ceiling. In such cases, the ceiling should be replaced with gypsum wallboard.

TABLE 24.4   Safe Room Characteristics

- Readily accessible to all people who are to be sheltered
- More tightly constructed than other rooms in the building
- Capable of being tightly sealed very rapidly
- Protected access to drinking water and toilets

TABLE 24.5   Steps for Preparing a Safe Room or Building to Shelter-in-Place

- Seal unintentional openings reducing the air exchange rate of the envelope
- Facilitate rapid closing of the envelope and fan deactivation
- Allow use of air-conditioning while sheltering without reducing the protection level
- Add internal (recirculating) filtration

Facilitating Rapid Sheltering

Capability to rapidly turn off all fans and shut all doors is important, especially in large buildings and complexes. Single-switch control of fans can be incorporated through use relays or digital control systems. Closing all doors quickly in a large building requires a notification system, such as a public-address system and an emergency action plan. Training and drills for building occupants will speed a more effective response.

Facilitating Rapid Exhaust

For internal releases, it is important to have the capability to rapidly exhaust a building. Single-switch control of fans and dampers can be incorporated through use relays or a digital control system. Rapid exhaust is also valuable for sheltering-in-place following the passage of an external contaminant cloud.

Use of Air-Conditioning

Standard air-conditioning and heating systems cannot be operated while sheltering-in-place because fans directly or indirectly introduce outside air. If many people are confined in a room or building without air-conditioning or air movement in hot weather, conditions can cause people to leave the shelter or safe room before safe conditions are ensured.

To install an air-conditioning/heating system that can be safely operated in sheltering mode, the air-handling unit (AHU) must serve the safe room exclusively. Both the air-handling unit and the return ducts must be located within the safe room, with the AHU in an interior mechanical closet and the return ducts beneath a hard ceiling.

The system must also have a reliable damper system for cutting off outside air to the AHU. This normally requires a triple-damper set, two dampers in line with a relief damper between the two, which opens when the other two close. Alternatively, a split system can be installed, one that does not introduce fresh air in either the normal or protective mode.

Internal Filtration

Internal filtration involves the use of indoor air purifiers or indoor air-quality units, which are commercially available. These can be ceiling-mounted, duct-mounted, or freestanding floor or table units having both a HEPA filter and adsorber. The HEPA filter increases protection that sheltering provides against aerosols, and the adsorber increases the protection against some toxic chemicals (those of relatively low vapor pressure). Filtration does not provide a benefit for all chemicals.

DECONTAMINATION

Decontamination is the process of making a building, occupants, and contents safe by removing, destroying, or reducing contaminants to an acceptable level. Decontamination may be required to return a building to normal operation after a toxic agent has been released in or near it.

If chemical or biological agents are released into a building, a portion of the contaminants will be purged by the normal exchange of air with the outdoors, and a portion will be retained in the building by the following processes:

- Chemical agents in the liquid phase will be absorbed by materials of the building and will desorb slowly over time.
- Chemical agents in the gas phase will be absorbed or adsorbed by materials of the building and will desorb slowly over time.

- Aerosols will settle onto surfaces at a rate dependent on aerodynamic particle size and air movement and may be re-aerosolized with the movement of people, air, and equipment in the building.

Unless measures are taken to purge, decontaminate, or contain agents immediately after release, the agent can be transported to and deposited onto inaccessible surfaces in the building, complicating the process of decontamination.

Decontamination involves removing and neutralizing agents. Procedures for decontamination include removing the agent with soap and water, and using complex procedures for neutralization, cleaning, or accelerated desorption.

To minimize retention and facilitate decontamination, building design should:

- Make surfaces and materials in the building less absorbent
- Provide decontamination access to all surfaces where agents are likely be deposited
- Provide that design areas can accommodate large volumes of water, to be used during decontamination

Making surfaces less absorbent requires minimizing use of carpeting, curtains, and fabric wall coverings. Open-face insulation should be avoided in ducts and plenums.

Plastics, polymers, paints, and sealants used in the building should be selected for chemical agent resistance in order to prevent chemical agent absorption. The practicality of doing so is limited, as agent-resistant materials may not have acceptable physical properties, availability, cost, and aesthetic qualities. Chemical agent resistance is defined by the rate at which a material absorbs chemical agents. Many plastics and elastomers readily absorb chemical agents, which are strong solvents. The need for resistance to chemical agents applies whether the material is likely to be exposed to an agent in the form of liquid or vapor.

Access to ducts and plenums is the principal consideration for making surfaces accessible for decontamination. Access ports should be located to facilitate cleaning of ducts and plenums.

The decontamination process for people is generally the same whether the agent is chemical or biological. People exposed to an agent must remove clothing, at least the outer layer of clothing, and wash or decontaminate areas of the body not covered by protective clothing at the time of exposure. Complete decontamination involves removing all clothing (for disposal or decontamination) and showering with soap and warm water followed by dressing in clean clothing.

Showering removes fine particles (biological and radiological agents) and chemical agent vapors or gases loosely held by the hair and skin and liquid chemical agent. Washing with soap does not remove liquid agents absorbed by the skin, but can prevent further absorption. Whether the removal of a liquid agent prevents injury depends mainly upon the time the agent has remained on the skin.

Fine particles deposited on clothing can be re-aerosolized by the motion of removing the clothing; therefore, the process of clothing removal, showering, and removing the protective mask must be done in sequence, maintaining respiratory protection and controlled ventilation to prevent the person's exposure to re-aerosolized agent. An effect similar to re-aerosolization occurs following exposure to chemical agent. Agent sorbed by the outer garments desorbs for a period of time after exposure.

Decontamination Space Planning

Specialized building areas may be required to accommodate personnel decontamination. These areas should be properly ventilated and planned in a one-way circulation route, enabling someone to enter from a contamination zone with soiled clothes, remove them and dispose of them appropriately, shower, disinfect, and change into clean clothes. Spaces would include decontamination areas, shower, changing and clean dressing rooms, with soiled disposal and clean storage areas. The space programming and circulation planning concepts are similar to those required for entering and leaving hospital operating room suites, central sterile supply areas, and laboratory clean rooms.

Avoiding cross contamination is essential to maintaining clean and dirty areas and containing toxic materials.

Decontamination Processes

Several methods are available for decontamination, including physical, chemical, and thermal processes. Physical processes remove agents from surfaces. When a physical process is used, another means of decontamination is necessary for detoxification. High-pressure systems, sorbents (simple inert), and solvent washes are examples of physical processes.

Sorbent technology involves materials that physically remove liquid chemicals from surfaces, including skin. Synthetic sorbents adsorb liquids, and natural sorbents absorb them. The state of the liquid after sorption depends on the type of sorbent material used.

Use of a solvent to remove a contaminant is a physical, rather than a chemical, process. Chemical agents are removed from a surface by washing molecules away using water, alcohol, Freon, diesel fuel, etc. In this process, the agent is diluted, not detoxified, and there may be residues left behind in cracks, pits, joints, etc. Solvents are often applied in an open environment using pressurized sprayers. The runoff from a solvent decontamination must be collected in order to minimize the areas contaminated. Solvent wash technology can also be used in an enclosed environment to decontaminate automobile interiors, portable communications equipment, or electronic devices. In a closed system, solvents can be heated or used with ultrasonic or supersonic sprays to increase their decontamination effectiveness. After a decontamination cycle, solvents can be recycled for further use in additional cycles before being discarded and detoxified.

Water and carbon dioxide sprayed at high pressures are used to physically remove agents from surfaces. Chemical agents can be removed from surfaces with water pressures less than 3000 pounds per square inch; however, removing agents from surfaces is highly dependent upon the nature of the surfaces. Flat, smooth surfaces can be more readily decontaminated than irregular, porous surfaces using water sprays. Additives can be mixed with water to improve the performance of a water jet. A HEPA-vacuuming system was reported effective in the removal and sampling of spores in the Hart Senate Office Building, in Washington, D.C., in fall 2001.

Chemical processes involve the use of reactive or catalytic chemicals (sorbents) to neutralize CB contaminants. A reactive sorbent adsorbs the agent and then chemically detoxifies it. Reactive sorbents have been prepared by soaking simple sorbents in alkaline solutions and loading the matrix with caustic material. Once sorbed into the sorbent matrix, the agent encounters the alkaline medium, reacts with it, and is destroyed. A second approach for reactive sorbents is to prepare a polymeric material with reactive groups attached to the polymeric backbone. In this case, the agent is sorbed by the polymeric matrix, encounters the reactive group, and is neutralized by it. A third approach is to use microcrystalline metal oxides such as aluminum oxide or magnesium oxide. Other examples of the chemical processes include sodium hypochlorite (i.e., bleach) and hydrogen peroxide–based systems.

Thermal processes remove chemical agents through vaporization. Another means of decontamination is necessary for agent detoxification. Thermal processes are not considered to be an effective decontamination means for biological warfare agents because of low operating temperatures.

EFFECTS ON BUILDING SYSTEMS

Architectural and mechanical engineering design systems affect a building's protective capability against CB agents (Table 24.6).

ARCHITECTURAL DESIGN

Several architectural design measures will reduce the potential for agents to enter or spread through a building if released in or near a building.

TABLE 24.6   Architectural and Engineering Design Elements Affecting Protective Capabilities against Chemical and Biological Agents

- Air intakes, air wells, and penetrations
- Tight building envelope
- High threat areas and spaces, such as mailrooms, lobbies, receiving areas
- Access control and entry screening areas
- Vestibules
- Mechanical rooms
- High-efficiency filter unit

Securing Air Intakes, Air Wells, and Penetrations

Fresh-air intakes should be located on the roof or the highest practical portion of the facility. The intakes should be made inaccessible to unauthorized people and secured by access-control equipment or devices.

Air wells within height or range of an object thrown from the ground or an adjacent building should be secured with chain-link fabric enclosures or sloped grating to prevent a grenade from discharging its contents into an air intake.

Penetrations at ground level, including exhaust fans, mail slots, dryer vents, and others should be avoided. Such penetrations may allow the direct introduction of hazardous materials from unsecured areas outside the building.

Tightening the Building Envelope

Producing overpressure with filtered makeup air yields the highest level of protection against outdoor sources of hazardous materials. To achieve such protection economically requires a tight envelope. Seams, joints, and penetrations of the building shell should be sealed to the maximum extent practicable, and continuous air leakage control barriers should be used in areas that define the protective envelope.

Air leakage (blower door) testing should be performed after construction to verify leakage rates and sealing effectiveness to ensure that the filtration system has sufficient capacity for pressurization. Pressurization may not be practical in buildings with high exhaust flows. The capability to adjust exhaust flows is a means for applying overpressure in heightened threat conditions. This is done by closing exhaust dampers, reducing airflow rates from or deenergizing exhaust fans.

Isolation of High-Threat Areas

Isolating spaces with a higher potential for an internal release is effective for limiting the spread of hazardous materials if an internal release occurs. These spaces, such as the mailroom, lobby, and loading dock, should be planned to be fully isolated through several design elements (Table 24.7).

Isolating separate HVAC zones minimizes transport from an internal release and provides some benefit against an outdoor release as it increases internal resistance to air movement caused by natural forces, reducing the rate of infiltration. Isolation of zones requires full-height walls between each zone and the adjacent zone and hallway doors.

Accommodations for Access Control and Entry Screening

To prevent a container of hazardous material or a dissemination device from being brought into a building requires a staffed access-control point and security screening equipment for people, mail,

TABLE 24.7   **Design Elements for Isolating Spaces with High Potential for Chemical-Biological Release**

- Design in full-height walls between adjacent zones.
- The air-handling unit should serve only that space, such as a separate zone.
- These spaces should have slightly negative pressure relative to the rest of the building by use of an exhaust fan or system balancing.
- Although the magnitude of the negative pressure may vary with room volume, the exhaust system should be designed to maintain a 100-foot/minimum air velocity through any open doorway, such as a vestibule or revolving door.

and supplies. Entry screening provides deterrence and a means of detecting containers containing hazardous materials. An x-ray system and metal detector, standard equipment for secure office buildings, provide the capability for identifying containers that may be concealed in hand-carried items or packages. Effective nonintrusive detection for CB agents is not available as of this writing.

Vestibules

Entrances should be designed with integral vestibules to minimize infiltration by stack and wind pressures. Vestibules should incorporate leakage-control doors for main entrances, entrances from garages, delivery entrances, and loading docks.

Secured Mechanical Rooms

Mechanical rooms should have access control to ensure the security of ventilation equipment. Doors to mechanical rooms should be constructed of metal, without windows, and with proper security locks. Stairways and exterior ladders to the roof should also be access controlled.

MECHANICAL AND ELECTRICAL ENGINEERING

Mechanical and electrical building systems play a vital life safety role in protecting buildings and occupants from chemical and biological contamination.

Enhanced Sheltering-in-Place Capability

To maximize protection attainable against short-duration outdoor hazards for which there is some form of warning, a building should incorporate a control system to close all boundary dampers and turn off all outside air fans and exhaust fans with a master switch. This allows the building envelope to be tightened rapidly for sheltering-in-place. Fresh air intakes and other ventilation system penetrations of the protected area should incorporate low-leakage damper assemblies.

High-Efficiency Filter Units

When a high-efficiency filter unit is installed outside the protective envelope or in an unprotected mechanical room, it should be configured with the fan upstream of the filters (blow-through configuration). The fan should be downstream of the filters (draw-through) when installed inside the protective envelope or in a protected pressurized mechanical room. Protected mechanical rooms have the same overpressure requirements as the protected area.

High-efficiency filtration systems can be employed either in standby mode, as with a safe room, or a continuous-operation mode. The cost benefit of the standby system is in reduced costs of operation and maintenance by reducing the frequency of replacing filters and reducing power consumption. However, this also reduces the benefit of the protective system because protection is governed by the capability to detect all threat agents and to have reliable forewarning.

A HEPA filter unit should be configured to achieve a uniform seal to the air-handling unit so that the overall leakage rate (bypass) at peripheral seals will be less than 0.01 percent. The HEPA filtration system housing should be of continuously welded construction and designed for an internal static pressure of 10 inches, water gauge (iwg). The HEPA filtration system should be subjected to a factory mounting frame leakage test per ASME N510. Pressure sensors or gauges should be installed with the HEPA filters to indicate when the filters should be changed as a result of dust loading.

Depending upon atmospheric pollutants, continuously operated high-efficiency filtration systems generally require roughing filters with an average efficiency of 25 to 30 percent when tested in accordance with ASHRAE 52.1. A prefilter or intermediate filter should be placed after the roughing filter but before the HEPA filter and have an average efficiency of 80 to 85 percent.

For continuously operating systems, the capacity of the filter unit necessary for pressurization is the sum of the leakage rate of the protected envelope at the design overpressure and the ventilation air intake rate needed for exhaust requirements. The blower of the filter unit should be selected to accommodate the total static pressure with loaded particulate filters, ductwork system pressure losses, and required overpressure.

After installation, a high-efficiency filtration system should be subjected to a mechanical leak test using a test gas and an aerosol. An independent testing agency should conduct the field-testing in accordance with ASME N510. This test may require an inlet port for upstream challenge and downstream sample ports in the ductwork. Such ports should be located to achieve good mixing, as required by ASME N509 and ASME N510.

If the protective system is configured as a standby system, low-leakage dampers should be used for transitioning from normal ventilation to protected mode. Low-leakage dampers should also be used on air intakes and exhaust systems to achieve the highest levels of protection in sheltering-in-place. These dampers should have an air leakage rate no greater than 4 scfm per square foot of damper area at a differential pressure of 1 iwg. The air intake and exhaust dampers on the boundary of the protective envelope should be configured to fail to the closed position if power is lost.

OPERATIONS AND MAINTENANCE

A protective system that includes high-efficiency filtration equipment, detection equipment, and decontamination equipment requires a protective action plan and an operation and maintenance manual for systems specific to CB protection.

A protective-action plan describes procedures and responsibilities for decision-making and protective response when hazardous conditions occur. It includes procedures for determining if and when a hazard exists such as deciding upon the best course of action to protect building occupants, such as sheltering-in-place, evacuation, or purging, based on available knowledge of conditions. An operation and maintenance manual for the protective system should contain:

- Operating instructions
- Preventive maintenance information
- Troubleshooting procedures
- Spare parts list

The manual should include:

- A description of each of the main components, including the filter units, detectors, control panels, dampers, position switches, circuit breakers, terminal panels, controllers, and pressure sensors

- Technical information on the filter unit and certifications of filter unit configuration, in-place leak testing, and flow and balance testing

- Detailed instructions and diagrams of controls and dampers to allow the user to locate the components and employ visual indicators for ensuring proper operation

- Troubleshooting guide for user repair actions and specialized repair actions by maintenance personnel

- Maintenance instructions, which should include step-by-step procedures for removing, replacing, and testing components, assemblies and subassemblies, that are subject to wear, malfunction, frequent replacement, damage, and testing

- A list of spare parts, expendable supplies, special tools, and equipment to have immediately on hand for maintaining the system

Maintenance instructions should state the maximum allowable pressure drop across HEPA filters and prefilters, which accumulate dust and develop a higher resistance to flow over time. To minimize the impact of filter resistance on flow rate, periodic tests should be specified for measuring the pressure drop across the filter system and change filters or adjust the manual flow control damper of the fan to maintain the design airflow.

Each time high-efficiency filters are installed, in-place filter leak testing is advisable to verify there are no substantial leaks between the mounting frame and housing or within the mounting frame, that there are no bypasses, and the filters have not been damaged. Testing is performed in accordance with American National Standard ASME N510, "Testing of Nuclear Air Treatment Systems."

The replacement cycle for military-grade adsorbers is 3 to 4 years, depending upon local air quality. HEPA filters without a prefilter can become fully loaded after 9 months of continuous use. Use of a prefilter extends the life of the HEPA filter to about 2 to 2.5 years of continuous use.

Air intakes and dampers to be closed in a CB event should be routinely checked for proper operation. The mechanical spaces in which CB filtration equipment is installed should include space for easy access and filter replacement. Detectors and air samplers used for the detection system require scheduled maintenance based on the vendor's recommended maintenance plan.

CASE STUDY: CB PROTECTION SYSTEM PROTOTYPE

This section describes a case study of a CB building-protection system incorporating all relevant subsystems to illustrate how the basic elements can be integrated. The protective system was installed in an office building under the Smart Building Program initiated in 1999 as a technology demonstration by the Defense Threat Reduction Agency. The objective was to install a system in an existing building that would automatically respond to a CB threat.

The six-story building, Social Hall Plaza, in Salt Lake City, Utah, housed the joint operations center during the 2002 Winter Olympics (Fig. 24.1).

Among the design goals of the Smart Building system were:

- Modularity and transportability, enabling the system to be quickly installed and easily removed from an existing building

- Use of only commercial off-the-shelf components in a modular unit that could be scaled to suit a future application

Capabilities of this system include:

- Filtered air for pressurization

- An array of sensors for chemical, biological, and radiological agents

- Emergency decontamination provisions for people entering the protective envelope

- An advanced control system integrating all system components

- Physical security regulating vehicle and pedestrian traffic in and around the building

FIGURE 24.1   Social Hall Plaza, Salt Lake City, Utah. This site, known as a Smart Building, was selected as a case study of collective protection, and was used during the 2002 Winter Olympics. (*Source: Battelle; Client: Defense Threat Reduction Agency; photographer: Bill Jackson, Battelle.*)

The CB system and related architectural, mechanical, electrical, and structural modifications provided positive-pressure collective protection to the top two floors (floors 5 and 6). This protective system operated continuously for the duration of the 2002 Olympics. An additional emergency electrical generator was installed to prevent loss of protection in the event of a line power failure.

Facilities were provided for decontamination of personnel entering the fifth and sixth floors in case of a large-scale CB release. A CB detection system, using multiple detectors and multiple technologies to maximize both sensitivity and selectivity to potential threats, was installed in the building and at selected exterior sites.

Physical security for the building consisted of temporary water-filled crash barriers outside the building, electronic access controls, and security checkpoints at all building entrances.

THE COLLECTIVE PROTECTION SYSTEM

The filtration system consisted of two parallel modular units, each supplying 10,000 cfm of filtered air to the protective envelope (Fig. 24.2).

This flow rate was sufficient to maintain positive pressure of approximately 0.1 iwg in the 60,000-square-foot protective envelope. Each filter unit consisted of a prefilter, one axial fan with variable frequency drive, and a set of ten 1000-cfm filter housings for the radial-flow filters. Each housing contained, in parallel, five M98 military-grade filter sets with the adsorber of ASZM-TEDA carbon; each set was rated at 200 cfm. Each unit was installed in a standard MilVan transport container and provided with a prefilter containing standard 20 percent ASHRAE air filters to protect the fans and filters from damage or premature clogging. The two 10,000-cfm modular filter systems were designed and fabricated by Battelle at engineering sites in Bel Air and Aberdeen, Maryland.

A steel platform was mounted on the roof to support the modular air-filtration system supplying purified air to the fifth and sixth floors. Interior modifications included extensive sealing measures to reduce air leakage from the protective envelope of the two floors. Mechanical rooms were constructed on both floors, and two air-handling units were installed in each mechanical room to provide cooling and recirculation in the protective envelope after it was isolated from the main HVAC system.

A gas-fired boiler was mounted on the rooftop support frame near the supply duct to heat the filtered air to a minimum of 55°F (or as specified). In-place leak testing was conducted on the filter units according to standard procedures (filtration system leakage not to exceed 0.03 percent for particulates and 0.1 percent for a test gas at full nominal airflow rate). This leak testing was conducted before the modular units left the fabrication site and again after they were installed on the Smart Building.

FIGURE 24.2 Smart Building, Salt Lake City, Utah. Photograph of collective protection system mounted on the building roof. (*Source: Battelle; Client: Defense Threat Reduction Agency; photographer: Bill Jackson, Battelle.*)

THE DETECTION SYSTEM

The CB detection system was designed to detect chemical warfare agents, a limited number of toxic industrial chemicals, biological warfare agents, and radioactive aerosols.

Based on a detailed market study and the specific requirements of this program, two types of commercially available chemical detectors were selected, one based on ion mobility spectrometry (IMS) technology and another on surface acoustic wave (SAW) technology. A dual-technology approach to chemical detection was chosen to provide improved sensitivity and selectivity and a means of minimizing false detection alarms. There were no false alarms from chemical detectors during the demonstration.

Inside the building, detectors were located at points selected to provide early detection of toxic vapors and to help determine the release location by the sequence of detector responses. Outside the building, chemical and radiological detectors were positioned on surrounding buildings to detect and evaluate an external airborne threat with a warning that would be sufficient to implement an appropriate building response.

Gamma detectors were used for detection of radiological threats. Alpha, beta, and neutron radiological threats would also produce sufficient gamma radiation to be detected. The sensitivity of the detectors was adjustable, an essential feature because at maximum sensitivity, the radiation detector was found to alarm when any person walking past the building had undergone recent medical isotope treatments or diagnosis.

Employed for detection of biological agents was the joint biological point detection system (JBPDS), a semiautomated self-contained system designed for the U.S. Department of Defense (Fig. 24.3).

This detection system operates by sampling the air continuously to measure and identify changes in certain parameters associated with the presence of biological aerosols. If such a change occurs (possibly several times a day), the system automatically alerts the operator, takes an air sample, and subjects the sample to a series of steps to detect any of the selected sets of threat organisms. The system also retains samples dissolved in water so an operator can perform a confirmatory test on site and can send a sample to a medical laboratory for definitive analysis.

As a separate confirmation means of detecting biological agents, two air-sampling canisters were installed in the building penthouse return-air plenum. One system was set to draw background air samples periodically from the building, and the other system was set to draw a single sample whenever a detector alarm occurred. The background canisters were changed once a week, and the single sample canister was changed each time an alarm occurred.

FIGURE 24.3 Smart Building, Salt Lake City, Utah. Photograph of biological detector located in the HVAC system mixing plenum. (*Source: Battelle; Client: Defense Threat Reduction Agency; photographer: Bill Jackson, Battelle.*)

THE CONTROL SYSTEM

The system control room was established on the sixth floor to monitor and control all critical parameters of the protective system. Emergency response procedures were developed and installed on an interactive database for instant reference and guidance.

The system also enabled protection at a lower level to other floors of the building. The HVAC system serving floors 1 through 4 was set to respond automatically in the event of a detector alarm. That is, the response to detecting contamination inside the building was to exhaust the air directly from the potentially contaminated zones, minimizing the potential for spread to other zones. If a detector indicated contamination outdoors, the control system would automatically place the building into sheltering mode, minimizing the introduction of outside air.

Control room operators responded to detector alarms by immediately investigating to determine whether the response was a true positive or a false positive. This confirmation process was assisted by queries to other sensors and detectors in and around the building, including 16 closed-circuit television cameras that could be controlled to display on control room monitors.

Communication capability was maintained with lobby security personnel, the receptionists, the CCTV control center (with access to many additional cameras), and the JBPDS operators. Control room operators were prepared to respond to problems indicated by sensors, detectors, and building pressure monitors. Provisions were also made to monitor incidents and alerts occurring throughout the city. The control room Internet connection accessed the networking software used by the joint operations center team. All relevant police and fire activity was posted on the network in real time. Intelligence bulletins and cautions were posted to maintain the focus of an alert on areas of potential threat.

Modifications were made to the building fire alarm system, as coordinated with the state fire marshal, to allow the filtration system fans and air-handling units in the protective envelope to continue functioning following a fire alarm on a lower floor. A fire alarm annunciator panel was installed in the control room, and direct communication with fire department personnel would be established immediately upon their arrival to ensure the safety of all personnel on the fifth and sixth floors. All air-handling units associated with the positive pressure collective protection system could be shut down from the control room, by direction of the fire department.

The control system for the Smart Building employed touch-screen monitors to display and adjust critical building parameters using a set of detector-control icons and a set of CCTV monitor selection icons.

Windows on each screen were used to display critical parameters related to the systems displayed on that screen. Touching an icon on any screen would activate the associated device display. For example, touching a CCTV icon would cause the image from that camera to be displayed on the number-one video monitor in the control room. Touching a detector icon would cause the full status of that detector to be displayed on the screen. Touching any place other than an icon on any of the floor plan screens would automatically zoom in on the point touched, giving an enlarged view of the zone.

THE DECONTAMINATION SYSTEM

Mantraps, airlocks (to prevent loss of positive pressure and infiltration of contaminated air), and decontamination rooms (tiled shower and changing rooms, equipped with disposable garments and contaminated waste containers) were installed at the elevator lobby entries to the fifth and sixth floors.

The decontamination capability also included trained decontamination teams with supplies of decontaminants, hand-held detectors, and detailed procedures for personnel decontamination. Training was provided by military personnel who supported the operation on site continuously throughout the Olympics. They were equipped with decontamination kits and handheld radiation detectors and chemical detectors. A training video was produced to introduce employees of the fifth and sixth floors to the concepts of personnel decontamination.

SYSTEM PERFORMANCE

The Smart Building Program employed a first-generation system. It was initially intended to be a technology demonstration, but the events of September 11, 2001, led to placing more emphasis on sustaining operational functionality throughout the 2002 Winter Olympics. The filtration system operated continuously throughout the events, and at the conclusion, a U.S. Army laboratory tested the filter capacity and determined the remaining life was at least 98 percent.

The chemical detectors also operated continuously, although they were not designed for continuous, long-term operation. These detectors required occasional resetting, adjustment, and repair; however, there were no false alarms, and they did not fail to detect any actual toxic chemical vapors, as far as can be determined. Once their sensitivity was adjusted to the proper level, the radiological detectors performed without fault, with no false alarms or failures to detect noted. Units of the JBPDS functioned continuously and performed within their specified limits. There were a number of aerosol indications that resulted in the automatic collection and analysis of air samples, and the operators were able to resolve each of the indications.

The control system was required to integrate the signals from all the detectors and sensors, monitor the building HVAC, and control the filtration system. The software development for these tasks continued throughout the operational interval. Essential functions were operational, but refinements were applied continuously.

Independent diagnostic testing of the levels of protection afforded by the protective envelope and the HVAC controls was performed by an independent organization. This testing involved the use of tracer gases and multiple sensor arrays. Preliminary test results indicate that the protective envelope was not breached when the building HVAC system was operated through the range of ventilation settings programmed into the building protection control system.

A 1000-kilowatt diesel generator was installed to provide emergency electrical power for the systems of the protective envelope. This was enough to maintain essential operations, including computer workstations, heating and air-conditioning, and both air-filtration modules. Critical computers, especially those monitoring building controls, were equipped with uninterruptible power supplies and were tested to confirm that the momentary delay from line power failure to full diesel generator power would not affect the continuous operation of the system. The building had an existing emergency generator, but it was capable of providing only minimal power for safety and security.

A 2000-gallon fuel tank was installed in the parking garage to supply the diesel generator with fuel for 24 hours of operation. Refueling could be accomplished from outside the building as necessary. As a diagnostic and confidence check, the emergency generator was programmed to automatically start and run for 20 minutes once each week.

APPLICABILITY OF CB PROTECTION SYSTEMS

The applicability of a particular building protection strategy and system design is determined by a number of factors including threat, vulnerability, the level of protection required, user requirements, cost, and other considerations (Table 24.8).

System design is primarily driven by the threat and vulnerability assessment. The threat assessment serves to identify the potential agent types, delivery mechanisms, and release locations of concern whereas the vulnerability assessment identifies the strengths and weaknesses of the building design, equipment, supplies, personnel, training, and other relevant assets. The assessment results determine the required protection system components. A comprehensive threat and vulnerability assessment should be conducted prior to initiation of system design.

TABLE 24.8   Strategy and System Design Factors

Parameter	System design factors
Threat	• Potential agent types • Delivery mechanisms • Release locations
Vulnerability	• Building design • Equipment • Supplies • Personnel • Training • Other relevant assets
Level of protection required	• Determine sections of building or complex that will be protected • Determine whether continuous or standby • Determine period of time protection will be afforded
User requirements	• Operations • Maintenance • Regulations • Other issues
Cost	• Capital • Operations and maintenance (O&M)

The level of protection required is determined by building stakeholders. Although affected by the threat, vulnerability assessment, and budget considerations, the level of protection required is not a purely objective decision. The selected system may be simplistic and low cost, or highly complex, comprehensive, and costly. Building stakeholders must address issues such as which sections of a building or building complex will be protected, whether the protection system will be continuous or standby, and the period of time protection will be afforded.

User requirements related to operations, maintenance, regulations, and other issues also affect system design. CB protection systems can be burdensome to building operators and maintenance staff. For example, collective protection airlocks may significantly affect the entry and exit rates of building occupants, and advanced filters and detectors may have high operation and maintenance costs. CB protection requirements may also oppose relevant regulations and standards, such as those associated with energy efficiency.

Comprehensive CB building protection can be extremely costly and therefore, system design is often driven by cost. For example, biological detectors may cost in excess of $250,000 (in 2003 dollars) and high-grade filters in excess of $25 per cfm of capacity. As is typical with most security systems, retrofitting the system is more expensive than integrating the system during building construction.

CONCLUSION

The threat to buildings and building occupants is continuously evolving. Although physical threats remain the main threat to building security, chemical and biological threats have become a key consideration to building protection planning. CB terrorism includes a broad array of chemical and biological agents and toxic industrial chemicals that may be delivered to a building via air, water, food, or surfaces.

CB protection systems for buildings range from simplistic, low-cost protective measures, such as sheltering-in-place, to complex and costly integrated positive-pressure collective protection systems coupled with advanced control and early warning systems. The applicability of a building protection strategy and system design is determined by threat, vulnerability, desired protection level, user requirements, cost, and other site- and owner-specific considerations.

Although recognized standards for designing and constructing a CB building protection system do not generally exist, several ongoing government research and development programs are developing standards and requirements.

ACKNOWLEDGMENTS

Contributors from Battelle Memorial Institute's Engineering Applications and Operations in Aberdeen, Maryland, who assisted with writing the text include:

- Richard Arcilesi, Principal Research Scientist
- Dr. Ken Ewing, Senior Research Scientist
- Thomas Kuchar, Program Manager
- James Risser, Program Manager
- Robert Rudolph, Chief Engineer
- Leo Saubier, Senior Research Scientist
- Timothy Stickler, Program Manager

Contributors from Battelle Memorial Institute in Aberdeen, Maryland, who assisted with preparation of the text:

- Heather Gatta, Administrative Assistant
- Alice Vickers, Administrative Assistant

Contributors from the Defense Threat Reduction Agency in Virginia:

- Robert Kehlet, Division Director
- Dr. Richard Lewis, Senior Program Manager

GLOSSARY

activated carbon Carbon that has been treated to develop an extensive network of micropores for the filtration of certain chemical compounds. It includes a wide range of amorphous carbon-based materials prepared to exhibit a high degree of porosity and an extended interparticulate surface area. The surface area of activated carbon is very large because it includes the walls of the submicroscopic pore structure.

active system A building protection system that remains in standby mode until activated by detection of a hazardous condition.

adsorption The process of trapping molecules within the pores of a microporous solid such as activated carbon, whereby a thin layer of molecules adheres to the surface as a result of atomic forces holding the atoms.

ASZM-TEDA Carbon, activated, impregnated, copper-silver-zinc-molybdenum-triethylenediamine. The ASZM-TEDA coating is patented by the United States Army and is used for chemical protection.

collective protection Methodical approach for protecting a building or shelter from CB contamination. Primary benefit is that persons within the space can continue to carry out their duties during a CB event, without wearing masks or protective garments.

decontamination The process of making a person, object, or area safe by absorbing, destroying, neutralizing, or removing chemical or biological agents or by removing radioactive material on or around it.

impregnated carbon An activated carbon chemically impregnated to increase its performance efficiency and adsorptive capacity for many gases that are difficult to adsorb onto base products. The impregnant may be a reagent that chemically converts a pollutant to a harmless or adsorbable product or may be a catalyst.

passive systems The protection systems that operate continuously and do not rely on detection systems.

protection factor A measure of the protection that a building protection system affords—calculated as the ratio of external dose and internal dose.

sorption Association of a (gas phase or aqueous) substance with a solid material, by surface attachment (adsorption) or dissolution and migration into the solid phase (absorption).

vapor density The weight of a vapor or gas compared to the weight of an equal volume of air; an expression of the density of the vapor or gas. Materials lighter than air have vapor densities less than 1.0 (e.g., acetylene, methane, hydrogen). Materials heavier than air (e.g., propane, hydrogen sulfide, ethane, butane, chlorine, sulfur dioxide) have vapor densities greater than 1.0.

volatility The property that describes how easily a substance will vaporize (turn into a gas or vapor). A volatile substance can be defined as (1) a substance that evaporates readily at normal temperatures and/or (2) one that has a measurable vapor pressure.

BIBLIOGRAPHY

Brletich, Nancy, Mary Jo Waters, Gregory Bowen, Mary Frances Tracy, *Worldwide Chemical Detection Equipment Handbook,* Chemical Warfare/Chemical and Biological Defense Information Analysis Center, Aberdeen Proving Ground, Md., AD-D754461, ISBN 1-888727-00-4, Oct. 1995.

Corps of Engineers Engineering Technical Letter (ETL) 1110-3-498, *Design of Collective Protection Shelters to Resist Chemical, Biological and Radiological (CB) Agents.* U.S. Army Corps of Engineers Protective Design Center, Omaha, Neb.

Fatah, A. A., J. A. Barrett, R. D. Arcilesi, K. J. Ewing, C. H. Lattin, and M. S. Helinski, *An Introduction to Biological Agent Detection Equipment for Emergency First Responders,* NIJ Guide 101-00, vols. 1 and 2, 2001.

Fatah, A. A., J. A. Barrett, R. D. Arcilesi, K. J. Ewing, C. H. Lattin, and M. S. Helinski, *Guide for the Selection of Chemical Agent and Toxic Industrial Material Detection Equipment for Emergency First Responders,* NIJ Guide 100-00, vols. 1 and 2, 2000.

Hunt, Robert E., Timothy Hayes, and Warren B. Carroll, *Guidelines for Mass Casualty Decontamination During a Terrorist Chemical Agent Incident,* Battelle, Columbus, Ohio, Sept. 1999.

Janney, Charles, et al., *Test Report, System Effectiveness Test of Home/Commercial Portable Air Cleaners,* CBIAC Report, Apr. 27, 2000, U.S. Army SBCCOM, Aberdeen Proving Ground, Md.

McKee, C. B., Lisa Collins, Jennifer Keetley, Dr. Howard Bausum, Terry Besch, Craig Moss, and Francis Hoin, *The Medical NBC Battlebook*, USACHPPM Technical Guide 244, July 1999.

National Academy of Sciences, *Chemical and Biological Terrorism: Research and Development to Improve Civilian Medical Response to Chemical and Biological Terrorism Incidents*, National Academy Press, Washington, D.C. 1999.

National Institute of Justice, *An Introduction to Biological Agent Detection Equipment for Emergency First Responders,* NIJ Guide 101-00, Law Enforcement and Corrections Standards and Testing Program, Washington, D.C., Dec. 2001.

National Institute of Justice, *Guide for the Selection of Chemical Agent and Toxic Industrial Material Detection Equipment for Emergency First Responders,* Law Enforcement and Corrections, Standards and Testing Program, Washington, D.C., June 2000.

National Institute of Justice, *Guide for the Selection of Chemical and Biological Decontamination Equipment for Emergency First Responders,* Law Enforcement and Corrections, Standards and Testing Program, Washington, D.C., Oct. 2001.

Rossman, Richard, et al., *Test Report, System Effectiveness Test of Commercial Recirculation Air Cleaners,* CBIAC Report, May 31, 2002, U.S. Army SBCCOM, Aberdeen Proving Ground, Md.

Rudolph, Robert C., et al., *Chemical Stockpile Emergency Preparedness Program (CSEPP) Protective Envelope Sealing Study Report,* CBIAC Report, Feb. 10, 1999, U.S. Army Edgewood Chemical and Biological Center (ECBC), Aberdeen Proving Ground, Md.

U.S. Army Field Manual 3-6, U.S. Air Force Manual 105-7, U.S. Marine Corps Fleet Marine Force Manual 7-11H, "Field Behavior of NBC Agents (Including Smoke and Incendiaries)," Washington, D.C., November 3, 1986.

U.S. Army Field Manual 3-9, U.S. Navy Publication P-467, U.S. Air Force Manual 355-7, "Potential Military Chemical/Biological Agents and Compounds," Washington, D.C., December 12, 1990.

Yang, Y. C., J. A. Baker, and J. R. Ward, *Decontamination of Chemical Warfare Agents, Chem. Rev,* vol. 92, 1992.

INTERNET RESOURCES

Battelle Memorial Institute
www.battelle.org

Chemical and Biological Information
 Analysis Center (CBIAC)
 www.cbiac.org

CHAPTER 25
CONSTRUCTION COST ESTIMATING FOR SECURITY-RELATED PROJECTS

Elizabeth J. Heider, AIA
Vice President, Skanska USA Building Inc.
Alexandria, Virginia

There is no such thing as absolute value in this world. You can only estimate what a thing is worth to you.
CHARLES DUDLEY WARNER (1829–1950)
U.S. editor and essayist

Construction costs, and premiums involved for security design, are of primary concern to owners, design professionals, and builders. After risk analysis and vulnerability assessments are conducted, and security related design and construction recommendations are identified, building owners must ensure that their project goals and budgets will be met. To maximize budget control, security design recommendations should be defined and evaluated during early project phases.

Hardening of buildings, and related security needs, often result in added costs for new construction and retrofit projects. Security-related costs address the elements needed to secure a building from specific terrorist threats, such as blast, and chemical or biological agents, since projects must comply with applicable building and life safety codes. A standardized approach to identifying and estimating security design elements allows building owners to determine the level of risk they wish to assume, and closely monitor construction costs.

BUDGETING

For public projects, especially federal government facilities, fixed capital construction budgets are often determined by long-range legislative appropriations. These fixed budgets essentially determine security risk levels a building project will be designed to sustain. Within this framework, the project team must identify risks and analyze threats, develop prioritized recommendations, incorporate them into the project design, and identify corresponding costs. Security-related features may also be driven by agency design standards and guidelines for a proposed site and building project. At the state and municipal levels, agencies may be ordered to increase building security based on threat alerts or law enforcement requests, requiring managers to shift funds from one agency or program to another in order to cover additional security construction costs.

Privately owned and funded building projects generally have a different budgeting process, and owners may have different reasons for implementing security design features, in addition to maintaining life safety. These reasons may include enhancing or maintaining real estate market values,

TABLE 25.1   Identifying Security Costs in Construction Projects

1. Perform a threat analysis to determine potential building vulnerabilities.
2. Determine which threats are already addressed in the project scope.
3. Scope addressable threats that are either cost related or non-cost related.
4. Identify measures to address construction cost-related threats.
5. Define the scope of work necessary to implement identified recommendations.
6. Identify alternative approaches.
7. Prepare documents in sufficient detail to allow each security measure and alternative approach to be priced. Associated costs should not include work that would otherwise be provided. For example, the cost of a rolling garage door should not be provided as part of the Site Perimeter Vehicular Entry measure if it would have been included otherwise.
8. Prepare an estimate for each approach.
9. Evaluate the cost of each measure against security benefits to determine best value measures. Best value describes measures providing the greatest protection for the lowest cost, or protection from the greatest threats at the lowest cost.
10. Prioritize measures in order of necessity, and those advised by standards and guidelines.
11. Incorporate as many measures into the project as funding permits, starting with highest priorities and adding other measures in order of best value.

attracting federal agencies, federal contractors, global corporations, and other high profile tenants needing security features, minimizing insurance and liability costs, and responding to local law enforcement and building department recommendations developed after September 11, 2001. All of these factors influence the extent and urgency of security-related construction costs. (Table 25.1).

THREATS

The most common threat types are terrorism, criminal, environmental, and infrastructure failure, or service interruption. This analysis focuses on terrorism, and related blast and chemical or biological threats, since most projects must comply with codes and standards addressing health, life safety, and welfare during emergencies and natural disasters. Based on an understanding of threats and vulnerabilities, design professionals and building owners should identify design elements needed to secure a building from the site perimeter inward. Costs for technology systems are not addressed here, because of the many variables involved with product selection, quantity, quality, and placement. However, security technology should be considered in total project costs and annual facility operational budgets.

SECURITY DESIGN AND CONSTRUCTION COSTS

The following section discusses cost considerations for nine security measures. All pricing reflects rough order-of-magnitude or ballpark costs to demonstrate the relative costs of each measure. This information reflects costs used by public agencies to benchmark construction projects in early planning phases. Actual costs may vary significantly and should be developed for each individual project.

Pricing assumes a construction start date of March 2004 for projects located in the Washington, D.C., metropolitan area. Adjusting numbers to reflect locations outside Washington could increase or decrease these costs by as much as 20 percent. Notable exceptions are New York City, with a location adjustment factor of approximately 140 percent, and the state of Alaska, with a location adjustment factor of approximately 133 percent. In addition to adjustments to reflect different project locations, costs must be adjusted to reflect the construction start date. Escalation has averaged between 2 and 3 percent per annum in most U.S. locations between 1998 and 2004. The location adjustment data is derived by averaging factors developed by RS Means and Marshall & Swift and adjusted to a reference location of Washington, D.C. (Table 25.2).

These terrorism-related security measures do not include costs for work addressing criminal or natural threats, or conventional features for certain building types. For example, secure glazing costs reflect incremental premiums for blast-resistant glazing above and beyond conventional window costs, not the total blast-resistant glazing cost.

All costs presented are based on new construction, as retrofit projects vary widely in scope and existing conditions and should be considered individually. For example, window replacement and progressive collapse design for existing buildings will likely be more costly than for new construction, because both areas depend on the strength and characteristics of existing structural and foundation systems.

TABLE 25.2   Location Factor Table for Cost Estimating

Range of location factors	+/–20%		
New York City	140%		

Location	Location factor	Location	Location factor
State averages, %			
Alabama	82	Montana	91
Alaska	133	Nebraska	90
Arizona	91	Nevada	105
Arkansas	80	New Hampshire	100
California	112	New Jersey	121
Colorado	97	Mexico	90
Connecticut	113	New York	113
Washington, DC	100	North Carolina	80
Delaware	107	North Dakota	91
Florida	85	Ohio	101
Georgia	84	Oklahoma	83
Hawaii	133	Oregon	106
Idaho	95	Pennsylvania	102
Illinois	105	Puerto Rico	94
Indiana	97	Rhode Island	110
Iowa	96	South Carolina	79
Kansas	90	South Dakota	86
Kentucky	90	Tennessee	85
Louisiana	83	Texas	82
Maine	95	Utah	93
Maryland	97	Vermont	93
Massachusetts	113	Virginia	88
Michigan	102	Washington	107
Minnesota	106	West Virginia	97
Mississippi	78	Wisconsin	103
Missouri	99	Wyoming	87

Source: RS Means and Marshall & Swift.

TABLE 25.3   Construction Cost Estimating Security Design Elements

1. Standoff distance
2. Site perimeter with vehicular entry
3. Site perimeter surveillance
4. Lobby
5. Loading docks and mailrooms
6. Progressive collapse
7. Building exteriors and windows
8. Roof
9. Mechanical, electrical, fire protection, and life safety systems

Construction cost estimating for security-related construction projects relies on several benchmark items, covering exterior and interior security design elements (Table 25.3).

In the following examples, a brief description of each security measure is given, along with assumptions made regarding scope of work and a potential cost impact. Cost impact is presented in terms of dollars per gross square foot of building area. To derive a total ballpark cost using these costs, apply the following formula:

Unit cost × location factor × escalation to date of construction start × gross area in square feet

The cost to implement a perimeter to establish a standoff distance (as defined in Item 1) for a 250,000 gross square feet (GSF) building with a 2003 start, to be built in New York City in 2005 would be the range of:

$0.75 (Unit cost) × 140% (location factor) × 1.03 × 1.03
(2 years' escalation to 2005) × 250,000 GSF or approximately $280,000

to

$1.75 (Unit cost) × 140% (location factor) × 1.03 × 1.03
(2 years' escalation to 2005) × 250,000 GSF or approximately $650,000

As a rule of thumb, high-rise projects with a gross area of approximately 400,000 GSF and a height of 10 to 19 floors above grade would tend to fall in the low end of the range. Mid-rise projects with a gross area of approximately 200,000 GSF and a height of 5 to 9 floors above grade would tend to fall in the middle of the range. Low-rise projects with a gross area of approximately 100,000 GSF and a height of 1 to 4 floors above grade would tend to fall in the high end of the range. Since the example references a mid-rise building, it is reasonable to assume that the cost would be in the region of $465,000. Note that the sums are rounded to the nearest $10,000 to reflect the roughness of these estimates.

SECURITY DESIGN ELEMENTS

Standoff Distance

Standoff distance refers to a building setback from roadways, vehicular circulation routes, and overall site perimeter, and is often achieved using plazas and landscaped areas. The greater the standoff distance, the less a building exterior needs to be hardened against blast, thereby potentially reducing costs for materials and systems. As standoff distance increases, so does the site area and site perimeter (Fig. 25.1).

Assumptions

- A 50-foot standoff distance, with barrier-type bollards where traffic intersections create a high-risk area is in place.
- A 6-foot nonclimbable fence in planted areas secures part of the perimeter.

Potential Cost Impact.   Between $0.75 per GSF and $1.75 per GSF.

Site Perimeter with Vehicular Entry

On-site personnel who monitor the vehicular entrance to a site will control an array of equipment and are housed in a small structure.

Assumptions

- A combination of security booths, barrier-type cable arms, hydraulic wedges, and security-control bollards are provided.

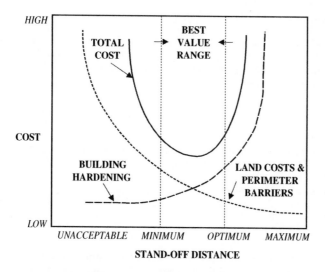

FIGURE 25.1 Relationships between land costs and perimeter barriers and building hardening costs. A balance between the two yields best value. (*Source: Joe Smith, Applied Research Associates.*)

Potential Cost Impact. $1.25 per GSF to $2.50 per GSF.

Site Perimeter Surveillance

Site perimeter surveillance is achieved through minimum lighting levels and cameras. An oddly configured site or a site with a standoff distance greater than 50 feet would be more costly than this example.

Assumptions

- Add security cameras and lighting at the site perimeter to provide illuminance of 5 footcandles.
- A 50-foot standoff distance is in place.

Potential Cost Impact. $0.75 per GSF to $1.50 per GSF.

Lobby

The cost model assumes the lobby already includes magnetometers located close to the main entry doors. The incremental cost to provide lobby security measures will be higher on a cost per GSF basis. Entrance lobby size is disproportionately large than for a low-rise building and disproportionately small for a high-rise building.

Assumptions

- Building system utility lines do not pass through or underneath the lobby.
- Provision of a 10-inch-thick reinforced concrete ceiling, floor and wall slab with No. 4 reinforcing bars 12 inches on center each way, each face, outboard of the magnetometer.
- All lobby columns are hardened to provide a 6-inch minimum standoff with steel jackets.
- All lobby doors and storefront outboard of the magnetometer are blast resistant.
- Doors are to be UL752 level 3 rated with door sweeps and seal.
- This hardening is intended to bring the secure threshold into the building and up to the magnetometer barrier, where portable explosive devices could be detected.
- The total building heating, ventilation, and air-conditioning (HVAC) costs are increased by 12 percent to provide a separate system serving the lobby area.

Potential Cost Impact. $3.00 per GSF to $8.00 per GSF.

Loading Docks and Mailrooms

The loading dock and mailroom areas already include colocated magnetometers at the building perimeter. The loading dock and mailroom are used for official use only. Rooms are hardened, to bring the secure threshold into the building and up to the magnetometer barrier, where portable explosive devices can be detected.

Assumptions

- The assumptions are the same as for the lobby.
- The costs per gross square foot to harden the loading dock and mailroom are lower than the lobby because of the smaller total net area of the loading dock and mailrooms.

Potential Cost Impact. $1.25 per GSF to $2.00 per GSF.

Progressive Collapse

Progressive collapse-resistant design requires stronger, heavier structural systems and assumes that any perimeter column may fail without the structure yielding to progressive collapse.

Assumptions

- Increase in the tonnage of steel required to harden the structure. This applies to new construction only.

Potential Cost Impact. $1.00 per GSF to $2.00 per GSF.

Building Exteriors and Windows

Blast-resistant glazing is one of the costliest security requirements. Cost is influenced by the amount of glazing on a building exterior, known as the *skin*. Costs are based on a skin ratio of approximately 50 to 60 percent. The skin ratio is the quantity of exterior closure or skin on a building divided by the total gross area of the project constructed above ground.

Window types, such as punched, ribbon, or curtain wall, will also impact costs. The cost to harden punched windows is often less costly than to harden ribbon windows or curtain wall. The technology is constantly changing and with increased demand, costs may decrease.

Assumptions

- A 50-foot standoff is in place.
- Construction is designed to withstand a blast with an effective force of 4 pounds per square inch (PSI).
- The building structure is strong enough to support blast-resistant window frames.
- An allowance of $2.00 per SF of precast area is included to reinforce a blast-resistant precast panel.
- The precast panel is 7 to 8 inches thick, is no greater than 20 feet wide, is internally reinforced with No. 6 reinforcing bars at one foot on center in the vertical direction, and two bars in the horizontal direction at panel mid-thickness.
- The precast panel is connected with one gravity and one lateral connection at two feet on center.
- The glazing assumes a maximum window lite size of 4'-0" by 5'-6".

- The glazing is a 1" insulated unit with ¼" heat-strengthened glass on the exterior, a ½" airspace and ¼" laminated annealed glass on the interior.
- All glazing has a minimum bite of ¾".
- Structural silicon sealant is specified.

Potential Cost Impact. $8.75 per GSF to $12.00 per GSF.

Roof

The roof of a low-rise building (four stories or fewer) will be hardened. A high-rise building (nine floors or more) would not require hardening, as it would be above the zone of influence, or the reach of an explosion to inflict damage.

Assumptions

- Provide a structural concrete roof slab reinforced by No. 4 reinforcing bars each direction, each side of the slab.

Potential Cost Impact. $0.75 per GSF to $1.75 per GSF.

Mechanical, Electrical, Fire Protection, and Life Safety Systems

Critical building systems are hardened.

Assumptions

- Walls around utility feeds, emergency generator and day tank, fire pump room, uninterruptible power system (UPS) room, and fire control room are hardened and flexible connections are provided.
- Air intakes are relocated above the fourth floor.
- Egress stairs are pressurized and equipped with smoke evacuation systems.
- The day tank is up-sized to provide eight hours of emergency operation.

Potential Cost Impact. $0.10 per GSF to $0.25 per GSF.

CONCLUSION

Determining security-related construction costs is a complex task based on many criteria from location, materials, building type, and owner to design, technology, and operational policies and procedures. During planning and design, owners must determine how their annual operational costs will balance against a one-time capital construction cost investment.

This analysis has presented typical costs for an order-of-magnitude pricing approach. As owners and design team members review security measures, the following considerations apply:

- Develop a risk-and-threat assessment to identify security measures early on during planning and design.
- Identify the cost of each measure, and prioritize the recommended elements for each project.
- Estimate each project individually, as unique conditions will apply by location, schedule, materials, and many other factors. Actual costs may vary significantly.
- Identify how to fund security design measures as part of the overall security budget.

- Apply costs indicated in this analysis to new construction projects. Renovation and retrofitting costs vary widely, based on existing conditions and many other criteria.
- Factor in first-time and ongoing maintenance costs for technology systems as well as operational security staffing for a total security budget.

By effectively integrating security costs in project budgets during early planning stages, owners and project team members will be able to achieve more effective security design and maintain a greater level of budget control on complex construction projects.

ACKNOWLEDGMENTS

PCC Construction Components, Gaithersburg, Maryland

GLOSSARY

zone of influence   The reach of an explosion to inflict damage.

INTERNET RESOURCES

Building Design & Construction
www.bdcmag.com

Construction Regional Publications:

- *California Construction*
- *Colorado Construction*
- *Intermountain Construction*
- *Louisiana Contractor*
- *Midwest Construction*
- *New York Construction News*
- *Northwest Construction*
- *Southeast Construction*
- *Southwest Contractor*
- *Texas Construction*

www.regionalpublications.construction.com

Construction Specifier
www.csinet.org/specify/index.htm

Construction Specifications Institute (CSI)
www.csinet.org

Design•Build
www.designbuildmag.com

Dodge Construction Reports, construction cost data, estimating information
www.dodge.construction.com

Marshall & Swift, cost estimating
www.marshallswift.com/index.asp

McGraw-Hill Construction, includes many industry links
www.construction.com

Norment/Norshield Security Products, manufacturers of blast and ballistic glazing and security devices
www.norshieldsecurity.com

PCC Construction Components, cost and installation methods of blast-resistant glazing
www.teamPCC.com

RS Means, construction cost data information
www.rsmeans.com

Skanska USA Building Inc.
www.skanskausa.com

CHAPTER 26

CONSTRUCTION: EMERGENCY RESPONSE LESSONS LEARNED FROM SEPTEMBER 11, 2001

Lewis J. Mintzer

(Formerly Director of Business Development)
AMEC Construction Management Inc.
New York, New York

> *The knowledge of all things is possible*
> LEONARDO DA VINCI (1452–1519)
> *Italian engineer, painter, & sculptor*

The terrorist attacks at the World Trade Center in New York City and at the Pentagon in Washington D.C., on September 11, 2001, resulted in a new awareness of vulnerability within the United States. Immediately after the attacks, public agencies and private industry focused on disaster recovery, business continuity, and increased homeland security (Figs. 26.1 to 26.6).

AMEC Construction Management mobilized at the World Trade Center and the Pentagon after the attacks to provide emergency response services. Both sites required daily coordination and spur-of-the-moment planning with legions of subcontractors, engineers, police, firefighters, city officials, and federal regulatory, military, and investigative personnel. The lessons learned from these experiences provide a guide for emergency response, especially where evacuation, rescue, and demolition are required.

After the attacks, AMEC ("the company") recorded actions by employees involved at both sites. Within two months, videotaped interviews were conducted with many individuals employed at either site. Interviewees discussed how they learned about the events of 9/11, how they mobilized, and how and why they took the actions they did. When respondents addressed how they had to make quick decisions in the first hours through the first few weeks after the incidents, the common theme emerging from the interviews centered on what people learned from dealing with an incident of such monumental proportions.

From the videotaped staff interviews, review of internal newsletters, and follow-up discussions, a "lessons learned" theme evolved. This information was documented and organized for use by others in the future, in the event of subsequent catastrophic emergencies.

THE PENTAGON: EMERGENCY REPAIR AND RESTORATION

AMEC had been working at the Pentagon before September 11th on the renovation and restoration of Wedge One, located on the southwest side of the Pentagon and encompassing five floors, totaling

FIGURE 26.1 Pentagon demolition, E-ring, October 19, 2001. (*Source: AMEC Construction Management Inc.*)

FIGURE 26.2 Pentagon demolition, E-ring, October 19, 2001. (*Source: AMEC Construction Management Inc.*)

FIGURE 26.3 Pentagon demolition, C-ring, October 23, 2001. (*Source: AMEC Construction Management Inc.*)

FIGURE 26-4 Pentagon demolition, C-ring, October 23, 2001. (*Source: AMEC Construction Management Inc.*)

FIGURE 26.5 Pentagon demolition, October 19, 2001. (*Source: AMEC Construction Management Inc.*)

1.2 million square feet. Blast-resistant windows and a steel-reinforcing system were installed along the exterior wall. This system was credited with saving a number of lives when the plane hit the building.

The plane's point of impact at the Pentagon was the junction of the strengthened Wedge One and Wedge Two, but most of the walls and windows of Wedge One remained intact. The company responded to the attack within minutes by rescuing survivors, constructing isolation barriers, installing shoring in portions of impacted areas, supplying debris removal equipment, and establishing an emergency communications system that was later adopted by several federal government entities on the project.

Environmental work included extensive asbestos and mold remediation. The expedited asbestos abatement effort involved 400,000 square feet of office space and the management of 400 asbestos workers, plus respiratory training and protection for 600 employees. Mold began growing rapidly after the flames were doused, affecting nearly a million square feet of the

FIGURE 26.6 Initial efforts at the Pentagon after September 11, 2001; aerial view of demolition. (*Source: AMEC Construction Management Inc.*)

facility. Air filtration was implemented to arrest mold growth, saving millions of dollars in tenant repair costs.

Other environmental services included ambient air-quality management; lead paint abatement; PCB and mercury assessment; smoke, soot, and debris management; jet fuel and petroleum assessment; and the development of mail-handling procedures to safeguard Pentagon project workers from the threat of anthrax contamination.

With demolition and debris removal completed in late November 2001, well ahead of the estimated four- to seven-month schedule, workers immediately began on the "Phoenix Project" phase, to rebuild structurally damaged areas.

The pouring of concrete columns and other activities topped out in April 2002. On June 11, 2002, exactly nine months after the attack, the final limestone slab was fitted into place on the building exterior. Completion of the façade meant work could begin on finishing the interior walls, wiring, and fixtures, enabling personnel to be back at their desks within one year after the attack.

By mid-year 2002, only three lost-time injuries were recorded at the Pentagon, despite extremely dangerous conditions, especially at the project onset. None of the injuries were permanent or life threatening; the most serious was a broken hand. Intense safety supervision, augmented by weekly and sometimes daily safety meetings with subcontractors, was provided.

In March 2002, the U.S. Congress unanimously passed a resolution praising AMEC's recovery and repair at the Pentagon. House Resolution 368 applauded the speed of both the demolition and rebuilding phases, as well as the dedication and long hours of the workers.

THE WORLD TRADE CENTER EMERGENCY RECOVERY

Within hours of the collapse of the two towers at the World Trade Center (WTC) in New York City's Lower Manhattan, the City of New York called upon AMEC to assist in the demolition and cleanup of Tower One and the Customs Building (known as WTC 6) on a time-and-materials basis (Figs. 26.7 and 26.8). AMEC mobilized a field staff on September 12, 2001, and established a 24-hour-a-day, seven-day-a-week (24/7) operation to remove debris from the site (Figs. 26.9 and 26.10).

The company employed over 100 ironworkers to burn the steel into manageable pieces, 30 operators to run and maintain four cranes, and four primary subcontractors to remove debris from the site and truck it to the approved debris station, a barging operation on the Hudson River (Fig. 26.11).

FIGURE 26.7 Members of the New York Police Department (NYPD) and construction crews assess the scene at the World Trade Center site on September 30, 2001. (*Source: AMEC Construction Management Inc.*)

FIGURE 26.8 Construction workers at the World Trade Center site on September 30, 2001. (*Source: AMEC Construction Management Inc.*)

FIGURE 26.9 Smoldering buildings and construction demolition equipment seen from above at the World Trade Center site on October 5, 2001. (*Source: AMEC Construction Management Inc.*)

FIGURE 26.10 Construction crew cleaning up the World Trade Center site on November 10, 2001. (*Source: AMEC Construction Management Inc.*)

FIGURE 26.11 Demolition of the World Trade Center building façade on November 10, 2001. (*Source: AMEC Construction Management Inc.*)

FIGURE 26.12 The hulking façade of the World Trade Center dwarfs construction demolition equipment on November 10, 2001. (*Source: AMEC Construction Management Inc.*)

AMEC Earth and Environmental assumed responsibility for on-site health and safety and ensured that each AMEC worker or subcontractor had the required personal protective equipment to work safely in the World Trade Center site. AMEC Technologies established a database and Web-based project management system to keep track of materials, manpower, and reporting requirements for the various agencies on site.

Initially, the most difficult challenge was immediately mobilizing a huge amount of manpower and heavy machinery (Fig. 26.12). Solid, long-standing relationships with subcontractors, trade unions, and the City of New York made this possible.

One of the major construction challenges at the World Trade Center site, which came to be known as ground zero, concerned maintaining the existing foundations around the site perimeter. The complex was originally built on landfill material and was protected from the Hudson River by a slurry wall. If the wall collapsed when the rest of the underground rubble was removed, the foundations of other buildings at the site would have been compromised. To safeguard the wall, workers performed the delicate task of installing more than a thousand tiebacks as they progressed underground. Tiebacks are steel cables extending at an angle from the slurry wall to bedrock.

Early in the project, deep pits in the slurry wall made it impossible for cranes and heavy equipment to reach the North Tower and other areas of the WTC site. This problem was solved by using steel columns and beams pulled from the debris to serve as the foundation for makeshift bridges and platforms, enabling equipment to move directly to what remained of the buildings (Figs. 26.13 and 24 14).

LESSONS LEARNED

The following information is adapted from *Lessons Learned: Emergency Responses to the World Trade Center and the Pentagon Attacks,* a guide published by AMEC in March 2002, primarily for internal use, based on the company's experience. This informational handbook was distributed to all employees with a role in emergency response, and does not constitute official corporate policy. Two main elements are as follows:

- Timeline Checklist providing emergency response guidelines based on the number of hours after the emergency event.
- Responsibility Matrix designating the responsible person who should lead, support, or implement each activity.

FIGURE 26.13 Aerial view of cleanup and demolition at the World Trade Center site on November 27, 2001. (*Source: AMEC Construction Management Inc.*)

FIGURE 26.14 Demolition and cleanup at the World Trade Center site on November 27, 2001. (*Source: AMEC Construction Management Inc.*)

EMERGENCY RESPONSE

These lessons learned are intended as guidelines for emergency response situations where construction management and related services may be required. This checklist is based on the experience of AMEC Construction Management ("the CM") at the World Trade Center and Pentagon after the September 11, 2001 terrorist attacks.

Definition of an Emergency

An emergency response can be triggered by a variety of activities, actions, or natural disasters These activities cover work sites where there is a contractual relationship with a client or owner and in situations where the CM needs to be prepared to respond to city, state, federal, or private client requests for emergency response. The following events may initiate an emergency response:

1. War
2. Terrorist activity
3. Riot
4. Political unrest
5. Earthquake
6. Volcano
7. Hurricane
8. Fire
9. Landslide
10. Flooding
11. Other adverse weather conditions, explosions, and accidents

Methodology

The *Lessons Learned* handbook is a compilation of data, notes, interviews, published material, and a review of videotapes arranged by the company to poll the personal experiences of employees from the CM and Earth and Environmental on the WTC and Pentagon projects (Fig. 26.15).

Lessons for the Construction Industry

The emergency response lessons have been divided into the following criteria and checklists:

General Emergency Response Activities.   This classification represents basic proactive measures that should be practiced or implemented to better prepare for similar events in the future. These measures should be regarded as basic principles applicable to any emergency response (Table 26.1).

Lessons Learned—Immediate Emergency Response Activities—First 48 Hours.   These are immediate actions to address the catastrophic event. Depending on the event, this time frame may be totally focused on a rescue and recovery mission (Tables 26.2 and 26.3).

FIGURE 26.15   Demolition and cleanup at the World Trade Center site on January 8, 2002. (*Source: AMEC Construction Management Inc.*)

TABLE 26.1 General Emergency Response Activities

Scope, schedule, budget, cost	1. Scope, schedule, and budget of assignment are typically not known.
Project management, resources, and coordination	1. For active and current job sites, an evacuation plan should be implemented and understood by the project team. 2. Define a standard composition of a typical emergency response team. This should typically include, at a minimum, the territory manager, project executive, senior project manager, project superintendent, and a representative from the Earth and Environmental division. 3. Maintain a solid relationship with subcontractors, trade unions, and the city in which services are being provided. 4. Develop and define a list of local subcontractors and suppliers with adequate resources to deal with an emergency. Suppliers of personnel protective equipment, such as safety glasses, respirators, gloves, and boots should be identified. Inquire about normal stock inventory for these suppliers and their ability to respond to emergencies. 5. Identify the local, state, and federal offices in the area and the key decision-making officials. They should already be identified in the contact listing. 6. Develop material checklists for immediate assembly and distribution to a typical emergency site, to include household items such as stationery, cups, coffee, first aid equipment, and medications.
QA/QC/safety	1. Continue to practice a safe and high-quality work environment. Adhere to all safety job requirements and to any documented safety and QA/QC procedures.

Source: AMEC Construction Management Inc.

Lessons Learned—Follow-Up Emergency Response Activities—48 Hours to 2 Weeks. These represent activities ideally considered and implemented in the first 48 hours. However, depending upon the magnitude of the event and prioritization of activities, they will more likely be addressed after a few days (Table 26.4).

The data collection process revealed that these activities are categorized into typical construction management components:

- Scope, Schedule, Budget, and Cost Concerns
- Project Management, Resources, and Coordination
- Quality Assurance, Quality Control (QA/QC), and Safety

The Emergency Response Responsibility Matrix (Tables 26.5 and 26.6) summarizes the activities and designates those who are responsible for leading, implementing, and supporting each activity. This matrix should be used as a guideline only, since each emergency response is unique and may require different parties to take appropriate action, based on immediate project needs.

CONCLUSION

The events related to the terrorist attacks on September 11, 2001, at the World Trade Center and the Pentagon created an unparalleled challenge of how construction managers can effectively and promptly respond to emergency situations and partner with public agencies to save lives and minimize further damage. (Fig. 26.16) The lessons learned from on-site experience at both locations

FIGURE 26.16 Construction crews continue to clear the World Trade Center site on January 8, 2002. View is looking west, toward the World Financial Center and the glass-enclosed Winter Garden, between the two towers. (*Source: AMEC Construction Management Inc.*)

FIGURE 26.17 The World Trade Center site, looking south, as crews complete their task. The World Financial Center is seen at grade level on the right. (*Source: AMEC Construction Management Inc.*)

provide a valuable emergency response planning guide for construction managers, contractors, and public officials charged with organizing response teams (Fig. 26.17).

ACKNOWLEDGMENTS

AMEC Construction Management Inc.

- John D. Onnembo, Jr., Esq., Senior Vice President and General Counsel, New York, New York
- Mitch Becker, former President and CEO, New York, New York
- Jake Bliek, Vice President, Chantilly, Virginia
- Ed Brundage, Vice President Business Development, Chantilly, Virginia
- David Kersey, Vice President, Bethesda, Maryland
- Josh Ofrane, former Marketing Coordinator, New York, New York

Material in this chapter has been adapted, with permission, from *Lessons Learned: Emergency Responses to the World Trade Center and the Pentagon Attacks,* a handbook published by AMEC Construction Management Inc. in March 2002, for internal use.

TABLE 26.2   Immediate Emergency Response Activities: The First 48 Hours, Part A

Scope, schedule, budget, cost	1. Establish an emergency telephone number with 24-hour coverage. 2. Consider innovative, resourceful, and unique approaches to each emergency response. 3. Logistically dissect the project into separate elements and components. 4. Prepare the organization to address a 24-hour-a-day/7-day-a-week (24/7) emergency operation. 5. Establish a secondary team to deal with shift work. This team should include managers, superintendents, and clerical support. (*Note:* everyone who responded to the WTC had to stay all night and longer until replacements were provided.) 6. Assign someone to supervise the documentation process of hours, labor, equipment, etc., so costs for the assignment can be equitably reimbursed at a later date.
Project management and resources	1. The territory manager or his designee should take charge of the emergency and inform each member of the specifics of the emergency. 2. Define or assign the leader and the team as soon as possible. Place a premium on experience and those who are battle-tested. 3. Implement the Emergency Response organization and emphasize specific roles and responsibilities so assignments are clear. 4. The territory manager (or designee) should contact the people at the corporate office and notify them of the situation and company involvement in the emergency. 5. The corporate office will notify the corporate safety director of the emergency. He will contact the territorial manager immediately upon notification. 6. Develop and distribute an organization chart illustrating clear lines of authority and responsibility. 7. Establish clear lines of communication between the emergency location and the territorial office. 8. Develop a list of personnel within the territory with specialized skills in demolition, heavy structural work, mechanical and electrical expertise. Include personnel from affiliate companies. 9. Establish a system of locating and contacting the key members of the Emergency Response Team at all times. A listing of home, office, and portable cell phones and beepers should be available. (*Note:* Cell phones did not work in all cases at the WTC.)

Source: AMEC Construction Management Inc.

INTERNET RESOURCES

AMEC Construction Management Inc.
www.amec.com

Engineering News Record
www.enr.com

New York Construction News
www.newyorkconstructionnews.com

TABLE 26.3   Immediate Emergency Response Activities: The First 48 Hours, Part B

Coordination	1. Obtain an emergency contact number for all subcontractors.
	2. The locations of the Emergency Response Team members must be known at all times by a dedicated individual who takes control of this responsibility.
	3. Team members should regard all specific project information as confidential. General information such as project name, client, location, or value of the project may be approved for release upon review and approval by the client.
	4. Do not discuss the project with the media. A designated point person is assigned to deal with all media inquiries.
	5. The territorial manager should establish the company's contractual relationship with the appropriate government agency. Contact corporate counsel prior to acceptance and execution of any contract with a government agency. Insurance coverage details should be addressed as soon as possible.

	6. The typical chain of command regarding outside forces in order of priority is as follows:
	  1. Fire Department—Chief
	  2. Firefighters
	  3. Police/FBI
	  4. Military
	  5. Ownership Group

	7. Make provisions for the project team to receive food and beverages.
	8. Photography documentation must be performed. Establish tight control of release of such photography.
QA/QC/safety	1. Address exposure to hazardous materials and obtain specific information for the best way to deal with them from the appropriate sources.
	2. Identify potential hazards and which divisions will be responsible for addressing them.
	3. Discuss concerns with the project manager regarding potential hazards (health and safety, data management, air quality).
	4. Have an up-to-date evacuation (escape route) plan of the job site. Include primary and secondary meeting places in the event of an emergency.
	5. Get map of emergency areas and support areas.
	6. Ensure and monitor distribution of safety hats, safety glasses, and respirators to workers, police, firefighters, military, and city officials.

Source: AMEC Construction Management Inc.

TABLE 26.4   Follow-Up Emergency Response: 48 Hours to 2 Weeks

Scope, schedule, budget, cost	1. Identify utilities posing further danger to the site. 2. Follow procedures and control the process for ordering materials. 3. Adhere to all contractual requirements regarding scope, authorization, payment, insurance, and indemnification. 4. Assess, be flexible, and implement nontradiational (demolition) approaches. (A cleanup crew from Washington National Airport worked at the Pentagon. Steel beams from the WTC debris were used as a makeshift bridge foundation to move equipment.) 5. Encourage open dialogue to generate assessment of all viable options and determine the concerns and advantages of each option. 6. Schedule daily meetings to coordinate all parties. 7. Ensure that workers do not stay around after their shift. 8. Document all activities, personnel, and equipment to get properly compensated and eliminate and reduce redundant activities.
Project management, resources, coordination	1. All Emergency Response Team members should familiarize themselves with the Corporate Crisis Management Plan. 2. The secretary should track and be aware of the locations of Emergency Response Team members at all times. 3. Institute a badging and sign-in/sign-out procedure. 4. Set up a local rest area, such as an apartment or hotel for individuals to rest, shower, change, and relax during off-hours. 5. Identify competitors and subcontractors who can assist, besides the standard list of engineers. 6. Employees need to be identifiable—they should all wear shirts and hardhats displaying the company logo. 7. Employees should carry personal identification on them, including blood type and emergency contact information. 8. Ensure the on-site field office is staffed with phones, local network, Internet, and a direct link to the main office. 9. Ensure that the team is prepared on all items before any client meetings. 10. Meet regularly with the client to address mutual concerns and corrective actions. 11. Superintendents must make a conscious effort to continue to communicate regularly and effectively with team members. 12. Provide Employee Assistance Programs for outreach. Anticipate psychological stress of the assignment, fatigue, anger, etc. 13. If more than one emergency response site occurs simultaneously, maintain a bulletin board of activities at the other job site. 14. Anticipate that public or government clients are likely to "think outside the government box" to accelerate emergency work.
QA/QC/safety	1. Develop a customized health and safety plan, to cover all aspects of the job, ranging from truck-spill prevention to boot-wash contamination. 2. Perform weekly risk assessments. 3. Hold regular safety meetings. Short daily meetings may be appropriate. 4. Assess likely weather conditions and potential adverse effects on the project. 5. Monitor the workers. Workers should monitor each other and report any unsafe situations. Project management should also monitor the workers.

Source: AMEC Construction Management Inc.

TABLE 26.5   Emergency Response Responsibility Matrix: General Emergency Response and First 48 Hours

EMERGENCY RESPONSE RESPONSIBILITY MATRIX

ACTIVITIES	COO	TM	EXEC	PM	SUPT	BUS MGR	HR	OFF MGR	LEGAL	MIS	E&E	SAFETY	ADMIN	CORP PR	QA/QC
GENERAL EMERGENCY RESPONSE															
Evacuation plan					I								L/S		
Define standard make-up of team			S	L/I	S										
Maintain solid relationship with sub and unions		S		S	L/I										
List local suppliers and contractors			L	I	S	S									
Identify local, state, federal offices			L	S/I											
Practice a safe work environment	X	X	X	X	X	X	X	X	X	X	X	X	X	X	X
FIRST 48 HOURS															
Establish 24 hr. emergency phone coverage								L/I/S							
Consider innovation, resourcefulness, uniqueness	X	X	X	X	X	X	X	X	X	X	X	X	X	X	X
Dissect the project into its elements			S	L	S										
Address 24 hr./7 day week operation				L	S			S							
Assign secondary team				L	S			S							
Documentation of hours, machinery, etc.				S	S	S	S	S	S		S	S	L/I	S	
Inform team members of specifics		L		S	S			S		S					
Assign the leader	S	L													
Develop/Implement emergency response organization		L/I	S	S	S										
Contact corporate office		L													
Contact corporate Safety Director		L	S/I												
Develop/Distribute organization chart		L	S/I												
Communicate to territory office				L											
Develop list of employees with specialized skills			L/I	S	S			S							
Develop list of home, phone, cell, beeper numbers				L				L/I/S							
Develop list of sub emergency contact numbers				L				S/I							
Know whereabouts of emergency response team				L				S/I							
Keep project information confidential	X	X	X	X	X	X	X	X	X	X	X	X	X	X	X
Response to media inquiries	S	S	S	S	S	S	S	S	S	S	S	S		L/I	
Contractual relationshipw/clientor agency			L/I	S											
Know the chain of command for outside forces	X	X	X	X	X	X	X	X	X	X	X	X	X	X	X
Documentation of photography/Release of photography				L	S					S		S			
Contact Environmental for exposure to hazmats															
Identify potential hazards					S						L/I				
Discuss concerns with pm regarding potential hazards					S						L/I				
Have up-to-date escape route				S	L/I										
Obtain map of emergency and support areas				S	L/I										
Distribute safety equipment to all participants								L/I				S			

Source: AMEC Construction Management Inc.

TABLE 26.6   **Emergency Response Responsibility Matrix: 48 Hours to 2 Weeks**

EMERGENCY RESPONSE RESPONSIBILITY MATRIX

ACTIVITIES	COO	TM	EXEC	PM	SUPT	BUS MGR	HR	OFF MGR	LEGAL	MIS	E&E	SAFETY	ADMIN	CORP PR	QA/QC
48 HOURS TO 2 WEEKS															
Identify utilities					L/I/S										
Order materials					S			L/I							
Adhere to all contractual requirements			S	L	I	I	I	I	I	I	I	I	I	I	I
Continue to assess-innovation				?											
Encourage open dialogue	S	S	S	L/I	S										
Set up daily meetings to coordinate all parties				L/I	S										
Make sure workers leave after shift					S			L/I							
Document all activities				L	L	S	S	S	S	S	S	S	S	S	I
Familiarization with company crisis plan	X	X	X	X	X	X	X	X	X	X	X	X	X	X	X
Whereabouts should be known at all times					L/I/S	S	S	S	S	S	S	S	S	S	S
Institute a badging and sign-in/sign-out procedure								L/I/S							
Set up local rest area					S			L/I							
Identify other competitors, subs who can assist			L	I	S										
Wear shirts and hardhats with company logo	X	X	X	X	X	X	X	X	X	X	X	X	X	X	X
Carry personal id/blood card/emergency contact info	X	X	X	X	X	X	X	X	X	X	X	X	X	X	X
On-site field office equipped					S			L/I							
Prepare in advance to any client meetings	S	S	S	L/I	S	S	S	S	S	S	S	S	S	S	S
Meet regularly with client	S	S	S	L/I	S										
Communicate with all team members	S	S	S	L/I	S	S	S	S	S	S	S	S	S	S	S
Employee assistance outreach				S	S		L/I								
Maintain a bulletin board of other site activities					L/S										
Develop a customized health and safety plan				S	S							L/I			
Weekly risk assessments															
Safety meetings				S	S							S	L/I		
Assess likely weather conditions					L/I							S	S		
Monitor the workers				L											

Codes

L = Lead, S = Support, I = Implement, X = Equal Participation
COO = Chief Operating Officer, TM = Territory Manager, EXEC = Project Executive, PM = Project Manager, SUPT = Superintendent
HR = Human Resources, E&E = AMEC Earth & Environmental Division

THIS MATRIX REPRESENTS A GENERAL DISTRIBUTION OF RESPONSIBILITIES WHICH WILL REQUIRE CUSTOMIZATION FOR INDIVIDUAL EMERGENCY

Source: AMEC Construction Management Inc.

TECHNOLOGY AND MATERIALS

CHAPTER 27
SECURITY TECHNOLOGY

William G. Sewell, RCDD

Senior Vice President, DMJM Technology
Arlington, Virginia

Urban anonymity, the idea that people won't know what you're doing or who you are, will, one hundred years from now, look like a small window in history—the 19th and 20th centuries.
ARNO PENZIAS (B. 1933)
American physicist, 1978 Nobel Prize Winner in Physics

The best-performing security sensor is a highly trained, dedicated human being. Human senses cover the necessary operations: sight, hearing, smell, touch, taste, feeling, and a voice to sound an alarm and remain vigilant. The human brain can process input from all senses simultaneously and make decisions based on inferences and subtle environmental changes.

Putting people in place to monitor and secure facilities is an expensive proposition. Security guards and cruising patrols can be a costly component of facility operations. Every security post, staffed 24 hours a day, 7 days a week (24/7), represents several full-time employee positions, whether in-house personnel or outsourced to private companies. When salaries, fringe benefits, and related costs are calculated over a year or longer, costs rapidly add up for each position. Minimizing the number of full-time security officer posts or employees allows building owners to reduce operational costs. As a result, by reducing staff costs as well as taking advantage of the many enhanced capabilities of twenty-first-century technology, security technology programs have become an essential and cost-effective strategy for many building owners.

Since the events of September 11, 2001, manufacturers have refined and upgraded many types of technology to address terrorism threats, including video processing, detection sensor technology, computer programs that manage and monitor systems, and the ability to send alerts to security personnel. Understanding the various types of technology systems, their capabilities, and applications is important when planning a technology program that is part of a comprehensive security plan (Table 27.1).

SECURITY SYSTEMS TECHNOLOGY

Technology is most effectively applied to deter, detect, delay, and assess an enemy's attack. An integrated security system has several elements (Fig. 27.1).

Deterrence and Delay

Deterrence is the ability to cause an intruder to abandon an attack or go elsewhere and leave a facility unharmed. Technology can deter intruders by being visible, or by creating the perception of a security

TABLE 27.1   Overview of Security Technology Applications

Type	Characteristics
Fence technology: • Passive: Chain link, wood, steel, concrete • Active: Electric fences, pulsed, fiber-optic	Provides perimeter and site security
Access control: • Combination locks • Keypad • Magnetic strip access card • Proximity card reader • Card reader and keypad combination	Deters an intruder from entering a facility. When several methods are combined, can deny or delay access, except through a central control point.
Biometric technology: • Hand geometry • Fingerprints • Iris scan • Retinal scan • Facial recognition	Verifies information on an access card against unique individual features.
Revolving door portal	Prevents tailgating, ensures that only one person enters an area at one time.
Weapons detection: • Magnetometers • Metal detectors • Hand wands	Detect weapons, metal objects, and hazardous materials, frequently used in airports and public lobbies.
Industrial and transportation applications: • Explosive detection systems (EDS) • Explosive trace detector (ETD) • Truck and cargo freight scanners	Screens air passengers, baggage, and cargo for explosive materials. Screens trucks and cargo freight for hazardous materials.
CCTV video technology capabilities: • Visible and infrared spectrum • Digital and analog formats • Indoor and outdoor use • Pan-tilt-zoom (PTZ) cameras • Monitors integrated with other systems	Photographs and records images with cameras. Images are displayed on a console and may be stored for future use.

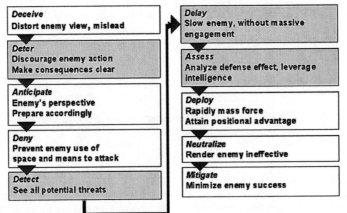

FIGURE 27.1 The elements of an integrated security system.

presence within a facility. If an avenue of attack has a highly visible detector, such as a closed-circuit television (CCTV) camera, an attacker who doesn't want to get caught is less likely to try to penetrate a facility at that point. Highly visible detection devices suggest that other devices are also present, thus prompting intruders to move on.

A determined terrorist who is willing to sacrifice his or her life is impossible to deter without great expense. Any situation or location will always carry some risk. Building owners and facility managers must determine the risk levels they are willing to assume.

Deterrence falls into two categories:

- Physical deterrence, such as fences, walls, and barriers.
- Deterrence systems, such as devices that prevent intruders from gaining easy access. They will cause most intruders to think twice before attacking a facility.

Both fences and deterrence systems can delay entry by an intruder. When fitted with detection devices, fences will detect an attack in progress and alert security personnel to respond.

FENCE TECHNOLOGY

The first line of facility defense is at the site perimeter. Expensive technologies available to the military, known as "beyond the fence line technology," can detect intrusion before arrival at the perimeter. This application assumes a large budget, a highly secure facility with a sterile area around the perimeter, and the capability to apply deadly force. However, this technology is seldom found around a typical commercial, institutional, or industrial facility. Fences are categorized as active and passive.

- Passive fences are traditionally made of chain link, wood, steel, concrete, or other materials.
- Active fences, such as electric fences, utilize technology to detect and deter intruders.

Electric Fences

The earliest electric fences consisted of three or four strands of wire set on insulators, used primarily to control cattle and other large animals. They kept trespassers out of fields and private areas. Eventually, electric fences were used in military and government installations. Characteristics of electric fences include the following:

- Can be dangerous or lethal
- Can't distinguish between a threat and a person who unintentionally wanders into them
- Are expensive to operate because they depend on a constant flow of electricity

Pulsed electric fences can be placed in conjunction with a standard chain link or other kind of fence. In such cases, horizontal wires in the fence carry very short pulses of high voltage. When touched, the pulses are strong enough to cause a person to retreat, but are not strong enough to cause permanent injury. The fence sends an alarm to a monitoring point and can be integrated with a camera system to provide visual verification of the intruder. In most applications, this fence configuration is installed behind a passive fence to prevent anyone from making accidental contact (Fig. 27.2).

Fiber-Optic Technology

Fiber-optic fence technology is designed to detect an intruder and send an alarm to a monitoring point. Fiber-optic cables are woven through the fence or buried under the fence line. The light traveling down the fiber behaves predictably, and when the fiber is disturbed, a detector sends a signal, triggering an alarm.

FIGURE 27.2   Powered fence behind a standard chain link fence. (*Gallagher Corporation.*)

ACCESS CONTROL TECHNOLOGY

- Access control deters an intruder from entering a facility, especially when combined with walls, fences, or other structures to deny or delay access, except through the control point. The key to access control is ensuring that technology will positively identify those presenting themselves for access and exclude those who are unauthorized to enter. This operation is simple in concept, but difficult in execution. Various forms of access control technology are available and widely used among all building types, including the following:
- Combination locks
- Keypad
- Magnetic strip access card
- Proximity card reader
- Card reader and keypad combination

Combination Locks

One of the oldest technologies still in use, after the traditional key style, is the combination lock, such as those found on safes or vaults. This number-based technology evolved into an electro-mechanical push-button combination lock (Fig. 27.3).

Keypads

Keypads evolved from the push-button combination lock. The keypad unit is connected electrically to a locking solenoid. When the correct code is entered on the keypad, the solenoid retracts, allowing the door or window to be opened (Fig. 27.4).

Access Cards

Access cards are another widely used access control technology. The card is shown to a person who either allows the cardholder to pass, or not. This approach requires security personnel to monitor access, which can result in high operational costs. When several access points must be monitored, costs can be prohibitive. For this reason, automated card readers were developed.

FIGURE 27.3 Electromechanical push-button combination lock. (*Cypher Lock.*)

FIGURE 27.4 Electromechanical keypad unit. (*Ademco.*)

FIGURE 27.5 Combination cardswipe and keypad. (*Ademco.*)

One of the most popular card readers is the magnetic strip reader, or mag-swipe card reader. This reader has a magnetic head, similar to a tape recorder head, and reads information encoded on a magnetic strip, attached to the access card (Fig. 27.5).

Another type of access card is the proximity card reader, or "prox card." This reader uses radio frequency (RF) technology to read an encoded device inside the card at a distance up to eight feet from the reader. These readers support a higher throughput, or volume of visitors, since users don't have to put their card in place and move it in a certain way. Additionally, since there is no physical contact between the reader and the card, there is less wear, and both the cards and readers last longer.

To add another level of security, card readers and keypads are often tied together, requiring someone to present a card to the reader and enter an access code. Both inputs must match before the lock is opened.

Card reader systems may be vulnerable because cards can be stolen, loaned, or lost and the person who has possession of the card has access to a facility, whether authorized or not. When access control systems combine a keypad with a card reader, access is prevented when cards are lost or stolen. However, this does not prevent a person from loaning his or her card and the access code to someone who would otherwise not have access to a facility.

BIOMETRIC TECHNOLOGY

Various devices have been developed to check information on the access card against unique individual physical features, known as biometric scanners. Common types of biometric scanners include the following:

- Hand geometry
- Fingerprints
- Iris scan
- Retinal scan
- Facial recognition

Hand Geometry

Hand geometry devices measure the width, length, and general shape of a human hand. The system is programmed when a person places his or her hand on a master reader, which then looks at several parameters of hand geometry and stores them in a database. The data record is associated with a key code, or access card, so that when a person enters the code or swipes the card, he or she must put his or her hand on the reader and both inputs must match before access is granted (Fig. 27.6).

Environmental conditions must be considered when designing systems with hand geometry readers, which require people to put bare skin against the reader surface. In hot climates, hands may get burned when touching the hot surface. Outdoor cold climates may cause skin to freeze and stick to the reader. Under these extreme conditions, other means of access control should be used.

Fingerprint Recognition

Fingerprint recognition systems are widely accepted because of their accuracy. Applications include positive ID for cashing personal checks, credit card verification, and access control. Fingerprint readers are more accurate than hand geometry readers because they take more readings against unique biological characteristics, resulting in a lower error rate. Error generates an access denied response, so a high error rate can be frustrating to users (Fig. 27.7).

Facial Recognition

Facial recognition systems were developed in the early 1990s, but have not been as widely used as other systems because they rely on heat characteristics that are inconsistent from day to day and by location. These systems are constantly being improved and tested, so they should not be ruled out. However, more reliable technology is readily available (Fig. 27.8).

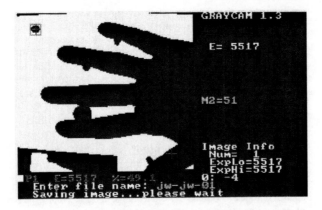

FIGURE 27.6 Hand geometry data. (*DMJM Technology.*)

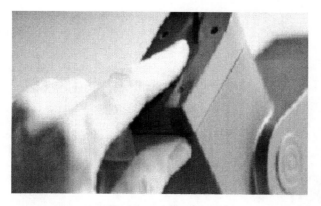

FIGURE 27.7 Fingerprint reader. (*Photo Source: Federal Aviation Administration.*)

FIGURE 27.8 Desktop facial recognition unit. (*Photo source: Federal Aviation Administration.*)

Iris Scan Technology

Iris scan technology is one of the most highly regarded and accurate systems. This technology is based on the unique characteristics of the iris in the eye of every individual. Iris scan devices have different looks and shapes. Some wall-mounted units look like vanity mirrors, while others are desktop units (Fig. 27.9).

These units scan the iris and compare the results to a base scan for the individual. They are entered into a key code or card swipe code, similar to hand geometry or fingerprint scanner operations. The error rate for iris scanners is very low compared to other devices, making this technology the most efficient of available access control solutions.

SECURITY BREACHES

One of the most common security breaches, known as tailgating, occurs when an authorized person opens a door or portal, and another person enters at the same time before the door closes. A number of doors and portals can either detect or prevent tailgating. The most effective method is using a revolving door portal that only allows passage of one person at a time. Other portals allow faster throughput and close when detecting more than one person in the lane (Fig. 27.10).

In some high-security applications, access control is an integrated solution combining an access control device with a portal that will deny access to unauthorized persons and trap the individuals inside. These mantraps hold the unauthorized persons until a security response team arrives to let them out and either establish their identity or take them into custody.

FIGURE 27.9 Wall-mounted iris scan terminal. (*Photo source: Federal Aviation Administration.*)

Detection and Assessment

Detection is the sweet spot for technology. Security devices extend and multiply the senses of the personnel managing a facility. Technology can:

- *See,* through cameras and video processing
- *Hear,* through listening devices
- *Smell,* by smoke and gas analysis and detection

FIGURE 27.10 Mantrap style iris scan system. (*Photo source: Federal Aviation Administration.*)

- *Feel*, through vibration sensors
- *Detect*, explosive materials and weapons hidden in bags or on a person

Connecting devices to computers provides a first filter to eliminate false alarms or events that are not threats. Computers can accept several inputs, make decisions, and display preprogrammed alarms.

An electronic contact detecting a door being opened may swing a camera to look at the door, while a video processor assesses the priority of the alarm and routes information to different devices, depending on the required response.

WEAPONS DETECTION TECHNOLOGY

Magnetometers and metal detectors are common detection devices found at airports and most government building lobbies, especially at federal facilities. Unlike most technologies, newer magnetometers are increasing, rather than decreasing, in size, thus requiring more floor area and clearance space in building lobbies. Designers should keep this in mind when planning lobby circulation in high-profile, high-risk facilities.

A metal detector is shaped like a doorway, allowing a person to walk through and be screened by a magnetic field located inside the doorway. When a metal object passes through, the field is disturbed and sensors sound an alarm. The field is adjustable, allowing concentration on areas more likely to detect weapons, such as pockets and the waist area. Areas unlikely or impossible to carry a weapon, such as the head, can be ignored. Sensitivity can be adjusted during high alerts or in response to likely threats (Fig. 27.11).

Hand wands, also used in airports, are secondary scanning devices when the walkthrough metal detector senses an object registering over the alarm threshold. Both the walkthrough device and the handheld wand can be used in any kind of facility, to prevent weapons or other contraband from being brought inside the building (Fig. 27.12).

INDUSTRIAL AND TRANSPORTATION APPLICATIONS

The events of September 11, 2001, created a new urgency and need for enhanced technology to screen air passenger baggage for explosives and trucks and cargo freight for explosives and hazardous materials. Three types of detection systems include:

- Explosive detection systems (EDS)
- Explosive trace detector (ETD)
- Truck and cargo freight scanners

Explosive Detection Technology

Explosive detection has become an integral part of air travel, after September 11, 2001, when the U.S. Congress mandated 100 percent baggage screening in all airports nationwide. Explosive detection systems are highly complex machines using a combination of x-ray, computerized tomography (CT),

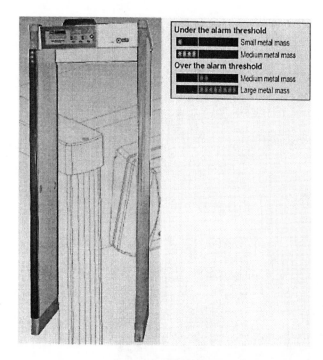

FIGURE 27.11 Walkthrough metal detection portal with alarm panel. (*Ceta.*)

FIGURE 27.12 Handheld metal detection wand. (*Ceta.*)

and gas analysis to look inside baggage. The systems are connected to a computer seeking predetermined suspicious shapes and are programmed to alert screeners when they appear. Highly trained operators look for shapes that could be explosives, weapons, contraband, or other dangerous materials (Fig. 27.13).

A smaller unit, called the explosive trace detector, is sometimes used to inspect regular baggage, hand-carried bags, or packages for traces of explosives that might indicate that an item contains a dangerous device or dangerous materials. Because of its sensitivity, the ETD may detect when people carrying packages may have worked with explosives or dangerous materials recently, even though they don't have any with them.

To activate the device, the operator wipes a cloth swab over the bag or package. If the bag contains explosive materials, traces of the materials will likely be present on the outside and the swab will pick up small bits of the material. The swab is placed into a chamber, where the chemistry of the swab is analyzed, and the analysis results are compared to a database of known dangerous materials (Fig. 27.14).

Cargo and Shipping Security

Scanning large crates, boxes, and cargo before they are loaded onto aircraft, ships, or trucks is another vital aspect of technology and homeland security. Trucks can also be scanned when they are already en route to a destination. Cargo scanning, based on baggage screening technology, is used at European

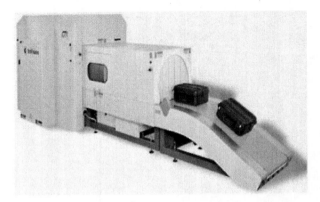

FIGURE 27.13 Explosive detection system used to screen airport baggage. (*Ceta.*)

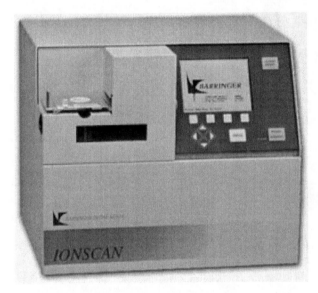

FIGURE 27.14 Explosive trace detector. (*L3 Communications.*)

airports and U.S. ports. Cargo screening is similar to baggage screening, but at an increased scale, to accommodate large cargo containers (Fig. 27.15).

Protecting highways and cities from truck explosives and hazardous materials requires integrating technology with law enforcement procedures and policy directives from agencies and jurisdictions with transportation oversight. Scanning technology for semi trailer trucks and shipping cargo is available. These large scanning devices can be portable, mounted on a vehicle, or stationary and built into a cargo-processing facility (Figs. 27.16 and 27.17).

VIDEO TECHNOLOGY

Detecting people trying to enter a facility or move into unauthorized areas can be accomplished in several ways. Cameras are available to operate in both the visible and infrared areas of the spectrum. Video camera technology has been around for decades and has changed from analog to digital formats.

FIGURE 27.15 A cargo container scanning system scans for explosives, drugs, and other contraband, prior to being loaded onto an aircraft. (*L3 Communications.*)

FIGURE 27.16 Vehicle-mounted scanning device. Truck (on right) being examined by a mobile x-ray scanner in the truck on the left. (*L3 Communications.*)

FIGURE 27.17 The results of the truck scan shows computers inside the truck packed with drugs and an automatic weapon hidden beneath the floor of the truck. These devices can see into the engine to detect explosives and contraband hidden inside the engine block. (*L3 Communications.*)

Digital images lend themselves to computer analysis and manipulation, making them both powerful and somewhat risky to use as evidence. The flexibility available with digital images makes them susceptible to manipulation through video editing software. Video files must be saved and stored to ensure their integrity, especially if they are to be used in court as evidence. Computers can analyze an image in real time and detect when someone in the frame has left a package unattended. The system will call the operator's attention to the possible threat.

Many cameras and housings are designed for indoor or outdoor use, sheltered by the camera housing. The housing lens or window can be equipped with an optional heater to keep the glass clear in cold or humid conditions, particularly when mounted outdoors. The housing can be equipped with the ability to pan back and forth, and to tilt up and down via remote control, enabling the operator and monitors to view any direction. The cameras can also zoom in on objects. The pan-tilt-zoom capability is often referred to as a PTZ camera (Fig. 27.18).

Newer, smaller video technology enables cameras to be less intrusive because they are less obvious. These cameras are found in nearly every building type, from casinos to grocery stores, and are available in PTZ versions. Because they are small and agile, they can move quickly and be preset through software to look at certain scenes with the touch of a button (Fig. 27.19).

FIGURE 27.18 Standard wall-mounted surveillance camera. (*Pelco.*)

EMERGENCY RESPONSE

First responders must have reliable technology to send and receive messages within and around a facility during emergencies. The effectiveness of handheld radio technology used by emergency personnel was a serious issue of concern during and after evacuation of the World Trade Center Twin Towers on September 11, 2001. Failure of the technology to operate in a given environment and incompatibility among several systems and manufacturers may have contributed to loss of life by firefighters on upper levels of the towers who were unable to receive word about the events unfolding on the ground and in the adjacent tower. As a result of this technology failure, a lesson learned from September 11th concerns refinement, testing, and compatibility of handheld portable radio technology.

FIGURE 27.19 Dome camera. (*Pelco.*)

Although fire and police departments use these applications routinely, the technology is also essential for corporate security and facility security management. This technology should include radio communication within the facility and radio and hard-line communication capability to local law enforcement and medical response teams.

EMERGENCY OPERATIONS CENTER

Technology plays an important role in efficient operations or how building owners or agencies choose to run their organizations. Emergency operations centers (EOC) are the primary response facilities serving as information collection and dissemination points for cities, counties, states, and private-sector facilities and campuswide organizations. EOC technology ranges from radio consoles and video display positions to access control head-end equipment. In large EOC facilities, such as those within major cities or counties, banks of incoming telephone lines and computer-aided dispatch (CAD) systems connect municipal agencies to each other and to state and federal authorities when emergency assistance is critical.

Avoiding information overload should be considered during systems planning and facility design to keep operators alert. For example, a security professional sitting in front of eight or more monitors with nine-inch screens will quickly ignore some monitors because there are too many to watch. These systems must have built-in intelligence to assist security personnel in doing their job most efficiently. Providing a large event monitor is one solution, allowing each camera to feed into a small monitor, and installing a single large monitor to display events on a rotating view basis.

Case Studies: A Typical Operation Center

As an example, assume one operation center is monitoring five external doors, five entry corridors, two loading docks, four computer spaces, a lobby, four views of the parking deck, and three different spaces in the executive suite, for a total of 24 different areas. This is considered a small installation, compared to many corporate or government buildings (Fig. 27.20).

- An event is detected by another device, such as a door contact, motion sensor, glass break sensor, or other sensing device.
- The video camera controller is programmed with preset positions to point a camera at the area around the sensing device.
- When the device is triggered, the camera swings to the preset location and the camera output is switched to the large event monitor as the device alarm sounds, alerting the guard to an event in progress.

In a real-life example, the following might happen: The operations center as described above monitors 24 cameras. One camera is installed in the loading dock and patrols, or automatically swings back and forth over, the dock area. The dock has a roll-up door for trucks, a standard size door with a vision panel, a receiving office with a window overlooking the dock, and a standard door between the dock and the rest of the building.

- An intruder sneaks up to the outside door, looks through the window, and waits for the camera to swing away from the door as it continues on patrol. The intruder forces the door open, expecting to sneak over to the receiving office before the camera swings back. As soon as the intruder opens the door, door contacts prompt the camera to swing immediately to a preset position and view the door.
- At the same time, an audible alarm sounds in the operations center, and the view from the door camera appears on the large event monitor.
- The security officer in the operations center checks the scene and immediately summons a response. This systems integration is relatively easy, inexpensive, prudent, and often a requirement for system design.

Another integrated systems design approach might eliminate most multiple monitors and program cameras to allow events to trigger alarms, causing video to be displayed. Since no video is displayed unless an event triggers a sensor, hundreds of sensors would need to be installed to cover every contingency. Video processing can allow events to trigger changes in the video picture.

FIGURE 27.20 Operations center, with control monitoring of over 100 camera inputs on multiple CCTV monitors. (*Lenel.*)

- If a camera is observing a scene and there is no change in the image, the camera output is not sent back to the operations center. When the image changes, such as a door opening or someone walking into the frame, the camera sends an alarm to the operations center, downloads the previous several seconds of video, and begins live video streaming to the monitors.

- This approach saves bandwidth in the transmission line, storage space on the server, and sends information to be analyzed when the information is important.

- Because there is less information to monitor and interpret, fewer people are required and operational costs are significantly reduced, whereas the security operation becomes more effective (Fig. 27.21).

TECHNOLOGY PLANNING

With so many choices available in the marketplace, the most challenging issue facing building owners, facility managers, and their security planning team or committee concerns selecting and installing appropriate technology systems and determining how much is enough. Specifying suitable technology systems is essential to meeting facility needs and security goals.

Facility and corporate security managers should consider hiring a security consultant before starting the technology assessment and planning process. The consultant should be independent of any manufacturer or equipment reseller to provide an unbiased viewpoint and suggest the best system capabilities, at the best price, matched to facility needs. Ideally, a consultant should have at least five years' experience in the security industry and experience in a number of similar installations. The broader the consultant's experience, the more likely an owner will get a balanced viewpoint and insight into a broad range of technologies.

Technology planning begins with a thorough vulnerability assessment of a site or facility. The assessment should follow a structured approach, consisting of the following:

- Cataloging assets
- Characterizing the facility
- Pairing assets with vulnerabilities
- Prioritizing threat mitigation

FIGURE 27.21   Integrated system brings alarm and camera inputs to a single PC monitor. (*Lenel.*)

Each mitigation element has a cost; total costs must be balanced against the project implementation budget. Tradeoffs must often be established to balance affordable technologies against desired security levels.

TECHNOLOGY SYSTEM DESIGN

System design reflects the facility needs identified in the vulnerability assessment. Technology planning must consider staff capabilities to operate and maintain any systems installed. For example, designing a system in which each camera has its own CCTV monitor is technically possible and may even be the least expensive approach. However, when the number of cameras reaches 16 or more, one person cannot effectively monitor all the information displayed. The solution may be either to add more staff or develop a different design. Technology system design considerations include the following:

- Cost
- Sophistication of operator
- Training programs to use system
- System complexity

During design, each vulnerability and mitigation element is matched to an appropriate technology system. The system should be designed to integrate the facility and the application, based on best practices and technical judgments.

- Some operational scenarios require separate and continual monitoring of certain assets, while others allow integration of several cameras onto a single screen.
- Integrating video cameras, video processing, and intrusion detection systems can be achieved so that an intrusion event will sound an alarm, swing a camera, zoom the picture, and process the video, all without human intervention.
- Businesses may seek to secure their intellectual property, data, and e-mail systems from disaster, loss, and unwanted hackers or intruders (Table 27.2).

OPERATIONS

Operations, when combined with facility design, must enable personnel to respond efficiently to any security event. Ergonomics are important because operators often sit for long periods of time monitoring cameras and alarm screens. Well-designed consoles that include the integration of sensors, displays, and computer systems make the operator's job more effective and less tedious (Fig. 27.22).

TABLE 27.2   Business Security Challenges

- Disaster protection and business continuity
- Reliable backup of critical business systems and data
- Reducing computer spam
- Virus scanning for incoming e-mail
- Computer network security

FIGURE 27.22 U.S. government security command and control center. (*DMJM Technology.*)

CONCLUSION

Technology can support the needs of building owners and facility managers by reducing risk and enhancing employee and tenant safety, while controlling operational costs. A successful technology implementation plan clearly defines:

- Assets to be protected
- Threats and risks to assets
- Mitigation measures to provide the desired level of protection

Security technology is constantly evolving with new features and advances to streamline routine operations. Selection, specification, and installation of technology are often less expensive in the long run than hiring three shifts of full-time security staff.

A comprehensive security plan effectively integrates technology with facility design, operational policies, and procedures. Access control, when combined with appropriate technology, provides positive identification of people and goods entering a facility and ensures that security policies and procedures are implemented and monitored.

When researching technology needs, alternatives and options must be explored to ensure that recommended solutions meet functional, operational, and budget goals (Table 27.3). Determining security needs includes:

- Developing a vulnerability analysis
- Performing a risk assessment
- Defining technology requirements
- Designing systems
- Managing implementation

Through methodical analysis of site-specific facility risks, needs, budgets, personnel capabilities, and operational protocols, developing a comprehensive technology system is among the most important accomplishments any building owner or manager can undertake for their facility.

Table 27.3 Security Technology Planning Checklist

1. Identify assets to be protected
2. Categorize assets: critical, essential, important, nonessential
3. Identify threats
4. Identify risks
5. Review existing technologies, policies, procedures
6. Establish system requirements
7. Determine technology budget
8. Define system approach
9. Complete system design
10. Examine alternatives
11. Complete final design
12. Issue competitive system request for proposal (RFP)

ACKNOWLEDGMENTS

- Mel Daley, Director, Corporate Security, Philip Morris USA, Richmond, Virginia
- Donald J. Dwore, FAIA, Principal, Spillis Candela DMJM Design, Coral Gables, Florida
- Tim O'Leary, Executive Assistant, DMJM Technology, Arlington, Virginia
- Scott Rice, Federal Sales Manager, Lenel Systems, York, Pennsylvania
- Colleen Sewell, Leesburg, Virginia
- Lyna Shirley, Marketing and Business Manager, DMJM Technology, Arlington, Virginia
- Alexandra Spencer, Media Relations Officer, DMJM/DMJM + HARRIS, Los Angeles, California
- Dr. Christer Wilkinson, Project Manager, DMJM System Solutions, Phoenix, Arizona

INTERNET RESOURCES

ADEMCO Group
www.ademco.com

American Society of Industrial Security (ASIS)
www.asisonline.org

DMJM Technology
www.dmjm.com

Gallagher, Inc.
www.powerfence.com

Homeland Defense Journal
www.homelanddefensejournal.com

Invision
www.invision.com

Johnson Controls, Inc.
www.johnsoncontrols.com

L3 Communications Corp
www.l-3comm.com

Lenel Systems International
www.lenel.com

Pelco Video Security Systems
www.pelco.com

Smiths Detection
www.smithsdetection.com

Security Management Magazine
www.securitymanagement.com

CHAPTER 28

SELECTING AND SPECIFYING SECURITY TECHNOLOGY PRODUCTS: A PRIMER FOR BUILDING OWNERS AND FACILITY MANAGERS

Francis J. Sheridan, AIA

Director, NYS Department of Correctional Services
Division of Facilities Planning and Development
Albany, New York

Security can only be achieved through constant change,
through discarding old ideas that have outlived their
usefulness and adapting others to current facts.
WILLIAM O. DOUGLAS *(1898–1980)*
U.S. Supreme Court Justice

Building owners, landlords, and facility managers have a special interest in ensuring that the security and technology products purchased and installed in their facilities will function properly, and be efficiently maintained on a long-term basis. Public agencies and private sector organizations will benefit from a structured process to identify, evaluate, and recommend appropriate security and technology products. Using lessons learned from one of the largest state correctional agencies in the United States, building owners and operators (to be referred to as owners) can effectively and successfully evaluate, select, and specify security technology products to meet the unique needs of their building and security programs, regardless of building type.

Few building types deal more with operational security and technology products on a daily basis than state and federal prisons and local jails, known collectively as correctional facilities. The policies and procedures described in this section are based on the case studies and experience of the New York State Department of Correctional Services, in Albany, New York, a state agency that has purchased and installed security and products for nearly 200 years (Fig. 28.1).

Whether owners are responsible for a single facility, a campus consisting of several different building types, such as college or office park; or a multisite system seeking to standardize products and operations, such as a national company with manufacturing plants, state university or prison system, facility managers and administrators must be cognizant that the choices they make relating to security technology and policies may someday have life and death implications. The most effective comprehensive security programs are tailored to meet an organization's mission and goals by integrating design, technology, and operations (Fig. 28.2).

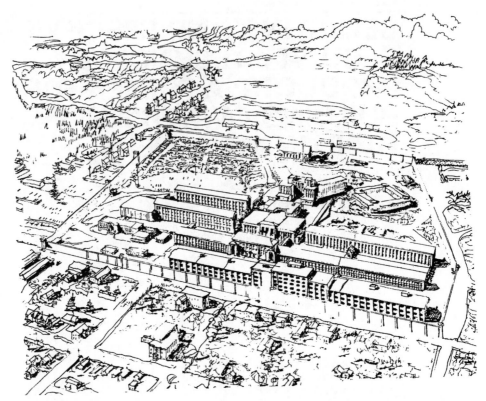

FIGURE 28.1 Birdseye view of a typical older state correctional facility campus. (*Pen and ink drawing: Francis J. Sheridan, AIA.*)

FIGURE 28.2 Main building of a state correctional facility, typically housing visitor screening and administration functions. (*Pen and ink drawing: Francis J. Sheridan, AIA.*)

BACKGROUND

The New York State Department of Correctional Services (NYS DOCS) is responsible for confinement and habitation of approximately 66,000 inmates at 70 correctional facility campuses, consisting of 3300 buildings and 36 million square feet. Like many correctional agencies, the department deals with high security on a daily basis (Fig. 28.3). For this reason, procedures must be in place for selecting and specifying security technology.

Use of technology products to support security is relatively new to the corrections arena. As a result of the many items coming out on the market during the early 1980s, and to determine which best addressed security needs, the department formalized a selection and specification process for security technology, equipment, and products (Fig. 28.4).

Based on the experience of securing and housing inmates for almost 200 years, the NYS DOCS identified four elements, and the level of participation necessary for selecting and specifying products leading to a successful security technology program. These elements are applicable to organizations responsible for protecting people, assets, and property (Table 28.1):

EXECUTIVE INVOLVEMENT

Building owners and managers should be involved and understand the process of product selection and specifications.

Meaningful involvement among building owners and managers is essential to a successful technology program. After September 11, 2001, increased security throughout society is a twenty-first century reality. Administrators and managers in the public and private sectors, especially those who are not architects, engineers, or electronic experts, may not be familiar with the many available security technology options, and thus may be reluctant to learn more about the many products on the market.

However, it is incumbent on building owners, managers, and those responsible for facility operations to understand the process of how to get the technology they want, because these are the people ultimately responsible for the safety and security of employees, visitors, and facilities.

Understanding the need for an evaluation process will help owners analyze security technology choices and select appropriate products for each operation. From perimeter security and intrusion alarm systems, to access control, closed circuit television (CCTV), and management information

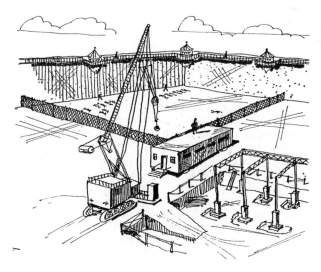

FIGURE 28.3 Construction projects within prison walls require daily security screening of all construction crews, equipment and vehicles entering and leaving the site. (*Pen and ink drawing: Francis J. Sheridan, AIA.*)

FIGURE 28.4 Guard towers are one of several perimeter security and surveillance system components in correctional facilities. Many sophisticated security technology options are available, and require rigorous testing and evaluation. (*Pen and ink drawing: Francis J. Sheridan, AIA.*)

TABLE 28.1 Four Elements for a Successful Security Technology Program

Element	Program description
1. Executive involvement	Building owners and managers need to be involved and understand the process of selection and specifying.
2. Committee involvement	Organize a product evaluation committee.
3. Staff involvement	Overcoming hurdles in the selection and specifying process.
4. Operational involvement	Develop and maintain emergency control plans.

systems (MIS), the process of selecting and specifying high-technology products is not as complicated as some may believe.

Security program selection is an executive level decision made by facility managers and owners involved with operations. For example, when planning a new facility, owners, users, and various stakeholders collaborate on decisions pertaining to space needs, adjacencies, functional relationships, the need for single offices, office landscaping, conference rooms, carpeting, colors, types of windows, doors, private toilets, gang toilets, and other details. Security systems depend on a number of factors, especially within correctional and government facilities (Table 28.2). Facility managers and building owners should not leave these decisions to the consultant design team of architects and engineers. Generally, owners discuss operational philosophies with design consultants, including where employees are located and housed, how employees move throughout a building or within a facility campus, how activities are programmed during day and evening hours, and the security levels needed. These policy and purchasing decisions cannot be left solely to outside consultants, architects, and engineers. Consultants are a resource, and can provide professional advice and experience for owners to consider (Fig. 28.5).

FIGURE 28.5 Executives discussing operational philosophies with consultant. (*All photos courtesy of NYS DOCS.*)

TABLE 28.2   Ten Factors Impacting Facility Security Systems

1. An organization's mission
2. Nature of potential threats, based on a threat assessment
3. Security classification
4. Staffing patterns
5. Emergency response time
6. Operational philosophy and methods
7. Programs
8. Staff training
9. Budgets
10. Maintenance policies

However, building owners and managers know how they want to operate and maintain their physical plants, and therefore, must be involved in security technology selection. Key issues include

- Intrusion alarm systems necessary to protect the facility
- Access control, locking systems, internal security, communications, fire safety systems, and management information systems best suited for a single facility and a system of campus-based facilities

COMMITTEE INVOLVEMENT

Product evaluation process

Field-testing all products for a predetermined length of time before specifying is the best way to ensure that they are appropriate for a facility installation and security program.

Organizing a product evaluation committee (PEC) is an effective way to review and analyze technology products. The committee composition depends on an organization's security mission and goals. Ideally, the chief executive officer (CEO) or a top-level manager designates the members who are best qualified and available to serve. As with any committee, those with an interest, prior background, and need to gain additional knowledge about a subject are often the most effective participants (Table 28.3).

The primary goal of the product evaluation committee is to review suitability of technology products, equipment, and systems, on the basis of programmatic needs and cost. The PEC offers an

TABLE 28.3 Product Evaluation Committee Testing Process

1. Organize product evaluation committee.
2. Establish benefits of a PEC.
3. Set up the committee.
4. Determine committee responsibilities.
5. Create review process.
6. Establish evaluation process.
7. Determine decision making process.
8. Implement recommendations.

opportunity to ensure that a comprehensive approach is taken in meeting the organization's security needs system-wide, while considering the unique concerns of an individual facility's physical plants, operations, extreme climates, or local environmental conditions (Tables 28.4 and 28.5).

All products are prescreened by committee members to determine whether they merit further research and review. Once interest is established in a product, a presentation is scheduled and either a site visit or field-test is arranged. Manufacturers often agree to loan their products for testing and evaluation at no cost, especially to large organizations and agencies. Testing schedules, locations, and procedures are determined by the committee. Tests are generally empirical in nature and attempt to verify or disprove manufacturers' claims, as well as determine product suitability for the organization's use.

The reporting process enables the CEO to remain aware of products to be evaluated, rejected, and recommended for use. Committee recommendations are submitted to the CEO, or a designated manager, for consideration.

TABLE 28.4 Technology and Equipment Subject to Product Evaluation Reviews: Access Control Equipment to Locking Systems

Category	Equipment Examples
1. Access control equipment	• Key control systems • Card access systems • Biometric access systems
2. ADA compliance equipment	• Handicap equipment • Toilets, sinks, grab bars
3. Contraband detectors (Fig. 28.6)	• Walk-through and handheld metal detectors • Package x-ray equipment (Fig. 28.7) • Drug detection equipment, ion spectrometry type • Explosive detection equipment (Fig. 28.8)
4. Biometric technology	• Fingerprinting • Facial recognition • Iris identification • Hand scanning • Voice recognition
5. CCTV equipment (Fig. 28.9)	• CCTV cameras and control systems • CCTV digital recording systems • Covert surveillance equipment • Audio monitoring equipment
6. Communications systems	• Intercom and public address systems • Telephone and paging systems • Computer networking and internet based systems • Radios and man down systems
7. Drug screening systems	• Quick test systems • Test cup, test strip
8. Inmate monitoring systems	• Inmate tracking systems for use within a facility • Remote offender monitoring systems
9. Lighting equipment	• Portable emergency equipment • Maximum-, medium-rated fixture types • Perimeter lighting
10. Locking systems	• Maximum, medium, minimum security locks • Detention doors construction • Bar gate construction • Electric control mechanisms • Electric control systems • Pneumatic locking systems • Hydraulic locking system

TABLE 28.5 Technology and Equipment Subject to Product Evaluation Reviews: Perimeter Intrusion Detection Systems to Security Personal Equipment

Category	Equipment Examples
11. Perimeter intrusion detection systems	• Taut wire • Fence-mounted shaker systems • Microwave and infrared systems • Video motion detection systems • Buried cable systems • Fiber optic mesh system • Interior motion detection system • Heartbeat detection systems • Field motion detection systems • Seismic detection systems • Control system—integrated vs. standalone • Electric fences—lethal vs. nonlethal
12. Security barrier systems	• Razor coil and fencing • Security walls and ceilings • Security windows • Security glazing—ballistic and breakout ratings (Figs. 28.10 and 28.11) • Security fasteners
13. Security personal equipment	• Body armor—ballistic and stab type • Weapons—handgun, rifle (Fig. 28.12) • Nonlethal weapons—stun guns, pepper spray, batons • Safety equipment, frisk gloves, flashlights • Gas masks

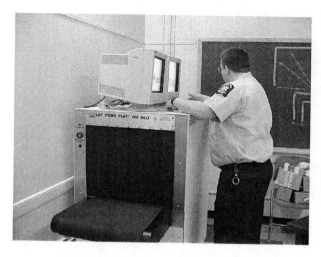

FIGURE 28.6 Evaluating package x-ray equipment a NYS DOCS test site. (*NYS DOCS.*)

FIGURE 28.7 Example of contraband found in inmate package from DOCS testing. (*NYS DOCS.*)

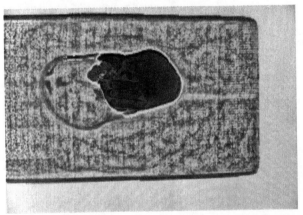

FIGURE 28.8 Example of sample bomb through an x-ray machine. (*NYS DOCS.*)

AFIGURE 28.9 CCTV and communications equipment installation at a typical correctional facility. (*NYS DOCS.*)

FIGURE 28.10 Evaluating breakout level of security glazing. (*NYS DOCS.*)

FIGURE 28.11 Evaluating security glazing ballistic rating. (*NYS DOCS.*)

FIGURE 28.12 Evaluating handguns at a NYS DOCS test site. (*NYS DOCS.*)

ORGANIZE PRODUCT EVALUATION COMMITTEE (PEC)

Create a security technology assessment program that serves as a central information and reference source for the organization (Tables 28.6 and 28.7).

- Define PEC responsibilities for evaluating and implementing technology products, systems, and equipment (Tables 28.8 to 28.10).
- Determine areas in which security technology reviews have been focused.

Facility managers and building owners cannot relinquish operational decisions to consultants or manufacturers. As the user, owners must be involved in the decision-making process because they are ultimately responsible for the security and safety of employees and visitors (Table 28.11).

TABLE 28.6 Benefits of a Product Evaluation Committee

1. Provides a means of evaluating new equipment and technology and disseminating the results.
2. Ensures that individual items of equipment are suitable for use (production units not prototype).
3. Ensures that equipment provides a performance level consistent with the level of security, control, safety, and durability required, i.e. maximum, medium, minimum security.
4. Ensures consistency in technology used throughout the organization.
5. Helps procurement officials make informed purchasing decisions based on performance and reliability, not solely on low bid.

TABLE 28.7 Setting Up the Product Evaluation Committee

1. Secure top-down support, which is needed for the committee to be successful.
2. Obtain endorsement and organization-wide support from the CEO to support the process.
3. Designating a committee chair who holds the keys to success: assessing the organization's technological needs, setting priorities and procedures for items to be evaluated and tested.
4. Appoint committee members based on their expertise and willingness to serve.
5. Create a multidisciplinary committee, a diverse group composed of different disciplines within the organization: security staff, executive staff, MIS, support operations, facilities planning.
6. Consult as necessary with outside architects and engineers, if the organization uses consultants.

TABLE 28.8 Responsibilities of the Committee

1. Reviews, from a program and cost basis, suitability of products and other types of high-expense, high-technology systems and equipment.
2. Ensure that a comprehensive approach is taken in meeting the organization's needs system-wide, while considering the uniqueness of each individual facility's physical plant, operations, and climatic extremes of the environs in which they are located.

TABLE 28.9   Create a Committee Review Process

1. The committee meets on a monthly basis and has a present agenda to review old business (products under review) and new business (new product review or vendor presentation).
2. All products are prescreened by committee members to determine whether they merit further research and review.
3. Once an interest is established in a product, a presentation is scheduled and either a site visit or field test is arranged

TABLE 28.10   Establish an Evaluation Process

1. If the committee expresses further interest in the product, the manufacturer is invited to participate in a testing and evaluation program.
2. Manufacturers agree to loan the organization products for testing and evaluation at no cost.
3. Testing schedules, locations, and procedures are determined by the committee.
4. Tests are generally empirical in nature and attempt to verify or disprove manufacturers' claims, as well as determine the products suitability for the rganization's use.

TABLE 28.11   Determine a Decision-Making Process

1. Committee reviews test data, then makes a recommendation (to CEO's designee) to approve or disapprove the product for organization use.
2. If the CEO designee concurs, the committee's recommendation is forwarded to the CEO for consideration.
3. The final outcome (approval or disapproval) is added to the organization's internal document.
4. The internal document is a history of products tested, date and location tested, and approval status.
5. Product description and final recommendation are forwarded to procurement staff and the organization's consulting design architects and engineers, as required.

STAFF INVOLVEMENT

Overcoming hurdles in the selection and specifying process

Managers should be aware that implementing the latest security measures might raise concerns among staff. The following are considerations to be addressed (Table 28.12).

Encountering and Anticipating Staff Resistance to Change

Understand that people are often resistant to change. Many feel threatened that technology will be used to replace them or make their jobs obsolete.

TABLE 28.12   Staff Involvement

1. Staff resistance to change.
2. Vendor did not deliver what salesperson promised.
3. Technology quickly becomes obsolete and costly to replace.
4. Staff not trained to operate and maintain.
5. Low bid must be accepted.

- Increase efficiency with proper use of technology, by enabling managers to do more with existing staffing levels.
- Be aware that staff may consider technology as a means of evaluating performance, such as camera systems in high-risk, high-security areas.
- Include staff in the implementation of technology. Review their needs and ask the people who will be affected by technology for their input regarding applications. The people who will be using technology know best how it will help in their duties.
- Help users better understand technology and related capabilities, and they will be less resistant to change.
- Create a collaborative process and involve users in technology selection and testing.
- Implement technology wisely. Tailor technology to suit operations; don't allow technology to dictate operations. Put technology to work for you, not against you.
- Provide constant technology training for staff. Set up programs to refresh previously trained and new personnel. When organizations offer staff training, they invest in human resources. Trained people are an extremely valuable resource which technology cannot replace. Technology cannot work well if it is not utilized properly by staff.

When Vendors Do Not Deliver

When manufacturers and vendors do not deliver service as promised, owners can take the necessary steps:

- Determine facility needs. Owners should review their operations and develop specifications for the types of technologies required at their facilities. Owners should not rely on vendors to decide on what is needed.
- Utilize staff to evaluate technology and products. Test before specifying and installation.
- Have programs in place allowing staff to monitor technology installation. Try to identify problems early, before they become impediments to operations.
- Insist on seeing other operational systems previously installed at other facilities and locations. Speak to users, not just managers, on site visits. The user's perspective is often different from management and may provide insight into how the technology will work with those who use and maintain it on a daily basis.
- Expect what you ordered. If the technology installed is not what was ordered or anticipated, owners should be firm with the vendor. Often, with extra effort, vendors can reconfigure technology to meet facility needs.
- Write specifications and contracts to put the burden on the vendor to perform. Owners, not the contractor, should remain in the driver's seat.

Technology Quickly Becomes Obsolete

- Purchase technology wisely. Determine present and future security needs and tailor systems accordingly. Biggest, fastest, and latest is not always the best way to go.
- Avoid custom-made products designed for only for one facility's use. Should the manufacturer go out of business, the technology could not be supported and serviced. Use standard products from reliable sources whenever possible.
- Build and maintain relationships with manufacturers, not just technology integrators. Manufacturers often notify steady customers about new designs and possible phase-out of old technologies with advance warning. Maintaining these relationships will allow managers to plan for the future and not be caught in situations requiring costly system replacement.

- If a new product is being developed, manufacturers will often work with their steady customers to ensure that new products will work and retrofit with older models. For example, upon request, one security vendor designed their new technology to retrofit with all their existing equipment and has incorporated the new design into their standard product line.

- Consider the life cycle of equipment when purchasing. Procure sufficient replacement parts at time of product installation to ensure against obsolescence.

Training Is Needed

- Have installer of technology provide training upon completion of work.

- Develop a system operations and maintenance training program for staff as an ongoing process to compensate for staff turnover.

- Utilize video training and maintain up-to-date product manuals and records. Utilize manufacturer-based training programs when available.

- Develop a competent team of people who can maintain technology products. This may not be possible at every facility. At multiple facilities run by the same organization, establish and disseminate an on-call list of regional resource people.

- If an in-house maintenance team is not an option, service agreements must be considered, but they can be costly. If service contracts are selected, contracts should state the exact number of years to be covered at the time of purchase of the technology. This price is best determined up front, rather than later, or after a certain brand of equipment is installed.

- Implement technology that is both operator- and maintenance-friendly.

How to Deal with Low Bid

- Develop tight specifications, which will meet short- and long-term needs.

- Develop strict performance criteria for technologies, which must be met by the bidder.

- Develop an experience specification for the successful bidder, which must be met and which ensures well-trained installers and proper installation.

- By developing this experience specification, it is possible to weed out unqualified bidders and help ensure that the end product is at an acceptable standard of quality.

Generally, organizations benefit from a cadre of in-house technology specialists familiar with various technologies. Specialists can interface with consultants, contractors, vendors, and the organization's facility managers to ensure that major technology investments are beneficial and cost effective.

OPERATIONAL INVOLVEMENT

Develop and maintain emergency control plans.

After the owners and facility managers have identified, purchased, and installed high-technology equipment, systems, and technology, they must develop and implement policies and procedures for rapid response to emergencies, problems, and catastrophic events (Table 28.13). These problems can range from terrorism and crime, to workplace violence, natural disasters, weather conditions, environmental, and biohazard threats. Every facility, whether in the public or private sector, must be prepared for the unexpected by developing an emergency control plan to deal with a variety of situations (Tables 28.14 to 28.18).

TABLE 28.13   Operational Involvement

1. Develop an emergency control plan.
2. Establish a facility communication center.
3. Develop mutual aid agreements.
4. Develop postemergency procedures.

TABLE 28.14   Establish a Facility Communication Center

1. Locate the facility communications center in a secure area with inside and outside telephone lines, radio communication equipment, fax machine, and tape recorder.
2. Forward observers close to the scene to observe events and be in constant contact with facility communication center.
3. Communication center point person in constant contact with forward observer and CEO.
4. Communications recorder should be programmed to log all events and provide stenographer assistance.

TABLE 28.15   How to Develop an Effective Emergency Plan

1. Keep the emergency control plans in a ready emergency data (RED) book.
2. Ensure that all supervisors are kept aware of and have access to the facility RED book.
3. Develop a procedure to create guidelines and maintain emergency control plans.
4. Provide prompt and decisive action in the event of an emergency, such as a disturbance, fire, explosion, hostage-taking incident, terrorist action, natural disaster, or bomb threat.
5. Assign the highest-ranking official at each facility to develop plans to prevent, and when necessary, to control emergencies.
6. Include personnel lists and telephone numbers in the RED book.
7. Test equipment and procedures regularly throughout the year.
8. Conduct various training exercises to ensure that all staff members understand emergency plans, including response activities, equipment location, and medical plans.
9. Provide for communications and the recording of events during an emergency.
10. Train key personnel to be familiar with CCTV and camera operations.
11. Ensure that emergency plans include necessary procedures, outside resources, prevention, recovery, and communication protocols (Table 28.16).

TABLE 28.16   Ten Components of an Emergency Plan

1. Employee procedures and drills for preparation
2. Outside emergency resources
3. Contact names and phone numbers of appropriate public agencies
4. Facility resources
5. Prevention of disturbances
6. Disturbance control procedures
7. Disaster planning for fire, explosion, chemical or biological threats, and medical response
8. Recovery procedures in case of disruption of services
9. Dissemination of emergency information
10. Procedures during natural disasters, such as hurricanes, earthquakes, blizzards, and tornadoes.

TABLE 28.17 Develop Mutual Aid Agreements

Prepare for emergencies by developing mutual aid agreements with local agencies:

1. Police department or local coordinating public safety agency
2. Fire department
3. County emergency services coordinator
4. Hospitals
5. Ambulance service

TABLE 28.18 How to Develop Postemergency Procedures

1. Investigate and determine cause of incident.
2. Determine if security weaknesses exist with facility, procedures, staff, and technology.
3. Evaluate physical plant for any renovation and repairs needed.
4. Assess if any legal action is required.
5. Review if any further changes to the emergency plan and RED book are necessary.

CONCLUSION

A successful security technology program starts with executive direction, support, and staff commitment to the program, and ends with an emergency control plan to deal with any adverse situation. The important points for building owners, facility managers, landlords, and officials at any agency, organization, or facility to remember are as follows:

- Research ways to develop a viable decision-making process to meet organizational needs.
- Ensure that all stakeholders in the system or organization are involved in the process.
- Visit other jurisdictions, cities, facilities, or similar building types to see what others have done. Be willing to learn from their experience, or inexperience, as the case may be.
- Meet with and listen carefully to salespeople who market technology products. They are generally very knowledgeable individuals who are interested in selling their product, but also can be extremely helpful in assisting owners in identifying security needs.
- Listen carefully to those who use and maintain technology systems. Ascertain if they have confidence in the system and various capabilities under all conditions.
- Consider that the axiom "what you see is what you spec" is very true in the selection of technological components and systems. Ultimately, building owners and facility managers must make the final choices—not the consultant, salesperson, operator, or maintenance staff.

Security technology can be a cost-effective means of assisting building owners and managers in performing their jobs and meeting their organizational missions and goals. This operational aspect should receive the same, if not more, attention to detail as other organizational programs and activities. Ideally, organizations should have people on staff qualified to deal with consultants, contractors, vendors, and internal operational concerns. The time is always right for developing a product evaluation committee to analyze products, implement selection, and specify security technology.

Lastly, owners and managers must remember the following: it's your program, your facility, your operation, and you must make the final decisions which can someday result in life-or-death situations involving your staff, visitors, family, and friends.

ACKNOWLEDGMENTS

Contributors from the New York State Department of Correctional Services, Division of Facilities Planning and Development, Albany, New York include:

- Thomas P. McQuade, Electronic Engineer
- Jane Carrara, Executive Assistant

All photos are courtesy of NYS DOCS. Individuals appear in photos with permission.

BIBLIOGRAPHY

Nadel, Barbara A., "Correctional Facility Design," in *Time Saver Standards for Building Types,* 4th ed., M. J. Crosbie and J. De Chiara (eds.), McGraw-Hill, New York, 2001.

Nadel, Barbara A., "Security and Technology: 21st Century Trends." *The Construction Specifier,* Construction Specifications Institute, Alexandria, Va., April 2001.

Sheridan, Francis J., "The Quiet Resource," *Corrections Today,* American Correctional Association, Lantham, Md., April 2000.

Sheridan, Francis J., "Architects Change the Way Prisons in '90s Are Designed to Meet Need for More Space," *Capital District Business Review,* February 9, 1998. http://albany.bizjournals.com/albany/stories/1998/02/09/focus4.html

Sheridan, Francis J., "Technology Selection is Your Responsibility," *Corrections Today,* American Correctional Association, 1993.

Sheridan, Francis J., "Exterior Electronic Intrusion Detection Security Perimeters," *Corrections Today,* American Correctional Association, 1990.

INTERNET RESOURCES

American Correctional Association (ACA)
www.aca.org

American Institute of Architects
Committee on Architecture for Justice
(AIA CAJ)
www.aia.org; www.aia.org/caj

American Jail Association (AJA)
www.aja.org

American Jails
www.aja.org

Construction Specifications Institute (CSI)
www.csinet.org

Construction Specifier
www.csinet.org

Correctional News
www.correctionalnews.com

Corrections Connection
www.correctionsconnection.com

Corrections Forum
www.correctionsforum.com

Corrections Today
www.aca.org/publications/ctmagazine.asp

National Law Enforcement and Corrections
Technology Center (NLECTC): A Program of
the National Institute of Justice
1. National Center; 800-248-2742;
www.nlectc.org
2. NLECTC West; El Segundo, CA; 888-548-
1618; nlectc@law-west.org
3. Border Research and Technology Center, San
Diego, CA; 619-685-1491;
brtcchrisa@aol.com
4. NLECTC Rocky Mountain; Denver, CO; 800-
416-8086; nlectc@du.edu
5. NLECTC Northeast; Rome, NY; 888-338-
0584; nlectc_ne@rl.af.mil
6. Office of Law Enforcement Standards;
Gaithersburg, MD; 301-975-2757;
oles@nist.gov
7. Office of Law Enforcement Technology,
Commercialization; Wheeling, WV; 800-678-
6882; oletc@nttc.edu
8. NLECTC Southeast; Charleston, SC; 800-
292-4385; nlectc-se@awod.com

CHAPTER 29
GLAZING AND SECURITY GLASS APPLICATIONS

F. John W. Bush
Director of Laminated Products and Development
Oldcastle Glass
Sunrise, Florida

Sue Steinberg
Vice President, Corporate Communications
Oldcastle Glass
Santa Monica, California

Catherine Kaliniak
Public Relations Consultant to Oldcastle Glass
McLean, Virginia

There is no right to strike against the public safety by any-body, anywhere, anytime.

CALVIN COOLIDGE (1872–1933)
30th U.S. president, in a telegram, 1919

Ever since the 1995 bombing of Oklahoma City's Alfred P. Murrah Federal Building and the tragic events of September 11, 2001, public and private sector groups in the United States have taken steps to mitigate the loss of life and property damage resulting from attacks against Americans at home and abroad. Around the world, Israel, Germany, the United Kingdom, and other countries have long experienced terrorist attacks on people and property, prompting them to address security issues (Fig. 29.1).

Building owners seeking to protect occupants, employees, assets, and structures must first conduct a risk assessment and vulnerability analysis, in collaboration with a security consultant and the design team, to determine potential threats. Based on location, function, neighboring uses, tenants, site conditions, and other related factors, each facility may be subject to a unique range of threats. Owners must determine the level of risk they are willing to assume, and what they can afford to spend to achieve a realistic security level. Potential threats include

- Direct attack, such as attempted robbery, kidnapping, or assault
- Indirect attack, when a building nearby is targeted for attack

Threat assessments should be performed at the earliest possible stages of project development, to ensure that appropriate protection is planned, designed, and specified within the budget, rather than applied later as an afterthought. Addressing threats and related security design elements during

FIGURE 29.1 Government Building in Haifa, Israel, built with blast windows using a cable catch system. Shown: *Blast-Tec™ Energy-Absorbing* Cable Catch System (EACCS). (*Source: Oldcastle-Arpal, LLC.*)

subsequent project stages may result in significant design changes and additional unanticipated costs. To best assist owners in meeting security needs, building designers and specifiers should, at minimum, be familiar with

- The need for a threat assessment, and an understanding of the implications
- Different types of protection available
- Techniques to harden buildings
- Materials to minimize fatalities through flying glass shards in the event of a blast

LAMINATED GLASS

Laminated glass is often an appropriate choice to protect against several types of threats. The effects of blasts, burglaries, and hurricanes can be mitigated with similar glass construction, tailored to meet specific needs. With the ability to add tinted glass, reflective coatings, silk-screened patterns and pigmented interlayers, laminated glass can address aesthetic, security, and performance needs (Table 29.1).

Laminated glass is manufactured by permanently bonding two or more plies of clear, tinted, low-E, patterned, wired, or reflective glass with one or more layers of polyvinyl butyral (PVB) sheets. The glass can be annealed, heat-strengthened, or fully tempered, and the plies can vary in thickness. Levels of protection can be achieved with different laminated glass configurations (Table 29.2).

TABLE 29.1   Summary of Laminated Glass Types for Different Threats and Typical Applications

Laminated glass by threat	Typical application
1. Blast-resistant	• High-risk or high-profile buildings containing tenants likely to be targets, government facilities, large glass facades, and curtain walls
2. Burglary-resistant	• Stores, retail centers, commercial office buildings, and residential use
3. Forced-entry-resistant	• Correctional facilities, buildings subject to civil disturbances, high-risk commercial buildings, banks, and jewelry stores
4. Ballistic (bullet) resistant	• Protection of individuals located behind the glass in guard booths, guard offices, and banks
5. Hurricane impact resistant	• Coastal zones susceptible to hurricane force winds, especially the southeastern United States and Caribbean
6. Earthquake and seismic resistant	• Areas prone to high-magnitude earthquakes, especially California and the western United States

TABLE 29.2   Laminated Glass: Summary of Security Performance

Nominal thickness	Configuration	Safety		Security			Hurricane		Other performance		
		CPSC Cat. 1	CPSC Cat. 2	ASTM F1233 Cl. 1	UL 972	Blast resistance	Small missile	Large missile	Seismic	Sound control	UV screening
1/4"	1/8"-0.015"-1/8"	*								*	*
1/4"	1/8"-0.030"-1/8"	*	*						*	*	*
5/16"	1/8"-0.060"-1/8"	*	*	*	*	*	*		*	*	*
5/16"	1/8"-0.090"-1/8"	*	*	*	*	*	*	*	*	*	*
3/8"	3/16"-0.015"–3/16"	*								*	*
3/8"	3/16"-0.030"–3/16"	*	*						*	*	*
7/16"	3/16"-0.060"–3/16"	*	*	*	*	*	*		*	*	*
7/16"	3/16"-0.090"-3/16"	*	*	*	*	*	*	*	*	*	*
1/2"	1/4"-0.015"-1/4"	*								*	*
1/2"	1/4"-0.030"-1/4"	*	*						*	*	*
9/16"	1/4"-0.060"-1/4"	*	*	*	*	*	*		*	*	*
9/16"	1/4"-0.090"-1/4"	*	*	*	*	*	*	*	*	*	*

Source: Oldcastle Glass.

BLAST MITIGATION

The primary challenge of blast-resistant glazing design is to eliminate hazards created by glazing systems as a result of a blast event. The effects of a blast, and the ensuing pressure wave, cause devastation in the immediate vicinity, and can cause tremendous damage miles from the target site. Extensive research and testing have been conducted on the effects of blast on structures. Test results indicate that the intended target is severely impacted, and peripheral damage can occur from flying glass debris reaching blocks away from the original blast site. These conditions occurred after the 1995 bombing of the Alfred P. Murrah Federal Building in Oklahoma City (Table 29.3).

When designing for blast protection, the goal is to create a unified building envelope, where the window and the wall are designed to similar capacities. A failing wall with an intact window or a standing wall with a window no longer in the opening are not desirable performance outcomes.

TABLE 29.3   Lessons Learned from Oklahoma City: Glazing

The 1995 bombing of the Alfred P. Murrah Federal Building killed 168 people and caused numerous injuries. This event underscored the need for blast-resistant glazing design. According to "Glass-Related Injuries in Oklahoma City Bombing," a study published in the *Journal of Performance of Constructed Facilities*, by the American Society of Civil Engineers, injuries in explosions result directly and indirectly from window glass failure, when glass shards fly from windows, causing lacerations and abrasions to victims.

Glass-related injury victims were found in nearby buildings, especially those located near glazed outside walls. Data indicated that over one-quarter of glass-related injury victims in adjacent buildings were positioned within five feet of glazed fenestration, and almost one-half of glass-related injury victims were located within 10 feet of a glazed fenestration wall.

Along with abrasions and lacerations, many victims suffered hearing problems because glazing failed to maintain window closure, exposing them to shock from the blast wave. Subsequent analysis of injuries to building occupants prompted the federal government and the construction industry to test and develop blast-resistant glazing to protect building occupants.

Use of laminated glass, as a component of blast-resistant glazing design and window systems, is an effective method of reducing glass-related injuries to building occupants.

Source: American Society of Civil Engineers Web site, Publications, *Vulnerability and Protection of Infrastructure Systems: The State of the Art.*

To provide the highest levels of blast protection for building occupants and those in the vicinity, laminated glass, using 0.060- and 0.090-inch PVB interlayer, is designed to hold glass fragments together. This interlayer stretches and absorbs much of the blast energy. To gain the greatest effect, the laminated glass must be properly installed with structural silicone in a frame system securing the glass.

As with all laminated glazing, glass can be tinted or reflective, and plies of glass can be annealed or heat-strengthened. For optimal results, tempered laminated glass should not be used in these instances. When insulating glass features are required for thermal performance, both lites of the insulated glass unit should be laminated to ensure maximum protection for occupants and passers by outside the building. If only one lite in the unit is to be laminated, the interior lite should be laminated to protect people inside the building.

Buildings considered targets are likely to be subjected to much larger blast pressures and may require a window framing system capable of resisting the intense pressure wave. The frame is an integral part of the blastmitigation glazing system. If glazing is made very stiff, the entire blast load is transferred to the building, resulting in damage to the structural integrity of the building.

Window Film

Window film, also known as antishatter film (ASF), applied to existing glazing is a temporary, low-cost solution providing limited protection to building occupants in the event of a blast (Table 29.4).

Blast Windows

Aluminum-based window systems, containing energy-absorbing devices concealed within the window structure, are commonly known as blast windows. With energy-absorbing, blast-resistant window systems, the frame and the laminated glass absorb energy without transferring loads onto the building structure (Table 29.5).

In retrofit projects, blast-resistant window systems can significantly reduce or eliminate the need for building reinforcement, allowing installation to be completed in a short time with minimal disruption. Blast windows are suitable for high-risk, high-profile buildings considered potential targets; for projects where budget constraints or other concerns limit window replacement options; and, where large glass facades, storefronts, and curtain walls are involved (Fig. 29.2).

TABLE 29.4   Window Film Characteristics

- Low cost
- Temporary solution
- Quick fix application
- Suitable for existing glazing
- Minimum interruption of daily operations
- Used as a stand-alone application, protects mainly against collateral damage
- Not an efficient blast mitigation design solution if a building is an actual target

Source: Oldcastle-Arpal, LLC.

TABLE 29.5   Advantages of Energy-Absorbing, Blast-Resistant Window Design Technology

- Minimal load transfer to window openings
- Eliminates heavy glazing units and massive framing
- Eliminates additional reinforcement of openings in retrofit projects
- Reduces hazards to people and building occupants
- Engineering flexibility allows most architectural design specifications
- Allows egress from building after a blast event, even if the window is deformed and cannot open properly (emergency personnel and equipment required.)

Source: Oldcastle-Arpal, LLC.

FIGURE 29.2   Test performance conditions with a high-performance cable catch window system, designed for low to high levels of blast loads. Shown: *Blast-Tec*™ Arpal 9.85CE fixed window. (*Source: Oldcastle-Arpal, LLC.*)

Some blast window frames look like regular window units and can complement the aesthetics of existing buildings and new construction. Commonly used in historic preservation applications, the energy-absorbing mechanisms enable installation in existing walls, without the need for costly structural reinforcement. Installation can readily occur without disrupting existing building components and in occupied buildings (Fig. 29.3).

Testing Windows in "Soft" Walls

The goal for protecting people in buildings is achieving a similar blast capacity for windows and walls, thereby creating a unified blast-resistant structural envelope. Blast windows are available for retrofit projects requiring protection for medium to high blast levels, especially for buildings with soft and brittle masonry construction. When struck by blast impulse pressure, the windows will "give," transferring only minimal loads to the surrounding walls.

Window behavior is affected by charge weight and standoff distance. Extensive testing allows forecasting and extrapolation of window behavior under different combinations of charge and standoff. Testing in concrete structures and vulnerable masonry walls, such as red clay hollow tiles and concrete masonry units (CMU) is a way to determine window performance under certain construction conditions (Fig. 29.4).

Cable Catch Window System

A blast-resistant window system absorbs most blast energy through a process of controlled collapse. While protecting against blast, certain types and models of available high performance, energy-absorbing blast windows are equipped with a thin cable stretched between the window jambs.

During a blast, antishatter film or laminated glass hits the cable, activating the energy-absorbing components located within the window jambs. The jambs deflect and shear the hooks holding them into the opening. This system allows the glass to be caught, rather than sheared or sliced; thus protecting building occupants and interior surroundings from flying glass and other blast hazards. The cable catch window system is a cost-efficient solution for new construction or retrofit projects (Fig. 29.5).

FIGURE 29.3 The IRS Building, Washington, D.C. This federal building used blast windows behind existing windows to maintain the historic appearance and provide blast protection, energy conservation, and sound reduction qualities. Shown: *Blast-Tec*™ Arpal 9.48, *Energy-Absorbing* Operable Internal Blast Window. (*Source: Oldcastle-Arpal, LLC.*)

FIGURE 29.4 This test performance shows three operable blast-resistant windows in a single red clay hollow tile masonry wall opening. The wall approached design capacity, as indicated by the severe crack. The window bowing inward is still considered "in the opening," and remains anchored in place and in the frame. Shown: *Blast-Tec*™ Arpal 9.80. (*Source: Oldcastle-Arpal, LLC.*)

FIGURE 29.5 Test performance conditions with a high-performance cable catch window system, designed for low to high levels of blast loads. Shown: *Blast-Tec*™ Arpal 9.10 *Energy-Absorbing* Cable Catch System (EACCS). (*Source: Oldcastle-Arpal, LLC.*)

Blast Doors

Blast-resistant doors are most effective as emergency exits where a panic device is specified and handicapped accessibility is required. They are appropriate for new construction and renovations, especially with soft and brittle masonry walls, often found in retrofit projects, because structural reinforcement is not required for installation (Fig. 29.6).

BURGLARY RESISTANCE

Laminated glass, composed of layers, can provide the necessary deterrent to a burglary attack. Typically, a burglary attempt is made using a blunt instrument, with the goal of a quick break-in, fast grab, and speedy exit before alarms or people alert the police. Even if the interlayer is successfully broken through, the small hole must also be enlarged to gain quick access or to remove property. By then, the intruder may have caused enough noise to be noticed and would hastily retreat to avoid apprehension. Because laminated glass installations frustrate the opportunist thief, this material is ideal for stores, retail centers, offices, and residential use. Two recognized industry standards apply to burglary-resistant glazing (Table 29.6).

FORCED-ENTRY RESISTANCE

The experienced attacker has a specific target in mind and comes prepared with various tools and an opportunistic time frame ranging from several minutes to as much as an hour. Originally created to foil prison breaks, forced-entry-resistant glazing was designed to withstand weapons obtained in prison and concealed on the inmate. Later uses included structures potentially threatened by civil disturbances. These same applications can be found in high-risk security buildings, such as banks and jewelry stores.

FIGURE 29.6   Hinged blast-resistant doors can be installed in a stand-alone mode or within a glass wall, storefront, or curtain wall. This blast door meets the Department of Defense Anti-Terrorism Construction Standard by opening to the outside. Shown: *Blast-Tec™* Arpal 9.90 Hinged Door. (*Source: Oldcastle-Arpal, LLC.*)

Security measures call for the laminated glazing materials to consist of many layers, with at least one layer comprised of the toughest clear plastic, polycarbonate; otherwise known as glass-clad polycarbonates. Polycarbonate has 250 times the impact strength of glass. To ensure maximum forced-entry resistance, both the inner and outer plies of the laminate are glass to provide the durability that polycarbonate alone cannot offer. The polycarbonate is laminated to the outer glass plies using an aliphatic urethane interlayer. Sheets of aliphatic urethane bond the layers of polycarbonate permanently together (Fig. 29.7).

Lighter weight laminates with multiple plies of polycarbonate containing no glass offer extreme levels of forced-entry protection. These lighter weight laminates are also effective for bullet-resistant protection, as the lack of glass prevents spalling. Composite materials with several thin layers bonded together present a greater attack-resistance than one thick layer. The external faces of polycarbonate are treated with a mar-resistant hard coating for durability, but this is not recommended for external use.

Several standards exist, with glazing manufacturers offering materials meeting different levels within each standard (Table 29.7).

TABLE 29.6   Burglary-Resistant Glazing Industry Standards

Standard	Criteria
Underwriters Laboratory (UL)	Underwriters Laboratory's standard test method for this type of glazing, UL 972, *Burglary Resistant Glazing,* specifies a number of ball-drop impacts to simulate scientifically a blunt instrument attack. Generally, laminated glass with a minimum of 0.060-inch polyvinyl butyral interlayer meets this standard.
ASTM International	ASTM International advances a similar standard, ASTM F1233, with Class 1 related to 10 impacts with a ball-peen hammer.

Source: Oldcastle Glass.

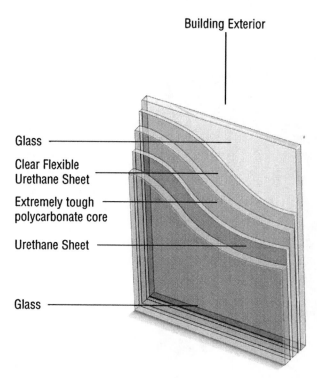

FIGURE 29.7   Forced-entry laminated glass combines multiple layers of glass and polycarbonate to achieve protection. (*Source: Oldcastle Glass.*)

BALLISTIC RESISTANCE

The need for glazing materials protecting against ballistic attacks falls into two categories:

- A robbery where a handgun is used to secure property
- An assault upon an individual to injure or kill

The goal of bullet-resistant glazing is twofold:

- Prevent penetration by bullets
- Limit the amount of spall, which are small pieces of flying glass shards leaving the rear face as a result of the impact

Limiting spall is a priority, because this application often protects individuals located directly behind the glazing, such as in a guard office or booth, or a bank (Fig. 29.8).

TABLE 29.7   **Forced-Entry Resistance Glazing Industry Standards**

Standard	Criteria
H.P. White Laboratories	HP Laboratories standard and test method, HP White TP 0500, *Transparent Materials for Use in Forced Entry or Containment Barriers.*
Walker, McGough, Foltz and Lyeria test	An old, almost obsolete, standard developed by an architectural firm; still common in specifications.
ASTM International	ASTM F1233, Class 2 through 5.

Source: Oldcastle Glass.

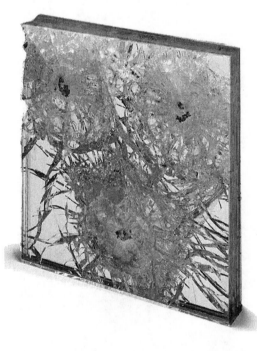

FIGURE 29.8   Ballistic-resistant glass, showing a successful test result. (*Source: Oldcastle Glass.*)

Bullet-resistant glazing manufacturers have achieved this performance level by adding a thin layer of glass for low-spall glazing, or a polycarbonate with a scratch-resistant coating that does not produce spall. All bullet-resistant glazing has an attack side and a protective side. The asymmetrical glass must be positioned and installed correctly for correct performance (Figs. 29.9 and 29.10).

Sustained physical attack is not necessarily fully protected by bullet-resistant glazing, though products with polycarbonate provide increased resistance. Since glass works in conjunction with the frames, the frames must also be bullet-resistant and able to support adequately the glazing to withstand attacks. If the glazing is removed from the frame opening, the level of protection is significantly impacted.

The glazing industry has established several standards and performance criteria, each with a number of levels relating to the weapon used, ranging from a 9-millimeter handgun to a 7.62-millimeter military rifle. Bullet speed, number of shots, bullet type and range, and shot pattern are all detailed in the standards (Tables 29.8 and 29.9).

HURRICANE IMPACT RESISTANCE

Hurricane impact-resistant glass is a laminated product used as part of a door or window system, especially in coastal zones susceptible to hurricane force winds (Fig. 29.11). After the significant damage caused by Hurricane Andrew in 1992, the South Florida Building Code (subsequently replaced by the Florida Building Code) developed several glazing performance criteria and testing standards used by the industry (Tables 29.10 to 29.12).

Since the initial testing and resulting ASTM E1996, *Performance of Exterior Windows, Curtain Walls, Doors and Storm Shutters Impacted by Wind-Borne Debris in Hurricanes,* five different levels of impact related to the building type and wind speed have been produced. Several grades and thicknesses

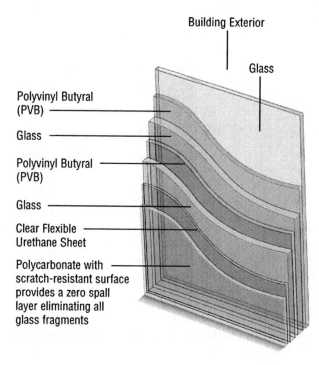

FIGURE 29.9 Ballistic-resistant zero-spall laminated glass section. (*Source: Oldcastle Glass.*)

Building Exterior

Glass

Polyvinyl Butyral (PVB)

Glass

Polyvinyl Butyral (PVB)

Glass

Clear Flexible Urethane Sheet

Polycarbonate with scratch-resistant surface provides a zero spall layer eliminating all glass fragments

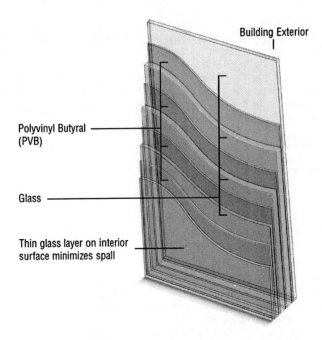

FIGURE 29.10 Ballistic-resistant low-spall laminated glass section. (*Source: Oldcastle Glass.*)

TABLE 29.8 **Bullet-Resistant Glazing Industry Standards**

Standard	Criteria
Underwriters Laboratory (UL)	UL 752, *Bullet Resistant Materials* featuring eight levels, has become the most widely accepted standard in North America.
H.P. White Laboratories	HP White, HPW-TP 500, with five levels.
National Institute of Justice (NIJ)	National Institute of Justice, NIJ 01078.01, with six levels.

Source: Oldcastle Glass.

TABLE 29.9 **Bullet-Resistant Glazing Testing Standards**

UL 752 test summary		HP White test summary (HPW-TP-0500)		National Institute of Justice (NIJ Standard 0108.01)	
Level	Weapon	Level	Weapon	Level	Weapon
1	9 mm	A	38 Special	1	38 Special
2	357 Magnum	B	9 mm	2A	.357 Magnum/9mm-LV
3	.44 Magnum	C	.44 Magnum	2	.357 Magnum/9mm-HV
4	.30-06	D	7.62 mm	3A	.44 Magnum/9mm
5	7.62 mm	E	.30-.06 AP	3	7.62 mm
6	9mm			4	.30-.06
7	5.56 mm				
8	7.62 mm				

Source: Oldcastle Glass.

FIGURE 29.11 Hurricane impact-resistant glass performance test. This glass was impacted by a 9-lb wooden 2- × 4-in test missile fired out of a cannon at 50 feet per second (33 mph). Designed to withstand hurricane wind forces of up to 140 mph, the glass is cracked but remains intact, due to a resilient interlayer preventing penetration. Shown: StormGlass™. (*Source: Oldcastle Glass.*)

TABLE 29.10   Lessons Learned from Hurricane Andrew in South Florida, 1992

In August 1992, Hurricane Andrew caused unprecedented economic devastation throughout the southern Florida peninsula, south-central Louisiana, and the northwestern Bahamas. According to the National Hurricane Center and the National Weather Service, damage in the United States was estimated at $25 billion, one of the costliest natural disasters in U.S. history. Indirect and other costs exceeded $40 billion. The Hurricane Insurance Information Center reported that Floridians filed more than 725,000 insurance claims resulting from Andrew's damage.

The glazing industry learned that pressurization following damage to windows and doors was the main cause of failure. Wind-borne debris caused windows to crack from impact, with high wind pressure produced from cyclic wind loads, forcing most glass to separate from frames.

As a result, the need arose to produce a glazing system resistant to debris carried by high winds and able to withstand a minimum of 9000 cyclic-pressure loads without glass rupturing or being removed from the frame. Four wind zone categories resulted from testing as identified under ASTM E1996 (Table 29.11). Initial testing was part of the South Florida Building Code (replaced by the Florida Building Code), with two impact levels—small and large missile (Table 29.12).

Sources: Oldcastle Glass and the National Hurricane Service.

TABLE 29.11   Wind Zone Categories Resulting from Testing as Identified under ASTM E1996

Wind zone	Wind speed
1	110-120mph+ (Hawaii)
2	120-130mph more than 1 mile from coast
3	130-140mph or 120-140 within 1 mile of coast
4	Greater than 140mph (south Florida)

Source: Oldcastle Glass.

of interlayers are being applied in hurricane-impacted areas. In testing, products have been subjected to high wind pressures representative of the extreme wind zone of Florida. Window units, featuring both noncaptured and captured glazing systems, have met the most stringent design standards established in the south Florida region, in many cases for design pressures in excess of 100 pounds per square foot (psf).

TABLE 29.12 Large and Small Missile-Impact Testing Performance Criteria from the Florida Building Code

Impact level	Testing performance criteria
Large missile	• Requires glazing to resist the penetration of a nine pound wood two-by-four traveling at 50 feet per second or 33 mph. These impacts are followed by 9000 inward- and outward-acting pressure cycles. • To meet large missile criteria, laminated glass with 0.090-inch PVB interlayer is typically sufficient for glass sizes up to about 25 square feet with design pressure up to 65 psf. • For higher performance needs, such as curtain wall, storefront, and large residential applications, laminated glass containing interlayers much stiffer than regular PVB to sustain greater design pressures are called for, with areas up to and exceeding 50 square feet. These products are usually laminated between two lites of 3/16-inch or 1/4-inch heat-strengthened or tempered glass.
Small missile	• Requires 2-gram steel ball bearings traveling at 130 feet per second. These impacts are followed by 9000 inward- and outward-acting pressure cycles. • To meet the small missile-impact and cycling test criteria, laminated glass with 0.060-inch PVB interlayer is standard. • For highest performance, the outer lite of glass should be tempered and the inner lite heat-strengthened.

Source: Oldcastle Glass.

EARTHQUAKES AND SEISMIC DESIGN

Earthquakes tend to cause movement or distortion in window sashes or frames, resulting in a change in angularity of corners, known as racking, in buildings. High-rise curtain wall systems, with the increased potential for flying and falling glass, are especially problematic during earthquakes.

Following the devastating earthquakes in Mexico in 1985, and in San Francisco in 1989, glass damage from earthquakes was studied extensively. Two major factors should be considered when evaluating earthquake damage:

• How glass systems perform and respond to racking

• How glazing performs after it has cracked from frame movement

Frames are integral to any earthquake-resistant glazing system. Forces impacting the frame cause significant deflection, such as interstory drift, and result in cracking glass. Despite extensive studies in this area, major building codes do not address these issues. Areas that are covered in industry standards include

• The American Architectural Manufacturing Association (AAMA) has developed a test method, AAMA 501.4, focusing on serviceability, which does not address life safety.

• The National Earthquake Hazards Reduction Program (NEHRP) guidelines, published by the Federal Emergency Management Agency, cover life safety and ensure that glass fallout does not occur due to building frame movement.

• The *International Building Code* (IBC), 2003 edition, refers to seismic design provisions contained in ASCE 7-02 (*Minimum Design Loads for Buildings and Other Structures*).

• ASCE 7-02, in turn, refers to AAMA 501.6-01 (*Recommended Dynamic Test Method for Determining the Seismic Drift Causing Glass Fallout from a Wall System*).

Based on established performance criteria and standards, architects, engineers, and designers can mitigate damage by addressing frame and glazing issues (Table 29.13).

Seismic glazing should be designed to minimize racking when floor slabs move sideways and cause glass-structured building openings to shift. During significant seismic activity, glass openings

TABLE 29.13   Seismic Design Considerations for Window Systems and Glazing

1. Flexible frames to accommodate racking without damage or serviceability
2. Adequate glass to frame clearances
3. Laminated glass in annealed or heat-strengthened constructions, either monolithic or in an insulating glass unit
4. Bottom and side blocks
5. Silicone glazing

Source: Oldcastle Glass.

often break. Laminated glass performs well under these circumstances. To prevent glass fragments from injuring occupants, laminated glass with tough plastic interlayers of either 0.030- or 0.060-inch provide adequate glass retention. The interlayers keep glass fragments together, and prevent the opening from expanding, curbing further damage from weather or looters. Both lites of insulating glass units should be laminated.

CONCLUSION

The Ultimate Security is your understanding of reality.
H. STANLEY JUDD
Author, film producer, and
communictions consultant

Glazing types are selected based on potential threats and vulnerabilities, as determined by building owners, security consultants, and project design teams. Energy conservation and sound reduction qualities should also be considered during selection and specification of glazing materials and products.

With laminated safety glass, the choice is a multifunctional glazing material suitable for a variety of applications, especially in commercial, institutional, and residential settings. Varying the amount and type of interlayer in the laminated glass product can provide resistance to threats and impacts, such as blast, burglary, forced entry, ballistics, hurricanes, and earthquakes.

Laminated glass typically breaks safely and remains intact within a building opening, eliminating the need for boarding up broken openings after a break, and resisting further damage by rain, wind, and looting. This unique quality is achieved through a plastic interlayer, which minimizes splinters and glass fragments, and can protect against occupant injury and property damage.

Blast-resistant window systems are effective ways to minimize injuries to building occupants resulting from flying glass shards, especially in buildings believed to be blast targets. Burglary-resistant glazing provides protection against other threats. Bullet-resistant glass is thicker, more rigid, and less flexible to absorb high winds and blasts. If ballistic and blast resistance are both desired, window frames and anchoring systems will be more substantial to absorb blast loads. Hurricane and seismic impact-resistant glazing systems are also available to meet climate- and geographic-specific needs. Early consideration of the security level and environmental threats will minimize budget concerns and reduce project completion time, while providing the highest available safety and security protection.

ACKNOWLEDGMENTS

- Peter Fillmore, President, Oldcastle-Arpal, LLC, Arlington, Virginia
- Moty Emek, Chief Technology Officer, Oldcastle-Arpal, LLC, Arlington, Virginia

GLOSSARY

annealing The process of controlled cooling to prevent residual stresses during the manufacturing of float glass. Reannealing is the process of removing objectionable stresses in glass by reheating to a suitable temperature followed by controlled cooling.

bullet-resistant glass A multiple lamination of glass and plastic that is designed to resist penetration from medium-to-superpower small arms and high-power rifles and to minimize spall.

deflection (center of glass) The amount of bending movement of the center of a glass lite perpendicular to the plane of the glass surface under an applied load.

deflection (framing member) The amount of bending movement of any part of a structural member perpendicular to the axis of the member under an applied load.

fenestration Any glass panel, window, door, curtain wall, or skylight unit on the exterior of a building.

glass clad polycarbonate One or more lites of flat glass bonded with an aliphatic urethane interlayer to one or more sheets of extruded polycarbonate in a pressure/temperature/vacuum laminating process.

glazing (noun) A generic term used to describe an infill material such as glass and panels.

glazing (verb) The process of installing an infill material into prepared openings such as windows, door panels, and partitions.

insulating glass unit Two or more lites of glass spaced apart and hermetically sealed to form a single-glazed unit with an air space between each lite. (Commonly called IG units.)

interlayer Any material used to bond two lites of glass and/or plastic together to form a laminate.

laminated glass Two or more lites of glass permanently bonded together with one or more interlayers.

lite Another term for a pane of glass. Sometimes spelled "light" in the industry literature, but spelled "lite" in this text to avoid confusion with light as in "visible light."

PVB Abbreviation for polyvinyl butyral, an extruded polymer sheet used to laminate glass.

racking A movement or distortion of sash or frames causing a change in angularity of corners.

spall Small fragments or splinters of glass, flying or dropping off the rear face of a glazing product following impact on the outer face. Often referred to in relation to bullet-resistant glass.

unit Term normally used to refer to one single assembly of insulating glass.

BIBLIOGRAPHY

American Society of Civil Engineers, *Minimum Design Loads for Buildings and Other Structures,* SEI/ASCE 7-02, Reston, Va., 2003

Norville, H. S., and Conrath, E. J., Considerations for blast-resistant glazing design. *J. Archit. Eng.,* **7**(3): 80–86 (2001). http://ascestore.aip.org/OA_HTML/asce_ciriac_abs.jsp

Norville, H. S., Harvill, N., Conrath, E. J., Shariat, S., and Mallonee, S., Glass-related injuries in Oklahoma City bombing. *J. Perform. Constr. Facil.,* **13**(2): 50–56 (1999). http://ascestore.aip.org/OA_HTML/asce_ciriac_abs.jsp

Rappaport, Ed, *Preliminary Report, Hurricane Andrew 16-28 August 1992.* National Hurricane Center, December 10, 1993. http://www.nhc.noaa.gov/1992andrew.html

INTERNET RESOURCES

American Architectural Manufacturing
Association (AAMA)
www.aamanet.org

American Society of Civil Engineers (ASCE)
www.asce.org

American Society for Testing and Materials
(ASTM)
www.astm.org

Building Officials & Code Administration,
International Inc. (BOCA)
www.bocai.org

Construction Specifications Institute (CSI)
www.csinet.org

Factory Mutual Research Corp (FM)
www.fmglobal.com

Federal Emergency Management Agency
(FEMA)
www.fema.gov/hazards/earthquakes

Florida Building Code
www.floridabuilding.org

Glass Association of North America (GANA)
www.glasswebsite.com

HP White
www.hpwhite.com

International Code Council (ICC)
www.iccsafe.org

National Glass Association (NGA)
www.glass.org

National Institute of Building Sciences (NIBS)
www.nibs.org

National Institute of Justice (NIJ)
www.ojp.usdoj.gov/nij/welcome.html

Oldcastle Glass, Inc.
www.OldcastleGlass.com

Oldcastle-Arpal, LLC
www.Oldcastle-Arpal.com

Portals for Glass Industry
www.glassfiles.com or www.glassonweb.com

Protective Glazing Council (PGC)
www.protectiveglazing.org

Underwriters Laboratories (UL)
www.ul.com

P · A · R · T · 6

CODES AND LIABILITY

CHAPTER 30

CODES, STANDARDS, AND GUIDELINES FOR SECURITY PLANNING AND DESIGN

Walter "Skip" Adams, CPP
Senior Security Consultant, Sako & Associates, Inc.
New York, New York

Deborah A. Somers
Senior Security Consultant, Sako & Associates, Inc.
Arlington Heights, Illinois

I have been often considering how it came to pass that the
dexterity of mankind in evil should always outgrow not only
the prudence and caution of private persons, but the continual
expedients of the wisest law contrived to prevent it.
                    JONATHAN SWIFT (1667–1745)
                              English satirist

Since the earliest civilizations in history, legal codes, laws, ordinances, and edicts have guided the way people led their lives, built their homes, and ran their businesses. The Bible and other scholarly books in many religions and cultures set forth rules for living and working within the built environment. The Industrial Revolution prompted workplace reform, led to new regulations, and increased attention to worker health and life safety. Modern building codes evolved over time, and continue to evolve, based on technological advancements, such as the elevator and, most importantly, as a means to protect human health, welfare, and life safety.

After the events of September 11, 2001, design professionals, elected officials, building owners, and the public saw a need to revisit egress, security, and life safety provisions in structures housing workplaces, especially commercial office buildings. Unlike many nationally and locally accepted fire protection, engineering, and building codes, standards, and health care guidelines, no single security code exists, applicable to privately owned structures, regardless of building or occupancy type. Increased security, specifically in the private sector, is generally a requirement determined and implemented by building owners and their project teams. Federal facilities at various agencies have clearly defined criteria for their security design and operational standards, but most state and local government facilities do not.

Security planning and design are multidisciplinary, relying on a combination of established national standards, best practices, and operational activities. Collectively, these benchmarks create a baseline for design professionals, building owners, and facility managers to use when enhancing building security. Understanding the types of available standards and how they best apply to each building type and owner is an important first step for developing a comprehensive security plan and an effective emergency response. The three most important security plan objectives are to:

- Protect assets
- Protect lives
- Maintain operations

Standards typically include model codes, specifications, rules, guidelines, certifications, and other criteria established to measure product quality, services, or system performance levels. Security standards may also apply to security products, services, architectural and engineering design features, and the professional practice of security principles within the built environment.

THREATS ADDRESSED BY SECURITY STANDARDS

The decision by building owners, corporations, landlords, and tenants to integrate security measures into commercial facilities in the United States is often based on the following criteria:

- Corporate risk management policy
- Corporate security standards
- Functions performed in or near the facility

Applying security threat countermeasures to commercial buildings is mostly a voluntary effort, with the exception of buildings that house government-related agencies and subcontractors.

Traditional Threats

Security countermeasures have addressed crimes that are traditionally considered threats against people and property, including burglary, larceny, assault (including battery, sexual assault, homicide, etc.), robbery, theft, and arson.

Economic crimes and concerns, related to the workplace or to certain types of business, have increased since the 1990s, such as:

- Employee time stealing
- Computer-related crime
- Industrial espionage
- Executive protection
- Workplace violence

Even after the 1993 bombing of the World Trade Center and the 1995 bombing of the Alfred P. Murrah Federal Building in Oklahoma City, terrorism was not considered a major concern among most building owners, landlords, facility managers, and corporate security departments. Until the attacks of September 11, 2001, terrorism threats were considered statistically insignificant among security professionals. However, the loss of life and destruction from the Murrah Federal Building attack prompted the U.S. General Services Administration (GSA) to develop guidelines assessing security needs on federal properties. During this time, the private sector did little to address security needs in commercial buildings.

Since 2001 heightened interest in world events, dangers posed by global forces, and the potential impact of terrorism on populations, structures, and a personal sense of well-being have been among the primary concerns of public and private-sector building owners. Traditional threats against people and property are unlikely to diminish, while terrorism threats, alerts, and warnings are likely to increase. As a result, architects, engineers, planners, construction professionals, owners, and facility managers involved with buildings in the United States, or with structures owned and operated by American interests outside the United States, need reliable resources, guidelines, and standards to assist in developing secure buildings and sites.

BRIEF HISTORY OF BUILDING CODES AND STANDARDS

The earliest forms of building codes and standards date as far back as the Mesopotamians in 1800 B.C. The Code of Hammurabi, the earliest legal code known in its entirety, is a collection of laws and edicts developed by the Babylonian king Hammurabi.

Since then, standards have evolved for health, welfare, and life safety in the workplace and for the general public. The Romans established many projects to increase public health and safety, including a system of aqueducts to carry and distribute fresh water throughout the city. Many other civilizations similarly contributed to public safety and welfare of their citizens.

The advent of the Industrial Revolution prompted development of new codes and standards. Workers flocked from subsistence farms into crowded, dangerous mills and mines. Tragic events connected with these new workplaces eventually led to reforms. During the latter part of the nineteenth century, governments, insurers, labor unions, professional organizations, and ad hoc watchdog groups developed more statutory rules, regulations, and performance standards addressing the hazards accompanying progress and economic development.

During the twentieth century, high-rise buildings and sprawling manufacturing plants altered life in ways unimaginable to preceding generations. Even though these advancements offered benefits to society, they also introduced new life safety and health hazards to workers and building occupants. To address these hazards, city and state governments established modern building codes, supported by insurers, professional organizations, and ad hoc watchdog groups who worked to develop performance standards for building construction and life safety. Architects, engineers, planners, designers, construction professionals, consultants, building owners, and operators concerned with creating safe and secure environments utilized codes and standards to meet their design goals and protect themselves from liability issues.

Nevertheless, security requirements are the least clear-cut of all codes and standards applicable to the design and construction industry. Security practice as a professional discipline appears to lack accessible, established criteria, supporting guidelines, and statutory code requirements.

Implementing Security Guidelines

Commercial building owners and operators often perceive fire protection, life safety, and security issues as a single concern. The National Fire Protection Association (NFPA) Life Safety Code is widely adopted by municipalities as a commercial building construction and operating standard for fire protection and life safety. However, equivalent security references do not exist for mixed-use buildings, schools, corporate headquarters, civic centers, arenas, hospitals, transportation centers, parking garages, and most other building types. There are no statutory or regulatory standards binding under the law. Virtually no standards, applied by either agreement or consent, delineate acceptable commercial building security measures.

Mandating security standards applicable to all buildings is difficult because security design addresses project-specific building programs and site analysis criteria, and considers the activities, functions, operations, and behavior of people within and near the project site. The project team and the building owner must identify proposed functional and space programs before the security plan can adequately address design, technology, and operational elements.

Early involvement of the security team during the programming and design process will encourage development of cost-effective security design and technology options. Owners must be alert to the impact that new tenants or access points may have on a facility security plan, as any significant changes in pedestrian and vehicular traffic could warrant significant modifications to the plan. A few exceptions of regulatory standards and guidelines exist within the commercial sector (Table 30.1).

TABLE 30.1   Regulatory Standards and Guidelines within the Commercial Sector

Building type	Regulatory standards
Nuclear power facilities	• Security may be mandated when extremely hazardous processes occur within a facility, such as nuclear power generation. The U.S. Nuclear Regulatory Commission (NRC) is an independent agency established by the Energy Reorganization Act of 1974 to regulate civilian use of nuclear materials. The NRC has established, among many other requirements, mandatory security measures to protect facilities and guard against removal or release of radioactive materials from the site.
Banks	• The Banking Act of 1968 imposes physical security requirements on banking institutions.
High-value goods	• High-value product manufacturers or retailers may be required by their insurers to institute certain electronic security measures in order to get insurance coverage. Jewelers are a prime example.
Drugs	• The Drug Enforcement Agency (DEA) through The Controlled Substances Act established requirements for electronic security measures that must be implemented to protect Schedule I and Schedule II substances.
Classified material	• Commercial enterprises providing services to a government agency and handling classified materials as an integral part of those services must meet minimum security provisions.

Beyond the examples cited above, no single entity has the authority to mandate security provisions in the commercial sector. Applying security measures in commercial buildings where no classified information is stored or processed, where no fiduciary activities occur, and where no high-risk activities are performed has mostly been an owner's or landlord's choice. The deciding factors are likely based on corporate risk management policies and insurance requirements.

Choosing to Secure a Building

Since security requirements are likely not mandatory, choosing to incorporate security measures in a commercial environment should depend on the probable risks, threats, and projected consequences. A thorough threat assessment should be the basis for selecting appropriate security measures. As part of standard risk management functions, corporate or in-house security departments may choose to proactively address identified risks with preventive measures. The threat assessment will most likely result in a narrative report with a table outlining levels of threats and consequences. Projecting the likely threats and consequences allows a security planner to recommend prioritized expenditures on mitigation factors (Table 30.2).

Abatement, or efforts to prevent a loss from occurring, is a countermeasure in response to an identified risk. Abatement is one example of a risk management method. Other methods of addressing risk include:

- *Transfer*. Insurance-related.
- *Avoidance*. Get rid of the asset.
- *Spreading*. Spreading risk among several departments.
- *Acceptance*. Do nothing.

These methods are typically not in the purview of the security manager, whose job is to identify threats, vulnerabilities, consequences, available countermeasures, and potential for mitigating risks. The decision-making process is highly subjective, with potential for error from identifying and quantifying threat assessments to selecting suitable countermeasures for implementation.

TABLE 30.2   Sample Threat Assessment List Evaluating Potential Risks, Threat Levels, and Consequence Levels

Risk	Threat	Consequences
Theft	High	Low
Armed intruders	Low	High
Arson	Low/medium	Medium/high
Parcel bomb	Medium/high	High
Vehicle bomb	Medium/high	High
Hostage taking	Medium/high	High
Shooting /sniper	Medium/high	High
Chemical agent	Medium/high	High
Biological agent	High	High
Radiological agent	Low/medium	High
Sabotage	Medium/high	High
Food/water contamination	Medium/high	High
Civil disturbance /protesters	Low/medium	Low/medium
Cyber attacks	Medium/high	Medium/high
Classified materials theft/destruction	Low/medium	Medium/high
Disgruntled employee	Medium/high	Medium/high

Without benchmarking references or widely accepted standards, effective programs may be increasingly dependent upon a mixture of the seasoned security manager's experienced eye and corporate guidelines. As a result, the lack of security codes and standards in the corporate and commercial sector is a growing concern among security industry professionals.

SECURITY CODES AND STANDARDS

To reap the benefits of any existing regulatory guidance, building owners, architects, engineers, designers, consultants, developers, and facility managers must assemble and adapt information from varying sources to design building security measures. Until statutory or minimal consensual regulatory standards for commercial buildings are developed, those concerned with security design must navigate through a maze of existing government guidelines, best practices recommended by security professionals and other professional organizations, and lists of technical security products offered by manufacturers.

Codes, industry standards, and guidelines typically address performance criteria, quality of materials and construction methods, and life safety issues. Conflicting interdisciplinary requirements must be coordinated. For example, security systems that control or restrict access may conflict with life safety requirements. Security design should conform to relevant industry standards wherever possible.

Several organizations, standards, and regulations represent the most commonly used and widely accepted industry standards. Some are legally binding, and others are noncompulsory expert advice (Table 30.3).

FEDERAL REGULATIONS

Many U.S. federal agencies have developed their own security standards and guidelines, addressing agency-related missions and goals. Federal regulatory codes are frequently aimed at high-risk activities that could adversely impact public safety or national security. Some of these standards may be applicable to private sector or state and local government facilities.

TABLE 30.3 Most Commonly Used and Widely Accepted Industry Security Standards

Security design component	Professional organizations and pertinent regulations
Building materials and performance criteria	• National Building Officials Code Administration (BOCA)
Lighting standards and practices	• The Illuminating Engineering Society
Fire and life safety standards	• The National Fire Protection Association (NFPA) • Occupational Safety and Health Act (OSHA)
Electronic engineering standards, components, and product performance	• Institute of Electrical and Electronics Engineers (IEEE) • National Electric Code (NEC) • National Electrical Manufacturers Association (NEMA) • The Electronic Industries Association (EIA) • International Electrotechnical Commission (IEC) • The International Organization for Standardization (ISO) • Underwriters Laboratories (UL)
Electronic product safety and application	• Underwriters Laboratories (UL) • Factory Mutual Research Corporation (FM) (*Note:* Underwriters Laboratories and Factory Mutual Research Corporation have a strong influence on commercial security measures because insurers tie policy issuance and insurance costs to the use of UL- or FM-approved materials and standardized practices.)
Accessibility	• American National Standards Institute (ANSI) • Americans with Disabilities Act (ADA)
Communications	• Federal Communications Commission (FCC)
Security consulting and management practices	• The American Society for Industrial Security (ASIS) • The International Association of Professional Security Consultants (IAPSC)

The Department of Homeland Security and its components will likely be a source for regulatory guidance as the agency evolves. Federal statutory and regulatory standards are published in the Code of Federal Regulations (CFR). Annual updates may be obtained through the U.S. General Services Administration.

While many federal regulations are helpful for determining best practices, they must necessarily be interpreted in order to apply to commercial buildings. For example, the U.S. Department of Defense regulation may specify shatter-resistant film of a certain thickness for application on exterior glass windows. The entire commercial building design team, together with the building owner or operator, would determine whether that aspect of the regulation is suitable, given the risk, threat, and vulnerabilities of the commercial property.

The list of federal security regulations provides an overview, by agency, of available standards suitable for adaptation to commercial use. This list is by no means exhaustive and the standards are subject to modifications and revisions at any time. Checking with the appropriate agency for the latest versions of regulatory guidelines is strongly advised before commencing related design and construction (Table 30.4)

Local Codes

Codes assure safety standards for personnel and assets. Local building and fire codes contain detailed formats outlining minimum performance and design criteria for structures. The codes are developed and enforced at the local city, village, and county levels, but follow a widely recognized best practices format. Most localities do not have security provisions within local building codes. However, some codes may reference life safety measures, such as door locking relating to use of electronic access control systems.

TABLE 30.4 Federal Regulations and Guidelines Suitable for Adaptation to Commercial Use

Agency	Regulation description
U.S. General Services Administration (GSA)	*Facilities Standards for the Public Buildings Service,* a detailed design and construction guide for federal facilities, offers recommendations readily applicable to commercial and mixed-use office buildings.
Department of Defense (DoD)	The Unified Facilities Criteria (UFC 4-010-01) provides Department of Defense Minimum Antiterrorism Standards for new construction and significant renovations; and design philosophy, strategies, and assumptions for military construction.
Department of State	*Countering Terrorism,* the Bureau of Diplomatic Security guideline, contains suggestions for U.S. business representatives abroad. Suggestions are mostly operational and are applicable to many building types.
Department of Health and Human Services (DHHS)	Laboratories storing and using certain types of agents and organisms must adhere to guidelines promulgated by DHHS through the Centers for Disease Control and Prevention (CDC) and National Institutes of Health (NIH). These biosafety guidelines address facility design and construction, equipment needs, and facility operations. See DHHS (NIOSH) Pub. No. 2002-139.
Department of Defense, Department of Energy, U.S. Nuclear Regulatory Commission, and Central Intelligence Agency	The National Industrial Security Program Operating Manual (NISPOM) prescribes requirements, restrictions, and safeguards to ensure that contractors protect classified information.
Department of Treasury	U.S. Customs publishes standards serving as models for cargo security best practices.
Federal Monetary and Banking Agencies	The Bank Protection Act of 1968 includes amendments and standards addressing intrusion and robbery alarm systems, lighting, locks, surveillance, vault, and safe requirements.
National Institute of Standards and Technology (NIST)	FIPS 31 is a guideline for Automatic Data Processing, Physical Security, and Risk Management.
Nuclear Regulatory Commission (NRC)	The NRC standards and regulations describe entry and exit controls to protected areas, material access areas, locks, perimeter intrusion alarm system, security equipment, key and lock controls, and protection against vehicular ramming and explosives.

Note: All regulations are subject to revisions and modifications.

Self-Imposed Guidelines

Some industries have chosen to develop their own nonbinding guidelines, rather than have them imposed by the government. For example, the U.S. Department of Transportation, within the Department of Homeland Security, regulates transport of certain chemicals, but tools are also available to help transportation specialists and plant managers. Industry groups, such as the American Chemistry Council, the Chlorine Institute, Synthetic Organic Chemical Manufacturers Association, the National Association of Chemical Distributors, and others, developed these standards.

Self-imposed security guidelines and safety practices are valuable resources because the most qualified and knowledgeable industry professionals often develop them. The danger is that new security requirements, additional production costs, or displacement will inhibit adaptation, as long as security measures are voluntary.

CHARTING A COURSE OF ACTION

Building owners and managers often view security provisions as optional costs, especially since most are not required by code. However, owners will typically pay for security in order to avoid liability, to add value, or to maintain critical and necessary operations. Examples of necessary operations include maternity ward infant protection systems in hospitals, warehouses with valuable inventory, and data centers housing essential or sensitive information.

Building owners, operators, and landlords understand the need for heightened security concerns among tenants stemming from terrorist threats, workplace violence, and crime. These security concerns should be shared with architects, engineers, designers, and construction professionals during the earliest phases of the programming and planning process. Owners must decide on the level of risk that they are willing to assume and work with the project team to determine appropriate security goals. Owners must also ensure that facility operations do not conflict with the comprehensive security plan.

Increased global concern about terrorist threats indicates that the trend toward enhanced security design, technology, and operations will likely remain strong. Implementing prescriptive codes could potentially reduce duplicative efforts, decrease waste associated with companies paying for useless provisions, and standardize the quality of expectations in the design and construction arena. Regardless of any potential life safety and security code provisions that address architectural and engineering design, a comprehensive security plan that integrates design, technology, and building operations is still the best protection for building owners.

Until a series of prescriptive codes is developed and made available for widespread, standard application, building owners, operators, and managers seeking to enhance security measures on their properties should develop a comprehensive security plan. (Table 30.5) Other tasks may require working with in-house professionals or outside consultants:

- Examine corporate security standards for applicability to site planning and building design.
- Assess the likely threats using a template developed by the corporate security department or a qualified professional consulting firm.
- Ascertain the security design experience and qualifications of architectural, engineering, and security consulting firms under consideration for selection in new construction or renovation projects. The firms and proposed team members should demonstrate appropriate, relevant experience and knowledge of essential security design elements (Table 30.6).

VIABLE OPTIONS FOR SECURITY CODES

The primary motives for development of security codes are to:

- Clarify conditions prior to identifying the need for security measures
- Develop viable options to address an identified threat
- Reduce duplication of effort
- Decrease waste
- Standardize quality

To further efforts in developing security standards for the commercial building sector, the following suggestions merit consideration:

- Use federal mandates for security provisions critical to emergency response at applicable facilities. Limited federal funding would ideally offset implementation costs.
- Implement federal recommendations for more in-depth security provisions, organized according to building type, function, and likely threat, for state and local homeland security, and counter-terrorism

TABLE 30.5   Ten Steps to a Comprehensive Security Plan

1. Assume incidents or attacks will occur and plan accordingly.
2. Identify threats by predicting the most likely attacks or incidents. The main objectives of an effective emergency response, which is part of any security plan, should be to protect lives, protect assets, and maintain operations.
3. Identify facility vulnerabilities with respect to the likely threats.
4. Maximize design features to improve security. Examples:
   - Minimize number of entryways
   - Protect utility areas from tampering and explosions
   - Harden mail and delivery facilities for blast resistance
   - Design architectural landscaping to prevent ramming
   - Provide adequate setback from roads, parking areas, and other facilities
   - Build space to accommodate security functions, such as a control station, inspection area, and badging operations
5. Select appropriate technology systems to address vulnerabilities. Examples:
   - Access control
   - Door alarms
   - Communications capabilities
   - Surveillance
   - Lighting
6. Use consistent standard operations, policies, and procedures to enhance the security plan, such as:
   - Key control
   - Identification card issuance and use
   - Hiring practices
   - Visitor policy
   - Mailroom and delivery policies
   - Computer security
7. Demonstrate genuine support for standard operations, policies, and procedures from the top down.
8. Develop and institute mandatory employee security training.
9. Develop an emergency response plan. Start by identifying who has the authority to initiate an emergency response and why.
10. Train, practice, evaluate, and refine the emergency response plan at least annually.

---

efforts. The federal government is best suited to this task, as several federal agencies have comprehensive guidelines suitable for adaptation by state and local government agencies.

- Encourage states to adapt federal recommendations, as applicable to local conditions, and mandate compliance. States could execute periodic inspections and compliance tracking.

- Provide incentives for local governments to assist in documenting compliance. For example, if state provisions have clear criteria, local governments could collect compliance statements from builders. However, if localities are responsible for approvals, they might have to train staff engineers; especially those already performing building code inspections, to handle security inspections. As a result, localities might be forced to hire more staff, a potential financial burden.

- Encourage states to provide incentives to building owners who voluntarily pay to be accredited by a security professional. Increased security and emergency response preparedness benefit employees, the community, and neighbors of the facility. Accreditation criteria should stress police and fire coordination and provisions supporting emergency personnel.

- Encourage architects, engineers, and design and construction professionals to be familiar with fundamental security design concepts, codes, and standards, especially pertaining to specific building types they are involved with, as part of maintaining professional licensure, and as part of the licensing examinations.

- Educate design and construction professionals in schools, professional conferences, and continuing education courses, about security design and related industry codes and standards.

Whether any future mandatory security codes exist as a stand-alone regulatory document, or are integrated into other life safety codes, components for standard documentation might include:

- Categorization tools, enabling building owners and operators to classify their facility based upon location, function, occupancy, risk, and public accessibility
- Baseline provisions required for all facilities to ensure a reasonable security level
- Architectural and engineering design recommendations
- Technology, such as security systems, communications, and data
- Operations, policies, and procedures

CONCLUSION

No one could have predicted, planned for, or counteracted the use of airplanes as missiles targeted at the World Trade Center's Twin Towers on September 11, 2001, and the resulting loss of approximately 3000 lives. However, many security lessons may be learned from these attacks, especially regarding commercial buildings (Tables 30.7 and 30.8).

Designing, installing, and maintaining security systems are significant expenses for commercial property owners. Without any binding codes or mandates addressing comprehensive security systems in the private sector, building owners must rely on recommendations from consultants and in-house security professionals. Ultimately, however, in the public and private sectors, owners determine their security needs, select and specify technology, and justify associated costs. Industry groups, design professionals, and public officials may eventually develop mandatory security codes for commercial buildings. However, a significant body of resources, from the public and private sectors, is available for adaptation to commercial use.

The tragic events of September 11, 2001, underscored the lack of, and the potential need for, baseline security codes and standards appropriate for private-sector commercial, institutional, and industrial buildings falling outside the mandates of government security guidelines. Design and construction professionals, facility managers, and building owners should remain aware of proposed changes to national, state, and local codes and standards to accommodate security provisions.

Until security guidelines are formally integrated with existing codes and standards, building owners and design professionals should become familiar with and routinely implement the best security

TABLE 30.7   Lessons Learned from 9/11: Security Planning

The most urgent lessons for design and construction professionals, building owners, and facility operators as a result of the attacks on September 11, 2001, and from other terrorist attacks directed at American facilities and operations, are the need to plan and design for security and emergency response operations.

- Coordinate a quality security system by integrating architectural design, technological devices, and operational activities.
- Develop a list of likely threats to be mitigated, specific to every site and function. Mitigating threats requires dedicating money to address security vulnerabilities.
- Hire an experienced professional to perform vulnerability assessments, whenever possible. Look for relevant certifications from industry organizations.
- Hire an experienced security professional to adapt best practices from regulated organizations, such as the Department of Defense, into the commercial building security design. Maintain documentation regarding which standards and best practices were implemented, should proof be required for insurance or liability purposes at a later date. Keep record copies at an off-site location from the building being covered.
- Understand that security emergencies cannot be predicted, nor can they all be prevented. Security plans mitigate risk and represent a tradeoff between operational freedom and restriction. Building owners must make informed decisions about the amount of risk that they are willing to accept and cover all related security costs.

TABLE 30.8 Lessons Learned from 9/11: Emergency Planning

The events of September 11th highlighted the need for building owners and managers to plan emergency response operations.

- Invest the time and effort required for planning emergency response. Plan for worst-case scenarios such as:
  - Power outages, including emergency backups, which render alarms, communications, elevators, lights, and electronic systems useless
  - Circumstances where key coordination people are unavailable or inaccessible
  - A chaotic, noisy, confusing, frightening, life-threatening situation
- Determine how security systems will function in emergency response efforts. For example, card access systems can provide a list of who is in the building, which is critical rescue information during emergencies. Plan to use such information in emergency response plans, which may require programming remote access of the electronic information.
- Recognize that preparedness is paramount, time-consuming, tedious, and sometimes costly. Sound emergency plans take time and effort to develop. Government organizations, like the Federal Emergency Management Agency (FEMA), publish helpful guidelines.
- Emergency plans are most useful if they are well designed, accurate, trained, rehearsed, and evaluated. Regular testing is the most effective way to assess emergency plan accuracy.
- Document the tests and promptly remediate any identified problems.
- Find innovative ways to multiply security system capabilities.
- Include employees and tenants in the security plan by fostering personal ownership of the workplace, living area, and common public spaces. Tenants walking through a lobby three times daily are more apt to notice an unusual package, a surveillance attempt, or a person who doesn't belong.

design and operational practices to ensure the health and life safety of their employees, tenants, and communities.

INTERNET RESOURCES

American Chemistry Council (ACC)
www.americanchemistry.com

American National Standards Institute (ANSI)
www.ansi.org

American Society for Industrial Security (ASIS)
www.asisonline.org

American Society for Testing and Materials (ASTM)
www.astm.org

Centers for Disease Control and Prevention (CDC)
www.cdc.gov

Chlorine Institute (CI)
www.cl2.com

Electronic Industries Alliance (Association) (EIA)
www.eia.org

Factory Mutual Research Corp (FM)
www.fmglobal.com

Illuminating Engineering Society of North America (IESNA)
www.iesna.org

Institute of Electrical and Electronics Engineers (IEEE)
www.ieee.org

International Code Council (ICC)
www.iccsafe.org

International Electrotechnical Commission (IEC)
www.iec.ch

International Organization for Standardization (ISO)
www.iso.org

National Association of Chemical Distributors (NACD)
www.nacd.com

National Electrical Manufacturers Association (NEMA)
www.nema.org

National Fire Protection Association (NFPA)
www.nfpa.org

National Institute of Standards and
Technology (NIST)
www.nist.gov

National Institutes of Health (NIH)
www.nih.gov

Sako & Associates, Inc.
www.sakosecurity.com

Synthetic Organic Chemical Manufacturers
Association (SOCMA)
www.socma.com

Underwriters Laboratories (UL)
www.ul.com

U.S. Customs Service (USCS)
U.S. Department of Treasury
www.customs.ustreas.gov

U.S. Department of Defense (USDoD)
www.defenselink.mil/pubs/

U.S. Department of Health and Human
Services (USDHHS)
www.os.dhhs.gov

U.S. Department of Homeland Security
(USDHS)
www.dhs.gov

U.S. Department of Justice (USDOJ)
Drug Enforcement Administration (DEA)
www.dea.gov

U.S. Department of State (USDOS)
http://www.state.gov/

U.S. General Services Administration
(USGSA)
Public Building Service
www.gsa.gov

U.S. Nuclear Regulatory Commission
(USNRC)
Office of Public Affairs (OPA)
www.nrc.gov

CHAPTER 31
LIABILITY EXPOSURE AFTER SEPTEMBER 11, 2001

Michael S. Zetlin, Esq.
Partner, Zetlin & De Chiara LLP
New York, New York

Noelle Lilien, Esq.
Attorney, Zetlin & De Chiara LLP
New York, New York

In a time of turbulence and change, it is more true today than ever that knowledge is power.
JOHN F. KENNEDY (1917–1963)
35th U.S. president

The tragic events of September 11, 2001, resulted in enhanced security building design and increased liability exposure for architects and engineers. The devastating terrorist attacks at the World Trade Center and the Pentagon in 2001 transformed operations within the American business arena, the workplace, and especially within the design and construction community.

Before 9/11, security was not a priority for most design professionals, except for those designing government and civic buildings, where security has long been included in project planning, design, and specifications. Since then, design professionals, especially those practicing within the commercial and institutional markets, must adapt to the changing environment and incorporate security features into facility planning and design.

The primary driver for this change is the enhanced risk of litigation, a familiar subject to most private-sector design professionals. Increasingly, design professionals are targets of litigation that arises from new construction development, who have to spend disproportionate amounts of time with lawyers, defending their assets and reputations against malpractice, personal injury, and other claims. Design professionals schooled in aesthetics are increasingly familiar with legal terms such as "negligent performance of professional services," "errors and omissions," and "negligent design." Most sobering are increased professional liability insurance premiums resulting from litigation. Litigation is expensive—in both actual and distraction costs—even when the design professional ultimately prevails.

The challenge facing design professionals is determining what measures should be taken to protect them from liability after 9/11. Federal, state, and local governments, trade organizations, academics, and the media focus on security features to be included in building design projects. However, with major national studies in different stages of completion, and with the courts yet to provide guidance on the responsibilities of architects and engineers after 9/11, the design community is largely operating in a zone of uncertainty.

This chapter will identify and clarify issues related to security design and liability for design professionals, by explaining liability sources, by providing insight into how design professionals' responsibilities may have changed since 9/11, and by suggesting steps for design professionals to minimize future litigation risk.

LIABILITY SOURCES

Although multiple areas of potential liability exist for design professionals, including breach of contract and negligent misrepresentation, claims based on negligent design pose the greatest litigation risk to design professionals after 9/11. The key determinant for establishing liability for negligent design is whether the architect or engineer has met the requisite standard of care in performing his or her services. The question is whether the services were performed in a manner consistent with the training, experience, and skill of similar design professionals operating under similar circumstances.

The standard of care is a fluid and amorphous concept and not easily defined. The standard of care is based on reasonable forseeability of a risk, which is measured by

- The risk of an accident occurring
- The magnitude of the harm should the risk materialize
- The availability of alternatives that would prevent the accident

Reasonable care is determined by balancing the likelihood of harm and the gravity of the harm if it happens, against the burden of the precaution, which would be effective to avoid the harm.

For example, a design professional who is designing a grandstand for an outdoor event must consider the possibility that a thunderstorm could strike and high winds could topple the grandstand, causing serious injuries to visitors. In light of the risk that a thunderstorm could occur while the grandstand is occupied, the design professional is further required to consider ways to make the grandstand as safe as possible in light of the risk that is posed. If the design professional fails to identify the risk and fails to take precautions to minimize the risk, the design professional will have breached the standard of care.

Whether a design professional has met the standard of care is usually proven by competing expert witness testimony at trial. The experts will explain their views on the prevailing standards of safety and design in a geographic area, or practice specialty, and then demonstrate how the design professional being sued either met or failed to meet that standard.

NAVIGATING THE STANDARD OF CARE POST-9/11

Although no consensus exists on the post-9/11 standard of care for design professionals, it appears that buildings designed in urban areas require greater attention to security details and design features, because of greater terrorism risks. For guidance in determining the prevailing standards of safety, design professionals should consider building codes, proposed codes and recommendations, as well as the protective features that other design professionals and government agencies are including in similar building types and design projects.

To minimize risk, an architect must consider building codes as the minimum baseline against which actions will be measured. Failure to comply with building codes is considered to be negligence per se in some jurisdictions, that is, the court will presume that the design professional was negligent if he or she violates the building code. However, a design professional who ignores foreseeable risks or fails to make improvements that should have been made under the circumstances may be exposed to liability for failing to meet the required standard of care, even if he or she follows the building code to the letter. In these circumstances, a court will compare the design professional's behavior against the higher standard of what a similarly situated design professional, with knowledge of the same risks, would have done under the circumstances. For example, a Michigan court decided that an architect breached the standard of care when designing a swimming facility even though the architect complied with governmental and industry standards.

This is particularly true in the case of 9/11, where the standard of care is evolving, and will continue to evolve even after municipalities revise their building codes in an attempt to protect urban infrastructure against future attacks. Codes or standards of safety proposed by governmental bodies or by private-sector associations can provide guidance for design professionals of the appropriate standard of care, even though the codes and standards lack the force of law. They define prevailing industry practices and importantly, at trial, provide support for expert witnesses concerning the proper standard of care.

After 9/11, several large United States cities reviewed their building codes and proposed amendments. In March 2003, the New York Task Force on Building Codes issued a report with several recommendations (Table 31.1).

Since 9/11, the Federal Emergency Management Agency (FEMA) and the National Institute of Science and Technology (NIST) have taken the lead on behalf of the federal government by initiating studies and issuing preliminary recommendations regarding increased building safety and security measures. These studies and recommendations cover areas such as structural engineering, fireproofing, and egress (Table 31.2).

In addition to building codes, proposed codes, and recommendations from government or private organizations, design professionals should also review and be familiar with industry standards, case studies, and best practices regarding security design since 9/11.

Across the United States, design professionals responded to the World Trade Center disaster with increased attention to all aspects of building safety, incorporating security features into design projects to improve structural integrity, fire prevention, blast resistance, and communication systems. Since the standard of care is slowly evolving, design professionals must remain informed of changing codes, regulations, standards, and security design trends (Table 31.3).

TABLE 31.1 9/11 Lessons Learned from World Trade Center: Recommendations of the New York Task Force on Building Codes

1. Enhancing robustness of structures so that damage is minimized in the event of an attack and the structure resists progressive collapse.
2. Prohibiting the use of open web bar trusses in new commercial high-rise construction.
3. Encouraging the use of impact-resistant materials in the construction of stair and elevator shaft enclosures.
4. Encouraging the inclusion of more stairwells or wider stairwells in buildings.
5. Prohibiting the use of scissors stairs in high-rise commercial buildings with a floor plate of over 10,000 square feet.
6. Improving the marking of the egress path, doors, and stairs with photo-luminescent materials and retro-fitting existing exit signs with either battery or generator backup power.
7. Requiring controlled inspection to ensure that fireproofing is fully intact on all structural building members exposed by subsequent renovations to ensure continued compliance with applicable code requirements.
8. Requiring all high-rise commercial buildings over 100 feet high without automatic sprinkler protection to install a sprinkler system throughout the building within 15 years.
9. Enhancing fire department emergency response communications in high-rise commercial buildings.
10. Requiring air intakes in all new construction to be located at least 20 feet above grade and away from exhaust discharges or off-street loading bays.

Source: City of New York, Department of Buildings, Recommendations by the World Trade Center Building Code Task Force, 2003.

TABLE 31.2   FEMA's Preliminary Recommendations for Increased Building Safety and Security

Security element	Preliminary recommendation
Structural engineering	• Structural framing systems need redundancy and robustness, so that alternative paths of additional capacity are available for transmitting loads when building damage occurs. • Connection performance under impact loads and during fire loads needs to be analytically understood and quantified for improved design capabilities and performance as critical components in structural frames.
Fireproofing	• Fireproofing needs to adhere under impact and fire conditions that deform steel members, so that coatings remain on steel and provide intended protection.
Egress systems	• Existing egress systems in use should be evaluated for redundancy and robustness, providing egress when building damage occurs, including the issues of transfer floors, stair spacing and locations, and stairwell enclosure impact resistance.

Source: Federal Emergency Management Agency.

MINIMIZE RISK

On any project, owners seek to minimize cost. However, architects and engineers, aware of standards and best practices by other design professionals, cannot allow an owner's financial interests to dictate security design components. While not all suggested security features must be incorporated into a building project, ideally, the owner should be ultimately responsible for making decisions and bearing the risks of making the wrong decision regarding security design.

Design professionals can best protect themselves from such risk at the outset of the engagement, when the owner and the design professional are negotiating the allocation of risk between them for the project. There are many factors that will influence which party will bear a greater proportion of the risk, such as the project size, financial sophistication of the parties, and the experience and negotiating skill of legal counsel. However, there are three contractual provisions that any design professional should insist on prior to accepting an engagement. Incorporating these provisions will make explicit the allocation of the risk between the owner and the design professional (Table 31.4).

First, the design professional should require that the owner agree to retain a security or protective design consultant who will conduct a formal vulnerability assessment of the proposed building against a terrorist attack. Even though many firms began offering vulnerability assessments after 9/11, owners should retain firms with extensive experience in the vulnerability assessment field, such as firms that have worked on secure facilities for the U.S. General Services Administration (GSA) or the State Department (Table 31.5).

Based on the findings and factors analyzed for the vulnerability assessment, security or protective design consultants will work with the owner and the design team to recommend appropriate security features to be incorporated into the project design.

An owner focused on minimizing costs may not be inclined to allocate resources for a vulnerability assessment, and some negotiation may be required to persuade the owner to agree to conduct an assessment. However, the assessment is in the owner's best interest, since conducting a vulnerability assessment and employing methods to enhance building safety will benefit the owner in several ways:

• Enhancing building security through design will minimize damage in the event of a terrorist attack or similar catastrophic event, thus reducing personal injuries, property damage, and the owner's litigation risk.

• From a marketing perspective, security features will attract tenants who are concerned about safety.

• A design that incorporates security features may reduce insurance premiums and financing costs.

An owner may not agree to incorporate all recommendations included in a vulnerability assessment or may not even agree to conduct a vulnerability assessment. If an owner does not agree to conduct a vulnerability assessment, the design professional's standard of care would dictate the recommendations

TABLE 31.3   Case Studies: Integrating Security Elements into Buildings in Design and Construction

Security element	Project and security features
Blast-resistant structural elements	• The Time Warner Headquarters, at Manhattan's Columbus Circle, was modified for enhanced security. The number of structural columns encased in concrete was increased, allowing the building greater capability to withstand a blast or fire.
Communications systems	• The owners installed systems to improve communications between the fire department and other rescue personnel.
Blast-resistant structural elements	• At Manhattan's CIBC Tower, steel plates were welded to structural columns to resist lateral forces of a bomb blast.
Blast-resistant glazing applications	• Shatterproof glass was installed on the building's lower floors.
Blast-resistant structural elements	• In Chicago's Loop, the design of a 50-story high-rise was entirely revamped after September 11 because the original design called for a stilt-like base with exposed struts.

Source: Eric Lipton and James Glanz, "9/11 Prompts New Caution in the Design of U.S. Skyscrapers," *New York Times,* Sept. 9, 2002, and Zetlin & De Chiara LLP.

TABLE 31.4   Three Contractual Provisions Design Professionals Should Insist on Prior to Accepting an Engagement

1. Require that the owner retain a security or protective design consultant.
2. Negotiate an indemnity provision in contracts, so the owner will indemnify the design professional from any claims arising from the owner's failure to conduct a vulnerability assessment or integrate security recommendations on the project.
3. Retain the right to terminate a contract if the owner fails to include recommended security elements, or if there may be substantial risk.

Source: Zetlin & De Chiara LLP.

TABLE 31.5   Key Factors Analyzed by Security Consultants during Vulnerability Assessments

• Profile of all building tenants
• Building location, especially proximity to landmarks and government buildings
• Actual threats received
• Physical vulnerabilities, including underground parking garages and loading docks
• Proximity to street and public access

Source: Zetlin & De Chiara LLP.

regarding safety, based on his or her knowledge of risks under similar circumstances. The owner may choose to decline to incorporate the recommendations, but ultimately the owner's business decision may determine that costs of security features outweigh the risk.

In all these cases, design professionals should negotiate for an indemnity provision in their contracts by which the owner will indemnify them for any claims arising in connection with the owner's failure to:

• Conduct a vulnerability assessment

• Include recommendations resulting from a vulnerability assessment in the project design

- Include recommendations from the design professional in lieu of a vulnerability assessment in the design

Lastly, since the owner's decision to incorporate recommended security features into a design will be determined after the contract has been executed and after the design professional has started developing the project, the design professional may want to have the right to terminate the contract if

- The owner ultimately decides not to incorporate recommended security features.
- The design professional in his or her judgment believes failure to include such recommendations poses a substantial risk.

Whether or not the owner agrees to the indemnification or termination provisions, the design professional should

- Notify the owner about security recommendations, in writing
- Document the owner's decision to forgo a vulnerability assessment or decision not to incorporate security recommendations

SAMPLE LETTERS

Sending letters pertaining to security provisions, like the samples set forth here, may help a design professional establish entitlement to indemnification should a claim arise (Tables 31.6 to 31.9). These letters may also help establish that the design professional did notify the owner of certain risks and will help document that the owner assumed the risks by failing to implement security design features on the project.

THE LEGISLATIVE IMPACT OF SEPTEMBER 11, 2001

After 9/11, the need for Good Samaritan laws covering design professionals who volunteer during rescue and recovery activities and terrorism insurance became important issues within the design and construction communities.

Good Samaritan Laws

The tragedies of 9/11 shed light on the need for a Good Samaritan law for architects and engineers. In the days and hours following the terrorist attacks on 9/11 in Lower Manhattan, hundreds of engineers and architects volunteered in search-and-rescue efforts. These architects and engineers were called upon by overwhelmed government agencies to provide their professional opinions about the structural stability of buildings, roadways, tunnels, and other infrastructures. However, liability issues arose, highlighting the need for Good Samaritan laws, offering immunity in certain cases to design professionals (Table 31.10).

The National Society of Professional Engineers professional policy includes a Model Engineers' Good Samaritan Act (Table 31.13).

TERRORISM INSURANCE

Before 9/11, coverage for acts of terrorism was generally included as part of a business's property and casualty insurance policy. Acts of terrorism were not included or were excluded in most poli-

TABLE 31.6   Sample Letter from Design Professional to Building Owner, Recommending that the Owner Retain a Protective Design Consultant and Conduct a Vulnerability Assessment

Playingitsafe & Associates Consulting Engineers
8000 S. Stony Island Avenue
Chicago, Illinois 60617

January 7, 2004

Mr. R. U. Wize
Allbright Properties Limited
875 Lakeshore Drive
Chicago, Illinois 60611

Re: Vulnerability Assessment for Burlington West Office Tower

Dear Mr. Wize:

We are pleased to submit the annexed proposal in connection with the Burlington West Office Tower Project.

In light of the uncertainty that has arisen as a result of recent terrorist activity and heightened threat levels, we strongly recommend that you retain a protective design consultant to conduct a vulnerability assessment for the Burlington West Tower property. The vulnerability assessment will provide us with guidance regarding the types of security features that should be considered as we develop the building design.

Please confirm that you plan to retain a protective design consultant to conduct a vulnerability assessment. If you are not familiar with any experienced protective design consultants, we will be glad to suggest firms for you to consider. After the assessment is completed, we will be available to meet with you and the consultant to discuss any design-related security issues identified during the assessment.

Please call me at your earliest convenience if you have any questions.

Very truly yours,

U. R. Playingitsafe

Note: These letters are for illustrative purposes only, and should not be relied on without consulting appropriate legal counsel and the laws of the governing jurisdiction.
Source: Zetlin & De Chiara LLP.

cies. After 9/11, insurance carriers announced that they would exclude coverage for acts of terrorism from their property insurance policies because they were unable to price such coverage. As a result, terrorism insurance was either unobtainable or prohibitively expensive. This change effectively discouraged owners and developers from constructing new projects. Lobbying from the insurance industry and construction trade groups resulted in federal legislation, the Terrorism Risk Insurance Act, signed in late 2002, which addressed these issues (Table 31.14).

CONCLUSION

September 11, 2001, had a profound effect on the design and construction community. Since 9/11, design professionals have been forced to examine security issues and to consider what steps they

TABLE 31.7   Sample Letter from Design Professional to Building Owner, Confirming Receipt of Vulnerability Assessment Report

---

Playingitsafe & Associates Consulting Engineers
8000 S. Stony Island Avenue
Chicago, Illinois 60617

March 25, 2004

Mr. R. U. Wize
Allbright Properties Limited
875 Lakeshore Drive
Chicago, Illinois 60611

Re: Vulnerability Assessment for Burlington West Office Tower

Dear Mr. Wize:

This will confirm that we received the vulnerability assessment report from your security consultant, _____ Associates. As you may know, the report contains recommendations that exceed any requirements contained in structural engineering codes or guidelines. We recognize that these suggestions may increase the cost of the project. To the extent that these measures are implemented, however, they will help guard against loss of life and will enhance the security of the structure in the event of a terrorist attack.

We would like to schedule a meeting with you, at your earliest convenience, to discuss the suggested security measures you would like us to incorporate into the design.

Very truly yours,

U. R. Playingitsafe

Note: These letters are for illustrative purposes only, and should not be relied on without consulting appropriate legal counsel and the laws of the governing jurisdiction.
Source: Zetlin & De Chiara LLP.

should take to protect themselves from liability risks. With limited exceptions, governmental entities have not revised building codes, and the courts have not yet addressed the extent to which the standard of care has evolved since 9/11.

Nevertheless, savvy design professionals can minimize their liability exposure by understanding sources of potential liability, appreciating how their responsibilities as design professionals may have changed since 9/11, and allocating risk during contract drafting and negotiation.

ACKNOWLEDGMENTS

• Timothy Hegarty, Esq., Lori Schwarz, Esq., Scott Winikow, Esq., Liliana Martire, Esq., Michelle Fiorito, Esq., and Mark Khmelnitskiy, of Zetlin & De Chiara, LLP, New York City, New York

TABLE 31.8   Sample Letter from Design Professional to Building Owner, Confirming Security Design Elements to Be Incorporated in Design Project

Playitsafe & Associates Consulting Engineers
8000 S. Stony Island Avenue
Chicago, Illinois 60617

June 13, 2004

Mr. R. U. Wize
Allbright Properties Limited
875 Lakeshore Drive
Chicago, Illinois 60611

Re: Vulnerability Assessment for Burlington West Office Tower

Dear Mr. Wize:

Based on the discussion at our meeting held yesterday, we will proceed with the design for the Burlington Office Tower Project. As you directed, we will incorporate the following security measures into the design:

1. Structural redundancy in exit stairwells
2. Enhanced blast protection in loading docks
3. Isolated mailroom
4. Blast protection on street level

Please contact us as soon as possible if you decide to incorporate any of the other options outlined by the protective design consultant.

Very truly yours,

U. R. Playingitsafe

Note: These letters are for illustrative purposes only, and should not be relied on without consulting appropriate legal counsel and the laws of the governing jurisdiction.
Source: Zetlin & De Chiara LLP.

- Tod Rittenhouse, PE, Principal, Weidlinger Associates, Inc., New York, New York
- Thomas G. Coghlan, President, Design Insurance Agency, Inc., New York, New York

BIBLIOGRAPHY

City of New York, Department of Buildings, Recommendations by the World Trade Center Building Code Task Force, February 14, 2003.

Federal Emergency Management Agency, *World Trade Center Building Performance Study,* chap. 8-1, May 1, 2002.

TABLE 31.9   Sample Letter from Design Professional to Building Owner Acknowledging that Owner Declined Vulnerability Assessment, and Offering Security Design Recommendations

---

Playingitsafe & Associates Consulting Engineers
8000 S. Stony Island Avenue
Chicago, Illinois 60617

December 23, 2004

Mr. R. U. Wize
Allbright Properties Limited
875 Lakeshore Drive
Chicago, Illinois 60611

Re: Vulnerability Assessment for Burlington West Office Tower

Dear Mr. Wize:

We understand your concerns regarding the cost of performing a vulnerability assessment in connection with this project. While we would prefer to have an expert conduct an assessment, we are not aware of any requirement that you do so. We are offering below some options that you may wish to consider to guard against security-related threats. These options are not intended as a substitute for a full vulnerability assessment.

These options include:
1. Redundancy in structural framing systems so that alternative capacity is available for transmitting loads if building damage occurs
2. Improved fireproofing on steel members
3. Redundancy and robustness in egress pathways and stairwell enclosure impact resistance
4. Above grade location of air intake
5. Enhanced blast protection in delivery bays
6. Mailroom remote and with enhanced blast protection
7. Support beams encased in plywood or concrete

Please contact me so that we can schedule a meeting to discuss how these security recommendations can be incorporated into the project's design.

Very truly yours,

U. R. Playingitsafe

Note: These letters are for illustrative purposes only, and should not be relied on without consulting appropriate legal counsel and the laws of the governing jurisdiction.
Source: Zetlin & De Chiara LLP.

Feld, Daniel E., "Admissibility in Evidence, on Issue of Negligence, of Codes or Standards of Safety Issued or Sponsored by Governmental Body or by Voluntary Association," *American Law Reports* 1974. (Explains that codes and standards proposed by governmental bodies or voluntary associations can provide guidance regarding the standard of care even if such proposed codes or standards lack the force of law).

Lipton, Eric, and James Glanz, "9/11 Prompts New Caution in the Design of U.S. Skyscrapers," *New York Times*, Sept. 9, 2002, sec. A, p. 1. (Provides comprehensive discussion regarding trend toward incorporating security

TABLE 31.10   9/11 Lessons Learned: Engineers and Architects' Good Samaritan Laws

After the events of September 11, volunteer architects and engineers in and around New York City risked their own personal safety for the sake of helping others. However, these volunteers faced substantial liability exposure because they were personally liable for any claims that may have arisen as a result of the services they provided. As volunteers, they were not covered by their employers' professional liability policies.

As of 2004, only 14 states, representing 28 percent of the United States, provide immunity for architects and engineers who volunteer in response to emergency situations (Table 31.11). In contrast, most states have enacted Good Samaritan statutes immunizing Certified First Responders and Emergency Medical Technicians (EMTs), as well as doctors, nurses, dentists, physical therapists, and physicians' assistants from liability if they render first aid or treatment in the event of an emergency.

Design professionals can lend support to Good Samaritan laws for engineers and architects. The American Society of Consulting Engineers (ASCE) developed a sample letter sent to New York State Legislators after 9/11/01 advocating for such a law (Table 31.12).

Source: Zetlin & De Chiara LLP.

TABLE 31.11   States Providing Immunity for Volunteer Architects and Engineers in Response to Emergency Situations*

Note: Most states have enacted Good Samaritan statutes protecting certified first responders, medical professionals, and emergency medical technicians (EMTs) from liability if they render first aid or treatment during an emergency.

1. California	6. Kentucky	11. North Dakota
2. Colorado	7. Louisiana	12. Oregon
3. Connecticut	8. Maryland	13. Virginia
4. Florida	9. New Mexico	14. Washington
5. Georgia	10. North Carolina	

*As of 2004, subject to change.
Source: Zetlin & De Chiara LLP and NSPE.

features into new designs in the wake of September 11, 2001, and discussion of Time Warner Headquarters, CIBC Headquarters, and skyscraper in Chicago's loop).

Related Legal Periodicals

Acret, James, *Violation of Statute Is Negligence Per Se*, 1 Construction Law Digests 13.4 (2002).

Farrug. Eugene J., *The Necessity of Expert Testimony in Establishing the Standard of Care for Design Professionals*, 38 DPLLR 873 (1989).

Nischwitz, Jeffrey L. *The Crumbling Tower of Architectural Immunity: Evolution and Expansion of the Liability to Third Parties*, 45 Ohio St. L.J. 217 (1984).

Schoenhaus, Robert M., *Necessity of Expert Testimony to Show Malpractice of Architect*, 3 A.L.R. 4th 1023 (1981).

Williams, Peg A., *Causes of Action Against Architect or Engineer for Negligence in the Preparation of Plans and Specifications*, 5 Causes of Action 329 (2001).

Wright, Murray H., and David E. Boelzner, *Quantifying Liability under the Architect's Standard of Care*, 29 U. Rich. L. Rev. 1471 (1995).

Zupanec, Donald M., *Architect's Liability for Personal Injury or Death Allegedly Caused by Improper or Defective Plans or Design*, 97 A.L.R.3d 455 (1980).

TABLE 31.12 Sample Letter to State Legislator for Good Samaritan Law

The Honorable [*member's name*]
Member of the Assembly
[*address*]

Re: Engineers and Architects Good Samaritan Act [*Bill number (if applicable)*]

Dear [*Legislator's Name*],

I am writing on behalf of the [*name of organization*] to request a meeting with you or a member of your staff to discuss legislation providing Good Samaritan protection for engineers and architects who volunteer during times of emergency.

The [*organization*] has [*number*] members living in the [*location*] Metropolitan Area, [*number*] members statewide, and [*number*] nationwide. During the days, weeks and months following September 11, 2001, over 200 [*organization*] members worked around the clock at Ground Zero [*or other disaster site*]. The events of September 11, 2001 demonstrated the importance of having access to the [*engineering/architectural*] expertise of individual volunteer [*engineers/architects*] and the [*engineering/architectural*] community during a large-scale disaster.

Engineers and architects volunteering in response to emergencies deserve immunity from professional liability. Engineers or architects who are called upon to volunteer during an emergency risk physical injury when they lend a hand. However, by volunteering in an emergency, design professionals expose themselves to tremendous personal liability for any claims that may arise in connection with their voluntary services. As a result, engineers and architects who volunteer in response to emergencies risk their lives and their personal assets, home and financial security.

Good Samaritan laws protecting practicing professional engineers and architects have been enacted in California and many other states. The laws were passed because lawmakers recognized that: (1) government agencies rely on volunteer engineers and architects after emergencies like earthquakes and terrorist attacks; and (2) engineers and architects deserve liability protection while performing work under harrowing conditions.

We advocate Good Samaritan protection for volunteer engineers and architects under certain critical, but very limited circumstances. The passage of this bill will ensure that engineers and architects continue to provide voluntary services in the event of any future emergency. We strongly endorse [*legislation number*], and request that you support this legislation. We welcome the opportunity to discuss Good Samaritan legislation for architects and engineers. Please contact me at [*telephone number*] to arrange a meeting with you.

Very truly yours,
Design Professional's Name

Source: ASCE and Zetlin & De Chiara LLP.

Case Index

Cachick v. United States, 161 F.Supp. 15 (S.D. Illinois, 1958) (explaining that a design professional breaches the standard of care if he or she fails to identify risk and fails to take precautions to minimize risk).

Fransisco v. Manson, Jackson & Kane, Inc., 145 Mich.App. 255, 261, 377 N.W.2d 313, 317 (1985) (holding architect liable for negligence despite his compliance with building codes).

Micallef v. Miele, 39 N.Y.2d 376, 348 N.E.2d 571 (1976) (setting forth reasonable care analysis).

TABLE 31.13   **National Society of Professional Engineers (NSPE) Model Good Samaritan Act, as Part of a Professional Policy**

The National Society of Professional Engineers professional policy includes a Model Engineers' Good Samaritan Act, as follows:

A professional engineer who voluntarily provides engineering services in response to a natural disaster or other catastrophic event will not be liable for any personal injury, wrongful death, property damage, or other loss caused by a professional engineer's acts, errors or omissions in the performance of such services. Immunity from liability would not be applied in cases of wanton, willful, or intentional misconduct. The immunity applies to services that are provided during the emergency or within 90 days following the end of the period for an emergency, disaster, or catastrophic event, unless extended by an executive order issued by the Governor under the Governor's emergency executive powers.

Source: NSPE and Zetlin & De Chiara LLP.

TABLE 31.14   **9/11 Lessons Learned: Terrorism Insurance Coverage**

The events of 9/11 caused insurance companies to exclude coverage for terrorism acts, rendering such coverage unobtainable or prohibitively expensive. To remedy this situation, the insurance industry and construction trade groups pushed for federal legislation to provide financial assistance from the federal government in the event of another terrorist attack. The bill's proponents hoped it would spur development and create new construction jobs.

On November 26, 2002, the Terrorism Risk Insurance Act, or H.R. 3210 (the "Act") was signed into law. The Act provides coverage for catastrophic losses from terrorist attacks. The Act provides that the federal government would create a one-year program (with a two-year extension) whereby the government would provide up to $100 billion in loans to the insurance industry to cover losses from future terrorist attacks. The loans would cover 90 percent of claims above $1 billion in industry losses. Under the Act, the federal liability would be capped at $90 billion in the first year, $87.5 billion in the second year and $85 billion in the third year.

Source: Zetlin & De Chiara LLP.

INTERNET RESOURCES

American Bar Association (ABA)
www.abanet.org

American Bar Association (ABA)
 Construction Industry Forum
http://www.abanet.org/forums/construction/
 home.html

American Institute of Architects (AIA)
www.aia.org

American Society of Civil Engineers (ASCE)
www.asce.org

Architectural Record
www.architecturalrecord.com

The Association of the Bar of the City
 of New York
www.abcny.org

The Construction Lawyer
American Bar Association (ABA) Forum
Committee on the Construction Industry
www.abanet.org/abapubs/periodicals/const-
law2.html

Council on Tall Buildings and Urban Habitat
(CTBUH)
www.ctbuh.org

Engineering News Record
www.enr.com

Federal Emergency Management Agency
(FEMA)
www.fema.gov

National Institute of Science and
  Technology (NIST)
World Trade Center Investigative Team
www.wtc@nist.gov

National Society of Professional Engineers
www.nspe.org

New York City Department of Buildings
  (NYC DOB)
http://home.nyc.gov/html/dob/home.html

New York Construction News
www.newyork.construction.com

The New York Law Journal
www.law.com/ny

Skyscraper Safety Campaign
www.skyscrapersafety.com

U.S. Department of Homeland Security
  (US DHS)
www.dhs.gov

Zetlin & De Chiara LLP
www.zdlaw.com

INDEX

Dated Events

1972 events, Munich Olympics, **1.**13
1983 events, American embassy (Beirut) attack, **22.**3
1992 events, Hurricane Andrew, **1.**36, **12.**11–**12.**12, **19.**2, **29.**13
1993 events, WTC (World Trade Center) bombing, **1.**9–**1.**10, **4.**3–**4.**4, **22.**3
1995 events. *See also* Benchmark event lessons
   Alfred P. Murrah Federal Building bombing, **1.**7–**1.**11, **1.**15, **1.**22–**1.**23, **1.**30, **1.**37, **2.**14–**2.**15, **4.**3–**4.**4, **7.**1–**7.**3, **22.**3, **22.**7–**22.**8, **22.**15, **22.**19, **29.**1–**29.**4, **30.**4
   Tokyo subway sarin gas attack, **1.**31–**1.**32
1996 events, Khobar Towers bombing, **1.**9–**1.**10
1997 events. *See also* Benchmark event lessons
   Columbine High School shootings, **1.**27, **20.**1–**20.**2
   Great Plains floods, **1.**21, **12.**8
2000 events, California and New Mexico wildfires, **1.**21, **12.**16–**12.**17
2001 events. *See also* Benchmark event lessons
   anthrax letters and contaminations, **1.**32, **21.**2, **24.**13
   September 11 terrorist events, **1.**3–**1.**40, **4.**4–**4.**7, **4.**13, **8.**2–**8.**5, **8.**8–**8.**11, **8.**19–**8.**26, **9.**6–**9.**8, **11.**1–**11.**5, **12.**26, **13.**5, **14.**1–**14.**2, **18.**11–**18.**12, **19.**1–**19.**3, **21.**2, **23.**1, **23.**7, **24.**2, **27.**3, **28.**3–**28.**4, **29.**1–**29.**2, **30.**3–**30.**4, **30.**12, **31.**1–**31.**14

A

AAMA (American Architectural Manufacturing Association), **29.**14
Abatement, **30.**6–**30.**7
Abnormal loads, **22.**5–**22.**6
Abruzzo, John, **1.**29, **22.**3–**22.**21
Academic institutions, **3.**13, **18.**1–**18.**16, **20.**1–**20.**16. *See also under individual topics*
   research facilities, **18.**1–**18.**16
   responsibility determinations for, **3.**13
   schools, **20.**1–**20.**16
Acceptance, **30.**6–**30.**7

Access-related issues. *See also under individual topics*
   access points, **2.**29
   biometrics, **27.**7–**27.**9
   booths, **7.**19–**7.**20
   cards and card readers, **27.**6–**27.**7
   CB (chemical and biological) protection designs and, **24.**14–**24.**15
   for clinics, **21.**3
   combination locks, **27.**6
   for courtrooms, **6.**23
   electronic systems, **7.**22
   for employees, **7.**7
   for entrances, **19.**8–**19.**10
   entry controls. *See* Entry controls
   historic preservation guidance, **9.**26–**9.**30
   keypads, **27.**6
   for mechanical and electrical rooms, **18.**10–**18.**11
   for religious institutions and community centers, **17.**5–**17.**6
   service access controls, **19.**8–**19.**10
   technology and, **27.**6–**27.**9
   tiered systems, **18.**4
   for visitors, **7.**7
   for women's health centers, **21.**3
Activated carbon, **24.**24
Active systems, **24.**24
Acute care hospitals, **8.**1–**8.**3
ADA (Americans with Disabilities Act), **6.**14–**6.**15, **30.**8
Adams, Ansel, **1.**39
Adams, Walter, **1.**37, **30.**3–**30.**14
Adjacent opening seals, **8.**15
ADL (Anti-Defamation League), **1.**25, **17.**1–**17.**18
Administration and record keeping issues, **12.**25
Administrative areas, **20.**13
Adsorption, **24.**24
AHJ (authorities having jurisdiction), **8.**30
AHUs (air-handling units), **8.**16–**8.**17, **24.**11
   for health care facilities, **8.**16–**8.**17
   for safe rooms, **24.**11
AIA (American Institute of Architects), **12.**19
Airborne contaminants, **18.**11

Air filtration. *See* Filters and filtration
Airflow management, **24.**9–**24.**10
Air intake and air well securing techniques, **24.**14
Alarms and alarm systems, **7.**24–**7.**25, **15.**3, **17.**7–**17.**8
Alderson, Caroline R., **1.**17, **9.**1–**9.**36
Alfonse M. D'Amato U.S. courthouse and Federal Building (Islip, NY), **14.**18–**14.**21
Alfred P. Murrah Federal Building bombing, 1995, **1.**7–**1.**11, **1.**15, **1.**22–**1.**23, **1.**30, **1.**37, **4.**3–**4.**4, **7.**1–**7.**3, **22.**3, **22.**7–**22.**8, **22.**15, **22.**19, **30.**4
AMEC Construction Management, **1.**33, **26.**1–**26.**16
American Chemistry Council, **30.**9
American embassy (Beirut) attack, 1983, **22.**3
American Heritage Dictionary of the English Language, **19.**1
American Red Cross, **12.**6–**12.**7
Ammonium nitrate and fuel oil, **2.**22
Analyses, **4.**9–**4.**12. *See also* Risk and vulnerability assessments; Threat assessments
Ancillary public areas, **8.**27
Anderson, Gerald, **1.**13, **4.**3–**4.**17
Andrew (hurricane), 1992, **1.**36, **12.**11–**12.**12, **19.**2, **29.**13
Annealing processes, **29.**16
ANSI (American National Standards Institute), **30.**8
Anthrax letters and contaminations, **1.**32, **21.**2, **24.**13
Applicability issues, **24.**22–**24.**23
Arenas, sports facilities, convention centers, and performing arts facilities, **4.**3–**4.**18
  ATF (Bureau of Alcohol, Tobacco, and Firearms) and, **4.**5
  benchmark event lessons for, **1.**13–**1.**14, **4.**3–**4.**6, **4.**13
  event security planning for, **4.**13
  facility types, **4.**12
  FBI (Federal Bureau of Investigation) and, **4.**5
  IAAM (International Association of Assembly Managers) protocols for, **4.**7
  insurance issue design responses for, **4.**5–**4.**7
    architectural planning, **4.**5–**4.**7
    life safety codes, **4.**7
    mechanical engineering systems, **4.**7
    overviews and summaries of, **4.**5
    site planning, **4.**5–**4.**7
    technology, **4.**7
  NSSEs (National Security Special Events), **4.**13–**4.**16
    crowd management for, **4.**14–**4.**15
    design checklists for, **4.**15
    final security details for, **4.**16
    overviews and summaries of, **4.**13–**4.**14
    screenings for, **4.**14
    security levels for, **4.**13, **4.**15
  overviews and summaries of, **4.**3–**4.**5, **4.**16
  reference resources (print and internet) for, **4.**16–**4.**17

Arenas, sports facilities, convention centers, and performing arts facilities (*Cont.*):
  risk and vulnerability assessments for, **4.**9–**4.**12
    design and construction emergencies and, **4.**10–**4.**11
    emergency estimate probabilities and, **4.**11
    facility design criteria and, **4.**11–**4.**12
    FEMA (Federal Emergency Management Agency) and, **4.**10–**4.**11
    geographic impacts and, **4.**10
    Guide for Business and Industry and, **4.**10–**4.**11
    human errors and, **4.**10
    internal *vs.* external resources and, **4.**11
    overviews and summaries of, **4.**9
    potential business impacts and, **4.**11
    potential emergencies and, **4.**10
    potential human impacts and, **4.**11
    potential property impacts and, **4.**11
    shelter area proximities and, **4.**11
    technological impacts and, **4.**10
    vulnerability analyses charts, **4.**10–**4.**11
  threat level assessments for, **4.**8–**4.**9
    level 1 (low degree of risk), **4.**9
    level 2 (guarded degree of risk), **4.**9
    level 3 (elevated degree of risk), **4.**8–**4.**9
    level 4 (high degree of risk), **4.**8
    overviews and summaries of, **4.**8
  USSS (U.S. Secret Service) and, **4.**5
Arm drop barrier systems, **7.**17–**7.**18
  fixed, **7.**17–**7.**18
  portable, **7.**17
Armed intruder checklists, **21.**13
Army Corps of Engineers, **7.**3–**7.**4, **24.**6–**24.**7
Arraignment areas, **6.**23
Art Commission, City of New York, **1.**23, **16.**1–**16.**2, **16.**8–**16.**9
ASCE (American Society of Civil Engineers), **2.**22–**2.**23, **29.**14–**29.**16
ASF (antishatter film), **2.**25, **29.**4–**29.**5
ASHRAE (American Society of Heating Refrigeration and Air Conditioning Engineers), **1.**26–**1.**27, **18.**11–**18.**14, **24.**5–**24.**6, **26.**16–**26.**19
  filters, **24.**5–**24.**6, **24.**16–**24.**19
  guidelines and standards of, **1.**26–**1.**27, **18.**11–**18.**14
  overviews and summaries of, **1.**26–**1.**27
ASIS (American Society for Industrial Security), **30.**8
Assessments, **2.**5–**2.**8, **4.**9–**4.**12, **12.**20–**12.**27. *See also* Risk and vulnerability assessments; Threat assessments
  damage, **12.**20–**12.**22
  insurance coverage, **12.**26–**12.**27
  overviews and summaries of, **4.**9–**4.**12
  security, **2.**5–**2.**8
ASTM International, **29.**9–**29.**13
ASZM-TEDA coatings, **24.**6, **24.**18–**24.**19, **24.**24

ATF (Bureau of Alcohol, Tobacco, and Firearms), **4.**5

Attorney/defendant interview rooms, **6.**18

Audio detectors, **15.**4

Audits, **3.**9–**3.**10

Authors. *See also under individual names*

of chapters

Abruzzo, John, **22.**3–**22.**21

Adams, Walter, **30.**3–**30.**14

ADL (Anti-Defamation League), **17.**1–**17.**18

Alderson, Caroline R., **9.**1–**9.**36

Anderson, Gerald, **4.**3–**4.**17

Bershad, Deborah, **16.**1–**16.**9

Blewett, William K., **24.**1–**24.**25

Blurock, Thomas, **20.**1–**20.**15

Bush, F. John W., **29.**1–**29.**18

Calabrese, Joseph, **18.**1–**18.**15

Campbell, David R., **6.**1–**6.**24

Galioto, Carl, **5.**1–**5.**10

Gaughan, Regis, **18.**1–**18.**15

Gunning, Jeffrey J., **19.**1–**19.**14

Harris, James W., **11.**1–**11.**6

Heider, Elizabeth J., **25.**3–**25.**10

Hlushko, Andrew, **23.**1–**23.**16

Jandura, Kenneth J., **6.**1–**6.**24

Janus, Michael C., **24.**1–**24.**25

Jones, Casey L., **14.**1–**14.**34

Josal, Lance K., **19.**1–**19.**14

Jung, Thomas M., **8.**1–**8.**32

Kaliniak, Catherine, **29.**1–**29.**18

Kelly, Terri, **3.**1–**3.**15

Leach, Terri, **7.**1–**7.**29

Lilien, Noelle, **31.**1–**31.**14

McCarthy, Bill, **2.**1–**2.**30

Mintzer, Lewis J., **26.**1–**26.**16

Nadel, Barbara A., **1.**3–**1.**40, **12.**1–**12.**32, **13.**1–**13.**10, **21.**1–**21.**15

Park, Sharon C., **9.**1–**9.**36

Phifer, Jean Parker, **16.**1–**16.**9

Rosenblatt, Arthur, **15.**1–**15.**6

Schultz, Bradley D., **10.**1–**10.**8

Sewell, Bill, **27.**3–**27.**19

Sheridan, Francis J., **28.**1–**28.**18

Simons, Russ, **4.**3–**4.**17

Somers, Deborah A., **30.**3–**30.**14

Stark, Stanley, **18.**1–**18.**15

Steinberg, Sue, **29.**1–**29.**18

Thompson, David, **2.**1–**2.**30

Tomasetti, Richard L., **22.**3–**22.**21

Zetlin, Michael, **31.**1–**31.**14

of quotations

Adams, Ansel, **1.**39

Brake, Pete, **7.**1

Breyer, Stephen, **14.**1

Burke, Edmund, **8.**1, **8.**28

Burnham, Daniel, **21.**1

Buscaglia, Leo, **12.**1

Calhoun, Jr., John C., **1.**29

Authors, of quotations (*Cont.*):

Churchill, Winston, **1.**3

Coolidge, Calvin, **29.**1

De Becker, Gavin, **6.**1, **13.**1

De Saint-Exupery, Antoine, **1.**33

Douglas, William O., **28.**1

Duncan, Donnie, **4.**3

editors, *American Heritage Dictionary of the English Language*, **19.**1

Einstein, Albert, **18.**14

Feiner, Edward A., **1.**6

Feynman, Richard, **8.**28

Ford, Henry, **23.**1

Gandhi, Mahatma, **20.**1

Gwathmey, Charles, **9.**1

Harper, Charles, **12.**12

Hickman, Tim, **4.**3

Hillel, **17.**1

Hoover, Herbert, **1.**32

Hugo, Victor, **12.**16

Jacobs, Jane, **3.**1

Jefferson, Thomas, **1.**33

Judd, H. Stanley, **29.**15

Kennedy, John F., **1.**6, **23.**1, **31.**1

Locke, John, **16.**7

McCormick, John, **12.**7

Moynihan, Daniel Patrick, **1.**5–**1.**6, **5.**1, **19.**1

Mumford, Lewis, **1.**12

Ozenfant, Amedee, **16.**1

Penzias, Arno, **27.**3

PPGG (Planned Parenthood Golden Gate), **21.**1

Roosevelt, Eleanor, **21.**1

Roosevelt, Franklin D., **1.**3, **24.**1

Roosevelt, Theodore, **1.**37, **11.**1

Santayana, George, **1.**3

Shakespeare, William, **6.**1

Strife, Eric, **10.**1

Swift, Jonathan, **30.**3

Tetreau, Jean, **8.**28

Warner, Charles Dudley, **25.**3

Weisberg, Sarelle T., **1.**8

Wells, H. G., **22.**3

Wilde, Oscar, **24.**1

Wilkinson, Paul, **4.**5

Williams, Scott, **4.**4

Woodcock, Douglas P., **6.**1

Avoidance, **30.**6–**30.**7

Axial tension, **22.**20

B

Background checks, **1.**18, **10.**4

Back-up systems and redundancy, **18.**13

BAER (banned area emergency rehabilitation) teams, **12.**16

Balanced magnetic contact switches, **15.**4

Ballasts, **7.**10

Ballistic resistance, **6.**21, **29.**3, **29.**10–**29.**14
  ballistic-resistant millwork, **6.**21
  large *vs.* small missile impacts, **29.**14
  overviews and summaries of, **29.**3, **29.**10–**29.**12,
    29.14
Banking Act, **30.**6
Barriers, **6.**4, **7.**16–**7.**18, **9.**11–**9.**15, **19.**13, **20.**4–**20.**5
  arm drop systems, **7.**17–**7.**18
  concealed drum, **6.**4
  fences and fencing. *See* Fences and fencing
  historic preservation guidance for, **9.**11–**9.**15
  for schools, **20.**4–**20.**5
  vehicle, **7.**16–**7.**17, **19.**13
Battelle Eastern Science and Technology Center, **1.**31
Battelle Memorial Institute, **24.**23–**24.**24
BCCs (building control centers), **18.**5–**18.**6
Beams, **15.**5, **22.**13–**22.**14
  photoelectric, **15.**5
  structural, **22.**13–**22.**14
    beam-to-beam connections, **22.**13–**22.**14
    beam-to-column connections, **22.**13–**22.**14
Beirut embassy attack, 2003, **22.**3
Benches, judge, **6.**20–**6.**22
Benchmark event lessons, **1.**3–**1.**40, **26.**1–**26.**16. *See
    also under individual topics*
  building security theory and practice and, **1.**8
  construction-related considerations and, **1.**32–**1.**33
  cost estimations and, **1.**32–**1.**33
  CPTED (crime prevention through environmental
    design) and, **1.**12, **1.**27
  for disaster planning, response, and recovery,
    1.7–**1.**8, **1.**19–**1.**20, **12.**7–**12.**8, **12.**11–**12.**12,
    12.16–**12.**17, **12.**26
  for egress systems, **5.**1, **5.**4, **5.**6–**5.**8
  emergency responses and, **26.**1–**26.**16
  engineering-related considerations of, **1.**29–**1.**30,
    1.29–**1.**32
  events. *See also under individual events*
    1972, Munich Olympics, **1.**13
    1983, American embassy (Beirut) attack, **22.**3
    1992, Hurricane Andrew, **1.**36, **12.**11–**12.**12,
      19.2, **29.**13
    1993, WTC (World Trade Center) bombing,
      1.9–**1.**10, **4.**3–**4.**4, **22.**3
    1995, Alfred P. Murrah Federal Building bomb-
      ing, **1.**7–**1.**11, **1.**15, **1.**22–**1.**23, **1.**30, **1.**37,
      4.3–**4.**4, **7.**1–**7.**3, **9.**4, **9.**26, **14.**2, **22.**3,
      22.7–**22.**8, **22.**15, **22.**19, **29.**1–**29.**4, **30.**4
    1995, Tokyo subway sarin gas attack, **1.**31–**1.**32
    1996, Khobar Towers bombing, **1.**9–**1.**10
    1997, Columbine High School shootings, **1.**27,
      20.1–**20.**2
    1997, Great Plains floods, **1.**21, **12.**8
    2000, California and New Mexico wildfires,
      1.21, **12.**16–**12.**17
    2001, anthrax letters and contamination, **1.**32,
      21.2, **24.**13

Benchmark event lessons, events, (*Cont.*):
    2001 (September 11), Pentagon building terrorist
      event, **1.**4, **1.**17–**1.**18, **1.**30, **1.**34–**1.**35, **8.**2,
      9.1, **22.**12, **26.**1–**26.**4
    2001 (September 11), terrorist events, **1.**3–**1.**40,
      4.4–**4.**7, **4.**13, **11.**1–**11.**5, **12.**26, **13.**5,
      18.11–**18.**12, **19.**1–**19.**3, **21.**2, **23.**1, **23.**7,
      24.2, **27.**3, **28.**3–**28.**4, **30.**3–**30.**4, **30.**12,
      31.1–**31.**14
    2001 (September 11), WTC (World Trade
      Center) towers terrorist event, **1.**3–**1.**40,
      5.1, **5.**4, **5.**6–**5.**7, **10.**4, **11.**2, **13.**7, **18.**1,
      18.11, **22.**3, **22.**12, **23.**3, **23.**11, **24.**2, **24.**21,
      26.1–**26.**16, **30.**12–**30.**13
    2003, blackout, **12.**7
    terrorist events, listings of, **1.**9
    workplace shootings, **13.**8
  for facility types. *See also under individual facilities*
    arenas, sports facilities, convention centers, and
      performing arts facilities, **1.**13–**1.**14,
      4.3–**4.**6, **4.**13
    commercial high-rises, **1.**14–**1.**15, **5.**1, **5.**4,
      5.6–**5.**8
    correction facilities, **1.**35–**1.**36
    courthouses, **1.**15
    federally owned/leased buildings, **1.**15
    health care facilities, **1.**15–**1.**16, **8.**2–**8.**11,
      8.19–**8.**26
    hospitality facilities, **1.**18–**1.**19, **10.**1–**10.**2, **10.**4
    industrial facilities and office buildings, **1.**21,
      13.5, **13.**7
    multifamily housing, **1.**19, **11.**1
    museums and cultural facilities, **1.**23
    religious institutions and cultural centers,
      1.25–**1.**26
    research facilities, **1.**26–**1.**27, **18.**1, **18.**11–**18.**14
    retail facilities and destinations, **1.**27,
      19.1.–**19.**3
    women's health centers, **1.**27–**1.**28
  for glazing and security glass applications,
    1.36–**1.**37, **29.**1–**29.**4, **29.**13–**29.**15
  guidelines, standards, and codes and, **1.**37–**1.**38,
    30.3–**30.**4, **30.**12–**30.**13
  historic preservation guidance and, **1.**17–**1.**18,
    9.1–**9.**2, **9.**4, **9.**6, **9.**8, **9.**26, **9.**31
  liability exposures and, **31.**1–**31.**14
  for lobbies, **1.**22–**1.**23, **14.**1–**14.**2
  master planning and, **1.**11–**1.**12, **2.**1–**2.**2
  overviews and summaries of, **1.**3–**1.**40
  for perimeters, **1.**23, **16.**2
  for product selection and specification, **28.**3–**28.**4
  for protection designs. *See also under individual
      designs*
    CB (chemical and biological), **1.**31–**1.**32, **24.**2,
      24.13, **24.**21
    mechanical, electrical, and fire, **1.**30–**1.**31, **23.**1,
      23.3, **23.**7, **23.**15

Benchmark event lessons, for protection designs, (*Cont.*):
    structural, **1.30–1.31, 22.3–22.4, 22.7–22.8, 22.12, 22.15,** 22.19**–22.20**
    reference resources (print and internet) for, **1.39–1.40**
    for security technology, **1.33–1.37, 27.3, 27.10**
    security *vs.* free society balances and, **1.5–1.7**
    transparent security and, **1.8–1.12**
Berm and blast wall construction, **2.19, 9.33**
Bershad, Deborah, **1.23, 16.1–16.9**
Best practices, schools, **20.4–20.5**
BICs (building information cards), **23.7–23.9**
Big box retailers, **19.13**
Biohazard threat checklists, **21.10**
Biological protection designs, **24.1–24.26.** *See also* CB (chemical and biological) protection designs
Biometrics, **6.9, 18.9–18.10, 27.7–27.9**
    facial recognition, **27.8**
    fingerprint recognition, **27.8–27.9**
    hand geometry, **27.8**
    iris scans, **27.9**
    overviews and summaries of, **27.7–27.8**
    readers, **6.9, 18.9–18.10**
Bite, **22.20**
Blackouts, **1.17, 1.20, 8.22–8.23**
BLASTOP (computer program), **7.15**
Blast-related issues, **2.19, 2.21–2.29, 7.13–7.15, 9.21–9.23, 17.13–17.15, 22.10–22.11, 29.3–29.8**
    blast analyses, **2.29**
    blast designs, **2.21–2.23, 22.10–22.11**
        blast hazard injuries and, **2.22**
        blast loads and, **22.10–22.11**
        criteria for, **2.22**
        master planning for, **2.21–2.23**
        overviews and summaries of, **2.21–2.22**
        progressive collapse and, **2.22–2.23**
        structural framing systems and, **2.23**
    blast mitigation, **2.19, 2.25, 9.21–9.23, 29.3–29.8**
        ASF (antishatter film), **29.4–29.5**
        blast curtains, **2.25, 9.21–9.23**
        blast doors, **29.8**
        blast shades, **9.21–9.23**
        blast windows, **29.3–29.7**
        cable catch window systems, **29.2, 29.6–29.7**
        overviews and summaries of, **29.3–29.4**
        soft wall testing, **29.6**
        wall construction, **2.19**
    car and truck bombs, **17.13**
    for courthouses, **6.11**
    protection criteria, **7.13**
    suicide bombers, **17.13–17.15**
Blewett, William K., **1.31, 24.1–24.25**
Bloomberg, Michael R., **13.5**
Blue Heron Nature Park, **16.5**
Blurock, Thomas, **1.27, 20.1–20.15**

BMBL (Biosafety in Microbiological and Biomedical Laboratories), **18.2**
BOCA (Building Officials Code Administration), **30.8**
Bollards, **6.4, 9.33**
Bomb threat checklists, **21.10–21.11**
Booths, **7.19–7.20**
Bradley, Laura, **16.**6
Brake, Pete, **7.**1
Breaches, **27.9–27.10**
    detection and assessment of, **27.9–27.10**
    overviews and summaries of, **27.9**
Breyer, Stephen, **14.1**
Briefing areas, **8.27**
Brisance, **1.30, 22.15, 22.20**
Brown, Terrance J., **1.20**
Budgeting, **25.3–25.4.** *See also* Cost estimations
Building entry controls, **7.18–7.20.** *See also* Entry controls
Building envelopes, **18.6–18.7, 24.14**
Building management systems, **18.13–18.14**
Building security. *See also under individual topics*
    code and liability aspects of, **30.1–31.14**
        guidelines, standards, and codes, **30.3–30.14**
        liability exposures, **31.1–31.14**
    construction aspects of, **26.1–26.16**
        cost estimations, **25.3–25.10**
        emergency response lessons, **26.1–26.16**
    engineering aspects of, **22.1–24.26**
        CB (chemical and biological) protection designs, **24.1–24.26**
        mechanical, electrical, and fire protection designs, **23.1–23.16**
        structural protection designs, **22.3–22.22**
    planning and design aspects of, **4.1–21.16**
        for arenas, sports facilities, convention centers, and performing arts facilities, **4.3–4.18**
        for commercial high-rise egress systems, **5.1–5.10**
        for courthouses, **6.1–6.24**
        disaster planning, response, and recovery, **12.1.–12.32**
        for federally owned/leased buildings, **7.1–7.30**
        for health care facilities, **8.1–8.32**
        historic preservation guidance, **9.1–9.36**
        for hospitality facilities, **10.1–10.8**
        for industrial facilities and office buildings, **13.1–13.10**
        for lobbies, **14.1–14.34**
        for multifamily housing, **11.1–11.6**
        for museums and cultural facilities, **15.1–15.6**
        for perimeters, **16.1–16.10**
        for religious institutions and community centers, **17.1–17.18**
        for research facilities, **18.1–18.16**
        for retail facilities and destinations, **19.1–19.14**
        for schools, **20.1–20.16**
        for women's health centers, **21.1–21.16**

Building security (*Cont.*):
　　technology and materials aspects of, **27.1–29.18**
　　　glazing and security glass applications, **29.1–29.18**
　　　product selection and specification, **28.1–28.18**
　　　security technology, **27.3–27.20**
　　transparent security aspects of, **1.1–3.16**
　　　benchmark event lessons, **1.3–1.40**
　　　CPTED (crime prevention through environmental
　　　　design), **3.1–3.16**
　　　master planning, **2.1–2.30**
Built-up sections, **22.14**
Bullet-resistant glass, **29.16**
Burglary deterrence and resistance, **12.2–12.3**, **29.3**,
　　29.8–29.9
Burke, Edmund, **8.1**, **8.28**
Burnham, Daniel, **21.1**
Buscaglia, Leo, **12.1**
Bus drop-off/pick-up zones, **20.7–20.8**
Bush, F. John W., **1.36**, **29.1–29.18**
Bush, George W., **18.1**
Business communities, responsibilities, **3.13**
Business disaster planning, response, and recovery,
　　12.1.–12.32. *See also* Disaster planning,
　　response, and recovery
Business impacts, potential, **4.11**
Butyric acid attack checklists, **21.10**
Byron G. Rogers Federal Building (Denver, CO),
　　14.14, **14.17–14.19**

C

Cable catch window systems, **29.2**, **29.6–29.7**
Calabrese, Joseph, **1.26**, **18.1–18.15**
CALAs (controlled access laboratory areas), **18.8–18.9**
Calhoun, Jr., John C., **1.29**
California and New Mexico wildfires, 2000, **1.21**,
　　12.16–12.17
Campbell, David R., **1.15**, **6.1–6.24**
Canizaro Cawthon Davis, **14**.17
Cannon Design, **14**.21
Capital improvement programs, **3.11–3.12**
Car and truck bombs, **17.13**
Cards and card readers, **6.9**, **18.9–18.10**, **23.7–23.9**,
　　27.6–27.7
　　BICs (building information cards), **23.7–23.9**
　　readers and, **6.9**, **18.9–18.10**, **27.6–27.7**
Cargo freight scanners, **27.10–27.12**
Case index, liability exposures, **31.12–31.13**
Case studies, **16.2–16.8**, **24.17–24.20**
　　of CB (chemical and biological) protection
　　　designs, **24.17–24.20**
　　of fences and fencing, **16.3–16.4**, **16.7–16.8**
　　of gates, **16.5–16.8**
　　of liability exposures, **31.5**
　　of lobbies, **14.10–14.30**
　　of perimeters, **16.2–16.8**
Casinos. *See* Gaming properties
Casuto, Morris, **1.25**

Catch systems, **22.17–22.18**, **29.2**, **29.6–29.7**
CB (chemical and biological) protection designs,
　　24.1–24.26
　　airflow management and, **24.9–24.10**
　　applicability issues for, **24.22–24.23**
　　architectural design measures for, **24.13–24.15**
　　　access controls and, **24.14–24.15**
　　　air intake and air well securing techniques, **24.14**
　　　building envelope tightening, **24.14**
　　　entrance screening and, **24.14–24.15**
　　　health care facilities and, **8.14**
　　　high-threat area isolation, **24.14**
　　　overviews and summaries of, **24.13–24.15**
　　　penetrations and, **24.14**
　　　secured mechanical rooms, **24.15**
　　　vestibules, **24.15**
　　benchmark event lessons for, **1.31–1.32**
　　building system effects of, **24.13–24.14**
　　case studies of, **24.17–24.20**
　　collective protection and air filtration, **24.4–24.7**,
　　　24.18
　　　aerosol filters, **24.5**
　　　chemical agent filters, **24.4–24.5**
　　　external (makeup air) filtration, **24.6**
　　　filter integrations, **24.5–24.6**
　　　HEPA (high-efficiency particulate air) filters,
　　　　24.4–24.6, **24.11**
　　　internal (recirculated air) filtration, **24.6–24.7**,
　　　　24.11
　　　overviews and summaries of, **24.4**
　　　systems for, **24.18**
　　　UVGI (ultraviolet germicidal irradiation)
　　　　systems, **24.5**
　　control systems, **24.20–24.21**
　　decontamination, **24.11–24.13**, **24.21**
　　　overviews and summaries of, **24.11–24.12**
　　　processes of, **24.13**
　　　space planning for, **24.12–24.13**
　　　systems for, **24.21**
　　Defense Threat Reduction Agency and,
　　　24.17–24.18
　　detection systems, **24.7–24.9**, **24.19–24.20**
　　　for biological agents, **24.8–24.9**
　　　flame photometry and, **24.8**
　　　GC (gas chromatography) and, **24.8**
　　　IMS (ion mobility spectrometry) and, **24.8**
　　　long-range monitoring systems, **24.9**
　　　MS (mass spectrometry) and, **24.8**
　　　overviews and summaries of, **24.7**
　　　point detectors, **24.8–24.9**
　　　SAWs (surface acoustic waves) and, **24.8**
　　disaster planning, response, and recovery and,
　　　12.5–12.6
　　historical perspectives of, **24.2–24.3**
　　mechanical and electrical engineering systems for,
　　　24.15–24.16
　　　enhanced sheltering-in-place capabilities, **24.15**

CB (chemical and biological) protection designs, mechanical and electrical engineering systems for (*Cont.*):
 high-efficiency particulate (HEPA) filters and, **24.15–24.16**
 overviews and summaries of, **24.15**
 operations and maintenance for, **24.16–24.17**
 overviews and summaries of, **24.1–24.3**, **24.23**
 protection system components, **24.3–24.4**
 reference resources (print and internet) for, **24.25**
 safe rooms, **24.10–24.11**
  AHUs (air-handling units) for, **24.11**
  internal filtration for, **24.11**
  overviews and summaries of, **24.10**
  rapid exhaust facilitation for, **24.11**
  rapid sheltering facilitation for, **24.11**
  sealing of, **24.10–24.11**
 Smart Building Program and, **24.17–24.22**
 Social Hall Plaza (Salt Lake City, UT), **24.17–24.18**
 strategies for, **24.22**
 system performance and, **24.21–24.22**
 terminology for, **24.24**
 threat assessments for, **24.2–24.3**
CCTV (closed-circuit television), **2.18–2.19**, **7.25–7.27**, **18.8–18.10**
CDC (Centers for Disease Control and Prevention), **18.2**
Cells, holding, **6.17–6.19**
Central control rooms, **6.17–6.18**
CFR (Code of Federal Regulations), **7.3**, **18.2**, **30.7–30.9**
Checklists. *See also under individual topics*
 for community security measures, **11.5**
 for contractors and employees, **11.3**
 for floods and tsunamis, **12.9–12.10**
 for hardened elements, **18.7**
 for home security, **12.3**
 for hurricanes, **12.12**
 for internal reporting, **11.2**
 for law enforcement cooperation, **11.3–11.4**
 for master planning, **2.7**
 for mechanical, electrical, and fire protection designs, **23.2**
 for media fact sheets, **12.28**
 for multifamily housing, **11.2–11.5**
 for NSSEs (National Security Special Events), **4.15**
 for operational management, **11.2**
 for operations security, **2.11**
 for perimeter security, **2.10**
 for policies and procedures, **19.12**
 for power outages, **12.5–12.7**
 for procedures, **21.8**
 for research facilities, **18.7**
 for residents, **11.2–11.3**
  application verification, **11.3**
  communications, **11.2**

Checklists (*Cont.*):
 for retail facilities and destinations, **19.12**
 for risk and vulnerability assessments, **23.2**
 for schools, **20.2**, **20.6**, **20.8**, **20.9**, **20.11**
  grounds and buildings, **20.9**
  policies, **20.2**
  programming, planning, and design issues, **20.11**
  site planning, **20.6**
  vehicular circulation and traffic elements, **20.8**
 for security assessment elements, **2.7**
 for security surveys, **2.10**
 for security technology, **27.19**
 for site planning, **2.10**, **7.5**
 for tornadoes and high winds, **12.14–12.15**
 for unit inspections, **11.3**
 for women's health centers, **21.7–21.13**
  biohazard threats, **21.10**
  bomb threats, **21.10–21.11**
  butyric acid attacks, **21.10**
  e-mail threats, **21.12**
  fires, **21.12**
  hostile clients, **21.12**
  procedures, **21.8**
  protesters, **21.13**
  reference, **21.7**
  robberies and armed intruders, **21.13**
  stalking and following, **21.14**
  suspicious packages and mail, **21.14**
Chemical agent filters, **24.4–24.5**
Chlorine Institute, **30.9**
Chromatography, gas, **24.8**
Churchill, Winston, **1.3**
CIA (Central Intelligence Agency), **7.3**, **30.8**
Circuiting requirements, lighting, **7.12**
Circulation, traffic. *See* Vehicular circulation and traffic elements
Civil liberties issues, schools, **20.2–20.3**
Classrooms. *See also* Schools
 portable, **20.10**
 programming, planning, and design issues for, **20.14**
Clients, hostile, **21.12**
Clinical laboratories, **8.24**
Code and liability issues, **30.1–31.14**. *See also under individual topics*
 guidelines, standards, and codes, **30.3–30.14**
 liability exposures, **31.1–31.14**
Cogeneration power systems, **8.21–8.22**
Cold and hot zones, **8.15**
Collapse, progressive, **7.13–7.14**. *See also* Progressive collapse
Collective protection and air filtration, **24.4–24.18**. *See also* Filters and filtration
 aerosol filters, **24.5**
 CB (chemical and biological) protection designs for, **24.4–24.7**, **24.18**

Collective protection and air filtration (*Cont.*):
  chemical agent filters, **24.4–24.5**
  external (makeup air) filtration, **24.6**
  filter integrations, **24.5–24.6**
  HEPA (high-efficiency particulate air) filters,
    24.4–24.6, 24.11
  internal (recirculated air) filtration, **24.6–24.7,
    24.11**
  overviews and summaries of, **24.4**
  systems for, **24.18**
  UVGI (ultraviolet germicidal irradiation) systems,
    24.5
Columbine High School shootings, 1997, **1.27,
  20.1–20.2**
Columns, **22.12–22.14, 22.20**
  beam-to-column connections, **22.13–22.14**
  splices, **22.12–22.13, 22.20**
Combination locks, **27.6**
Commercial developers, responsibilities of, **3.13**
Commercial high-rise egress systems, **5.1–5.10**
  benchmark event lessons for, **1.14–1.15, 5.1, 5.4,
    5.6–5.8**
  evacuation statistics for, **5.8**
  high-rise towers, typical, **5.2–5.5**
    building services for, **5.2**
    enhanced egress stairs for, **5.5**
    floor plates for, **5.7**
    lighting issues of, **5.4**
    overviews and summaries of, **5.2–5.3**
    safe areas and life safety plans for, **5.2–5.4**
    tenant space planning for, **5.2**
  New York City Building Code and, **5.2–5.4**
  overviews and summaries of, **5.1–5.2, 5.6–5.9**
  redundancy for, **5.6**
  reference resources (print and internet) for,
    5.9–5.10
  stair preparations, **5.2**
  tenability of, **5.6**
  terminology for, **5.1**
  vertical transportation systems for, **5.6**
Common areas, schools, **20.13**
Communications-related issues, **7.27, 11.2, 12.29,
  28.14**
  communication centers, **28.14**
  communications systems, **7.27**
  crisis management and public relations, **12.29**
  overviews and summaries of, **11.2**
Community centers, **17.1–17.18.** *See also* Religious
    institutions and community centers
Community involvement, **3.5, 28.5–28.6**
Community security measures, **11.5**
Compartmentalization, **8.11**
Compatible technology, **1.16**
Concealed drum barriers, **6.4**
Concrete construction, **22.14–22.16**
  brisance, **22.15, 22.20**
  enhancements of, **22.15–22.16**
  limited ductility, **22.15**

Concrete construction (*Cont.*):
  overviews and summaries of, **22.14**
  shear failures, **22.14–22.15, 22.20**
Connections, structural, **22.13–22.14**
  beam-to-beam, **22.13–22.14**
  beam-to-column, **22.13–22.14**
Connectivity, wireless, **23.10**
Construction aspects, **25.1–26.16.** *See also under
    individual topics*
  cost estimations, **25.3–25.10**
  emergency response lessons, **4.10–4.11,
    26.1–26.16**
  master planning and, **2.23–2.26**
Contact sensors, **15.3–15.4**
Contact switches, magnetic, **15.3–15.4**
  balanced, **15.4**
  simple, **15.3**
Contaminants, airborne, **18.11**
Contamination protection, health care facilities,
  8.23–8.24
Control booths, **7.19–7.20**
Control rooms, **6.17–6.18**
CONUS *vs.* OCONUS terrorist groups, **22.6**
Convention centers, **4.3–4.18.** *See also* Arenas, sports
    facilities, convention centers, and performing
    arts facilities
Coolidge, Calvin, **29.1**
Corrections facilities, **1.35–1.36, 28.1–28.18**
Corridors, courthouses, **6.16–6.17**
Cost estimations, **25.3–25.10**
  benchmark event lessons for, **1.32–1.33**
  budgeting and, **25.3–25.4**
  elements of, **25.5–25.9**
  formulae for, **25.6**
  location factors and, **25.5**
  overviews and summaries of, **25.3–25.4,
    25.9–25.10**
  reference resources (internet) for, **25.10**
  for risk and vulnerability assessments,
    2.13–2.14
  for security designs, **25.5–25.9**
    building exteriors, **25.8–25.9**
    loading docks, **25.8**
    lobbies, **25.7.** *See also* Lobbies
    mail rooms, **25.8**
    mechanical, electrical, fire protection, and life
      safety systems, **25.9**
    overviews and summaries of, **25.5**
    progressive collapse, **25.8**
    roofs, **25.9**
    site perimeters, **25.6–25.7**
    standoff distances, **25.6–25.7**
    surveillance, **25.5**
    vehicular entries, **25.6–25.7**
    windows and glazing, **25.8–25.9**
  terminology for, **25.8**
  for threats, **25.4**
  zones of influence and, **25.10**

Courthouses, **6.**1–**6.**24
    benchmark event lessons for, **1.**15
    case studies of, **14.**10–**14.**30
        Alfonse M. D'Amato U.S. courthouse and Federal
            Building (Islip, NY), **14.**18, **14.**20–**14.**23
        John Joseph Moakley U.S. Courthouse (Boston,
            MA), **14.**11–**14.**14
        Lloyd D. George U.S. Courthouse (Las Vegas,
            NV), **14.**21, **14.**23–**14.**24
        Sam M. Gibbons U.S. Courthouse (Tampa, FL),
            14.28, **14.**31–**14.**32
        Thomas F. Eagleton U.S. Courthouse (St. Louis,
            MO), **14.**27–**14.**30
        U.S. Federal Courthouse (Covington, KY),
            14.14–**14.**16
        U.S. Federal Courthouse (Gulfport, MS), **14.**17,
            14.19–**14.**21
    courtrooms, **6.**18–**6.**23
        access to, **6.**23
        arraignments and, **6.**23
        ballistic-resistant millwork, **6.**21
        fire release doors, **6.**23
        furnishings for, **6.**22–**6.**23
        high security issues, **6.**21
        judge benches, **6.**20–**6.**22
        jury boxes, **6.**20–**6.**21
        jury deliberation rooms, **6.**23
        overviews and summaries of, **6.**18–**6.**19
        public seating, **6.**21
        sightlines, **6.**19–**6.**21
        technology for, **6.**22
    interiors, **6.**12–**6.**23
        ADA (American with Disabilities Act) and,
            6.14–**6.**15
        attorney/defendant interview rooms, **6.**18
        central control rooms, **6.**17–**6.**18
        corridors, **6.**16–**6.**17
        courtrooms, **6.**18–**6.**23
        floor blocking diagrams for, **6.**14
        holding cells, **6.**17–**6.**19
        interface zones, **6.**18
        overviews and summaries of, **6.**12
        private zones, **6.**16–**6.**17
        public zones and corridors, **6.**12–**6.**13
        screening stations, **6.**15–**6.**16
        secure zones, **6.**17
        stacking diagrams for, **6.**13
        surveillance systems, **6.**16
    overviews and summaries of, **6.**1–**6.**3, **6.**23–**6.**24
    perimeters and exteriors, **6.**7–**6.**12
        air intake vents, **6.**10
        biometric readers for, **6.**9
        blast-resistant designs, **6.**11
        card readers for, **6.**9
        loading docks, **6.**10
        overviews and summaries of, **6.**7–**6.**8
        sally ports, **6.**8–**6.**10
        trash receptacles, **6.**11–**6.**12

Courthouses, perimeters and exteriors (*Cont.*):
        windows and glazing, **6.**10–**6.**11
    planning committee roles, **6.**2
    reference resources (print and internet) for, **6.**24
    site planning, **6.**3–**6.**7
        for access, **6.**3–**6.**4
        bollards and, **6.**4
        for circulation, **6.**3–**6.**4
        concealed drum barriers and, **6.**4
        for duress, **6.**5
        landscaping and, **6.**6
        lighting and, **6.**7
        overviews and summaries of, **6.**3
        for parking (public, private, and secure), **6.**5–**6.**6
        signage and, **6.**4
        standoffs and standoff distances and, **6.**6
        surveillance and, **6.**4–**6.**5
        utilities and, **6.**7
    types of, **6.**2
Courtrooms, **6.**18–**6.**23. *See also* Courthouses
Coverage assessments, insurance, **12.**26–**12.**27
CPTED (crime prevention through environmental
        design), **3.**1–**3.**16
    addressing crime with, **3.**6–**3.**10
        audits, **3.**9–**3.**10
        demographic changes, **3.**6
        existing land uses, **3.**6
        overviews and summaries of, **3.**6
        planning, **3.**9–**3.**10
        policies, **3.**6–**3.**7
        site characteristics, **3.**6
        stakeholders and participants, **3.**8
        strategy design and evaluation, **3.**7–**3.**8
        team establishments, **3.**9
        traffic and transit issues, **3.**6
    benchmark event lessons for, **1.**12, **1.**27
    benefits of, **3.**3
    capital improvement programs for, **3.**11–**3.**12
    community connections of, **3.**5
    definitions of, **2.**29, **3.**1, **19.**3
    development regulations for, **3.**10–**3.**11
        landscape ordinances, **3.**11
        overviews and summaries of, **3.**10
        standards and guidelines and, **3.**11
        subdivision ordinances, **3.**10–**3.**11
        zoning ordinances, **3.**10
    disaster planning, response, and recovery and,
        12.3–**12.**4
    elements of, **3.**2–**3.**5
    goals and objectives of, **3.**12
    historical perspectives of, **3.**3–**3.**5
    master planning for, **2.**5
    occupancy and, **3.**15
    overviews and summaries of, **3.**1–**3.**5
    project planning and, **3.**14–**3.**15
    reference resources (print and internet) for, **3.**15
    for religious institutions and community centers,
        17.1

CPTED (crime prevention through environmental design) (*Cont.*):
  responsibility determinations for, **3.12–3.15**
    of academic institutions, **3.13**
    of architects and designers, **3.13**
    of business communities, **3.13**
    of housing and commercial developers, **3.13**
    of legal communities, **3.13–3.14**
    of neighborhoods, **3.14**
    overviews and summaries of, **3.12**
    of public agencies, **3.12–3.13**
    of special expertise companies, **3.13**
    of utilities, **3.13**
  for retail facilities and destinations, **19.5–19.7**
  for schools, **20.4–20.5**
  site selection and, **13.1–13.4**
  theory and practice of, **3.3–3.4**
Credentialed professionals management, **8.8**
Criminal threats, **2.9**
Crisis management and public relations, **12.27–12.29**
  communication and, **12.29**
  control and, **12.29**
  honesty and, **12.29**
  media fact sheet checklists, **12.28**
  overviews and summaries of, **12.27**
  preparation and, **12.28**
  research and information dissemination and, **12.28**
  technical expertise and, **12.27**
Critical asset identification, **2.6–2.8**
Crowd management, **4.14–4.15**
Cultural facilities, **4.3–15.6**. *See also under individual topics*
  for arenas, sports facilities, convention centers, and performing arts facilities, **4.3–4.18**
  museums and cultural facilities, **15.1–15.6**
Curtains, blast, **2.25**, **9.21–9.23**
CWAs (chemical warfare agents), **24.2–24.3**

D
Damage assessments, **12.20–12.22**
Da Vinci, Leonardo, **26.1**
Dead loads, **22.20**
DEA (Drug Enforcement Agency), **30.6**
Death and Life of Great American Cities, **1.12**, **2.5**, **3.1**
De Becker, Gavin, **6.1**, **13.1**
Decontamination, **8.14–8.15**, **24.11–24.13**, **24.21–24.24**
  facility designs for, **8.14–8.15**
    adjacent opening seals, **8.15**
    hot and cold zones, **8.15**
    overviews and summaries of, **8.14**
  overviews and summaries of, **24.11–24.12**
  processes of, **24.13**
  space planning for, **24.12–24.13**
  systems for, **24.21–24.24**
Defendant/attorney interview rooms, **6.18**

Defense Threat Reduction Agency, **24.17–24.18**, **24.24**
Defensible Space, Crime Prevention Through Urban Design, **2.5**
Defensive tiers, **2.5**
Deflection, **29.16**
Delay and deterrence, **27.3**, **27.5**
Deliberation rooms, **6.23**
Demographic changes, **3.6**
Dennis, Donna, **16.3**
Department of Agriculture, **18.1**
Department of Education, **20.3**
Department of Energy, **7.8**, **30.8**
Department of Homeland Security, **1.13**, **2.6**, **4.9**, **7.2–7.3**, **9.4**, **11.1–11.2**, **30.8–30.9**
Department of State, **7.3**, **7.16**, **12.4–12.5**, **22.5**, **30.8–30.9**
Department of the Interior, **1.17**
Department of Transportation, **30.8–30.9**
Department of Treasury, **11.4**, **30.8–30.9**
De Saint-Exupery, Antoine, **1.33**
Design and construction emergencies, **4.10–4.11**
Designing for Security: Using Art and Design to Improve Security, **16.1–16.2**, **16.8–16.9**
Designing Safer Communities, **3.15**
Design Notebook for Federal Building Lobby Security, **14.32–14.33**
Designs. *See also under individual topics*
  CPTED (crime prevention through environmental design), **3.1–3.16**
  planning and design aspects, **4.1–21.16**
  protection, **22.1–24.26**
    CB (chemical and biological), **24.1–24.26**
    mechanical, electrical, and fire, **23.1–23.16**
    structural, **22.3–22.22**
Desks, security, **9.26–9.27**
Destinations, retail, **19.1–19.14**. *See also* Retail facilities and destinations
Detectors and detection systems. *See also under individual topics*
  alarm elements for, **15.3**
  audio, **15.4**
  for breaches, **27.9–27.10**
  contact sensors, **15.3–15.4**
  discriminators, **15.4**
  ETDs (explosive trace detectors), **27.10–27.11**
  glass break detectors, **15.4**
  glass window bugs, **15.4**
  magnetic contact switches, **15.3–15.4**
    balanced, **15.4**
    simple, **15.3**
  metal, **7.18**
  metal detectors, **14.9**
  microswitches, **15.4**
  motion, **15.5**
  for museums and cultural facilities, **15.2–15.5**
  overviews and summaries of, **15.2–15.3**

Detectors and detection systems (*Cont.*):
photoelectric beams, **15.**5
plunger switches, **15.**4
pressure-sensitive mats, **15.**5
shock and impact sensors, **15.**4
systems. *See also under individual systems*
for biological agents, **24.**8–**24.**9
CB (chemical and biological) protection designs
for, **24.**7–**24.**9
EDSs (explosive detection systems),
27.10–**27.**11
flame photometry and, **24.**8
foil tape, **15.**4
GC (gas chromatography) and, **24.**8
IMS (ion mobility spectrometry) and, **24.**8
intrusion detection, **7.**22–**7.**27
lacing, **15.**5
LEL (lower explosion limit) detection, **18.**12
long-range monitoring, **24.**9
MS (mass spectrometry), **24.**8
overviews and summaries of, **24.**7
point detectors, **24.**8–**24.**9
SAWs (surface acoustic waves) and, **24.**8
truck and cargo freight scanners, **27.**10–**27.**12
vibrators, **15.**4
for weapons, **27.**10
x-ray machines, **14.**9
Deterrence and delay, **27.**3, **27.**5
Developers, responsibilities of, **3.**13
Development regulations, **3.**10–**3.**11
landscape ordinances, **3.**11
overviews and summaries of, **3.**10
subdivision ordinances, **3.**10–**3.**11
zoning ordinances, **3.**10
DHHS (Department of Health and Human Services),
18.1, **30.**8–**30.**9
Disaster planning, response, and recovery,
12.1.–**12.**32
benchmark event lessons for, **1.**7–**1.**8,
1.19–**1.**20, **12.**7–**12.**8, **12.**11–**12.**12,
12.16–**12.**17, **12.**26
for burglary deterrence, **12.**2–**12.**3
for businesses, **12.**2, **12.**22–**12.**26
administration and record keeping, **12.**25
business-home shared concerns, **12.**2
direction and control issues, **12.**25
emergency management plans, **12.**25
life safety issues, **12.**25
overviews and summaries of, **12.**22
property and records protection, **12.**26
recovery and restoration, **12.**26
risk and vulnerability assessments, **12.**24
business-home shared concerns for, **12.**2
for CB (chemical and biological) hazards,
12.5–**12.**6
checklists for, **12.**3, **12.**5–**12.**6, **12.**9–**12.**10, **12.**12,
12.14–**12.**15, **12.**20, **12.**24–**12.**28

Disaster planning, response, and recovery (*Cont.*):
CPTED (crime prevention through environmental
design) and, **12.**3–**12.**4. *See also* CPTED
(crime prevention through environmental
design)
crisis management and public relations and,
12.27–**12.**29
communication and, **12.**29
control and, **12.**29
honesty and, **12.**29
media fact sheet checklists, **12.**28
overviews and summaries of, **12.**27
preparation and, **12.**28
research and information dissemination and,
12.28
technical expertise and, **12.**27
disaster response issues, **12.**19–**12.**20
damage assessments, **12.**20–**12.**22
response efforts, **12.**19
response teams, **12.**19–**12.**20
emergency management processes, **12.**23
fire-resistant planning and design, **12.**18–**12.**19
building materials and maintenance, **12.**18
life safety issues, **12.**19
overviews and summaries of, **12.**18
site designs and vegetation, **12.**18
water supplies, **12.**18
for floods and tsunamis, **12.**7–**12.**9, **12.**7–**12.**10
checklists for, **12.**9–**12.**10
flood water recovery, **12.**9–**12.**10
overviews and summaries of, **12.**7–**12.**10
for health care facilities, **8.**12–**8.**13
home security checklists for, **12.**3
for hurricanes, **12.**11–**12.**12
checklists for, **12.**12
Hurricane Andrew, **12.**11–**12.**12
National Hurricane Center, **12.**11–**12.**12
overviews and summaries of, **12.**11
Stafford-Simpson classification scale, **12.**11
indemnification language, **12.**22–**12.**23
insurance coverage assessments for, **12.**26–**12.**27
for natural disasters, **12.**6–**12.**7
overviews and summaries of, **12.**1–**12.**2
for power outages, **12.**5–**12.**7
checklists for, **12.**6–**12.**7
overviews and summaries of, **12.**5–**12.**6
reference resources (print and internet) for,
12.29–**12.**32
risk and vulnerability assessments, **12.**24
safe rooms and, **12.**4–**12.**5
for terrorist-related disasters, **12.**5
for tornadoes and high winds, **12.**12–**12.**16
checklists for, **12.**14–**12.**15
design and construction issues for, **12.**13–**12.**14
F-scale, **12.**13–**12.**14
in-residence shelters, **12.**15–**12.**16
overviews and summaries of, **12.**12–**12.**13

Disaster planning, response, and recovery (*Cont.*):
  volunteer services for, **12.**20–**12.**22
  for wildfires, **12.**16–**12.**17
Discriminators, audio, **15.**4
DOA (Department of Agriculture), **18.**1
Docks, loading, **25.**8
DoD (Department of Defense), **2.**6, **7.**3, **7.**14, **9.**4, **24.**19–**24.**20, **30.**8–**30.**9
DOJ (Department of Justice), **3.**5, **7.**1–**7.**4, **22.**3–**22.**4
Doors, **6.**23, **7.**6–**7.**7, **17.**10, **29.**8
DOP (dispersed oil particulate) filters, **23.**11–**23.**12
Douglas, William O., **28.**1
Downtown properties, hospitality facilities, **10.**6
Drop-off/pick-up zones, schools, **20.**7–**20.**8
Ductility, limited, **22.**15
Duncan, Donnie, **4.**3
Duress alarm systems, **7.**24–**7.**25

E

Earthquake and seismic designs, **29.**3, **29.**14–**29.**15
Eastmont Mall Planned Parenthood, **21.**4–**21.**6
Eddy Street Planned Parenthood Clinic, **21.**5
ED (emergency department) terrorism responses, **8.**12–**8.**14
EDSs (explosive detection systems), **27.**10–**27.**11
EECS (electronic entry control systems), **7.**18
Egress systems, high-rise, **5.**1–**5.**10. *See also* Commercial high-rise egress systems
EIA (Electronic Industries Association), **30.**8
Einstein, Albert, **18.**14
Electrical and mechanical room access, **18.**10–**18.**11
Electrical protection designs, **23.**1–**23.**16. *See also* Mechanical, electrical, and fire protection designs
Electrical systems, **8.**21–**8.**23, **18.**12–**18.**13, **25.**9
  cost estimations for, **25.**9
  for health care facilities, **8.**21–**8.**23
  for research facilities, **18.**12–**18.**13
Electric/powered fences, **27.**5–**27.**6
Electronic access systems, **7.**22
Electronic building protection, **15.**2–**15.**3. *See also* Detectors and detection systems
Electronic SCCs (security control centers), **7.**21–**7.**23
Electrostatic filters, **23.**11–**23.**12
Elevated degree of risk (threat level 3), **4.**8–**4.**9
E-mail threat checklist, **21.**12
Emergency control plans, **2.**28, **28.**13–**28.**14
Emergency response lessons, **26.**1–**26.**16. *See also* Benchmark event lessons
  AMEC Construction Management and, **26.**1–**26.**16
  emergency responses, **26.**8–**26.**15
    activities for, **26.**9–**26.**13
    emergency, definitions of, **26.**8–**26.**9
    methodologies for, **26.**9
    overviews and summaries of, **26.**8–**26.**9
    responsibility matrices for, **26.**15–**26.**16
  EOCs (emergency operations centers) and, **27.**14–**27.**16

Emergency response lessons (*Cont.*):
  Lessons Learned: Emergency Responses to the World Trade Center and the Pentagon Attacks, **26.**7–**26.**16
  overviews and summaries of, **26.**1, **26.**10–**26.**11
  Pentagon building lessons, **26.**1–**26.**4
  reference resources (internet) for, **26.**12
  routes, emergency vehicles, **20.**7
  for schools, **20.**7
  security concerns, emergency *vs.* traditional, **19.**2–**19.**3
  WTC (World Trade Center) lessons, **26.**1–**26.**16
Employee-related issues. *See* Workplace-related issues
Enclosed malls, **19.**3
Engineering aspects, **22.**1–**24.**26
  CB (chemical and biological) protection designs, **24.**1–**24.**26
  mechanical, electrical, and fire protection designs, **23.**1–**23.**16
  structural protection designs, **22.**3–**22.**22
Enhanced egress stairs, **5.**5
Enhanced sheltering-in-place capabilities, **24.**15
Entrances. *See also under individual topics*
  CB (chemical and biological) protection designs for, **24.**14–**24.**15
  entrance, waiting, and registration areas, **21.**4–**21.**6
  entrance-exit separations, **14.**3
  vs. exits, **20.**4–**20.**5
  for federally owned/leased buildings, **7.**6
  for hospitality facilities, **10.**4
  to lobbies, **14.**3–**14.**4
  for malls, **19.**9
  overviews and summaries of, **19.**7–**19.**8
  for parking garages, **19.**9
  queuing spaces, **14.**3–**14.**4
  for retail facilities and destinations, **19.**7–**19.**10
  schools, **20.**4–**20.**5, **20.**9
  screening and, **24.**14–**24.**15
  service access control for, **19.**8–**19.**10
  service entry points, **19.**10
  for women's health centers, **21.**4–**21.**6
Entry controls. *See also under individual topics*
  access and. *See* Access-related issues
  control booths, **7.**19–**7.**20
  detectors and. *See* Detectors and detection systems
  EECS (electronic entry control systems), **7.**18
  for federally owned/leased buildings, **7.**15–**7.**20
  IDSs (intrusion detection systems), **7.**18
  overviews and summaries of, **7.**18
  for perimeters, **7.**15–**7.**18
    fences and fencing, **7.**17–**7.**18
    fixed arm drop barrier systems, **7.**17–**7.**18
    overviews and summaries of, **7.**15–**7.**16
    portable arm drop barrier systems, **7.**17
    vehicle barriers, **7.**16–**7.**17
  x-ray machines, **7.**18–**7.**19

Envelopes, building, **18.6–18.**7, **24.**14
Environmental designs, **3.**1–**3.**16. *See also* CPTED
   (crime prevention through environmental design)
Environmental threats, **2.**9
EOCs (emergency operations centers), **27.**14–**27.**16
EOMs (emergency operations manuals), **2.**28
Epigraphs. *See* Quotations
Essential generator loads, **18.**13
Estimations, cost, **25.**3–**25.**10. *See also* Cost
   estimations
ETDs (explosive trace detectors), **27.**10–**27.**11
ETRPs (explosive threat response plans), **17.**12–**17.**13
Evacuation practice drills, **1.**10
Evacuation statistics, **5.**8
Evaluation processes, **28.**5–**28.**10
Event planning, **4.**13
Event recording, real-time, **7.**25
Events, benchmark, **1.**3–**1.**40, **26.**1–**26.**16. *See also*
   Benchmark event lessons
Executive involvement, **28.**3–**28.**5
Exhaust, rapid, **24.**11
Existing land uses, **3.**6
Exits *vs.* entrances, **14.**3, **20.**4–**20.**5. *See also*
   Entrances
Explosion detection technology, **27.**10–**27.**11
Explosions, LEL (lower explosion limit) detection
   systems, **18.**12
Exposures, liability, **31.**1–**31.**14. *See also* Liability-
   related issues
Exterior wall systems, **6.**7–**6.**12, **9.**15–**9.**19,
   22.16–**22.**20, **25.**8–**25.**9
   catch systems, **22.**17–**22.**18
   courthouses, **6.**7–**6.**12
   fenestration, glass, **22.**16–**22.**17, **22.**20
   historic preservation guidance for, **9.**15–**9.**19
   overviews and summaries of, **22.**16, **25.**8–**25.**9
   structural protection designs for, **22.**16–**22.**19
   window performance criteria, **22.**18
External factors, definitions of, **2.**29
External (makeup air) filtration, **24.**6
External *vs.* internal resources, **4.**11

F

FACEA (Freedom to Access Clinic Entrances Act),
   1.28, **21.**3
Facial recognition, **10.**7, **27.**8
Facility communication centers, **28.**14
Fact sheets, media, **12.**28
Failures, shear, **22.**14–**22.**15, **22.**20
Fall hazards, **10.**8
FBI (Federal Bureau of Investigation), **4.**5, **4.**8–**4.**9,
   11.1–**11.**3
FCC (Federal Communications Commission), **30.**8
Federal Buildings, **9.**1–**9.**36, **14.**1–**14.**34
Federally owned/leased buildings, **7.**1–**7.**30
   benchmark event lessons for, **1.**15
   blast protection criteria for, **7.**13

Federally owned/leased buildings (*Cont.*):
   building entry control for, **7.**18–**7.**20
      EECS (electronic entry control systems), **7.**18
      entry control booths, **7.**19–**7.**20
      IDSs (intrusion detection systems), **7.**18
      metal detectors, **7.**18
      overviews and summaries of, **7.**18
      x-ray machines, **7.**18–**7.**19
   design elements for, **7.**5–**7.**7
      doors, **7.**6–**7.**7
      employee access, **7.**7
      entrances and entry points, **7.**6
      guard services, **7.**6
      listing of, **7.**6
      overviews and summaries of, **7.**5–**7.**6
      parking, **7.**6–**7.**7
      security design checklist, **7.**5
      site planning checklist, **7.**5
      visitor access, **7.**7
      walls, windows, and openings, **7.**7–**7.**8
   design guidelines for, **7.**4–**7.**5
      overviews and summaries of, **7.**4
      planning and design, **7.**4–**7.**5
   electronic access systems for, **7.**22
   electronic security for, **7.**21–**7.**22
   guidelines, standards, and codes for, **7.**1–**7.**2,
      7.28–**7.**29
      listing of, **7.**28–**7.**29
      overviews and summaries of, **7.**1–**7.**2, **7.**28–**7.**29
      USDOJ (U.S. Department of Justice) and,
         7.1–**7.**3
      Vulnerability Assessment of Federal Buildings,
         7.1–**7.**2
   intrusion detection systems for, **7.**22–**7.**27
      CCTV (closed circuit television) and, **7.**25–**7.**27
      communications systems and, **7.**27
      duress alarm systems, **7.**24–**7.**25
      electronic access systems and, **7.**22
      electronic SCCs (security control centers) and,
         7.23
      historical recording and, **7.**27
      overviews and summaries of, **7.**22
      real-time event recording and, **7.**25
      SMSs (security management systems) and,
         7.22–**7.**25
      VIISs (video imaging and identification
         systems) and, **7.**25
   lighting for, **7.**8–**7.**9
      ballasts, **7.**10
      circuiting requirements of, **7.**12
      controls, **7.**12
      fixture performance and, **7.**11
      flexibility characteristics of, **7.**12
      fluorescent lamps, **7.**9
      HPS (high-pressure sodium) lamps, **7.**9
      lamp selection, **7.**9
      light fixtures, **7.**10

Federally owned/leased buildings, lighting for (*Cont.*):
  luminaire mounting heights and locations, **7**.12
  maintenance for, **7**.10–**7**.11
  metal halide lamps, **7**.9
  obstructions of, **7**.11–**7**.12
  optical controls, **7**.11
  overviews and summaries of, **7**.8
  sources and source types for, **7**.9–**7**.11
  surface reflectance for, **7**.12
  systems, **7**.11–**7**.12
  uniformity issues of, **7**.11
 overviews and summaries of, **7**.1, **7**.27
 perimeter entry controls for, **7**.15–**7**.18
  fences and fencing, **7**.17–**7**.18
  fixed arm drop barrier systems, **7**.17–**7**.18
  overviews and summaries of, **7**.15–**7**.16
  portable arm drop barrier systems, **7**.17
  vehicle barriers, **7**.16–**7**.17
 progressive collapse of, **7**.13–**7**.14
  DoD (Department of Defense) Interim
    Antiterrorism/Force Protection construction
    Standards and, **7**.14
  overviews and summaries of, **7**.13–**7**.14
  structural member response limits and, **7**.14
 reference resources (print and internet) for, **7**.28
 SCCs (security control centers) for, **7**.20
 security levels for, **7**.2–**7**.3, **7**.13
  Department of Homeland Security and, **7**.2–**7**.3
  FPS (U.S. Federal Protective Services) and,
    7.2–**7**.3
  GSA (U.S. General Services Administration)
    and, **7**.2–**7**.3, **7**.13–**7**.15
  ISC (Interagency Security Committee) and, **7**.3,
    7.13
  overviews and summaries, **7**.2–**7**.3
  protection levels and, **7**.13
 VIISs (video imaging and identification systems)
    and, **7**.25
 vulnerability assessments for, **7**.3
 windows and glazing for, **7**.14–**7**.16
  low and low/medium protection levels,
    7.14–**7**.15
  medium and high protection levels, **7**.14–**7**.16
  overviews and summaries of, **7**.14
Feiner, Edward A., **1**.6
FEMA (Federal Emergency Management Agency),
  4.10–**4**.11, **12**.4–**12**.5, **31**.3–**31**.4
Fences and fencing. *See also under individual topics*
 case studies of, **16**.3–**16**.4, **16**.7–**16**.8
 electric/powered, **27**.5–**27**.6
 for federally owned/leased buildings, **7**.17–**7**.18
 fiber-optic, **27**.5
 master planning for, **2**.16–**2**.17
 overviews and summaries of, **27**.5
 for playfields, **20**.6–**20**.7
 for religious institutions and community centers,
  17.10–**17**.11

Fences and fencing (*Cont.*):
 for schools, **20**.4–**20**.5
 technology-related issues of, **27**.5–**27**.6
Fenestration, **22**.16–**22**.17, **22**.20, **29**.16
Feynman, Richard, **8**.28
Fiber-optic fences, **27**.5
Film, antishatter, **2**.25, **29**.4–**29**.5
Filters and filtration, **24**.4–**24**.18
 aerosol, **24**.5
 airflow management and, **24**.9–**24**.10
 chemical agent, **24**.4–**24**.5
 collective protection and, **24**.4–**24**.7, **24**.18
 external (makeup air) filtration, **24**.6
 HEPA (high-efficiency particulate air), **24**.4–**24**.6,
  24.11, **24**.15–**24**.16
 integrations of, **24**.5–**24**.6
 internal (recirculated air) filtration, **24**.6–**24**.7, **24**.11
 overviews and summaries of, **24**.4
 for safe rooms, **24**.10–**24**.11
 systems for, **24**.18
 UVGI (ultraviolet germicidal irradiation) systems,
  24.5
Fingerprint recognition, **27**.8–**27**.9
Fire doors, **17**.10
Fire protection designs, **23**.1–**23**.16, **25**.9. *See also*
  Mechanical, electrical, and fire protection
  designs
Fire release doors, **6**.23
Fire-resistance planning issues, **12**.18–**12**.19
 building materials and maintenance, **12**.18
 disaster planning, response, and recovery for,
  12.18–**12**.19
 life safety issues, **12**.19
 overviews and summaries of, **12**.18
 site designs and vegetation, **12**.18
 water supplies, **12**.18
First Impressions program, **14**.2
FISA (Foreign Intelligence Surveillance Act), **11**.4
Fixed arm drop barrier systems, **7**.17–**7**.18
Fixtures, light, **7**.10–**7**.11
Flame photometry, **24**.8
Flexibility, **7**.12, **8**.18
 of lighting, **7**.12
 of space, **8**.18
Flexural properties, **22**.20
Floods and tsunamis, **12**.7–**12**.10
 checklists for, **12**.9–**12**.10
 disaster planning, response, and recovery for,
  12.7–**12**.9
 flood water recovery, **12**.9–**12**.10
 overviews and summaries of, **12**.7–**12**.10
Floors, **5**.7, **6**.14
 blocking diagrams of, **6**.14
 floor plates, **5**.7
Fluorescent lamps, **7**.9
Flying glass hazards, **9**.20
FM (Factory Mutual Research Corporation), **30**.8

Foil tape detector systems, **15.**4
Following and stalking checklists, **21.**14
Forced-entry resistance, **29.**8–**29.**10
Ford, Henry, **23.**1
Formulae, cost estimations, **25.**6
Fougeron, Anne, **1.**28
FPS (Federal Protective Services), **7.**2–**7.**3, **14.**1–**14.**2
Framing systems, structural, **2.**23
Free society-security balances, **1.**5–**1.**7
Free zones, lobbies, **14.**4–**14.**5
Freight scanners, **27.**10–**27.**12
Fruin, J. J., **5.**3
F-scale, tornadoes, **12.**13–**12.**14
Fujita, T. Theodore, **12.**13

G

Galioto, Carl, **1.**14, **5.**1–**5.**10
Gallerias, **19.**3
Gaming properties, **10.**6–**10.**7
  facial recognition technology, **10.**7
  mantraps for, **10.**7
  slots and gaming machines in, **10.**6–**10.**7
Gandhi, Mahatma, **20.**1
Garages, parking. *See* Parking
Gates, **16.**5–**16.**8
Gaughan, Regis, **1.**26, **18.**1–**18.**15
GC (gas chromatography), **24.**8
Generator loads, **18.**13
Gensler, **14.**14, **14.**22, **14.**25
Geographic impacts, **4.**10
Geometry, hand, **27.**8
Gift of Fear, **13.**1
Glass. *See also* Windows and glazing
  break detectors for, **15.**4
  fenestration, **22.**16–**22.**17, **22.**20
  flying glass hazards, **9.**20
  glazing and security glass applications, **29.**1–**29.**18.
    See also Glazing and security glass applications
  security, **29.**1–**29.**18
  window bugs, **15.**4
Glass clad polycarbonate, **29.**16
GLASTOP (computer program), **7.**15
Glazing and security glass applications, **29.**1–**29.**18.
  See also Windows and glazing
  for ballistic resistance, **29.**3, **29.**10–**29.**16
    large *vs.* small missile impacts, **29.**14
    overviews and summaries of, **29.**10–**29.**12,
      29.14, **29.**16
  benchmark event lessons for, **1.**36–**1.**37, **29.**1–**29.**4,
    29.13–**29.**15
  for blast mitigation, **9.**20–**9.**21, **29.**3–**29.**8
    ASF (antishatter film), **9.**20–**9.**21, **29.**4–**29.**5
    blast doors, **29.**8
    blast windows, **29.**3–**29.**7
    cable catch window systems for, **29.**2, **29.**6–**29.**7
    overviews and summaries of, **29.**3–**29.**4
    soft wall testing for, **29.**6

Glazing and security glass applications (*Cont.*):
  for burglary resistance, **29.**3, **29.**8–**29.**9
  for courthouses, **6.**10–**6.**11
  earthquake and seismic designs and, **29.**3,
    29.14–**29.**15
  for forced-entry resistance, **29.**8–**29.**10
  guidelines, standards, and codes for, **29.**9–**29.**16
    AAMA (American Architectural Manufacturing
      Association) and, **29.**14
    ASCE (American Society of Civil Engineers)
      and, **29.**14–**29.**16
    ASTM International, **29.**9–**29.**13
    H.P. White Laboratories, **29.**9–**29.**10, **29.**12
    IBC (International Building Code), **29.**14
    NEHRP (National Earthquake Hazards
      Reduction Program) guidelines, **29.**14
    NIJ (National Institute of Justice), **29.**12
    South Florida Building Code, **29.**11–**29.**13
    UL (Underwriters Laboratory), **29.**9, **29.**12
  historical preservation guidance for, **9.**19–**9.**23
  for hurricane impact resistance, **29.**3, **29.**11–**29.**14
  laminated glass, **29.**2–**29.**3
    overviews and summaries of, **29.**2–**29.**3
    security performances of, **29.**3
    types of, **29.**3
  overviews and summaries of, **29.**1–**29.**2
  planning issues for, **2.**24
  reference resources (print and internet) for,
    29.16–**29.**17
  replacement glazing, **9.**20–**9.**21
  terminology for, **29.**16
Glossaries. *See* Terminology
Goldstone and Hinz, **16.**3
Good Samaritan laws, **1.**20–**1.**21, **1.**38, **31.**6, **31.**11
Governmental departments and bodies. *See* U.S.
  governmental departments and bodies
Graffiti controls, **20.**9–**20.**10
Gravity load systems, **22.**7
Great Plains floods, 1997, **1.**21, **12.**8
Green field selection criteria, **18.**3
Grounds and buildings, schools, **20.**8–**20.**10
  checklists for, **20.**9
  entrances, **20.**9
  graffiti controls for, **20.**9–**20.**10
  overviews and summaries of, **20.**8–**20.**10
  portable classrooms, **20.**10
  site lighting, **20.**10
GSA (General Services Administration), **1.**5–**1.**7,
  1.17, **2.**5–**2.**6, **4.**12, **7.**2–**7.**3, **7.**13–**7.**16, **9.**4,
  14.1–**14.**4, **22.**9, **22.**18, **22.**28, **23.**10–**23.**11,
  30.4–**30.**5, **30.**9, **31.**4–**31.**5
Guarded degree of risk (threat level 2), **4.**9
Guard houses, **2.**19, **9.**10–**9.**11
Guard services, **7.**6
Guide for Business and Industry, **4.**10–**4.**11
Guidelines, standards, and codes, **30.**3–**30.**14
  benchmark event lessons for, **30.**3–**30.**4, **30.**12–**30.**13

Guidelines, standards, and codes (*Cont.*):
benefits of, **30**.7
codes. *See also under individual topics*
 BOCA (Building Officials Code Administration)
  and, **30**.8
 CFR (Code of Federal Regulations), **7**.3, **18**.2,
  30.7–**30**.9
 Code of Hammurabi, **30**.3–**30**.14
 IBC (International Building Code), **18**.12, **23**.3,
  29.14
 local, **30**.8–**30**.9
 NEC (National Electric Code), **18**.12
 New York City Building Code, **5**.2–**5**.4, **23**.3,
  31.3
 New York State Task Force on Buildings Codes
  and, **31**.3
 South Florida Building Code, **29**.11–**29**.13
development regulations, **3**.10–**3**.11
 landscape ordinances, **3**.11
 overviews and summaries of, **3**.10
 subdivision ordinances, **3**.10–**3**.11
 zoning ordinances, **3**.10
for facility types. *See also under individual topics*
 commercial high-rise egress systems, **5**.2–**5**.4
 federally owned/leased buildings, **7**.1–**7**.2,
  7.28–**7**.29
 research facilities, **18**.2
 women's health centers, **21**.7–**21**.15
for glazing and security glass applications, **29**.9
goals and objectives of, **30**.10–**30**.12
historical perspectives of, **30**.5–**30**.7
for historic preservation, **9**.2–**9**.5, **9**.34
of independent agencies and organizations. *See
 also under individual topics*
 AAMA (American Architectural Manufacturing
  Association), **29**.14
 American Chemistry Council, **30**.9
 ANSI (American National Standards Institute),
  30.8
 ASCE (American Society of Civil Engineers),
  2.22–**2**.23, **29**.14–**29**.16
 ASHRAE (American Society of Heating
  Refrigeration and Air Conditioning
  Engineers), **18**.11–**18**.14
 ASIS (American Society for Industrial Security),
  30.8
 ASTM International, **29**.9–**29**.13
 Chlorine Institute, **30**.9
 EIA (Electronic Industries Association), **30**.8
 FM (Factory Mutual Research Corporation), **30**.8
 H.P. White Laboratories, **29**.9–**29**.10, **29**.12
 IAPSC (International Association of
  Professional Security Consultants), **30**.8
 IEC (International Electrotechnical
  Commission), **30**.8
 IEEE (Institute of Electrical And Electronics
  Engineers), **30**.8

Guidelines, standards, and codes, of independent
 agencies and organizations (*Cont.*):
 Illuminating Engineering Society, **30**.8
 ISO (International Organization for
  Standardization), **30**.8
 National Association of Chemical Distributors,
  30.9
 NEHRP (National Earthquake Hazards
  Reduction Program) guidelines, **29**.14
 NEMA (National Electrical Manufacturers
  Association), **30**.8
 NFPA (National Fire Protection Association),
  23.3, **30**.5–**30**.8
 NIST (National Institute of Standards and
  Technology), **30**.9
 Synthetic Organic Chemical Manufacturers
  Association, **30**.9
 UL (Underwriters Laboratory), **29**.9, **29**.12, **30**.8
 Walker, McGough, Foltz, and Lyeria tests, **29**.10
industry standards, **30**.8
Interim Antiterrorism/Force Protection
 Construction Standards, **7**.14
laws and legislation. *See also under individual topics*
 ADA (Americans with Disabilities Act), **30**.8
 Banking Act (1968), **30**.6
 Energy Reorganization Act (1974), **30**.6
 National Historical Preservation Act, **9**.3
 OSHA (Occupational Safety and Health Act),
  30.8
liability exposures and, **31**.1–**31**.14
listing of, **30**.6
for lobbies, **14**.1–**14**.2
for mechanical, electrical, and fire protection
 designs, **23**.2–**23**.3
overviews and summaries of, **23**.2–**23**.3
for planning processes, **30**.10–**30**.11
reference resources (internet) for, **30**.13–**30**.14
rehabilitation standards, **9**.3
Security Design Guidelines, **9**.4
security reference guidelines, **21**.7–**21**.15
self-imposed guidelines, **30**.9
Standards for Rehabilitation, **9**.3–**9**.4
threat assessments and, **30**.4–**30**.5, **30**.7
UFAS (Uniform Federal Accessibility Standards),
 7.6
of U.S. governmental departments and bodies.
 See also U.S. governmental departments
 and bodies
 DEA (Drug Enforcement Agency), **30**.6
 Department of Homeland Security, **9**.4, **30**.9
 Department of State, **30**.9
 Department of Treasury, **30**.9
 DHHS (Department of Health and Human
  Services), **30**.9
 DoD (Department of Defense), **30**.9
 FCC (Federal Communications Commission),
  30.8

Guidelines, standards, and codes, of independent
  agencies and organizations, of U.S. govern-
  mental departments and bodies (*Cont.*):
  FPS (Federal Protective Service) and, **14.1–14.**2
  GSA (General Services Administration), **9.**4,
    14.1–14.2, **30.**9
  ISC (Interagency Security Committee), **9.3–9.**4
  National Park Service, **9.**4
  NCPC (National Capital Planning Committee),
    9.4
  NCR (Nuclear Regulatory Commission), **30.**9
  NIJ (National Institute of Justice), **29.**12
  PBS (Public Buildings Service), **14.**1
  Secretary of the Interior, **9.3–9.**4
  USMS (U.S. Marshal Service), **14.1–14.**2
Guiding Principles for Federal Architecture, **1.**6
Gunning, Jeffrey J., **1.**27, **19.1–19.**14
Gwathmey, Charles, **9.**1

H
Hallways, schools, **20.12–20.**13
Hammurabi, Code of, **30.**5
Hand geometry, **27.**8
Hardened elements, **18.**7, **22.**4
Hardening, **1.**26, **2.**29
Harper, Charles F., **1.**20, **12.**12
Harris, James W., **1.**19, **11.1–11.**6
Harrison, Dian J., **1.**28
Harry Campbell Associates, **14.**21
HAZL (computer program), **7.**15
Health care facilities, **8.1–8.**32
  acute care hospitals, **8.1–8.**3
  AHJ (authorities having jurisdiction) and, **8.**30
  ancillary public areas, **8.**27
  benchmark event lessons for, **1.15–1.**16, **8.2–8.**11,
    8.19–8.26
  building systems for, **8.10–8.**11
    compartmentalization and, **8.**11
    emergency systems, **8.**11
    HVAC (heating, ventilation, and air conditioning)
      systems, **8.**11
    overviews and summaries of, **8.**10
  clinical laboratories, **8.**24
  contamination protection for, **8.23–8.**24
  decontamination facility designs, **8.14–8.**15
    adjacent opening seals, **8.**15
    hot and cold zones, **8.**15
    overviews and summaries of, **8.**14
  ED (emergency department) terrorism responses,
    8.12–8.14
    for CBR (chemical, biological, and radiological)
      agents, **8.**14
    decontamination, **8.13–8.**14
    disaster planning, **8.12–8.**13
    overviews and summaries of, **8.12–8.**13
  electrical service for, **8.21–8.**23
    cogeneration power systems, **8.21–8.**22

Health care facilities, electrical service for (*Cont.*):
    emergency power, **8.21–8.**22
    large-scale blackouts and, **8.22–8.**23
    overviews and summaries of, **8.**21
  emergency response roles of, **8.**4
  facility-specific issues, **8.5–8.**9
    credentialed professionals and volunteer
      management, **8.**8
    Homeland Security Advisory System and,
      8.5–8.9
    ICS (incident command system) protocol,
      8.5–8.9, **8.**30
    overviews and summaries of, **8.**5
    patient tracking and record keeping, **8.**9
    technology ad equipment compatibilities, **8.**8
  hospital infrastructures, **8.20–8.**21
  impact factors for, **8.**2
  infection control for, **8.15–8.**18, **8.**30
    airborne infection isolation and ventilation, **8.**16
    air handling systems, **8.16–8.**17
    contaminated material disposal and disinfection,
      8.17–8.18
    infection control risk assessments, **8.**30
    isolation rooms, **8.**17
    overviews and summaries of, **8.**15
    PPE (personal protective equipment), **8.**17
    space flexibility, **8.**18
    syndrome surveillance protocols, **8.15–8.**16
    waiting areas for, **8.**16
  media briefing areas of, **8.**27
  mobile units, **8.25–8.**26
  mortuaries, **8.**24
  nursing homes, **8.3–8.**4
  overviews and summaries of, **8.1–8.**3, **8.28–8.**30
  patient care nursing units, **8.18–8.**20
    ICUs (intensive care units), **8.**20
    M/Ss (medical/surgical units), **8.19–8.**20
    nurseries and maternity units, **8.**19
    overviews and summaries of, **8.18–8.**19
  planning and design issues for, **8.11–8.**12
    circulation, **8.**12
    critical program elements, **8.**12
    overviews and summaries of, **8.**11
    site selection, **8.**12
  recovery times and, **8.25–8.**26
  reference resources (print and internet), **8.30–8.**31
  regional perspectives of, **8.4–8.**6, **8.**30
    HERDS (Hospital Emergency Response Data
      System) and, **8.5–8.**6, **8.**30
    New York State DOH (Department of Health)
      and, **8.5–8.**6
    overviews and summaries of, **8.4–8.**5
    regional health care resources, **8.**5
    regional planning, **8.**5
  security control for, **8.26–8.**27
  surge capacities of, **8.**18, **8.24–8.**26
  terminology for, **8.**30

Health care facilities (*Cont.*):
threat assessments for, **8.4**
victim and missing persons status issues, **8.27**
vulnerability assessments for, **8.9–8.10**
overviews and summaries of, **8.9**
planning teams for, **8.10**
site and perimeter security, **8.10**
water service for, **8.22–8.23**
women's health centers, **21.1–21.16**. *See also*
Women's health centers
Heider, Elizabeth J., **1.32**, **25.3–25.10**
HEPA (high-efficiency particulate air) filters,
24.4–24.6, **24.11**, **24.15–24.16**
HERDS (Hospital Emergency Response Data
System), **8.5–8.6**, **8.30**
Heritage protection, **9.2**. *See also* Historic preservation
guidance
Hickman, Tim, **4.3**
High degree of risk (threat level 4), **4.8**
High-rise egress systems, **5.1–5.10**. *See also*
Commercial high-rise egress systems
High security issues, courtrooms, **6.21**
High-threat area isolation, **24.14**
High winds and tornadoes, **12.12–12.16**. *See also*
Tornadoes and high winds
Hillel, **17.1**
Historical perspectives, **3.3–3.5**, **24.2–24.3**, **30.5–30.7**
of CB (chemical and biological) protection
designs, **24.2–24.3**
of CPTED (crime prevention through environmental design), **3.3–3.5**
of guidelines, standards, and codes, **30.5–30.7**
of product selection and specification, **28.3**
Historical recording issues, **7.27**
Historic American Building Survey, **9.5–9.6**
Historic preservation guidance, **9.1–9.36**
benchmark event lessons and, **1.17–1.18**, **9.1–9.2**,
9.4, **9.6**, **9.8**, **9.26**, **9.31**
for building exteriors, **9.15–9.19**
guidelines, standards, and codes and, **9.2–9.5**, **9.34**
checklists for, **9.4–9.5**
of Department of Homeland Security, **9.4**
design standards, **9.3–9.4**
of DoD (U.S. Department of Defense), **9.4**
of DOJ (U.S. Department of Justice), **9.4**
of GSA (U.S. General Services Administration),
9.4, **9.13–9.14**
of ISC (Interagency Security Committee),
9.3–9.4
life safety, **9.7**
listing of, **9.34**
for modifications to historic structures, **9.5**
of National Historical Preservation Act, **9.3**
of National Park Service, **9.4**
of NCPC (National Capital Planning
Committee), **9.4**
overviews and summaries of, **9.4**

Historic preservation guidance, guidelines, standards,
and codes and (*Cont.*):
rehabilitation standards, **9.3**
Security Design Guidelines, **9.4**
Standards for Rehabilitation, **9.3–9.4**
of U.S. Secretary of the Interior, **9.3–9.4**
for interiors, **9.23–9.26**
overviews and summaries of, **9.23–9.24**
wall liners, **9.24–9.26**
wall treatments, **9.24**
for lobby screening and circulation control,
9.26–9.30
overviews and summaries of, **9.26**
plans for, **9.30**
public amenities and, **9.30**
screening alternatives, **9.27**
security desks, **9.26–9.27**
off-site alternatives, **9.8**
operational improvements, **9.6–9.7**
overviews and summaries of, **9.1–9.2**, **9.27**, **9.31**
physical planning changes, **9.8–9.9**
postdisaster planning, **9.7–9.8**
protection planning, **9.1–9.6**
documentation for, **9.5–9.6**
evaluation and, **9.6**
heritage protection and, **9.2**
heritage resource information for, **9.2**
Historic American Building Survey and, **9.5–9.6**
historic resource values and, **9.2**
historic structure reports for, **9.6**
National Register of Historic Places and, **9.5–9.6**
overviews and summaries of, **9.1–9.5**
principles of, **9.2**
public safety and, **9.2**
standoffs and standoff distances for, **9.34**
reference resources (print and internet) for,
9.34–9.35
site-specific issues, **9.8–9.15**
barriers, **9.11–9.15**
guard houses, **9.10–9.11**
lighting, **9.8–9.10**
overviews and summaries of, **9.8**
passive security elements, **9.14**
perimeters, **9.15–9.16**
security performance elements, **9.9**
set-back requirements, **9.9**
surveillance cameras, **9.8–9.10**
terminology for, **9.33–9.34**
for windows, **9.19–9.23**
blast curtains and blast shades, **9.21–9.23**
flying glass hazards, **9.20**
laminated glass storm windows, **9.23**
overviews and summaries, **9.19–9.20**
replacement glazing, **9.20–9.21**
window films, **9.20–9.21**
Hlushko, Andrew, **1.30**, **23.1–23.16**
HOK, **14.27**, **14.28**, **16.8**

Holding cells, **6.**17–**6.**19
Home disaster planning, response, and recovery, **12.**1–**12.**32. *See also* Disaster planning, response, and recovery
Homeland Security Advisory System, **8.**5–**8.**9
Home security checklists, **12.**3
Hoover, Herbert, **1.**32
Hospitality facilities, **10.**1–**10.**8
    background checks and, **10.**4
    benchmark event lessons for, **1.**18–**1.**19, **10.**4
    biological hazards and, **10.**5
    command centers for, **10.**5–**10.**6
    design issues for, **10.**3–**10.**7
        general, **10.**3–**10.**6
        overviews and summaries of, **10.**3, **10.**6
        specific, **10.**6–**10.**7
    downtown properties, **10.**6
    emergency power and, **10.**5
    entrances for, **10.**4
    gaming properties, **10.**6–**10.**7
        facial recognition technology, **10.**7
        mantraps for, **10.**7
        overviews and summaries of, **10.**6
        slots and gaming machines in, **10.**6–**10.**7
    hotels and resorts, **10.**2, **10.**6
    large properties, **10.**6
    litigation issues for, **10.**7–**10.**8
        overviews and summaries of, **10.**7–**10.**8
        slip and fall hazards, **10.**8
    loading docks for, **10.**4
    lobbies and lobby areas of, **10.**4
    money areas of, **10.**5
    operational issues for, **10.**2–**10.**5
        industrial intelligence, **10.**3
        overviews and summaries of, **10.**2
        workforce- and employee-related, **10.**3–**10.**5
    overviews and summaries, **10.**1, **10.**8
    parking garages for, **10.**3–**10.**4
    reference resources (internet) for, **10.**8
    surveillance issues for, **10.**4
    threat assessments for, **10.**1–**10.**2
        of locations, **10.**1–**10.**2
        overviews and summaries of, **10.**1
        of ownership, **10.**2
        of threat types, **10.**2
Hospitals, **8.**1–**8.**32. *See also* Health care facilities
Hostile client checklist, **21.**12
Hot and cold zones, **8.**15
Hotels and resorts, **10.**2, **10.**6
Housing. *See also under individual topics*
    developers, responsibilities, **3.**13
    disaster planning, response, and recovery, **12.**1–**12.**32
    multifamily, **11.**1–**11.**6
H.P. White Laboratories, **29.**9–**29.**10, **29.**12
HPS (high-pressure sodium) lamps, **7.**9
HUD (Department of Housing and Urban Development), **11.**2–**11.**3

Hugo, Victor, **12.**16
Human errors, **4.**10
Human impacts, potential, **4.**11
Hurricanes, **12.**11–**12.**12, **29.**3, **29.**11–**29.**14
    checklists for, **12.**12
    disaster planning, response, and recovery and, **12.**11–**12.**12
        Hurricane Andrew, **12.**11–**12.**12
        hurricane impact resistance, **29.**3, **29.**11–**29.**14
        National Hurricane Center, **12.**11–**12.**12
        overviews and summaries of, **12.**11
        Stafford-Simpson classification scale, **12.**11
HVAC (heating, ventilation, and air conditioning) systems
    for health care facilities, **8.**11, **18.**11–**18.**12

I

IAAM (International Association of Assembly Managers), **1.**13, **4.**7
IAPSC (International Association of Professional Security Consultants), **30.**8
IBC (International Building Code), **18.**12, **23.**3, **29.**14
ICS (incident command system) protocol, **8.**5–**8.**9, **8.**30
ICUs (intensive care units), **8.**20
Identifications systems, **7.**25
IDSs (intrusion detection systems), **7.**18
IEC (International Electrotechnical Commission), **30.**8
IEEE (Institute of Electrical And Electronics Engineers), **30.**8
IFMA (International Facility Management Association), **13.**8–**13.**9
Illegitimate *vs.* legitimate users, **19.**3
Illuminating Engineering Society, **30.**8
Immunity-related issues, **31.**11
Impregnated carbon, **24.**24
IMS (ion mobility spectrometry), **24.**8
Indemnification language, **12.**22–**12.**23
Industrial facilities and office buildings, **13.**1–**13.**10
    benchmark event lessons for, **1.**21, **13.**5, **13.**7
    disaster planning for, **12.**1–**12.**32, **13.**7–**13.**8. *See also* disaster planning, response, and recovery
    federally owned/leased, **7.**1–**7.**30. *See also* Federally owned/leased buildings
    overviews and summaries of, **13.**1, **13.**9
    policies for, **13.**4–**13.**6
        consistent, **13.**4–**13.**5
        establishment of, **13.**5–**13.**6
        screening, **13.**5
    reference resources (print and internet) for, **13.**10
    site selection for, **13.**1–**13.**4
        CPTED (crime prevention through environmental design) and, **13.**1–**13.**4
        facility operations, **13.**3–**13.**4
        liability issues, **13.**2
        lighting, **13.**3

Industrial facilities and office buildings, site selection
for (*Cont.*):
overviews and summaries of, **13.1**–**13.2**
parking garages and lots, **13.3**
perimeter security, **13.3**
physical plants, **13.3**
workplace-related issues for, **13.8**–**13.9**
IFMA (International Facility Management
Association) and, **13.8**
workplace shootings, **13.8**
workplace threats, **13.8**–**13.9**
workplace violence, **13.8**
Industrial intelligence, **10.3**
Industry standards, **30.8**
Infection control, **8.15**–**8.18**, **8.30**
Influence areas, **22.7**–**22.8**
Information cards, buildings, **23.7**–**23.9**
Information dissemination and research, **12.28**
Infrastructure, **2.9**, **2.25**–**2.29**
elements of, **2.25**–**2.29**
failure threats to, **2.9**
In-residence shelters, **12.15**–**12.16**
Insulating glass units, **29.16**
Insurance issue responses, **1.38**, **4.5**–**4.7**, **23.10**,
31.6–**31.7**, **31.13**
architectural planning, **4.5**–**4.7**
coverage assessments, **12.26**–**12.27**
life safety codes, **4.7**
mechanical engineering systems, **4.7**
overviews and summaries of, **4.5**, **23.10**
site planning, **4.5**–**4.7**
technology, **4.7**
terrorism insurance, **1.38**, **31.6**–**31.7**, **31.13**
Intakes, air, **24.14**
Integrations, filters, **24.5**–**24.6**
Interface zones, **6.18**
Interim Antiterrorism/Force Protection construction
Standards, DoD (Department of Defense), **7.14**
Interiors, **6.12**–**6.23**, **9.23**–**9.26**
courthouses, **6.12**–**6.23**
historic preservation guidance for, **9.23**–**9.26**
Interlayers, glass, **29.16**
Internal (recirculated air) filtration, **24.6**–**24.7**, **24.11**
Internal reporting checklists, **11.2**
Internal *vs.* external resources, **4.11**
Internet reference resources. *See also under individual
topics*
for arenas, sports facilities, convention centers, and
performing arts facilities, **4.17**
for benchmark event lessons, **1.40**
for CB (chemical and biological) protection
designs, **24.25**
for commercial high-rise egress systems, **5.9**–**5.10**
for cost estimations, **25.10**
for courthouses, **6.24**
for CPTED (crime prevention through
environmental design), **3.15**

Internet reference resources (*Cont.*):
for disaster planning, response, and recovery,
12.30–**12.32**
for emergency response lessons, **26.12**
for federally owned/leased buildings, **7.28**
for glazing and security glass applications, **29.17**
for health care facilities, **8.31**
for historic preservation guidance, **9.35**
for hospitality facilities, **10.8**
for industrial facilities and office buildings,
13.10
for liability exposures, **31.13**–**31.14**
for lobbies, **14.33**–**14.34**
for master planning, **2.30**
for mechanical, electrical, and fire protection
designs, **23.16**
for multifamily housing, **11.6**
for perimeters, **16.9**
for product selection and specification, **28.16**
for religious institutions and community centers,
17.17
for retail facilities and destinations, **19.14**
for schools, **20.15**
for security technology, **27.19**
for structural protection designs, **22.21**
for women's health centers, **21.15**
Interview rooms, **6.18**
Intruders, armed, **21.13**
Intrusion detection systems, **7.22**–**7.27**
CCTV (closed circuit television) and, **7.25**–**7.27**
communications systems and, **7.27**
duress alarm systems, **7.24**–**7.25**
electronic access systems and, **7.22**
electronic SCCs (security control centers), **7.23**
for federally owned/leased buildings, **7.22**–**7.27**
historical recording and, **7.27**
overviews and summaries of, **7.22**
real-time event recording and, **7.25**
SMSs (security management systems) and,
7.22–**7.25**
Iris scans, **27.9**
IRS (Internal Revenue Service), **7.3**–**7.4**
ISC (Interagency Security Committee), **7.3**, **7.13**,
9.3–**9.4**, **22.3**–**22.4**
ISO (International Organization for Standardization),
30.8
Isolation, **8.17**, **24.14**
of high-threat areas, **24.14**
rooms, **8.17**

J

Jacobs, Jane, **1.12**, **2.5**, **3.1**, **3.4**
Jandura, Kenneth J., **1.15**, **6.1**–**6.24**
Janus, Michael C., **1.31**, **24.1**–**24.25**
Jaudon, Valerie, **16.7**
Jefferson, Thomas, **1.33**
Jeffrey, C. Ray, **3.1**, **3.4**

John Joseph Moakley U.S. Courthouse (Boston, MA), **14.**11–**14.**14
Jones, Casey L., **1.**22, **14.**1–**14.**34
Josal, Lance K., **1.**27, **19.**1–**19.**14
Judd, H. Stanley, **29.**15
Judge benches, **6.**20–**6.**22
Jung, Thomas, **1.**16, **8.**1–**8.**32
Jury boxes, **6.**20–**6.**21
Jury deliberation rooms, **6.**23

K

Kaliniak, Catherine, **1.**36, **29.**1–**29.**18
Keeping Your Jewish Institution Safe, **17.**17
Kelly, Terri, **1.**12, **3.**1–**3.**15
Kennedy, John F., **1.**6, **23.**1, **31.**1
KEVLAR, **2.**25, **9.**21
Key controls and locks, **17.**6–**17.**7
Keypads, **27.**6
Khobar Towers bombing, 1996, **1.**9–**1.**10

L

Laboratories, clinical, **8.**24
Lacing systems, **15.**5
Laminated glass, **29.**2–**29.**3, **29.**16
   definitions of, **29.**16
   overviews and summaries of, **29.**2–**29.**3
   security performances of, **29.**3
   types of, **29.**3
Lamps, **7.**9
Landscape ordinances, **3.**11
Large properties, hospitality facilities, **10.**6
Large-scale blackouts, **8.**22–**8.**23
Large *vs.* small missile impacts, **29.**14
Large *vs.* small schools, **20.**3
Lateral load systems, **22.**8
Lavatories. *See* Toilet rooms and lavatories, schools
Law enforcement cooperation, **11.**3–**11.**4
Leach, Terry L., **1.**15, **7.**1–**7.**29
Leased buildings, federal, **7.**1–**7.**29. *See also* Federally owned/leased buildings
LEED (Leadership in Energy Environmental Design)-certified buildings, **1.**14
Legal communities, responsibilities of, **3.**13–**3.**14
Legitimate *vs.* illegitimate users, **19.**3
LEL (lower explosion limit) detection systems, **18.**12
Lessons, benchmark events, **1.**3–**1.**40, **26.**1–**26.**16. *See also* Benchmark event lessons
Lessons Learned: Emergency Responses to the World Trade Center and the Pentagon Attacks, **26.**7–**26.**16
Letters (sample), liability exposures, **31.**6–**31.**12
Liability-related issues. *See also under individual topics*
   indemnification language, **12.**22–**12.**23
   insurance issue responses, **23.**10

Liability-related issues (*Cont.*):
   liability exposures, **31.**1–**31.**14
      benchmark event lessons for, **31.**1–**31.**14
      case index for, **31.**12–**31.**13
      case studies of, **31.**5
      FEMA (Federal Emergency Management Agency) and, **31.**3–**31.**4
      Good Samaritan laws and, **31.**6, **31.**11
      immunity-related issues and, **31.**11
      legislation for, **31.**6
      liability sources, **31.**2
      Model Engineers' Good Samaritan Act, **31.**6, **31.**13
      New York City Building Code and, **31.**3
      New York State Task Force on Buildings Codes and, **31.**3
      NIST (National Institute of Science and Technology) and, **31.**3
      NSPE (National Society of Professional Engineers) and, **31.**6, **31.**13
      overviews and summaries of, **31.**1–**31.**2
      reference resources (print and internet) for, **31.**9–**31.**14
      risk and vulnerability assessments for, **31.**5
      risk minimization, **31.**4–**31.**6
      sample letters for, **31.**6–**31.**12
      standard of care navigation for, **31.**2–**31.**4
      terrorism insurance for, **31.**6–**31.**7, **31.**13
      U.S. GSA (General Services Administration) and, **31.**4–**31.**5
   for schools, **20.**2–**20.**3
   for site selection, **13.**2
Life safety issues, **4.**7, **5.**2–**5.**4, **12.**19, **12.**25, **25.**9
   cost estimates for, **25.**9
   disaster planning, response, and recovery and, **12.**25
   for fire-resistant planning and design, **12.**19
   guidelines, standards, and codes for, **4.**7
   historic preservation and, **9.**7
   safe areas and, **5.**2–**5.**4
   systems for, **25.**9
Lighting, **5.**4, **7.**8–**7.**12
   ballasts, **7.**10
   circuiting requirements of, **7.**12
   for commercial high-rise egress systems, **5.**4
   for federally owned/leased buildings, **7.**8–**7.**9
   fixtures, **7.**10–**7.**11
   flexibility characteristics of, **7.**12
   fluorescent lamps, **7.**9
   for high-rise towers, **5.**4
   historic preservation guidance for, **9.**8–**9.**10
   HPS (high-pressure sodium) lamps, **7.**9
   light sources, **7.**8–**7.**9
   luminaire mounting heights and locations, **7.**12
   maintenance for, **7.**10–**7.**11
   metal halide lamps, **7.**9
   obstructions of, **7.**11–**7.**12
   optical controls for, **7.**11
   overviews and summaries of, **7.**8

Lighting (*Cont.*):
  performance and, **7.**11
  for religious institutions and community centers, **17.**11
  selection criteria for, **7.**9
  sources and source types for, **7.**8–**7.**11
  source types, **7.**9–**7.**11
  surface reflectance for, **7.**12
  uniformity issues of, **7.**11
Lilien, Noelle, **1.**37, **31.**1–**31.**14
Limited ductility, **22.**15
Liners, walls, **9.**24–**9.**26
Line-X, **2.**25
Lites, definitions of, **29.**16
Litigation issues, **10.**7–**10.**8
  for hospitality facilities, **10.**7–**10.**8
  slip and fall hazards, **10.**8
Live loads, **22.**20
Lloyd D. George U.S. Courthouse (Las Vegas, NV),
    14.21, **14.**23–**14.**24
Loading docks, **2.**26, **6.**10, **10.**4, **25.**8
Loads, **18.**13, **22.**5–**22.**11
  abnormal, **22.**5–**22.**6
  blast, **22.**10–**22.**11
  generator, **18.**13
  gravity load systems, **22.**7
  lateral load systems, **22.**8
Lobbies, **14.**1–**14.**34
  benchmark event lessons for, **1.**22–**1.**23, **14.**1–**14.**2
  case studies of, **14.**10–**14.**30
    Alfonse M. D'Amato U.S. courthouse and Federal
        Building (Islip, NY), **14.**18, **14.**20–**14.**23
    Byron G. Rogers Federal Building (Denver, CO),
        14.14, **14.**17–**14.**19
    John Joseph Moakley U.S. Courthouse (Boston,
        MA), **14.**11–**14.**14
    Lloyd D. George U.S. Courthouse (Las Vegas,
        NV), **14.**21–**14.**22
    overviews and summaries of, **14.**10–**14.**11
    Peter Rodino Jr. Federal Building (Newark, NJ),
        14.22, **14.**25–**14.**26
    Sam M. Gibbons U.S. Courthouse (Tampa, FL),
        14.28, **14.**31–**14.**32
    Thomas F. Eagleton U.S. Courthouse (St. Louis,
        MO), **14.**27–**14.**30
    U.S. Courthouse (Gulfport, MS), **14.**17,
        14.19–**14.**21
    U.S. Federal Courthouse (Covington, KY),
        14.14–**14.**16
    William S. Moorhead Federal Building
        (Pittsburgh, PA), **14.**25–**14.**28
  cost estimations for, **25.**7
  *Design Notebook for Federal Building Lobby
      Security* and, **14.**32–**14.**33
  entrances to, **14.**3–**14.**4
    entrance-exit separations, **14.**3
    overviews and summaries of, **14.**3
    queuing spaces, **14.**3–**14.**4

Lobbies (*Cont.*):
  First Impressions program, **14.**2
  free zones for, **14.**4–**14.**5
  guidelines, standards, and codes for, **14.**1–**14.**2,
      14.33–**14.**34
    of FPS (Federal Protective Service), **14.**1–**14.**2
    of GSA (U.S. General Services Administration),
        14.1–**14.**2
    listing of, **14.**33–**14.**34
    of PBS (Public Buildings Service), **14.**1
    of USMS (U.S. Marshal Service), **14.**1–**14.**2
  historic preservation guidance for, **9.**26–**9.**30
  overviews and summaries of, **14.**1–**14.**2. **14.**30
  reference resources (print and internet), **14.**33–**14.**34
  screening stations for, **14.**5–**14.**8
    overviews and summaries of, **14.**5–**14.**7
    station arrangement and operations, **14.**7–**14.**8
  technology and equipment for, **14.**9–**14.**10
    metal detectors, **14.**9
    overviews and summaries of, **14.**9
    secure areas, **14.**9–**14.**10
    x-ray machines, **14.**9
Local codes, **30.**8–**30.**9
Location factors, cost estimations, **25.**5
Locke, John, **16.**7
Locker rooms, **20.**14
Lockers, schools, **20.**13–**20.**14
Locks and key controls, **17.**6–**17.**7, **27.**6
Long-range monitoring systems, **24.**9
Low degree of risk (threat level 1), **4.**9
Luminaire mounting heights and locations, **7.**12

M

Magnetic contact switches, **15.**3–**15.**4
  balanced, **15.**4
  simple, **15.**3
Magnetometers, **14.**12, **27.**10
Main street retail facilities, **19.**3–**19.**5
Makeup air filtration, **24.**6
Mall entrances, **19.**9
Management systems, building, **18.**13–**18.**14
Mantraps, **10.**7
Masonry walls, **22.**19
Master planning, **2.**1–**2.**30
  benchmark event lessons for, **1.**11–**1.**12, **2.**1–**2.**2
  for blast designs, **2.**21–**2.**23
    blast hazard injuries and, **2.**22
    criteria for, **2.**22
    overviews and summaries of, **2.**21–**2.**22
    progressive collapse and, **2.**22–**2.**23
    structural framing systems and, **2.**23
  characteristics of, **2.**4
  construction site issues of, **2.**23–**2.**26
    blast curtains, **2.**25
    building planning, **2.**26
    exterior wall construction, **2.**23–**2.**24
    infrastructure elements, **2.**25–**2.**26

Master planning, construction site issues of (*Cont.*):
loading docks, **2**.26
mullion and window support systems, **2**.24–**2**.25
overviews and summaries of, **2**.23
roofs and roofing, **2**.26
window film, **2**.25
windows, **2**.24
CPTED (crime prevention through environmental design) and, **2**.5. *See also* CPTED (crime prevention through environmental design)
goals and objectives of, **2**.2–**2**.5
operational issues for, **2**.27–**2**.28
emergency planning, **2**.28
overviews and summaries of, **2**.27–**2**.28
security officers and personnel, **2**.27–**2**.28
staff training, **2**.28
overviews and summaries of, **2**.1–**2**.2, **2**.28
processes for, **2**.3
reference resources (print and internet) for, **2**.30
risk and vulnerability assessments, **2**.9–**2**.14
consequences of, **2**.12
cost-related issues of, **2**.13–**2**.14
critical nature of, **2**.11–**2**.12
elements of, **2**.15
mitigation-related issues, **2**.12–**2**.13
occurrence probabilities and impacts, **2**.12
overviews and summaries of, **2**.9–**2**.11
security deficiencies and, **2**.11
special issues of, **2**.11
threat types, **2**.12
threat verification, **2**.12
security assessment elements for, **2**.5–**2**.8
checklists for, **2**.7
critical asset identification, **2**.6–**2**.8
defensive tiers (rings of defense), **2**.5
overviews and summaries of, **2**.5–**2**.6
performance criteria, **2**.6–**2**.7
solutions implementation, **2**.6
threat assessments and, **2**.8–**2**.9
for security solutions, **2**.14–**2**.22
berm and blast wall construction for, **2**.19
CCTV (closed circuit television), **2**.18–**2**.19
fences and fencing for, **2**.16–**2**.17
MIFs (material/mail inspection facilities) for, **2**.17, **2**.20–**2**.21
overviews and summaries of, **2**.14
for parking, **2**.17–**2**.18
for perimeters (inner), **2**.14
for perimeters (outer), **2**.14
security posts and guard houses for, **2**.19
SOCs (security operations centers) for, **2**.20
VCCs (visitor control centers), **2**.20
vehicle barriers for, **2**.18
for vehicular circulation, **2**.16–**2**.17
vetting areas for, **2**.19
security surveys and, **2**.8–**2**.9
building security checklists, **2**.10

Master planning, security surveys and (*Cont.*):
criminal threats, **2**.9
elements of, **2**.9–**2**.11
environmental threats, **2**.9
infrastructure failure threats, **2**.9
operations security checklists, **2**.11
overviews and summaries of, **2**.8–**2**.9
secure perimeter checklists, **2**.10
service interruption threats, **2**.9
site planning checklists, **2**.10
terrorism threats, **2**.8
teams for, **2**.2–**2**.3
technology and, **2**.26–**2**.27
terminology for, **2**.29
U.S. governmental departments and bodies and
Department of Homeland Security, **2**.6
DoD (Department of Defense), **2**.6
GSA (General Services Administration), **2**.5–**2**.6
Materials and technology aspects, **27**.1–**29**.18. *See also under individual topics*
glazing and security glass applications, **29**.1–**29**.18
product selection and specification, **28**.1–**28**.18
security technology, **27**.3–**27**.20
Maternity units, **8**.19
Mats, pressure-sensitive, **15**.5
McCarthy, Bill, **1**.11, **2**.1–**2**.30
McCormick, John, **12**.7
Mechanical, electrical, and fire protection designs, **23**.1–**23**.16
benchmark event lessons for, **1**.30–**1**.31, **23**.1, **23**.3, **23**.7, **23**.15
BICs (building information cards) and, **23**.7–**23**.9
CB (chemical and biological) protection designs and, **24**.15–**24**.16
cost estimations for, **25**.9
electrical services, **23**.3–**23**.5
fire alarm systems, **23**.7–**23**.10
fire suppression systems, **23**.5–**23**.7
guidelines, standards, and codes for, **23**.2–**23**.3
ICC (International Building Code), **23**.3
New York City Building Code, **23**.3
NFPA (National Electrical Code), **23**.3
overviews and summaries of, **23**.2–**23**.3
insurance issue responses for, **23**.10
overviews and summaries of, **23**.1–**23**.2, **23**.15
reference resources (print and internet) for, **23**.15–**23**.16
risk and vulnerability assessments for, **23**.1–**23**.2, **23**.2
checklists for, **23**.2
overview and summaries of, **23**.1–**23**.2
smoke management systems, **23**.14–**23**.15
ventilation systems, **23**.10–**23**.14
water services, **23**.3–**24**.5
wireless connectivity and, **23**.10
Mechanical rooms, **18**.10–**18**.11, **24**.15
access to, **18**.10–**18**.11

Mechanical rooms (*Cont.*):
  CB (chemical and biological) protection designs
    for, **24**.15
Media briefing areas, **8**.27
Media fact sheet checklists, **12**.28
Medical facilities, **8**.1–**8**.32, **21**.1–**21**.16. *See also
    under individual topics*
  health care facilities, **8**.1–**8**.32
  women's health centers, **21**.1–**21**.16
Membrane behaviors, **22**.20
Metal detectors, **7**.18, **14**.9, **27**.10
Metal halide lamps, **7**.9
Microswitches, **15**.4
MIFs (material/mail inspection facilities), **2**.17,
    2.20–**2**.21
Millwork, ballistic-resistant, **6**.21
*Minimum Design Loads for Buildings and Other
    Structures,* **22**.6
Mintzer, Lewis J., **1**.33, **26**.1–**26**.16
Missile impacts, large *vs.* small, **29**.14
Missing person and victim status issues, **8**.27
Mitigation, blasts, **29**.3–**29**.8. *See also* Blast-related
    issues
Mitigation-related issues, **2**.12–**2**.13
Mobile health care units, **8**.25–**8**.26
Model Engineers' Good Samaritan Act, **31**.6, **31**.13
Modifications, historic structures, **9**.5. *See also*
    Historic preservation guidance
Moment continuity, **22**.20
Money areas, **10**.5
Mounting heights and locations, luminaire, **7**.12
Moynihan, Daniel Patrick, **1**.5–**1**.6, **5**.1, **19**.1
MS (mass spectrometry), **24**.8
M/Ss (medical/surgical units), **8**.19–**8**.20
MTA (Metropolitan Transportation Authority),
    16.6–**16**.7
MTBF (mean time between failures), **23**.1–**23**.2
MTTR (mean time to repair), **23**.1–**23**.2
Mullion and window support systems, **2**.24–**2**.25
Multifamily housing, **11**.1–**11**.6
  benchmark event lessons for, **1**.19, **11**.1
  checklists for, **11**.2–**11**.5
    community security measures, **11**.5
    contractors and employees, **11**.3
    internal reporting, **11**.2
    law enforcement cooperation, **11**.3–**11**.4
    operational management, **11**.2
    resident application verification, **11**.3–**11**.4
    resident communications, **11**.2
    unit inspections, **11**.3
  FISA (Foreign Intelligence Surveillance Act) and,
    11.4
  NMHC/NAA JLP (National Multi Housing
    Council/National Apartment Association Joint
    Legislative Program) and, **11**.1–**11**.5
  overviews and summaries of, **11**.1, **11**.5
  PATRIOT/USA Act and, **11**.4
  reference resources (print and internet) for, **11**.5–**11**.6

Multiple perimeters, **20**.4–**20**.5
Mumford, Lewis, **1**.12
Munich Olympics, 1972, **1**.13
Museums and cultural facilities, **15**.1–**15**.6
  assessments for, **15**.2–**15**.3
    security surveys, **15**.2–**15**.3
    threat, **15**.2–**15**.3
  benchmark event lessons for, **1**.23
  detectors for, **15**.2–**15**.5
    alarm elements, **15**.3
    audio discriminators, **15**.4
    audio glass break detectors, **15**.4
    contact sensors, **15**.3–**15**.4
    foil tape systems, **15**.4
    glass window bugs, **15**.4
    lacing systems, **15**.5
    magnetic contact switches, balanced, **15**.4
    magnetic contact switches, simple, **15**.3
    microswitches, **15**.4
    motion, **15**.5
    overviews and summaries of, **15**.2–**15**.3
    photoelectric beams, **15**.5
    plunger switches, **15**.4
    pressure-sensitive mats, **15**.5
    shock and impact sensors, **15**.4
    vibrators, **15**.4
  electronic building protection for, **15**.2–**15**.3
  operational issues for, **15**.6
  overviews and summaries of, **15**.1–**15**.2, **15**.6
  reference resources (print) for, **15**.6
Musica, Frank D., **1**.20
Mutual aid agreements, **28**.15

N

Nadel, Barbara A., **1**.3–**1**.40, **12**.1–**12**.32, **13**.1–**13**.10,
    21.1–**21**.15
  benchmark event lessons and, **1**.3–**1**.40
  disaster planning, response, and recovery and,
    12.1–**12**.32
  industrial facilities and office buildings and,
    13.1–**13**.10
  women's health centers and, **21**.1–**21**.15
National Association of Chemical Distributors, **30**.9
National Capital Planning Commission, **9**.33
National Capital Urban Design and Security Plan,
    16.1–**16**.2
National Clearing House for Educational Facilities
    and, **20**.2–**20**.3, **20**.6
National Conference of State Historical Preservation
    Officers, **9**.32
National Crime Prevention Council, **3**.15
National Flood Insurance Program, **12**.8
National Historical Preservation Act, **9**.3
National Hurricane Center, **12**.11–**12**.12, **29**.13
National Register of Historic Places, **9**.5–**9**.6
National Weather Service, **29**.13
Natural disasters, **12**.6–**12**.7
Navigation, standard of care, **31**.2–**31**.4

NCPC (National Capital Planning Committee), **9**.4
NCPC (National Crime Prevention Council), **1**.12
NCR (Nuclear Regulatory Commission), **30**.9
NEC (National Electric Code), **18**.12
NEHRP (National Earthquake Hazards Reduction Program) guidelines, **29**.14
Neighborhood-related responsibilities, **3**.14
NEMA (National Electrical Manufacturers Association), **30**.8
Newman, Oscar, **2**.5, **3**.4–**3**.5
New Mexico wildfires, 2000, **1**.21, **12**.16–**12**.17
New York Aquarium, **16**.3–**16**.4
New York City Board of Education, **16**.8
New York City Building Code, **5**.2–**5**.4, **23**.3, **31**.3
New York City Department of Parks and Recreation, **16**.5
New York City Task Force on Buildings Codes, **1**.14–**1**.15, **31**.3
New York State DOH (Department of Health) and, **8**.5–**8**.6
NFPA (National Fire Protection Association), **23**.3, **30**.5–**30**.8
NIH (National Institute of Health), **18**.2
NIJ (National Institute of Justice), **29**.12
NIST (National Institute of Science and Technology), **30**.9, **31**.3
NMHC/NAA JLP (National Multi Housing Council/National Apartment Association Joint Legislative Program), **11**.1–**11**.5
NRC (Nuclear Regulatory Commission), **30**.6–**30**.9
NSPE (National Society of Professional Engineers), **31**.6, **31**.13
NSSEs (National Security Special Events), **4**.13–**4**.16
  crowd management for, **4**.14–**4**.15
  design checklists for, **4**.15
  final security details for, **4**.16
  overviews and summaries of, **1**.13–**1**.14, **4**.13–**4**.14
  screenings for, **4**.14
  security levels for, **4**.13, **4**.15
Nurseries and maternity units, **8**.19
Nursing homes, **8**.3–**8**.4
Nursing units, **8**.18–**8**.20
NYS DOCS (New York State Department of Correctional Services), **28**.1–**28**.18

O

Obsolescence issues, **28**.12–**28**.13
Occupancy issues, **3**.15
Occurrence probabilities and impacts, **2**.12
OCUNUS *vs.* CONUS terrorist groups, **22**.6
Office buildings, **13**.1–**13**.10. *See also* Industrial facilities and office buildings
Oklahoma City bombing, 1995, **1**.7–**1**.11, **1**.15, **1**.22–**1**.23, **1**.30, **1**.37, **4**.3–**4**.4, **7**.1–**7**.3, **22**.3, **22**.7–**22**.8, **22**.15, **22**.19, **30**.4
Operational issues. *See also under individual topics*
  historic preservation guidance and, **9**.6–**9**.7
  for hospitality facilities, **10**.2–**10**.3

Operational issues (*Cont.*):
  master planning and, **2**.27–**2**.28
  for museums and cultural facilities, **15**.6
  operational management, **11**.2, **28**.13–**28**.15
  operations, definitions of, **2**.29, **19**.3
  operations security checklists, **2**.11
  product selection and specification, **28**.13–**28**.15
  for retail facilities and destinations, **19**.11–**19**.12
Optical controls, lighting, **7**.11
OSHA (Occupational Safety and Health Act), **30**.8
Outline of History, **22**.3
Ownership-related issues, hospitality facilities, **10**.2
Ozenfant, Amedee, **16**.1

P

Parent drop-off/pick-up zones, **20**.7–**20**.8
Park, Sharon C., **1**.17, **9**.1–**9**.36
Parking, **6**.5–**6**.6. *See also under individual topics*
  for courthouses, **6**.5–**6**.6
  for federally owned/leased buildings, **7**.6–**7**.7
  garages and lots, **10**.3–**10**.4, **13**.3, **19**.9
  for hospitality facilities, **10**.3–**10**.4
  master planning for, **2**.17–**2**.18
  for schools, **20**.8
  site selection for, **13**.3
  for women's health centers, **21**.3–**21**.4
Passive systems, **9**.14, **24**.24
Patient care nursing units, **8**.18–**8**.20
Patient tracking and record keeping, **8**.9
PATRIOT/USA Act, **11**.4, **18**.1
Patterns of Global Terrorism, **22**.5
Pauls, J.L., **5**.3
PBS (Public Buildings Service), **14**.1
PECs (product evaluation committees), **28**.6–**28**.10
Pei Cobb Freed & Partners, **14**.11
Penetrations, **20**.4–**20**.5, **24**.14
Pentagon (2001 terrorist event), **1**.4, **1**.17–**1**.18, **1**.30, **1**.34, **7**.3, **22**.12, **26**.1–**26**.4
Penzias, Arno, **27**.3
Percent for Art program, **1**.23, **16**.2
Performance criteria, **2**.6–**2**.7
Performance of Exterior Windows, Curtain Walls, Doors and Storm Shutters by Wind-Borne Debris in Hurricanes, **29**.11–**29**.12
Performing arts facilities, **4**.3–**4**.18. *See also* Arenas, sports facilities, convention centers, and performing arts facilities
Perimeters, **7**.15–**7**.18, **16**.1–**16**.10
  Art Commission, City of New York and, **16**.1–**16**.2, **16**.8–**16**.9
  benchmark event lessons for, **16**.2
  buildings as, **20**.4
  case studies of, **16**.2–**16**.8
    Blue Heron Nature Park, **16**.5
    fences and fencing, **16**.3–**16**.4, **16**.7–**16**.8
    gates, **16**.5–**16**.7
    MTA (Metropolitan Transportation Authority), **16**.6–**16**.7

Perimeters, case studies of (*Cont.*):
New York Aquarium, **16.3–16.4**
overviews and summaries of, **16.2–16.3**
PS (Public School) 234, New York City,
16.3–16.4
Studio Museum in Harlem, **16.7**
Townsend Harris High School, **16.8**
walls, **16.3**
checklists for, **2.10**
cost estimations for, **25.6–25.7**
courthouses, **6.7–6.12**
definitions of, **2.29**
designs for, **16.1–16.2**
overviews and summaries of, **16.1–16.2**
Percent for Art program and, **16.2**
quality of, **16.2**
entry controls for, **7.15–7.18**
fixed arm drop barrier systems, **7.17–7.18**
overviews and summaries of, **7.15–7.16**
portable arm drop barrier systems, **7.17**
vehicle barriers, **7.16–7.17**
of federally owned/leased buildings, **7.15–7.18**
fences and fencing for, **7.17–7.18**, **20.4–20.7**
overviews and summaries of, **7.17–7.18**
for playfields, **20.6–20.7**
in schools, **20.4–20.7**
guidelines for, **16.1–16.2**
*Designing for Security: Using Art and Design to
Improve Security* and, **16.1–16.2**, **16.8–16.9**
*National Capital Urban Design and Security
Plan,* **16.1–16.2**
inner, **2.14**
master planning for, **2.14**
multiple, **20.4–20.5**
outer, **2.14**
overviews and summaries of, **16.1**
reference resources (print and internet) for, **16.9**
for schools, **20.4**
site selection and, **13.3**
Personnel screenings, **18.10**
Peter Rodino Jr. Federal Building (Newark, NJ),
14.22, **14.**25–**14.**26
Phifer, Jean Parker, **1.**23, **16.1–16.**9
Phoenix Project, **3.**2
Photoelectric beams, **15.**5
Photolaser scanning, **9.**33
Photometry, flame, **24.**8
Physical plants, site selection, **13.**3
Pick-up zones. *See* Drop-off/pick-up zones, schools
Planning and design aspects, **4.1–21.**16. *See also
under individual topics*
for arenas, sports facilities, convention centers, and
performing arts facilities, **4.**3–**4.**18
for commercial high-rise egress systems, **5.1–5.**10
for courthouses, **6.1–6.**24
for CPTED (crime prevention through environmental design), **3.**9–**3.**10, **3.**14–**3.**15

Planning and design aspects (*Cont.*):
disaster planning, response, and recovery,
12.1.–**12.**32
emergency control plan development and maintenance, **2.**28, **28.**13–**28.**14
for federally owned/leased buildings, **7.1–7.**30
for health care facilities, **8.1–8.**32
historic preservation guidance, **9.1–9.**36
for hospitality facilities, **10.1–10.**8
for industrial facilities and office buildings,
13.1–13.10
for lobbies, **14.1–14.**34
master planning, **2.1–2.**30
for multifamily housing, **11.1–11.**6
for museums and cultural facilities, **15.1–15.**6
for perimeters, **16.1–16.**10
plan elements, **18.**3
for religious institutions and community centers,
17.1–17.18
for research facilities, **18.1–18.**16, **18.**2–**18.**3
for retail facilities and destinations, **19.1–19.**14
for schools, **20.1–20.**16
for security technology, **27.**16–**27.**17
Plates, floor, **5.**7
Playfields, schools, **20.**6–**20.**7
Plinths, **9.**34
Point detectors, **24.**8–**24.**9
Policy-related issues. *See also under individual topics*
civil liberties issues and, **20.**2–**20.**3
for CPTED (crime prevention through environmental design), **3.**6–**3.**7
for industrial facilities and office buildings,
13.4–**13.**6
liability exposures and, **31.1–31.**14
policies, definitions of, **2.**29
for schools, **20.1–20.**3
for women's health centers, **21.**7
Portable arm drop barrier systems, **7.**17
Portable classrooms, **20.**10
Postdisaster planning, **9.**7–**9.**8
Postemergency procedures development, **28.**16
Potential impacts, **4.**10–**4.**11
business, **4.**11
emergency, **4.**10
human, **4.**11
property, **4.**11
Powered/electric fences, **27.**5–**27.**6
Power outages, **12.**5–**12.**7
PPE (personal protective equipment), **8.**17
PPGG (Planned Parenthood Golden Gate), **1.**28, **21.**1,
21.7–**21.**8, **21.**15
Practice drills, evacuations, **1.**10
Preservation, historic, **9.1–9.**36. *See also* Historic
preservation guidance
Pressure-sensitive mats, **15.**5
Print reference resources. *See also under
individual topics*

Print reference resources (*Cont.*):
  for arenas, sports facilities, convention centers, and performing arts facilities, **4**.16
  for benchmark event lessons, **1**.39–**1**.40
  for CB (chemical and biological) protection designs, **24**.25
  for commercial high-rise egress systems, **5**.9
  for courthouses, **6**.24
  for CPTED (crime prevention through environmental design), **3**.15
  for disaster planning, response, and recovery, **12**.29–**12**.30
  for federally owned/leased buildings, **7**.28
  for glazing and security glass applications, **29**.16
  for health care facilities, **8**.30
  for historic preservation guidance, **9**.34–**9**.35
  for industrial facilities and office buildings, **13**.10
  for liability exposures, **31**.9–**31**.13
  for lobbies, **14**.33–**14**.34
  for master planning, **2**.30
  for mechanical, electrical, and fire protection designs, **23**.15–**23**.16
  for multifamily housing, **11**.5–**11**.6
  for museums and cultural facilities, **15**.6
  for perimeters, **16**.9
  for product selection and specification, **28**.16
  for retail facilities and destinations, **19**.14
  for schools, **20**.15
  for structural protection designs, **22**.20–**22**.21
  for women's health centers, **21**.15
Private zones, **6**.16–**6**.17
Product selection and specification, **28**.1–**28**.18
  benchmark event lessons for, **28**.3–**28**.4
  community involvement in, **28**.5–**28**.6
  correctional facilities and, **28**.1–**28**.18
  evaluation processes for, **28**.5–**28**.10
    benefits of, **28**.10
    overviews and summaries of, **28**.5–**28**.6
    PECs (product evaluation committees) and, **28**.5–**28**.11
    technology and equipment subject to evaluation, **28**.6–**28**.9
  executive involvement in, **28**.3–**28**.5
  historical perspectives of, **28**.3
  implementation factors and, **28**.5
  low bid considerations of, **28**.13
  NYS DOCS (New York State Department of Correctional Services) and, **28**.1–**28**.18
  operational involvement in, **28**.13–**28**.15
    emergency control plan development and maintenance, **28**.13–**28**.14
    facility communication centers, **28**.14
    mutual aid agreements, **28**.15
    postemergency procedures development, **28**.16
  overviews and summaries of, **28**.1–**28**.4, **28**.15–**28**.16
  reference resources (print and internet) for, **28**.16

Product selection and specification (*Cont.*):
  staff involvement in, **28**.11–**28**.13
    overviews and summaries of, **28**.10–**28**.12
    staff resistance and, **28**.10–**28**.12
    staff training and, **28**.13
  technology obsolescence issues and, **28**.12–**28**.13
  technology program elements, **28**.4–**28**.5
  vendor-related issues of, **28**.12
Programming, planning, and design issues, **20**.10–**20**.14
  administrative areas, **20**.13
  checklists for, **20**.11
  circulation systems, **20**.10–**20**.11
  classrooms, **20**.14
  common areas, **20**.13
  elements of, **20**.12
  hallways, **20**.12–**20**.13
  locker rooms, **20**.14
  lockers, **20**.13–**20**.14
  overviews and summaries of, **20**.10
  for schools, **20**.10–**20**.14
  supervision and, **20**.12–**20**.13
  surveillance maximization and, **20**.13
  toilet rooms, **20**.14
Progressive collapse, **7**.13–**7**.14
  blast designs and, **2**.22–**2**.23
  cost estimations and, **25**.8
  definitions of, **2**.29, **22**.20
  DoD (Department of Defense) Interim Antiterrorism/Force Protection construction Standards and, **7**.14
  of federally owned/leased buildings, **7**.13–**7**.14
  master planning and, **2**.22–**2**.23
  overviews and summaries of, **7**.13–**7**.14
  structural member response limits and, **7**.14
  structural protection designs and, **22**.5–**22**.6, **22**.20
Property and records protection, **12**.26
Property impacts, potential, **4**.11
Protection designs, **22**.1–**24**.26. *See also under individual topics*
  CB (chemical and biological) protection designs, **24**.1–**24**.26
  mechanical, electrical, and fire protection designs, **23**.1–**23**.16
  structural protection designs, **22**.3–**22**.22
Protection levels, **7**.13
Protester checklists, **21**.13
PS (Public School) 234, New York City, **16**.3–**16**.4
Public agencies, responsibilities of, **3**.12–**3**.13
Public areas, ancillary, **8**.27
Public Health Security and Bioterrorism Preparedness and Response Act, **18**.1
Public relations, **12**.27–**12**.29. *See also* Crisis management and public relations
Public seating, courtrooms, **6**.21
PVB (polyvinyl butyral), **29**.2–**29**.3, **29**.16

Q

Queuing spaces, **14.3–14.**4

Quotations. *See also under individual authors and titles*
authors of
Adams, Ansel, **1.**39
anonymous, **18.**1
Brake, Pete, **7.**1
Breyer, Stephen, **14.**1
Burke, Edmund, **8.**1, **8.**28
Burnham, Daniel, **21.**1
Buscaglia, Leo, **12.**1
Calhoun, Jr., John C., **1.**29
Churchill, Winston, **1.**3
Coolidge, Calvin, **29.**1
Da Vinci, Leonardo, **26.**1
De Becker, Gavin, **6.**1, **13.**1
De Saint-Exupery, Antoine, **1.**33
Douglas, William O., **28.**1
Duncan, Donnie, **4.**3
editors, *American Heritage Dictionary of the English Language,* **19.**1
Einstein, Albert, **18.**14
Feiner, Edward A., **1.**6
Feynman, Richard, **8.**28
Ford, Henry, **23.**1
Gandhi, Mahatma, **20.**1
Gwathmey, Charles, **9.**1
Harper, Charles, **12.**12
Hickman, Tim, **4.**3
Hillel, **17.**1
Hoover, Herbert, **1.**32
Hugo, Victor, **12.**16
Jacobs, Jane, **3.**1
Jefferson, Thomas, **1.**33
Judd, H. Stanley, **29.**15
Kennedy, John F., **1.**6, **23.**1, **31.**1
Locke, John, **16.**7
McCormick, John, **12.**7
Moynihan, Daniel Patrick, **1.**5–**1.**6, **5.**1
Mumford, Lewis, **1.**12
Ozenfant, Amedee, **16.**1
Penzias, Arno, **27.**3
PPGG (Planned Parenthood Golden Gate), **21.**1
Roosevelt, Franklin D., **1.**3, **24.**1
Roosevelt, Theodore, **1.**37, **11.**1
Santayana, George, **1.**3
Shakespeare, William, **6.**1
Sills, Beverly, **15.**1
Strife, Eric, **10.**1
Swift, Jonathan, **30.**3
Tetreau, Jean, **8.**28
Warner, Charles Dudley, **25.**3
Weisberg, Samuel, **1.**8
Wells, H. G., **22.**3
Wilde, Oscar, **24.**1
Wilkinson, Paul, **4.**5

Quotations, authors of (*Cont.*):
Williams, Scott, **4.**4
Woodcock, Douglas P., **6.**1
cited from
American Heritage Dictionary of the English Language, **19.**1
Death and Life of Great American Cities, **3.**1
Gift of Fear, The, **13.**1
Outline of History, **22.**3
Security Reference Guide, **21.**1

R

Racking, **29.**16
Rapid exhaust facilitation, **24.**11
Rapid sheltering facilitation for, **24.**11
Readers, **6.**9, **18.**9–**18.**10, **27.**6–**27.**7
biometric, **6.**9, **18.**9–**18.**10
card, **6.**9, **18.**9–**18.**10, **27.**6–**27.**7
Real-time event recording, **7.**25
Recirculated air filtration, **24.**6–**24.**7, **24.**11
Recording, **7.**25–**7.**27
historical, **7.**27
real-time event recording, **7.**25
Record keeping and protection, **12.**25–**12.**26
Recovery times, **8.**25–**8.**26
Red Cross, **12.**6–**12.**7
Redundancy, **5.**6, **18.**13, **22.**4, **22.**9–**22.**10
back-up systems and, **18.**13, **22.**4
of egress systems, **5.**6
structural, **22.**9–**22.**10
Reference resources. *See also under individual topics*
Internet
for arenas, sports facilities, convention centers, and performing arts facilities, **4.**17
for benchmark event lessons, **1.**40
for CB (chemical and biological) protection designs, **24.**25
for commercial high-rise egress systems, **5.**9–**5.**10
for cost estimations, **25.**10
for courthouses, **6.**24
for CPTED (crime prevention through environmental design), **3.**15
for disaster planning, response, and recovery, **12.**30–**12.**32
for emergency response lessons, **26.**12
for federally owned/leased buildings, **7.**28
for glazing and security glass applications, **29.**17
for health care facilities, **8.**31
for historic preservation guidance, **9.**35
for hospitality facilities, **10.**8
for industrial facilities and office buildings, **13.**10
for liability exposures, **31.**13–**31.**14
for lobbies, **14.**33–**14.**34
for master planning, **2.**30
for mechanical, electrical, and fire protection designs, **23.**16

Reference resources, Internet (*Cont.*):
    for multifamily housing, **11.**6
    for perimeters, **16.**9
    for product selection and specification, **28.**16
    for religious institutions and community centers,
        17.17
    for retail facilities and destinations, **19.**14
    for schools, **20.**15
    for security technology, **27.**19
    for structural protection designs, **22.**21
    for women's health centers, **21.**15
  print
    for arenas, sports facilities, convention centers,
        and performing arts facilities, **4.**16
    for benchmark event lessons, **1.**39–**1.**40
    case index, liability exposures, **31.**12–**31.**13
    for CB (chemical and biological) protection
        designs, **24.**25
    for commercial high-rise egress systems, **5.**9
    for courthouses, **6.**24
    for CPTED (crime prevention through environ-
        mental design), **3.**15
    for disaster planning, response, and recovery,
        12.29–**12.**30
    for federally owned/leased buildings, **7.**28
    for glazing and security glass applications, **29.**16
    for health care facilities, **8.**30
    for historic preservation guidance, **9.**34–**9.**35
    for industrial facilities and office buildings,
        13.10
    for liability exposures, **31.**9–**31.**13
    for lobbies, **14.**33–**14.**34
    for master planning, **2.**30
    for mechanical, electrical, and fire protection
        designs, **23.**15–**23.**16
    for multifamily housing, **11.**5–**11.**6
    for museums and cultural facilities, **15.**6
    for perimeters, **16.**9
    for product selection and specification, **28.**16
    for retail facilities and destinations, **19.**14
    for schools, **20.**15
    for structural protection designs, **22.**20–**22.**21
    for women's health centers, **21.**15
Reflectance, surface, **7.**12
Regional perspectives, health care facilities, **8.**4–**8.**6,
    8.30
Regional retail facilities, **19.**5
Registration and waiting areas, **21.**4–**21.**6
Rehabilitation standards, **9.**3
Religious institutions and community centers,
    17.1–**17.**18
  benchmark event lessons for, **1.**25–**1.**26
  CPTED (crime prevention through environmental
    design) for, **17.**1
  overviews and summaries of, **17.**1
  physical security of, **17.**4–**17.**6, **17.**16
    access controls, **17.**5–**17.**6

Religious institutions and community centers, physical
    security of (*Cont.*):
    alarms and alarm systems, **17.**7–**17.**8
    car and truck bombs and, **17.**13
    disaster recovery planning, **17.**16
    ETRPs (explosive threat response plans),
        17.12–**17.**13
    fences and fencing, **17.**10–**17.**11
    fire doors, **17.**10
    key controls and locks, **17.**6–**17.**7
    overviews and summaries of, **17.**4–**17.**5
    protective devices, **17.**7–**17.**8
    protective lighting, **17.**11
    suicide bombers and, **17.**13–**17.**15
    target hardening and, **17.**15–**17.**16
    technology selection, **17.**8
    windows and doors, **17.**9–**17.**10
    WMDs (weapons of mass destruction) and, **17.**13
  reference resources (internet) for, **17.**17
  security philosophies for, **17.**1–**17.**2
  security plans for, **17.**2–**17.**4
Replacement glazing, **9.**20–**9.**21
Research and information dissemination, **12.**28
Research facilities, **18.**1–**18.**16
  ASHRAE (American Society of Heating
    Refrigeration and Air Conditioning Engineers)
    guidelines and standards for, **18.**11–**18.**14
    building management systems, **18.**13–**18.**14
    electrical systems, **18.**12–**18.**13
    essential generator loads, **18.**13
    HVAC systems, **18.**11–**18.**12
    IBC (International Building Code) and, **18.**12
    LEL (lower explosion limit) detection systems,
        18.12
    NEC (National Electric Code) and, **18.**12
    overviews and summaries of, **18.**11
    redundancy and back-up systems, **18.**13
    systems architecture, **18.**12
  BCCs (building control centers) for, **18.**5–**18.**6
  benchmark event lessons for, **18.**11–**18.**14
  building envelopes of, **18.**6–**18.**8
    hardened element checklists for, **18.**7
    overviews and summaries of, **18.**6–**18.**8
  DHHS (U.S. Department of Health and Human
    Services) and, **18.**1
  guidelines and standards for, **18.**2, **18.**11–**18.**14
  overviews and summaries of, **18.**1–**18.**2, **18.**14
  PATRIOT ACT/USA and, **18.**1
  perimeters, site, **18.**4–**18.**5
  Public Health Security and Bioterrorism
    Preparedness and Response Act, **18.**1
  reference resources (print and internet) for,
    18.14–**18.**15
  SCCs (security control centers) for, **18.**5–**18.**7
  security planning for, **18.**2–**18.**3
    BMBL (Biosafety in Microbiological and
        Biomedical Laboratories) and, **18.**2

Research facilities, security planning for (*Cont.*):
  CDC (Centers for Disease Control and Prevention) and, **18.**2
  CFR (Code of Federal Regulations) 73, **18.**2
  design teams for, **18.**2
  guidelines and standards, **18.**2
  NIH (National Institute of Health) and, **18.**2
  overviews and summaries of, **18.**2–**18.**3
  plan elements, **18.**3
  threat assessments and analyses for, **18.**2–**18.**3
  security system technologies for, **18.**8–**18.**10
    biometric readers, **18.**9–**18.**10
    CALAs (controlled access laboratory areas), **18.**8–**18.**9
    card readers, **18.**9–**18.**10
    CCTV (closed-circuit television and digital recording), **18.**8–**18.**10
    listing of, **18.**8
    overviews and summaries of, **18.**8
  SEOPs (Standard or emergency operating procedure) for, **18.**1–**18.**2
  site and facility locations, **18.**3–**18.**4
    green field selection criteria for, **18.**3
    overviews and summaries of, **18.**3–**18.**4
  system controls for, **18.**10–**18.**11
    mechanical and electrical room access, **18.**10–**18.**11
    overviews and summaries of, **18.**10
    personnel screenings, **18.**10
  tiered access control systems, **18.**4
  U.S. Department of Agriculture and, **18.**1
Resident application verification, **11.**3
Resistance. *See also under individual topics*
  ballistic, **29.**3, **29.**10–**29.**12
  burglary, **29.**3, **29.**8–**29.**9
  forced-entry, **29.**8–**29.**10
  hurricane impacts, **29.**3, **29.**11–**29.**14
  of staff, **28.**10–**28.**12
Resorts. *See* Hotels and resorts
Resources, internal *vs.* external, **4.**11
Response limits, structural members, **7.**14
Response teams, **12.**19–**12.**20
Responsibility determinations, **3.**12–**3.**15, **26.**14–**26.**15
  of academic institutions, **3.**13
  of architects and designers, **3.**13
  of business communities, **3.**13
  of housing and commercial developers, **3.**13
  of legal communities, **3.**13–**3.**14
  matrices for, **26.**15–**26.**16
  of neighborhoods, **3.**14
  overviews and summaries of, **3.**12
  of public agencies, **3.**12–**3.**13
  of special expertise companies, **3.**13
Retail facilities and destinations, **19.**1–**19.**14
  benchmark event lessons for, **1.**27, **19.**1.–**19.**3
  building systems for, **19.**10–**19.**11
  building types, **19.**3–**19.**4

Retail facilities and destinations (*Cont.*):
  CPTED (crime prevention through environmental design) for, **19.**5–**19.**7
  entrances for, **19.**7–**19.**10
    mall entrances, **19.**9
    overviews and summaries of, **19.**7–**19.**8
    parking garages, **19.**9
    service access control, **19.**8–**19.**10
    service entry points, **19.**10
    technology applications, **19.**10
  management strategies for, **19.**6–**19.**7
    designs, **19.**7
    overviews and summaries of, **19.**6
    site planning and landscaping checklists for, **19.**7–**19.**8
  operational issues for, **19.**11–**19.**12
    management, **19.**6–**19.**7, **19.**11
    overviews and summaries of, **19.**11
    policies and procedures checklists, **19.**12
    tenant participation, **19.**11–**19.**12
  overviews and summaries of, **19.**1–**19.**2, **19.**12
  references resources (print and internet) for, **19.**14
  risks and vulnerabilities assessments for, **19.**3–**19.**5
    overviews and summaries of, **19.**3–**19.**5
    regional facilities, **19.**5
    suburban facilities, **19.**5
    urban and main street facilities, **19.**4–**19.**5
  terminology for, **19.**3
  traditional *vs.* emerging security concerns of, **19.**2–**19.**3
  wayfinding for, **19.**10–**19.**11
Retrofit improvements, **22.**19
Riccardi, Paul V., **1.**20
Richard Dattner Architect, **16.**3
Richard Meier & Partners, Architects, **14.**18
Rings of defense/defensive tiers, **2.**5
Risk and vulnerability assessments. *See also under individual topics*
  arenas, sports facilities, convention centers, and performing arts facilities, **4.**9–**4.**12
  of breaches, **27.**9–**27.**10
  checklists for, **23.**2
  consequences of, **2.**12
  cost-related issues of, **2.**13–**2.**14
  critical nature of, **2.**11–**2.**12
  design and construction emergencies and, **4.**10–**4.**11
  disaster planning, response, and recovery and, **12.**24
  elements of, **2.**15
  emergency estimate probabilities and, **4.**11
  facility design criteria, **4.**11–**4.**12
  FEMA (Federal Emergency Management Agency) and, **4.**10–**4.**11
  geographic impacts and, **4.**10
  human errors and, **4.**10
  internal *vs.* external resources and, **4.**11
  liability exposures and, **31.**5
  master planning for, **2.**9–**2.**14

Risk and vulnerability assessments (*Cont.*):
  for mechanical, electrical, and fire protection
    designs, **23.1–23.2**
  mitigation-related issues, **2.12–2.13**
  occurrence probabilities and impacts, **2.12**
  overviews and summaries of, **2.9–2.11, 4.9,
    23.1–23.2**
  potential business impact and, **4.11**
  potential emergencies and, **4.10**
  potential human impact and, **4.11**
  potential property impact and, **4.11**
  for retail facilities and destinations, **19.3–19.5**
  risk minimization and, **31.4–31.6**
  security deficiencies and, **2.11**
  shelter area proximities and, **4.11**
  special issues of, **2.11**
  technological impact and, **4.10**
  threat levels, **4.8–4.9**. *See also* Threat assessments
  vulnerability analyses charts, **4.10–4.11**
*Risk Management Guidance for Health and Safety
  under Extraordinary Incidents,* **1.26–1.27**
R.M.Kliment & Frances Halsband Architects,
  14.17
Robbery and armed intruder checklists, **21.13**
Rogers Marvel Architects, **16.7**
Roofs and roofing, **2.26, 20.4–20.5, 25.9**
  configurations, **20.4–20.5**
  cost estimations for, **25.9**
  master planning for, **2.26**
Roosevelt, Eleanor, **21.1**
Roosevelt, Franklin D., **1.3, 24.1**
Roosevelt, Theodore, **1.37, 11.1**
Rosenblatt, Arthur, **1.23, 15.1–15.6**

S

Safe areas, **5.2–5.4**
Safe rooms, **12.4–12.5, 24.10–24.11**
  AHUs (air-handling units) for, **24.11**
  CB (chemical and biological) protection designs
    for, **24.10–24.11**
  internal filtration for, **24.11**
  overviews and summaries of, **24.10**
  rapid exhaust facilitation for, **24.11**
  rapid sheltering facilitation for, **24.11**
  sealing of, **24.10–24.11**
SAFEVU (computer program), **7.15**
Sally ports, **6.8.–6.9**
Sam M. Gibbons U.S. Courthouse (Tampa FL),
  14.28, 14.30–14.31
Sample letters, liability exposures, **31.6–31.12**
Santayana, George, **1.3**
Sarin gas attack, Tokyo subway, **1.31–1.32**
Sasaki, Toshio, **16.3**
SAWs (surface acoustic waves), **24.8**
Scaled distances, **2.29**
Scanners, truck and cargo freight, **27.10–27.12**
Scans, iris, **27.9**
SCCs (security control centers), **7.20, 7.23**

Schools, **20.1–20.16**
  emergency management centers, **1.27**
  event lessons learned and, **20.1–20.2**
  grounds and buildings, **20.8–20.10**
    checklists for, **20.9**
    entrances, **20.9**
    graffiti controls for, **20.9–20.10**
    overviews and summaries of, **20.8–20.10**
    portable classrooms, **20.10**
    site lighting, **20.10**
  National Clearing House for Educational Facilities
    and, **20.2–20.3, 20.6**
  overviews and summaries of, **20.1, 20.15**
  policies for, **20.1–20.3**
    checklists for, **20.2**
    liability and civil liberties issues and, **20.2–20.3**
    overviews and summaries of, **20.1–20.3**
  programming, planning, and design issues for,
    20.10–20.14
    administrative areas, **20.13**
    checklists for, **20.11**
    circulation systems, **20.10–20.11**
    classrooms, **20.14**
    common areas, **20.13**
    elements of, **20.12**
    hallways, **20.12–20.13**
    locker rooms, **20.14**
    lockers, **20.13–20.14**
    overviews and summaries of, **20.10**
    supervision and, **20.12–20.13**
    surveillance maximization and, **20.13**
    toilet rooms, **20.14**
  reference resources (print and internet) for, **20.15**
  site planning for, **20.5–20.7**
    checklists for, **20.6**
    overviews and summaries of, **20.5–20.6**
    playfield design, **20.7**
    playfield fencing, **20.6–20.7**
    supervision and, **20.7**
  small *vs.* large, **20.3**
  strategies for, **20.4–20.5**
    best practices, **20.4–20.5**
    building penetrations and openings, **20.4–20.5**
    buildings as perimeters, **20.4**
    CPTED (crime prevention through environmental
      design), **20.4–20.5**
    entrances *vs.* exits, **20.4–20.5**
    fencing and barriers, **20.4–20.5**
    multiple perimeters, **20.4–20.5**
    overviews and summaries of, **20.4**
    perimeter controls, **20.4**
    roof configurations, **20.4–20.5**
    sight line maximization, **20.4–20.5**
  U.S. Department of Education and, **20.3**
  vehicular circulation and traffic elements for,
    20.7–20.8
    bus drop-off/pick-up zones, **20.7–20.8**
    checklists for, **20.8**

Schools, vehicular circulation and traffic elements
for (*Cont.*):
emergency vehicle routes, **20.**7
overviews and summaries of, **20.**7
parent drop-off/pick-up zones, **20.**7–**20.**8
parking, **20.**8
traffic circulation, **20.**8
Schultz, Bradley D., **1.**18, **10.**1–**10.**8
Screenings. *See also under individual topics*
CB (chemical and biological) protection designs
for, **24.**14–**24.**15
historic preservation guidance for, **9.**26–**9.**30
for industrial facilities and office buildings, **13.**5
for NSSEs (National Security Special Events), **4.**14
personnel screenings, **18.**10
policies for, **13.**5
screening stations, **14.**5–**14.**8
courthouses, **6.**15–**6.**16
for lobbies, **14.**5–**14.**8
overviews and summaries of, **14.**5–**14.**7
station arrangement and operations, **14.**7–**14.**8
security desks, **9.**26–**9.**27
Seals, **8.**15, **24.**10–**24.**11
for adjacent openings, **8.**15
for safe rooms, **24.**10–**24.**11
Secretary of the Interior, **9.**3–**9.**4
Secure zones, **6.**17
Security, building. *See* Building security
Security assessment elements, **2.**5–**2.**8
checklists for, **2.**7
critical asset identification, **2.**6–**2.**8
defensive tiers (rings of defense), **2.**5
overviews and summaries of, **2.**5–**2.**6
performance criteria, **2.**6–**2.**7
solutions implementation, **2.**6
Security design elements, **25.**3–**25.**10
building exteriors, **25.**8–**25.**9
cost estimations for, **25.**3–**25.**10
loading docks, **25.**8
lobbies, **14.**1–**14.**34, **25.**7. *See also* Lobbies
overviews and summaries of, **25.**4–**25.**5
progressive collapse, **25.**7
roofs, **25.**9
site perimeters, **25.**6–**25.**7
standoff distances, **25.**6–**25.**7
surveillance, **25.**7
vehicle entries, **25.**6–**25.**7
Security Design Guidelines, **9.**4
Security desks, **9.**26–**9.**27
Security glass applications, **29.**1–**29.**18. *See also*
Windows and glazing
Security levels, **4.**13, **4.**15, **7.**2–**7.**3, **7.**13
for federally owned/leased buildings, **7.**2–**7.**3, **7.**13
for NSSEs (National Security Special Events),
4.13, **4.**15
Security officers and personnel, **2.**27–**2.**28
Security posts and guard houses, **2.**19

Security Reference Guide, Planned Parenthood
Golden Gate, **21.**1
Security surveys, **2.**8–**2.**9
Security technology, **27.**3–**27.**20
access control, **27.**6–**27.**9
access cards and card readers for, **27.**6–**27.**7
combination locks for, **27.**6
keypads for, **27.**6
overviews and summaries of, **27.**6
benchmark event lessons for, **27.**3, **27.**10
biometrics, **18.**9–**18.**10, **27.**7–**27.**9
biometric readers, **18.**9–**18.**10
facial recognition, **27.**8
fingerprint recognition, **27.**8–**27.**9
hand geometry, **27.**8
iris scans, **27.**9
overviews and summaries of, **27.**7–**27.**8
breaches and, **27.**9–**27.**10
detection and assessment of, **27.**9–**27.**10
overviews and summaries of, **27.**9
CALAs (controlled access laboratory areas),
18.8–**18.**9
card readers, **18.**9–**18.**10
CCTV (closed-circuit television and digital
recording), **18.**8–**18.**10
checklists for, **27.**19
definition of, **19.**3
emergency responses, **27.**14
entrances, **19.**10
EOCs (emergency operations centers),
27.14–**27.**16
fences and fencing, **27.**5–**27.**6
electric/powered, **27.**5–**27.**6
fiber-optic, **27.**5
overviews and summaries of, **27.**5
industrial and transportation applications,
27.10–**27.**12
EDSs (explosive detection systems),
27.10–**27.**11
ETDs (explosive trace detectors), **27.**10–**27.**11
explosive detection, **27.**10–**27.**11
overviews and summaries of, **27.**10
truck and cargo freight scanners, **27.**10–**27.**12
insurance issue design responses for, **4.**7
operations, **27.**17–**27.**18
overviews and summaries of, **27.**3, **27.**18
planning for, **27.**16–**27.**17
reference resources (internet) for, **27.**19
for research facilities, **18.**8–**18.**10
retail facilities and destinations, **19.**10
risk and vulnerability assessments and, **4.**10
security systems, **27.**3–**27.**4, **27.**17
applications for, **27.**4
designs for, **27.**17, **27.**19
deterrence and delay, **27.**3, **27.**5
integrated, **27.**4
overviews and summaries of, **27.**3–**27.**4

Security technology (*Cont.*):
    video, **27.**12–**27.**14
    weapons detection, **27.**10
    for women's health centers, **21.**6
Semihardened façades, **2.**29
Sensors. *See also* Detectors and detection systems
    contact, **15.**3–**15.**4
    shock and impact sensors, **15.**4
SEOPs (Standard or emergency operating procedure),
    18.1–**18.**2
Service interruption threats, **2.**9
Setback requirements, **9.**9
Sewell, William G., **1.**34, **27.**3–**27.**19
Shades, blast, **9.**21–**9.**23
Shakespeare, William, **6.**1
Shear failures, **22.**14–**22.**15, **22.**20
Sheinberg, Steven C., **1.**25
Shelter area proximities, **4.**11
Sheltering, **24.**11–**24.**15
    enhanced sheltering-in-place capabilities, **24.**15
    rapid, **24.**11
Shelters, in-residence, **12.**15–**12.**16
Sheridan, Francis J., **1.**35, **28.**1–**28.**18
Sherman-Carter-Barnhart, **14.**14
Shootings, workplace, **13.**8
Sightlines, **6.**19–**6.**21, **20.**4–**20.**5
    courtrooms, **6.**19–**6.**21
    maximization of, **20.**4–**20.**5
Signage, **6.**4
Sills, Beverly, **15.**1
Simons, Russ, **1.**13, **4.**3–**4.**17
Simple magnetic contact switches, **15.**3
Site perimeters. *See* Perimeters
Site selection and planning. *See also under individual*
    topics
    for courthouses, **6.**3–**6.**7
    CPTED (crime prevention through environmental
        design) and, **3.**6, **13.**1–**13.**4
    facility operations and, **13.**3–**13.**4
    green field selection criteria for, **18.**3
    for industrial facilities and office buildings, **13.**1–**13.**4
    insurance issue responses for, **4.**5–**4.**7
    liability issues of, **13.**2
    lighting and, **13.**3, **20.**10
    overviews and summaries of, **13.**1–**13.**2, **18.**3–**18.**4
    for parking garages and lots, **13.**3
    perimeter security of, **13.**3
    for physical plants, **13.**3
    for research facilities, **18.**3
    for schools, **20.**5–**20.**7
        checklists for, **20.**6
        overviews and summaries of, **20.**5–**20.**6
        playfield design, **20.**7
        playfield fencing, **20.**6–**20.**7
        supervision and, **20.**7
    for women's health centers, **21.**3–**21.**4
Situational crime reduction, **19.**3

Slepian, Barnett, **1.**28, **21.**2
Slip and fall hazards, **10.**8
Slots and gaming machines, **10.**6–**10.**7
Small *vs.* large missile impacts, **29.**14
Small *vs.* large schools, **20.**3
Smart Building Program, **24.**17–**24.**22
Smoke management systems, **23.**14–**23.**15
SMSs (security management systems), **7.**22–**7.**25
Social Hall Plaza (Salt Lake City, Utah), **24.**17–**24.**18
SOCs (security operations centers), **2.**20
Soft wall testing, **29.**6
Solutions, master planning, **2.**6, **2.**14–**2.**22
Somers, Deborah A., **1.**37, **30.**3–**30.**14
Sorption, **24.**24
Sources and source types, lighting, **7.**8–**7.**11, **7.**9–**7.**11
South Florida Building Code, **29.**11–**29.**13
Space flexibility, **8.**18
Spalls, **29.**16
Special expertise companies, responsibilities of, **3.**13
Spector Group, **14.**18
Spectrometry, mass *vs.* ion mobility, **24.**8
Splices, column, **22.**12–**22.**13
Sports facilities, **4.**3–**4.**18. *See also* Arenas, sports
    facilities, convention centers, and performing
    arts facilities
Spreading, **30.**6–**30.**7
Stacking diagrams, courthouses, **6.**13
Staff involvement issues, **28.**10–**28.**13
    overviews and summaries of, **28.**10–**28.**12
    staff resistance, **28.**10–**28.**12
    staff training, **2.**28, **28.**10–**28.**12
Stafford-Simpson hurricane classification scale, **12.**11
Stairs, **5.**2–**5.**5
    enhanced egress, **5.**5
    preparations for, **5.**2
Stakeholder-related issues, **3.**8
Stalking and following checklists, **21.**14
Standard of care navigation, **31.**2–**31.**4
Standards, **30.**3–**30.**14. *See also* Guidelines, standards,
    and codes
Standards for Rehabilitation, **9.**3–**9.**4
Standoffs and standoff distances, **2.**29, **9.**34, **22.**4,
    22.20, **25.**4–**25.**6
Stark, Stanley, **1.**26, **18.**1–**18.**15
Steel construction, **22.**11–**22.**14
    beam-to-beam connections, **22.**13–**22.**14
    beam-to-column connections, **22.**13–**22.**14
    built-up sections, **22.**14
    column splices, **22.**12–**22.**13
    overviews and summaries of, **22.**11–**22.**12
    structural protection designs for, **22.**11–**22.**14
Steinberg, Sue, **1.**36, **29.**1–**29.**18
Strategy design and evaluation, **3.**7–**3.**8, **20.**4–**20.**5
Strife, Eric, **10.**1
Strip centers, **19.**3
Structural framing systems, **2.**23
Structural member response limits, **7.**14

Structural protection designs, **22.**3–**22.**22
 abnormal loads and, **22.**5–**22.**6
 benchmark event lessons for, **1.**30–**1.**31, **22.**3–**22.**4,
  22.7–**22.**8, **22.**12, **22.**15, **22.**19–**22.**20
 blast loads and, **22.**10–**22.**11
 concrete construction and, **22.**14–**22.**16
  brisance, **22.**15, **22.**20
  enhancements of, **22.**15–**22.**16
  limited ductility, **22.**15
  overviews and summaries of, **22.**14
  shear failures, **22.**14–**22.**15, **22.**20
 enhancements for, **22.**16
 for exterior wall systems, **22.**16–**22.**19
  catch systems, **22.**17–**22.**18
  fenestration, glass, **22.**16–**22.**17, **22.**20
  overviews and summaries of, **22.**16
  window performance criteria, **22.**18
 GSA (U.S. General Services Administration) and,
  22.9, **22.**18
 ISC (Interagency Security Committee) and,
  22.3–**22.**4
 for masonry walls, **22.**19
 overviews and summaries of, **22.**3–**22.**4,
  22.19–**22.**20
 progressive collapse and, **22.**5–**22.**6, **22.**20
 reference resources (print and internet) for,
  22.20–**22.**21
 retrofit improvements and, **22.**19
 steel construction and, **22.**11–**22.**14
  beam-to-beam connections, **22.**13–**22.**14
  beam-to-column connections, **22.**13–**22.**14
  built-up sections, **22.**14
  column splices, **22.**12–**22.**13
  overviews and summaries of, **22.**11–**22.**12
 strategies for, **22.**4–**22.**5
  hardening, **22.**4
  overviews and summaries of, **22.**4–**22.**5
  redundant systems, **22.**4
  standoffs and standoff distances, **22.**4, **22.**20
 structural redundancy for, **22.**9–**22.**10
 systems for, **22.**6–**22.**8
  gravity load systems, **22.**7
  influence areas, **22.**7–**22.**8
  lateral load systems, **22.**8
 terminology for, **22.**20
 terrorist organizations and, **22.**6
 transparent security, **22.**4
 U.S. Department of State and, **22.**5
 USDOJ (U.S. Department of Justice) and,
  22.3–**22.**4
 vulnerable construction features and, **22.**12
Structural redundancy, **22.**9–**22.**10
Studio Museum in Harlem, **16.**7
Subdivision ordinances, **3.**10–**3.**11
Suburban retail facilities, **19.**5
Suicide bombers, **17.**13–**17.**15
Supervision issues, schools, **20.**7, **20.**12–**20.**13

Surface reflectance, lighting, **7.**12
Surge capacities, **8.**18, **8.**24–**8.**26
Surveillance systems. *See also under individual topics*
 cost estimations and, **25.**7
 for courthouses, **6.**4–**6.**5, **6.**16
 historic preservation guidance for, **9.**8–**9.**10
 for hospitality facilities, **10.**4
 in schools, **20.**13
Surveys, security, **2.**8–**2.**9, **15.**2–**15.**3
Suspicious package and mail checklists, **21.**14
Swift, Jonathan, **30.**3
Syndrome surveillance protocols, **8.**15–**8.**16
Synthetic Organic Chemical Manufacturers
 Association, **30.**9

T

Target hardening, **1.**26
Teams, **2.**2–**2.**3, **3.**9, **18.**2
Technical expertise, **12.**27
Technology and materials aspects, **27.**1–**29.**18. *See
 also under individual topics*
 benchmark event lessons for, **1.**33–**1.**37
 for compatibility issues of, **8.**8
 for courtrooms, **6.**22
 definitions of, **2.**29
 glazing and security glass applications,
  29.1–**29.**18
 for health care facilities, **8.**8
 for lobbies, **14.**9–**14.**10
 master planning for, **2.**26–**2.**27
 product selection and specification, **28.**1–**28.**18
 for religious institutions and community centers,
  17.8
 security technology, **27.**3–**27.**20
 x-ray machines, **14.**9
Tenability, commercial high-rise egress systems, **5.**6
Tenant participation, **19.**11–**19.**12
Terminology. *See also under individual topics*
 for CB (chemical and biological) protection
  designs, **24.**24
 for commercial high-rise egress systems, **5.**1
 for glazing and security glass applications, **29.**16
 for historic preservation guidance, **9.**33–**9.**34
 for master planning, **2.**29
 for retail facilities and destinations, **19.**3
 for structural protection designs, **22.**20
Terrorism, **1.**38, **19.**13, **22.**6, **31.**6–**31.**13
 assessments for, **22.**6
 definitions of, **19.**13
 insurance, **1.**38, **31.**6–**31.**7, **31.**13
 terrorist organizations, **22.**6
Terrorism Risk Assurance Act, **1.**38
Tetreau, Jean, **8.**28
Theory and practice issues, **1.**8
Thomas F. Eagleton U.S. Courthouse (St. Louis, MO),
 14.27–**14.**30
Thompson, David, **1.**11, **2.**1–**2.**30

Threat assessments. *See also under individual topics*
  biohazard threat checklists, **21.**10
  bomb threat checklists, **21.**10–**21.**11
  butyric acid attack checklists, **21.**10
  for CB (chemical and biological) protection
      designs, **24.**2–**24.**3
  cost estimations for, **25.**4
  criminal-related, **2.**9
  e-mail threat checklists, **21.**12
  environmental, **2.**9
  for health care facilities, **8.**4
  for hospitality facilities, **10.**1–**10.**2
  infrastructure failures, **2.**9
  master planning for, **2.**8–**2.**9
  for museums and cultural facilities, **15.**2–**15.**3
  protester checklists, **21.**13
  for research facilities, **18.**2–**18.**3
  robbery and armed intruder checklists, **21.**13
  service interruptions, **2.**9
  stalking and following checklists, **21.**14
  suspicious package and mail checklists, **21.**14
  terrorist assessments, **22.**6
  threat level assessments, **4.**8–**4.**9
      level 1 (low degree of risk), **4.**9
      level 2 (guarded degree of risk), **4.**9
      level 3 (elevated degree of risk), **4.**8–**4.**9
      level 4 (high degree of risk), **4.**8
  threat types, **2.**12, **10.**2
  threat verification, **2.**12
  for women's health centers, **21.**2–**21.**3
  for workplace threats, **13.**8–**13.**9
TICs (toxic industrial chemicals), **24.**2–**24.**3,
      24.7–**24.**8
Tiered access control systems, **18.**4
Toilet rooms and lavatories, schools, **20.**14
Tokyo subway sarin gas attack, **1.**31–**1.**32
Tomasetti, Richard L., **1.**29, **22.**3–**22.**21
Tornadoes and high winds, **12.**12–**12.**16
  checklists for, **12.**14–**12.**15
  design and construction issues for, **12.**13–**12.**14
  disaster planning, response, and recovery for,
      12.12–**12.**16
  F-scale, **12.**13–**12.**14
  in-residence shelters, **12.**15–**12.**16
  overviews and summaries of, **12.**12–**12.**13
Townsend Harris High School, **16.**8
Trace detectors, explosive, **27.**10–**27.**11
Traditional *vs.* emerging security concerns, **19.**2–**19.**3
Transfer, **30.**6–**30.**7
*Transparent Materials for Use in Forced Entry or
      Containment Barriers,* **29.**10
Transparent security aspects, **1.**1–**3.**16. *See also
      under individual topics*
  benchmark event lessons, **1.**3–**1.**40
  CPTED (crime prevention through environmental
      design), **3.**1–**3.**16
  master planning, **2.**1–**2.**30

Trash receptacles, **6.**11–**6.**12
Truck and car bombs, **17.**13
Truck and cargo freight scanners, **27.**10–**27.**12
Tsunamis, **12.**7–**12.**9. *See also* Floods and tsunamis

U

UFAS (Uniform Federal Accessibility Standards), **7.**6
UL (Underwriters Laboratory), **29.**9, **29.**12, **30.**8
Unit inspections, **11.**3
Units, glass, **29.**16
Urban and main street retail facilities, **19.**4–**19.**5
U.S. governmental departments and bodies. *See also
      under individual departments and bodies*
  Army Corps of Engineers, **7.**3–**7.**4, **24.**6–**24.**7
  ATF (Bureau of Alcohol, Tobacco, and Firearms),
      4.5
  CDC (Centers for Disease Control and Prevention),
      18.2
  CIA (Central Intelligence Agency), **7.**3, **30.**8
  DEA (Drug Enforcement Agency), **30.**6
  Department of Agriculture and, **18.**1
  Department of Education, **20.**3
  Department of Energy, **7.**8, **30.**8
  Department of Homeland Security, **1.**13, **2.**6, **4.**9,
      7.2–**7.**3, **9.**4, **11.**1–**11.**2, **30.**8–**30.**9
  Department of State, **7.**3, **7.**16, **12.**4–**12.**5, **22.**5,
      30.8–**30.**9
  Department of the Interior, **1.**17
  Department of Transportation, **30.**8–**30.**9
  Department of Treasury, **11.**4, **30.**8–**30.**9
  DHHS (Department of Health and Human
      Services), **18.**1, **30.**8–**30.**9
  DOA (Department of Agriculture), **18.**1
  DoD (Department of Defense), **2.**6, **7.**3, **7.**14, **9.**4,
      24.19–**24.**20, **30.**8–**30.**9
  FBI (Federal Bureau of Investigation), **4.**5,
      4.8–**4.**9, **11.**1–**11.**3
  FCC (Federal Communications Commission), **30.**8
  federal courthouses, **14.**14–**14.**18
  FEMA (Federal Emergency Management Agency),
      4.10–**4.**11, **12.**4–**12.**5, **31.**3–**31.**4
  FPS (Federal Protective Services), **7.**2–**7.**3,
      14.1–**14.**2
  GSA (General Services Administration), **1.**5–**1.**7,
      1.17, **2.**5–**2.**6, **4.**12, **7.**2–**7.**3, **7.**13–**7.**16, **9.**4,
      14.1–**14.**2, **22.**9, **22.**18, **22.**28, **23.**10–**23.**11,
      30.4–**30.**5, **30.**9, **31.**4–**31.**5
  HUD (Department of Housing and Urban
      Development), **11.**2–**11.**3
  IRS (Internal Revenue Service), **7.**3–**7.**4
  ISC (Interagency Security Committee), **7.**3, **7.**13,
      9.3–**9.**4, **22.**3–**22.**4
  National Hurricane Center, **29.**13
  National Park Service, **9.**4
  National Weather Service, **29.**13
  NCPC (National Capital Planning Committee), **9.**4
  NIH (National Institute of Health), **18.**2

U.S. governmental departments and bodies (*Cont.*):
NIJ (National Institute of Justice), **29**.12
NRC (Nuclear Regulatory Commission), **30**.6–**30**.9
PBS (Public Buildings Service), **14**.1
Pentagon, **7**.3, **26**.1–**26**.4
Secretary of the Interior, **9**.3–**9**.4
USDOJ (Department of Justice), **3**.5, **7**.1–**7**.4, **9**.4, **22**.3–**22**.4
USMS (U.S. Marshal Service), **14**.1–**14**.2
USSS (United States Secret Service), **4**.5, **4**.8–**4**.9, **4**.15
UVGI (ultraviolet germicidal irradiation) systems, **24**.5

V

Vapor density, **24**.24
V-bed filters, **24**.6
VCCs (visitor control centers), **2**.20
Vegetation and site designs, **12**.18
Vehicular circulation and traffic elements, **2**.16–**2**.17, **7**.16–**7**.17, **19**.13, **20**.7–**20**.8, **25**.6–**25**.7
master planning for, **2**.16–**2**.17
parking, **20**.8. *See also* Parking
for schools, **20**.7–**20**.8
bus drop-off/pick-up zones, **20**.7–**20**.8
checklists for, **20**.8
emergency vehicle routes, **20**.7
overviews and summaries of, **20**.7
parent drop-off/pick-up zones, **20**.7–**20**.8
parking, **20**.8
traffic circulation, **20**.8
vehicle barriers, **2**.18, **2**.29, **7**.16–**7**.17, **9**.11–**9**.15, **19**.13
vehicle entries, cost estimations for, **25**.6–**25**.7
Vendor-related issues, **28**.12
Ventilation systems, **23**.10–**23**.14
Vertical transportation systems, **5**.6
Vestibules, **24**.15
Vetting areas and processes, **2**.19, **2**.29
Vibrator detectors, **15**.4
Victim and missing persons status issues, **8**.27
Video systems and technology, **7**.25, **18**.8–**18**.10, **27**.12–**27**.14
CCTV (closed-circuit television and digital recording), **2**.18–**2**.19, **18**.8–**18**.10
imaging and identification systems, **7**.25
overviews and summaries of, **27**.12–**27**.14
VIISs (video imaging and identification systems), **7**.25
Violent incidents, **13**.8, **21**.2
at women's health centers, **21**.2
in workplaces, **13**.8
Visitor access, **7**.7
Volatility, **24**.24
Volunteer management, **8**.8
Volunteer services, **1**.20–**1**.21, **8**.8, **12**.20–**12**.22

Vulnerability assessments, **4**.9–**4**.12. *See also* Risk and vulnerability assessments
for health care facilities, **8**.9–**8**.10

W

Waiting and registration areas, **8**.16, **21**.4–**21**.6
Walker, McGough, Foltz, and Lyeria tests, **29**.10
Walls, **7**.7–**7**.8, **16**.3, **22**.16–**22**.19
berm and blast wall construction, **2**.19
case studies of, **16**.3
exterior wall systems, **22**.16–**22**.19
historic preservation guidance, **9**.24–**9**.26
liners for, **9**.24–**9**.26
masonry, **22**.19
overviews and summaries of, **7**.7–**7**.8
soft wall testing, blasts, **29**.6
Warner, Charles Dudley, **25**.3
Water recovery, flood, **12**.9–**12**.10
Water services, **8**.22–**8**.23, **12**.18, **23**.3–**24**.5
Wayfinding, **19**.10–**19**.11
Weapons detection, **27**.10
Weisberg, Sarelle T., **1**.8
Wells, H. G., **22**.3
White (H.P.) Laboratories, **29**.9–**29**.10, **29**.12
Wilde, Oscar, **24**.1
Wildfires, **12**.16–**12**.17
Wilkinson, Paul, **4**.5
William S. Moorhead Federal Building (Pittsburgh, PA), **14**.25–**14**.28
Williams, Scott, **4**.4
Wilson, Fred, **16**.8
Wilson, Therese, **1**.28
WINDAS (computer program), **7**.15
Windows and glazing. *See also under individual topics*
blast windows, **29**.3–**29**.7
for courthouses, **6**.10–**6**.11
for federally owned/leased buildings, **7**.7–**7**.8, **7**.14–**7**.16
glass, **15**.4, **22**.16–**22**.17, **22**.20
break detectors, **15**.4
fenestration, **22**.16–**22**.17, **22**.20
window bugs, **15**.4
glazing and security glass applications, **29**.1–**29**.18
historic preservation guidance for, **9**.19–**9**.23
mullion and window support systems, **2**.24–**2**.25
overviews and summaries of, **7**.14
performance criteria for, **22**.18
protection levels and, **7**.14–**7**.16
low and low/medium, **7**.14–**7**.15
medium and high, **7**.14–**7**.16
window film, **2**.25
WINLAC (computer program), **7**.15
Wireless connectivity, **23**.10
WMDs (weapons of mass destruction), **17**.13
Women's health centers, **21**.1–**21**.16
benchmark event lessons for, **1**.27–**1**.28
design issues for, **21**.3–**21**.6

Women's health centers, design issues for (*Cont.*):
    clinic access, **21.**3
    entrance, waiting, and registration areas, **21.**4–**21.**6
    interiors and technology, **21.**6
    parking, **21.**3–**21.**4
    site planning and selection, **21.**3–**21.**4
    Eastmont Mall Planned Parenthood, **21.**4–**21.**6
    Eddy Street Planned Parenthood Clinic, **21.**5
    vs. health care facilities, **8.**1–**8.**32. *See also* Health
        care facilities
    overviews and summaries of, **21.**1, **21.**15
    policies and procedures for, **21.**7
    PPGG (Planned Parenthood Golden Gate) and,
        21.1, **21.**7–**21.**8, **21.**15
    reference resources (print and internet) for, **21.**15
    security reference guidelines for, **21.**7–**21.**15
        biohazard threat checklists, **21.**10
        bomb threat checklists, **21.**10–**21.**11
        butyric acid attack checklists, **21.**10
        e-mail threat checklists, **21.**12
        fire checklists, **21.**12
        forms for, **21.**8–**21.**9, **21.**11
        hostile client checklists, **21.**12
        overviews and summaries of, **21.**7
        procedures checklists, **21.**8
        protester checklists, **21.**13
        reference checklists, **21.**7
        robbery and armed intruder checklists, **21.**13
        stalking and following checklists, **21.**14
        suspicious package and mail checklists, **21.**14
    threats against, **21.**2–**21.**3
        FACEA (Freedom to Access Clinic Entrances
            Act), **21.**3
        overviews and summaries of, **21.**2–**21.**3
        threat types, **21.**2

Women's health centers (*Cont.*):
    violent incidents and, **21.**2
Woodcock, Douglas P., **6.**1
Workplace-related issues, **7.**7, **10.**3–**10.**5, **11.**3,
    13.8–**13.**9, **18.**10
    background checks, **10.**4
    contractors and employees, **11.**3
    employee access, **7.**7
    for hospitality facilities, **10.**3–**10.**4
    for industrial facilities and office buildings, **13.**8–**13.**9
    personnel screenings, **18.**10
    shootings, **13.**8
    threats, **13.**8–**13.**9
    violence, **13.**8
WTC (World Trade Center)
    1993, bombing, **1.**9–**1.**10, **4.**3–**4.**4, **22.**3
    2001 (September 11) terrorist event, **1.**3–**1.**40, **5.**1,
        5.4, **5.**6–**5.**7, **10.**4, **11.**2, **13.**7, **22.**3, **22.**12, **23.**3,
        23.11, **24.**2, **24.**21, **26.**1–**26.**16, **30.**12–**30.**13

X

X-ray machines, **7.**18–**7.**19, **14.**9. *See also* Metal
    detectors

Z

Zetlin, Michael S., **1.**37, **31.**1–**31.**14
Zones, **6.**16–**6.**18, **8.**15, **25.**10
    drop-off/pick-up. *See* Drop-off/pick-up zones,
        schools
    hot and cold, **8.**15
    interface, **6.**18
    private, **6.**16–**6.**17
    secure, **6.**17
    zones of influence, **25.**10
Zoning ordinances, **3.**10